Power
Tools for
Technical
Communication

Power Tools for Technical Communication

David A. McMurrey

THOMSON
———✦———
WADSWORTH

Australia   Canada   Mexico   Singapore   Spain   United Kingdom   United States

Power Tools for Technical Communication
David A. McMurrey

Publisher: *Earl McPeek*
Acquisitions Editors: *Julie McBurney, Bill Hoffman*
Market Strategist: *John Meyers*
Project Manager: *Andrea Archer*

Cover: *Graphic World Publishing Services*

Printed in the United States of America
6 7 8 9 10   06 05

For more information contact Wadsworth, 25 Thomson Place, Boston, MA 02210 USA, or you can visit our Internet site at http://www.wadsworth.com

ISBN: 0-1550-6898-9

Library of Congress Catalog Card Number: 2001087280

Preface

Whether you are a student or an instructor of technical writing, you'll want to read the following. It shows you how to use this book and discusses its main concepts and organization.

WHAT'S THIS BOOK ABOUT—WHO'S IT FOR?

This book is for students and teachers in introductory technical-writing courses—courses that are required in the technical majors such as the following:

Academic Majors Commonly Requiring Technical Writing

Aerospace engineering	Kinesiology
Air conditioning technology	Landscaping
Automotive technology	Legal assistant programs
Building construction technologies	Medical laboratory technology
Commercial arts	Nursing
Consumer electronics technology	Occupational therapy
Criminal justice	Office administration
Diagnostic medical imaging (radiology, sonography)	Pharmacy technology
Emergency medical (paramedic) technology	Physical fitness technology
Engineering—all kinds!	Physical therapy
Engineering design graphics	Quality assurance
Fire protection technology	Semiconductor manufacturing technology
Geomatics	Space science
Heating and refrigeration technology	Surgical technology
Industrial supervision	Waste water treatment
Information records management	Welding technology
International business	

The focus of this book is people pursuing their own study programs and students coming to introductory technical-writing courses from other majors. Therefore, this book doesn't say much about issues such as workplace culture, professional ethics, and other such currently popular issues.

These are best left to the faculty in students' majors. For example, professionals in the healthcare field are far better positioned to address the culture and the ethics of their workplaces such as the hospital, the clinic, the agency, and the home-healthcare setting.

Instead, this book focuses on writing—technical writing. It focuses on design, format, style, structures, and applications of technical writing. It focuses on strategies and tools you can use to produce excellent technical documents in any of the common delivery methods. "Documents" refers to all manner of technical reports, proposals, instructions, and user guides, as well as business letters, memos, and e-mail containing technical material. "Delivery methods" refers not just to printed documents, but to oral-presentation delivery as well as delivery over the World Wide Web.

Instead of forcing you into a theory-now writing-later approach, this book groups topics by type (as shown in the following table), making it easier for you to construct your own preferred sequence. Like a hypertext in print, the chapters in this book can be used in practically *any* order you wish. Few technical-writing instructors or students use their textbooks in the published order anyway.

Topics Covered in *Power Tools*
(chapter numbers are shown in parentheses)

Part I: Practice Projects	Part I: Real-World Projects	Part II: Document-Design Tools	Part III: Document-Delivery Tools	Parts IV–V: Project-Development Tools
Description (1)	Site, accident, trip, field reports (1)	Headings (7)	Informal reports (1, 15)	Audience and task analysis (19)
Process (2)	Product specifications (1)	Lists (8)	Business-letter reports (2, 15)	Team writing (22)
Cause-effect (3)	Instructions (2)	Notices (9)	Memo reports	Organization at **www. io .com/~hcexres/power_ tools/organization.html**
				Sentence-style at **www.io.com/~hcexres/ power_tools/sentence_ style.html**

Continued

Topics Covered in *Power Tools* — *continued*
(chapter numbers are shown in parentheses)

Part I: Practice Projects	Part I: Real-World Projects	Part II: Document-Design Tools	Part III: Document-Delivery Tools	Parts IV–V: Project-Development Tools
Comparison (4)	Recommendation, evaluation, feasibility reports (4)	Tables (10)	Formal reports (15)	Grammar, usage, punctuation (B, C)
Definition (5)	Background reports (5)	Charts (10)	Oral reports (16)	Transitions at **www.io .com/~hcexres/power_ tools/transitions.html**
Classification (5)	Proposals (6)	Illustrative graphics (11)	Web-page documents (17)	Mechanics: abbreviations, symbols, numbers (A)
Persuasion, argumentation (6)	Progress reports (6)	Highlighting (12)		Topics at **www.io .com/~hcexres/power_ tools/topics.html**
	Inquiry, complaint, adjustment letters (13)			Narrowing at **www.io .com/~hcexres/power_ tools/narrowing.html**
	Resumes, application letters (14)			Outlining at **www.io .com/~hcexres/power_ tools/outlining.htm**

HOW DO YOU USE THIS BOOK?

This book is *not* designed to be read or used from cover to cover. It is *not* set up to be read in the order that the chapters are listed in the table contents. It's *not* designed to take you on a lengthy lock-step tour of theory and concepts before you get to do any actual writing.

Chapter sequences. Instead, this book is designed so that you can sequence chapters according to what you need to study, what you are ready to study, and which technical-writing projects you are interested in. Conceptual issues such as audience or page design are much more meaningful in the context of a writing project in which you use those concepts. When you are engaged in an actual technical-writing project, bookish issues like audience, transitions, organization, headings, lists, graphics, and collaboration all of a sudden have immediate relevance. However, if you studied audience six weeks ago, you are not likely remember much about it or put it into practice effectively.

Project approach. Instead of forcing you into a long march through theory, this book enables you to design your study program according to increasingly challenging projects. Select projects that are interesting and relevant. If you have already studied description, process, comparison, and definition, skip those portions of the chapters and move right into workplace projects such as instructions, proposals, and background reports. To supplement those projects, select the nonproject chapters that go best with them. For example:

- Course startup: about technical writing (Introduction) and workplace writing (Chapter 22).
- Audience analysis (Chapter 19) with definition writing (Chapter 5).

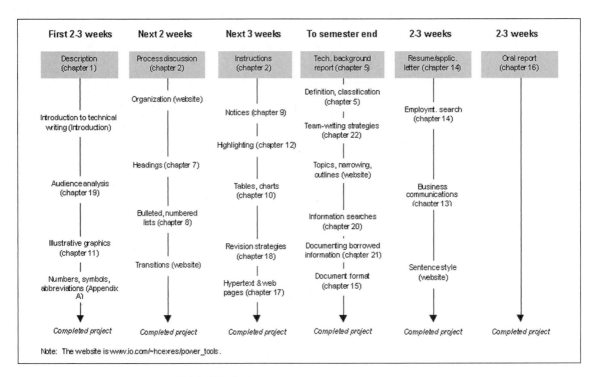

FIGURE P-1

Ideas for interlacing chapters of this book. The six projects shown above use almost all of the chapters in this book and take up about 14 to 16 weeks total. In each you begin with a project—something that addresses a real or realistic need or problem in the workplace. For additional ideas, see the instructor's manual or **www.io.com/~hcexres/power_tools**.

- Graphics (Chapter 11) with descriptions (Chapter 1).
- Lists and notices (Chapter 9) with instructions (Chapter 2).
- Information search (Chapter 20) and documentation of borrowed information (Chapter 21) with the formal technical report (Chapters 5 and 15).
- Tables, graphs, and charts (Chapter 10) with recommendation reports (Chapter 4).

No doubt you'll find many other combinations and sequences that fit your learning or teaching needs. That's one of the main reasons that chapters in this book are grouped rather than sequenced. For additional ideas on combining and sequencing chapters, see Figure P-1.

All theory—no play. If you've ever looked in technical-writing textbooks, you've noticed that the common sequence of chapters looks like what is shown in Figure P-2. You've got to learn *all* the basics before you can start practicing an art or skill, right? Yes indeed, if you are studying something such as medical procedures. For example, you don't get to

COMMON CHAPTER SEQUENCING: OTHER TECHNICAL-WRITING BOOKS

Chapters in this book corresponding to the following topics are indicated in parentheses:

1. *Technical writing*—About the subject and the field (Introduction).
2. *Audience*—The essential focus of all technical writing (Chapter 19).
3. *Workplace context*—Use and importance of technical writing in a broad range of fields, professions, occupations, and disciplines (Introduction and Chapter 22).
4. *Qualities of good technical writing*—Importance of direct, succinct, readable writing (Introduction).
5. *Ethics*—Ethical problems in technical writing and professions in general (throughout).
6. *International communication*—Considerations for writing for audiences in other cultures (references in Chapter 13)
7. *Page design and graphics*—Page layout, typography, headings, lists, illustrations (Part 2 chapters).
8. *Arrangement and organizational patterns*—Description, definition, process, general-to-specific, problem-solution, and others (Part 1 chapters).
9. *Information gathering*—Using the library and the Internet as well as direct information-gathering methods (Chapter 20).
10. *Citing sources of borrowed information*—Using APA, MLA, IEEE (Chapter 21).
11. *Revision*—Substantive editing, copyediting, proofreading (Chapter 18).
12. *Applications*—Only after all of the above have been presented do you get to actually write documents such as instructions, reports, letters, memos (Part 1 Chapters).

FIGURE P-2

Common chapter sequencing in technical-writing textbooks. Eventually, you get to write.

"revise" if, while trying to start an IV, you give your patient an embolism. However, you can practice activities like writing, cooking, painting, singing, composing, and sports in a safe environment, where it's okay if your first efforts aren't perfect or fully informed of all available theory. It's okay to "mess up." (Of course, cooking might be a problem—who wants to waste good food?) In these areas you can learn a little, get some practice using what you just learned, and repeat the process again and again. If you try to swallow the theory whole, you'll gag—you won't remember much of it or put much of it into practice. It's like memorizing a whole box of German vocabulary cards without ever practicing reading, speaking, or writing the language.

Workplace writing. This book acknowledges that most technical-writing students are not in workplace situations that provide good contexts for the writing projects discussed here. That's a problem because technical writing is all about workplace writing and solving workplace problems using the tools of technical writing. Faced with this dilemma, we try to find real situations in which descriptions, definitions, instructions, and other types of documents are needed. But more often we have to invent realistic situations. Sometimes that means starting with an interesting topic and working "backwards" to a realistic workplace situation in which that topic would be featured.

Infrastructures. The first seven chapters of this book—Part I, "Project Tools for Technical Writers"—rely on the concept of infrastructure. The infrastructure of a society is its water, sewage, electrical, and gas systems; its system of roads and bridges, as well as mundane things like garbage collection, mail delivery, telephones, and so on. These are the backbone, the skeletal structure of a society. Without them, a modern society doesn't work. When they are working, we hardly notice them. They exist as if underneath—"infra"—to the surfaces of our society. Information structures such as description, classification, comparison, process, cause-effect discussion, and definition exist "underneath" the applications of technical writing—such as instructions, user guides, feasibility and recommendation reports, technical background reports, and other such technical documents. You rarely find a "pure" description or "pure" classification—instead, they are internal to the application—"infra." When these infrastructures inform a technical-writing application, they undergo a good many transformations: they lose the pure characteristics of organization and content described in Part I.

Infrastructures are important—they give you starting points, models, patterns with which to begin building technical documents. Infrastructures can be mixed and matched in an infinite variety of ways. For example, you can write a process discussion using the structure of a description; one by one, you can trace the events of the process through the components of the device. In the end, who cares whether we call it a process description or a physical description as long as it meets the needs of the audience and supports the purpose of the document?

WHAT'S IN THIS BOOK—WHAT'S DISTINCTIVE?

Obviously, the chapter organization of this book and its project approach are some of its most distinctive features. This book contains just about everything you expect to see in a technical-writing textbook, but there are some new features.

Topic boxes. Every chapter begins with a box full of Web links to important science or technology issues such as photovoltaics, nanotechnology, and global warming. Technical-writing courses are great opportunities to explore these areas. Where else can you explore such a broad range of science and technology? (If you prefer not having to type those URLs, see **www.io.com/~hcexres/power_tools**.)

Step-by-step "tools" approach. Everywhere you'll find specific steps for using document-design "tools" such as headings, lists, tables, graphs, charts, hypertext, and Web pages. You'll see specific steps for thinking of projects, narrowing and outlining topics, checking organization and transitions, working in writing teams, developing instructions, planning recommendation reports, using presentation software (such as Lotus Freelance Graphics or Microsoft PowerPoint), and more.

Student writing with annotations. Just about all of the examples in this book have student names associated with them—students from Austin Community College; University of Texas at Austin; Baker University in Baldwin City, Kansas; Kennesaw State University; Coastal Carolina College; and my own private online courses. These examples give you a realistic sense of what can reasonably be expected of students in introductory technical-writing courses—people at the beginning of their careers, taking courses, often holding down jobs, and taking care of families. And these examples are annotated—marginal comments point out key features in the examples.

Separate chapters on headings, lists, notices, and highlighting. Notice the page-design chapters in Part II. Elements like headings, bulleted and numbered lists, tables, special notices, graphics, and highlighting get their own chapters.

Step-by-step software procedures. It's about time we integrate software tasks such as creating numbered lists, tables, templates, styles, and other such essentials into our introductory technical-writing studies. In this book, you'll see steps for these tasks using Corel WordPerfect 8, Lotus Word Pro 9, Microsoft Word 97, Excel 97, Jasc's Paint Shop Pro 6, Lotus 1-2-3, and Freelance Graphics 9.

These applications were some of the leading software applications as of early 2000. However, Sun Microsystem's StarOffice is an interesting late entry into the software wars. It is available for free download at www.sun.com/staroffice. It includes word-processing, database, spreadsheet, graphics presentation, and groupware applications that are similar to Microsoft Office 97, Lotus SmartSuite 8, and Corel Suite 8.

Hypertext introduction. Built into this book is a belief that you will soon be creating Web pages as routinely as print documents. For this new medium, the concept of hypertext and the strategies for developing it are essential. You'll find a whole chapter on hypertext as well as steps for creating it and an example scenario.

HTML instruction for creating Web pages. In this book, you'll find directions not only for creating the obligatory bare-bones Web page but directions for using HTML to create headings, lists, notices, tables, graphics, highlighting, frames, and other important page-design elements. You'll find these directions in the chapters where they apply. For example, in the tables chapter, you'll not only read about designing tables but also about creating tables with HTML.

Note: This book is loaded with URLs—addresses to Web sites. It's very likely some will have changed by the time you read this book. Please see **www.io.com/~hcexres/power_tools** for updated URLs.

ACKNOWLEDGEMENTS

Thanks to Claire Brantley, Harcourt acquisitions editor, for spotting my online textbook on the World Wide Web and convincing me that printed textbooks are still needed; Julie McBurney and Bill Hoffman, subsequent editors, Marsena Konkle, development editor, and Keith Roberts of Graphic World Publishing Services for getting me through this project. I couldn't have done this without my family—specifically Patrick, Jane, and Phoebe. I also owe a deep debt of gratitude to Katherine Staples for rescuing me from The Machine; my friends and colleagues at IBM Corporation, Dell Computer, and Tivoli Systems who taught me a great deal about technical writing in the trenches. I also owe much coffee-based inspiration to the Java Café (the one on Metric), the Spider House (near the UT campus), Mojo Café (on the Drag), the Upper Crust Café, and Austin's Capital Metro bus system. And finally, thanks to the many technical-writing students, both those who wrote the examples and graciously agreed to let me adapt them here, as well as the many others who've helped me understand what works, and what doesn't, in the technical-writing classroom.

Table of Contents

Technical Writing: An Introduction

TECHNICAL COMMUNICATION

The technical communication profession is well-represented on the World Wide Web. Explore these links to find out what you could be getting into:

Society for Technical Communications (STC)—the largest professional organization for technical communicators. **www.stc.org**

Allyn & Bacon TechCommunity—an excellent guide to all things technical writing. **www.abacon.com/techcommunity**

The Institute of Electrical and Electronics Engineers Professional Communications Society (IEEE PCS)—the technical-communications arm of the international engineers society. **www.ieeepcs.org**

About.com. Technical writing—Gabriel Conroy, about.com guide—an equally excellent resource for all things technical writing. **techwriting.about.com/arts/techwriting**

TECHWR-L Mailing List Archive—search the archives of this mailing list and see what practicing technical writers talk about. **www.documentation.com/archives/techwrit/techwrit-l/ techwrit-l.htm**

Technical Communications Resources on the World Wide Web, developed by Teresa Ashley, Reference Librarian, Austin Community College. **library.austin.cc.tx.us/research/w3/voc_tech/tcm/tcm.htm**

Accessed January 3, 2001.

If you are just getting started with technical writing, you probably have the same questions that are addressed in this introduction:

- What is technical writing?
- What kind of writing is technical writing?
- Who are technical writers and what do they do?
- Why are there technical writing courses?

From the outset, however, understand that the point of this book, and of technical writing courses, is not to turn you into a full-time professional technical writer. If you are interested in that—great! Take a look at the resources in the box on page 1. The technical communication profession is a good one—plenty of interesting work, lots of new technology, plenty of rewards, and, oh yes, pretty good pay and benefits. As we plunge deeper and deeper into the high-tech revolution, technical writers will be more in demand and their work will be more diverse and interesting.

Although this book certainly can give you a good start in a technical writing career, its purpose is to show you some skills, techniques, concepts, and examples that will be valuable no matter what field, profession, or occupation you enter.

WHAT IS TECHNICAL WRITING, OR TECHNICAL COMMUNICATION?

Professional technical communicators prefer the term "technical communication" because the profession involves much more than writing. It involves communicating technical information through whichever communication tools do the job best. These tools include not only writing, but graphics, animation, video, and audio. Thus, even though "technical communication" is a mouthful, it more accurately describes what professionals in this field do. The following offers pieces of a definition of technical communication:

- communicates technical information
- has a specific purpose
- geared to the needs of a specific audience
- occurs in a specific workplace situation
- uses the communication tools that work best

Consider the definition in the following table part by part:

Defining Technical Communication

Communication	This definition uses *communication* rather than *writing* because technical communicators use not only words, but pictures, animation, sound, and video to present information.
Technical	The term *technical* refers not just to computers and electronics but to any body of knowledge, any craft or expertise not commonly understood. Thus, *technical* can refer not only to rocket science, but to carpentry, plumbing, auto repair, hair styling, gardening, cooking, welding, nursing, massage therapy, restaurant management, acupuncture and acupressure, music recording, accounting, commercial graphics, and many other fields, as well as to the fields we commonly think of as "technical," such as brain surgery, electronics, and—yes—rocket science.
Information	*Information* in the technical world includes user guides (how to operate something), reference manuals (details on a process, concept, or the functions of a product), quick-reference guides, installation guides, troubleshooting guides, recommendation reports, background reports, progress reports, proposals, research reports, and so on. Business letters, memos, and e-mail also may contain technical material.
Specific purpose	What is provided is not just information but information with a specific purpose for a specific set of readers. The purpose can be informative (what is this thing?), instructive (how do I use this thing?), or persuasive (I recommend we use this thing!). Technical communication is rarely literary (no sonnets in user guides) or expressive (no blowing off steam about the klugey product).
Specific audience	Audiences of technical communication are not only rocket scientists and brain surgeons, but ordinary people who may be "out of their depth" or "in over their heads." The users of technical information range from beginners to seasoned veterans. The most interesting challenges are those in which you must convey technical information to beginners and novices. That's why it's often best not to be an expert on a science or technology topic when you are writing for beginning and intermediate readers.
Needs	Audiences of technical writing have specific needs for information. They may need background on a topic, instructions for equipment, or recommendations on which product to purchase. They may need to know the structure or operation of equipment, or the causes or effects of a phenomenon. They may need a recommendation on which product to purchase or an evaluation of how well a program is working.
Specific situation	Most technical writing occurs within a specific framework in which a customer or client expects (and may even be paying for) the information. The information has direct professional, business, or industrial applications. It solves a workplace problem, responds to a need, or addresses an opportunity.
Tools	Technical communicators use a variety of communication methods to convey their message: words, sounds, images, and video. This information appears in print, online, and on screen. Technical writers may find themselves using FrameMaker to develop a printed book, ForeHELP to develop online helps, Dreamweaver to develop a Web site, Photoshop to create images, After Effects to create animation, and audio and video tools to create tutorials that run on a VCR.

WHAT KIND OF WRITING IS TECHNICAL WRITING?

It's too easy to pass off technical writing as factual, objective writing with lots of numbers and symbols. From the preceding, you already know that technical communication is not just informative or instructional but also seeks to convince or persuade.

Technical Texts

examples

Research reports. One of the classics of technical writing has long been the scientific research report. Traditionally, this type of report stays totally emotionless, uses exact words, loads sentences with statistical detail, interprets or speculates only in specially marked parts of the report, and uses all passive voice in an effort to sound objective.

The number of dead birds found on mortality plots did not differ from reference plots at $P = 0.05$ but did differ at $P = 0.10$ ($G = 2.982$, 1 df, $0.05 < P < 0.10$). While habitat type (i.e. agricultural vs. CRP) did not influence the number of dead birds found on mortality plots ($G = 0.53$, 1 df, $P > 0.05$; Table 1), end turbines (turbines at the end of a turbine string) were associated with a disproportionate number of dead birds ($G = 5.05$, 1 df, $P \leq 0.05$; Table 1). The seasonal mortality pattern did not differ from random at $P = 0.10$ ($G = 7.04$, 3 df, $0.50 < P < 0.10$). Mortality was higher than expected by chance in spring.[1]

[1] Adapted with permission from Robert G. Osborn, et al., "Bird Mortality Associated with Wind Turbines at the Buffalo Ridge Wind Resource Area, Minnesota," *American Midland Naturalist* 143 (2000):41-52.

User guides. Another of the "classics" of technical writing is the user guide—in other words, instructions. Unlike the scientific research report, user guides have become personal, direct, helpful, and friendly (but considerably short of Mister Rogers' neighborhood).

Configuring the program. Eudora needs only a little information to get you ready to start sending and receiving e-mail:

Click **Tools** and then select **Options** as shown in Figure 1. Eudora opens a dialog box with several option categories.

Choose the **Getting Started** icon in the Categories column.

Enter your POP Account in the space provided.

Note: If you are not sure what your POP account name is, contact your Internet service provider. Typically it's your user name.

Online helps. Online helps are those windows of quick reminders or quick helps you get when you press the Help button on most software applications. Helps differ from user-guide information in that they are shorter, serving more to remind than to teach. This difference is subtle, but compare this FTP help information to the Eudora user-guide information just above: helps are shorter and less explanatory.

Transferring Files or Folders

To transfer files or folders:

1. Select the files or folders on the source system.
2. Open the folder to which you want to transfer files on the destination system.
3. Select the file transfer mode.

Continued

Technical Texts cont'd.

4. Transfer the files using the left and right arrow buttons located between the list boxes.

Click the left arrow button to transfer files from the remote to the local system.

Click the right arrow button to transfer files from the local system to the FTP site.[2]

[2] Adapted with permission from Michael Caldwell, former technical writing student at Austin Community College.

Technical-support writing. With increasingly high-tech products going to nontechnical consumers, answering consumer telephone and e-mail problems has become an employment growth area. This writing is primarily internal: technical-support people write up problem–solution summaries and add them to a database that other technical-support people can use. (And increasingly, these same problem–solution databases are made available online to consumers.)

Problem: The battery pack cannot be fully charged in 3.5 hours by the power-off charging method.

Action: The battery pack might be over-discharged. Do the following:

1. Turn off the computer.
2. Make sure that the over-discharged battery pack is in the computer.
3. Connect the AC Adapter to the computer and let it charge.

If the battery pack cannot be fully charged in 24 hours, use a new battery pack.

Reference information. Reference information is encyclopedia-style information, typically presented in tables or alphabetically. It doesn't teach you how to use something; it tells you what the settings, features, modes, and variables are and what their effects are. In the example to the right, the reference information explains the function and format of one of many Perl command-line options. The complete set of options is arranged alphabetically. In contrast, user guides take a step-by-step, hand-holding approach.

-v Option

The -v option specifies which version of Perl is running on your machine. When the Perl interpreter sees this option, it prints information on itself and then exits without running your program. For example:

```
$ perl -v test1
```

produces output similar to the following:

```
This is perl, version 5.001

Copyright (c) 1987-1994, Larry Wall

Perl may be copied only under the terms of
either the Artistic License or the GNU
General Public License, which may be found
in the Perl 5.0 source kit.
```
[3]

[3] Adapted with permission from Red Hat, Inc.

Consumer literature. Government agencies and non-profit organizations often find themselves in the business of conveying technical information about environmental issues, regulations, and product safety

The average American household generates 15 pounds of household hazardous waste (HHW) each year. Our homes contain an average of 3 to 8 gallons of hazardous materials in kitchens, bathrooms,

Continued

Technical Texts cont'd.

concerns. This material is distributed to the public—in other words, consumers.

Information like the example here is indeed technical, but it is presented in such a way that ordinary citizens not only understand it, but feel obligated to comply with it.

garages, and basements. A four-city study, conducted by the University of Arizona, found the following proportions of HHW in the waste stream:

- household maintenance items 36.6 percent (paints, thinners, adhesives, etc.)
- household batteries 18.6 percent
- cosmetics 12.1 percent (includes nail polish and removers)
- cleaners 11.5 percent (includes polishes and oven cleaners)
- automotive items 10.5 percent (mostly motor oil)
- yard items 4.1 percent (includes pesticides, pet supplies, fertilizers)
- hobby/other 3.4 percent (pool chemicals, art supplies, etc.)
- pharmaceuticals 3.2 percent

These household hazardous wastes are sometimes disposed of improperly by individuals pouring wastes down the drain, on the ground, into storm sewers, or putting them out with the trash. The dangers of such disposal methods may not be immediately obvious, but certain types of household hazardous waste have the potential to cause physical injury to sanitation workers; contaminate septic tanks or wastewater treatment systems if poured down drains or toilets; and contaminate drinking water supplies below unlined landfills. They can also present hazards to children and pets if left around the house.[4]

[4] Adapted with permission from Texas Natural Resource Conservation Commission.

Consultant technical writing. Consultants regularly get involved in technical writing—in some cases, it's their primary work-getting tool and their primary work output. Consider proposals: they seek approval or contracts to do work and are typically loaded with technical information. Consider recommendation and feasibility reports: they advise recipients to take one course of action or another and pile on plenty of technical information to support that advice.

Jamie

Accuracy. Accuracy is the most significant consideration; without it, the program is useless. Dragon Systems' NaturallySpeaking scored highest on all of the accuracy tests performed by *PC Magazine* and was unequivocally selected as the Editors' Choice. In their tests, the average accuracy was 91% and at times was considerably greater [1].

Average accuracy for L&H Voice Xpress was 87% [2]. Accuracy for IBM's ViaVoice tested at 85% [14], and Philips FreeSpeech98 was 80% [15].

Although Dragon Systems' NaturallySpeaking is considerably more expensive, its accuracy, speed, ease of use, and flexibility justify the extra expense.[5]

[5] Adapted with permission from Dr. Pat Roach, former online technical writing student.

Continued

Technical Texts cont'd.

Marketing literature. Technical writers also get involved in marketing literature—product brochures and specifications, for example. This field is often called "marketing communication," or "marcom" for short. Marketing people, product planners, and technical writers team up to develop promotional literature for their products. In marketing-oriented technical writing, you see all the common inducements, promotion, and language that you would expect to see in any written advertisement.

Red Hat Linux 6.1

for Intel (x86), Alpha, and SPARC® platforms

Release 6.1 takes ease of installation to a new standard for Linux, and provides the workstation, server, and customer service features that are important to you. Red Hat delivers third party applications for personal productivity, all of the Internet server favorites such as Apache, SAMBA, and SendMail, and fast FTP access to updates from priority.redhat.com.

New Features:

- New, easier installation
- High availability clustering
- Enhanced systems management with LDAP integration
- Easy connection to the Internet with the new PPP Dialer
- Choice of KDE or GNOME default desktop[6]

[6] Adapted with permission from Red Hat, Inc.

Technical journalism. You've probably read plenty of newspaper and magazine articles on science and technology topics. The writers of this material are also "technical writers," although they may prefer the term "technical journalists." This form seeks to entertain as much as to inform. If you write about nanotechnology for *Omni* (a popular mainstream magazine devoted to science and technology topics), you want readers to go "Gee—wow!" as much as to feel more informed.

Notice in this example how the technical journalist highlights the human element and the excitement brought on by the impact of this discovery.

When Kary Mullis was a second-year grad student at Berkeley he wrote a paper called "The Cosmological Significance of Time Reversal," about how half the matter in the universe is going backwards in time. He sent it to *Nature* and they published it immediately, attributing it to a "Dr. Mullis." In 1983, 10 years after receiving his doctorate in biochemistry, a 39-year-old Mullis sent *Nature* another paper about a technique called polymerase chain reaction (PCR) that essentially amplifies DNA, enabling scientists to make millions of copies of a DNA molecule in an incredibly short time. *Nature* rejected it. Then *Science* rejected it. Over the next 10 years, however, the science world became convinced that PCR was the biggest advancement in molecular biology in decades. In 1993, Mullis was awarded a Nobel Prize in chemistry for an invention that shed new light on the quest to decode DNA.

From the moment he conceived of PCR, while gliding along the highway through the mountains of Northern California, Mullis knew the epic implications. He describes his revelation in his book, *Dancing Naked in the Mind Field*: "PCR was a chemical procedure that would make the structures of the molecules of our genes as easy to see as billboards in the desert and as easy to manipulate as Tinkertoys. . . ."[7]

[7] Adapted with permission from www.feedmag.com.

WHO ARE TECHNICAL WRITERS—WHERE ARE THEY?

Many people work part-time as technical writers—some are not even aware of it. Maybe even you are a technical writer and don't know it!

Part-time technical writers. Plenty of ordinary people in a wide variety of professions and occupations do part-time technical writing. They must routinely convey information about their expertise to others—often to others who are not experts. How these part-timers convey that technical information has much to do with the success of a project or the well-being of an organization or a community, not to mention their own professional and financial well-being. Communities, organizations, projects, and individuals cannot be successful without successful communication, including successful technical communication. Just about every technical profession involves a good measure of technical writing. That's one big reason why there are technical writing courses.

Practical Ethics: An Introduction

In church or in a business-ethics course, you'd not be surprised to hear the question: "What is the right or moral thing to do?" Because you're in neither place, you might be surprised or even a little annoyed to find that even in a technical writing course you must face ethical considerations. But it's true. As a technical writer, you might be expected to fudge test results in a report to the FDA. You might be tempted to suggest that a colleague's innovative idea is your own. You might neglect to mention the risks when writing about the benefits of a product. These are all situations in which that pesky question rears its head: "What is the right or moral thing to do?"

This question has been debated for centuries, and the answer is rarely easy or straightforward. Many companies and professional associations have ethical guidelines for their employees and members that can help. The matter can sometimes be resolved by simply considering the legal consequences of certain behavior.

However, Sam Dragga, a technical communications scholar, asked 48 technical communicators how they made moral choices and found that, for them, the process was "fluid and dynamic" rather than defined by critical thinking techniques or codes of conduct. Dragga reported that "while simple or unimportant issues may be decided individually according to conscience, complicated and critical issues are usually discussed with trusted colleagues or supervisors."[8] In other words, no textbook or theory on ethics can prepare you for every ethical situation, but at least you won't have to face these situations alone.

Scattered throughout this book are boxes titled "Practical Ethics" in which you will find scenarios describing typical dilemmas faced by technical communicators. You won't find hard and fast answers in this book, but the process of awakening your conscience to the possibility of such dilemmas and discussing them with others in your class or workplace will help you to contend with whatever dilemmas the future may throw your way.

[8] From Sam Dragga, "A Question of Ethics: Lessons from Technical Communicators on the Job," *Technical Communication Quarterly* 6 (1997): 2, 162.

Full-time professional technical writers. There are plenty of full-time professionals who consciously describe themselves as "technical writers" and "technical communicators." The classic technical writers work in places like Dell, IBM, Hewlett-Packard, Microsoft, Adobe, Motorola, and Compaq, where they develop user guides, online helps, and Web pages for hardware and software products. However, technical writers also work in plenty of noncomputer companies such as Boeing, Lockheed, Caterpillar, and General Motors. Look around: any expensive, complex equipment has a user guide or reference manual associated with it. Guess who wrote them!

Academic, government, research-oriented technical writers. Plenty of technical writers work in government agencies and academic institutions. Good examples are technical writers at the Texas Natural Resource Conservation Commission who write brochures, guides, and reports concerning environmental issues for the public. They also get involved in developing research reports, grant proposals, and other such materials.

Freelance technical writers. Lots of technical writers work freelance, usually specializing in a particular industry such as computers, aerospace, heavy machinery, or medicine. They work right alongside the full-timers doing similar tasks, but only for a set period of time.

Technical journalists. Some technical writers double as journalists. They write magazine and journal articles about various aspects of science, technology, medicine, health, and other such areas. As mentioned earlier, they often bring out the excitement of new developments in science and technology.

WHAT DO TECHNICAL WRITERS DO?

What do technical writers do? The answer is obvious—they write! Right? Actually, studies of full-time technical writers show that they write for only about one-fourth of the time they spend on the job.[9] The rest of the time is taken up in research, project meetings, and interviews with developers and engineers. They spend time sending and answering e-mail and working with prototypes of products they are documenting. If they are not documenting a product, they may be spending their time gathering and analyzing data for reports and interviewing the experts.

Experts are important to technical writers. Technical writers cannot stay at the same level of expertise with product developers, engineers, and research scientists. Instead, they rely on those people for information and reviews. Technical writers are a different kind of expert: they are experts in communication, document design, usability, and audience analysis. In this respect, when you study technical writing you play a role like that of the full-time technical writer. You start with a workplace requirement and you carefully analyze your audience. You are probably not an expert on your topic so you must find information, interview experts, and do other sorts of research—just like a technical writer.

WHY ARE THERE TECHNICAL-WRITING COURSES?

The need for technical writing courses should be obvious by now.

Employer demands. Leaders in every field, profession, and occupation demand good writing skills in their employees. Such skills are critical to the

[9] Jonathan Price and Henry Korman, *How to Communicate Technical Information* (Redwood City, CA: Benjamin/Cummings, 1993).

success and well-being of communities, organizations, professions, projects and individuals. General writing skills are one thing, but the skills you get in a technical writing course are more directly focused on scientific and technical needs. That's why most technical majors require technical writing courses.

Vital tool for any professional. Engineers, for example, tell us that they spend 20 to 40 percent of their work time writing memos, letters, e-mail, reports, and proposals. They also say that this percentage increases as they are promoted. And finally, they say that they wish they had had more writing courses in college.[10] In one survey, more than half of the graduates in technically oriented majors (for example, engineering, science, nursing) said that the ability to write well is of "great" or "critical" importance, and nearly all said that the ability to write well is important.[11] And it's not just the engineers: in a survey of graduates in a range of professional fields, three-fourths of the respondents rated writing as "very important," the highest rating possible.[12]

Powerful tool for other courses. Don't delay your technical writing course until the very last semester. Technical writing skills are valuable in writing projects you do for other courses. Knowing how to prepare a report, use headings and lists, construct tables and graphics, control highlighting, and make the finished product readable and professional looking—these are invaluable skills in academic courses as well as in the workplace.

Chance to explore science and technology. Practicality aside, a technical communication course can be one of the most stimulating of your academic career. Where else can you explore topics like the ones sprinkled throughout this book—extraterrestrial intelligence, global warming, electronic game design, wind energy, solar power, recycling, time travel, computer viruses, cloning, fractals, human expeditions to Mars, photovoltaics, brain research, nanotechnology, and so on? Where else are you challenged to explain how a light bulb works, how an acoustic speaker produces sound, how a photovoltaic device generates electricity from the sun, how a CD-ROM holds over 600 megabytes of sound or data, how a television produces color and images on screen, how a computer adds two simple numbers, or why the sky is blue?

WORKSHOP: TECHNICAL COMMUNICATION

Here are some suggestions for exploring technical communication in the workplace:

1. *Interview professionals.* Interview professionals in your field concerning the amount of writing they do, the types and purposes of the

---

[10] David Beer and David McMurrey, *Guide to Writing as an Engineer* (New York: Wiley, 1997).
[11] Paul V. Anderson, "What Survey Research Tells Us about Writing at Work," in *Writing in Nonacademic Settings* ed. Lee Odell and Dixie Goswami (New York: Guilford, 1985), 3–85.
[12] Lorie Roth, "Education Makes a Difference: Results of a Survey of Writing on the Job," *Technical Communication Quarterly* 2 (1993): 177–184.

writing they do, the importance of that writing, and any recommendations they may have for you or your technical writing instructor. Consider designing a questionnaire that you can send to professionals or fill out as you interview them.

2. *Analyze an organization chart for written work.* Get together with two or three other students in your field or major, draw up an organization chart typical of companies or agencies in your field, and identify the kinds of writing that employees located at various areas in that organization do. Identify who writes what to whom, and the purposes and characteristics of that writing. Don't forget to identify writing that stays within an area of the organization and writing that travels outside of the organization (for example, to customers or the public).

3. *Analyze samples of technical writing.* Find two or three examples of technical writing that are dramatically different—in terms of content, approach, intended audience, technical level, design, and so on. Define the audience, purpose, and situation of these examples.

4. *Compare technical writing for different audiences.* Find two technical documents on the same subject—one written for experts, the other written for novices (people untrained or inexperienced in the subject matter). Identify what the novice version does to help readers understand the subject matter; identify what the expert version *doesn't* do.

5. *Analyze a technical document from another field.* Find a technical document, written for an expert audience, in some other field that you know little or nothing about. Identify what the writer could do to enable you to understand that document, noting things like definitions, historical background, examples, and so on.

6. *Summarize your findings.* As directed by your technical writing instructor, select one of the preceding workshops and summarize your findings in a memo to your technical writing class. Better yet, meet with two or three other students, consolidate your findings, and team-write the memo.

PART I

Project Tools for Technical Writers

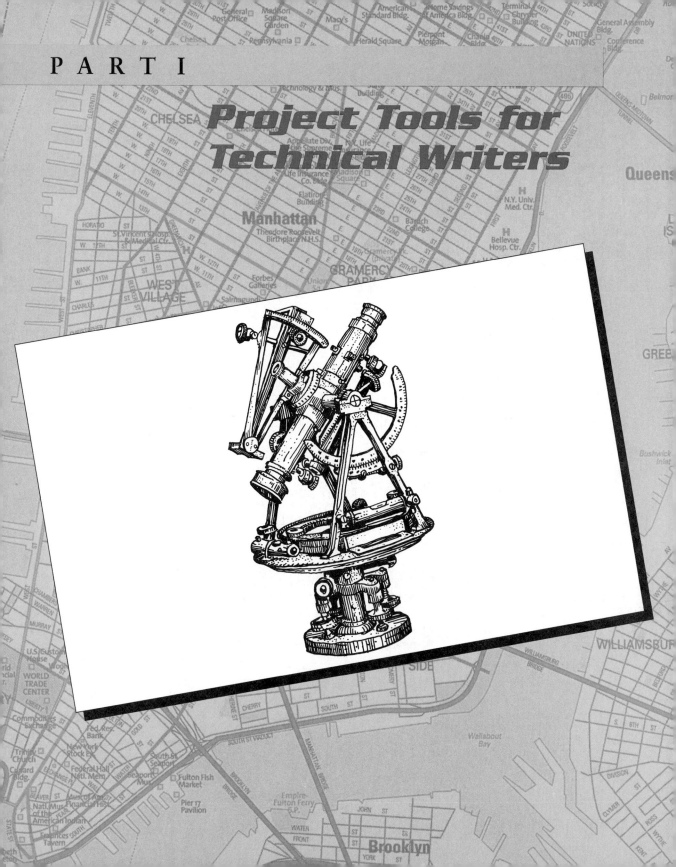

CHAPTER 1

Description: Product Specifications and Informal Reports

SOLAR POWER: SOLAR AUTOMOBILES

On the Internet you'll find plenty of activity involving uses of solar energy. Particularly exciting is the ongoing work to develop viable solar-powered automobiles.

Matt's Solar Car Page. **www-lips.ece.utexas.edu/~delayman/solar.html**

Junior Solar Sprint. **www.nrel.gov/education**

NREL Hybrid Electric Vehicle Program. **www.ott.doe.gov/hev/**

University of British Columbia, Solar Car Project.
www.physics.ubc.ca/~solarcar/raven/default.html

Mr. Solar Home Page. **www.mrsolar.com**

Photovoltaic Power Resource Site. **www.pvpower.com**

U.S. Department of Energy, Energy Efficiency and Renewable Energy Network Solar Buildings Home page.
www.eren.doe.gov/solarbuildings

Solar car page of Samer Abou-Sweid, mechanical engineering student at the University of Western Ontario.
publish.uwo.ca/~syabousw/ElectricCars.html

Accessed January 4, 2001.

Many applications of technical writing rely on description as an essential infrastructure. As you know from the Preface, an *infrastructure* in this context is a special combination of content and organization that enables a technical document to do its work. A *description* is a special combination of physical, quantifiable details with part-by-part organization. The applications covered in this chapter—product specifications and informal reports—commonly use description as their infrastructure.

This chapter shows you how to write descriptions and then how to construct product specifications and informal reports with description built in as the infrastructure.

Note:
- If you are new to this book, see "How Do You Use This Book?" in the Preface.
- For additional examples of the documents discussed in this chapter, see **www.io.com/~hcexres/power_tools/examples**. On this Web site you will also find an additional example of technical writing: a bid specification for the construction of single-story purple martin birdhouses.

HOW DO YOU WRITE A DESCRIPTION?

Before getting into the details of new-product specifications and informal reports, take a moment to review description, the essential infrastructure used in these documents. In this context, *description* means the presentation of physical, quantifiable details about some object. Physical details include color, shape, size, texture, materials of construction, ingredients, weight, height, width, depth, and so on. Quantifiable details are those you can count or measure, such as the number of trees on a vacant lot, the number of inhabitants of a city, geographical locations, or distances.

One of the best, most organized ways to present this physical, quantifiable detail is the *part-by-part approach* (see Figure 1-1). Think of the simple wooden pencil. You can describe the lead, the wooden barrel, the eraser, and that metal clip that holds the barrel and eraser together.

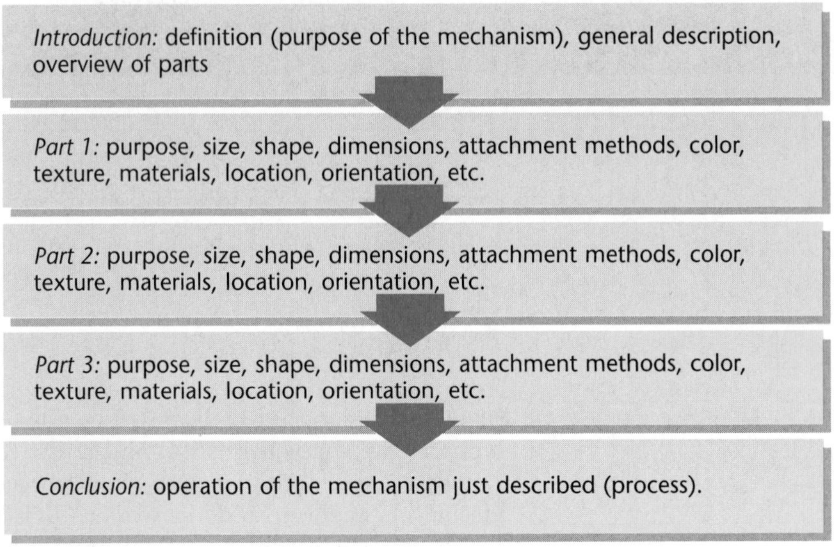

Introduction: definition (purpose of the mechanism), general description, overview of parts

Part 1: purpose, size, shape, dimensions, attachment methods, color, texture, materials, location, orientation, etc.

Part 2: purpose, size, shape, dimensions, attachment methods, color, texture, materials, location, orientation, etc.

Part 3: purpose, size, shape, dimensions, attachment methods, color, texture, materials, location, orientation, etc.

Conclusion: operation of the mechanism just described (process).

FIGURE 1-1

Part-by-part description. Describing part by part enables you to take a more organized approach to description. Describe each part in one or more sentences or in one or more paragraphs.

Describe each of these parts separately in a sentence or two, or even a whole paragraph.

Of course, there are other ways to organize a description. Sometimes the thing you want to describe does not divide as neatly into parts as does the wooden pencil. For example, describing a vacant lot for real estate purposes might work better with the *characteristics approach*—location, dimensions, vegetation, structures, soil, and so on.

The following steps walk you through the important phases in writing a simple description using the part-by-part approach. To get a sense of how the steps work in a writing project, we follow a single example through all of the steps.

1. **Find a simple project involving description.** Try finding a situation in which specific readers need a description. For example, insurance adjusters need flood damage descriptions and real estate investors need property descriptions. But why would anyone need descriptions of bottle openers, corkscrews, sunglasses, coffee cups, or wooden pencils? One possibility is product specification. In manufacturing, marketing specialists need descriptions for advertisement planning; manufacturing specialists, for planning the manufacture of the product; financial specialists, for planning production costs and projected revenues. (Having trouble thinking of a topic? See **www.io.com/ ~hcexres/power_tools/topics.html**.)

Imagine that you've decided to describe a bow saw—the kind of saw used to cut tree limbs. It has very coarse teeth that quickly rip through wood. Why is this description needed? Let's use the product specification idea: your company is developing a new bow saw. All interested parties in the company need to do their respective planning work in relation to this new product. They all need a description of the product for their marketing, manufacturing, financial, packaging, and distribution planning.

2. **Define the purpose and audience for the project.** The next step is to clarify the purpose and audience. (See Chapter 19 on analyzing audiences and adapting to them.) If you've found a real or realistic situation for a description, then your audience and purpose are almost defined already.

For this bow saw description, picture an audience of marketing, manufacturing, financial, and distribution planners. Marketing people need information for advertisements and catalogs. Manufacturing people need to know dimensions and materials of construction. Financial planners need information for projecting manufacturing costs and potential revenues. Distribution planners need information such as size, dimensions, and weight to plan packaging and distribution. To simplify matters, let's write the bow saw description for manufacturing planners only.

3. **Research the thing you are describing.** Early in a project, you may need to research the object you've chosen to describe. In particular, you'll need part names and various specifications. Listed below are resources that contain labeled pictures of thousands of objects. These resources explain the processes by which equipment works and you'll find plenty of terminology about parts and construction.

Brain, Marshall. *How Stuff Works:* **www.howstuffworks.com**
Clarke, Donald, Ed. *The Encyclopedia of How It Works: From Abacus to Zoom Lens.*
Clarke, Donald, and Mark Dartford. *The New Illustrated Science and Invention Encyclopedia: The New How It Works.*
Corbeil, Jean Claude, Ed., Ariane Archambault. *Macmillan Visual Dictionary*
Macaulay, David, and Neil Ardley. *The New Way Things Work.*
Sutton, Caroline. *How Do They Do That? Wonders of the Modern World Explained.*

If you searched the Web on bow saws, you'd probably be surprised at how much you'd find. Much of course is advertisement. Still, you can find some nice images to borrow (legally, if you cite the source) as well as dimensions and other specifications.

4. **Plan and develop graphics.** Try to visualize the graphics needed in your description. Use the strategies in Chapter 10 and Chapter 11 to plan the drawings, diagrams, photos, and charts you need to include.

> A good graphic for the bow saw description is obviously a labeled drawing of the bow saw itself, and perhaps also a close-up of the saw blade showing the teeth. Because specifications are important for this description, label the drawing with various measurements (lengths and widths of the parts of the bow saw).

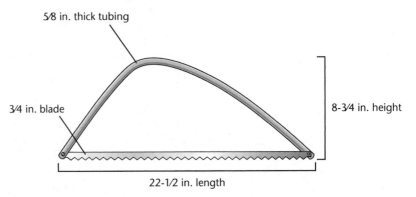

5. **Identify the parts and subparts.** Make a list of the parts whose descriptions best meet the needs of your audience. For this practice description, try to discuss at least four parts of the item. Omit unimportant parts such as electrical cords. Don't forget to list important subparts. For example, a description of a mechanical pencil would include details on the subparts of the lead-advancing mechanism.

> How many parts does this bow saw have? Two? Three? First, there is the saw blade with its jagged teeth. There is also the C-shaped handle—or should it be called the frame, or the brace? You'll have to research that one. This particular bow saw has a plastic or rubber grip on part of the handle.

6. **Plan the overall description.** You'll also need an overall description of the object. Think of that wooden pencil. Describing the parts is not enough; you still need to describe characteristics that the part-by-part descriptions cannot address, such as the overall length and the overall weight. The overall description may also need a definition of the thing you are describing.

> The overall description of the bow saw must include its fully assembled weight, length, and height. Define it according to how and why the bow saw is useful.

7. **Plan the description of each part.** One of the next steps is to decide the order in which to describe each part and whether to spend a few sentences or an entire paragraph on each part.

In this example description, describe each part in a separate paragraph:
- *Saw blade*—explain its purpose; provide details on its length, height, and width; its materials of construction and color; and precise details about the saw teeth.
- *Handle*—explain its purpose; describe its length, shape, color, materials of construction, and its diameter; include details as to where and how much it angles and where and how much it tapers. Also explain how the saw blade is attached.
- *Grip*—explain its purpose, and then describe the grip in terms of its materials of construction, length, thickness, color, and method of attachment to the handle.

8. **Sketch the headings you'll use.** If your description is going to be more than two or three paragraphs, use headings (see Chapter 7). If you describe each part in one or more separate paragraphs, create a heading to identify each part.

For the description of the bow saw, let's use "Saw blade," "Handle," and "Grip" as the headings to introduce the description of these parts.

9. **Select the sources of description.** One problem with practice descriptions is that they fail to provide enough descriptive detail. Use the sources of description listed in the table on page 20 as a way of thinking of that extra detail. These sources are like tools you can use to develop a description to its fullest.

This bow saw description obviously does not need to draw on all of these sources of description. Include details as to its size, shape, color, finish, texture, weight, methods of attachment, materials of construction, and pattern (in the handle or of the teeth). Anything else?

10. **Plan an introduction.** Introductions must indicate the *topic* and *purpose* of the document and provide an overview of what will be discussed. Also included must be an *audience identifier* to help readers decide whether the information is suited to their needs, interests, and knowledge level. Descriptions should also include a list of parts to be described and an *overall description*.

Imagine that you've written a short paragraph on each of the parts of the bow saw, along with the overall description. For the introduction, indicate the topic, audience, and purpose—an informative description to enable manufacturing planners to develop plans to

Sources of Description

Source of description	Comments
Purpose	How is the item used? What are it applications?
Size	How big or small is it? Can you compare its size to something familiar?
Shape	How is it shaped? Can you compare its shape to something familiar?
Color	What are its colors?
Texture, finish	How does it feel to the touch—rough, smooth, grainy, wavy? How does it look—shiny, glossy, dark, dull?
Dimensions	What are its length, height, width, depth?
Weight	How much does it weigh?
Materials of construction	What materials are used in its construction—wood, steel, aluminum, cardboard?
Ingredients	If it is something that is mixed, what are the ingredients?
Methods of attachment	How are the different parts attached—glued, welded, bolted or screwed on, nailed in?
Location, orientation of parts	What's the orientation of the parts to each other—above, below, to the left, to the right, within?
Age	How old is it?
Temperature	Is temperature an important descriptive detail?
Moisture content	What's the percentage of water content?
Amounts	How many are there?
Capacity	How much can it hold?
Volume	What are the various measurements of volume related to it?
Smell, odor	What does it smell like?
Pattern, design	Does it have a certain pattern or design associated with it?

manufacture the bow saw. Define the bow saw and discuss its uses. Indicate that you are about to provide a part-by-part description and list the parts to be described. Because the overall description is brief, include it in the introduction.

11. Consider the format. For this simple project, you don't need the elaborate report formats shown in Chapter 15. Instead, use the format of the example description of the flashlight at the end of this chapter.

Purpose: This description begins the overall purpose of the thing to be described.

Sources of description: Notice the different sources used here: output (in watts and voltage); construction components (arrays, subarrays, panels, cells); orientation (southerly direction and 40° tilt); quantities (100 kw, 3000 panels, 10 cells, 3 panels); dimensions (inches); other components (inverters, transformers, feed lines, meters); financial details and percentages.

Illustration: Wouldn't it help to have a diagram that illustrated the relationships of the panels, arrays, subarrays, sections, and cells here?

Source: U.S. Department of Energy. History of the Beverly, Massachusetts Photovoltaic Array www.eren.doe.gov/solarnow/beverly.htm

Beverly High School in Beverly, Massachusetts, uses a system of solar photovoltaic flat-plate panels to generate its electricity needs. Currently, this system produces 100 kw, but could produce considerably more with some simple modifications. The Beverly photovoltaic system is made up of more than 3,000 panels. Each panel contains 10 photovoltaic cells. The photovoltaic array is made up of separate subarrays of photovoltaic modules deployed in rows on a southerly facing slope. Each subarray is made from 3 standalone (but electrically integral) sections called panels, supported by a portable mechanical jack. Although the panels can be manually tilted to follow the path of the sun, they have been put in a stationary position that optimizes their exposure to the sun. Each panel measures 292 inches by 93 inches and contains 10 photovoltaic cells. The power generated by these panels is transmitted at 4160 v from the inverters and a step-up transformer to the main 4160 v utility feed line into the school. Separate meters are used to measure power bought from or sold to the local utility. At the optimum tilt angle—about 40 degrees—the array provides about 14% of the annual school load. This amounts to annual energy savings of between $8,000–$16,000.

FIGURE 1-2

Description using the part-by-part approach. Although this description is a single paragraph, you can see where the description of each part begins and ends.

Use a descriptive title centered at the top of the page and second- and third-level headings. Use lists, illustrations, tables, and citations of your borrowed information sources, as necessary.

This bow saw description is an initial overview of the product idea, not likely to require more than two pages. Let's use the memo format, with "Working description of the new bow saw product" in the subject line. Use headings, subheadings, lists, graphics, and tables in this memo just as you would in any report.

12. Review and revise your rough draft. Use the strategies in Chapter 18 to systematically review and revise your description. Use the top-down approach described in Chapter 18: start by reviewing for audience, purpose, and situation; then move on to content, organization, and transitions; then work with headings, lists, tables, and graphics; then sentence style revision and technical style; and finally grammar, usage, spelling, and punctuation problems.

Understanding the essential infrastructure (description) will enable you to write heavily detailed but well organized technical documents such as those discussed in the next sections of this chapter.

HOW DO YOU WRITE PRODUCT SPECIFICATIONS?

Specifications describe purchaser requirements for products, projects, and services. If a local garden store hired you to build birdhouses that it would sell, the store owner would give you specifications as to the dimensions, materials, and construction of those birdhouses. As shown in Figure 1-3, some specifications are just tables of numbers and words, requiring little actual writing.

Specifications not only describe the physical characteristics of something. They also specify *operational* characteristics: how the thing will run or work,

Specifications: Chickadee Birdhouse	
Type of bird	Chickadee
Floor	5-1/2″ × 4″
Front	8″ × 5-1/2″
Sides (2)	8″ × 5-1/2″
Back	11″ × 5-1/2″
Entrance hole	1-1/8″ centered 1″ below the top of the front piece
Material	Ash
Construction	Brass screws (not nails or glue)

FIGURE 1-3

Specifications for a birdhouse. Some specifications do not require writing, just tables of numbers and words, as in these specifications for chickadee birdhouses.

Texas Native Sun II (developed by the Longhorn Solar Race Car Team at the University of Texas, Austin)	
Chassis	1″ OD T6 Aluminum, 48 lbs.
Suspension	Front: unequal length, double-wishbone with coil overdamper; Rear: trailing arm with coil overdamper
Body	3/8″ balsa wood sandwiched with 0.02″ carbon fiber
Drive train	DC brushless motor with chain-drive transmission to rear wheel
Speed	55 mph (cruising)
Dimensions	Width: 1.9 m (74.8″) Height: 1.2 m (46″) Length: 4.4 m (173.2″)
Weight	1000 lbs.
Solar cells	792 cells, 14% efficient, terrestrial-grade silicon
Array area	8 m^2 (89 ft^2)
Peak array output	1.1 Kw

FIGURE 1-4

Specifications for a solar race car. Notice that the specifications for speed and output are operational characteristics. The rest are construction specifications.

how it will hold up under certain kinds of wear and tear, and so on. Specifications like these can also be captured in table form, as Figure 1-4 shows. Some specifications are performance or operationally oriented only. That is, they specify how the product or service should perform but say nothing about its materials, constructions, dimensions, or other such details.

Precise, clear writing is critical in specifications. If the product is not built "to spec" or if the product or service does not perform "to spec," someone could be headed for a lawsuit. That's one reason why specifications have a particular style, format, and organization and why some technical writers spend their whole careers as specification writers. If specification writing is so specialized, why consider it here? It's an excellent challenge to your ability to describe with great precision. Here are some characteristics to notice about specifications:

- Use decimal-style numbering for sections and each individual detailed specification.
- Use exact numbers for measurements and other such details. Use numerals rather than words for numbers.
- Include operational specifications as well as physical ones, as necessary.
- Use "shall" to indicate requirements.
- Use precise language that cannot be interpreted in multiple ways. In other words, avoid ambiguity.
- Use a terse writing style. Incomplete sentences and omission of understood words are acceptable. (A great chance to use fragments!)
- Be careful with pronouns such as "it" or "they" and conjunctions such as "which" and "that." Make sure there is no doubt of what pronouns refer to and what modifiers modify.
- Make sure your specifications are complete in terms of their expected purpose: for example, be sure to specify the grade and thickness of wood for those birdhouses.

The following walks you through the most important steps in writing a simple set of specifications. To get a sense of how these steps work in an actual writing project, we'll follow another example throughout.

1. Find a project requiring specifications. When you study technical writing, you must often "work backwards" from a topic you want to write about to the reasons for writing about it and the people for whom you write. If you can find someone in need of specifications, great! For example, your next door neighbor may want a deck. Write the specifications capturing the exact design and dimensions your neighbor wants. However, if your neighbor already has a deck, find a simple object for which someone might require specifications. Simple things like cabinets, shelves, gardens, fences, woodsheds, or doghouses work just fine.

Imagine you want to write construction specifications for that chickadee house with the dimensions shown in Figure 1-3. These will be design and construction specifications like those in the example specifications shown at **www.io.com/~hcexres/power_tools/examples**.

2. **Define the purpose, audience, and situation.** Specifications provide excellent practice in adjusting your writing to a specific audience, purpose, and situation. The customer has specific requirements as to what the product or service should be and how it should work. It's your job to capture those physical and operating characteristics in your specifications.

   Why write specifications for a chickadee birdhouse? Imagine that you work at a wildlife center whose owner wants to sell all sorts of wildlife products, such a birdhouses. She wants you to write specifications for chickadee birdhouses as well as other products to be sold at the center. She will then send out these specifications to craftspeople who will bid on the construction work for these wildlife shelters. Thus your specifications capture your boss's ideas as to the design of these products and enable craftspeople to bid on these building projects.

3. **Write the scope and definitions sections as necessary.** A *scope statement* defines what you will specify, what you will not specify, and who will have which roles and responsibilities. A *definitions section* establishes the meanings of any terms that you use in a specialized way. If these sections are short enough, they can be consolidated into the introduction, or combined into a section of their own.

   In the scope and responsibilities section, define what the contractor must do and what happens if the contractor must deviate from the specs. In the definitions section, explain who the "contractor," "bidder," "client," and "owner" are. Ensure that the contractor knows what you mean by such terms as "wood," "screws," and "glue."

4. **Provide a general description of the product or service.** Include an overall description of the product or service. In the design section, the part-by-part description cannot address overall details such as overall length, width, height and other such details. These are addressed in the overall description.

   Let's provide a brief description of the completed chickadee house: how tall, wide, and deep it is; where the entrance hole is located; and so on. If possible, supply a labeled drawing as well.

5. **Write a materials sections, if needed.** Consider including a section specifying requirements for materials to be used. What kind of wood, hardware, nails, screws, glue, paint, plastic, and so on will be

necessary? If these materials are easy enough to specify in the design section, you can dispense with a separate materials section.

In these specifications, be sure to "spec out" the materials you expect the contractor to use. What type of wood? What type of fasteners? If wood screws, what type and size? If glue must be used, what type or brand?

6. Write the design section. The design section contains the most excruciatingly detailed and precise writing you may ever do. In this section, you proceed part by part specifying dimensions, clearances, materials of construction, attachment methods, and so on.

Now comes the hard part. In the design section, you'll wear out the word *shall*. Use the same approach that you see in the example specs shown at **www.io.com/~hcexres/power_tools/examples**. Each main part is introduced, and its specifications and its attachment to other parts are explained. Notice that each sentence uses decimal numbering. If several statements must be made about an individual part, those statements are indented and given lower-level decimal numbering.

7. Write an operating characteristics section, if needed. The type of specifications discussed here are primarily for the design and construction of a product. But even this type must include requirements for operation. For example, how much load can the product bear? If some part slides in and out, should it slide smoothly without binding? Certain characteristics cannot be specified physically with numbers, dimensions, materials, and so on. You must state *operational requirements* instead.

Fortunately, the specifications for the chickadee birdhouses need no operating instructions. The craftspeople will bang these birdhouses out and then the nature center will sell them. Purchasers will need to know how to set up these birdhouses, where to place them, and how to clean them periodically; but those are instructions, and that's another chapter (Chapter 2 to be precise).

8. Write the introduction for your specifications. In an introduction to specifications, you can state the purpose of the document, the product or service to be described, the recipient or customer of these specifications, and any administrative details such as cost or project dates relating to the project.

In a simple introduction, state who owns the specifications as well as the design and the finished chickadee houses. Also provide an overview. For example, state that these specifications contain scope and responsibilities statements, definitions, materials requirements, design specifications, and inspection requirements.

9. **Consider the format.** See the various report formats shown in Chapter 15. Typically, specifications are a separate formal document with a cover letter or memo attached to the front.

    Write the chickadee house specifications as a separate document. Use headings, subheadings, lists, graphics, and tables in this document just as you would in any other technical document. Attach a simple cover memo, addressed to the owner of the wildlife center, stating that the specifications she requested are attached and that she should let you know if she finds any problems with them.

10. **Review and revise your rough draft.** Use the strategies in Chapter 18 to systematically review and revise your specifications. Use the top-down approach described in that chapter: start by reviewing for audience, purpose, and situation; then moving on to content, organization, transitions; then headings, lists, tables, graphics; then on to sentence style revision, technical style; and finally grammar, usage, spelling, and punctuation problems.

HOW DO YOU WRITE INFORMAL REPORTS?

If you browse a big stack of technical writing textbooks (and there are plenty), you'll see a category of reports loosely called "informal," made up of things like site reports, inspection reports, accident reports, field trip reports, investigation reports, and so on. These informal reports are rather similar: they have description as their primary infrastructure; and they are usually written internally. But before starting, consider these distinctions:

■ **Site and inspection reports.** A site or inspection report is a description of a site: a building, a lot, a facility, equipment, and so on. It provides objective details important to a particular audience, for example, realtors. If it evaluates whether the property is a good investment, it is a recommendation or evaluation report, discussed in Chapter 4.

■ **Accident reports.** The accident report takes the site report several steps further. Not only does it describe something (in this case, an accident), it may also delve into the causes of that accident. In this case, you use the strategies for discussing causes and effects discussed in Chapter 3. Discussing causes and effects naturally forces you to write about *processes:* event-by-event discussions of how the accident occurred. See strategies for discussing processes in Chapter 2.

■ **Trip reports.** Trip reports can be the least descriptive, and they overlap the other informal reports discussed here. If you went to a professional conference or industry exposition you might be expected to turn in a summary of your observations (along with the expense report). Plenty of description would be needed and the report might read more like a narrative (in which case, you'd use the strategies for writing about processes presented in Chapter 2).

■ **Investigative, analytical reports.** Another type of informal report not only describes and considers causes, problems, and solutions, but also includes some research to determine whether those causes or solutions are in fact the most likely or the most effective. In this case, the report uses the strategies of primary research report, presented in Chapter 3.

Here are the essential steps and considerations for writing an informal report.

1. **Find a project for an informal report.** Use the definitions of the different informal reports to get some ideas. For example, you could go inspect a building, a vacant lot, some equipment, or you could go inspect a wrecked car or flood damage.

   Imagine that you work for the police department and have been assigned the task of describing a car accident and doing some preliminary speculations as to the causes.

2. **Identify and analyze the audience, purpose, and situation.** You're lucky if you work in a situation in which your job is to write informal reports. If not, work backward to define an audience and situation. For example, if you inspect a vacant lot, you might be working for a real estate investment company. If you inspect flood or tornado damage, you might be doing so for an insurance adjustment company.

Practical Ethics: Biased Language

Nobody wants to be reduced to a stereotype, especially when it comes to race, age, religion, gender, or physical status. Stereotyping people isn't courteous, and from a practical writing standpoint, readers who feel they're being unfairly stereotyped simply won't listen to what you're trying to communicate.

There are very few instances in which it's even necessary to mention a person's nationality, disability, or religion. The authors of *The Business Writer's Handbook* point out that "identifying people by such categories is simply not relevant in most workplace writing. Telling readers than an engineer is Native American or that a professor is African-American almost never conveys useful information."[1] Mentioning this type of information has the added negative impact of implying that it's unusual for people of a certain background to hold these positions. This implication is both untrue and offensive.

If you work for a company that is expanding into new territory and you have to write an informative memo acquainting salespeople with the demographics of this territory, facts about culture, religion, and age might be relevant and necessary. In this case (and others like it), take the time to choose descriptive words that inform without being derogatory. Use *Native American* instead of *Indian*, *mentally handicapped* instead of *retarded*, *Christian* instead of *Bible thumper*.

Taking care to avoid biased language will go far in assuring that whatever you write will be received openly by a wide and diverse audience. It's only common sense.

[1] Alred, Gerald, Brusaw, and Oliu. *The Business Writer's Handbook*. New York: St. Martin's Press, 2000, p. 75.

Your audience is the police department and, potentially, insurance representatives and those involved in the accident. Each of these sets of readers has different interests and needs. Each group uses different language, although the special terminology used by the police and insurance agents is likely to be similar and nearly unintelligible to the third group—those involved in the accident. Your report must be understood by all three audiences.

3. **Do the necessary research and investigation.** A nice thing about informal reports is that you get out of the house, the dorm, or the library. Take your camera, tape measure, and notebook to the site and record as much detail as you can—whatever is relevant to your audience, purpose, and situation.

How do you reconstruct the accident? You use police accident reports, visit the scene of the accident, and conduct interviews. You may need to review city traffic ordinances in case the accident falls into a gray area between multiple laws.

4. **Identify the things you must describe.** For most descriptions, you must use the part-by-part or characteristics approach. How does that work in terms of a building, for example? Describe the location and the surroundings; then the exterior, breaking that down in roof, siding, windows, doors, and so on; then the individual rooms; and finally infrastructural things such as plumbing, electrical, and heating and cooling systems.

You must describe the location where the accident occurred and the damage to the vehicles. You may also need to describe the injuries received by those involved.

5. **If narration is needed, discuss the events step by step.** You may need to provide a brief narration of what you did or what happened. For example, if you went to an exposition or took a tour of a facility, describe what you saw event by event.

In the accident report, attempt to reconstruct and then narrate the accident, step by step. This will be a challenge: you'll get different information from the people involved. You might even need to interview witnesses to the accident for their perception.

6. **If causal discussion is needed, identify the related causes.** Your job may be more than just a site description. You may have to determine what caused the problem at that site; for example, damage caused by a flood, fire, mudslide, or structural collapse. If so, describe the damage in one section. In another section, either (a) compare the possible causes, attempting to determine the primary

one, or (b) carefully walk through the obvious cause step by step, event by event.

Obviously, determining the causes of the car accident will be an important part of your work on this project. Ultimately, who was at fault and why?

7. If primary research is needed, set up and collect data from your research. Instead of speculating on causes or the solutions, you may have to confirm your viewpoint through experiments. If so, design the report like a primary research report: discuss your experimental method, data, conclusions, and recommendation. See Chapter 3 for discussion and examples.

This accident report doesn't seem to require primary research, but don't dismiss the possibility outright. What if the accident occurred at a tricky intersection at which many other accidents have occurred? If so, interview locals to see what they think. Perhaps run some informal experiments to see if you have any problems at the intersection. Observe traffic at the intersection to see if a high rate of near-accidents occurs.

8. Organize and rough-draft your informal report. Once you've identified all the pieces of information that must go into your informal report, find a way to organize it. The best plan may be to start with objective descriptive and narrative information and then move on to interpretive discussion such as causes and effects.

In this accident report, create a section that narrates the accident neutrally, without interpretation, and then describes the damage. Then summarize the different perspectives on the accident from the different parties involved, including witnesses. End with your view of what happened and why it happened.

9. Consider the format. Chapter 15 shows that you can design an informal report for e-mail or as a memorandum or a business letter. It can be a separate report with a cover letter or memo, an oral report, or it can be posted on the World Wide Web. The informal report at the end of this chapter is a self-contained memo written from one member of an engineering consulting firm to another. If the description is more than three pages, consider using a cover memo or letter and making the report a separate, attached document.

In the accident report, use the business letter format; this communication goes to different people in different organizations. After the introductory paragraph, use "Accident: Events and Damage" as the heading for objective narration of the accident and the objective description of the damage. To introduce the summary of the different viewpoints, use "Different Perspectives" as the heading. For your interpretation and conclusion, use "Conclusions" as the heading. Throughout, use lists, graphics, and tables in this letter just as you would in a report.

10. **Review and revise your rough draft.** Use the strategies in Chapter 18 to systematically review and revise your informal report. Use the top-down approach described in Chapter 18: start by reviewing for audience, purpose, and situation; then moving on to content, organization, transitions; then headings, lists, tables, graphics; then on to sentence style revision, technical style; and finally grammar, usage, spelling, and punctuation problems.

WORKSHOP: DESCRIPTION

Here are some additional ideas for practicing the concepts, tools, and strategies in this chapter:

1. *Identify parts.* The part-by-part approach is one of the keys to writing detailed, well-organized descriptions. See how many parts you can name for one or more of the following objects:

Bicycle without gears or hand brakes	A flower	Molly bolt
Ordinary pliers	An ant	Spray bottle
Classroom desk-chair	Reading glasses	TV remote

2. *Plan the sources of description.* For one or more of the objects for which you just listed parts, make a list of the sources of description you would use to describe those parts.

3. *Identify sources of description.* Take a look at the following description and list the sources of description you see.

The CheapTech BikeLite is simply a battery-powered light source which can be attached to a bicycle for visibility when riding at night. As it uses light-emitting diodes (LEDs) to provide its light, it is small (about 7 x 5 x 4 cm) and light enough (approximately 60 g including the battery) to be detached and slipped into the rider's pocket when not in use. The BikeLite consists of two major parts: the LED unit, which contains five LEDs together with the necessary electronics and battery; and the mounting bracket, which is used to fix the BikeLite on to a bicycle frame. The LED unit is detachable, and is fixed to the bracket using a plastic clip. If required, the clip can also be used to fix the unit to a belt or other article of clothing.

4. *Write a brief description.* Take a look at the instructions and specifications for creating any of the following, and write a detailed description of the completed item:

   House for American robins and barn swallows:
   http://www.npwrc.usgs.gov/resource/tools/ndblinds/robin.htm
   House Wren, Black-capped Chickadee, White-breasted Nuthatch:
   http://www.npwrc.usgs.gov/resource/tools/ndblinds/houswren.htm
   Or any of the nesting structures or feeders you like at
   http://www.npwrc.usgs.gov/resource/tools/ndblinds/ndblinds.htm,
   made available by the U.S. Geological Survey's Northern Prairie Wildlife Center.

5. *Plan a site or accident report.* Imagine that you must write a site or accident report on one of the topics listed below. What are the parts or characteristics you'd use for the descriptive sections of that report?

Hurricane damage	Tornado damage	Flood damage
Vacant lot	Used automobile	Rental property
Potential office space	Street needing repair	Technology exposition

Title: The title for this description is bold, centered, a few point sizes larger than the regular text. Notice that the title is not just "Workhorse Flashlight" but includes the fact that this is a "technical description." Make sure your titles capture both the topic and focus of the information that follow.

Notice that there is no Introduction heading. In a short document like this, it ought to be obvious that the paragraph following the title is introductory.

Introduction: The introduction to this technical description does two essential things: (a) provides a general description of the flashlight and (b) provides a list of its parts, which doubles as an overview of the sections to follow.

In-sentence list: This is an example of an in-sentence list. Notice that lowercase letters are used and that the letters are enclosed on both sides with parentheses. (See Chapter 8 for more on lists.)

Figure title: Notice the figure title. It is centered below the figure and italicized, making it distinct from regular text and headings. Don't just number figures—include a descriptive title as well.

Second-level heading: Because this is a short document, first-level headings are not necessary. (For more on headings, see Chapter 7.)

Third-level heading: These are used for the two paragraphs describing the subparts of the body of the flashlight.

TECHNICAL DESCRIPTION

Workhorse Flashlight[2]

The Workhorse is a hand-sized plastic flashlight that fits into most automobile glove compartments. The Workhorse's overall length is 6 inches, with a diameter of 2 inches at the head of the flashlight, tapering to 1-1/4 inches in diameter at the battery compartment. The cylindrically shaped body of the Workhorse is made of matte black, high-impact plastic, ribbed for a secure handgrip. The Workhorse flashlight consists of two major parts: (a) the body, containing battery compartment and switch; and (b) the bulb assembly, containing the reflector, the bulb, and the connector. The flashlight is powered by two 1.5-volt, C-size batteries. (See Figure 1 for an illustration of the fully assembled flashlight.)

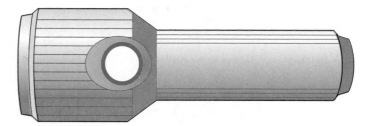

Figure 1. Fully Assembled Flashlight

Body

The body of the Workhorse Flashlight is 5-5/8 inches, with a diameter of 2 inches at the screw, or head end, tapering to 1-1/4 inches at the battery compartment. The interior of the screw end is threaded, allowing for connection with the bulb assembly. (See Figure 2 for an illustration of the complete flashlight assembly.)

Battery compartment. The battery compartment holds the batteries, the power source for the flashlight. The compartment is cylindrical, 3-1/2 inches long and 1-1/4 inches in diameter, with a coiled metal spring on the interior of the closed end, and 1/4-inch wide strip of

[2] Many thanks to Mary Bailey, former technical writing student at Austin Community College for this technical description and permission to adapt it here.

Numbers: Notice that throughout this description, numbers (digits) are used, instead of words, for many of the numerical values. Values like 2 inches, 6 inches, and 1.5 volts are exact amounts and also key values. In technical writing, use digits rather than words for these situations. (Notice however, in the introduction that the word "two" is used in "two major parts." That's because the value is not important even though it is exact. (For more on digits versus words for numbers, see Appendix A.)

Fractions: Hyphenate a whole number followed by a fraction, as you see here. Doing so prevents that momentary confusion: for example, is it 1-1/2 or 11/2?

gold-colored metal running along one interior side of the compartment. The compartment holds two 1.5 volt C batteries, in a stacked position, with the negative end of the lowermost battery in contact with the spring and the positive end of the lowermost battery supporting the negative end of the uppermost battery. The open end of the battery compartment closes with the insertion of the bulb assembly.

Switch. The switch turns the flashlight on and off. It is located on the body of the Workhorse 1-1/2 inches from the screw end. The switch is made of white plastic, designed to be activated with the thumb of the hand holding the flashlight. When the switch is pushed forward, toward the larger end of the flashlight, the light turns on. When the switch is returned to the original position, the light turns off.

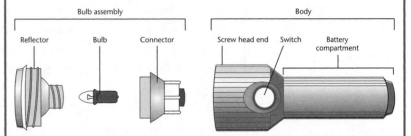

Figure 2. Components of the Workhorse Flashlight

Bulb Assembly

The bulb assembly of the flashlight consists of the reflector, the bulb, and the connector. When fully assembled, the bulb assembly is 2 inches long, with a diameter of 2 inches at the reflector end reducing to 3/4 inch at the contact end of the connector. The bulb assembly completes the flashlight by screwing into the end, or head end of the body of the flashlight.

Descriptive detail: Notice how much detail is provided in this description. Even so, plenty more could be added.

Part-by-part and subpart-by-subpart description: Notice that each part and each subpart is described separately in its own paragraph.

Reflector. The reflector magnifies and projects the light generated by the battery powered bulb. When viewed from the larger end, the reflector consists of a transparent flat plastic cover over a chrome colored reflective plastic concavity with a central hole. The elements are permanently attached together and housed in matte black plastic. The reflector screws into the connector on one end, and

Third-level headings. Notice how the subsections of the bulb-assembly description are introduced by third-level headings. See Chapter 7 for more on headings.

Sources of description: Consider the different types of descriptive detail used here: contents (subparts), length, diameter, width, shape, attachment methods, color, materials of construction, relationship of the parts, location.

With the description complete, the concluding paragraph focuses on function and use.

the midsection of the reflector provides the main screw for attachment to the flashlight body.

Bulb. The light source for the Workhorse is a glass bulb, 1/2-inch long, permanently fused onto a cylindrical metal base 1/2-inch long and 3/8-inch in diameter. The bottom of the metal base has a protrusion, providing the electrical connection between the bulb and connector. The bulb itself contains a metallic filament, one-half the length of the glass portion of the bulb, surrounded, at a point halfway up the length, by a clouded white plastic-like material.

Connector. The connector connects the reflector and bulb to the battery power source. The connector is made of black plastic, ringed with a metallic collar 3/8-inch wide. The closed end of the connector is mounted with a 5/6-inch-square gold-colored metal strip. The metal strip facilitates the connection between the bulb and the batteries. The open end of the connector is threaded to allow joining with the bulb and reflector.

When fully assembled, the Workhorse Flashlight is a sturdy, easily held tool providing light sufficient for regular outdoor and emergency use. The compact size makes the flashlight easily portable, and batteries and bulb are readily accessible for replacement.

DATE: June 15, 2000[3]

TO: Maury Hughes, Jr., Principal

Hughes Energy Consultants

FROM: Carrie Hughes Brown, HVAC Specialist

SUBJ: Report on my trip to the Ann Arbor energy-efficient housing study

Maury, I have just returned from the second trip you requested that I make to the prototype energy-efficient housing project in Ann Arbor, Michigan. I arrived May 25, interviewed the key players, inspected the prototype, took notes and photos, and returned June 6. The following is a brief summary of what I observed.

Standard House Prototype

As you'll recall from my previous visit, the prototype residence was designed as a standard home. Its characteristics included the following.

Internal, usable	2,450 square feet floor area
Internal, usable	29,960 cubic feet building volume
Occupancy	4 people
Appliances	Typical refrigerator, freezer, range, range hood, microwave, toaster, dishwasher, sump pump, washing machine, dryer, computer, 2 televisions, 3 radios, garbage disposal
Utilities	Municipal water, natural gas water heater, furnace, central air-conditioning unit
Building structure	Lumber construction with fasteners, braces, drywall, exterior sheathing and siding, brick facing, vapor barriers, trim, adhesives, and paint
Walls and insulation	2 × 4 wood frame construction, 16″ on center with 3.5″ of rolled bat glass wool insulation; 0.5″ of drywall finishing on interior wall, polyisocyanurate sheathing; 8″ sprayed fiberglass insulation in ceiling

[3] Information contained in this report was adapted with permission from the U.S. Department of Energy. "History of the Beverly, Massachusetts Photovoltaic Array," **www.eren.doe.gov/solarnow/beverly.htm.** Some details have been changed to fit this context. *Accessed July 7, 2000.*

Floors	2 × 10 floor joists on 12″ centers, 0.75 OSB carpet, vinyl and ceramic tile floor covering
Windows	Double-glazed, double-hung windows with PVC frames, window glass thickness 1/8″
Roof/ceiling	Wood trusses, deck lumber, weathering materials
Electrical	Wiring meets electrical code; typical number of outlets and switches
Water	Noninsulated copper piping for hot and cold water throughout
Lighting	Incandescent lighting throughout, except for closets
Foundation	Gravel substrate, concrete foundation, drainage system
Furniture	None included for this study

For more detail, see the November 19, 1999 memo I sent you last year. If you can't readily put your hands on that memo, just holler—I'll print you another copy.

Modification for the Energy-Efficient Prototype Home
Now, as you know, they completed the setup of the standard house and had collected data on it by the end of 1999. Since that time, they have been redesigning the house for energy efficiency. As a result of my interviews with Emily Bergstrom and inspections of the new model, I can provide this quick summary of what they've done to the standard-home prototype.

- To improve thermal performance of the envelope, they have substituted fiberglass insulation with cellulose and increased thickness by creating a 2 × 4 wall.
- To reduce energy consumption by wall infiltration, they have reduced infiltrate from an average of 0.67 ACH to 0.35 with caulking and sprayed-in cellulose.
- To increase the R-value from 12 (in the original standard home design) to 60 in this energy-efficient version, they have substituted fiberglass insulation with cellulose and increased thickness of roof insulation by modifying the roof to accommodate that extra thickness.

Headings: Notice the use of headings in this memo. They enable readers to skip uninteresting sections and go the information they want. For example, the particular recipient of this memo would probably remember every detail of the prototype. (For more on headings, see Chapter 7.)

Bulleted lists: To make the discussion of modification more readable and scannable, the writer uses the bulleted list format. (For more on lists, see Chapter 8.)

Parallelism: Notice how each bulleted-list item begins with an infinitive phrase ("to") followed by the main clause. (For more on parallelism, see Appendix C.)

- To increase solar gain associated with the windows while reducing heating, they have increased window area from 337 square feet to 490 square feet, using double-low E/argon).
- To reduce primary energy consumption, they have exchanged electrical appliances with those using natural gas. They have tried to use high-efficiency appliances everywhere else in the house as well. They believe this will cut primary energy consumption by a factor of 3.
- Also to reduce energy consumption, they have replaced all incandescent bulbs with fluorescent ones.
- To allow for full winter sun exposure but to cut out significant amounts of summer sun, they have redesigned to increase overhang on all windows.
- To reduce natural gas consumption for water heating by a projected 40%, they have installed a system that uses a heat-transfer coil to recover waste heat from disposed-of hot water. In other words, they are pre-heating water to the water heater.

Numbers: Notice in the descriptive text of this report how often numerals—digits instead of words—are used. In technical writing, use digits for exact, important values. (For more on numbers versus words, see Appendix A.)

Obviously, the next phase of this study will be to collect data on the energy performance of this new design. Because of the improved thermal envelope and the more efficient HVAC system, they expect a significant reduction in natural gas consumption—as much as 70%. For the same reasons, they expect as much as 50% reduction in electricity consumption.

Even so, there is some concern that these savings will not be enough compared with expenditures for the long-term: the 50-year life cycle of the residence. I suggested to Emily that they may be using the wrong modeling formula, but we will need to hold off until they collect sufficient data over the next year.

Report types: This short, informal report is partly a "trip report" and partly a "site report." The writer narrates what she did on this trip and describes what she saw.

I'll keep in touch with Emily. Let me know if you need any other information on this project.

CHAPTER 2

Processes: Instructions, Policies, and Procedures

take art of 3/6

MARS AND THE HUMAN EXPLORATION OF MARS

Much has been learned about the famous red planet from recent Pathfinder and Voyager expeditions. Much more will be learned if the planned human expeditions to Mars happen, as described in some of the following links:

Mars Exploration Program (provided by JPL and NASA). **mars.nlanr.net** or **mars.jpl.nasa.gov**

Center for Mars Exploration. From NASA's Ames Research Center. **cmex-www.arc.nasa.gov**

Fifth International Conference on Mars. **mars.nlanr.net/mep/themes/future.html**

The Mars Society. **www.marssociety.org**

Whole Mars Catalog. **www.spaceref.com/mars**

On the Question of the Mars Meteorite. **cass.jsc.nasa.gov/lpi/meteorites/mars_meteorite.html**

Exploring Mars: NASA Educational Brief. **cass.jsc.nasa.gov/expmars/edbrief/edbrief.html**

The Lunar and Planetary Institute. Exploring Mars. **www.lpi.usra.edu/expmars/expmars.html**

Space Science Adventures from the Search for Extraterrestrial Intelligence (SETI) Institute. **www.seti.org/game**

The Space Settlement FAQ. **members.aol.com/oscarcombs/spacsetl.htm**

Accessed January 8, 2001.

Instructions and policy-and-procedure documents both have process at their core. A *process* is a series of actions or events that accomplish something. Photosynthesis is a natural process occurring in plants. The cycle of seasons is another process. In addition to natural biological processes, there are mechanical processes, for example, the way a combustion engine works, the way a solar cell produces electricity, and so on.

As you know from the Preface, most technical documents are based on one or a combination of *infrastructures*—elemental structuring principles that enable those technical documents to do their job. The infrastructure essential in instructions and policy-and-procedure documents is the process. To enable people to understand processes and procedures, you must break the event or action into its units: its steps, phases, or events.

This chapter shows you how to write about processes and then how to build processes into the infrastructure of instructions and policy-and-procedure documents.

Note:
■ If you are new to this book, see "How Do You Use This Book?" in the Preface.
■ For additional examples of the documents discussed in this chapter, see **www.io.com/~hcexres/power_tools/examples**.

WHAT IS A PROCESS?

Before getting into instructions and policy-and-procedure documents, take a moment to learn or to review the idea of processes, that essential infrastructure used in these kinds of technical documents. The worlds of science and technology are fascinated by how things happen; in other words, processes. A process is a series of events or actions that occur over time and that accomplish something. Processes occur in the natural and mechanical worlds; these processes are for the most part repetitive or repeatable, for example, photosynthesis or mitosis. Processes also occur in the human social world. Although many of these are repeated, you can also treat one-time-only events, such as the first walk on the moon, as processes. Other processes are plans, such as the expedition to Mars that haven't happened yet. The *step-by-step approach* is key to writing about processes: you must carefully discuss each step, phase, action, or event in a process.

As Chapter 3 on causal discussion explains, discussions of processes and discussions of causes and effects are often hard to differentiate. In fact, it's almost impossible to discuss causes and effects without discussion of process, the events within which the causes and effects are working. To avoid splitting hairs, let's say that the discussion of a process is organized by the steps, phases, or events and that the main focus is the narration of the events within that process.

HOW DO YOU WRITE ABOUT PROCESSES?

Let's walk through the most important steps in writing about processes. To provide a sense of how these steps work in an actual writing project, we'll follow an example through each of the steps.

1. **Find a project involving discussion of a simple process.** Try to find a situation in which a specific group of readers needs an explanation of a noninstructional process. It's easy to think of encyclopedia-style processes such as those involving automotive technology, electronics, computers, agriculture, medicine, and natural phenomena. You can find plenty of processes around your house, garage, or yard, but why would anyone want one of those processes discussed? (For more ideas on topics, see **www.io.com/~hcexres/power_tools/topics.html**.)

   Instead of all the usual processes explained in any encyclopedia—mitosis, photosynthesis, water cycle, gestation of an embryo—how about a process discussion that people you know will actually use? Imagine you are interning at the microprocessor plant of Advanced Micro Devices (AMD). To orient other interns, you could write about the process used to produce Athlon 1HGz chips. This would be very useful in getting new interns up to speed. But that's a huge project. Instead, how about a process-oriented discussion of NASA's plans to put human beings on Mars and the activities planned while there?

2. **Define the purpose and audience for this project.** The next step is to clarify the purpose and audience for your process discussion. (See Chapter 19 for audience-analysis strategies.) If you've started with a real set of readers in a real situation, this step is easy. To discuss AMD's process for producing the Athlon chip for new interns, you can adapt your writing exactly to the typical knowledge and needs of new interns.

As often happens when you are studying technical writing, you must work backward from a topic that interests you to the situation in which a document involving that topic is needed. Who wants to read about NASA's plans for a human expedition to Mars and why? If you searched the World Wide Web for this information as of early 2000, you wouldn't exactly have gone into orbit with the fragmented, highly technical material you found. But NASA takes a keen interest in making good information available to the public, which will build excitement for its projects. As a member of the Mars Society, you are concerned about the quality of information about the expedition that is currently available. You recognize the need for good information about the expedition. Your purpose is primarily informative, though a persuasive aim lurks in your project to get people enthusiastic about the Mars expedition and to support it.

3. **Do some research.** To write about even a simple process, you may need to do some research to gather information on the process you are writing about. There are also some wonderful books that focus directly on processes:

Brain, Marshall. *How Stuff Works*: **www.howstuffworks.com**

Clarke, Donald, Ed. *The Encyclopedia of How It Works*

Corbeil, Jean Claude, Ed., Ariane Archambault. *Macmillan Visual Dictionary*

Macaulay, David, and Neil Ardley. *The New Way Things Work.*

Sutton, Caroline. *How Do They Do That? Wonders of the Modern World Explained.*

If you did some searching on Mars, and the human exploration of Mars in particular, you'd find plenty of material, as you can see in the topic box at the beginning of this chapter. As of the year 2000, the information is quite formal: lots of passive voice and a general "personless" style of writing. It would be a challenge to present this information in a way that would be understandable and interesting to the target audience, another example of why technical writers are so necessary.

4. **Plan and develop graphics.** Early in this project, try to visualize the graphics your process discussion will need. Use the strategies in Chapter 10 and Chapter 11 to plan the drawings, diagrams, photos, and charts you may need.

Graphics will be a fun part of this project. NASA provides plenty of photos of Mars, the stages of the expedition, diagrams of the trajectories, timelines, and much more. It's certainly legal for you to use these materials; just remember to cite your sources (where you found the material). Downloading, importing, sizing, cropping, and

Introduction: definition of the process (non-instructional), overview of the steps or phases.

Step 1: definition or overview of the step; events occurring in the step; causes and effects related to these events.

Step 2: definition or overview of the step; events occurring in the step; causes and effects related to these events.

Step 3: definition or overview of the step; events occurring in the step; causes and effects related to these events.

Conclusion

FIGURE 2-1

Step-by-step process discussion. Discuss each step or phase in a sentence—or, better yet, a paragraph of its own.

positioning graphics in your documents can be challenging; see Chapter 11 for these techniques.

5. Identify the main steps or phases in the process. With your topic, purpose, and audience defined, identify the important steps in your process.

If you succeed in disentangling NASA's information on the Mars expedition, you'll see that the expedition is tentatively designed around six launches. The first three put supplies, equipment, and shelter in place. Systems for producing oxygen, fuel, power, and even food will be functioning by the time people arrive. The plans for growing food on Mars are worthy of a technical report in their own right, not to mention the plans for scientific analyses of conditions on Mars. The best way to structure this discussion is to have a section for each launch; in other words, each main phase.

6. Discuss each step or phase separately. Now you're ready to begin writing the actual process discussion one step at a time. If your readers only want a paragraph on the entire process, spend no more than a sentence per step. If they want more detail, explain each step in one or more full paragraphs.

Each section will discuss when that launch begins and ends and what it accomplishes. You could probably write a separate report on each launch, but your readers want just an overview. How long will it take for a launch to get to Mars? How will the nuclear power plant be set up, checked out, and made operational? And just what do they plan to grow on Mars? In any case, spend a sentence or two per launch; or, if you've got more room, spend a paragraph per launch. Notice how each step is represented as a separate paragraph in the diagram in Figure 2-1.

7. **Identify any other necessary sections.** When you've written, or at least planned, the discussion of the process phases, consider what nonprocess information readers may need to understand the process better. Do they need background or conceptual information before getting into the process itself?

   It won't work to dive right into the first launch. Consider the possibilities: where will they land; why was that site chosen; why is the expedition being planned in the first place; what are the goals; will it really happen, or will there be public opposition to such an expensive project?

8. **Sketch the headings you'll use.** If your process discussion takes more than two or three paragraphs, use headings (see Chapter 7). If you discuss each step in one or more separate paragraphs, create a heading to identify each step.

   For the discussion of the Mars expedition, you'll want to use a descriptive heading to introduce each of the phases of the expedition.

9. **Plan an introduction.** It's best to write, or at least plan, the essential parts first—steps, phases, or events—followed by the supplementary materials like those mentioned in a preceding step. Only then write or plan the introduction. In it, indicate the topic, purpose, and intended audience and provide an overview of what you'll cover.

   For the Mars expedition, get phrases such as "NASA's plans for the human exploration of Mars" into the first few lines. Find a clever way of implying that the discussion is aimed at a high school–level audience, but without specifically saying so. Finally, indicate that you plan to discuss the purpose, schedule, and activities for each launch.

10. **Consider adding a conclusion.** Good possibilities for conclusions might be to discuss the causes or effects of the process or a description of the end result produced by the process.

    For a conclusion to this discussion of NASA's plans for the human exploration of Mars, one obvious concern might be whether these plans will ever be carried out. Addressing this issue briefly and generally would be a good way to finish up. Another possibility would be a brief, general discussion of the outcomes of the expedition. What will we discover there? What will we get for all those billions of tax dollars?

The process here is the sequence of planned expeditions to Mars. Each expedition is like a step. Notice that the individual expeditions are discussed one by one in order.

Notice the strong transition words ("begin," "following," "next step"): they alert readers that a new step or phase is about to be discussed. (For more on transitions, see Chapter 20.)

This discussion would be more readable if it used a numbered list for each of the expeditions, and possibly an italicized label using the name of the spacecraft.

In the first decade of the next millennium, Mars will be the destination for a number of expeditions currently planned by the United States, Russia, and Japan. Because of the relationship of the orbits of Mars and Earth, the optimum launch "window" for expeditions to Mars occurs every 26 months. NASA hopes to launch spacecraft to Mars during every available window between now and 2005. The sequence of missions will begin in 1999 with the launch of Mars Polar Lander to be launched January 3, 1999 and land on Mars December 3, 1999. It will carry a microphone for listening for sounds on the Martian surface. Following the Polar Lander will be the March and April 2001 launches of the Mars Survey Orbiter and Lander, respectively. The Orbiter will orbit Mars for three years, analyzing the planet's surface and measuring the radiation environment; the Lander will study soil and atmospheric conditions on the surface of Mars. The next step will be the Mars Surveyor to be launched in 2003, which will feature a lander and a rover. The rover will travel 10 km searching for organic materials and signs of life using a sampling arm to gather Martian rock and soil. The lander will be equipped with an imaging system, radiation monitors, and instrumentation to study the physical and chemical properties of the soil gathered by the rover. Sometime between July and August 2005, the Mars Surveyor will be launched. Its purpose will be to gather samples collected and stored by the Mars Surveyor 2001 or 2003 missions and bring them back to Earth. NASA has not targeted a human expedition to Mars until 2012.

FIGURE 2-2
Example process discussion. The sequence of expeditions to Mars planned by NASA are steps in the process, that process being the exploration of Mars.

Take a look at the single paragraph process discussion in Figure 2-2. Even though it's only one paragraph, you can see exactly how each step begins and ends, as well as the introduction and conclusion.

11. Consider the format. For this simple project, you are not likely to need the elaborate report formats shown in Chapter 15. Instead, use the format you see for the process example at the end of this chapter. Begin with a descriptive title centered at the top of the page, and use second- and third-level headings. Use lists, notices, illustrations, tables, highlighting, and documentation (citations of your borrowed information sources) as necessary.

12. Review and revise your rough draft. Use the strategies in Chapter 18 to systematically review and revise your process discussion. Use the top-down approach described in Chapter 18: start by reviewing for audience, purpose, and situation; then move on to content, organization, and transitions; then check headings, lists, tables, and graphics; then examine sentence-style revision and technical style; and finally, review grammatical, spelling, and punctuation problems.

HOW DO YOU WRITE INSTRUCTIONS?

Instructions (or procedures) show people how to do something step by step. They provide step-by-step explanations of how to do things, operate things, repair things, or construct things. The following sections walk you through the important steps for developing instructions.

1. **Find a project for instructions.** Find a smallish device around your apartment or house that needs instructions. Look for a simple software application in need of a user guide. If you are interested in taking on something more complex but don't want to write 150 pages, select essential tasks, or perhaps a set of advanced tasks, from an application (for example, Jasc's Paint Shop Pro.)

   Imagine that you are charged with the task of writing a set of instructions for the typical toy watch with the LED display and two buttons. Admittedly, such watches do not come with instructions. You're expected to fumble around until you figure it out. Our user-friendly toy watch company will eliminate the fumbling and provide simple instructions!

2. **Define the purpose and audience.** The next step is to decide on a purpose and an audience for this process discussion.

   Is the audience for these instructions a 5-year-old, or is it really parents? If grown-ups read the manual only as a last resort, we certainly can't expect preschoolers to read it. As is the practice with instructions, assume an eighth-grade reading level. Picture an audience with lots of little distractions, under pressure to make the watch work before somebody starts crying.

3. **Define the tasks.** When you write instructions, you must perform a *task analysis*. Identify the common tasks that readers want to perform with the mechanism. See Chapter 19 for details on task analysis.

   The tasks for the toy watch are simple:
   ■ Set the time, which actually has these subtasks: setting the hour, setting the minute, setting AM/PM.
   ■ Set the date, which has these subtasks: setting the month, setting the day of the month, and setting the year.
   ■ Make it glow in the dark.
   ■ Change the battery? Not likely—the battery will outlast the toy watch.

4. **Do some research.** When you write instructions, much of your research is hands-on: you observe yourself performing the tasks so that you can write about them. Research into print materials may also be necessary: for example, you may need to research organic pest-control methods for a backyard-gardening manual.

In this case, your only research will be to confirm your understanding of how to set the time and date of the toy watch. Be aware of the mistakes you make; your readers will probably make the same ones. Include them as notes in your instructions. You could research how LEDs work, but neither the kids nor their parents will be interested.

5. **List the equipment and supplies needed.** For some instructions, you must list the equipment (tools such as screwdrivers, rulers, hammers, scissors) and the supplies (consumables such as tape, nails, ingredients) that readers will need to gather. Present this list before

Practical Ethics: Making Ethical Decisions

 Regardless of your future profession, you will be confronted with ethical decisions. In fact, you've probably already made numerous decisions on the job that call for ethical judgments without even realizing it. Have you ever taken a pen from work to use at home? Have you ever used e-mail or surfed the Web on company time? More than likely you didn't have any problem determining whether your behavior was ethical or not, if you even stopped to question yourself.

But what you consider good behavior might be unethical or wrong in another person's eyes. What then?

Academics and philosophers have struggled with these questions for years, proposing many different models to help people determine what is ethical and what isn't. Pagano[1] suggests using the following six questions:

- Is it legal?
- Does the decision produce the greatest good for the greatest number of people?
- Do you want this to be a universal stand?
- What if it appeared on TV? Would you be proud?
- Do you want the same to happen to you?
- Get a second opinion from a close friend who has no investment in the outcome.

To these six questions, Sturges[2] adds: if something isn't considered ethical by society as a whole, is social deviance justified? Likewise, if something isn't legal, is civil disobedience justified?

Consider the following situation. You are the manager of a company where customers mail in their checks once they receive a bill from your accountant. You need to write a policy about what to do when a customer overpays by a few dollars. Should the accountant take the time to write out a check and mail a refund? Or should the customer's bill be raised to match the payment so your books balance? What specific amount justifies the resources it requires (in postage and in employee hours) to send a refund—$1, $3, $5? Would the criteria offered by Pagano and Sturges help you decide? What personal guidelines would you use to determine whether an action is ethical or not?

[1] Pagano, A. "Criteria for Ethical Decision Making in Managerial Situations," *Proc. Nat. Acad. of Management*, New Orleans, 1987, pp 1–12.

[2] David Sturges, "Overcoming the Ethical Dilemma: Communication Decisions in the Ethic Ecosystem," *IEEE Transactions on Professional Communication* 35 (1992): 1, 44–50.

the procedure under its own heading with a lead-in such as "Before beginning, gather the following items."

The only items people will need in order to use the toy watch are the toy watch itself and maybe a pencil to press the buttons. These are so incidental you don't need a list.

6. **Plan the special notices.** Notices are those specially formatted warnings, cautions, and dangers commonly found in instructions. They keep people from hurting themselves, damaging equipment, or ruining the procedure, and they defend manufacturers from lawsuits. See Chapter 9 for details.

For the toy watch instructions, there are some obvious notices: don't submerge it in water, don't throw it or stomp on it, and don't eat it. But consider the "gotchas" you experienced when you were learning how to use the watch yourself. For example, after you set the time or date, you need to keep pressing the MODE button until you return to full display of date and time. Also, you needn't worry about leaving the watch glowing in the dark all night: it automatically turns off after 10 minutes.

7. **Plan the highlighting scheme.** Instructions commonly use special effects like bold, italics, and alternate fonts to cue readers about the meaning and context of elements such as button names, displayed information, and text that readers must type. Use special effects carefully, consistently, and with restraint. To plan a highlighting strategy, see Chapter 12.

Even the toy watch instructions need some highlighting. For the three buttons—MODE, SET, and ☺ (glow)—you could use some combination of small caps, bold, or sans serif font (such as Arial, to contrast with the Times New Roman used in regular text). You could highlight instances in which you refer to something displayed in the LED. Perhaps you could find a font resembling the typical design of LED numbers and letters or just use a font like Courier New, which looks typewritten.

8. **Plan and develop graphics.** Illustrations are important in instructions. They show readers locations of buttons, knobs, dials, and components. They show the orientation of hands in relation to the components as well as before-and-after views. Illustrations show the essential objects and the essential actions involved in the procedure. Use the strategies in Chapter 11 to plan the drawings, diagrams, and photos you may need to include.

The toy watch instructions need only a few illustrations. The most important will be a diagram of the watch with the MODE, SET, and ☺ (glow) buttons labeled. Consider one or more diagrams illustrating the LED when you are setting the date or time. For example, when you press the MODE button once, the LED displays a blinking numeral for the hour.

9. **Plan the terminology.** Readers are dismayed when different words are used to refer to the same thing. In the computer world, "hard drive," "hard file," and "fixed disk" all refer to the same thing, sometimes even within the same document! The same happens with "display," "screen," and "monitor." "Press," "depress," "hit," "strike," and "mash" have all been used to refer to the simple action of pressing a key on a keyboard. Avoid making up words, using inappropriate words, and using words above the appropriate reading level. Can you guess what "deiconify" refers to? What's happening when a computer "warps," "barfs," "relinquishes," "disengages," or "actuates" something. Define any specialized or potentially unfamiliar terminology (see Chapter 5).

   With the toy watch instructions, let's stick with "press" as the verb for the buttons (not "push" or "poke"). Should you refer to the LED as the "screen," "display," or "window"? Use the word parents will most likely recognize, but avoid "LED." Call the three buttons "buttons" and not "keys" or "switches." When something shows up in the LED, say that it "is displayed" rather than "appears" or "shows." Even though the glow button is labeled with the ☺ symbol, call it the GLOW button.

10. **Identify the main headings.** For instructions, plan the headings (see Chapter 7 for the format and style for headings).

    For these instructions, you need three main headings: "How to Set the Date," "How to Set the Time," and "How to Illuminate the Watch Face." You could use gerund phrasing, "Setting the Time"; or you could use imperative phrasing, "Set the Time." But use just one of these styles of phrasing; keep headings parallel in phrasing (see Appendix C). For instructions, use task-oriented phrasing for headings: headings like "Time," "Date," or "Glow" don't convey that a procedure is about to be discussed.

11. **Plan or write the step-by-step procedures.** If you've done all of the preceding, you're more than ready to start writing. It's a good strategy to plan or write the step-by-step procedures first. That way, you can determine what other noninstructional information is needed. When you write procedures, use numbered lists for sequential steps. For nonsequential steps, use bulleted lists. For example, troubleshooting steps are nonsequential: readers try different ways to fix a problem, but in no necessary order. (See Chapter 8 on lists.) In your procedure section, begin each task with a task-phrased heading. Introduce the numbered or bulleted list of steps with a lead-in sentence.

For example, create a heading such as "Setting the Time." Beneath it, use a lead-in such as "To set the time:" followed by the step-by-step procedure. For each step in the procedure, use imperative phrasing: "Press the MODE button"; "Press the SET button." Supply additional explanatory detail as necessary: for example, "Press the MODE button until the hour number blinks."

12. **Develop and supplement each step as necessary.** Complex instructions typically need more than numbered steps. Some require background and theory before the procedures become meaningful. You may have used a custom-color tool on a computer. You push three little sliders until you get the color the way you want it. If you don't know the theory as to how colors are created using red, blue, and green or how saturation and hue influence the process, you might spend a whole day pushing those sliders around.

In some instructions, it's important to give readers before-and-after views of the project or equipment they are working on. For example, what should the computer screen look like before you press the Compile button; what should it look like after? Provide readers with information so that they can determine whether they've completed the task correctly. For example, how thick should the pancake batter be when you've mixed in all the ingredients?

Lucky for you, the toy watch requires no assembly and no theory! However, explain that in normal operation the colon between the time numerals blinks every second. When readers want to change the hour, they should press the Mode button until they see just the hour numeral flashing on the LED. These before-and-after views help readers know whether they are performing instructions correctly.

13. **Write an introduction.** Introductions to instructions must accomplish several important tasks: identify the procedure to be explained; indicate the knowledge, experience, and skills required to be able to understand the instructions; and provide an overview of what will be explained. (This overview doubles as a *scope* statement, indicating what will not be covered.)

The instructions for the toy watch hardly need much introduction. Picture a title, "Using the Warrior Princess Watch," followed by an introductory sentence such as "Anyone can set the date and time on the Warrior Princess Watch by following these easy instructions:" Despite its simplicity, this introductory sentence does identify audience skills needed as well as provide an overview.

14. **Consider adding a conclusion.** Instructions need little in the way of conclusions. However, some possibilities include telling readers how

to get additional information if they have a problem or what other interesting things they might try next.

If any conclusion is needed, it might be some comments about changing the battery, a technical support number, or perhaps a policy concerning malfunctioning watches. And of course, if Marketing requires it, you may have to add a customer-cordiality note such as "Have fun with your Warrior Princess Watch!"

15. **Consider the format.** Instructions are formatted depending on how they will be used. For simple procedures that employees must follow, a memo or e-mail might work. For equipment instructions, laminating and posting them right next to the equipment might be a good idea. If the instructions are like directions that come with a product, design them like a small booklet complete with front and back covers and a table of contents.

If you want to turn the instructions for the Warrior Princess Watch into a user guide, include a front cover with the name of the watch and the words "Operating Instructions." Include a trademark symbol and product and document numbers. On the back cover, include something like "Printed in the U.S." and a publication date.

16. **Review and revise your rough draft.** Use the strategies in Chapter 18 to systematically review and revise your instructions. Use the top-down approach described in that chapter: start by reviewing for audience, purpose, and situation; then moving on to content, organization, transitions; then headings, lists, tables, graphics; sentence-style revision, technical style; and finally grammar, usage, spelling, and punctuation problems.

HOW DO YOU WRITE POLICIES AND PROCEDURES?

Policy and procedure manuals are another essential workplace document that make use of process as the essential infrastructure. In the following, you get an introduction to these manuals, their function in the workplace, and their contents and design.

About Policies and Procedures

Organizations use policies and procedures documents to record their rules and regulations: attendance policies, substance-abuse policies, work-flow procedures, and so on. Once recorded, the policies and procedures are there for everybody in the organization to refer to, and these documents become the means of settling most disputes within the organization. To distinguish between these two terms, *policies* are rule statements. Policies are like laws: for example, most organizations have antiharassment policies, which mimic actual government-legislated laws. *Procedures*, on the other hand, are the step-by-step methods of carrying out those policies. Of course, some policies do not require procedures. If the organization has a no-smoking policy, that's all that need be said. However, if someone breaks that policy, a procedure is needed for handling that situation.

Plan a Policies-and-Procedures Document

Writing a brief policies-and-procedures document is another good way to build your technical-writing skills. Keep in mind that the following does not give you the whole story. Here are some good resources for full coverage of policies-and-procedures manuals:

- *SOHO Guidebook: A Practical Guide to Starting, Running and Growing a Small Business*, available at **www.toolkit.cch.com**
- University of Virginia. Office of Environmental Health and Safety: Policies and Procedures. **keats.admin.virginia.edu/polproc/home.html**
- Stephen Page. *Establishing a System of Policies and Procedures.* A self-published book available at **www.companymanuals.com**
- About.com. *Employee Handbooks.* **humanresources.about.com/ business/humanresources/library/weekly/aa033199.htm**

The following walks you through the main steps in developing a simple policies-and-procedures document.

1. **Find a situation or organization needing policies and procedures.** A surprising number of small organizations lack policy-and-procedure manuals. Check your workplace to see if any such manual exists. There are also plenty of other inventive ways to find a situation in which you can write a relatively brief manual.

   Imagine that you live in an apartment with three other students. Some of you have had bad experiences with these situations in the past, and as a group you are determined not to repeat them. You want to set up policies for things like loud music, parties, drugs and alcohol, cooking, cleaning, groceries, and so on. As a group, you want to draft a set of policies and procedures that all agree to and will abide by.

2. **Identify the general policies the organization needs.** All organizations, no matter what their business, have general policies, such as those relating to sexual harassment, discrimination, smoking, drugs, alcohol, and absenteeism.

   Your apartment policy-and-procedure document will contain lots of policies. You and your apartment mates want to state policies on smoking, drugs, alcohol, loud music, television, parties, and general slovenliness. Violating certain policies will be grounds for getting kicked out of the apartment. Violating other policies will earn the culprit ingenious forms of punishment!

3. Identify the technical policies the organization needs. Some organizations must define policies relating to their specific work and the associated technology. For example, health care agencies have precise policies and procedures on how their health care professionals must wash their hands, dispose of syringes, draw blood, and so on. Software development companies have precise policies and procedures on how to protect the confidentiality of new products under development.

As mentioned earlier, your apartment policy-and-procedure document is likely to include all general policies. However, if the four of you have a small business that you run from the apartment, then you might need technical policies. For example, you might run a typing, formatting, and resume-writing service. You'll need policies and procedures on how you take in work, how you complete it, and how you ensure its quality.

4. State the purpose for each policy. Typically, it's not enough just to state the policy. You must also explain its purpose, its justification, and its importance.

The reason for the no-drugs policy has to do with everyone's fear of being arrested just because one individual has them hidden away in a closet. The groceries, cooking, and cleaning policies ensure that everyone pitches in. The "quality-assurance" policy specifies a series of steps to ensure that your resume work is satisfactory to customers and is free of "bugs."

5. Plan or write the procedures for each policy, as needed. As mentioned earlier, not all policies need procedures. For example, you don't need a procedure to tell people how to follow the no-smoking policy. But plenty of policies do require step-by-step procedures. Organizations want policies carried out a certain way. If it's a step-by-step procedure, use numbered lists. If it's a list of things to try or to consider, use bulleted lists. Be sure to use the style and format for lists presented in Chapter 8.

Consider the procedures for the policies on groceries, cooking, and cleaning. Menus must be planned, all must chip in to buy food, people have to cook, others have to clean up, and policies are needed for when individuals are absent. Apartment-cleaning procedures need to be developed. What will be done? How will it be done? When will it be done? (Who's going to scrub the potty?)

6. Write the definitions for each policy-procedure section, as needed. As you write policies and procedures, you'll notice that certain words and phrases are essential and must be defined carefully. For example, if the policy states "no smoking on premises," you must define what you mean by "premises." These definitions need to be placed before the procedure and after the policy.

As you develop your apartment policies and procedures, you'll find that plenty of terms must be defined. For example, what constitutes loud music? A certain number on the volume dial? How do you define messy? Or do you use a different term altogether?

7. **Cross-reference other policies.** As mentioned above, policies mimic laws. In some cases, they are based on existing federal, state, or local laws. When that's true, reference the law.

Your apartment policies-and-procedures document may not need cross-references. Of course, if you are pre-law, you'd cite the statutes on possession of drugs or city ordinances regarding noise levels. If you are in nursing school, you might want to cite health-related dangers of letting strange life forms grow in the refrigerator, the toilet, or the bathtub.

8. **Review and revise your rough draft.** Use the strategies in Chapter 18 to systematically review and revise your policies and procedures. Use the top-down approach described in Chapter 18: start by reviewing for audience, purpose, and situation; then moving on to content, organization, transitions; then headings, lists, tables, graphics; then on to sentence-style revision and technical style; and finally grammar, usage, spelling, and punctuation problems.

Considerations like these provide the nucleus of a policies-and-procedures document. If you are writing one for real, be sure to study some of the full-length published sources mentioned previously.

Design a Policies-and-Procedures Document

If you've developed or rough-drafted the information in the preceding, you're more than ready to write or complete your policies-and-procedures document.

Special design requirements.   You'll need to consider special design work for your policies-and-procedures document as follows:

- Begin each policy (including its purpose, definitions, procedures, and cross-references) on a new page.
- Use the decimal-style numbering as shown in the hand-washing procedures at the end of this chapter. This makes it easier to refer to specific sections of the policies-and-procedures document.
- Include dates at the end of each policy section. For example, note the date reviewed, date revised, or date effective. That way, people in the organization can tell whether a policy is up to date.

Packaging possibilities. Design your policies-and-procedures document according to how your organization will use it:

■ *Formal bound document with cover letter or memo.* The common way to design such a document is to print it out, put it in a ring binder, and give a copy to each employee. The ring binder enables you to issue change pages, rather than printing and redistributing the whole thing.

■ *Web page policies-and-procedures document.* As of 2000, organizations are publishing their policies-and-procedures manuals on the World Wide Web, specifically, on their intranets. Doing so saves time, paper, and money. Of course, employees must have ready access to computers and get used to using an online version of the manual. Also, the online manual must be designed well. See Chapter 17 for strategies on designing hypertext and Web pages.

Regardless of the packages you choose, use headings, lists, tables, and graphics just as you would in any other technical document. Take a look at the example policies-and-procedures document shown at the end of this chapter to get some ideas about how to design your own.

WORKSHOP: PROCESS, INSTRUCTIONS, POLICIES, AND PROCEDURES

Here are some additional ideas for practicing the concepts, tools, and strategies in this chapter:

1. *Identifying noninstructional processes.* Choose any three of the following topics and define as many processes associated with them as you can:

Real estate prices	Weather	Blood pressure
Sleep	Trees	Batteries
Marriage	Divorce	Cameras
Radios	Automobiles	Breakfast
Autumn	Employment	Painting or drawing
Gardening	Education	Cooking
Cats	Dogs	

2. *Identifying instructional processes.* Choose any three of the preceding topics and define as many instructional processes associated with them as you can.

3. *Defining noninstructional phases.* For those noninstructional processes you defined in Exercise 1, define as many of the phases as you can.

4. *Defining instructional tasks.* For those instructional processes you defined in Exercise 2, define as many of the tasks as you can.

5. *Defining instructional steps.* For any of the tasks you previously defined, identify as many of the individual steps as you can.

6. *Analyzing instructions and user guides.* Find several examples of instructions and user guides and compare them according to their use of numbered and bulleted lists, phrasing of headings, format and content of notices, use of highlighting, graphics, and other such detail.

7. *Defining policies and procedures.* Choose one of the following situations and define up to a half dozen policies; then define the procedures for each of those policies:

Employees' use of the World Wide Web during regular workday hours

Students living in an off-campus co-op

Employees' use of office telephones for private calls

Telephone help desk employees' interactions with customers

Students' use of computers in college computer labs

Employees holding parties on company property

Receptionists' interactions with customer phone calls and office visits

Students visiting the tutoring lab at school

Process: Processes can be repetitive events occurring in nature or in human society. You can treat future events as processes, such as the plan for the Mars Polar Lander. Notice the very careful phase-by-phase discussion of the mission plan from launch to first signal.

In-sentence list: The overview is presented in a four item in-sentence list in the introduction. Notice that both opening and closing parentheses are used. (For more on lists, see Chapter 8.)

By the time you read this, we may know what happened to the Mars Polar Lander. Contact with it was lost December 3, 1999 as it was entering the Martian atmosphere.

Organization by steps and phases. Notice that the writer has divided the mission into phases, beginning with the launch and ending with the first signal. Each of these phases is systematically discussed in its own separate section, under its own heading.

Headings: In this relatively short document, second-level headings are used to mark off the main phases of the Mars Polar Lander mission. (For more on headings, see Chapter 7.)

Audience: To promote the space program, NASA makes lots of information available to the public. Even though the audience is the taxpaying public, plenty of details here need some extra explaining for that audience. For example, what's the deal about the aeroshell? What is an "X-band transmitter" or a "medium-gain horn antenna"?

Mars Polar Lander: Mission Overview[3]

The Mars Polar Lander will settle onto the surface of the red planet, much as the Mars Pathfinder did in 1997. But instead of inflating airbags to bounce on the surface as it lands, the Mars Polar Lander will use retro-rockets to slow its descent, like the Viking landers of the 1970s. The following summarizes activities planned for the (1) launch, (2) entry, descent and landing, (3) post-landing, and (4) first signal. This summary will conclude with a brief overview of activities that are planned for the Mars Polar Lander.

Launch

The Mars Polar Lander is scheduled to launch January 3, 1999, at about 3:20 P.M. Eastern Standard Time on a Delta II rocket from Space Launch Complex 17B at Cape Canaveral Air Station, FL. The Delta II is a model 7425 with two liquid-fuel stages augmented by four strap-on solid-fuel boosters, and a third-stage Thiokol Star 48B solid-fuel booster. At the time of launch, the lander will be encased within an aeroshell attached to a round platform called the cruise stage. Because the lander's solar panels are folded up within the aeroshell, a second set of solar panels is located on the cruise stage to power the spacecraft during its inter-planetary cruise. Shortly after launch, these hinged solar panels will unfold, and the spacecraft will fire its thrusters to orient the solar panels toward the sun. Fifty-eight minutes after launch, the 112-foot-diameter (34-meter) antenna at the Deep Space Network complex in Canberra, Australia, should acquire the Polar Lander's signal.

Entry, Descent, and Landing

By the time it reaches Mars on December 3, 1999, the Polar Lander will have spent 11 months in cruise. Throughout the cruise, the spacecraft will be communicating with Earth using its X-band transmitter and the medium-gain horn antenna on the cruise stage.

Preparations for the lander's entry into the Martian atmosphere will begin 14 hours in advance, when the final tracking coverage of the cruise

[3] *Source:* Adapted from NASA's Mars Polar Lander/Deep Space 2: Press Kit December 1999 with permission. Original document at: **www.jpl.nasa.gov/marsnews/mplds2hq.pdf**

period begins. This is the final opportunity for ground controllers to gather navigation data before entry. About 18 hours before entry, software that normally puts the spacecraft in safe mode in reaction to unexpected events will be disabled for the remainder of the spacecraft's flight and its descent to the surface. Traveling at about 15,400 miles per hour (6.9 kilometers per second), the spacecraft will enter the upper fringe of Mars' atmosphere, as shown in Figure 1. Onboard accelerometers, sensitive enough to detect G forces as little as 3/100ths of Earth's gravity, will sense when friction from the atmosphere causes the lander to slow slightly. At this point, the lander will begin using its thrusters to keep the entry capsule aligned with its direction of travel.

The spacecraft's descent from the time it hits the upper atmosphere until it lands will take about 5 minutes and 30 seconds to accomplish. As it descends, the spacecraft will experience G forces up to 12 times Earth's gravity, while the temperature of its heat shield will rise to 3000° F (1650° C).

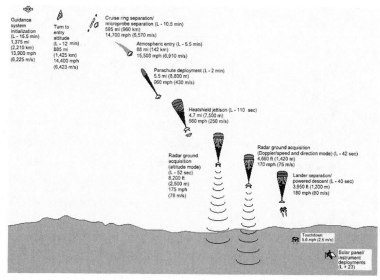

Figure 1. Mars Polar Lander — Entry, descent and landing phases.

About two minutes before landing, the lander's parachute will be fired from a mortar (or small cannon) when the spacecraft is moving at about 960 miles per hour (430 meters per second) some 4.5 miles (7.3 kilometers) above the surface. Ten seconds after the parachute opens, the

Future tense: Future tense is often abused—that is, used unnecessarily—in technical prose. However, in this context, there is no other choice. When this document was written, these events were still in the future.

Illustration: This illustration was in the original PDF file made available on the Web by NASA. To get it into another document, just take a screen capture of the page on which it occurs and then crop it to the desired size. (For more on screen captures, cropping, and graphics in general, see Chapter 11.)

Cross-references to illustrations: Notice that throughout this document direct cross-reference are made to figures, even if the figure occurs on the same page. This is standard good practice: draw the reader's attention to illustrations, tables, and charts and give them a clue as to what they contain and how are they are related.

Transitions: Notice how many words and phrases throughout this document alert us to where we are in this process: "14 hours in advance," "when," "About two minutes before landing," "Starting at about…," "before entry," "then," and so on. This document very carefully guides us through the events, alerting us to their interrelationships, sequencing, and timing. (For more on transitions, see Chapter 20.)

Mars Descent Imager will power on and the spacecraft's heat shield will jettison. The first descent image will be taken 0.3 seconds before heat-shield separation. The imager will take a total of about 30 pictures during the spacecraft's descent to the surface. About 70 to 100 seconds before landing, the lander legs will deploy; 1.5 seconds after that, the landing radar will activate. The radar will be able to gauge the spacecraft's altitude about 44 seconds after it is turned on, at an altitude of about 1.5 miles (2.5 kilometers) above the surface.

Shortly after radar ground acquisition, when the spacecraft is traveling at about 170 miles per hour (75 meters per second) some 4,600 feet (1.4 kilometers) above the surface, the thrusters that the spacecraft has used for maneuvers throughout its cruise will be turned off, and the backshell will separate from the lander. The descent engines will turn on one-half second later, turning the lander so that its flight path gradually becomes vertical. The pulse-modulated descent engines will maintain the spacecraft's orientation as it descends. The engines will fire to roll the lander to its proper orientation so that it lands with the solar panels in the best orientation to generate power as the Sun moves across the sky. The radar will turn off at an altitude of about 130 feet (40 meters) above the surface, and the spacecraft will continue using its gyros and accelerometers for inertial guidance as it lands.

Once the spacecraft reaches either an altitude of 40 feet (12 meters) or a velocity of 5.4 miles per hour (2.4 meters per second), the lander will drop straight down at a constant speed. The descent engines will turn off when touchdown is detected by sensors in the footpads. The engines will have been on for a total of about 40 seconds during final descent to the surface.

Post-Landing

The lander is expected to touch down at 12:01 P.M. Pacific Standard Time (PST) at the Mars landing site. (Because radio signals take 14 minutes to travel from Mars to Earth, during the landing the mission team will be watching events in Earth-received time, with landing noted at 12:15 P.M. To avoid confusion, all subsequent times of mission events

---

Dual measurements: Many technical documents, like this one, are written for international audiences. That means offering both British or American versions as well as international metric versions of the measurements.

Passive voice: Notice how much passive voice this document uses. In this context, it's the most efficient and effective way to write. For example, "descent engines will be turned off" is a passive-voice sentence. Little would be gained by rephrasing this sentence to read "NASA ground crew will turn descent engines off." In every instance of the passive voice in this document, we know full well who the agent of these activities is—people back on planet Earth.

Quotation marks: Quotation marks are used around "Earth-received time" because it is an unusual phrase and because it is defined at that point. The writer could have used italics instead (but not both quotation marks and italics) to highlight this phrase at its point of definition. Notice that later in this same document "sleeps" is also enclosed in quotation marks—an unusual usage indeed!

discussed below are stated in "Earth-received time," when a signal would be received on Earth. Actual events will have taken place on the spacecraft about 14 minutes earlier in each case.) The descent imager will be turned off 60 seconds after landing.

After waiting five minutes to allow for dust kicked up by the landing to settle, the lander's solar arrays will be unfolded. Eight minutes after landing, while the medium-gain antenna is being turned to point at Earth, the spacecraft's gyros will be used like compasses to determine which way is north. The spacecraft's inertial measurement units will then be powered off. (These components are shown in Figure 2.)

After gyrocompassing is completed, the medium-gain antenna will turn toward Earth. This antenna slew may take up to 16 minutes. A vertical scan will then be taken by the surface stereo imager before its boom is deployed. Both the meteorological and imager masts will then be raised.

Placement of illustrations: Place illustrations just after the point where they are relevant, as is done here. If an illustration just won't fit, bump it to the top of the next page, fill in the remaining white space with text, and set a cross-reference to the illustration (but do not include page reference).

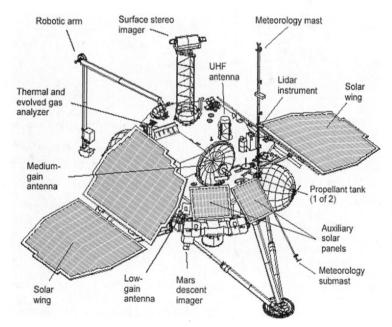

Figure 2. Mars Polar Lander spacecraft.

Introductory-element commas: Appendix B is adamant about punctuating any introductory element, no matter how short, with a comma. For example, "At 1:46 P.M. PST" is an introductory element. So is "To avoid confusion"

Numbers: As you would expect, this document contains plenty of numbers. For numbers that are both exact and essential, use digits. However if a number begins a sentence, spell it out. (For more on numbers versus digits, see Appendix A.)

Hyphens: Throughout this document, hyphens are used on compound modifiers before nouns: for example, "dish-shaped," "medium-gain," "low-resolution," and "black-and-white" are hyphenated. A good test for hyphens is to see if you can mis-read the phrase. For example, is it an "antenna shaped like a dish" or a "shaped antenna of the dish type"? Obviously it's the first interpretation. Not hyphenating the two words causes momentary hesitation; you want your technical writing to be as immediately understandable as possible. (For more on hyphens, see Appendix B.)

Final section: Although the primary focus of this document is "getting there," you can imagine readers feeling a little cheated by not getting some idea of what will happen while on Mars. This conclusion probably gives them enough of an idea.

First signal

The first opportunity to hear from the lander will take place when it begins transmitting directly to Earth using its dish-shaped medium-gain antenna about 23 minutes after landing. This signal is expected to be received at 12:39 P.M. PST. The transmission session will end 45 minutes later, or 1:24 P.M. PST, and will include engineering data on the lander's entry, descent and landing, as well as possible low-resolution black-and-white pictures from the undeployed camera on the lander's deck. At 1:46 P.M. PST, the lander will shut down and "sleep" for 4 hours and 40 minutes while its solar panels recharge its onboard battery.

Assuming that all is normal with the spacecraft, it will power up again at 6:26 P.M. PST and turn on its receiver. At this time, mission controllers expect that they will send the lander commands, such as what data rate to use for later radio transmissions. The receiver will continue listening for commands from Earth until 7:41 P.M. PST. At 8:09 P.M., the lander will begin transmitting to Earth until 10:45 P.M. After that session concludes, the lander will run through a sequence that takes about half an hour as it prepares to shut down for the night. At 11:24 P.M. PST the lander will power down.

Operations

Instead of a rover, the Mars Polar Lander is equipped with a robotic arm that will dig into the soil near the planet's south pole in search of subsurface water and fine-scale layering that may physically record past changes in climate. The lander will also conduct experiments on soil samples acquired by the robotic arm and dumped into small ovens, where the samples will be heated to drive off water and carbon dioxide. Surface temperatures, winds, pressure, and the amount of dust in the atmosphere will be measured on a daily basis, while a small microphone records the sounds of wind gusts and mechanical operations onboard the spacecraft.

Title: Notice that the title is precise about who should use this guide, what the document is (a "guide"), and even what version, release, and point release the guide is for.

Introduction: This introduction contains what we need to see in an introduction: subject matter of the document, audience skills needed, purpose of the document, and overview of what's contained.

Background: These instructions rightly use a background section to explain just what Eudora is and why you ought to be interested in it.

Headings: Because they are relatively short, these instructions use second- and third-level headings (as defined in Chapter 7 on headings). If you think of headings like items in an outline, "About Eudora Lite," "Setting Up Eudora" and "Using Eudora" would be I, II, and III. The subheadings beneath them would be A, B, and C.

Bulleted list: These items are in no necessary order. Therefore, use a bulleted list (see Chapter 8 for detailed discussion of lists).

Notice: To make this special point stand out, the writer uses the note format (see Chapter 9 for detailed discussion of notices).

Eudora Lite 1.5.4 for Windows 95:
Beginner's Guide[4]

This beginner's guide to Eudora Lite for Windows 95 covers everything you need to know to start using Eudora to send and receive e-mail, including program configuration and basic tasks involved in composing, sending, receiving and reading e-mail. To use this guide, you should be familiar with the basics of mouse operation and navigating the standard Windows interface.

About Eudora Lite

Eudora Lite is freeware (software that can be used at no cost) that offers essential e-mail utilities for managing electronic mail messages. Because the program uses the standard Windows interface, anyone familiar with the Windows environment should find Eudora easy to navigate. The application is designed to access POP servers—computers connected to a network or the Internet running software that sends, receives, and stores e-mail. Eudora handles communications between the remote POP server and your computer to send and receive e-mail.

Setting Up Eudora

Before you can begin using Eudora, make sure you have the right equipment and then configure Eudora.

Getting started. To use these instructions, you'll need the following.

- IBM PC-compatible computer running under Windows 95
- Installed copy of Eudora Lite application
- Internet access with a POP3 e-mail account.

Note: If you are not sure what kind of account you have, contact your Internet service provider (ISP). POP refers to the type of software used on the server where your e-mail is received and stored. Most e-mail today uses POP3 software.

---

[4] Many thanks to Michael Caldwell, former Austin Community College technical-writing student for these instructions and permission to adapt them here.

Highlighting: These instructions use bold, italics, and alternate fonts in one of the common industry-standard ways. Bold is used for interface buttons or options that users click. Arial font is used for example text to contrast to the Courier New.

Numbered lists: Notice that any sequential steps are formatted as numbered lists. This makes it easier for readers to follow.

Configuring the program. Before you can use Eudora for e-mail tasks, you must tell the program a few things about yourself and your account. If Eudora is not running, you should start it now.

1. Click **Tools** and then select **Options** as shown in Figure 1. Eudora opens a dialog box with several option categories.

2. Choose the **Getting Started** icon in the Categories column.

3. Enter your POP Account in the space provided.

Note: Your POP Account is your user name followed by the @ symbol and the name of your e-mail server. For example, if your user name is jdoe and your server is the.mail.com, enter jdoe@the.mail.com in the POP Account space.

4. Enter your actual name in the Real Name space. This name identifies you to your e-mail recipients.

5. Make sure the Winsock button is checked. When you've completed these settings, Eudora is ready to communicate with your e-mail server.

Illustrations: Create screen captures like this in Windows by pressing Alt+PrtSc and pasting the images into your document. Most software applications provide sizing and cropping tools to shape the image as necessary.

Figure titles: Notice that each figure in these instructions has a figure title, left-aligned below the figure. These identify the contents of the figure and make it easy to refer to the figure.

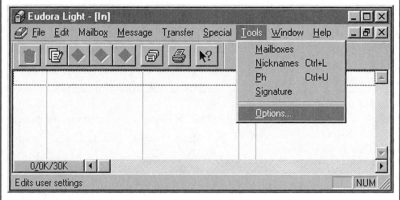

Figure 1. Tools Menu

Second-level headings: Notice that these instructions use two second-level headings—one for the Eudora-setup section and this one for the "Using Eudora" section.

Section overview: Occurring between the second- and third-level headings, these two sentences give you an overview of what's contained in this section. They also prevent you from having *stacked headings*—two or more consecutive headings without intervening text.

Using Eudora

Eudora is simply a program for managing e-mail. The following sections cover the basic steps for composing, sending, receiving, and reading your e-mail.

Composing and sending messages. Eudora provides a convenient facility for creating new e-mail messages, which are then sent out to the network. The steps, shown in Figure 2, are simple.

1. Click **Message** and then select **New Message**. The program will open a window in which you can address and compose the message.

2. Enter the e-mail address of your recipient in the To: field. Eudora always places the cursor in this position each time a new message window is opened. (To test your setup, send e-mail to your own e-mail address.)

3. Tab down to, or click on the Subject line. Type a subject for your message.

4. Tab down three times, or click on the body portion of the message box. Enter your message here.

5. When you have written your message, click on the **Send** button in the toolbar at the top of the message window. Eudora will contact your server and submit a copy of the message to be sent out on the Internet or network.

Caution: Be certain your message is ready for the rest of the world—you can't get it back once you press the **Send** button.

Highlighting: Notice that "Send" is bolded but "Subject" is not. That's because pressing **Send** makes things happen, whereas Subject is simply a label on the screen. Notice, also, that the capitalization style of these labels matches the style used in the program itself.

Caution notice: A caution notice is used here because dire consequences could occur if you pressed the **Send** button and mistakenly sent a message to the wrong people. As defined in Chapter 9, caution notices are for situations in which damage to data or equipment could occur. The wrong message sent to the wrong person might not damage data, but it could certainly damage something worse.

Illustrations: Notice the nice overlaid effect of these two screen captures. To do this, just paste both images in the same area of a document, and move one on top of the other to make them overlap. If the right image is not on top, right-click on the image you want, and select **Order→Bring to front** (in Word).

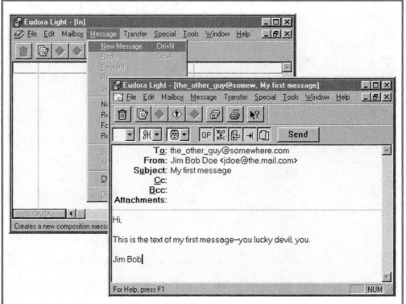

Figure 2. New Message Menu and Window.

Third-level headings: This section is made up of two subsections: composing and sending messages and receiving and reading messages. Third-level headings are used to indicate these subsections. (See Chapter 7 for details on third-level headings.) Notice the format of third-level headings: bold, ending with a period, and "run into" the paragraph. Notice that the sentence following the heading is not a grammatical part of the heading.

Receiving and reading messages. You can use Eudora to check your POP account for mail, copy new messages to your machine, and then read them.

Click **File** and then select **Check Mail.**

Enter your password when Eudora prompts for it. The program will establish contact with your server and check for new mail. If messages are present, Eudora will notify you and copy the e-mail to your In box to be read.

Note: If you do not know your password, contact your Internet Service Provider for help.

Hyphenation: "Double-click" is hyphenated because it is a verb compound that condenses a longer phrase.

Select a new message to be read. Figure 3 shows a listing of new messages in the In box. Double-click on any message to read it. The program will open a message window that contains the body of the mail (Figure 3).

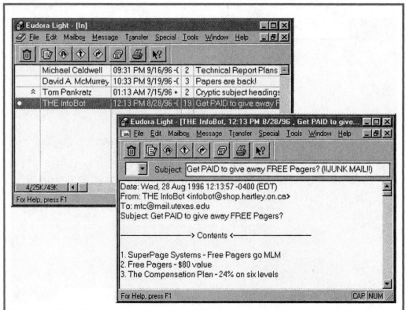

Figure 3. Checking for messages and reading messages.

Simple, consistent wording: Notice how many sentences are phrased the same way. This style is desirable in this context: it simplifies things for readers.

For other Eudora tasks, click **Help** in the menu bar to see the online helps.

CHAPTER 3

Causes and Effects: Primary Research Reports (Lab Reports)

GLOBAL WARMING

As you are probably all too aware, global warming is the term for the scary theory that human CO_2- and methane-producing activities have led and are leading to small increases in average global temperature, which may in turn have enormous consequences for our lives here on the planet—namely, drought, elevated sea levels, flooding, higher temperatures, reduced agriculture, increased tropical storm activity, and increased insect problems. You can read about both sides of this issue at these World Wide Web sites:

Cooler Heads Coalition or the National Consumer Coalition's Global Warming Information Page. **www.globalwarming.org/index.htm**. See its Web site at **www.globalwarming.org/science**

CNN's "Our Changing Climate" special. **www.cnn.com/SPECIALS/1997/global.warming**

Instant Expert's Guide to Global Warming. **www.heartland.org/studies/ieguide.htm** (From the Heartland Institute)

EPA Global Warming Site. **www.epa.gov/globalwarming**

Understanding Global Climate Change. What Is It? Kathy Finberg, FACSNET section editor. **www.facsnet.org/issues/specials/gcc/basic/carbon.php3** (From FACsNET)

EDF's Global & Regional Air Page. **www.edf.org/programs/GRAP/#warming**

WWF Climate Change Campaign Page. **www.panda.org/climate/**

Accessed January 11, 2001.

A *primary research report* is a report in which you gather your most important information directly from primary resources, such as the field or the laboratory, rather than published documents. While you summarize published information in the "literature" section of a primary research report, the most important information comes from surveys, samplings, questionnaires, tests, and experiments—original data that you generate, collect, and analyze. Because the primary research report focuses on why certain things happen, its infrastructure is some combination of causes and effects.

This chapter shows you how to write about causes and effects and then how to construct primary research reports in which you incorporate causes and effects as the infrastructure.

Note:

- If you are new to this book, see "How Do You Use This Book?" in the Preface.
- For additional examples of the documents discussed in this chapter, see **www.io.com/~hcexres/power_tools/examples**.

HOW DO YOU WRITE ABOUT CAUSES AND EFFECTS?

Before getting into the details of primary research reports, spend some time thinking about how to discuss causes and effects, which are central to the primary research report.

Defining types of causes and effects.   Defining causes and effects can be bewildering. Some create a telescoping effect, with one cause or effect leading to another and still another. Or the situation may have alternative causes associated with it that are controversial.

- *Telescoping causes.* Sometimes defining causes and effects only leads to additional causes and effects. Consider the sinking of the Titanic. What caused it? The mighty ship ran into an iceberg, which tore a big gash in its side. But why did it run into an iceberg? Was it a problem with the course, with the navigator, or with the lookouts? Why did the gash cause it to sink? After all, it was supposedly unsinkable. Notice how one question leads to another, just like a telescope being extended further and further.

■ *Alternative causes.* Some cause–effect discussions force you to consider competing alternative causes. Did the navigators of the Titanic plot a course through waters known to be filled with dangerous icebergs, thinking that the ship was invulnerable? Was the general attitude of the builders, owners, or crew nonchalant? Consider the example of global warming and the greenhouse effect. Some people refuse to accept the notion that the average temperature of our planet has risen and continues to rise. Others refuse to accept the notion that human activities are the primary cause of that temperature increase. Scientists debate over a host of causes, attempting to prove which are primary.

■ *Hypothetical, projected effects.* Another important form of cause–effect discussion has to do with predicted effects, results, or consequences. Predicted effects are based on current conditions: if this situation continues, that is going to happen. The perfect example is the Y2K problem that worried our technology-dependent society at the start of year 2000. Everything from no effect at all to disruption and chaos equal to the Great Depression and nuclear war was predicted because of the change of four little digits.

Discussing causes and effects. What happens when you actually write about causes and effects? Providing details on causes and effects is largely a matter of the following:

■ *Explaining processes (step-by-step events).* A causal discussion of the Titanic might discuss step by step how the ship set sail, how it charted its course, when it hit the iceberg, and how the ship slowly filled and then broke in half and sank. Causes and effects would be emphasized throughout.

■ *Providing descriptions (physical, visual, quantifiable details).* This same discussion might also include descriptions of the iceberg, the gash in the hull, and so on. The global warming discussion might include information about the CO_2 that has been produced and how it traps radiation in the atmosphere.

■ *Making comparisons, particularly to the familiar.* Help readers understand causes and effects by comparing them to something familiar. For example, the greenhouse effect—the much-debated, primary cause of global warming—is often compared to the way a closed automobile warms up by trapping heat.

■ *Discussing examples.* For certain causal discussions, reviewing examples helps. If you were focusing on the causes and effects of tornadoes, you might recount examples of the worst tornadoes, such as the one that struck Jarrell, Texas, in 1993.

Introduction: This discussion focuses on the effects of the increase of just a few degrees in average global temperature. Notice that the last sentence of the introduction provides an overview of the effects ("impacts") to be discussed.

Scientists are gradually moving toward a consensus that catastrophic environmental changes will occur in the 21st century. One manifestation of this concern is the United Nations' Intergovernmental Panel on Climate Change. The panel now predicts a global temperature increase of 1 to 3.5 degrees Centigrade in the next century, which would have dramatic effects on water, land, and the atmosphere.

Effect-by-effect discussion: Notice that this cause–effect discussion takes up one effect per paragraph, one at a time.

- *Impact on water.* According to projections from the Intergovernmental Panel on Climate Change, increased temperatures will cause increased melting of the Earth's polar ice caps, which in turn will cause the world's oceans to rise between 15 and 95 cm during the next hundred years. Low-elevation areas like Bangladesh may lose more than 20 percent of their usable land; cities like New Orleans may be underwater. Higher sea levels will also cause erosion of coastal areas, contaminate coastal water supplies, and increase damage caused by hurricanes.

Bulleted list: Bulleted-list items help differentiate the individual effects discussion. (Bullets are used rather than numbers because these effects are not in a required sequence.)

- *Impact on land.* Because higher temperatures in the next century will cause moisture in the soil to evaporate more rapidly, scientists predict reduced crop yields. As already demonstrated by the growth of the Sahara Desert, deserts worldwide are also expected to expand because of increasing global temperatures.

Labels: Each of these bulleted items starts with a label that identifies the topic of the item, like a mini-heading. Notice that the label is not a grammatical part of the rest of the bulleted item.

- *Impact on atmosphere.* The scientific community is uncertain, however, as to what will happen to the atmosphere because of these predicted increases in global temperatures. With the increased evaporation caused by higher temperatures, there should be an increase in cloud cover, which may cause a decrease in temperatures. However, that increased cloud cover may also have heat-trapping effect, which would cause a further increase in the average global temperature.

FIGURE 3-1

Short cause–effect discussion. Notice that this example discusses the effects ("impacts") one at a time, each in its own paragraph. Notice, also, how the bulleting and labeling make the individual effects more distinct.

- *Emphasizing keywords and transitions.* Also important in discussing causes and effects is emphasizing specific causes and specific effects. Phrases such as "The main cause of," "Another cause of," and "One of the most noticeable effects of" are cues to readers. Equally important are transitions. Words like "because," "as a result of," and "in turn" help readers see the connections between the causes and effects. Take a close look at Figure 3-1 to see how causes and effects are carefully named and how transitions emphasize these relationships.

Let's step through the important phases in writing cause–effect discussions. To give you a sense of how these steps work in an actual writing project, we'll follow a single example throughout.

1. **Find a simple project involving the discussion of causes, effects, or both.** It's easy enough to think of exercises such as why the sky is blue; what causes earthquakes, tornadoes, or hurricanes; why the sound of a large speeding vehicle is so shrill when it is approaching; or how acoustic speakers reproduce sound. How about starting with a real or realistic problem in the workplace? To write a simple cause–effect discussion, think of some specific situation that fits one of the following.

   - Define and discuss the causes of a problem.
   - Define and discuss the effects of that problem.
   - Define and discuss the solutions to a problem.

   (Having trouble thinking of a topic? See **www.io.com/~hcexres/ power_tools/topics.html.**)

   Assume that you must write the cause–effect section for a technical background report on global warming. This section has two parts: the first discusses the causes of global warming; the second discusses the effects. You are not going to get into solutions, at least in this section. You are just exploring the basic mechanism of global warming.

2. **Define an audience and purpose.** The next step is to decide on an audience and purpose for this cause–effect discussion. Who are your readers? Why do they need this information? What, if anything, can you assume about their background on the topic? (See Chapter 19 for strategies to use in analyzing audiences and adapting your writing to them.)

   Assume you are writing for an audience of investment advisors—individuals who advise investors about long-range investments. Obviously, these people need to know whether the global warming threat is just a gloom-and-doom scare or a no-nonsense reality. These investment advisors are not scientists or environmentalists. They are nonspecialist readers who need technical detail served up in a way that they can understand. Your purpose is to present the arguments for the global warming theory. Elsewhere in the report, you may get into the standard arguments against this theory.

3. **Do some research.** For even a simple cause or effect, you may need to do some research.

   If you did some research on global warming, you'd find lots of information, like the links at the beginning of this chapter. Activist groups such as the World Wildlife Federation and the Environmental Defense Fund believe that global warming is a serious threat. They have Web sites presenting their point of view. But the other side of the issue is well represented also—for example, the Cooler Heads Coalition, the National Consumer Coalition, and the Instant Experts Guide from the Heartland Institute.

4. **Plan and develop graphics and tables.** Early in this project, visualize the graphics this cause–effect discussion will need. Use the strategies in Chapter 11 to plan the drawings, photos, and charts you may need to include.

   Graphics for a global warming report might include a diagram of the earth showing how radiation is trapped in the atmosphere. You might also need a line graph depicting rising global temperature averages over the past century or a table showing how much our production of carbon dioxide (CO_2) has dramatically increased over the past century.

5. **Identify the causes.** With your topic, purpose, and audience defined, figure out the causes that must be discussed.

   For global warming, a variety of causes are cited, with human activities, of course, being the most debated. Practically any article, report, or book on this topic will show that among the most commonly cited causes are fuel combustion leading to increased CO_2; ranching, farming, and landfills leading to increased methane; land clearing leading to reduced consumption of CO_2; and heavy harvesting of marine organisms leading to increased plankton (CO_2 producers) in the oceans.

6. **Identify the effects.** With your topic, purpose, and audience defined, figure out the effects that must be discussed. Remember that the problem–solution discussion is practically the same as the cause–effect discussion.

   In this project, the effects of global warming are obviously, first and foremost, an overall rise in average global temperature ($1°F$ in the past century). Effects variously cited include a rise in sea levels (4 to 10 inches in the past century), reduction of glaciers and polar ice caps, increased tropical storm activity, drought, increased insect problems, hotter summers, and so on.

7. **Identify relationships between the causes and effects.** Once you've listed the causes and effects, think about how they are related. Does one cause lead to an effect that in turn becomes the cause of another effect? Are there multiple causes that have varying degrees of force?

Introduction: Explanation of the problem; overview of the causes to be discussed.	*Introduction:* Explanation of the problem; overview of the effects to be discussed.
Cause 1: Discuss how this cause is the main cause or a contributing cause; explain this cause using description or process.	*Effect 1:* Discuss how this effect is the main effect or an important one; explain this effect using description or process.
Cause 2: Discuss how this cause is another cause or a contributing cause; explain this cause using description or process.	*Effect 2:* Discuss how this effect is another main effect or an important one; explain this effect using description or process.
Cause 3: Discuss how this cause is another cause or a contributing cause; explain this cause using description or process.	*Effect 3:* Discuss how this effect is another main effect or an important one; explain this effect using description or process.
Conclusion	*Conclusion*

FIGURE 3-2
Cause–effect discussion. Here are two possibilities for structuring a cause-effect discussion. The idea is to discuss one cause or effect at a time. There are other possibilities: for example, a chain reaction in which one effect turns into a cause that, in turn, leads to another effect.

Some alleged causes of global warming precede others: melting of glaciers and the polar ice cap obviously precedes the rise in sea levels. The causes also vary in terms of their force and in terms of controversy. The same is true for effects: some are more powerful; some are more controversial. The cause–effect section in this global warming report must make these relationships clear.

8. **Discuss the causes and effects.** Take a rigorously organized approach to your discussion of the causes and effects. Discuss each one separately, in a sentence or two or in a paragraph or two (which is illustrated in Figure 3-2). As mentioned earlier, discussing causes and effects usually involves description, step-by-step process discussion, examples, and comparisons.

In this global warming report, use statistics to explain how the global temperature increase can be demonstrated. Do the same with increased sea levels. Perhaps provide comparisons of glaciers, sea levels, and temperatures a century ago and today. You might include a step-by-step discussion of how CO_2 traps heat in the atmosphere, if you believe that your bottom-line–minded investor audience would want this technical discussion. In any case, keep the discussion of the causes and effects separate. Be heavy handed with the transitions between the causes and effects. For example, use the phrase "Another cause considered important in the global. . ."

9. **Sketch the headings you'll use.** If you discuss each individual cause or effect in one or more paragraphs, create a heading for each one (see Chapter 7).

   For the global warming report, use a second-level heading to introduce the causes and another second-level heading to introduce the effects. Use third-level headings to introduce the discussion of the individual causes or effects.

10. **Plan an introduction.** Introductions must indicate the topic and purpose of the document and provide an overview of what will be discussed. In the case of causal discussions, provide an overview of the causes, effects, or both that you are about to discuss. Do the same if you plan to discuss problems and solutions or conditions and symptoms, which are causal discussions as well. Another element to consider is the *audience identifier,* which helps readers decide whether the information is suited to their needs, interests, and knowledge level.

    Imagine you've written the main text for this cause–effect section on global warming. Go back now and plan the introduction. Perhaps start with a warning: most of this part of the report is controversial; the goal is simply to present the theory. Perhaps provide a quick review of how global warming is defined. Be sure to indicate that causes will be discussed first and then effects. It may be heavy handed to list the causes and effects here. Just the words "causes" and "effects" should be enough.

11. **Consider adding a conclusion.** You can summarize the main points to refocus your readers, state a conclusion as to how serious a threat global warming is, or provide some general closing thoughts.

    For this conclusion, you might want to remind readers that most of what you've just presented is rather warmly debated (no pun intended). You might also point out that this field changes constantly. For example, a recent study indicated that receding glaciers are not necessarily proof of global warming. You might also review a list of major related questions about which scientists simply do not have a clue.

12. **Consider the format.** For this simple project, you don't need the elaborate report formats shown in Chapter 15. Instead, use the format you see in the cause–effect discussion of schizophrenia at the end of this chapter. Begin with a descriptive title centered at the top of the page, and use second- and third-level headings. Use lists, notices, illustrations, tables, highlighting, and documentation (citations of your borrowed information sources) as necessary.

13. Review and revise your rough draft. Use the strategies in Chapter 18 to systematically review and revise your cause–effect discussion. Use the top-down approach described in Chapter 18: start by reviewing for audience, purpose, and situation; then move on to content, organization, and transitions; then headings, lists, tables, and graphics; then sentence-style revision and technical style; and finally grammar, usage, spelling, and punctuation problems.

HOW DO YOU WRITE PRIMARY RESEARCH REPORTS?

Primary research reports are often called "empirical" research reports because they contain data gathered directly from experiment and observation rather than information gathered from printed or in-person sources. This section discusses the primary research report and then shows you how to plan, write, and design one. Because the primary research report seeks to determine why something happens or what will happen as a result, cause–effect discussion is its essential infrastructure.

The following sections guide you through contents and organization of the primary research report as well as the typical phases in its development. (Be sure to look at the example research report about bats at the end of the chapter, which illustrates most of the sections discussed in the following chapter tasks.)

1. Build a team? Primary research reports are good opportunities to work as a team. These types of reports are commonly developed by teams. The tasks required by most primary research reports take a lot of work.

2. Find a project requiring a primary research report. Throughout, this book emphasizes writing projects that solve real or realistic workplace problems. Primary research reports certainly do that, but they also venture into the realms of pure knowledge, where there is no immediate practical problem to be solved. However, someday someone may find practical applications for that knowledge. As you search for a project, or for people needing some research, remember that you're not limited to the traditional lab experiment. You can also do field research, involving surveys and questionnaires.

Imagine that you are an avid backyard gardener. Every summer you have problems with stinkbugs stinging your tomatoes and rendering many of them inedible. You learn from discussions with other backyard gardeners that your tomatoes are not the only victims. While doing some research on stinkbug control, you discover a journal that publishes experiments conducted by small-time gardeners. But nothing has been published on stinkbugs. Perfect! You'll run an experiment testing several methods of stinkbug control, collect the data, and write a report for that journal.

3. **Define an audience and purpose.** As with any technical-writing project, begin by developing an in-depth understanding of the situation requiring a report and of the needs, interests, and knowledge levels of the readers. Readers of primary research reports expect this sequence: problem, background, method, data, discussion, and conclusions. They also expect details that enable them to visualize or even run your experiment.

   The readers of the small-time gardening research journal are not scientists; they are not specialists in areas like botany, entomology, or chemistry. They are looking for practical solutions to their gardening problems, but they like the research format because of its emphasis on specific conditions, weather, localities, people, and success rates.

4. **Describe the problem and the background.** One of the first things to do, either in the introduction or in a separate section of its own, is to discuss the situation that has led to the research. For example, research may be lacking for your topic, or there may be conflicts in existing research. Explain this at the beginning of a primary research report.

   In your primary research report, you'll include a background section in which you first discuss the details of your stinkbug problem, then the difficulty of determining how to control it, and, finally, the lack of good information on this problem.

5. **Describe the purpose, objectives, and scope.** Toward the beginning of this type of report, discuss what you intended to do in the research project—what were your objectives? Also, explain the scope of your work—what were you not trying to do?

   Your purpose is to compare several methods of controlling stinkbugs. Because you are opposed to insecticides for simple backyard gardening, you limit your experiment to organic control methods.

6. **Plan the review of literature.** After you've established the basis for the project, summarize the literature relevant to it. Summarize the theory and research directly relevant to your project. Show how it contradicts itself or is inadequate

   On the Internet, in your library, in gardening stores, and among your gardening friends, you discover a wide range of ideas about how to control stinkbugs. For example, commercial growers raise "trap crops" that lure stinkbugs away from the main crop. There is also an organic method involving sabadilla. Summarize this literature and the opinions in a separate "literature review" section.

7. **Describe the materials, equipment, and facilities.** Remember that one of your goals in writing this type of report is to enable readers to

Practical Ethics: Omission

It is quite common—and even beneficial—to quote experts in technical documents. It is also quite common to condense a quote to fit the length and requirements of your report. You need to zero in on the shortest, most relevant statement the expert made and weed out anything extraneous. When you do this, it's important to let your readers know that you aren't using a full or complete quotation by using an ellipsis (. . .) to indicate exactly where words or phrases have been omitted.

According to the Modern Language Association (MLA), "Whenever you wish to omit a word, a phrase, a sentence, or more from a quoted passage, you should be guided by two principles: fairness to the author quoted and the grammatical integrity of your writing. A quotation should never be presented in a way that could cause a reader to misunderstand the sentence structure of the original source."[2]

When you are writing any type of technical document, you have to decide not only what portions of a quote to include, but also which facts to include. As a writer, part of your job is to sort through all the information available on a topic and to provide your audience with only what they need to know. It can be tempting to provide only the information you *want* to, but there are some ethical implications to doing so.

Imagine that Valentine's Day is nearing and you have to write about chocolate. As you browse the Internet for information, you find several reports that chocolate, similar to red wine, may reduce the risk of heart disease. If you write an enthusiastic report on the health benefits of chocolate without also pointing out the health risks associated with high-fat foods, you are not being fair to your audience.

Consider other situations in which you have an ethical obligation *not* to omit certain facts. You are a statistician hired by a drug company to report the results of a drug study to the FDA. Do you omit some of the side effects, or downplay the risks, in order to get the drug approved? Let's say the drug is approved by the FDA, side-effects and all, and you are in charge of publicity. What information will you include and what will you omit in the ad campaign aimed at doctors or the general public?

Another place to be careful about what you omit is the bibliography. Obviously, you cite resources that support your claims, but it's also important to include those sources that contain contrary information.

Being careful about what you omit not only makes your documents fair and balanced, but it's also a sign of professionalism.

[2] *Source:* Gibaldi, Joseph. *MLA Handbook for Writers of Research Papers.* New York: Modern Language Association of America, 1999, p. 85.

visualize or even repeat the research you performed. Therefore, you must discuss the equipment and facilities you used. Describe it in detail, providing brand names, model numbers, sizes, and other such specifications.

For this project, you'll enlist the help of several gardening friends. Each will raise the same variety of tomato, starting on the same day and using the same cultivation techniques. You'll compare soil samples and measure the amount of direct sunlight each garden gets. You'll try to ensure that these gardens are roughly the same in terms of soil, sunlight, and other such variables. Describe all of these efforts in a separate section of the primary research report.

8. **Explain your theory, methods, and procedures.** To enable readers to repeat your project, you must also explain the procedures or methods you used. Use the step-by-step format for this discussion. If you are testing a theory or basing your research on a theory, explain that as well.

   This section may so overlap the preceding section that you can combine them. This section will read like a log of what you and your fellow gardening researchers do from the time you prepare the soil, through planting, through the treatments including routine cultivation, to the end result—harvested tomatoes. As for "theory," you can discuss the strategy used in each control method: for example, one method may repel stinkbugs; another method may lure them to sacrificial plants; and one other method may kill them in some ingenious organic way.

9. **Present the results, findings, and data.** Critical to any primary research report is the data that you collect. You present it in tables, charts, and graphs (see Chapter 10) as well as in regular paragraphs. In any case, you don't interpret the data at this point. Just present it, without trying to explain it.

   How are you going to collect statistical data for this experiment? Count stinkbugs? Count the ruined tomatoes? Unfortunately, one of your research colleagues had to agree that her garden would be the "control" group—in other words, the garden in which no antistinkbug methods are used. You decide to count stinkbugs on three separate plants every third day and record your results. You can present the raw data in tables and perhaps use line graphs to show the comparisons more dramatically.

10. **Write the discussion, conclusions, and recommendations.** In primary research reports, you interpret or discuss your findings in a section separate from the one for data. This is the time to explain your data, interpret it, make recommendations, and state ideas for further research.

    Now you get to interpret your stinkbug numbers and make recommendations. Which control method worked best? Why did it work best? Can you identify conditions that may have "skewed" or distorted your findings? Based on your findings, how strong of a recommendation can you make for the winning stinkbug-control method?

11. **Format the list of information sources.** Ideally, a primary research report builds upon or adds to a body of knowledge. Your primary research report rests on top of all the work done by other researchers on the same topic. For that reason and others, you must list the sources of information you used or consulted in your project.

Create citations for each of the information sources that you used to research this project. In your relentless pursuit of the stinkbug, you consulted books, journal articles, agricultural reports, the Internet, local gardening stores, and fellow backyard gardeners. Make a citation for each of these that you in some way refer to, summarize, or quote.

12. **Plan the appendixes.** Create an appendix for your report for such things as the information sources, large tables of statistics, large illustrations or other kinds of graphics, or any other information that might be useful to readers but that doesn't fit in the main text. (See Chapter 15 for appendix format.)

In the appendixes of this report you might provide a map showing the locations of the gardens in your experiment and diagrams of each garden and its contents. If the data tables are too big for the body of the report, put them in an appendix as well.

13. **Write the introduction.** In the introduction to a primary research report, briefly state the problem your research addresses, the purpose of your research, perhaps the limitations of your findings, and an overview of the contents of the rest of the report.

In the introduction to the stinkbug research report, briefly refer to the stinkbug problem and the difficulty of finding a good solution (but keep it brief; you'll have a background section that goes into the details). State that this report presents findings, conclusions, and recommendations along with procedures. Perhaps mention also the scope of your report—that it's not rigorous experimental science.

14. **Plan the format.** Traditionally, a primary research report is written as an article to be published in a journal. The example primary research report at the end of this chapter uses that format. However, if you were doing this research for a client or employer, you could enclose the report within a business letter or memo. As Chapter 15 shows, you could make the report an attachment to a cover letter or memo, or you could integrate the report with the letter or memo into one self-contained whole.

Because you and your gardening friends hope to get this research report published in that journal, you write a cover letter to the editor of the journal. You make sure that the format of your research report is the same as that required by the journal.

15. **Review and revise your rough draft.** Use the strategies in Chapter 18 on reviewing and revising to systematically review and revise your primary research report. Use the top-down approach described in

Chapter 18: start by reviewing for audience, purpose, and situation; then moving on to content, organization, and transitions; then headings, lists, tables, and graphics; then on to sentence-style revision and technical style; and finally grammar, usage, spelling, and punctuation problems.

WORKSHOP: CAUSES, EFFECTS, PRIMARY RESEARCH REPORTS

Each writes their own draft then comb...

research disease

Here are some additional ideas for practicing the concepts, tools, and strategies in this chapter:

1. *Identifying causes.* Consider one or more of the following topics or situations and identify the possible causes—either sequential, telescoping, or controversial.

sneezing	ulcer	heart attack
red color of Mars	lightning	wind
snow	headache	migraine
stopped-up sink	common cold	overdraft at the bank
overheated car engine	car air conditioner not cooling	solar eclipse

Choose 1

Medical condition
Research causes
Audience — Blue Cross Blue Shield policy holders
newsletter

2. *Identifying effects.* Consider one or more of the preceding topics or situations, and identify the potential effects—either sequential, telescoping, or controversial.

3. *Experiments and surveys.* Consider any one of the following experiments or surveys. How would you structure the primary research report on that experiment? What would be the main sections and what would they contain?

Best varieties of tomatoes for your backyard garden

Most effective organic methods of pest control in backyard gardens

Online learning versus traditional classroom learning

Best storage medium for solar energy

Effects of free ridership on the use of mass transportation

Effects of melatonin on sleep behaviors

Dvorak keyboard versus the standard QWERTY keyboard

Productivity and in-house fitness/recreational facilities for employees

Why does batsaliva help w/ brain aneurisms?

Term to define: This discussion of schizophrenia is causal in that it focuses on a series of potential symptoms of the mental condition. A *symptom* is a type of effect, consequence, or result. The condition (cause) called schizophrenia produces these symptoms (effects).

Highlighting: The word "positive" is italicized to indicate that it is defined at that point in the document.

Bulleted-list overview: Notice that the symptoms are listed in a series of bullets, clearly indicating the organization of the upcoming discussion.

Headings: This is the first of the main headings in this discussion of the symptoms of schizophrenia. In the terminology used by the headings chapter (Chapter 7) this is a second-level heading. It is bold, left-aligned, and uses headline-style caps.

Neutral personal pronouns: A common problem is to write the sentence this way: "A person may feel that they . . .." The problem is that "person" is singular, and "they" is plural. The best solution is to rephrase with a plural noun, as is done here. (Phrasing it "A person may feel that he . . .." would be an instance of sexist language.)

Citations: This document uses the number system to indicate sources of borrowed information. The first bracketed number indicates the source number; the second indicates the page numbers on which the original information occurs. Go to the end of the document and find source 1 in the list of information sources.

CAUSE–EFFECT DISCUSSION

Symptoms of Type I Schizophrenia[3]

According to the American Psychiatric Association, the symptoms of schizophrenia that are considered *positive* are those that exhibit an excess, or addition, of expressions to the otherwise characteristic set of expressions that a person usually projects. A person must show continuous signs of these symptoms during a six-month period, and at least two of the symptoms must be present for a period of at least one month.

The main categories of symptoms associated with Type I Schizophrenia include:

- Disorganized speech
- Other-controlled cognitive processes
- Delusions
- Hallucinations

Disorganized Speech and Thought Processes

Disorganized speech is characterized by the inability to form continuous and coherent speech or to maintain a topic to its logical conclusion. It is common for schizophrenic individuals to make up words or phrases that have meaning only to themselves. People suffering from this symptom may also rhyme or echo previous statements [1:346-347].

Other-Controlled Cognitive Processes

A cognitive process is a thought process that the brain uses to organize and develop thoughts and ideas. Individuals with "other-controlled" cognitive processes may feel that their thoughts are controlled or influenced by an outside force, or that thoughts are put into (thought insertion) or taken out of (thought withdrawal) their heads [3].

[3] *Source:* Special thanks to Stephen B. Floyd, former Austin Community College technical writing student, for this cause–effect discussion and permission to adapt it here.

Delusions

Individuals suffering from delusions maintain ideas that are quite real to them but absurd to others. *Delusions* are false and irrational beliefs subscribed to by a person even when evidence to the contrary is produced. Delusions of persecution, grandeur, and control are a few of the most common types. Individuals may feel that they possess super-human powers such as the ability to communicate with alien forces on another planet, or they may believe they are being followed by the CIA, which intends to kill them.

Persecutory delusions involve the belief that others are spying on, spreading false rumors about, or planning to harm the person [2]. Forms of thought involve loosening of associations, in which ideas or thoughts shift from one subject to another [2].

Content and form of thought involve delusions that are often multiple, fragmented, or bizarre. Individuals may feel that their thoughts are being broadcast or controlled by a dead person.

Hallucinations

Hallucinations are distortions of perception initiated within the body, having no external basis. Hallucinations may involve one or all of the five senses of taste, smell, touch, sight, and hearing.

The most common hallucinations are *auditory*, in which people hear voices inside their own heads that no one else can hear. Auditory hallucinations can consist of single or multiple voices typically making insulting or demeaning remarks to the individual (you are no good, you are the devil, etc.) [3].

- *Tactile* (touch) hallucinations may take the form of tingling or burning, or the feeling of insects crawling just beneath the skin surface [1:347].
- *Somatic* (from the mind) hallucinations create sensations of internal organs moving or shifting.

Documentation: As shown in the bracketed citations on this page, you do not have to indicate the page number in all cases. (If you want to be nice to your readers, include them.)

Sexist language: Notice that throughout this document the writer carefully avoids using singular nouns that would, in turn, require a singular pronoun: "individuals" instead of "individual"; "people" instead of "person." Plurals enable the writer to use "they" or "them" instead of the sexist "he" or "him," the awkward "he/she," or the grammatically incorrect "they or them."

Bulleted lists: Notice the use of bullets to present the different types of hallucinations. Notice. also, that the name of each type is italicized to make it more readily accessible to readers. (For more on lists, see Chapter 8.)

- *Visual* hallucinations can manifest as distortions of colors, shapes, or visualization of objects that do not exist.
- *Gustatory* hallucinations are those in which individuals continually feel that their food tastes strange when in reality the food is perfectly normal.
- *Olfactory* hallucinations are those that delude individuals into the belief that they frequently smell poisonous smoke or decay [1].

Information Sources

1. Comer, Ronald J. *Fundamentals of Abnormal Psychology.* New York: W. H. Freeman, 1996.
2. *Diagnostic and Statistical Manual of Mental Health, DSMIII,* 3rd ed. Washington, D.C.: American Psychiatric Association, 1987.
3. Groningen University, Department of Social Psychiatry, *Schizophrenia,* 1996.

Information sources: At the end of the document is the information-sources list. Notice that it is arranged alphabetically by author's last name and numbered.

Primary research report: This example reports on research done to verify that bats roost on the ground in the winter. As you'll see, it's essentially a series of observations made during prescribed burns in a forested area. Source: "Bats Roosting in Deciduous Leaf Litter," *Bat Research News*, 40(3) (1999): 74–75.

Introduction and background: In a longer research report, you'd see a separate background section with its own heading. It would summarize the current knowledge about the topic, present the research question, and perhaps discuss the rationale for attempting to find answers for it.

In this case, the report is brief; an elaborate literature review is not needed. This introduction quickly refers to existing research ("recent surge of information . . ."), poses the research question ("little is known . . ."), and then states the purpose of this report ("Herein, we report . . .")

Writing style—point of view: While this report certainly has the atmosphere of traditional research-reporting style, notice that it is comfortable with the contemporary first-person style ("Herein, we report . . .," "We made 10 observations . . .," "On 16 February, we conducted . . . ."). Even so, this report still contains lots of passive voice: and rightly so, because we are more interested in the bats! But notice the reference to "researchers"—that's a little confusing. Same people?

Modifier problem: The traditional research writing style makes it easy to create dangling and misplaced modifiers. For example, the words "one bat was flushed while raking fire lines" suggest that bat was doing the raking. To fix this one, rewrite it as "one bat was flushed while the fire lines were being raked."

PRIMARY RESEARCH REPORT

Bats Roosting in Deciduous Leaf Litter[4]

Christopher E. Moorman,[1] Kevin R. Russell,[1] Michael A. Menzel,[2] Stephen M. Lehr,[1] Justin E. Ellenberger,[1] and D. H. Van Lear[1]

[1]Department of Forest Services, Clemson University, Clemson, SC 29634
and
[2]Division of Forestry, West Virginia University, Morgantown, WV 26506

Despite the recent surge of information concerning characteristics of roost sites used by tree-roosting bats during summer (for example, Crampton and Barclay, 1998; Menzel et al., 1998), little is known about roost sites used by bats during winter. During summer, some tree-roosting bats roost within the canopy of hardwood trees (Menzel et al., 1998). However, once leaves fall, deciduous trees may no longer be adequate as roost sites. Herein, we report observations that further support claims concerning use of litter on the forest floor by bats in winter.

Observations

We made 10 observations of bats in winter flying from deciduous leaf litter in three upland hardwood stands in the South Carolina Piedmont. The three stands were located on the Clemson University Experimental Forest ca. 4 miles N of Clemson, South Carolina. All observations were made in stands comprised predominately of mixed oaks (*Querus*) with lesser amounts of yellow poplar (*Liriodendron tulipifera*), hickory (*Carya*), and red maple (*Acer rubrum*). The understory was sparsely vegetated with isolated mountain laurel (*Kalimia latifolia*), red buckeye (*Aesculus sylvatica*), and American holly (*Ilex americana*). Depth of the litter layer in the three stands was ca. 7 cm.

A single bat was flushed from leaf litter on 5 January 1999, as several researchers walked near its location. Nine other observations were made while conducting low-intensity strip-head fires in 6 1-ha [hectare] plots

[4] *Source:* Thanks to the authors of this article and G. Roy Horst of *Bat Research News* for permission to adapt it here.

within the three stands. All burns were conducted on clear days. Bats roused during prescribed burns flew as the strip fires approached, and one bat was flushed while raking fire lines. Two or more of the researchers viewed each bat. Once bats were roused, they flew over the roost site for several seconds and disappeared into the canopy or smoke created by the fire. Because bats flew out of sight, some observations could have been on the same individual.

On 16 February, we conducted a prescribed fire at two plots bisected by a small perennial stream. The aspects and slope gradients of the two plots were 105° SSW and 280° WNW and 40% and 15%, respectively. At the time of the burn, ambient temperature was 18°C, and the minimum temperature the night previous was 2°C. Two bats flew from the forest floor of the SSW-facing slope, and three bats flushed from the WNW-facing slope. One of the bats on the WNW-facing plot flew from a location within 5 m of where the first bat was flushed on 5 January, suggesting that the individual may have returned after researchers left the area.

On 25 February, we conducted a second prescribed fire at two plots bisected by a different biennial stream. The aspects and slope gradients of the two plots were 45° NE and 216° SSW and 32% and 23%, respectively. Ambient temperature during the prescribed burn was 14°C, and minimum temperature the previous night was 0°C. Two bats were roused from the SSW-facing plot, but no bats were observed while burning the second plot.

On 23 March, a third prescribed burn was conducted at two plots bisected by a third small stream. Aspects and slopes of the two plots were 20° NNE and 210° SSW and 30% and 26%, respectively. While burning, ambient temperature was 22°C, and minimum temperature during the previous 24 hours was 4°C. One bat was flushed when fire lines were raked on the SSW-facing slope, and a second bat flew from the forest floor on the NNE-facing slope as the fires approached.

Numbers: Notice the contrasting use of numbers as words and as digits throughout this report. Any numerical value that is both exact and essential is displayed as a digit. Thus "5 "is used with "m"; "10" with "observations"; "7" with "cm"; "4" with "miles." But notice that words are used in "three upland hardwood stands" and "two plots." Although these are exact values, the writers don't view them as essential or critical enough to display as digits.

Content and organization: Although this is a brief and rather informal report, it still has the structure of the research report: it begins with a research question and literature review, provides details on observations, and begins discussing and concluding only in the final section. Throughout, related research is cited. Notice how carefully these writers avoid drawing conclusions or speculating on causes or effects in "Observations."

Latin abbreviations: Notice the use of "et al." It's Latin for "and others"; "al." is an abbreviation for "alia." "ca." stands for "circa" in Latin, or "about." Even though these are non-English words, their use is so common in this context they are not italicized. Although Latin abbreviations are generally not used, in this scientific context they are standard: for example, "i.e." and "e.g." are other commonly used Latin abbreviations.

Source citations: This report uses American Psychological Association style. If you want to see details on Brose and Van Lear, 1998, go to the literature-cited section at the end of this report: you'll see the title of the article and of the journal in which it appeared as well as dates. (Notice that if the author name is stated in the regular text, it can be omitted in the parenthetical citation.)

Documentation style: This report, published in *Bat Research News*, uses APA style. You can see that the in-text citations include names and years in parentheses. Notice that italics are not used on book and journal names but instead on species names only. That's the way these researchers want it!

Discussion and Conclusions

Although we were unable to make definitive identifications, we suggest the bats were eastern red bats (*Lasiurus borealis*). All were relatively large (i.e., larger than *Myotis*), and those seen up close were reddish. Saugey et al. (1989) also reported seeing bats "smoked" from their hibernation sites during a prescribed winter burn in Arkansas, and they believed the bats were eastern red bats resting in leaf litter on the forest floor. In 1993 and 1994, a female and male eastern red bat were radiotracked to a single site in hardwood-pine leaf litter on the forest floor (Saugey et al., 1998). Past reports were from the central United States, but our data indicate possible use of leaf litter by eastern red bats is more widespread geographically and may occur throughout the species' range.

Oak leaves dominated the litter layer of the plots prior to burns. No bats were flushed from up-slope portions of the stands, which typically contained fewer hardwoods and more pines (*Pinus*). Because of their color, insulatory properties, and resistance to decay, sites with well-developed hardwood litter, especially oak litter, may provide important wintering sites for eastern red bats. However, prescribed fires typically eliminate much forest-floor debris, including leaf litter and small woody debris. Therefore, fire likely renders the burned area temporarily inadequate for ground-roosting bats. Although prescribed fire traditionally has been used for pine management, recent research (Brose and Van Lear, 1998; Brose et al., 1999) indicates that fire is an essential ecological process in management of upland oaks during the regeneration phase. In light of our observations, further investigation of bat use of forest-floor debris is warranted, especially in areas where prescribed burning or other silvicultural manipulations are common.

Acknowledgements

We thank S. K. Cox, S. Perry, D. B. Vandermast, J. Albiston, and many undergraduates for assistance during prescribed burns. Prescribed fires were conducted for a project funded by McIntire–Stennis through Clemson University.

Literature Cited

Brose, P. H., and D. H. Van Lear. 1998. Response of hardwood advanced regeneration to seasonal prescribed fires in oak-dominated shelterwood stands. Canadian Journal of Forest Research, 28:331-339.

Brose, P. H., D. H. Van Lear, and R. Cooper. 1999. Using shelterwood harvests and prescribed fire to regenerate oaks on productive upland sites. Forest Ecology and Management, 113:125-141.

Crampton, L. H., and R. M. R. Barclay. 1998. Selection of roosting and foraging habitat by bats in different-aged mixed wood stands. Conservation Biology, 12:1347-1358.

Menzel, M. A., T. C. Carter, B. R. Chapman, and J. Laerm. 1998. Quantitative tree roosts used by red bats (*Lasirius borealis*) and Seminole bats (*L. seminolus*). Canadian Journal of Zoology, 76:630-634.

Saugey, D. A., D. R. Heath, and G. A. Heidt. 1989. The bats of the Quachita Mountains. Proceedings of the Arkansas Academy of Science, 43:71-77.

Saugey, D. A., R. L. Vaughn, B. G. Crump, and G. A. Heidt. 1998. Notes on the natural history of *Lasirius borealis* in Arkansas. Journal of the Arkansas Academy of Science, 52:92-98.

CHAPTER 4

Comparison: Recommendation, Evaluation, and Feasibility Reports

VOICE-RECOGNITION TECHNOLOGIES

Computers have come a long way in their ability to process and respond to normal human speech. But have they come far enough? The recommendation report on voice-recognition software at the end of this chapter considers that question. And for more information on this emerging technology, see these Web sites.

Beyond Recognition, to Understanding. MIT's Victor Zue.
www.speechtechmag.com/st.mag/st15/zue.htm

Speech's Holy Grail: The Present and Future of Large Vocabulary Continuous Speech. Peter Fleming and Robert Andersen.
www.speechtechmag.com/st.mag/st06/holygral.htm

Kimberly Patch & Eric Smalley, "Speech recognition makes some noise," February 2, 1998 (Vol. 20, Issue 5).
www.idg.net/new_docids/speech/heres/recognition/understand/ computer/overview/promise/anyway/new_docid_9-63999.html

Victor Zue, "Talking with Your Computer."
www.scientificamerican.com/1999/0899issue/0899zue.html

MIT's Spoken Language Systems (theses and papers).
www.sls.lcs.mit.edu/sls/publications/index.html

Accessed January 12, 2001.

Recommendation, evaluation, and feasibility reports are a loosely differentiated set of reports that compare carefully gathered information to pass judgment on products, properties, plans, or personnel. As you know from the Preface, most technical documents are based on one or more *infrastructures*—elemental structures that enable reports to do their job. The infrastructure essential to recommendation, evaluation, and feasibility reports is *comparison*. To make an intelligent choice from a set of options (such as products, properties, plans, organizations, or personnel), you have to compare those choices against a set of requirements and against each other.

This chapter shows you how to write comparisons and then how to construct recommendation, evaluation, and feasibility reports with comparison incorporated as the infrastructure.

Note:
▪ If you are new to this book, see "How Do You Use This Book?" in the Preface.
▪ For additional examples of the documents discussed in this chapter, see **www.io.com/~hcexres/power_tools/examples**.

HOW DO YOU WRITE A COMPARISON?

Before getting into the details of recommendation, evaluation, and feasibility reports, take a moment to review comparison—the essential infrastructure used in these types of reports. Although comparisons can be structured in a variety of ways, the *point-by-point approach* is usually the most effective. It forces you, the writer, to compare items systematically, one *point of comparison* at a time. For example, in a comparison of three speech-recognition software applications, you might first discuss the accuracy of the three applications, then the ease of use, then the cost, and so on. (These two approaches are illustrated in Figure 4-1.)

The opposite of the point-by-point approach is the *whole-to-whole approach*. It usually produces uneven, inconsistent, and incomplete comparisons. In the whole-to-whole approach, it's too easy to discuss one option, then the next, then the next, without ever directly comparing those options fully. (See the example of a point-to-point comparison in Figure 4-2.)

Let's walk through the important steps in writing comparisons using the point-by-point approach. To give you a sense of how these steps work in an actual writing project, we'll follow a single example throughout.

1. Find a situation requiring comparison of two or more items. Try to find a workplace situation in which a document containing comparison is needed. The comparison can be *informative*, to help readers understand the things being compared. For example, in the early days of the personal computer, word-processing applications were commonly compared with the typewriter. Comparisons can be

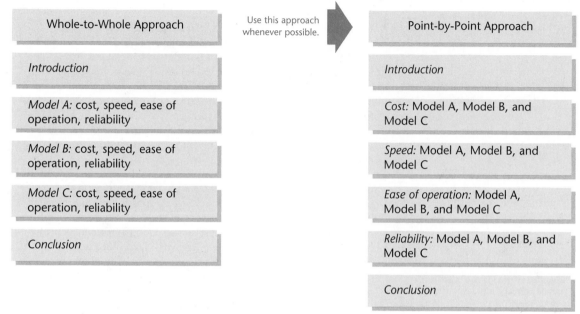

FIGURE 4-1

Different approaches to comparison. The whole-to-whole approach forces readers to make comparisons for themselves and easily becomes disorganized. The point-by-point approach systematically compares each item against one category, or point of comparison, at a time.

evaluative, to help readers decide whether to purchase, fund, implement, or continue something. Recommendation, feasibility, and evaluative reports are covered later in this chapter. (Having trouble thinking of a topic? See **www.io.com/~hcexres/power_tools/topics.html**.)

Imagine that you are part of a team developing a "white paper" on voice-recognition software for a state agency. The agency is considering the use of this software for its handicapped employees. One part of the project is to compare voice-recognition software to something familiar to help agency officials understand this software. Your comparison will be used in the "basics" section. The white paper will go on to discuss how the software works, how well it works, and other such issues.

2. **Choose what to compare.** You may already know what you are going to compare; for example, you might compare CD-ROMs to DVDs. However, if you want to compare something familiar to something unfamiliar, you may have some brainstorming to do. For example, what familiar item could you use for a comparison to superstrings (that strange concept with which physicists hope to develop the Grand Unified Theory)?

These paragraphs compare classical ("binary") logic and "fuzzy" logic.	One of the essential theories that makes technologies like voice-recognition software possible is fuzzy logic and fuzzy sets, an idea developed by Lotfi Zadeh in the mid-1960s.
Note how the two kinds of logic are compared, first, by how they deal with set; second, by how they process data; and, third, by how they are or can be used in applications.	The essential distinction between classical logic and fuzzy logic has to do with sets and membership in sets. In classical logic, an individual item either is or is not a member of a set. For example, a certain tree is either a member of the set of tall trees or not. In contrast, fuzzy logic offers a method for expressing the extent to which an individual item belongs to a set. Thus, fuzzy logic can state that a certain tree belongs "partly" to the set of tall trees and that that tree can be described as "fairly tall."
Notice that both kinds of logic get mentioned in each of the three paragraphs.	Fuzzy-logic systems process data in a markedly different way than do systems based on binary logic. Binary logic is limited to two values—1 or 0 (yes or no)—in expressing the possibility that an event will occur. On the other hand, fuzzy logic can express that possibility in varying degrees of truthfulness or falsehood ("maybe," "probably," "most likely," "not likely," "no way!"). In other words, fuzzy logic provides a system for expressing the probability of an event.
Notice the strong use of transition words that emphasize that a comparison is being made.	Applications that use fuzzy logic reach far beyond the capabilities of those that use classical binary logic. Starting out in the 1980s as an experimental technology, systems using fuzzy logic have become commercially viable in the 1990s. While systems using conventional binary logic had reached a dead end in areas such as speech and handwriting recognition, fuzzy-logic systems have enabled dramatic strides in these areas. Fuzzy systems are now used in camcorders, washing machines, and air-conditioning systems, among others. They are also used in Japan to control subways.

FIGURE 4-2
Short comparison. This example uses the point-by-point approach to compare classical, binary logic to "fuzzy" logic.

Just what can you compare voice-recognition software to? At first, you think you could compare training and using voice-recognition software to training a dog. Fetch! Exit! But that might not play well with state officials. Then you realize that this software is not merely about converting spoken words to text, but about interpreting and acting on requests. It's very much like interacting with a human assistant—and that's the analogy you decide to use.

3. **Define a purpose and audience.** The next step is to zero in on a purpose and an audience for this comparison. (See Chapter 19 for strategies to use in analyzing audiences and adapting your writing to them.) To keep this practice comparison simple, use an informative purpose and a nonspecialist audience. Either help readers understand both things being compared, or use an analogy to something familiar to help readers understand one of them.

The audience for your comparison is agency officials who are clueless about voice-recognition software. These readers are executives, though, in positions to approve the acquisition of this software for hundreds of handicapped state employees. These state officials have enough basic familiarity with computers to write documents. You know that they are interested in performance, results, and costs, and they are only minimally interested in technical details about how this software works. Your immediate purpose is to inform: these readers need to gain a reasonable level of understanding from your comparison. You also have another purpose lurking quietly in the background: you want those state officials to get interested and even excited about this software.

4. Do some research. To write even a simple comparison, you may need to do some research.

If you did some searching on voice-recognition software, you'd find advertisements from the major manufacturers of the software such as IBM, Dragon Systems, and others. However, you'd also find some interesting articles from *Scientific American* as well as general-discussion materials available from the manufacturers themselves. The technology is still so new as of the year 2000 that they must establish its credibility. You'd also find literature from places like MIT and AT&T Bell Labs.

5. Identify the points of comparison. With your purpose and audience defined, choose the points of comparison that meet the needs of the readers and enable a good discussion of the things being compared. Identify three, four, five, or more points of comparison— enough to bring out the comparison fully.

You can compare how voice-recognition systems and human assistants take in and interpret requests, how they must clarify those requests if something's amiss, select the correct domain of knowledge (for example, weather forecasts or flight schedules), formulate queries, communicate the results of queries, and so on.

6. Plan how to write each comparative point. Now you're ready to plan the actual comparison. Plan to spend one or more sentences, or a whole paragraph, comparing the items according to *one point of comparison at a time.*

Consider the paragraph on clarifying requests. You can compare how a human assistant might ask, "Did you say Boston or Austin?" to how voice-recognition software would need the same capability. Another comparative paragraph would discuss selection of domains. If you asked, "When's the next flight to Boston?" how would the software know to check flight schedules as opposed to weather forecasts? You can compare how a human assistant would do this to how the software does it.

7. **Plan and develop graphics.** Early in this project, visualize the graphics your comparison will need. Use the strategies in Chapter 10 and Chapter 11 to plan the drawings, diagrams, photos, tables, and charts you may need to include.

   Illustrative graphics for voice-recognition software may be hard to come by. You can show the basic setup: a microphone, a computer, and screen captures of the interface of the software. To help people understand the software, you might provide a flowchart of how speech is processed. Tables might be useful to present data on the performance of this software—different software packages, in particular.

8. **Sketch the headings you'll use.** If your comparison is more than two or three paragraphs, use headings (see Chapter 7). If you use one or more paragraphs to discuss individual points of comparison, create a heading for each one.

   Your points of comparison resemble the phases in the operation of voice-recognition software. You can use a heading for each point of comparison: "Input," "Interpretation," "Clarification," "Queries," "Action," and "Communication." Perhaps you can use a continuous example, such as asking a human assistant or the voice-recognition software about the next flight to Boston.

9. **Plan an introduction.** Save the introduction until after you've planned or drafted the main text of the comparison. In the introduction, indicate the purpose: to compare. List the items to be compared and the points of comparison you'll use, and provide some idea as to why the comparison is needed.

   In this introduction, indicate that you are going to provide a "nontechnical" overview of voice-recognition software by comparing it to interaction with a human assistant. Provide a general comparison: that using voice-recognition software is much like interacting with a human assistant.

10. **Consider adding a conclusion.** If your comparison doesn't "feel" complete after the final point of comparison, consider adding a summary that refocuses your readers, enabling them to finish reading with the right perspective.

    An obvious candidate for the conclusion would be to discuss the limitations of voice-recognition software—how it's *not* like a human assistant.

11. Consider the format. For this simple project, you are not likely to need the elaborate report formats shown in Chapter 15. Instead, use the format you see for the comparison of Mars and Earth at the end of this chapter. Begin with a descriptive title centered at the top of the page, and use second- and third-level headings. Use lists, notices, illustrations, tables, highlighting, and documentation (citations of your borrowed information sources) as necessary.

12. Review and revise your rough draft. Use the strategies in Chapter 18 to systematically review and revise your comparison. Use the top-down approach described in that chapter: start by reviewing for audience, purpose, and situation; then move on to content, organization, and transitions; then headings, lists, tables, and graphics; then sentence-style revision and technical style, and finally grammar, usage, spelling, and punctuation problems.

WHAT ARE RECOMMENDATION, EVALUATION, AND FEASIBILITY REPORTS?

Out in the real world you are not likely to find people who use the names of these types of reports with as much precision as we do here. The names—recommendation, evaluation, and feasibility reports—are interchangeable for most professionals. But making the following distinctions may help you to get a sense of the range of this important type of report:

■ *Recommendation report*—Compares two or more options (products, properties, plans, organizations, or personnel) against requirements and then recommends one option (the one that best meets the stated requirements), several options (the ones that meet the requirements but in different ways), or none.

■ *Evaluation report*—Compares individual products, plans, programs, properties, organizations, or personnel against requirements and makes an evaluative judgment—whether it met its expectations, or whether it is "good" or "useful."

■ *Feasibility report*—Makes an evaluative judgment as to whether a project is possible or worthwhile. Its essential task is to tell readers whether a project is "feasible"—whether it is technically, socially, economically, administratively, or environmentally possible or practical.

These reports are essential tools for consultants. Consultants typically study a problem and recommend a solution. They usually get their jobs by submitting proposals (covered in Chapter 6). When they get a contract, they do the research and, generally, submit one of the types of reports presented in this chapter.

HOW DO YOU WRITE A RECOMMENDATION REPORT?

Comparison is the essential infrastructure of recommendation, evaluation, and feasibility reports. It forces you to identify key requirements, which you translate into points of comparison and discuss one at a time. It forces you to give equal time to each item being compared and to state how each item meets the requirements. Writing these reports with comparison as the infrastructure shows readers how you reached your conclusions and recommendations. If they are skeptical, readers can use your comparative information to reach different conclusions and make their own decisions.

The following example walks you through the typical phases in developing this type of report. (Be sure to look at the recommendation report on voice-recognition software at the end of the chapter, which illustrates most of the sections discussed in the following.)

1. **Find a situation in need of a recommendation report.** The classic situation is an individual or organization making an expensive purchase decision. Try to find just such a situation, or invent a realistic one. In this type of report, you start with a problem or need and two or more products, services, or programs that might help. You compare those options and recommend one.

   Imagine that a professional organization of medical transcriptionists has commissioned you to study voice-recognition software (a still-emerging technology as of the year 2000). You might have to do a *feasibility study* as to whether this software is practical in terms of its usefulness, accuracy, and cost. You might have to do a *recommendation report* comparing different voice-recognition software packages against your clients' requirements. Or you might have to do an *evaluation report* in which you research some organization currently using voice-recognition software to determine whether it is working. In any case, the medical transcriptionist organization is paying your fee: you do the work they require.

2. **Define the audience and purpose.** As with any technical-writing project, you begin by developing an in-depth understanding of the situation requiring a report and of the needs, interests, and knowledge levels of the readers of that report. For a recommendation, evaluation, or feasibility report, study the problem or the opportunity that the audience is considering. Study these readers' goals and their requirements for reaching those goals. Understand their level of knowledge and experience in relation to the potential project and its technical aspects.

   This medical transcriptionist organization wants a recommendation as to which software application to use, apparently having made up its collective mind to use this software. You recognize that its members want to know how the software works, how well it works, how easy it is to learn and use, whether its benefits justify its cost, and so on.

3. **Build a team?** Recommendation reports, like primary research reports and proposals, are good opportunities to work as a team. Typically, there's more work to do than one individual can handle.

Writing on voice-recognition software will be no small project. You will have to research how this technology works, gather information about individual software products, review how this software is used in business and industry, collect evaluative information on how it performs, and more. You may have to reduce your coverage severely or put together a team of one or two others to share the workload.

4. **Describe the problem or opportunity.** In a recommendation, evaluation, or feasibility report, you focus on situations involving problems in need of solutions and opportunities for improvement. You must explain the situation that brought about the report; for example, an administrative decision, an organizational problem, or a request for proposals. Describe the project in your report in order to demonstrate your understanding of it and to reassure readers that you understand their situation. This section of your report also provides dates, names of individuals and organizations, contract numbers, and so on.

In this voice-recognition project, medical transcriptionists want to solve problems with slow, expensive, inaccurate medical transcription. They seek improvements in the efficiency and accuracy of their work. They want to know whether the software really works and which software package is the best for their needs. You might describe their current operations—how much manual transcription costs, how much time it takes, how much inaccuracy there is—in very specific statistical detail.

5. **Define the requirements and priorities.** In this type of report, you must research your readers' requirements and summarize them. Because you systematically compare the options one requirement at a time, you must have a section stating those requirements and their rationale. In the requirements section, include the following:

   - *Numeric requirements.* Some requirements are based on numbers, for example, costs, weight, height, and so on: "The maximum cost for the option is $2000."
   - *Yes/no requirements.* Other requirements are simply a yes/no; does the option have a certain feature or not? For example: "The option must have on-screen editing capabilities."
   - *Rating-based requirements.* Still other requirements rely on ratings by experts or typical users: "The option must have an ease-of-use rating of at least 4.0 on a 5.0 scale."

It's not enough just to define requirements. You must also establish *priorities*. These help you decide in cases where there is no clear cut best choice among options, as is usually the case. For example, how will you decide if one option has the lowest cost while another option has the best functions?

For this voice-recognition project, include requirements such as cost maximums, minimum ease-of-use ratings, and percentage-based efficiency improvements. State these requirements in specific statistical, yes/no, or ratings-based terms. Because accuracy is still the biggest issue in this emerging technology, define it as the top priority, ahead of cost and ease of learning and use.

6. **List and describe the options.** Discuss options that may solve the problems, exploit the opportunities, or meet the requirements. Explain how you narrowed the field of options to the ones you actually compare. Consider discussing each option. In a recommendation or feasibility report this discussion can be a separate section.

In the voice-recognition example, present the candidates just after the requirements section. Explain why you excluded other voice-recognition software packages. Explain how these candidates meet the minimal requirements presented in the requirements section.

7. **Consider including technical background.** For some reports, you must provide some technical background. That way, readers can understand related concepts and terminology as they are mentioned later in the report. Avoid including technical background that readers don't need. If you write the background section late in the project, you'll know which concepts, theory, and terminology readers need help with, and you can write the section accordingly.

In this report on voice-recognition software, it might not be a bad idea to discuss some theory: important aspects of human speech, techniques for sampling and recognizing speech, training methods used to accustom software to an individual's voice, and so on. Without this background, readers may have trouble understanding the comparative discussion. However, write this background after the comparison so that you focus strictly on background necessary for understanding the comparisons.

8. **Plan and write the point-by-point comparisons.** If you've done everything up to this point, you are ready to compare the options against the requirements and determine the best choice. The essential element, the heart of this type of report, is the comparison section. The point-by-point approach is critical in providing a systematic presentation of the strengths and weaknesses of the options being compared. (In the voice-recognition report at the end of this chapter, the heading "Points of Comparison" introduces the comparison.) To write an individual comparative section, be sure to do at least the following:

- Begin by stating the point of comparison and the related requirement.
- Compare and contrast the relevant details of each option related to the point of comparison. If one option is significantly less expensive, discuss reasons why that might be so. Explain whether the differences are significant.
- State which is the best option for the point of comparison. State this conclusion overtly; don't leave it to readers to figure out, no matter how obvious it may seem.

In the comparisons section of this recommendation report, compare the software products by accuracy, speed, ease of use, cost, and so on. In the processing speed comparison, state how fast each product can process human speech. Consider factors that might distort those speeds; for example, discuss whether one product takes more processing time but achieves greater accuracy. After this discussion, state a conclusion as to which product has the best speed. Qualify that statement if other factors make a difference. Follow this same pattern in each of the other comparative sections.

9. **Create a summary of conclusions.** Once you've finished the comparisons, copy the conclusions into a separate list of conclusions. Review these conclusions, apply the requirements and priorities you established earlier, and determine the overall best candidate. If you can't pick a winner, you may have to redefine your requirements and priorities. The list of conclusions is important for readers: they can scan it for the key facts and conclusions. (In the voice-recognition report at the end of this chapter, the conclusions summary is introduced by the heading "Executive Summary.") In a list of conclusions, state the following:

- State the important *primary conclusions*, those that you reach in each of the comparative sections. For example, one option may be the least expensive; another may have the highest ease-of-use ratings. These are primary conclusions.
- Also state *secondary conclusions*, those that apply the requirements and priorities to conflicting primary conclusions. Primary conclusions "conflict" when they point to different options as the best choice. One option may be the cheapest; another may be the easiest to use. What to do? Ideally, you've defined a priority that will help you decide.
- And last, state a *final conclusion*—that is, which option is the best choice based on the requirements and priorities. Remember that although an option may be the best choice, it may not necessarily be the one that you would recommend. One option may be the "best" among the options compared, but it might meet so few of the requirements that you could not recommend it.

Practical Ethics: Anecdotal Evidence

Anecdotes, or stories of personal experience, are powerful things. They are used in almost every form of communication to sell items ("I took this diet pill and lost two hundred pounds"), to illustrate a point, to persuade ("This is my experience and will be yours, too"), or to simply pique people's interest so they will listen or keep reading.

Using anecdotes in communication is perfectly legitimate, but they have limitations. Certainly, using anecdotes to create interest or make a topic more personal is often a good idea. Wouldn't you rather listen to a speaker who uses lively stories or interesting anecdotes rather than one who simply recites dry statistics? Most people would. However, when you are trying to inform or convince an audience of something important, hard evidence and statistics are far more credible than personal experience.

Let's say you tried a new brand of soap and your face broke out. There seems to be a definite cause and effect between the soap and your allergic reaction, and it makes sense that you would warn friends or family away from the soap based on your personal experience. But it is also possible that the allergic reaction was influenced by something you aren't aware of, like a change in your diet, a drug interaction, or the poison oak you inadvertently brushed up against. So to conclude that *no one* should be allowed to use or manufacture this soap is not a fair use of anecdotal evidence, and unless your personal experience is corroborated by outside sources, you probably won't get very far in lobbying for the soap's removal from the market.

When used correctly, either in personal situations or combined with scientific research, anecdotes are powerful tools of communication. If you are making recommendations or conclusions in a technical report, make sure you back up your anecdotes with solid research.

In the conclusions section for this recommendation report, repeat the key conclusions occurring in the comparison section: for example, which product had the best processing speed and best accuracy, was the least expensive, and so on. Those are the primary conclusions, as discussed earlier. Next, develop the secondary conclusions, indicating that you value the product with the best accuracy as opposed to the one with the lowest price. End with the final conclusion; that is, which voice-recognition software product is the best of the ones compared. Remember that this final conclusion is not necessarily a recommendation. Voice-recognition technology may not be mature enough to provide any real advantage for your readers.

10. **Create a summary table.** For most reports of this type, it helps to include a *summary table,* which is a table that summarizes all the key comparative information about the options. See the summary table in the voice-recognition report at the end of this chapter. Also, see Chapter 10, which discusses the basics of table design. Providing the summary table gives readers a different view of the same information presented in regular paragraph form; it's another way of ensuring that readers get your message.

In this voice-recognition software report, design a table with rows for the four software applications compared and columns for the comparisons. One column might be for cost; another for requirements; another for ease-of-use ratings; another for accuracy; and so on. This design enables readers to compare vertically.

11. Write the recommendation section. Although it may seem totally obvious, you must state your recommendation and the main conclusions that support that recommendation in a separate section of the report. Introduce the recommendation with a readily identifiable heading so that readers can find it as soon as they open your report.

In the report on voice-recognition software, you can state which software product you recommend and then review the three or four most important reasons why. These reasons will summarize the most important conclusions. Consider writing a conditional recommendation: for example, if the readers expect to use the software often for critical projects, they should purchase the most powerful software (which is also the most expensive). If not, they should purchase the less expensive product.

12. Format the list of information sources. As with any professional writing project, indicate the sources of information that you used to develop this report. Include not only printed sources (including product brochures) but Internet sources and informal, unpublished sources such as interviews. List them at the end of the report.

The information sources for this voice-recognition software report include the individuals you interviewed at the client's location, current users of the software, product specifications and brochures, manufacturers' sales representatives, magazine articles, and books on voice-recognition technology in general.

13. Create any necessary appendixes. Create an appendix for such things as information sources, large tables, large illustrations, or any other useful information that doesn't fit in the main text. In fact, you can move your background, descriptions, and comparisons to appendixes. That way, readers will see your conclusions and recommendations as soon as they open your report. (This approach is known as the "executive format" and is illustrated in the example recommendation report at the end of this chapter.)

In this example, you could include product specifications and brochures in one appendix, full-length examples of transcriptions in another, and detailed technical background in still another.

14. Write an introduction. Save your recommendation report's introduction to write when you are finished with the rest of the report.

An introduction is like a road map, and the process of writing is like finding your way—you can't create the road map until you've found your way. When you write the introduction, remember to indicate the topic, the purpose, and the intended readers—stating individuals' names or organization names, or both. Review the intended readers' needs for the information as well as their knowledge and background.

For the introduction, nothing is wrong with a straightforward, businesslike approach stating that the following is a report on voice-recognition software for medical transcription. For background, mention that this technology has advanced far enough that it now offers affordable recognition with reasonable accuracy. Perhaps mention that medical transcription is one field that needs such a solution. Continue by indicating the organization that commissioned the report, and indicate the purpose of the report. Include a quick in-sentence list of the report's contents: requirements, technical background, comparisons, conclusions, and recommendations.

15. Consider the format. Chapter 15 shows that you can design a recommendation report as a memorandum, a business letter, or a separate document with a cover memo or letter. The recommendation report on voice-recognition software at the end of this chapter is a separate document with a cover business letter.

Make this recommendation report a formal report with a transmittal letter attached to the front. It contains enough pages that the business-letter format won't work.

16. Review and revise your rough draft. Use the strategies in Chapter 18 to systematically review and revise your recommendation report. Use the top-down approach described in Chapter 18: start by reviewing audience, purpose, and situation; then move on to content, organization, and transitions; then headings, lists, tables, and graphics; then sentence-style revision and technical style, and finally grammar, usage, spelling, and punctuation problems.

HOW DO YOU WRITE FEASIBILITY AND EVALUATION REPORTS?

If you studied the preceding sections on how to structure a point-by-point comparison and how to develop a recommendation report, you already know how to write feasibility and evaluation reports. In these types of reports, you use comparison just as much as you do in recommendation reports.

Feasibility Reports

As explained earlier, a feasibility report tries to forecast whether a program or project will be feasible. *Feasibility*, in this context, focuses on whether a program or project is possible, practical, or both:

- *Technical feasibility*. Does the voice-recognition software really work? Does it give us the advantages we need or solve our problem? Will it really save substantial time, money, and headaches?
- *Financial feasibility*. Can we afford the software? Will it pay for itself in the proper amount of time? Are the advantages it brings worth the expense?
- *Social feasibility*. Will employees use the software? A better example in this case might be a municipal recycling program. Will people participate?
- *Administrative feasibility*. Is the idea legal? Does it conflict with existing regulations? Is there administrative capacity to handle it?

Obviously, individual feasibility studies needn't cover all these categories. For a feasibility report on whether a state agency should use voice-recognition software, we must show whether it really works, really provides significant advantages, is easy to learn and use, and is affordable. A feasibility report looks to the future and attempts to project whether an idea will work. Logically, the feasibility report precedes the recommendation report. A feasibility report tells us whether the plan will work and meet the needs. A recommendation report shows which option best meets that need. (In everyday practice, these two kinds of reports are often combined and may be called practically anything—even proposals.)

If you understand point-by-point comparison, you know how to structure a feasibility report: compare aspects of the program or project category by category against the requirements. If it meets enough of the requirements, the right requirements, or the right combination of the requirements, it's feasible.

Evaluation Reports

Whereas feasibility reports attempt to tell the future—will the program or project work?—evaluation reports study existing programs or projects to determine whether they are working. Requirements are essential for both types of reports. A feasibility report determines whether a program or project *will* meet a set of requirements. An evaluation report determines whether a program or project *is* meeting its requirements.

WORKSHOP: COMPARISON AND RECOMMENDATION REPORTS

Here are some additional ideas for practicing the concepts, tools, and strategies in this chapter:

1. *Points of comparison.* To ensure that you understand the idea of point-by-point comparison, develop at least four points of comparison for one or more of the following topics:

Internet service providers	Cordless or cellular phones	Collies and Irish setters
Minivans (for the family)	Garden irrigation systems	Microwave ovens
Lawn sprinklers	Tomato varieties	Shampoos and conditioners

2. *Recommendation, evaluation, and feasibility reports.* To ensure that you understand recommendation, evaluation, and feasibility reports, develop a project for each type of report using one or more of the following topics:

Cellular phones for employees	Speech-recognition software for visually impaired employees
Underground lawn irrigation systems	Software for correcting usage and punctuation errors for case-worker staff
Notebook computers for all seventh graders	Electric vehicles for college maintenance and security
Home-schooling using the Internet	Tax incentives for installing devices that save on utilities (water, wastewater, gas, electricity)
Solar power for a residence	
Program for free city-bus riding	

3. *Automobile recommendation.* Imagine that you are going to write a recommendation report on automobiles for people just like you. What would you use as your points of comparison? What would your requirements and priorities be?

4. *Feasibility of a new technology.* Think of some new or emerging technology, and imagine that you must write a feasibility report on it for some local government or business organization. How will you determine its feasibility in technological, social, administrative, or other terms?

5. *Evaluation of a program.* Think of a program that is currently running in local or regional government; for example, free bus service or city-wide recycling. Imagine that you have been hired to evaluate that program and write a report containing your findings and conclusions. What would you use as your requirements? How will you decide whether the program is working?

6. *Web format.* Find an existing, printed recommendation, evaluation, and feasibility report and convert it to a web-based report. Use either the frames approach (in which the link menu always appears in a frame) or the nonframes approach (in which the link menu appears in a separate file of its own). If you haven't learned enough HTML to do this yet, cut the report into chunks, handwrite the link menu and other navigational elements, and draw arrows from the links to their destinations.

Notice that the introduction makes it sound like this comparison occurs within a larger report. The topic of that report is most likely NASA plans for a manned mission to Mars.

Introduction and overview: Notice the strong overview sentence occurring in the introduction. It isn't exactly the style of writing you'd find in *People* magazine, but it gets the job done. People need to know what they are about to read—a road map of the topics about to be discussed.

Illustration: Notice that this illustration does not have a title. Because its content is obvious and because this is a short document, no title is needed.

Abbreviations: Notice in these paragraphs that abbreviations that do not spell a word are not punctuated with a period. Notice too that they are not written against the number they modify (written "solid"). Thus, you'd say that the polar radius of Mars is 3375 km (not 3375km).

Table discussion: Notice how the second paragraph repeats some of the detail in the first table. This kind of repetition is common and acceptable: you give readers two views of important information—one in the form of a table, another in regular text.

Point-by-point comparison method: Notice that this comparison does not have one big paragraph on Mars followed by another big paragraph on Earth. Instead the two planets are compared point by point: size, radius, orbit, length of year, temperature, atmosphere, length of day, and so on.

Comparison

Comparison: Mars and Earth

Any manned expedition to Mars must take into account the basic features of the planet *in comparison with* those of Earth. The following compares the two planets according to size, density, orbits, distances from the Sun, climate, atmosphere, and seasons.

12,756 km diameter

6,749 km diameter

Size. Mars is *smaller than* Earth in terms of its mass, volume, and equatorial radius. Mars is *just over half* the size of Earth, its equatorial radius being 3397 km to Earth's 6379 km. Because it is approximately one-and-a-half times *farther from* the Sun, the martian orbit is *longer than* Earth's and Mars is *cooler than* Earth. The martian year is 687 Earth days.

Temperature and atmosphere. The surface temperature on Mars is from $-17°$ C ($1°$ F) to $-107°$ C ($-178°$ F), although temperatures can reach as high as $27°$ C ($81°$ F) and as low as $-143°$ C ($-225°$ F). The atmosphere of Mars is composed chiefly of carbon dioxide (95.3%), nitrogen (2.7%) and argon (1.6%). The atmospheric pressure is *less than* 1/100th that of Earth, as shown in the following table:

Dual measurement style: Notice the standard presentation of measurements: the first is in standard international metric and the second is in English in parentheses.

Capitalization: Notice that not only Mars but Earth and Sun are capitalized. When the context is planets and astronomy in general, you capitalize names of all the "heavenly bodies."

Transitions: Comparisons need a lot of transition words, such as those highlighted in this example. (See **www.io.com/~hcexres/ power_tools/transitions.html** for more on transitions.)

Column alignment in tables: Notice the alignment in these tables: numerical data is right (or decimal) aligned and then centered within the column. Textual data is left aligned. (For more on tables, see Chapter 10.)

Headings: This comparison uses third-level headings to indicate the start of each new comparative point. (See Chapter 7 for more headings.)

Footnotes in tables: Notice the use of explanatory footnotes in this table. You could put this information in the column headings with Earth and Mars, but that would balloon those two cells and create an awkward table.

	Mars	Earth	Ratio (Mars/Earth)
Mass (1024 kg)	0.6419	5.9736	0.107
Volume (1010 km³)	16.318	108.321	0.151
Equatorial radius (km)	3397	6378	0.533
Polar radius (km)	3375	6356	0.531
Mean density (kg/m³)	3933	5520	0.713
Surface gravity (m/s²)	3.69	9.78	0.377

Orbit and seasons. Mars has seasons *similar to* those of Earth. The tilt of its rotational axis (axial inclination) to the plane of its orbit about the Sun is *about the same as* Earth's. However, *unlike* Earth, the strongly elliptical shape (eccentricity) of Mars' orbit means that the seasons on Mars are also affected by varying distances from the Sun. Because of Earth's almost circular orbit, our seasons result simply from the tilt of the Earth's rotational axis. *In contrast*, martian seasons are *about double the length* of those on Earth. However, a day on Mars is *roughly the same* length as a day on Earth: 24 hours, 37 min, and 23 sec—or 1.026 Earth days, as shown in the following table:

Seasons	Earth[1]	Mars[2]
Spring	93	171
Summer	94	199
Fall	89	171
Winter	89	146

[1] Measured in terms of the Northern Hemisphere.
[2] Measured in terms of Earth days.

Recommendation report: This report compares various voice-recognition software applications on the market and then recommends one over the others. Notice that it is not a feasibility report: it does not consider the overall practicality and effectiveness of this software.

Executive report design: Notice that this report starts with an executive summary made up of the key conclusions and recommendations. The background on voice-recognition software and product comparisons are considered appendixes, available if the executive readers want to read that detail. (This report would be bound and have a transmittal letter attached to the front cover. See Chapter 15 for more on report design.)

Primary conclusions: The first eight conclusions repeat what is stated in the product comparisons (in the appendixes). In fact, these conclusions are in the same order as the sections in which they are stated.

Secondary conclusions: With the primary conclusions stated, this writer moves on to the business of weighing cost against performance. One would expect more secondary conclusions here. For example, the writer could state that FreeSpeech98, despite its low cost, would simply be of no use in the environment the writer is considering.

Voice Recognition Software:
Recommendations for Medical Transcriptionists[1]

Executive Summary

From business, medical, and legal perspectives, the creation and maintenance of accurate, complete records are crucial. The primary downside to such thorough record-keeping includes: (1) the time required for dictation, (2) the costs in finding and hiring a competent medical transcriptionist, (3) the necessary delays between dictation and actual availability of the transcribed records, and (4) the time needed to proof and correct the transcriptionist's output.

Conclusions

To date, the weakest link in speech recognition technology has been accuracy. This technology is rapidly advancing, and current software has significantly improved within the last year. Can a voice recognition software program eliminate some of the problems occurring in conventional medical transcription? The following conclusions, along with the recommendation that follows, will help answer this question:

1. All of the programs specify system requirements that are well within the parameters of existing computer systems.
2. All of the programs integrate with Microsoft Word 97.
3. All of the programs can be installed by the average user with reasonable ease.
4. Dragon Systems' NaturallySpeaking Medical Suite is by far the most expensive voice recognition program. Whereas it is $1,243, including one year of technical support, the other three programs are all under $200, exclusive of support.
5. Philips does not include a microphone with its software as do the other three software companies, but purchasing a microphone does not increase the total cost appreciably. Dragon Systems' microphone

[1] Many thanks to Dr. Pat Roach, former online technical-writing student, for writing this recommendation report and for permission to adapt it here.

is considered more usable than the other microphones tested by *PC Magazine*.

6. Dragon Systems' NaturallySpeaking has accumulated a lengthy list of awards; no awards were found for the other three programs.

7. Dragon Systems' NaturallySpeaking Medical Suite with Add-On Vocabularies is easily customizable for most practices' needs for specialized medical vocabularies and medical forms.

8. Dragon Systems' NaturallySpeaking technology is the most accurate of the four programs tested.

9. Although Dragon Systems' NaturallySpeaking is considerably more expensive, its accuracy, speed, ease of use, and flexibility justify the extra expense.

Recommendation

Dragon Systems' NaturallySpeaking Medical Suite is strongly recommended for its superior accuracy, powerful customization features, and industry recognition and awards. No other product comes close, and its strong advantages justify its considerably higher price. Once the program has been customized, and the user has dictated for several weeks and become familiar with the software, acceptably accurate transcription and instantly available medical records should be possible with NaturallySpeaking Medical Suite, solving some of the record-keeping problems faced by most medical practices.

Recommendation: In the "Conclusions" section, the writer has not made a recommendation; all she has done is reach a conclusion as to the best product of the three compared. In this "Recommendation" section, the writer puts her professional standing on the line by recommending one of the products.

Page break: Notice that the executive summary ends with a full page break to mark the boundary between it and the appendixes.

Introduction: When you write the introduction, be sure to identify the situation, indicate the purpose, and provide an overview of what's to come, as this introduction does.

Background: This report rightly includes background on voice-recognition software. At the time this report was written, people did not know much about this technology. Also, this background section introduces key concepts and terminology to be used in the rest of the report.

Documentation: The bracketed numbers are citations of borrowed information. Go to the end of this report to see what source number 11 is. This style of indicating the source of borrowed information is the "number system." Variations of it are used in the Council of Biology Editors and Institute of Electrical and Electronics Engineers (IEEE)-styles.

Voice Recognition Software: Appendixes

With the recent, widely advertised breakthroughs in voice recognition software, many medical practices are considering its use for their transcription work. The expense, error rate, and record-completion delays associated with conventional transcription work have stimulated a search for better ways of accomplishing these essential record-keeping tasks. The following report reviews the capabilities and requirements of this new software and makes recommendations as to the best voice-recognition software on the market.

Several voice recognition products currently exist in the marketplace, and viable choices are greater in number than they were only a few years ago. Rapid changes have been fueled by the ever-increasing power and plummeting prices of desktop systems. Though room for improvement still exists, accuracy has advanced tremendously in a stunningly short time.

Voice Recognition Software: Background

The first software-only dictation product for personal computers, Dragon Systems' DragonDictate for Windows 1.0, using discrete speech recognition technology, was released in 1994. Discrete speech is a slow, unnatural means of dictation, requiring a pause after each and every word [11].

Two years later, IBM introduced the first continuous speech recognition software, its MedSpeak/Radiology. These systems had five-figure price tags and required expensive personal computers. Continuous speech technology allows its users to speak naturally and conversationally, relieving much of the tedium of discrete speech dictation [11].

Power devourers. With all of the complex selections and tremendous flexibility demanded of voice recognition software, it is small wonder that considerable computer muscle is required to run these programs. To take fullest advantage of current speech recognition programs, a personal computer with a minimum of a 300-MHz Pentium II processor is recommended. A separate 16-bit SoundBlaster-compatible card is also advisable because the sound cards that are bundled as part of a personal computer's motherboard can produce inferior results with voice recognition software [4].

Realistic reminders. Voice recognition technology has advanced impressively over the last year, with programs variously offering smarter speech recognition engines, larger active vocabularies, integration with the most popular word-processing programs, and improved accuracy. This report sorts through these features to find the most accurate program and the best value available and to determine if the accuracy supplied is acceptable at this time [4]. It is essential to remember the following:

- While voice recognition software has made enormous strides, it is not perfect. Dictated records, particularly in the first few weeks of use, must be sufficiently proofed while on screen.
- Because medical and legal requirements for obstetric and gynecologic records are exacting and extensive, considerable dictation is required. Dictation using voice recognition software is like many other things: practice makes all the difference. Tests by PC Magazine Labs showed that increased experience with dictation and with the software significantly increased accuracy [3].
- Be prepared to invest a few weeks of dictation time and practice with the software in order to see enhanced accuracy.

Stringent demands. Much is demanded of speech recognition programs. Accuracy is critical and speed is essential to any effective program. Added to these challenges is the enormous variation that exists among individual human speech patterns, pitch, rate, and inflection. These variations are an extraordinary test of the flexibility of any program. Voice recognition follows these steps:

1. Spoken words enter a microphone.
2. Audio is processed by the computer's sound card.

Numbered list: All of the preceding lists have been bulleted because the items were in no required order. Here the items are in a required order—specifically, the sequence of phases by which voice-recognition software processes human speech. (For more on lists, see Chapter 8.)

3. The software discriminates between lower-frequency vowels and higher-frequency consonants and compares the results with phonemes, the smallest building blocks of speech. The software then compares results to groups of phonemes, and then to actual words, determining the most likely match.

Contextual information is simultaneously processed in order to more accurately predict words that are most likely to be used next, such as the correct choice out of a selection of homonyms such as merry, marry, and Mary.

4. Selected words are arranged in the most probable sentence combinations.

5. The sentence is transferred to a word processing application [11].

Voice Recognition Software Requirements

Based on stated preferences and system specifications, the following requirements have been established for this study:

Bulleted lists: Notice how often this writer uses bullets in this report. To emphasize the cost differences between these programs, she creates four bullets. Notice also that this, as well as every other list in this report, is introduced by a lead-in punctuated with a colon.

- Because the goal is to save time and effort while enhancing results and decreasing the salary overhead incurred with a medical transcriptionist, continuous speech recognition software is preferred, rather than the slower, more unnatural and lower-priced discrete speech recognition software also on the market.
- The application must run on a Pentium-powered personal computer under Windows 95 and be capable of integration with Microsoft Word 97.
- The software program must be easily and successfully installed by any intermediate-level computer user in the office.
- The program must be one that can be learned and customized reasonably quickly by nearly anyone in the office.
- The cost limit is $1500.

Points of Comparison

The voice recognition software programs compared are Dragon Systems' NaturallySpeaking 3.0 Preferred Edition, IBM ViaVoice 98 Executive, L&H Voice Xpress Plus, and Philips FreeSpeech98. Discussion of Dragon Systems' NaturallySpeaking will also include its Medical Suite.

In-sentence list overview: The points of comparison are listed here using an "in-sentence" list. The third-level headings that follow are in the same order as the items in this list. Notice the format: the lead-in is a complete sentence and is punctuated with a colon, both opening and closing parentheses are used, and semicolons are used between the items because the items have their own internal commas. See Chapter 8 for more on lists.

Point-by-point comparisons: Typically, the best way to approach a recommendation report is to use comparison, and the best way to structure a comparison is the point-by-point approach. The points of comparison here include microphones, accuracy, cost, and so on. It would not work well to have separate sections on the Dragon System, the ViaVoice, and the FreeSpeech in which all details for each option were discussed.

Italics for magazine and journal names: It's standard to italicize the names of magazines and to put the articles within those magazines in quotation marks.

Eight categories of comparison will be made in order to effectively evaluate these competing programs: (1) accuracy; (2) minimum system requirements; (3) capacity to manage a specialized medical vocabulary and medical records; (4) integration with Microsoft Word; (5) ease and speed of installation, customization, and use; (6) industry ratings and awards; (7) inclusion of microphones; and (8) cost.

Industry ratings and awards. Only one of these products refers to and lists awards on its web site: Dragon Systems' NaturallySpeaking. None of the other three products has any such mention anywhere on its site, nor do any awards or industry recognition show up on multiple web searches for the products. Dragon Systems' web site lists over fifty awards, some of which are listed here:

- *PC Magazine, Editors' Choice*, October 1998; this particular article is referenced several times in this report [1,7].
- "The 12 Best PC Products on the Planet: Input Device Category." *PC/Computing: Time Capsule*, August 1998 [7].
- "World Class Award: Best Voice Recognition Software." *PC World*, June 1998 [7].
- "The Best New Products/Software." *BusinessWeek*, January 1998 [7].
- "The Best of 1997/Cybertech." *Time Magazine*, January 1998 [7].
- "5 Star Rating." *PC/Computing*, November 1997 [7].

While industry recognition and journalistic evaluations are not the only considerations, Dragon Systems boasts an impressive list of awards and ratings by prestigious periodicals.

Inclusion of microphones. As previously noted, a microphone is necessary for the capture of spoken words. Here's how the products compare:

- Dragon Systems ships with a VXI Parrott 10-3 microphone; *PC Magazine* notes that it is usable, comfortable, and performs well [5].

- IBM's ViaVoice and L&H Voice Xpress Plus both provide an Andrea NC-80 microphone, which *PC Magazine* states is not as comfortable as the XVI Parrott 10-3 [5].
- Philips FreeSpeech98 does not include a microphone; it recommends its own SpeechMike at an extra cost of $69.95 [5].

None of these are make-or-break details, but Dragon Systems has a slight edge in the reviews provided by *PC Magazine*.

Dragon Systems made an enormous stride in June 1997, when it released NaturallySpeaking, the first general-purpose, continuous speech software program. Much more affordable than earlier programs, it brought the realm of continuous speech recognition to a much wider range of users. Two months later, IBM released its competing continuous speech software, ViaVoice [10].

Accuracy. Accuracy is the most significant consideration; without it, any program is useless. Dragon Systems' NaturallySpeaking scored highest on all of the accuracy tests performed by *PC Magazine* and was unequivocally selected as the Editors' Choice. In these tests, the average accuracy was 91% and at times was considerably greater [1].

Average accuracy for L&H Voice Xpress was 87% [2]. Accuracy for IBM's ViaVoice tested at 85% [14], and Philips FreeSpeech98 was 80% [15].

At first glance these percentages, particularly the top two, may not seem significantly different. Consider, however, that for every 1,000 words, an accuracy rate of 87% means that 130 words must be corrected. An accuracy rate of 91% represents an average of 90 errors per 1,000 words, while an 80% rate means that 200 out of every 1,000 words must be corrected.

Thousands of words are dictated daily in this industry. Time is scarce and precious. Medicolegal conditions mandate that records must be

Pronouns and corporate nouns: Notice the use of "it" to refer to "Dragon Systems." Our tendency is to use "their," which creates a pronoun-reference problem. Another, more striking example of this problem is to refer to "IBM" as "they," "them," or "their."

Discussion of the comparative data: Notice that the writer doesn't merely throw out the numbers and move on. She explains how differences of 4 or 5 percentage points have a great impact on the effectiveness of this software.

exhaustively thorough and accurate. Under these rigorous circumstances, every percentage point counts, and Dragon Systems' NaturallySpeaking yields the highest accuracy.

Minimum system requirements. All four programs run on Pentium-powered personal computers utilizing Windows 95, 98 or NT 4.0 and require 16-bit SoundBlaster-compatible sound cards. Random access memory (RAM) requirements for software running under Windows NT are higher for all of these programs [5]. However, only the RAM required for Windows 95 is listed in the table below, as it is the operating system used in most practices. It is important to recall that, as noted earlier, significantly greater system resources are recommended to optimize performance. Given the sufficient system resources, none of these software programs should present a problem for existing systems.

Comparison of Minimum System Requirements [5]

Software	CPU	RAM (MB)	Hard Disk (MB)	L2 Cache
Dragon	Pentium/133MHz	32	180	None
Via Voice	Pentium/166MHz	40	180	256 KB
L&H	Pentium/166MHz	32	130	None
Philips	Pentium/166MHz	32	150	None

Capacity to manage a customizable, specialized medical vocabulary. Medicine in general, and each medical specialty in particular, has its own complex, specialized vocabulary, and the ability to manage that vocabulary is critical:

- Dragon Systems' NaturallySpeaking offers a so-called Medical Suite targeted to medical professionals and specified as an alternative to transcription. Marketing materials state that an extensive vocabulary of thousands of words, including medical procedures, terms, drugs, diagnoses, and symptoms, is included. The software allows creation of multiple vocabularies for specialty customization, if desired [8].
- IBM offers add-on VoiceType Vocabularies for use with ViaVoice. The medical vocabularies available are for Emergency Medicine Dictation

---

Individual conclusion: Notice the overtly stated conclusion here at the end of the section on accuracy, even though it's obvious from the numbers above. State these conclusions even if they seem totally obvious to you.

Tables: Notice the design of this table:

Instead of dragging all this information through the regular text, the writer presents it far more economically in the form of a table.

- The table title occurs in the first row, which spans all columns, and the source of the table is indicated in brackets at the end of the title.
- The column headings occur in the next row and are italicized.
- The column headings and the cells are left aligned. To some book designers, the columns for RAM and hard disk look bad. They'd prefer centering those columns under the headings. However, left alignment is common in table design, and it's certainly easier!
- This table is structured for vertical comparison, which is preferable according to conventional table-design wisdom. You scan downwards to see how the products compare in terms of RAM requirements.

However, if you had eight or more comparative categories, the table would fit better on the page if the four products acted as columns—in other words, turning the table 90 degrees.

and Radiology Dictation. No other specialty customization is available [13].

- L&H Voice Xpress and Philips FreeSpeech98 do not offer medical vocabularies, either as add-ons or bundled with the software [9,12].

Two of the four companies offer a product that provides medical terminology. IBM's emergency room and radiology add-on software is not applicable to the dictation needs of obstetric and gynecologic practices. Dragon Systems' NaturallySpeaking Medical Suite offers the same voice recognition technology as the previously mentioned NaturallySpeaking Preferred Edition, with the addition of extensive customizable medical terminology that can be tailored to specialty practices.

Integration with Microsoft Word. All four programs integrate with Word 97 and can therefore be used with existing word processing software [5].

Ease and speed of installation, customization and use. Each of the four programs uses "wizards" to install and configure hardware, and all programs support macros for frequently used phrases:

Quotation marks: The word "wizard" is in quotation marks because, at the time this report was written, this was a strange usage. The same is the case for the word "training." It's an odd and unfamiliar idea to think of "training" a software product.

- Dragon Systems' NaturallySpeaking uses its wizard to train the system to recognize the user's voice within 4 minutes. Material is provided so that about 30 minutes of reading aloud will improve accuracy [5]. Electronic medical documents can be analyzed automatically to "learn" new specialized terms and proper names. Its CommandWizard feature enables any user to create medical-specialty macros. Commonly used and required medical forms, electronically stored, can be called up readily with the user being prompted to fill out each section of a form [8].
- IBM's ViaVoice also trains the system by means of reading from selected texts for about 30 minutes, and its wizard adjusts microphone and speaker volume levels [5].
- L&H Voice Xpress Plus directs the user to read chapters of a book, and in *PC Magazine's* tests, about 75 minutes was required for the process [5].

Detailed comparisons and overt conclusions: In each comparative section, this writer states the comparative information, explores the reasons for and significance of the differences, and ends with an overt statement as to which product is best in terms of that comparison. As a writer, you must help readers understand the differences, whether they are significant, why they exist, and how they lead to a conclusion.

Bulleted lists for individual products: Notice how in these sections the writer uses a bulleted item for each product. This further increases the scannability of this document

- Philips FreeSpeech98 directs the user to read selected text for about 15 minutes; ten training topics are available for the user's review [15].

Installation of all of the programs appears straightforward, and the initial basic "training" is not excessively time consuming for any of the products. Although all provide macros, the medical customization features of Dragon Systems' product are considerably greater. Though they will initially require more time and document input, accuracy is increased, and for this reason, Dragon's software is recommended in this comparison.

Cost. Highly significant price differences exist among these programs:

- The Dragon Systems' NaturallySpeaking Preferred Edition tested by *PC Magazine*, October 1998, retails for $179 when purchased directly from Dragon or through resellers. However, NaturallySpeaking Medical Suite, preferable for medical practices, is $995. An add-on Medical Specialty Vocabulary is available for $49. One year of 800-number telephone support for all products is an additional $199, for a total cost of $1,243, exclusive of tax and shipping costs, for the Medical Suite [6].
- IBM's ViaVoice 98 Executive software program costs $150, and the medical specialty add-ons are $240. However, because these add-ons are for emergency medicine and radiology, they are of no use to many practices [13].
- L&H Voice Xpress Plus is $70 [5].
- Philips Free Speech98 costs $39 and does not include a microphone. A Philips SpeechMike can be ordered for $69.95, for a total cost of $108.95, exclusive of tax and shipping costs [5].

L&H offers the best price by far. IBM and Philips are roughly in the same ballpark. Dragon Systems' Preferred Edition is more expensive at $200, but not significantly so. The only medical software program customizable to a wide range of practices is Dragon Systems' Medical Suite, which, at $1,243, is over ten times the cost of Philips' software, though it includes one year of technical support.

References: This section lists all the information sources this writer directly drew on to create this report. The format of this list is the number system; it loosely follows CBE style. Although the references are alphabetized here, in some styles you list them in order of their first occurrence in the text.

Publication and access dates: Notice that both the date these web pages were published and the date this writer accessed them are shown. When you cite Internet sources of information, cite the date of publication that you find on the source. Typically, web pages have a publication date somewhere, often at the bottom. Also, you must indicate the date you accessed the source, as is done here.

No author: If you cannot find an author name, you can use the organization name, as is done here with Berkeley Voice Solutions and Dragon Systems. If it doesn't even have an organization name, use the title of the page.

Italics and quotation marks: Notice that the names of magazines are italicized and the titles of articles are in quotation marks.

References

All references are found online.

1. Alwang, Greg. "Editors' Choice." *PC Magazine Online.* October 20, 1998.
   www.zdnet.com/pcmag/features/speech98/edchoice.html Accessed 23 October 1998.
2. Alwang, Greg. "L&H Voice Xpress Plus 1.01." *PC Magazine Online.* October 20, 1998.
   www.zdnet.com/pcmag/features/speech98/rev3.html Accessed 23 October 1998.
3. Alwang, Greg. "Performance Tests." *PC Magazine Online.* October 20, 1998.
   www.zdnet.com/pcmag/features/speech98/perftest.html Accessed 23 October 1998.
4. Alwang, Greg. "Speech Recognition: Finding Its Voice." *ZDNN.* October 2, 1998. **www.zdnet.com/zdnn/stories/zdnn_display/ 0,3440,350879,00.html** Accessed 23 October 1998.
5. Alwang, Greg. "Summary of Features." *PC Magazine Online.* October 20, 1998.
   www.zdnet.com/pcmag/features/speech98/features.html Accessed 23 October 1998.
6. Berkeley Voice Solutions. "Products and Services." **www.pcvoice.com/products.html:** Accessed 21 October 1998.
7. Dragon Systems, Inc. "Dragon NaturallySpeaking Awards." **http:/www.dragonsys.com/news/awards.html** Accessed 21 October 1998.
8. Dragon Systems, Inc. "Dragon NaturallySpeaking Medical Suite." **www.dragonsys.com/products/medical.html** Accessed 21 October 1998.
9. Lernout & Hauspie. "L&H Online Store." **www.storefront.zbr.com/LHS-store:** Accessed 21 October 1998.
10. Munro, Jay. "Speech Technology Timeline." *PC Magazine Online.* March 10, 1998.
    www.zdnet.com/pcmag/features/speech/sb1.html Accessed 23 October 1998.
11. Munro, Jay. "Watch What You Say." *PC Magazine Online.* March 10, 1998. **www.zdnet.com/pcmag/features/speech/intro1.html** Accessed 23 October 1998.
12. Philips. "Philips Speech Processing." **www.speech.be.philips.com** Accessed 21 October 1998.
13. Provantage. "IBM VoiceType Dictation Vocabularies." **www.provantage.com/FP_09907.htm** Accessed 21 October 1998.
14. Stinson, Craig. "IBM ViaVoice 98 Executive." *PC Magazine Online.* October 20, 1998.
    www.zdnet.com/pcmag/features/speech98/rev2.html Accessed 23 October 1998.

15. Stinson, Craig. "Philips FreeSpeech98." *PC Magazine Online.* October 20, 1998. **www.zdnet.com/pcmag/features/speech98/rev4.html** Accessed 23 October 1998.

Definition and Classification: Background Reports

NANOTECHNOLOGY: MOLECULAR CIRCUITRY

Some believe that nanotechnology—manufacturing at the molecular level—will be the "next industrial revolution" and totally change our way of life. The following links take you to some highly visionary stuff related to this topic:

NanoTechnology Magazine. **www.nanozine.com**

Ralph C. Merkle's Nanotechnology site at Zyvex. "Nanotechnology." **www.zyvex.com/nano**

IBM Corporation. "Small Wonders: Positioning Progress, Atom by Atom." **www.research.ibm.com/nanoscience/index1.html**

Brilliant New World - HP Labs at the Forefront of Creating Nanotechnology. **www.hp.com/ghp/features/nano**

C.P. Collier, et al., "Electronically Configurable Molecular-Based Logic Gates," *Science,* 16 July 1999.

Hewlett-Packard. "Molecules That Compute." **www.hpl.hp.com/news/molecules_that_compute.html**

Accessed January 15, 2001.

If you've skimmed the chapters of Part I, you know that instructions show people how to do something, recommendation reports recommend one thing over another, and proposals attempt to convince readers to approve a project.

Background reports, on the other hand, are less easy to define. They also solve real workplace problems and respond to real workplace needs. They do so by focusing on a *topic*—a subject matter—in a way that meets a specific audience's needs. Definition and classification, the two infrastructures for this chapter, are essential in writing background reports.

This chapter shows you how to write definitions and classifications and then how to use them as infrastructures for technical background reports.

Note:
- If you are new to this book, see "How Do You Use This Book?" in the Preface.
- For additional examples of the documents discussed in this chapter, see **www.io.com/~hcexres/power_tools/examples**.

WHAT IS A DEFINITION AND HOW DO YOU WRITE ONE?

The technical and scientific worlds are loaded with unfamiliar terminology. For all those unfamiliar words, an important tool is definition. But defining a technical term is not always as easy as stating its synonym. Sometimes, a formal sentence definition, a full paragraph, or even an entire report may be necessary. In everyday use, definition means any sort of description or explanation. In this book, however, *definition* means the explanation of the meaning of a potentially unfamiliar word. As you can see in the following table, technical and scientific fields are loaded with such words.

Synonym Definitions

You can use a synonym—a simple, familiar word—to provide a quick on-the-spot definition of a potentially unfamiliar term. In these examples,

Field	Unfamiliar terms
Computers	Cache, bus, DRAM, binary, ASCII, file, FTP, Internet, client, server, virus, emulator, multi-tasking, parallel computing, relational database, terabyte.
Medicine	AIDS, HIV, pseudomonas, sickle cell anemia, asthma, hypertension, dyslexia, arthritis, PMS, schizophrenia, autism.
Economics	Recession, depression, inflation, venture capital, demand curve, amortization, M1, M2, M3, macroeconomics, microeconomics, hedging, monopoly.
Automotive technology	Drive train, disc brakes, cam, differential, fly wheel, fuel cell, power train, traction, planing, catalytic converter, desulfurization.
Agriculture	Hydroponics, organic, germplasm, floriculture, permaculture, viticulture, sustainable agriculture, desertification, terraforming.
Engineering	Stress, sheer, turbulence, intercalation compounds, optical tweezers, photonic devices, servo, composite, fiber optics, pneumatics, hydraulics, polymers.

notice how the following synonyms are introduced in parentheses, dashes, and clauses or phrases.

> One possibility of nanotechnology is "respirocytes" (artificial red blood cells) presented in an earlier issue of **nanozine.com**.

> Cryonics—freezing people for the future—involves replacing a human's blood and body water with chemicals to inhibit freezing damage and preserving them in liquid nitrogen (LN_2) at $-196°C$ ($-320°F$).
>
> An IBM research team from Zurich, Switzerland, created a fully functional abacus (an ancient device for calculation) that uses individual molecules as the "beads" for counting.
>
> The positional assembly required by nanotechnology requires molecular robotics—that is, robotic devices that are molecular both in size and precision.

Formal Sentence Definitions

You can use a full sentence to provide a more formal definition of a technical term. As illustrated in the following table, the *formal sentence definition* has a particular structure: it begins with the term being defined,

Raw materials		Formal Sentence Definition
Term	nanometer	A nanometer is a measurement that equals one billionth of a meter (3–4 atoms wide).
Category	measurement	
Differentiation	equals one billionth of a meter (3–4 atoms wide)	
Term	nanite	A nanite is a nanotechnology term for the microscopic combination of microscopic motors, gears, levers, bearing, plates, sensors, and power and communication cables with powerful microscopic computers.
Category	nanotechnology term	
Differentiation	for the microscopic combination of microscopic motors, gears, levers, bearing, plates, sensors, power and communication cables with powerful microscopic computers.	
Term	fractals	Fractals are geometric figures, just like rectangles, circles, and squares, possessing special properties that Euclidean geometrical figures do not have.
Category	geometric figures	
Differentiation	just like rectangles, circles, and squares, possessing special properties that Euclidean geometrical figures do not have.	

locates that term in a category, and then differentiates that term from the other members of that category.

Glossaries are home turf for formal sentence definitions—or should be. Use formal sentence definitions to write glossary entries such as in the following examples:

nanometer Measurement that equals one billionth of a meter (3-4 atoms wide).

nanite Microscopic combination of microscopic motors, gears, levers, bearing, plates, sensors, and power and communication cables with powerful microscopic computers. *See also* nanotechnology.

prion Microscopic protein particle similar to a virus but lacking nucleic acid; thought to be the infectious agent responsible for certain degenerative diseases of the nervous system. *See also* virus.

Formal sentence definition: Start by carefully defining nanotechnology.

Supplementary definition: Define unfamiliar terms in the formal definition (or any preceding text).

Process: Explain the basics of nanotechnology by focusing on the process: how it works.

Causes and effects: Explore the impacts that nanotechnology could have on society.

Nanotechnology is molecular manufacturing or, more simply, building things one atom or molecule at a time. A nanometer is one billionth of a meter (3 to 4 atoms wide). Utilizing the well-known physical properties of atoms and molecules, nanotechnology proposes the construction of nanosize devices possessing extraordinary properties. The trick is to manipulate atoms individually and place them exactly where needed to produce the desired structure. The anticipated payoff for mastering this technology is far beyond any human accomplishment so far. Technical feasibilities include self-assembling consumer goods, computers billions of times faster, extremely novel inventions (impossible today), safe and affordable space travel, medical nanotechnology (the virtual end to illness, aging, death), no more pollution, automatic cleanup of already existing pollution, molecular food syntheses (the end of famine and starvation), access to a superior education for every child on Earth, reintroduction of many extinct plants and animals, and terraforming here and throughout the solar system.

FIGURE 5-1

Short, extended definition. Notice how this extended definition briefly characterizes the process that nanotechnologists envision and then races headlong into the visionary effects of this idea on society.

```
fractals  Geometric figures, just like rectangles,
circles, and squares, possessing special properties
that Euclidean geometrical figures do not have.
```

Extended Definitions

An interesting challenge for you as a technical communicator is the *extended definition*—a definition taking up one or more paragraphs. Some technical terms simply need extra discussion because the audience or situation requires it. Terms like *artificial intelligence, World Wide Web, distance education, El Niño, global warming,* and the *Big Bang theory* all seem to need extra discussion to become fully meaningful to some readers.

Take a look at the extended definition in Figure 5-1. Notice that it is made up of description, process, cause-effect, classification, and comparison—whatever it takes to convey a full sense of the term. These are the *tools for definition*; they are listed in the table in the following pages. To get a sense of how to write an extended definition, let's walk through the important steps and follow an example project.

1. **Find a simple project requiring an extended definition.** Think of a practical situation requiring an extended definition. In past writing courses, you may have written definitions on things like freedom, democracy, socialism, home, happiness, and other such topics. That's *not* what we want here. For the technical-writing context, the term need not have to do with engineering, electronics, or computers; but it must have some specialization, substance, or practicality about it.

The following example scenario shows you one way to do that. (Having trouble thinking of a topic? See **www.io.com/~hcexres/ power_tools/topics.html**.)

Imagine you've just heard an exciting news clip on NPR about something called "nanotechnology." You know it involves building things at the molecular level and that it will somehow revolutionize the world. Checking the Internet, you find a startling amount of information about it. But can you imagine a practical situation in which an extended definition of nanotechnology would be needed? Can you imagine a real-world problem that could be solved with a document that, in part, defined this word?

2. **Define a purpose and an audience.** The next step is to decide on a purpose and an audience for this extended definition. (See Chapter 19 for strategies to use in analyzing audiences and adapting your writing to them.)

As a nonspecialist and beginner with this topic, you cannot expect to address researchers and experts. You need a nonspecialist audience that actively seeks this information. An audience of ordinary people with a casual interest in new technology won't work! But an audience with professional, governmental, business, or commercial interests will. Scenarios—such as a legislator considering a bill to fund increased research and development in nanotechnology, an investor considering investment in a start-up venture involving nanotechnology, or an association of nanotechnologists looking for a writer to explain nanotechnology to people in the right places—can give some context for an extended definition.

3. **Research the term.** Early on in this project, you may need to do some research on the term you've chosen to define.

If you did a search on nanotechnology, you'd find items like the ones listed in the topic box at the beginning of this chapter. You'd see that at least three individuals seem to be the pioneers: Ralph C. Merkle, K. Eric Drexler, and Richard Smalley. All have Web sites. Corporations like IBM and Hewlett-Packard are involved in, and have Web pages devoted to, nanotechnology. Likewise, numerous universities have Web pages showing their research involvement in this field.

4. **Write a formal sentence definition.** It's a good idea to start an extended definition with a formal sentence definition, discussed in the preceding pages of this chapter. A good formal sentence definition can set up the rest of the extended definition—elements in the formal sentence definition will probably need further discussion.

For nanotechnology, find a way to define the term in one sentence. As Figure 5-1 shows, it's a manufacturing process that builds things

Introduction: word to be defined; overview of discussion to follow.

Process: you might start by explaining how something works that is closely related to the term you are defining.

Description: you might follow by describing something closely related to the term you are defining.

Classification: if some aspect of the term divides into categories—and if discussing those categories helps readers—discuss them!

Causes and effects: you can also discuss causes, effects, or both, related to the term you are defining.

Conclusion

FIGURE 5-2
Extended definition—example. This diagram illustrates just one of many possibilities for structuring an extended definition. Each term will require its own combination of definition sources and its own sequence of those sources.

atom by atom. If possible, squeeze in something about how nano assemblers must be "self replicating" in order to build objects more efficiently. Can you also jam something about the revolutionary impact of this technology into this one formal sentence definition?

5. **Choose the tools for the extended definition.** Take a careful look at your formal sentence definition. Which of the definition tools does it seem to need? Think about the term itself. Which of the definition tools are most directly related to it? Which definition tools focus most on the key aspects of the term you are trying to define? (Figure 5-2 illustrates how these definition tools can work together in the paragraphs of an extended definition.)

In this example, you must explain the *process* of nanotechnological manufacturing. You'll need *comparison* to help readers to conceptualize a nanometer: if you blew up a baseball to the size of the Earth, the atoms would be the size of grapes. A discussion of the possibilities that nanotechnology raises is a discussion of its potential *effects*. *Classification* might be useful for exploring the potential social effects of nanotechnology in the fields of medicine, agriculture, space travel, manufacturing, and so on. This extended definition would need to consider *problems* as well—in other words, what's holding us back from realizing those visionary possibilities—as shown in table opposite.

6. **Plan and develop graphics.** In the early stages of this project, try to visualize the graphics your definition will need. Use the strategies

Tools for Extended Definition

Select the right combination of these tools to write extended definitions.

Extended definition tool	Description
Description	Provide descriptive detail about the term being defined (size, shape, dimensions, materials, ingredients, weight, density, location, methods of attachment, etc.)
Process	Explain the steps in one or more processes related to the term being defined.
Causes	Discuss causes related to the term being defined.
Effects	Discuss consequences, results, and effects related to the term being defined.
Problems	Discuss problems related to the term being defined.
Comparisons	Compare the term being defined to related or opposite things. Explore analogies involving the term.
Categories	Discuss the categories into which the term being defined can be divided; discuss the category to which the term being defined belongs.
Applications	Discuss the real-world uses of some aspect of the term you are defining.
Benefits, advantages	Discuss any benefits or advantages that are associated with the term you are defining.

in Chapters 10 and 11 to plan the drawings, diagrams, photos, and charts you may need to include.

If you explore Web sites focusing on nanotechnology, you'll encounter some rather bizarre graphics: 3-D animations depicting how something can be built molecule by molecule, illustrations of molecular nano assemblers, arrangements of atoms and molecules to create "Buckyballs" and "Buckytubes," and so on.

7. **Organize the materials you'll use to write the extended definition.** Once you have a good idea of how to discuss the term you are defining, one of the next steps is to plan a sequence for that discussion. If you are uneasy about organizing the parts of a discussion like this, take a look at **www.io.com/~hcexres/power_tools/ organization.html**. Here are some patterns that usually work:

Does this sequence for an extended definition of nanotechnology make sense? Start with the formal sentence definition, move on to an explanation of the manufacturing process, continue with a discussion of the applications of this technology, move onto the visionary projections of how nanotechnology will affect our society, then end with a discussion of what it's going to take to realize these visions.

8. **Sketch the headings you'll use and the contents they introduce.** If your definition exceeds two or three paragraphs, use headings (presented in Chapter 7). For example, use a heading to identify each of the individual sources of definition.

    For this definition, how about these headings: "Nanotechnology Manufacturing Process," "Nanotechnology Applications," "Nanotechnology: Impact on Society," and "Conclusion: What It's Going to Take"? Under the first heading would be a paragraph on how nanotechnological machines will build things; under the second heading, a paragraph on the applications of this technology; under the third, speculation on the social impact. The final paragraph would discuss how much research and development will be needed to realize the visions surrounding nanotechnology.

9. **Plan an introduction.** The best time to write an introduction is *after* you've written the body of a document. Remember that the job of an introduction is to announce the topic and purpose, indicate the audience, provide an overview of the rest of the discussion, but introduce only a minimum of background.

    With the body of this extended definition planned, or even written, start thinking about the introduction. A perky journalistic approach for our serious-minded legislators won't work. Instead, let's start with something about the excitement and confusion over nanotechnology. Then state the formal sentence definition. Finally, indicate the purpose and provide an overview of what follows.

10. **Plan a conclusion.** You'll probably need some sort of ending sentence or paragraph for your extended definition.

    For a discussion like this, you can discuss a related subtopic but in a brief, general way. For example, a brief general discussion of the barriers to nanotechnology might be a good way to conclude this extended definition.

11. **Consider the format.** For this simple project, you are not likely to need the elaborate report formats shown in Chapter 15. Instead, use the format you see for the example definition at the end of this chapter. Begin with a descriptive title centered at the top of the page, and use second- and third-level headings. Use lists, notices, illustrations, tables, highlighting, and documentation (citations of your borrowed information sources) as necessary.

12. Review and revise your rough draft. Use the strategies in Chapter 18 to systematically review and revise your definition. Use the top-down approach described in Chapter 18: start by reviewing for audience, purpose, and situation; then move on to content, organization, and transitions; then headings, lists, tables, and graphics; then sentence-style revision and technical style; and finally, grammar, usage, spelling, and punctuation problems.

WHAT IS A CLASSIFICATION AND HOW DO YOU WRITE ONE?

Classification, like definition, is an important infrastructure for supplying basic information about a technical subject. Classification actually means two things: determining the category to which an item belongs and dividing a topic into categories.

Location within a Category

In one of its senses, classification means deciding to which category an individual item belongs. Within corporations, you have to decide whether a document is "for internal use only," "confidential," or "confidential-restricted." A company may develop a new computer: is it a laptop, a notebook, a palm-top, or a finger-top?

To write about which category an item belongs to, use comparison. Define the characteristics of each category, and then compare the characteristics of the item to those of the categories. In the end, declare the item a member of one category, or make up a new category. An interesting example of this occurs in "Computer Viruses as Artificial Life" by Eugene H. Spafford of Purdue University (**www.alw.nih.gov/Security/FIRST/papers/virus/alife.ps**). He defines life as having a "pattern in space-time"; being able to self-reproduce, grow, expand, and evolve; having an interdependence of parts; being able to metabolize (that is, convert matter to energy); and so on. He then compares these characteristics one by one to computer viruses.

Division into Categories

In technical documents, particularly technical background reports, a common strategy is to divide the subject into categories and to discuss each one separately (see Figure 5-3).

However, you must use only one *basis of classification.* Look at the examples in the table on page 129.

The following walks you through the important steps in writing a classification. To get a sense of how these steps work in an actual writing project, we'll follow an example through each of these steps.

Classification: This classification discusses three categories of devices essential to the theory of nanotechnology.

Overview: Notice that the introduction lets you know that three types of devices will be discussed.

Bulleted list: To make the discussion of the three categories distinct, the writer uses bulleted items with italicized labels.

Transitions: Notice how much this writer repeats the words "type" and "essential." Notice also that key terms like "assembler" and "molecular computer" are used over and over again throughout. Synonyms would only confuse us!

Conclusion: This discussion ends with an overview of how these devices work together in the manufacturing process.

The theory of nanotechnology relies on three essential types of devices to build almost any chemically stable structure atom by atom. These three devices are defined according to the role they play in the molecular-level manufacturing process.

■ *Assemblers.* One essential type of device in the theory of nano-technology is the "assembler." It possesses a submicroscopic robotic "arm" under computer control that enables it to hold and position reactive compounds in precise locations at which desired chemical reactions can occur. Thus large, atomically precise objects can be built molecule by molecule through a sequence of precisely controlled chemical reactions. An essential characteristic of assemblers will be their ability to make copies of themselves. Vast armies of assemblers will be needed to build objects rapidly and cheaply.

■ *Molecular computers.* To direct the activities of assemblers, another essential type of device will be necessary: the molecular computer. With components a few atoms wide, though, a simple mechanical computer would fit within 1/100 of a cubic micron, many billions of times more compact than today's so-called micro-electronics. Even with a billion bytes of storage, a nanomechanical computer could fit in a box a micron wide, about the size of a bacterium. These molecular computers will be fast because, although their signals will move about 100,000 times slower than the signals in current computers, they will need to travel only 1/1,000,000 as far. Thus these "nanocomputers" may be thousands of times faster than current microcomputers.

■ *Disassemblers.* One last type of device that is essential in the theory of nanotechnology is the disassembler. While molecular computers will control molecular assemblers, providing the swift flow of instructions needed to direct the placement of vast numbers of atoms, disassemblers will help scientists and engineers analyze things. Disassemblers will use enzymes and chemical reactions to break bonds and thus take anything apart, a few atoms at a time. Moreover, they record what it removes layer by layer.

Assemblers, disassemblers, and nanocomputers will work together. For example, a molecular computer will direct the disassemblers to take apart an object and record its structure and then direct an assembler to use those recorded instructions in reverse to assemble perfect copies of that object.

FIGURE 5-3
Example classification. This definition discusses types of devices one by one. Notice that the "principle of classification" is explained in the introduction.

Subject	Basis of Classification	Categories
Lasers	Potential for injury to humans (also based on watts).	Classes I, II, IIIa, IIIb, IV
Solar water	How water (or heating element) is circulated.	Passive (gravity is used) and active (pumps are used)
Solar collectors	The design of the tubing through which water is circulated and heated.	Flat-plate, evacuated-tube, and parabolic solar collectors
Solar cookers	How sunlight is focused and collected in the cooker.	Box, parabolic, panel cookers
Schizophrenia	Commonly associated sets of behaviors.	Paranoid, catatonic, disorganized, residual, undifferentiated
Diabetes	Dependency on insulin.	Type I (insulin-dependent diabetes) and Type II (non–insulin-dependent diabetes)

1. **Find a simple project requiring a discussion of categories.** Try to find a practical situation in which you'd need to write about categories. To write a classification, you'll need to find a term that can readily be divided into categories, such as those shown in the preceding table. (Having trouble thinking of a topic? See **www.io.com/ ~hcexres/power_tools/topics.html.**)

   What's "categorizable" about nanotechnology? If you scan Web resources, you'll see lots of possibilities. Nanotechnologists divide human history into "bulk" and "molecular" technological methods. However, for an understanding of the fundamentals of nanotechnology, terms like "assembler," "disassembler," "replicator," and "meme" are essential and occur again and again in the literature on nanotechnology.

2. **Define a purpose and an audience.** The next step is to decide on a purpose and an audience for this classification. (See Chapter 19 for strategies to use in analyzing audiences and adapting your writing to them.)

   Imagine that this discussion will be a section in a technical report. But who wants such a report? Who's willing to pay thousands of dollars to research and write the report? What are their requirements in relation to this topic? Venture-capital investors are always a possibility; these executive-type readers need background to help them decide whether to invest. Legislators and other government officials are another possibility; perhaps they need background in order to consider research and development funding. They don't have time to surf the Web all night or sort through stacks of books and articles that are way over their heads. That's for you to do!

3. Research the topic. Early in this project, you may need to do some research.

As the topic box at the beginning of this chapter shows, the World Wide Web is loaded with material on nanotechnology. But use caution! Some of it is wildly visionary. You can start by searching the Web using the term "nanotechnology" with any of the major search engines. Also look at some "guide sites," and move on to some searches of online libraries, such as the Library of Congress. Also, use your local library to search for published magazine and journal articles on the topic. Don't forget government documents.

4. Plan and develop graphics. Early on in this project, visualize the graphics for your classification. Use the strategies in Chapter 10 and Chapter 11 to plan the tables, charts drawings, diagrams, and photos you may need to include.

As you research nanotechnology, you'll see plenty of possibilities for graphics. Of course, because nanotechnology is a molecular thing, most of the illustrations are conceptual drawings. Conceptual drawings of nanotechnology processes and objects will be essential in helping readers understand this topic.

5. Decide on a basis of classification. Before dividing a topic into categories, find a good basis of classification, one that fulfills your readers' needs and presents the topic in the most informative way. To do this, you may need to draft several lists of categories until you find the most useful one.

In nanotechnology, terms like "assembler," "disassembler," "replicator," and "meme" occur constantly. Are these types of devices, or are they concepts? If they are concepts, there's no classification—it's not a set of categories. But as it turns out, the first three terms are indeed essential categories of nanotechnological devices. Their basis of classification is function—the job they do in the manufacturing process.

6. Divide the topic into categories. If you've learned enough about your topic from your initial research or know enough about it already, divide it into categories. Remember to apply only one basis of classification—the one you developed in the preceding step.

When you review your resources, you see that "meme," as it is used by the writers involved in this technology, is really not a category of

Practical Ethics: Manipulating Photos

Photos always present an accurate picture of reality, right? Well, no. With a home computer, digital imaging software, and a few clicks, a photo can be manipulated to show what we want it to. Slim models become even slimmer, political enemies are removed from snapshots of historic meetings, people are added to a crowd, turning a few protesters into a mob. In the past it was possible to compare a photograph with its original negative to determine if it had been altered. Digital cameras make this impossible.

Not everyone uses the power of technology as a license to alter photos. "The most important relationship we have with our readers is that of trust," said Robert York, senior editor for visuals at the *San Diego Union-Tribune*. "And we are not going to do anything digitally in the pages of our newspaper that will compromise that trust. No single image or series of images would be worth that price."[1]

Retaining readers' trust involves more than saying no to digital manipulation. A conscious effort has to be made to size and crop photos so the essential content is left intact, eliminating only irrelevant clutter that would distract or confuse readers.

Let's say you're writing a detailed promotional report for an air-conditioning system. Your boss is concerned that the size of the unit will discourage consumers from considering it, especially because it is larger than that of the competition's unit. You are given a photo of the system to use, which includes a man, and the system comes up to his chest. If he wasn't in the picture, there would be nothing to visually establish the size of the unit. What would you do?

Would you use the entire photo or would you crop the man out? Would you state the dimensions in the caption below the photo or anywhere else in the report? What if your boss told you specifically to crop the photo and not mention the dimensions? How would you justify your answers? Reread York's quote above. Do you agree with his statement?

[1] Lubrano, Gina, "When Photographs Aren't What They Seem," *The San Diego Union-Tribune*, 29 November 1999, p. B-7.

nanotechnological devices. However, assembler, disassembler, and replicator are essential device types. Each has an important function in the business of nanotechnology.

7. Write a formal sentence definition of the topic and each of the categories. Start a classification with a formal sentence definition, discussed earlier in this chapter. Also define each of the categories. Put the definition of the topic in the introduction and the definitions of the individual categories in their respective body paragraphs.

Nanotechnology is manufacturing at the molecular level. However, you need to explain this idea further before it begins making sense to readers. An assembler, as its name implies, is a molecular-sized device that assembles objects atom by atom. A disassembler, as its name also implies, is a device that disassembles objects in order to analyze their structure and contents. A replicator is a molecular-sized device that can build replicas of itself that do useful work.

8. Use the tools for extended definition to discuss the categories. Take a careful look at your formal sentence definitions; which of

Introduction: discuss or define the set to which the categories belong; provide an overview of the categories you'll discuss and the basis of the classification.

Category 1: discuss this category using one or more of the definition sources discussed earlier in this chapter.

Category 2: discuss this category using one or more of the definition sources discussed earlier in this chapter.

Category 3: discuss this category using one or more of the definition sources discussed earlier in this chapter.

Conclusion

FIGURE 5-4
Classification (discussion of categories). In this diagram, categories are discussed one at a time, each in its own paragraph. Each of those paragraphs uses the strategies for extended definition to discuss the category.

the definition tools do they suggest? Return to the list of extended-definition tools in the preceding pages and pick the ones you need.

For example, in the paragraph on assemblers, you'll first need a *definition* of an assembler, then a discussion of the *process* by which it builds objects. Use an analogy to the process by which biological assemblers—cells—build objects. Consider discussing *effects*—the extraordinary impact that this new form of manufacturing could have on society. Problems—*causes*—that will hinder the progress of nanotechnologists will also be important. And finally, use plenty of *examples* throughout. (Figure 5-4 illustrates how these definition tools can work together in the paragraphs of a classification.)

9. **Sketch the headings you'll use.** For a classification of three or more paragraphs, use headings (see Chapter 7). If you discuss individual categories in one or more separate paragraphs, create a heading for each.

For this classification, the headings will obviously be something like "Assemblers," "Disassemblers," "Replicators," and so on, followed by at least a paragraph on each.

10. **Plan an introduction.** Introductions, as you know, indicate the topic to be discussed; indicate the readers and situation the document

is intended for; provide an overview of what is about to be discussed; and, only minimally, present background information (such as key concepts, definitions, or the importance of the topic). If you have a lot of background information, move it into a paragraph of its own following the introduction.

For a separate document on nanotechnology, the introduction must define the term. If this definition becomes too long, you may have to move it to a second paragraph and just sketch a definition in the introduction. You'll also need to indicate the audience—investors or legislators—in the introduction as well as the purpose.

11. Plan a conclusion. For the final section, summarize (pull together the essential ideas you've discussed), conclude (draw some logical conclusion based on what you've been discussing), discuss some final point but at a general level, or use some combination of these methods.

It might be useful to review the basic concepts previously discussed. After all, this topic will be rough going for many readers. A logical conclusion might comment on how soon we can expect nanotechnology to have an impact or whether it is a realistic possibility at all. A final-thought conclusion might discuss the problems that the future of nanotechnology faces, or perhaps the ethical questions it raises.

12. Consider the format. For this simple project, you are not likely to need the elaborate report formats shown in Chapter 15. Instead, use the format you see for the example classification of solar collectors at the end of this chapter. Begin with a descriptive title centered at the top of the page, and use second- and third-level headings. Use lists, notices, illustrations, tables, highlighting, and documentation (citations of your borrowed information sources) as necessary.

13. Review and revise your rough draft. Use the strategies in Chapter 18 to systematically review and revise your classification. Use the top-down approach described in that chapter: start by reviewing for audience, purpose, and situation; then move on to content, organization, and transitions; then headings, lists, tables, and graphics; then sentence-style revision and technical style; and finally grammar, usage, spelling, and punctuation problems.

HOW DO YOU WRITE TECHNICAL BACKGROUND REPORTS?

Technical background reports solve workplace problems by providing information on a topic, information for which readers have specific needs. For example, Hewlett-Packard made headlines in 1999 with its developments involving nanotechnology. Plenty of product planners sat up and wanted to know just what "nanotechnology" is. One solution is the background report, which does the research and then summarizes it for such clients. Its infrastructure is typically definition: to discuss a topic adequately, you must consider it from multiple angles such as description, process, classification, and so on.

Let's walk through the important steps in writing a technical background report and apply them to an example project along the way:

1. **Build a team?** As with primary research reports and recommendation reports, technical background reports are great opportunities to work as a team. These reports take a lot of brainstorming and a lot of work.

2. **Find a project requiring a background report.** One of the hardest tasks in writing a technical background report for a technical-writing course is finding a real or realistic project. Something like "a report for anybody who happens to be interested in advanced manufacturing techniques" just won't work. Use the suggestions in **www.io.com/ ~hcexres/power_tools/topics.html** for developing practical technical-writing projects that solve real problems. Look around you for people and organizations or consider legislators and other government officials; then think about new technologies and identify background information that would meet your audience's needs, help them make decisions, or help them solve problems.

   Imagine that you want to use your technical-writing course to find out about nanotechnology. The background report provides a good way to capture your findings in an introductory-type document. This report won't provide conclusions, recommendations, instructions, or other such information; it will just provide introductory, background information for readers to use according to their own needs.

3. **Analyze the audience and purpose.** Once you've found a situation involving a problem that can be solved, in part, by a background report, zero in on the audience. See Chapter 19 for strategies to use in identifying or inventing and then analyzing audiences. Zero in on the purpose as well. To do all this, you may need to do some preliminary reading to become familiar with the topic.

   Who wants to read our technical background report on nanotechnology? Who would, in fact, pay us to write such a report? Investors perhaps? As of the year 2000, practical applications of nanotechnology were a long way off. Explore the following ideas:
   - What about government officials? Nanotechnology research and development will need a strong financial boost; other countries might get ahead of us. Imagine that you are a member of a legislative research team that has been directed to develop a background report on nanotechnology for legislators.

- What about organizations promoting nanotechnology that need promotional literature? Obviously, they are the experts, but perhaps they are not the best people to write about it for general, non-specialist readers.
- What about marketing analysts and planners? They represent another possible set of readers.

The legislative research team provides a good scenario. Legislators want to promote increased research and development in nanotechnology and bring that activity to their home state. The readers may be lawyers, career politicians, or educators—but they are not rocket scientists, nor are they nanotechnologists!

4. **Choose the "packaging" for the report.** Think about the design—the "packaging"—you'll use for this report. Will it be a memo report, business-letter report, online report, e-mail report, or formal bound report? See Chapter 15 for details on these options. For a report like this one the format of the formal report, complete with cover letter and front and back matter elements, is probably the best choice. See example excerpts from a report on alternative energy resources for rural health clinics at the end of Chapter 15.

   This technical background report on nanotechnology will not be a short report, but neither will it run over 20 pages. Its primary audience is legislators who won't want lots of pages. A report this long will not work as a memo or letter report; it needs to be a formal report with a cover memo. The online format is not an option for our legislative readers; it must be a conventional printed, bound report.

5. **Narrow the topic for the report.** For practically any technical topic, you can write at least one large heavy book, if not multiple ones. But that's not what your readers want. They want you to do the legwork in the library, sift through all those books and articles to find the best ones, and then, in a nice tidy 20-page bundle, summarize the key information they need using words they can understand. See **www.io.com/~hcexres/power_tools/narrowing.html** for strategies to use in narrowing topics.

   Remember that narrowing means chopping out topics that readers don't want and adjusting the level of detail to their needs. Our legislative readers need to know about nanotechnology, but not in excruciating technical detail. They need to know its likely applications and the impact on society. They also need to know how far research and development has progressed and how soon practical results will emerge. They will want to know where the research is, who the competition is, what the costs are, and what the likely payoff is.

6. **Use the infrastructures to develop a tentative outline.** Infrastructures include description, process, causes, effects, definition,

classification, and persuasion. Each one requires certain kinds of content and certain kinds of organization, making them handy tools for developing outlines.

To explain what "manufacturing at the molecular level" means, you'll need a *process* description—a step-by-step explanation of how things can be built atom by atom. You'll need to include *causes and effects,* as well—just what will be the impact on society? Lots of *definitions* will be in order—what does the prefix *nano-* mean? In fact, the whole report will be essentially a big extended definition of nanotechnology. You may also need *description*—what will this equipment look like?

7. **Plan and develop graphics and tables.** As you research a topic, you'll see useful graphics and tables. Photocopy or download them and record complete bibliographic information for each one.

   ■ If the graphic is from a book, make a note of the author, title, page number, publisher, city of publication, and year.
   ■ If it's from an article, record the author, article title, magazine or journal name, date of the issue, volume and issue numbers (if applicable), and page number.
   ■ If it's from a Web page, record the author (if available) or organization, title of the page, URL, date you accessed the page, as well as the date of the last revision of the Web page.

   If you find that you must develop some of the graphics and tables yourself, get out your artist's beret, but also see Chapter 11 on illustrative graphics.

   For the nanotechnology project, you'll need flowcharts and diagrams of the manufacturing process. Tables will be good for showing expenditures on research and development as well as the projected impact on society.

8. **Set up a source list.** It's extremely annoying to have to go back and find bibliographic information on your sources. It takes time that you probably won't have, and inevitably you'll have trouble relocating some of your sources. Set up the sources list according to the format prescribed by the documentation style you are using.

9. **Review and revise your rough draft.** Use the strategies in Chapter 18 to systematically review and revise your definition. Use the top-down approach described there: start by reviewing for audience, purpose, and situation; then move on to content, organization, and transitions; then headings, lists, tables, and graphics; then sentence-style revision and technical style; and finally grammar, usage, spelling, and punctuation problems.

WORKSHOP: DEFINITION, CLASSIFICATION, BACKGROUND REPORTS

Here are some additional ideas for practicing the concepts, tools, and strategies in this chapter:

1. *Synonym definitions.* Rewrite the following sentences using the "raw materials" to create synonyms:

Base sentence:	One of the most important classes of disorders of the hematological system involves various types of anemia.
Raw material:	Anemia is a disorder of the red blood cells.
Base sentence:	Alzheimer's disease was first described in 1907 by Alos Alzheimer, a German physician.
Raw material:	Alzheimer's disease is defined as an adult-onset neurological disorder.
Base sentence:	Carbon dioxide is essential for photosynthesis.
Raw material:	Carbon dioxide is an odorless, colorless gas that constitutes about 0.035% of the atmosphere.
	Photosynthesis is the process by which the sun's energy is converted to forms usable by plants and animals.
Base sentence:	As of the 1980s, between 30 and 40 million metric tons of hazardous wastes were generated in the United States annually.
Raw material:	Hazardous waste can be defined as a substance that can cause serious, irreversible, or incapacitating illness as well as environmental damage if not handled properly.
Base sentence:	For example, gene therapy could provide medical treatment to eliminate sickle-cell disease.
Raw material:	Sickle-cell disease is a human genetic disorder involving red blood cells.

2. *Formal sentence definitions.* Use the following "raw material" to write formal sentence definitions:

Term	Raw materials
Solar collector	In a solar heating system, heats circulating water necessary for space heating. Uses layers of glass to trap heat.
Salt marshes	Low coastal grassland frequently overflowed by the tide; develop when the rate of sediment deposition is greater than the rate of land subsidence.

Continued

Term	Raw materials
Sickle-cell disease	Human genetic disorder; affects red blood cells; when red blood cells give up oxygen, they take on an elongated shape; elongated cells clog blood vessels and are less able to become re-oxygenated.
Greenhouse effect	The trapping of solar radiation into the lower atmosphere; makes Earth's surface warmer than it would be otherwise; caused by carbon dioxide in atmosphere block re-radiation of infrared heat back into space.
Hazardous waste	Can cause death or increase in serious, irreversible, or incapacitating illness; poses substantial threat to human health and the environment if improperly treated, transported, or disposed of.

3. *Tools for definition.* Take a look at the following extended definition and identify the tools for extended definition.

> Salt marshes are defined as low coastal grassland frequently overflowed by the tide. They form in lagoons, estuaries, and other sheltered coastal positions. They develop when the rate of sediment deposition is greater than the rate of land subsidence. Sediment deposited on the marsh surface follows a simple distribution pattern: larger, heavier sand grains are deposited close to the low tide mark, while lighter silt particles are carried further inland on the high tide. Mudflats form between the marshes and the sea, acting as a buffer and dissipating wave energy. Deep, branching drainage channels develop on the marsh, directing flood patterns and reducing the erosion from flood tides. The height of a salt marsh above sea level cannot exceed the level of the highest spring tide. If this limit is reached because of a drop in relative sea level, then the salt marsh will evolve into a brackish or freshwater marsh and eventually become coastal scrub or woodland. Normally, salt marshes are covered in rooted vegetation, mainly grass species, which are adapted to withstand periodic submergence in salt water. The plant roots anchor the surface of the sediment, increasing resistance to erosion in storm conditions. Plants on the marsh are distributed in characteristic zones, according to the level of salinity and frequency of submergence that

they are adapted to survive. Many salt marshes in
Europe are located in sparsely populated areas. In
the past they were often reclaimed from the sea to
be used for heavy industry and refuse disposal. The
increasing recognition of the importance of marshes
as a wildlife habitat has reduced the number of
reclamation and industrial schemes aimed at salt
marshes.

4. *Division into categories.* Divide one or more of the following topics
   into categories, types, and classes. (If you can't think of categories,
   look these topics up in any general encyclopedia.)

Primates	Telescopes	Industrial robots
Trees	Cancers	Solar energy devices
Clouds	Rocks	Shells
Hurricanes	Earthquakes	Pollution
Computers	Basic electronic components	Telephones
Solar eclipses	Food	Trauma

5. *Background reports—using infrastructures.* Consider one or more
   of the following topics for technical background reports. Which
   infrastructures would you use, and what would be their contents?

Continental drift for California home owners	Solar automobiles for college maintenance supervisor
Industrial waste disposal for a neighborhood association	Hypoglycemia for school counselors and advisors
Steroids for athletic coaches and trainers	Creationist theories for science faculty
Evolution theories for fundamentalist congregations	Fossils for the paleontology club
Loans for citizens	Energy-saving techniques for home owners

Definition: This extended definition focuses on "molecular manufacturing," the term that the author prefers to "nanotechnology."

Introduction: This document begins by discussing the current confusion about the meaning of the term. Following that is a formal sentence definition. The formal sentence spills over into the following sentence. The introduction ends with an overview of what the rest of this extended definition will cover.

Comparison: To establish the definition of molecular manufacturing more firmly, this next section contrasts molecular manufacturing to current manufacturing.

Classification: This extended definition uses classification to discuss essential types of molecular-manufacturing devices. Remember that in extended definition, you must select from the other kinds of writing discussed in Part I of this book.

EXTENDED DEFINITION
Molecular Manufacturing

Since nanotechnology has seized popular imagination, it has been used loosely to refer to research where dimensions, quantities, and locations are around 1,000 nanometers. However, the "nanotechnology" that leaders like K. Eric Drexler, Ralph C. Merkle, and others are talking about refers to a process in which essentially every atom can be put in the right place at manufacturing costs not greatly exceeding those of the required raw materials and energy. This makes possible the manufacture of almost anything for which we can provide detailed atomic specifications. Because their concept of nanotechnology refers to manufacturing atom by atom and molecule by molecule, leading nanoscientists sometimes prefer the term "molecular manufacturing." The following further explores this new technology and its applications [5].

Manufacturing Technologies: Current and Future

Merkle uses LEGOs to explain the basics of molecular manufacturing. Common forms of manufacturing such as casting, grinding, and milling manipulate atoms in what he calls "great thundering statistical herds." In current manufacturing methods, we can "push the LEGO blocks into great heaps and pile them up," but we cannot fit them together the way we want at the molecular level [5]. If we had a manufacturing process that gave us that level of control, we could rearrange the atoms in a chunk of coal to make a diamond or the atoms in ordinary sand to make a computer or the atoms in dirt and water to make potatoes. This is what Merkle and others call "molecular manufacturing."

An example illustrating this contrast is lithography, the essential manufacturing process used to build computer chips. Continued improvements in lithography have enabled us to work with dimensions less than one micron. But despite the improvements in computer hardware capability that submicron lithography has made possible, this manufacturing method will probably reach its fundamental limits in the first two decades of the 21st century. Merkle and others believe that nanotechnology will provide a "post-lithographic" manufacturing process. It will enable us to build inexpensive computer systems with "mole quantities of logic elements that are molecular in both size and precision" [5].

Molecular Manufacturing: Essential Components

Merkle identifies two concepts essential to molecular manufacturing: positional assembly and self-replication.

Headings: Because this is a relatively short document, it does not use first-level headings (unless you consider the title a first-level heading). In fact, you can imagine this entire document as a background section in a longer report on molecular manufacturing. In any case, a heading like "Molecular Manufacturing: Essential Components" is a second-level heading, as defined in Chapter 7. Headings like "Positional assembly" are third-level headings.

Positional assembly. To get "the right molecular parts in the right places," some form of positional assembly is required. This implies robotic devices that are molecular both in their size and precision. The idea of such devices, as strange as it may seem, is not new. Richard Feynman, considered one of the founding theorists of nanotechnology, introduced this idea in "There's Plenty of Room at the Bottom," his famous 1959 presentation to the American Physical Society: "The principles of physics, as far as I can see, do not speak against the possibility of maneuvering things atom by atom" [2]. According to Drexler, "Just as today's engineers build machinery as complex as player pianos and robot arms from ordinary motors, bearings, and moving parts, so tomorrow's biochemists will be able to use protein molecules as motors, bearings, and moving parts to build robot arms which will themselves be able to handle individual molecules" [1].

Direct quotations: This document uses more direct quotations than other documents in this book. Notice, however, that the quotations are always attributed to a source—you know who made the quoted statement. Notice, as well, that in every case the direct quotation has something individualistic about it. For example, the phrase "respectable speck" deserves quotation marks, but a "small dot" would not.

Self-replication. For objects to be manufactured inexpensively and efficiently, self-replicating components are also needed. This idea was originally put forth by John von Neumann in the 1940s. Such a device would make copies of itself and manufacture the desired objects [5]. In *Engines of Creation,* Drexler foresees replicators whose components will include molecular "tape" to supply instructions, a reader to translate those instructions into arm motions, and several assembler arms to hold and move workpieces. Drexler calculates that such a replicator will add up to one billion atoms or so and, working at one million atoms per second, will copy itself in one thousand seconds (about fifteen minutes). Working singly, a replicator would need a century to stack up enough copies to make a "respectable speck." But with replicators making copies of themselves, the process would produce a ton of copies in less than a day [1].

Molecular Manufacturing: Applications

When they discuss applications of molecular manufacturing, nanotechnologists such as Ralph C. Merkle, K. Eric Drexler, and Richard Smalley become downright visionary. Self-assembling consumer goods; computers billions of times faster; extraordinary inventions (impossible today); safe and affordable space travel; a virtual end to illness, aging, and death; no more pollution and automatic cleanup of already existing pollution; molecular food synthesis and thus the end of famine and starvation; access to a superior education for every child on Earth; reintroduction of many extinct plants and animals; terraforming on Earth and in the Solar System—these are the things they foresee [7].

Medicine. One of the most far-reaching applications is medical research. To treat disease, current medical technology uses techniques involving drugs, radiation, and surgery. These techniques are generally slow, tedious, and sometimes dangerous. Nanotechnological agents (often called "nanites") could perform the tasks of drugs, radiation, and surgery far better. Instead of relying on open heart surgery to remove a blockage in an artery, nanites could be inhaled and find their way through the body to the specified artery and pick apart the blockage without causing any harm. Some nanotechnologists believe that "nanomedicine" will enable people to live for indefinite amounts of time [4]. According to one nanomedicine researcher, Robert Freitas, nanomedicine, which he defines as "the ability to direct events in a controlled fashion at the cellular level," will be "the key that will unlock the indefinite extension of human health and the expansion of human abilities" [3].

Space exploration. Another area that will benefit from this new concept is space exploration and aerospace technology. Nanosystems could be used to manufacture the materials, fuel, and hardware needed in spacecraft. These materials would cost virtually nothing because nanites

---

Borrowed information: This definition uses the number system to identify the sources of information that were used. Remember that it does not matter whether the borrowed information is directly quoted, paraphrased, or summarized. It's still borrowed and needs "citations" to indicate the source. This document uses bracketed numbers to indicate the source.

Applications and effects: As an additional way of exploring the meaning of nanotechnology, this definition discusses applications and their effect on society. Thus short definitions, comparison and contrast, as well as cause and effect have all been used to extend this definition.

will be able to rearrange the molecules of any common substance into those of another. And these same processes can be used on other planets using common materials found there to create oxygen, food, and other substances needed to sustain human life. And if nanomedicine enables people to live practically forever, we'll need to settle other planets to keep from overpopulating Earth.

Computer industry. An area where nanotechnology may make its first practical impact is the computer industry. Nanosystems may enable the manufacture of computer chips with a cost of less than a dollar per pound, with operating frequencies of tens of gigahertz or more, with a size of roughly 10 nanometers per device, and with extraordinarily low energy requirements (or as Drexler puts it, "roughly the energy of a single air molecule bouncing around at room temperature") [6].

Conclusion: When?

When asked how soon these scientific miracles may happen, nano-technologists are the first to say that they just do not know. However, *Wired* magazine in 1995 assembled some of the top minds in nano-technology and asked them to estimate when certain critical events in the advance of nanotechnology might occur. Their predictions for when we might see the first molecular assembler (a device for position assembly discussed previously) ranged from 2000 to 2025; for a nano-computer, 2010-2100; for cell repair, 2018-2050; for a commercial product, 2000-2015; for laws regulating nanotechnology, 1998-2036 [6].

Information Sources

1. Drexler, K. Eric. *Engines of Creation: The Coming Era of Nano-technology.* 1 April 1997. **www.foresight.org/EOC**. Accessed 2000, February 28.
2. Feynman, Richard P. "There's Plenty of Room at the Bottom: An Invitation to Enter a New Field of Physics." 1959. **www.zyvex.com/nanotech/feynman.html**. Accessed 2000, February 28.
3. Freitas, Robert A. "Nanomedicine." 2000, January 28. **www.foresight.org/Nanomedicine**. Accessed 2000, February 28.
4. Hunter, Richard. "Nanotechnology and its Applications." No date. **www.personal.psu.edu/dept/scifi/science/articles/nano.html**. Accessed 2000, February 28.

Information sources: Occurring here at the end is the list of information sources used to write this document. The style used here is the number system. Notice that the items are alphabetized and numbered. Notice, as well, that quotation marks are used around article titles, whereas italics are used for book titles (even though they appear on the Web). And finally, these entries include both the publication date and the date the writer of this extended definition accessed them.

5. Merkle, Ralph C. "Nanotechnology." No date. **www.zyvex.com/nano**. Accessed 2000, February 28.
6. Merkle, Ralph C. "How long will it take to develop nanotechnology?" No date. **www.zyvex.com/nanotech/howlong.html**. Accessed 2000, February 28.
7. "What is Nanotechnology?" 2000 February 24. **nanozine.com/WHATNANO.HTM**. Accessed 2000, February 28.

Types of solar water heaters: This document, which could occur in a larger report on solar technology, presents two types of solar water heaters and then three types of solar collectors that can be used in those systems.

Introduction: Notice that this introduction begins with a bit of fanfare about solar water heaters and, then in the last sentence, provides an overview of what is going to be covered.

Second-level headings: Using the terminology presented in Chapter 7, this document uses two second-level headings: one for basic types of solar water heaters; the other for types of solar collectors.

Basis of classification: Notice that the basis for this classification of solar water heaters—the circulation method—is explained.

No stacked headings: If there were no text between the second-level heading, "Solar Water Heaters: Basic Types," and the third-level heading, "Active solar water heaters," we would have stacked headings on our hands! (See Chapter 7 for details.)

CLASSIFICATION

Solar Water Heaters: An Introduction[2]

Over a million homeowners and nearly a quarter of a million businesses in almost all climates across the United States use solar devices for their water-heating needs. In summer months, in most parts of the country, a solar system for a residential building can meet 100% of the water-heating requirements. In winter months, the system may meet only half the water-heating requirements; therefore, a backup heat source supplements the solar system. The following discussion introduces the two types of solar water heaters and the three basic types of solar collectors used in those heaters.

Solar Water Heaters: Basic Types

There are two broad categories of solar water heaters: active and passive. The essential difference is the method used to circulate water.

Active solar water heaters. Active solar water heaters use pumps to circulate water or some other fluid from the collectors, where it is heated by the sun, to the storage tank, where the water remains until needed. Active systems fall into two general groups based on freeze protection: those using a fluid with a low freezing point (such as propylene glycol) in the collector loop and those using water in the loop (which is automatically drained when the sun is not shining).

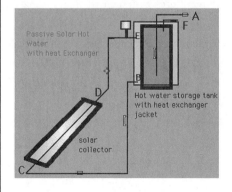

Passive Solar Hot Water with heat exchanger

Hot water storage tank with heat exchanger jacket

solar collector

Passive solar water-heating system.
Mr. Solar. Solar Water Heater. http://www.msolar.com/arthotwater.html

[2] Produced for the U.S. Department of Energy (DOE) by the National Renewable Energy Laboratory, a DOE national laboratory.

Third-level headings: These headings are "run in" to the paragraph and use sentence-style caps. (See Chapter 7 for information about third-level headings.)

Discussing categories: Notice that the paragraphs that discuss types do so, in this document, by explaining how they work (process), how they are constructed (description), and what's good and bad about them (causes, effects, and comparison).

Passive solar water heaters. Passive solar water heaters, which rely on gravity, are typically either integral collector/storage (ICS) systems or thermosyphon systems. The major advantage of these systems is that they don't use controls, pumps, sensors, or other mechanical parts, meaning that only minimal maintenance is required during their lifetime. They are less expensive than active solar systems and can only be used in warm sun-belt climates. Also, the roof structure must be able to support the load of the storage tanks used in passive systems.

Solar Collectors: Basic Types

One of three types of solar collectors can be selected for solar water-heating systems: flat-plate, evacuated-tube, and parabolic-trough collectors.

Flat-plate collectors. A flat-plate collector is basically a panel-shaped box containing fluid-filled tubes mounted on a dark-colored absorber. Suitable for both residential and nonresidential use, it can also operate well in a humid climate, where haze creates more diffuse, rather than direct, sunlight.

Evacuated-tube collectors. In an evacuated-tube collector, side-by-side tubes hold the fluid to be heated. Each tube is surrounded by an outer glass tube, and a vacuum between the inner and outer tubes provides good insulation to reduce heat loss. The collector operates at high temperatures with high efficiency using direct and diffuse light.

Parabolic-trough collectors. A parabolic-trough collector consists of a long U-shaped mirror that focuses the sun onto a fluid-filled tube along the center of the U-trough. This highly efficient system typically tracks the sun and requires direct, not diffuse, sunlight. The major use has been nonresidential or institutional applications such as prisons and hospitals.

CHAPTER 6

Persuasion: Proposals and Progress Reports

RECYCLING

Recycling is not necessarily the ecological sacred cow that you may think it is. There's plenty of opposition to it as some of the following Web pages indicate. Still, it is interesting to review just how well recycling is working and how much it has worked its way into our societal habits. Here are some Web sites that address these issue:

EPA Recycling site. **www.epa.gov/wastewise/recyclin.htm**

Links to Recycling sites. **www.epa.gov/wastewise/other.htm**

Richard A. Denison and John F. Ruston. "Recycling Is Not Garbage." **www.techreview.com/articles/oct97/recycle.html**

Recycling Isn't Garbage. **www.edf.org/issues/NYTrecycle.html**

John F. Ruston and Richard A. Denison. "Assessing the Full Costs and Benefits of Curbside Recycling." **www.edf.org/pubs/Reports/advrec.html**

"Environmental Life-Cycle Comparisons of Recycling, Landfilling and Incineration." From the *Annual Review of Energy and the Environment.* **www.edf.org/AboutEDF/denison.pdf**

Accessed January 12, 2001.

As you know from the Preface, most technical documents are based on one or a combination of *infrastructures*—elemental structures that enable those documents to do their job. The infrastructure essential in proposals and progress reports is *persuasion* (also known as *argumentation*). To convince people to hire you to do a project and to reassure them that the project is going well, you need persuasive strategies. This chapter reviews the common persuasive strategies and shows you how to write proposals and progress reports with those strategies built in.

Persuasion is certainly at the core of resumes and application letters as well as "problem communications" such as complaint, adjustment, and inquiry letters. However, this chapter is already splitting at its seams. For resumes and application letters, see Chapter 14, "Employment Search: Application Letters and Resumes." For problem communications such as complaint, adjustment, and inquiry letters, see Chapter 13, "Business Communications: Letters, Memos, e-mail."

Note:
▪ If you are new to this book, see "How Do You Use This Book?" in the Preface.
▪ For additional examples of the documents discussed in this chapter, see **www.io.com/~hcexres/power_tools/examples**.

WHAT ARE THE TOOLS FOR PERSUASION?

Before getting into the contents, organization, format, and style of the technical-writing applications covered in this chapter, review some of the basics of writing persuasively (see Figure 6-1 for an example). If you remember your Rhetoric and Composition 101, you know that several types of "appeals" are available for persuasive writing:

▪ *Logical appeal.* When you use reasons and arguments, backed up by facts and logic, to make your case, you are using the logical appeal. We normally think of the logical appeal as the only legitimate method of argument, but the "real world" shows us differently.
▪ *Emotional appeal.* When you attempt to rouse people's anger or sympathies in a persuasive effort, you are using an emotional appeal. A photo of a little girl fleeing from a burning village bombed by war planes or an oil-soaked seagull on a beach devastated by an oil spill are images that spark emotions like anger, horror, and sympathy; but they don't make a logical case for or against anything. These images may, however, capture readers' attention and cause them to pay more attention to the rest of your persuasive effort.
▪ *Personal appeal.* When you present your qualifications, experience, expertise, or wisdom, attempting to build readers' confidence, you are using the personal appeal. As with the emotional appeal, there is no logical justification for the personal appeal. It's like saying, "Trust me."

Main assertion: This paragraph begins with a straightforward thesis that recycling is not cost-efficient—that it costs too much.

Support: Relying primarily on the Tierney article, this writer goes through a series of reasons for the extra expense: extra city officials, public education programs, reduced efficiency of recycling pickup, and minimal market value for recyclables.

Direct quotations: Notice that this writer quotes two pithy phrases from Tierney's articles, quotations that carry some of the attitude and personality of the original author.

Documentation: Even if this writer had not quoted his source directly, he is still obligated to cite his source for the information he has borrowed.

One of the biggest problems with recycling is that it is not cost-efficient. In fact, recycling is a serious financial drain on all but a very few municipalities. As John Tierney pointed out in his 1996 *New York Times Magazine* article, collecting and handling a ton of recyclable materials is three times more expensive than putting them directly into a landfill. Why is that? Recycling programs require extra bureaucrats to manage them and enforcement officers to inspect people's recycling efforts and fine them if they are not complying. They require expensive public education campaigns to train people in the arduous process of sorting and storing their garbage correctly. (According to Tierney, "New Yorkers still don't know the rules.") Recycling programs are also more expensive because less garbage can be picked up at each stop. Tierney, in his aptly titled article, "Recycling Is Garbage," estimated that in 1996, New York City was spending more than $200 more to recycle a ton of glass, plastic, and metal than it would spend to bury the material in a landfill. He points out that market prices for recyclables has "rarely risen as high as zero." In fact, the city has to pay an additional $40 to get rid of valueless recyclables.

Source: John Tierney. "Recycling Is Garbage." *New York Times Magazine,* June 30, 1996: **www.igc.org/nrdc/nrdcpro/recyc/appenda.html**. Accessed January 18, 2000.

FIGURE 6-1

Single-paragraph example of persuasion. This paragraph would be one of several paragraphs attempting to discredit the recycling movement.

Despite that, readers sometimes want to know who you are and what gives you the right to speak so authoritatively on a subject. Just as the emotional appeal can be used legitimately to get readers to pay attention and care about your message, the right amount of personal appeal can build readers' confidence in you—or at least a willingness to hear you out.

You may also have encountered the *stylistic* appeal—the use of language and visual effects to increase the persuasive impact. For example, a glossy, fancy design for a resume can have as positive an impact as the content.

In your rhetoric and composition studies, you may also have encountered something called the Toulmin approach to persuasion. The complete system involves claims, grounds, warrant, backing, and rebuttal, but a particularly useful element is the *rebuttal*, and another known as the *concession*.

■ *Rebuttal.* In a rebuttal, you directly address counterarguments that your persuasive opponents might bring up. You show how they are wrong, or at least how they don't affect your overall argument. Picture yourself face to face with your persuasive opponents. What arguments are they going to come back at you with? How are you going to answer those arguments? In a *written* persuasive effort, you must simulate this back-and-forth, debate-style argumentative process. Imagine your opponents' counterarguments (arguments they might put forth against your position) and then imagine your own rebuttals (your answers to those counterarguments).

- *Concession.* In a concession, you acknowledge that certain opposing arguments have some validity, but you explain how they do not damage your overall argument. Concessions build personal appeal: they make you seem more open-minded.

- *Synthesis.* Modern rhetoricians urge us not to view the persuasive process as a win-lose, all-out war. When people are entrenched, they shut out the arguments of the other side. Such rigidity prevents us from resolving the issue and getting on with our lives. Instead, the process of counterargument, rebuttal, and concession should be sincere and continuous until all parties reach synthesis—a middle ground where they drop their weapons and agree.

You should also be aware of the logical fallacies commonly found in persuasive efforts:

- *Hasty generalizations.* When you draw a conclusion based on too little evidence, you make a hasty generalization. For example, if you conclude that there is a big social trend to return to the '70s look because you see two or three pairs of bellbottoms and paisley shirts one day, you've drawn a hasty generalization based on a very limited, incomplete sample.

- *Irrelevant, ad hominem arguments.* When you base all or part of your persuasive effort on your opponent's character, behavior, or past, that's an *ad hominem* argument (meaning "to the man" in Latin). If a middle-aged political candidate were attacked for smoking marijuana in college, that might be an irrelevant personal attack.

- *Bandwagon effect.* If you base all or part of your persuasive effort on the idea that "everybody's doing it," you're using the bandwagon effect. Commercial advertisement commonly uses this tactic: everybody's buying the product—so should you!

- *False causality.* If you argue that because one event came after another, the first event caused the second, you may be making an argument based on false causality. For example, imagine that your father joined IBM in 1984 as a regular employee and shortly thereafter the company began its historic slide to near-extinction. Imagine further that in 1995 he left the company, at which time the company began its remarkable comeback. Was it your dad who nearly brought the company to its knees? Did his departure save the company?

- *Oversimplistic, either-or arguments.* If you reduce the choices to the choice you favor and a totally unacceptable choice, you are using an oversimplistic, either-or argument. Advocates for a nuclear power plant might argue that either we build the thing or we go without electricity.

- *False analogies.* When you compare a situation to a simple object or process, that's an *analogy.* When you base an entire persuasive effort on an analogy, you may have problems. Some analogies are just wrong to begin with. And all analogies break down at some point. For example, arguments relating to global warming often use the analogy of how a car heats up when the windows are closed. The Vietnam war was justified using the analogy of how dominoes all topple over when they are lined up. Analogies can help readers understand, but not justify, an argument.

HOW DO YOU WRITE PERSUASIVELY?

Let's walk through the important steps in writing persuasively. For a sense of how these steps work in an actual writing project, we'll follow an example through each of the steps.

1. **Find a simple project requiring persuasive writing.** Finding a project for persuasion is like trying to pick a fight. Think of the main issues of the day—global warming, ozone-layer depletion, alternative fuels, mass transportation, pesticides, zero population growth, solar energy, cloning (bioengineering), abortion, effects of computer- and video-game violence, capital punishment, nuclear armaments, chemical warfare. Each of these topics has multiple issues that are hotly debated. Technical-writing courses are not the place for the common pro-and-con and letter-to-the-editor essays you may have written in past writing courses. However, these topics have a technical side that challenges your abilities as a technical writer, and several of the document types presented in this book use persuasion. (Still having trouble thinking of a topic? See **www.io.com/~hcexres/power_tools/ topics.html**.)

   Imagine that you are a member of a group advocating city-wide curb-side recycling—one in which the city picks up glass, metal, and paper "at the curb" at individual residences and offices. Your problem is to overcome people's opposition to and misunderstanding of recycling, as well as the inertia of city bureaucracy. Written documents will be only one part of the solution to this problem.

2. **Define a purpose and an audience.** The next step is to decide on a purpose and an audience for this persuasion. (See Chapter 19 for strategies to use in analyzing audiences and adapting your writing to them.)

   Assume a dual audience: one made up of ordinary citizens, the other made up of city officials. Your purpose is to convince them to begin serious consideration of a recycling program in the city. Appeal to these two audiences in distinctly different ways: ordinary citizens want to know if it's going to be a hassle, whether it will increase their utility bills, and so on. City officials want to know about these issues as well, but from an administrative point of view.

3. **Do some research.** To write persuasively about a topic, you may need to do a bit of research.

> In your local library, you might find government averages on municipal waste, percent of recyclable content, cost of landfill disposal, and so on. At city hall, city officials might give you this same data for your own city, including the costs of operating the landfill and its projected date of close. On the World Wide Web, you might be able to find case studies of cities currently operating recycling programs, enabling you to see how the programs work, how much they cost, how much they save, and how they are received by the citizens. This material would contribute to your logical appeals, although the bandwagon effect ("Other cities are doing it!") might creep in.

4. **Plan and develop graphics and tables.** Early in this project, visualize the graphics your persuasive argument will need. Use the strategies in Chapter 10 and Chapter 11 to plan the tables, charts, diagrams, and other graphics you may need to include.

> The most important nontextual information will be tables of statistics about municipal wastes, percent of recyclables, landfill costs, rate of landfill use, and potential costs of or revenue from recycling programs. For greater impact, you can represent this table data as charts or graphs. Also, recycling literature often contains flowcharts of waste cycling between factories, consumers, landfills, and recycling plants.

5. **Identify the main logical arguments.** With your topic, purpose, and audience defined, identify the most important arguments.

> What are the logical arguments for recycling—more specifically, a city-based curb-side recycling program? They range from altruistic (for the city, for the planet) to selfish (to reduce waste management costs, to decrease taxes). Which arguments you use depends on your readers. Altruistic arguments may be of no use to certain conservative or business readers or to city administrators, but they may be vital in getting ordinary citizens to back such the program.

6. **Discuss each argument separately, providing plenty of support.** You must prove each logical argument, using supporting data, reasoning, and examples. You can't just baldly state that something costs less, works better, provides benefits, and is acceptable to the public. You've got to prove it!

> In your persuasive effort to get the city to consider recycling, you might use the logical appeal that such a program would reduce landfill requirements. How can you prove that? Do some research. What

Practical Ethics: The "Good" Debate

 Do Americans expect presidents to act ethically both in and out of the Oval Office? It's a topic that has been hotly debated in recent years. Some believe a person's private behavior—ethical or not—affects the quality of their leadership, whereas others believe ethics and leadership are two separate issues.

How does this question relate to technical writing? In this course you're learning how to communicate effectively, and being an excellent communicator is often equated with good leadership. Thus you are dragged into the debate: do you have to be a good person in order to be a good writer or a good speaker?

The ethics argument extends back through the centuries. In an article published in *The South Atlantic Quarterly*, Richard Lanham outlines some of the most influential debaters of Quintilian's assertion that the *perfect* speaker must also be a good 'person.[1] Plato believed that intelligence and moral courage go hand in hand. A man named Peter Ramus said that although the ability to speak and write well "is a virtue, it is a virtue of the mind and the intelligence . . . whose followers can still be [people] of the utmost moral depravity."[2]

Contrast Martin Luther King Jr. with Adolf Hitler. They were both effective communicators and powerful leaders who spurred people into action. Obviously, one was a highly moral person while the other was not. But is this a formula? Does an unethical person automatically translate into unethical leadership and vice versa? Can you think of any people, famous or otherwise, who would refute this formula? Apply this question to yourself. How will your own ethics affect your communication, both on and off the job?

[1] Lanham, Richard A. "The 'Q' Question." *The South Atlantic Quarterly* 87:4, Fall 1988. Durham, NC: Duke University Press, pp 653–700.

[2] Ibid.

is the city's daily input to the landfill; what are the costs? Can you determine the percent made up by recyclables? If you can get believable numbers, calculate landfill savings in terms of volume and dollars.

7. **Consider emotional appeals.** At best, emotional appeals capture readers' attention and get them to care about the issue. At worst, they rouse strong emotions such as fear and anger, preventing readers from thinking clearly about an issue.

   What emotional appeals could you use for the recycling promotion? (Not that you actually would use them, of course.) Images of overflowing landfills might work; images of dwindling natural habitats, replete with deer, chipmunks, hummingbirds—these might work. Would they pull at the heart strings of your readers, or would readers cynically mutter "Give me a break"? How would you feel about using such tactics?

8. **Consider personal appeals.** Like emotional appeals, personal appeals have no logical relevance to an argument. If you use the personal appeal, you attempt to build readers' confidence in you as

someone who is knowledgeable and reliable. Citing years of experience and education is a common example of building a personal appeal.

What personal appeals could this recycling persuasion use? To get people to accept your data, cite believable sources, such as government reports or leading experts. To give yourself credibility, describe your past experience and training in this area. Perhaps also describe yourself as a long-time resident of the city. These appeals shouldn't have any relevance, but they may cause people to hear you out.

9. **Address any counterarguments.** It's a good idea to address counter arguments—objections people might raise in relation to your argument. Imagine people out there saying, "But—but—but—!" Discuss their counterarguments and show how they are wrong, how they can be addressed, or how they are irrelevant to your main point.

As for recycling programs, you must address the standard objections. *It's a hassle.* Your might counterargue that recycling is no more of a hassle than taking out the garbage. *It's a hassle sorting everything and keeping it in separate bins.* That one is easy—most recycling programs don't require sorting. *It's messy and attracts pests.* Hmmm, that's a hard one—time for some research.

10. **Sketch the headings you'll use.** If your persuasion is more than two or three paragraphs, use headings (presented in Chapter 7). If you present arguments one at a time in separate paragraphs, create a heading for each one.

For this persuasion, you might have headings to introduce each of your main arguments; for example, "Landfill Reduction," "Municipal Revenue," and so on.

11. **Plan an introduction.** In an introduction to a persuasive argument, you cannot start out guns blazing and swords rattling. It's not necessary to state your main argumentative point right away. Instead, just indicate the subject matter—not your main point about it. Your readers are more likely to hear you out.

Imagine that you've written the main sections of this persuasion. You have logical appeals, counterarguments, and possibly some personal and emotional appeals as well. Instead of demanding that the city adopt a recycling program, begin with a quiet purpose statement saying that this document "looks at" or "investigates" the possibilities for recycling. Indicate that this document is for both city officials and ordinary citizens. Provide an overview, indicating that you'll be discussing current and projected landfill use and associated costs, amount of recyclables in municipal waste, their recyclable value, potential revenue from a recycling program, costs of a recycling program, and necessary administrative and citizen participation in such a program.

12. **Write a conclusion.** In a persuasion, the final section is often a "true" conclusion. If you have not yet overtly stated your main argumentative point, now's the time. When you do, summarize the main arguments that support it.

   While the introduction may be the place for quiet understatement, the conclusion is the place to pound home your main point. Come out and state vigorously that the city should implement a recycling program and then summarize the main reasons why.

13. **Consider the format.** For this simple project, you are not likely to need the elaborate report formats shown in Chapter 15. Instead, use the format you see for the example persuasion at the end of this chapter. Begin with a descriptive title centered at the top of the page, and use second- and third-level headings. Use lists, notices, illustrations, tables, highlighting, and documentation (citations of your borrowed information sources) as necessary.

14. **Review and revise your rough draft.** Use the strategies in Chapter 18 to systematically review and revise your persuasion. Use the top-down approach described there: start by reviewing for audience, purpose, and situation; then move on to content, organization, and transitions; then headings, lists, tables, and graphics; then sentence-style revision and technical style; and finally grammar, usage, spelling, and punctuation problems.

HOW DO YOU WRITE A PROPOSAL?

Proposals are useful tools to get interesting, useful, and financially or professionally rewarding projects approved or under contract. The following sections discuss just what proposals are, how persuasion fits in, and how to plan and design a proposal.

About Proposals

People use the word "proposal" loosely in ordinary conversation. However, *proposal* here refers to a document that seeks to get its writer or its writer's company hired or approved to do a project. In a proposal, you seek to convince readers that you (or your organization) can do the project successfully and that you are the best choice for the project. Obviously, the proposal is a persuasive and even competitive document. Consider the following situations:

- A software development company needs a users' guide written for the new software application it is producing.
- A state agency needs someone to train its employees to convert their information to hypertext for the World Wide Web.

- To proceed with a doctoral thesis, a graduate student must prepare a proposal for approval by her committee.
- To write their technical reports, students in a technical-writing course must write proposals for approval by their instructor.

The software company and the state agency might issue a request for proposals (RFP), compare the proposals received, select the best one, and contact the proposal writer to arrange a contract.

Plan a Proposal

The following walks you through the important steps in writing a proposal. To see how these steps work in an actual writing project, we'll follow an example through each of the steps.

1. **Build a team?** Proposals are good opportunities to work in teams. In the professional world, plenty of proposals are developed by teams. In technical-writing courses, team-written proposals can be effective: proposals take a lot of brainstorming to plan; team members who work well together generally out-brainstorm individuals; and proposals take a lot of work to write.

2. **Think of a project for a proposal.** If you know people wanting to install a local area network in their company and you have that expertise, you've got an ideal, "real-world" situation for a proposal. However, you may not be so lucky as to have tailor-made projects just begging for proposals. Instead, you may have to use your imagination. If you know of an ongoing project, back up to the beginning and write your own proposal. Think of companies, agencies, or individuals in need of projects and write a proposal for one of them. Think of an interesting topic, and then imagine a related project that would call for a proposal. See **www.io.com/~hcexres/power_tools/topics.html** for other methods of finding and narrowing topic ideas.

   To get a sense of how to develop a proposal, imagine that you want to address urban recycling somehow. There are plenty of possibilities, as the following examples demonstrate:
   - You could research the feasibility of a successful recycling program in your hometown. Would it work? Would the public accept it? How much would it cost? Would it pay for itself or even bring in revenue?
   - You could develop a background report on recycling for city council members who need in-depth information to help in their decision making.
   - Consider this possibility: what about a case-study report in which you research several municipal recycling programs? Imagine that the city has sent out an RFP requesting just such a study.

3. **Define the problem or situation.** Proposals offer to undertake a project that will help the customer solve a problem or take advantage of an opportunity. To convince the customer that you, the proposal writer, understand it, include a section discussing your perspective on the problem or situation. In terms of persuasion, this builds personal appeal—readers' confidence in you.

> In this proposal project, the city is beginning an investigation of recycling. City planners want to know how other cities are doing with their programs. Imagine that the city has contracted out this case-study work. Someone else can do the travel, research, investigation, and writing. City planners want objective information rather than rah-rah promotion of recycling. To do this job correctly, you had better find a full spectrum of cases—not only cities with highly successful programs, but cities that have experienced problems or that have even abandoned their recycling programs.

4. **Describe a purpose and an audience.** To write a proposal that has a chance of winning the contract or gaining approval, carefully analyze the audience—the customers (the recipients of your proposal). Understand their technical level, and don't overshoot or undershoot it. Understand what they are looking for and what will convince them that your approach or your project is worthy of approval. See Chapter 19 for strategies for analyzing audiences.

> One of your audiences, city planners, will expect technical detail. City officials, on the other hand, may not want the detail but will want information for their decision making. These readers do not want rah-rah promotion of recycling. They want a report that saves them hours of travel, research, and analysis—a report that is the next best thing to being there themselves. Your other audience, ordinary citizens, wants to know if recycling is a hassle, if it's a mess, if it will save tax dollars, and so on.

5. **Describe your proposed project.** In your proposal, describe specifically what you propose to do. It's easy to get so caught up in "selling" your project that you neglect to explain what you actually propose to do (and not do).

> Your project will be to find up to a half-dozen cities with ongoing recycling programs and investigate how they are doing. In the "proposal" section, be careful to state that you intend to focus on cities similar to yours and to describe problems as well as successes.

6. **Describe some combination of the results, benefits, and feasibility of your proposed project.** Proposals can be categorized as *solicited* and *unsolicited*. Solicited proposals are requested by the

customer—for example, by means of an RFP. Unsolicited proposals have not been requested. They come in the mail or through the door unexpectedly. In an unsolicited proposal, you have to convince the customer that the proposed project should be done and that its results will be valuable. *Results* refer to what the customer will get from the proposed project. *Benefits* refer to the positive gains that the customer will get from the project. *Feasibility* refers to the likelihood of those benefits (for some projects, you can't guarantee the benefits).

In this solicited proposal, you don't need to "sell" the project much. Your customers have already perceived the need for this project, prompting them to issue the RFP.

7. **Describe your method and plan.** Some proposals must describe the method and the process that the proposer intends to use in the project. Doing so gives the customer an opportunity to visualize how the project will proceed and to compare different proposers' plans.

In this proposal, describe the procedures you'll use to do this research. Explain how you'll select the cities for case study. Emphasize that you intend to travel to these cities to get first-hand information.

8. **Create a tentative schedule for your project.** Most proposals contain a timeline for the proposed project. Identify the major milestones and establish either completion dates or completion time frames for them. Including the schedule builds personal appeal: it shows customers that you are organized and professional.

In this case-study project, ask for several weeks for local research, including research using the Internet and phone calls. At the end of this period, expect to have a list of candidate cities for case study. Block out another several weeks to narrow the field to those matching the criteria of similar-size cities whose recycling programs range from the successful to the not-so-successful. Next, define a period in which to gather information on these cities' recycling programs—perhaps a week per city. After this phase, come back to your home base and process the information you've gathered and write the report. Allot several weeks for this phase. What's left? A delivery date for the report, a meeting with the customers, a review period, and a final approval meeting will all need dates in the schedule as well.

9. **List your qualifications for the project and references.** An important function of the proposal is to present your qualifications for the project. You can briefly list your education, training, and work experience; you can attach your resume; or you can do both. References to past customers who have been satisfied with your work

may also be useful, as may pictures and descriptions of your past projects. Again, this material builds personal appeal.

If you are a student in a technical-writing course, the qualifications section may be a problem. What qualifications do you really have for this project: good intentions, strong work ethic, Internet savvy, good technical-writing skills, low rates? Some instructors may encourage you to invent a realistic set of qualifications—even your own consulting firm complete with logo and stationery! Spend some time identifying or researching the appropriate qualifications for this project.

10. **List the costs, fees, and necessary resources for your proposed project.** Some proposals show how much the project will cost, what resources will be needed, and so on. "Break out" the costs and hourly rates for the different types of work, as well as the costs for other project expenses. Even an internal project has costs; estimate your total hours, resources you'll need, and so on.

What will be the costs for this project? Costs may include gas mileage for getting to the local library, photocopying, or ordering government reports. Online research will cost in terms of connect time; you'll likely be ordering reports and articles over the Internet as well. You might search commercial databases, which will mean start-up and usage fees. As you identify cities suitable for case study, you'll start running up your long-distance bill. Then there will be travel costs: air fare, lodging, and meals. And finally in development of the final report, there will preparation costs, cost for graphics, binding, and so on. Most important are your professional hourly rates. How much will you charge by the hour, by the day, or by the job for your expertise? Break down the costs enough so that the potential customers see what they are paying for.

11. **Consider whether graphics or tables are needed.** Proposals are just as likely to need graphics and tables as any other technical document. In fact, including them will lend professionalism to your finished proposal. Maps, floor plans, sketches, flowcharts, and other such graphics can be good ways to convey information in your proposal. You can use tables to show your costs and fees, statistics about the problem, or project results. (See Chapter 11 for ideas and strategies for graphics; Chapter 10, for tables, charts, and graphs.)

This recycling proposal will need lots of tables showing municipal refuse amounts, percentage of recyclables recovered, costs of running recycling programs, revenue gained from such programs, landfill savings (in terms of dollars and volume), citizen participation, and attitudes toward recycling programs. Flowcharts may be a good way to depict how the individual cities process their recyclables. Photos of recycling facilities may also be useful.

12. Include other necessary supporting information. Certainly not all of the sections just described are needed in every proposal. Nor are they the only sections that may be needed; they are just the most common. Back away from this project occasionally, and imagine what your customer needs to approve your project or to select you to do the project. A proposal is persuasive effort. What else would help convince your readers: a tentative outline of the final report; a sketch of the finished project; samples of what the finished project will look like?

13. Consider the format. Chapter 15 shows that you can design a proposal as a memorandum, a business letter, or a separate document with a cover memo or letter. The proposal at the end of this chapter is a separate document with a cover business letter.

This proposal is an external document, written from your private organization to city planners. Thus, it must be either a self-contained, business-letter proposal or a separate formal proposal with a cover letter. Let's not weigh city planners down with a ton of verbiage (however recyclable it may be). Make this proposal a neat, concise, self-contained business letter.

14. Review and revise your rough draft. Use the strategies in Chapter 18 to systematically review and revise your proposal. Use the top-down approach described there: start by reviewing for audience, purpose, and situation; then move on to content, organization, and transitions; then headings, lists, tables, and graphics; then sentence-style revision and technical style; and finally grammar, usage, spelling, and punctuation problems.

HOW DO YOU WRITE A PROGRESS REPORT?

Progress reports are another interesting example of persuasion, although they are a quieter form than the proposal. The following discusses what progress reports are, how they function within a project, as well as how to plan and design progress reports.

About Progress Reports

When you are involved in a lengthy, complex, or expensive project, you must write regularly scheduled progress reports summarizing the status of the project. These reports are essentially persuasive: they seek to convince readers that you are handling the project competently and progressing smoothly, or that you are addressing problems responsibly. If there are problems, you are letting your customer know about them up front, rather than hiding them. Your customer can see your efforts to solve the problems and can even get involved. If the project is going smoothly, your customer can feel satisfied with your work. Progress reports also help you defend yourself or your organization in case you get blamed for something that is not your fault. For example, if your technical documentation contained serious inaccuracies because developers wouldn't take the time to review it, you could have stated that in your progress reports.

The essential information in a progress report includes a summary of the work completed, the work in progress, the work coming up, and an overall assessment of the status of the project. It answers the customer's question, "How is it going?" It also enables you to go on record by saying, "These are our concerns." Progress reports also contain other information such as schedules, outlines, drawings, expense reports, and early data and conclusions—whatever is needed to convey a full sense of the status of the project.

Plan a Progress Report

The following steps guide you through the important considerations in writing a progress report. To see how these steps work in an actual writing project, we'll follow a single example through each of the steps.

1. **Find a project for which you can write a progress report.** If you are not involved in a project, finding a project for a progress report in a technical-writing course can be a problem. Consider this: write about your progress on your semester technical report, usually assigned early in the semester and due toward the end of the semester. Perhaps you are involved in a team design project in your major, or in a project at work. Perhaps you are an intern at a major corporation involved in developing a new release of a product: try interviewing managers and developers on the status of the project (not a bad way to get to know some key players if you want to get hired full time).

   Imagine that you've chosen to write a progress report on your semester technical-report project. You're writing that report that you proposed back in the proposal section of this chapter—the case study of selected cities currently running recycling programs.

2. **Analyze the audience; review your purpose and objective.** Remember that your goals are not merely to report on the status of the project but to maintain good relations with your customer and to protect yourself. Remember, as well, that the actual reader of your progress report may not necessarily be at your technical level. Project managers do not necessarily have the technical depth, but they pay the bills!

Task	Sept. 25-Oct. 1	Oct. 2-Oct. 8	Oct. 9-Oct. 15	Oct. 16-Oct. 22	Oct. 23-Oct. 29	Oct. 30-Nov. 5	Nov. 6-Nov. 12	Nov. 13-Nov. 26
Prototype	▬							
Style guide		▬						
Graphics				▬	▬	▬	▬	
Rough-draft phase			▬	▬	▬			
Rough-draft review						▬		
Style-guide update					▬	▬		
Rough-draft revision							▬	
Final draft: edit/proof							▬	
Final-draft production								▬
Final-draft inspection								▬
Project upload								▬
Party at Jube's								▬

FIGURE 6-2

Gantt chart. Gantt charts are useful in projects where critical tasks must be complete before others can begin.

3. **Write a brief description of the project.** It's a good idea to include a descriptive overview of the project. That way your customers can see whether your idea of the project is the same as theirs. It also helps newcomers in the customer's organization understand what the project is about.

    In your description, explain that the purpose of the project is to provide city officials—in particular, city planners—detailed information on how recycling programs are doing in similar cities. Mention when the contract for this project was awarded to you and when the project is due, specifying dates and organization names.

4. **List of the main tasks in the project.** One good way to assess your progress is to create a task analysis of the project. List all the important tasks that you must complete in order to finish the project. Better yet, turn that list into a Gantt chart (as shown in Figure 6-2) that shows start and stop times for those tasks on an overall timeline.

    You know that this project requires that you do the following: search libraries and government documents for books, articles, reports, and other resources for specific municipal recycling programs; search the Internet for recycling sites, not just for cities involved in recycling but also organizations that promote or oppose recycling; select a half-dozen cities of similar size but with varying success with their recycling programs; find the right individuals in these cities to contact for detailed information; and get that information sent to you or travel to the cities to get it. Set up a Gantt chart showing the expected start and completion dates of each major task in your project.

5. **List what you have completed, what you are currently working on, and what you have left to do.** Assess your project in terms of completed tasks, current tasks, and future tasks. Be as specific and detailed as you can. Instead of saying that the questionnaire analysis took longer than expected, say that it required 21 hours over the projected 85.

   In your case-study project, imagine that you have completed your library and Internet searches; scanned what you found about cities involved in recycling programs; and selected the cities you want to research. Imagine that you are currently telephoning and e-mailing these cities to find the right departments and the right individuals who can help you get the information you need. You've gotten a wealth of information in the form of reports from one city and you've booked flight and hotel reservations to two others. The rest of the tasks are left to do.

6. **List major concerns and problems related to the project.** Spend some time thinking about what is not going so well in your project, what the problems are, and what unexpected things have happened. Perhaps certain important information has not yet arrived. Find a diplomatic way to describe these problems in the actual progress report—if you want to maintain good relations with your customer (internal or external).

   Imagine that you've not found any unsuccessful recycling programs to report on. Cities with successful programs are quite happy to show theirs off, but it's tough finding cities that are keeping quiet about their programs. How can you research abandoned recycling programs? Your contacts with the cities you are currently researching may help you find cities that show the other side of the story. Also, your contacts with government agencies, associations promoting or opposing recycling, and private consultants may help.

7. **Summarize project expenses, hours, and resources used.** Progress reports don't necessarily include expense reports. Your customer will be the one to stipulate what is included. Obviously, money, time, and other resources consumed to date are an important indicator of project status. If you do include such details, present them as tables (see Chapter 10 for details on designing tables).

   So far, you and your partners have worked 4 weeks and logged 390 hours. You've run up several hundred dollars of long-distance phone calls. You've purchased over a hundred dollars worth of books, articles, and reports, and you've done nearly a hundred dollars worth photocopying. You are paying one assistant to handle most of the photocopying, purchasing, and deliveries.

8. Summarize current outcomes, if applicable. For some projects, you may want to give your customers a glimpse of current results. If you are running an experiment, show the data you've collected so far. If you are designing or building something, provide photographs, drawings, diagrams, or blueprints. If you are writing a report, show the current outline.

In this project, there is not much for the customer to glimpse. However, you might provide a brief summary of the recycling operations of that one city you received materials on. You might also provide a list of the cities that you have selected for case study and briefly describe each one.

9. Write an overall, concluding summary of the project status. If you've assessed your project in terms of work completed, work on-going, work upcoming, expenses, resources used, and problems and concerns, you are ready to write a detailed, informed summary.

In your summary, you can honestly state that the project is going smoothly and is on schedule—with the exception of that one concern about locating recycling programs that are experiencing problems or that have been abandoned.

10. Plan the introduction. When you've rough-drafted or at least planned your progress report, it's time to write or plan the introduction. It may seem backward, but it's only then that you really know the topics you cover and the major points you make. In an introduction to a progress report, at least state the purpose of the document (to tell the customer about the status of the project) and provide an overview of what you'll cover.

Keep the introduction to this progress report brief. State that this is a progress report to bring the client up to date on the status of the survey of city recycling programs. Also state that you will describe the overall project, work completed, and work upcoming, and that you will assess the overall status of the project.

11. Consider the format. Chapter 15 demonstrates how to design a progress report as a memorandum, a business letter, or a separate document with a cover memo or letter. The progress report at the end of this chapter is a separate document with a cover business letter.

This progress report is an external document, written from your organization to city planners. Thus it must be either a self-contained, business-letter report or a separate formal report with a cover letter. Once again, let's take it easy on those city planners. Make this progress report a neat, concise, self-contained business letter.

12. Review and revise your rough draft. Use the strategies in Chapter 18 to systematically review and revise your progress report. Use the top-down approach described there: start by reviewing for audience, purpose, and situation; then move on to content, organization, and transitions; then headings, lists, tables, and graphics; then on to sentence-style revision and technical style; and finally grammar, usage, spelling, and punctuation problems.

WORKSHOP: PERSUASION, PROPOSALS, AND PROGRESS REPORTS

Here are some additional ideas for practicing the concepts, tools, and strategies in this chapter:

1. *Topics for persuasion.* Consider the following topics. What persuasive documents might be written involving these topics?

internet privacy	career planning
gene therapy	animal testing
Web site design	immigration

2. *Persuasive appeals.* For one of the persuasive projects you defined in the preceding item, make a list of the logical, emotional, and personal appeals you might use, along with any counterarguments you might have to address.

3. *Topics for proposals.* Consider the following topics. What sorts of proposals can you imagine for them? Who would be the recipients of these proposals?

life in extreme environments	climate changes
computers and elementary students	oceanic pollution
	lack of city recreational areas
sleep disorders	speech-recognition software
homeless people	

4. *Audiences for proposals.* Consider the following audiences. What sorts of proposals might they be interested in?

high school principals	city council members
technical-writing professors	political party leaders
senior citizens	parent–teacher association

board members for a battered
women center

neighborhood association
members

student council members

department head for city
planning

5. *Requests for proposals.* Consider the following organizations, agencies, and places. What sorts of requests for proposals (RFPs) might they issue?

Environmental Protection
Agency

Partners in Art Education

Habitat for Humanity

Senior Citizens Association

Center for Transportation and
the Environment

Department of Health and
Social Services

City Council

City Planning Department

6. *Tasks and proposals.* Choose one of the following simple projects, and then list the major tasks that the project would include and that you would describe in a proposal.

creating a program to encourage middle school students to
plan to attend college

obtaining computers for a
disadvantaged school

starting a community garden

holding an International Day at
your college

7. *Gantt charts.* For the task list you created in the preceding exercise, sketch a Gantt chart showing the start and end dates for each task in relation to the overall start and end dates for the project.

Persuasion in technical-writing
courses: As discussed in this
chapter, technical-writing courses
are not normally venues for the
standard editorial essay. At the
same time, you must be ready to
produce persuasive documents
with highly technical content,
such as this one.

Rebuttal and concession
approach: This report is structured
as a series of rebuttals to the
common objections to recycling.
The writer answers these objections one by one. Remember that
a rebuttal is an answer to an
objection or counterargument to
your point of view.

Title: Even the title is a rebuttal!

Introduction: Notice that in three
sentences, this introduction
creates some interest, indicates
the purpose of the document, and
provides an overview of what
follows.

Illustrations: Normally, in a
technical-writing context,
decoration has no place. But here,
it does. It reminds us of the
environment, endangered species,
and other such related matters.
And so does the inclusion of
illustrations of endangered species
created by eleven-year-olds.

First rebuttal: This writer begins
by countering what recycling
critics claim is the number one
problem with recycling—that it's a
hassle. He answers this claim by
showing how much recycling
activities have increased. Does this
rebuttal work?

PERSUASIVE TECHNICAL WRITING

Recycling: Not a Waste of Money or Time![3]

In the last decade of the 20th century, the recycling movement in the
U.S. has come under increasing attack from various parts of the media
and industry—even though the U.S. public has dramatically increased its
recycling activities in that same period. Any recycling start-up effort
must be aware of the arguments of these opponents. The following
reviews these arguments and explains how they are exaggerated or just
plain wrong.

Recycling Is a Hassle

The most common argument against recycling is that it's a hassle.
Opponents have always insisted that ordinary citizens would not take
the time to sort the recyclables from their trash.

"Karner Blue Butterfly," Charlene
Hanneman, Age 11, Wisconsin Rapids, WI.
Winner of Environmental Defense Fund's
Endangered Species Art Contest.

Despite these claims, the number of municipal curbside recycling collection programs climbed from about 1,000 to 8,817 during the period from
1988 to 1996, according to *BioCycle* magazine. Recycling programs like
these are now available to 51 percent of the population. Facilities for
composting yard trimmings grew from about 700 to 3,260 over the same

[3] Thanks to Richard A. Denison and John F. Ruston of the Environmental Defense Fund for
permission to adapt this article from Anti-Recycling Myths: "Commentary on Recycling is
Garbage" (John Tierney, *New York Times Magazine*, June 30, 1996): www.techreview.com/
articles/oct97/recycle.html.

period. These efforts complement more than 9,000 recycling drop-off centers and tens of thousands of workplace collection programs. According to the EPA, the nation recycled or composted 27 percent of its municipal solid waste in 1995, up from 9.6 percent in 1980.

Recycled Materials Are More Expensive to Use

Opponents typically characterize the recycling movement as misguided altruism that is both unnecessary and expensive. Certainly, the goals of the recycling movement have always included reducing environmental damage from activities such as strip mining and clear-cutting in favor of conserving energy, reducing pollution, and minimizing solid waste in manufacturing new products. However, a number of recent major studies have shown that recycled materials, because they have already been refined and processed, require less energy to use in manufacturing new products than do virgin materials, and produce less pollutants, which are expensive problems as well. (The studies were conducted by Argonne National Labs, the Department of Energy and Stanford Research Institute, the Sound Resource Management Group, Franklin Associates, Ltd., and the Tellus Institute.)

Recycling Means More Intrusion by Big Government

Another common argument against recycling is that it's just one more instance of big government intruding into every corner of our private lives. Actually, these arguments come primarily from think tanks, including the Competitive Enterprise Institute and the Cato Institute (both in Washington, D.C.), the Reason Foundation (in Santa Monica, Calif.), and the Waste Policy Center (in Leesburg, Va.)—all vigorous anti-recycling operations. These organizations are funded in part by companies in the packaging, consumer-product, and waste-management industries. These industries fear what might happen if consumers begin seeking environmentally friendly alternatives to these industries' products and services. Anti-recyclers maintain that government bureaucrats have imposed recycling on people against their will. They evoke images of Big Brother hiding behind every recycling bin. Yet several consumer researchers, such as the Rowland Company in New York, have found

---

Second rebuttal: The second argument against recycling involves economics. The writer counterargues by referring to studies that prove recycled materials are actually less expensive. (But wouldn't it help to see some numbers here?)

Third rebuttal: This objection to recycling jumps on the anti-government bandwagon. The writer answers this objection in two ways: first, that the objection is promoted by organizations that are corporations threatened by the recycling movement; and second, that surveys of public opinion have shown recycling is generally supported.

Transitions and lead-ins: Notice that the first sentence of just about every individual rebuttal section begins almost heavy handedly with words like "Another common objection to recycling...." Although this might seem repetitive, it guarantees that readers know where they've been, where they are, and where they are headed in this document.

that recycling enjoys strong support because people believe it is good for the environment and conserves resources—not because they feel they have been forced into recycling by government edict.

Recycling Is Expensive, Not Cost-Effective

The argument that recycling is too expensive and not cost-effective is not only wrong but devious. Approaching the question as accountants, we must determine whether adding recycling to a traditional waste-management system will increase the overall cost of the system over the long term. The answer, in large part, depends on the design and maturity of the recycling program and the rate of participation within the community.

Recycling-program maturity. Costs decline as programs mature and expand. New curbside recycling collection programs are typically inefficient because they duplicate existing trash-collection systems. In time, cities increase the efficiency of their recycling collection systems by changing truck designs, collection schedules, and truck routes. For example, Visalia, California, has developed a truck that collects refuse and recyclable materials simultaneously. And Fayetteville, Arkansas, has added curbside recycling with no increase in residential bills by cutting back waste collection from twice to once weekly.

Rate of participation. As citizen participation in recycling programs increases, costs go down. In cities with comparatively high levels of recycling, per-ton recycling collection costs are much lower than in cities with low recycling rates. A North Carolina Department of Environment, Health, and Natural Resources study found that in municipalities with recycling rates greater than 12 percent, the per-ton cost of recycling was lower than that for trash disposal. Higher recycling rates allow cities to use equipment more efficiently and generate greater revenues to offset collection costs. Adding in increased sales of recyclable materials and reductions in landfill disposal costs, high-recycling cities can break even or make money from recycling.

Second-level headings: Because it's relatively short, this document uses second-level headings (unless of course you consider the title a first-level heading). Notice the parallelism of the phrasing in these headings—they are all complete sentences.

Third-level headings: For longer sections, this writer uses third-level headings to indicate the topic of individual subsections. These are the "run-in" headings "Recycling-program maturity" and "Rate of participation." Notice that these headings are italicized, use sentence-style capitalization (first letter of first word only), end with a period, and are not a grammatical part of the sentence that follows.

Concession: Notice this example of concession. The recycling critics "rightly point out" that there are more trees in the U.S. than ever before. Concessions are a "yes-but" tactic: you agree with your opponent but then explain why that objection doesn't matter or misses the point (as in this example).

We're Not Running Out of Trees

Anti-recyclers rightly point out that more trees are growing in the U.S. than ever before and that new forests are started as soon as trees are cut. However, this perspective fails to take into account that in the southern United States, for example, where most of the trees used to make paper are grown, the proportion of pine forest in plantations has risen from 2.5 percent in 1950 to more than 40 percent in 1990, with a concomitant loss of natural pine forest. At this rate, the acreage of pine plantations will overtake that of natural pine forests in the South during the 1990s and will approach 70 percent of all pine forests in the next few decades. While pine plantations are excellent for growing wood, they are far less suited than natural forests are for providing animal habitat and preserving biodiversity. Paper recycling extends the overall supply of fiber and can thus help reduce the pressure to convert remaining natural forests to tree farms.

Conclusion

Recycling is not a threat to U.S. industry, an inconvenience, or another instance of big government invading private lives. We must get past these fears and half-truths and study how communities can improve efficiency and increase participation. Increasing the efficiency of municipal recycling, establishing price incentives, and capitalizing on the environmental and industrial benefits of recycling will enable recycling to meet its full potential.

References

John Tierney. "Recycling is Garbage." *New York Times Magazine*, June 30, 1996.
Richard A. Denison and John F. Ruston. "Anti-Recycling Myths." **www.edf.org/pubs/reports/armythfin.html**. See this source for all other references.

Situation: Shawn was not the type for imagining or inventing scenarios. Instead, he found a real situation in his college course work that needed some technical writing. He had observed that a certain key phase of the microchip-manufacturing process was not being addressed in his courses.

Memo format: The memo format is appropriate here in that an instructor and students can be considered as members of the same organization, making it an internal communication.

Subject line: Notice that the subject line identifies the topic and purpose of the memo. If "Proposal" were omitted, readers would wonder if this simple memo were going to discuss the whole of photolithography!

Introduction: In a business-like manner, the introductory paragraph states the purpose of the memo, refers to the context (the instructor's assignment), and then gives a brief overview of the contents of this memo.

Proposal

MEMORANDUM[4]

TO: David A. McMurrey, TCM 1603 instructor
FROM: Shawn Wolski, TCM 1603 student
DATE: June 21, 1998
SUBJECT: Proposal: role of photolithography in semiconductor
                     manufacturing

The following proposal is in response to your assignment, due June 21st. As I mentioned earlier, I intend to provide an informational view of contemporary microchip fabrication and the role of photolithography in that process. The following describes the problem, outlines the information I intend to present, and discusses the time and resources required to complete this project.

Background: class situation

My Semiconductor Manufacturing Technology (SMT) coursework emphasizes that photolithography is an important phase in the wafer-fabrication process. Because it is not presented in any of our courses, I will pursue this subject for my own benefit as well as for other SMT students. One of my SMT instructors has taken an interest in this project and may use it in his future courses.

Proposal: photolithography report

My proposed report will present the role of photolithography in the manufacture of semiconductors. The report will cover the basics of manufacturing microchips in a universal manufacturing process flow but will not reveal trade secrets of a particular company—such as the 1 GHz chip or the copper chips that IBM is developing. As you suggested, I'll zero in on the photolithography part of the process, supplying plenty of detail.

[4] Thanks to Shawn Wolski, former technical-writing student at Austin Community College, for this proposal and permission to adapt it here.

Proposal logic: As discussed in the chapter on proposals, this one begins by stating a problem (no coverage of the photolithography phase of the wafer-fabrication process), then proposes a solution (a report on this phase), and presents the benefits of such a project (better preparation of students entering this field).

Benefits of the report

The primary benefit I see from writing this report will be educational, for SMT students and others interested in the semiconductor manufacturing process. To my knowledge, this topic has not been addressed before. Another benefit is that this report will be written from a student's point of view, which will help other students better understand the process.

Procedure: developing the report

In writing the report, I will take the following steps to obtain information:

- My first sources will be my own textbooks and information that I can find in local libraries.
- I will also search for information on the Internet, either with search engines or with the addresses provided to me by others.
- I will solicit interviews from experts who work in wafer fabrication (fabs), plus information I can obtain from instructors.

These steps will help me determine why photolithography is so important.

Project description: In this classroom context, the writer is attempting to convince the instructor that his proposed project is a good one, worthy of approval. To ensure that the instructor agrees, this writer describes the final report and the graphics it will contain and provides an outline. To reassure the instructor that he can indeed accomplish this project, the writer includes a schedule, describes his background in relation to the report topic, lists information sources, and itemizes his expected expenses.

Description of the final report

The end product will consist of at least four single-spaced pages for the written version, and at least four files for the HTML version. I will discuss the microchip fabrication process flow and explain why photolithography is important to fab operations. I will include graphics illustrating the universal process flow and the role of photolithography in the microchip fabrication process. To clarify technical terms, I will append a glossary.

Graphics list: In a "real world" proposal, you might not be obliged to list the graphics you expect to include in a proposed document. However, in this classroom context, the instructor requires that the final report have graphics. And even a real-world customer might want to know about the graphics the writer expects to include; it's one more way for the customer to visualize the final product.

Graphics

The following is a tentative list of graphics I may use in this report:

CMOS process flow in wafer fabs	Graphic
Steps in manufacturing CMOS devices	Graphics (31 individual pictures)

Presence of photolithography in fabs	Graphic
Photolithography process	Graphics (10 individual pictures)
Condition of wafers: before/after patterning	Graphic
Importance of resolution and overlay	Graphic
Factors affecting wafers in photo	Graphic

This list of graphics will probably change, as I find graphics that better illustrate photolithography.

Projected Schedule

The following is a tentative schedule for the report:

June 21	Proposal uploaded; begin research.
July 07	Complete research in the library, on the Internet, and in textbooks.
July 19	Complete interviews and visits to wafer fabs.
August 06	Send draft to Dr. McMurrey for review.
August 09	Complete revisions and upload final copy of report.

This schedule is likely to change, but I do not foresee any problems in maintaining this timeline.

Qualifications for the proposed project

Here are my qualifications for this project:

- Currently an ACC student majoring in Semiconductor Manufacturing Technology; will receive my certification by early August of this year.
- Current grade point average in the program is 4.0 out of 4.0.
- Studies have included the basics of manufacturing industry operations, microchip manufacturing process flow, theories behind the processes in the manufacture of microchips, and basic electronics.
- Familiarity with both PC and Macintosh computers and with MS-DOS 6.22, Windows 3.11, Windows 95, and MacOS 8.1.

Headings: Because this is a rather brief document, first-level headings aren't needed. Instead, this proposal uses a series of second-level headings (as defined in Chapter 7).

My software knowledge includes Ami Pro 3.1, Lotus Word Pro 4.0 for Windows 95, and Netscape 4.05.

- Experienced Web page developer, having written personal Web pages since 1994.
- Experienced with graphics, using Jasc's Paint Shop Pro (3.11 to 5.0.)

Projected project expenses

The following is my anticipated breakdown of costs:

Internet service: AOL	5.60
Travel: Bastrop to Austin (round trip)	261.00
TOTAL	$266.60

The Internet service charge by AOL is based on the sum of accumulated time totaling 8 days at $21.00 a month for access. Travel expense is based on a total of 15 trips averaging 60 miles at 29 cents per mile.

Other expenses include the time required to research the report by other means previously mentioned, the time to format the report in both Lotus Word Pro and HTML, and the time involved in making the HTML version of the report available for viewing on the Internet.

Tentative report outline

I. Introduction

II. Microchip Fabrication
  A. General view of wafer fab
  B. CMOS process flow

III. Photolithography
  A. Process
  B. Effects on wafer
    1. Before patterning
    2. After patterning
  C. Effects on wafer fab operations
    1. System constraint (bottleneck)
    2. Center of fab

Outline: To enable the potential customer to visualize the finished project, this writer includes a tentative outline. Although this is obviously an instructor requirement, you can imagine a real-world proposal including an outline. It would provide customers one more way of visualizing the final product. (See **www.io.com/~hcexres/power_tools/outlining.html** for strategies and format for outlining.)

IV. Conclusion

    A. Summary of effects

    B. Emphasis on importance

Information sources: Obviously, a list of information sources is another instructor requirement. A real-world customer is not likely to care which information sources the writer uses, as long as they are reliable ones and as long as they contribute to an accurate and complete finished product.

Information sources

I have most of the basic theoretical knowledge required for this report. For the finer details, I can get what I need from my course work, textbooks, the library, instructors, the Internet, and experts in the microchip fabrication industry. I foresee little difficulty in using these sources for information.

Day, Richard, et al. *Sematech: Furnace Processes and Related Issues in Semiconductor Manufacturing.* Texas A&M University: Texas Engineering Extension Service, 1994.

Serda, Julian. *Semiconductor Manufacturing Technology II: Advanced Technology Education in Semiconductor Training.* Austin: AMD, 1997

Van Zant, Peter. *Microchip Fabrication.* New York: McGraw-Hill, 1997.

Feasibility of the project: In this final section, the proposal writer discusses whether he expects any major problems in the project, whether he can handle these problems, and whether the project will have the benefits he mentioned earlier. This is a common way to conclude a proposal, along with the encouragement to get in touch.

Feasibility of the project

I do not anticipate problems in obtaining the information I need for this report or in completing the report by the deadline.

The costs for this project, as stated above, are not a problem. They are already part of my educational expenses and won't affect my ability to finish this report. Photolithography, and in particular, its importance to the microchip manufacturing process, has not been addressed in the SMT program. This project will provide plenty of educational value, especially because this topic is part of the curriculum in the SMT major.

Please contact me if you have questions regarding the report. My home phone number is (555) 333-3333, and my e-mail address is wolfburg@america.net.

Proposal

Sarah Iyer[5]
311 Thornton Drive
Franklin, TX 00000
(000) 000-0000

January 31, 1999

David McMurrey, Director
Elevation Pointe on the Lake
12155 Cole Rd.
Salado, TX 75000
(000) 000-0000

SUBJ: Proposal to develop a handbook on communication and swallowing disorders in the elderly for use by nursing staff and aides.

The following proposal outlines the content of the handbook based on your announcement in the American Speech-Language and Hearing Association's newsletter. A description of the handbook, an outline, a list of graphics, information sources, a schedule for completion, and a bid are included in the proposal. Thank you for your time and consideration. You can reach me during business hours at (000) 000-0000.

Sincerely,

Sarah Iyer

Sarah Iyer
Enclosure

[5] Many thanks to Sarah Iyer, former online technical-writing student at Kennesaw State University, for this proposal and permission to adapt it here.

Cover business letter: This proposal writer chooses to attach a cover letter to her proposal and make the proposal a separate document. If she had chosen to use a self-contained business-letter format, she would move the signature block to the end of the proposal, delete the title (on the next page), and then merge the contents of the paragraph in the cover letter and the introductory paragraph on the next page.

Contents: Notice the contents of this letter. It states the purpose of the document to follow, gives an overview of the contents of the document to follow, and contact information for the author. Notice that these same contents are repeated in the introductory paragraph for the proposal proper on the next page. That's because the writer can't be sure if this cover letter will remain attached once it gets to the recipient.

Title: The title does two important things: it indicates that this is a proposal to develop a handbook and it indicates the subject matter of the proposed handbook.

Introduction: This introduction states the purpose of the document (this proposal), the writer's source of information about the project (an RFP), some promotion for the need for the handbook, and finally an overview of the contents of this proposal. Notice that this introduction doesn't begin with its own heading. Readers should be able to assume that the first paragraph following the title of a document is introductory.

Background on the need for the project: Most proposals should explain the need for the proposed project. Even if the client has requested proposals and thus fully understands the need, the review of the project rationale enables the client to see that this writer understands the need.

Description of the project: The need-for section is like a statement of a problem; this project-description section is like a discussion of the solution.

HANDBOOK PROPOSAL:

Communication and Swallowing Disorders in the Elderly

The following is a proposal to develop a handbook on communication and swallowing disorders in the elderly, for use by the nursing staff at Elevation Pointe on the Lake. This proposal is based on the RFP announced in the January issue of the American Speech-Language and Hearing Association's newsletter. The information provided in the handbook will be a valuable resource for your staff. The following proposal will provide information regarding the need for the handbook, a description of the proposed handbook, and the benefits of the handbook. An outline, a list of graphics, information sources, a schedule for completion, qualifications of the author, and costs will also be presented.

Need for the Handbook

Recent changes in the healthcare industry, specifically changes that affect long-term care facilities, have resulted in changes in the provision of therapy services. In the past, most long-term care facilities had access to a speech-language pathologist as a full-time employee or full-time contractor. Currently, many facilities have been forced to reduce the hours of their therapy staff. As a result, nurses and nurse aides may not have access to someone who can answer questions about communication and swallowing disorders. In turn, patients may have more difficulty expressing their needs and may also suffer unnecessarily from swallowing disorders.

Description of the Handbook

The handbook will address communication and swallowing disorders that are commonly found in long-term care facilities. It will provide basic definitions and a brief list of causes for each type of disorder. Signs or symptoms will be discussed to aid the nursing staff in identifying these disorders in their patients. General recommendations will be given to help the nursing staff communicate with patients and assist them during mealtimes. If patients are suspected of having any of these disorders, it is recommended that a physician and speech-language pathologist be notified.

Results, benefits, advantages, feasibility: After you've introduced the problem and proposed your solution, the next logical step is to discuss the outcomes and their likelihood. In this proposal, the writer explains how the use of her handbook will help in training efforts and in reference needs. Because the project has been requested, she does not have to address feasibility (that is, the likelihood of those benefits).

More description: To further enable her potential clients to visualize her approach to this project, this writer presents a tentative outline of the handbook she proposes to write. Following the outline, notice that the writer includes a special notice warning the potential client of the limitations of the handbook. (She's not promising to write a textbook!)

Outline format: Not sure about how to create outlines or how to format them? See **www.io.com/ ~hcexres/power_tools/ outlining.html**.

Benefits of the Handbook

The proposed handbook can be used as a teaching aid when training nurse aides, and as a reference for nurses and nurse aides who have completed training. The handbook can be used as a reference to answer questions when a speech-language pathologist is unavailable. In addition, it will provide recommendations on communication and swallowing disorders that would be beneficial to all residents of Elevation Pointe on the Lake.

Handbook Outline

The following is a tentative outline of the handbook:

I. Introduction
   A. Purpose
   B. Overview
II. Communication Disorders
   A. Expressive Language Disorders
      1. Definition
      2. Common Causes
      3. Signs or Symptoms
      4. General Recommendations
   B. Receptive Language Disorders
      1. Definition
      2. Common Causes
      3. Signs or Symptoms
      4. General Recommendations
   C. Voice Disorders
      1. Definition
      2. Common Causes
      3. Signs or Symptoms
      4. General Recommendations
   D. Hearing Loss
      1. Definition
      2. Common Causes
      3. Signs or Symptoms
      4. General Recommendations

III. Swallowing Disorders

    A. Definition

        1. Normal Swallowing Process

        2. Abnormal Swallowing Process

    B. Common Causes

    C. Signs or Symptoms

    D. General Recommendations

IV. Conclusion

Note: This handbook is not meant to substitute for or override a physician's evaluation or recommendations or a speech-language pathologist's evaluation or recommendations. It is meant as a brief introduction to communication and swallowing disorders and to aid nursing staff in identifying those patients who may require evaluation by a physician and a speech-language pathologist.

Graphics and Tables

A variety of graphics will be used to illustrate the concepts discussed in the handbook. A tentative list of graphics follows:

Prevalence of Communication Disorders in Long-Term Care Facilities	Pie Chart
Signs and Symptoms of Communication Disorders	Table
Recommendations for Communicating with Patients with Communication Disorders	Table
Prevalence of Swallowing Disorders in Long-Term Care Facilities	Pie Chart
Anatomy of the Head and Neck as it Relates to Swallowing	Schematic Drawing
Swallowing Problems in the Healthy and Frail Elderly Person	Table
Signs and Symptoms of Swallowing Disorders	Table
Recommendations for Assisting Patients with Swallowing Disorders	Table

Tentative graphics and tables: This writer includes a tentative list of the types of graphics and their content because it is her technical-writing instructor's requirement, not because it is a necessary element of this proposal. However, this list might be useful to the potential clients, giving them more insight into the design and contents of the proposed handbook.

Headings: Notice that this proposal uses second-level headings (see Chapter 7 for details). For a relatively short document such as this one, first-level headings are too elaborate.

Two-column list format: Secretly, this two-column list is a table. To save yourself more than a few headaches, format material like this as a table with the grid lines turned off. To do this in MS Word, select **Table→Table Auto Format→(none)**.

Tentative bibliography: As with the list of graphics, this section may not be essential to a proposal in the "real world." But you could make a case for its inclusion: what if this writer's information sources imply an approach that the potential client disapproves of? What if the writer has left out an important source in this field?

Bibliography format: The format here is roughly the Council of Biology Editors or the Institute of Electrical and Electronics Engineers style. Items are alphabetized and numbered; last name first; book and journal names italicized; concluding with the city of publication, publisher, and date of publication.

Schedule: When you write a proposal, think of every kind of information the potential client may need to understand how you'll do the project and why you're a good choice to do the project.

At this point in the proposal, the writer has presented a problem, proposed a solution in the form of a project, and explained the benefits of the proposed project. If the client has gotten interested, now's the time to get in the logistics of the proposed project: its schedule, the writer's qualifications, and costs.

Timeline or milestones: In most proposals, you'll need to indicate your schedule for the project, including due dates and major milestones leading up to that due date. If you can't specify actual dates, estimate days or weeks to complete the tasks.

Qualifications: In this context, the writer must explain her essential qualifications—what makes her right for this project. This part of a proposal is like a mini-resume. To further establish her qualifications, she could attach a complete resume (referring to it here), offer references who can attest to the quality of her work, or offer to provide a portfolio of her past work.

Tentative Bibliography

The bibliography will consist of textbooks and clinical manuals for speech-language pathologists. Pamphlets from the American Speech-Language and Hearing Association will also be used. Following is a tentative list:

1. Andrews, Moya L. *Manual of Voice Treatment: Pediatrics through Geriatrics.* San Diego, CA: Singular Publishing Group, 1995.
2. Burns, Martha, ed. *Clinical Management of Right Hemisphere Dysfunction.* Gaithersburg, MD: Aspen, 1985.
3. Chapey, Roberta, ed. *Language Intervention Strategies in Adult Aphasia.* Baltimore, MD: Williams & Wilkins, 1994.
4. Cherney, Leora Reiff, ed. *Clinical Management of Dysphagia in Adults and Children.* Gaithersburg, MD: Aspen, 1994.
5. Nicolosi, Lucille, Elizabeth Harryman, Janet Kresheck, eds. *Terminology of Communication Disorders: Speech-Language-Hearing.* Baltimore, MD: Williams & Wilkins, 1989.

Schedule

The handbook will be completed and a camera-ready copy along with electronic files will be delivered to your office on March 26, 1999. The following schedule lists milestones for completion of the handbook:

Approval to develop handbook	February 1
Research topics	Through February 15
Write first draft	Through March 1
Create graphics	Finish March 3
Complete first draft	Finish March 8
Send first draft for review to Elevation Pointe	March 9
Receive review comments from Elevation Pointe	March 19
Revise first draft	Finish March 25
Deliver handbook: camera-ready copy and files	March 26

Qualifications

As a speech-language pathologist, I have had specialized education and training for assessing and treating individuals with speech, language, and swallowing disorders. A brief summary of my education and experience follows:

- Texas license to practice Speech-Language Pathology
- Certificate of Clinical Competence by the American Speech-Language Hearing Association
- Two years professional experience in long-term care facilities
- M.S. Speech Language Pathology GPA 3.85/4.0
- B.S. Communication Disorders GPA 3.64/4.0

Costs: Notice that the cost for the proposed project is presented only at the end of the proposal. The writer has convinced the reader of the problem, described the solution (the proposed project), discussed the benefits of the proposed solution, discussed her schedule to complete the project, and her qualifications to do the project. Now and only now is the time to present the costs to do the project.

Notice that this writer does not throw out a single-figure cost to do the project. She breaks it out into the subcosts. She does not, however, provide the estimated hours or her hourly rate for any of the tasks.

Conclusion: This proposal ends with a brief conclusion in which the writer emphasizes that she has developed this proposal according to the specifications in the RFP, expresses her interest in doing the project, and encourages the potential client to get in touch so that they can move forward.

Remember that a proposal is not necessarily a contract. In this case, some additional details may need to be worked out, such as the logistics for the 10-hour maximum for client-requested changes. These additional details can be incorporated into a revision of this proposal or into a separate formal contract.

Cost

The total cost for researching, writing, editing, developing graphics, and revising to meet your requirements is $4,286. Please note that there is no charge for revisions according to your requirements, unless this work requires more than 10 hours. A breakdown of the total expenses follows:

Research	$500.00
Writing	$2,211.00
Editing	$325.00
Graphics	$1,250.00
Revision (according to client's requirements)	(no charge)
Total Expense	$4,286.00

Conclusion

I have developed this proposal based on your requirements listed in the RFP. However, if you need any additional information, please contact me. The information provided in the proposed handbook will be a valuable resource for your nursing staff in enabling them to improve daily communication and safety during mealtimes for all of your residents. I look forward to sharing the information I have gained through my formal education and work experience to benefit the nursing staff and residents at your facility.

Cover letter: This progress report begins with a cover letter, separate from the actual report itself.

Letterhead logo: Please note that "Progress Report" is not part of this letter. When you develop business-letter materials, try creating a letterhead design. This one uses Tekton, a larger type size, and bold-italics for the company name, and a smaller type size for the address.

Letter format: This letter uses the block format, in which all components start on the left margin. Notice the use of the subject line (Re:).

Contents: The cover letter identifies what is attached—a progress report. This letter reminds readers of the overall purpose of the project and briefly describes its contents. In the second paragraph, the writer mentions the purpose of the attached report and lists its essential contents.

Signature block: Notice the contents of the signature block: complimentary close, four lines for the signature, the typed name of the writer, organization name, and enclosure.

Progress Report

Nari Design

1007 Wormley Drive – Pflugerville, TX 70000

July 20, 1999

Suzanna Walters

435 77th and M Sts., NW

Washington, DC 20002

000-000-0000

Re: Progress report on the handbook for audience interpretation of advertising images·

Dear Ms. Walters:

I am pleased to update you on the status of the proposed handbook. As you know, public awareness of and sensitivity to advertisers' messages has become increasingly sophisticated as the influence of advertising has grown. For that reason then, it is a smart idea for image creators to understand what their target audiences perceive. This handbook will provide your staff with an introductory definition of media studies concepts and a sample ad analysis.

Attached is a status report of Nari Design's work on the project. In the report I discuss the following concepts: the intended audience, description of the work, an outline, a list of figures, and our overall appraisal of the project.

I am confident that my group will produce a handbook that will serve your organization's needs. If you have any questions, please feel free to contact me at 000-000-0000. ·

Sincerely,

Keerti Kharod

Keerti Kharod

Nari Design

Attachment: Progress Report

Report title: When you design a report that uses a cover letter or memo, create a full title and complete introduction for the report proper. Don't assume that the cover letter or memo will remain attached to the report.

Report introduction: As with the title, write the introduction as if the cover letter or memo were not attached. Identify the purpose and situation of the report and provide an overview of the report's contents.

Review of the project: This section summarizes the purpose of the project. Doing so serves several purposes: it enables clients to determine whether they are thinking the same way about the project as the writer, and it enables newcomers to get an introduction to the project.

Notice that the project description consists of several sections: a general review of its purpose and use, a discussion of the writer's assumptions about readers' knowledge, an outline, a list of information sources, and a list of graphics according to their content and type.

Audience and outline: Although the project is obviously for a technical-writing course, it still makes sense to include an audience description and an outline. That way, the clients—the people for whom this project is being done—have a chance to request changes.

PROGRESS REPORT:

Audience Perception of Advertisement Images

Nari Design was hired by Danuta Advertising to produce a handbook to address the relationship between the producers of images and the viewers, as well as to provide feedback from a typical target audience for a sample image. Following is a progress report on the handbook. It includes a description of the intended audience, a brief description of the proposed work, an outline for the handbook, a list of references and figures, and the overall status of the project. The overall status can be broken down into three primary tasks: (1) compilation of sources, (2) acquisition of suitable images (ads and graphics), and (3) development of the written text. Each section is accompanied by descriptions of the work completed and work remaining.

Description of the Proposed Work

The handbook will provide the reader with simple explanations about the impact of images on viewers. It can be used as an introductory resource for a novice designer, as well as a reference tool for expert artisans and marketing staff. It includes definitions of concepts and examples that relate to media studies. Though it is intended to be a reference guide, it can also be used to orient newcomers to concepts and methods in media studies.

This handbook will act as a guide to some of the implications of visual design elements for the general public. The latter part of the handbook will analyze an advertisement from the perspective of a target audience of young professional women. This analysis will provide your staff with an idea of what may be perceived through the advertisement. Resources for further study will be included in the reference notes.

Audience. The handbook will be written for the staff of Danuta Advertising. Readers should have experience with advertising in some form, whether in design, marketing, or audience analysis. The handbook will include concepts borrowed from sociology and anthropology, but no prior knowledge of these areas or media studies will be assumed on the part of your staff.

Outline. The handbook will be organized in an easy-to-follow format and written in simple, clear language. Following is the outline for the handbook:

I. Introduction
   - A. Purpose
   - B. Overview
II. Analyzing Images
   - A. Definition of Terms
     1. How does the advertisement speak to us?
     2. Who is the target audience?
   - B.   Encoding and Decoding
     1. Producer's perspective: goals, intentions
     2. Consumer's perspective: perceptions, inferences
III. Methods Used by Advertisers to Hail the Audience
   - A. Alienated spectators
   - B. Authenticity
   - C. Sign wars
   - D. Objectification
IV. Sample Analysis
   - A. Presentation of image
   - B. Critique/deconstruction of image
V. Conclusion

Bibliography. I've found good sources both in print and on the Internet. Here are the printed sources I've located:

Goldman, Robert, and Stephen Papson. *Sign Wars: The Cluttered Landscape of Advertising*. New York: Guilford Press, 1996.

Jaggar, Allison M., Ed. *Living With Contradictions: Controversies in Feminist Social Ethics*. Boulder: Westview Press, 1994.

Walters, Suzanna D. *Material Girls: Making Sense of Feminist Cultural Theory*. Berkeley: University of California Press, 1995.

Notice that the outline is carefully designed and avoids some common problems: first-level heads use initial caps on all main words (but not prepositions, articles, or other "little" words); second- and lower-level heads have initial caps on the first word only; there are no As without Bs, no 1s without 2s; alignment is carefully maintained; and the phrasing of items at the same level within the same section is carefully parallel (For more on outlining, see **www.io.com/ ~hcexres/power_tools/ outlining.html**.)

Bibliography: The style and format used for these items is Modern Language Association.

Reference to Internet items: Notice the format of the information sources found on the World Wide Web: as required by the MLA format, the author name is followed by the title of the page; that is followed by the full URL, which is followed by the date that this writer accessed that page.

These are the Internet sources I've located:

Cultural Studies Central. URL **www.culturalstudies.net/index.html** (visited January 10, 2000).

Maryland Theorists and Washington Consortium. URL **www.bsos.umd.edu/socy/theory/Theoryan.htm** (visited January 10, 2000).

Media and Communication Studies: News Media & Advertising. URL **media.ankara.edu.tr/~erdogan/newsad.html** (visited January 10, 2000).

MIT Libraries Ejournal Collection, Postmodern Culture, v.3, 1992–1993. URL **bion.mit.edu/ejournals/b/n-z/PMC/3/** (visited January 10, 2000).

List of graphics: Once again, this is a requirement from a technical-writing course, although a paying client might want to know these details as well. Knowing what graphics will be included in the project gives the client one more way of visualizing the final product, and one more way of asking for changes.

One of the easiest ways to create a two-column list like the graphics list is to create a two-column table in which you hide the grid lines. In MS Word, select **Table→Table AutoFormat** and then select **(none)**.

Status of the project: This is the main part of any progress report. Back in the introduction, the writer tells us she'll break this discussion into three areas. Here, she discusses the status of her work on each of these areas, in each case, summarizing work completed and work remaining.

Graphics.
These graphics will be included in the handbook.

Mapping the logic of the commodity sign	Illustration
Process of encoding and decoding	Illustration
Authenticity	Advertisement
Sign wars	Advertisement
Objectification	Advertisement

Compilation of Sources
We've gathered most of our information sources, but there are a few left.

Work completed. The resources to be used for the handbook have been narrowed to the list shown in the bibliography. While our definitions of the terms defined in the handbook are based on these sources, the interpretations of the images will be our own. This will demonstrate the practical application of media studies.

Work to be done. We are currently reviewing shorter articles that may supplement the resources shown above. They may be added to the bibliography.

Acquisition of Suitable Images (Ads and Graphics)

The graphics for this project are progressing nicely.

Work completed. After the proposal, we added a graphic that would explain encoding and decoding and removed two advertisements. I have included copies of our images (with brief explanations) for your perusal. Our goal is to place enough graphics in the handbook to make the text easier to understand.

Work to be done. The graphics have to be made print-ready. Right now they are in the forms of drawings, magazine advertisements, or GIF images. They must be given captions and placed appropriately in the text.

Written Text

Converting complex sociology into simple language has been most time-consuming.

Work completed. Because much of the writing depends on the images and figures presented in the text, the two must be finalized together. I have finished drafts for the advertisement images in the handbook, as well as the sample analysis of the advertisement at the end. I have also selected a title for the handbook: *Buying the Drama: Audience Perception of Advertisement Images.*

Work to be done. Once the sections of the handbook are compiled, we will proofread, edit, and format them.

Overall Appraisal

Overall status: Like most progress reports, this one ends with an overall appraisal of the project's status.

The project is coming together very well. The completed handbook promises to be a professional resource that will be useful for your staff. Right now I am confident that I will meet the August 4 deadline. However, if unforeseen circumstances cause any delay, I will notify you immediately.

If you have any questions or concerns about this progress report or the handbook, please call. I will be most happy to discuss the project with you. Our goal is to meet your needs and produce the best possible handbook for your company.

PART II

Document-Design Tools

CHAPTER 7

Headings  *centered*

BRAIN, SLEEP, AND DREAM RESEARCH

On the World Wide Web, you'll find plenty of interesting (and on-the-fringe) information about what's inside our heads as well as research on sleep and dreams.

Sleep from A to Zzz. ThinkQuest Web site entry by an international team of three high school students: **library.advanced.org/25553**

Archives Media: Sleep & Sleep Disorders. **www.stanford.edu/~dement/mediarc.html**

The Art & Science of Dreams. **www.suite101.com/article.cfm/science_of_dreams/13572**

International Institute for Dream Research. **www.dreamresearch.ca**

Circadian Rhythms. From About.com. **sleepdisorders.about.com/ health/diseases/sleepdisorders/msubcircadian.htm**

University of Virginia. Center for Biological Timing. **www.cbt.virginia.edu**

Sleep Disorder & Melatonin. From About.com. **sleepdisorders.about.com/health/diseases/sleepdisorders/ msubmelatonin.htm**

Neurosciences. From About.com. **neuroscience.about.com**

Harvard Medical School. The Whole Brain Atlas. **www.med.harvard.edu/AANLIB/home.html**

Paul Pietsch, Indiana University. "ShuffleBrain." **www.indiana.edu/~pietsch/home.html**

Christof Koch, California Institute of Technology. "Debunking the Digital Brain." **www.sciam.com/explorations/020397brain/ 020397explorations.html**

Accessed January 16, 2001.

Visual cues
—consistency

Headings are those titles and subtitles that you see inserted right in the running text of a document. They indicate the topic, purpose, or both, of the paragraphs that follow. Headings are one of the most powerful tools you can use in your technical, business, and scientific writing. They increase the readability, scannability, and the overall professionalism of your documents.

This chapter discusses the value of headings in technical writing and some basic design considerations for headings. It then shows you how to create and use headings. Included in this chapter are techniques for creating headings with Corel WordPerfect, Lotus Word Pro, Microsoft Word, and with HTML (for Web pages). For both word-processing software and for Web pages, you'll learn how to create *styles*, powerful tools that ensure consistency and increase efficiency.

WHAT ARE HEADINGS: WHAT ARE THEY GOOD FOR?

As mentioned in the preceding, headings are the titles and subtitles you see inserted into the text of documents that indicate the topic and purpose of the paragraphs that follow. Actually, the best analogy for headings is that they are like outline items that have been pumped into the text at the appropriate points. Reconstruct the outline you'd see for the headings in Figure 7-1.

As you can see in Figure 7-1, an individual heading indicates the topic of the one or more paragraphs that follow. Headings can be a powerful tool in your writing in a number of ways:

- *Provide an overview* of the document. Headings enable readers to scan an entire document and rapidly get a sense of what it covers.
- *Indicate the logic of the document.* Headings indicate the logic and structure of a document just the way outlines do.
- *Indicate the topic of the upcoming section.* An individual heading indicates the topic of the upcoming section (one or more paragraphs), helping to focus and guide readers' attention.

191

font / size & style

all caps?

First-level heading: This heading is centered and bold and uses a font that contrasts with the body text (14-point Arial as opposed to 12-point Times New Roman).

Arial + TNR common fonts

Serif + Sans serif

Placement of heading deliberate

II. SLEEP CYCLE

The following discusses the different types of sleep followed by the major types of sleep disorders. The normal sleep cycle consists of the following:

1. Stage 1 sleep is the initial stage people undergo when they fall asleep. It accounts for approximately 2% to 5% of a normal night's sleep.
2. Stage 2 sleep follows stage 1 sleep and accounts for approximately 45% to 55% of a normal night's sleep.
3. Stage 3 sleep is considered one of the "slow wave" sleep stages. In this stage, brain activity slows dramatically as the person progresses to stage 4 sleep.
4. Stage 4 sleep is the other phase of slow-wave sleep. In it, brain activity continues to slow dramatically. Slow-wave sleep patterns combine to account for 13% to 23% of a normal night's sleep.
5. Stage 5 is rapid eye movement (REM) sleep. It is a very active stage of sleep and accounts for 20% to 25% of a normal night's sleep.

Second-level heading: This heading is on the left margin, uses 12-point bold-italic Arial, and has a line above it. (For a ruled line in Word, choose **Format→Borders and Shading**; in Word Pro, choose **Text→Lines** and click on the appropriate icon. In WordPerfect, choose **Insert→Shape→Horizontal Line**.)

Types of Sleep

Researchers define two major types of sleep: active sleep and quiet sleep. Both are part of the overall sleep cycle.

Active sleep. In this type of sleep, breathing, heart rate, and brain wave activity quicken. Vivid dreams can occur. In this stage of sleep, rapid eye movement (REM) occurs. If you watch people in this stage, their eyes are moving rapidly. After REM stage, the body usually returns to stage 2 sleep.

Third-level headings: These headings are "run in" to the paragraph. They are **bold** (including the period). Notice that they are not a grammatical part of the sentence that follows.

Quiet sleep. The body cycles or "drifts" through the four stages of sleep: Stages 1, 2, 3, and 4, which are the quiet-sleep stages. Heart rate and respiration become slower. The body returns to stage 2 before moving into "active sleep."

FIGURE 7-1

Headings and outlines. Notice how headings are like outline items that have been inserted into the text at the points where they belong. Notice too that different formats are used to indicate the different levels of headings.

■ *Enable readers to read selectively, or to skip sections if they wish.* Technical, scientific, and business people rarely read documents straight through; they skip around, and they may not read certain sections at all. Headings enable them to do this type of selective reading.

- *Provide breaks and white space in dense text.* A nice side advantage of headings is that they break up text and add white space. While you shouldn't insert headings merely to create white space, functional headings do indeed increase overall readability, giving documents a less crowded, more open feel.
- *Keep readers focused.* Because headings indicate topics of upcoming sections and because readers can glance back at headings as they read, headings help keep readers oriented. Headings keep readers focused on the topic, on the sequence of topics, and on the logic of that sequence.
- *Keep the writer focused and organized.* Another side advantage of headings is that they keep you, the writer, more focused and organized as you write. Headings force you to stay on the topics you announce in those headings.

HOW DO YOU DESIGN HEADINGS?

To start using headings, you must first *design* them—that is, decide on their characteristics, such as font, face (bold, italics, underscore), size, capitalization, location on the page, and so on.

Levels of headings. Take a look at the headings used in the examples throughout this book. Notice that bold, italics, type size, alternate fonts, capitalization, and positioning on the page are all used to differentiate levels of headings. Levels of headings correspond to levels in an outline: roman-numeral sections are the highest level; capital-letter sections are next; arabic-numeral sections are next. The design of headings must visually indicate these levels. You ought to be able to look at an individual heading on a page and think, "Oh yes, this is a subsection of the such-and-such section that started on the preceding page."

To create good headings, you must have some basic skills in creating outlines: you must understand how items are grouped and sequenced logically and how certain groups of items are "subordinate" to others. For a review, see **www.io.com/~hcexres/power_tools/outlining.html**.

A common heading design. Most documents have a system of three to four levels of headings. Bold, italics, type size, alternate fonts, capitalization, and positioning on the page are used so that the different levels are distinct from each other. Take a look at the design of the headings in Figure 7-1:

- *First-level headings.* Use bold and a larger type size (specifically, Arial 14 point); also, make them bold and centered.
- *Second-level headings.* Use bold, italics, and a slightly smaller type size (specifically, Arial 12 point); make them flush to the left margin. (Optionally, use a solid ruled line across the page just above these headings.)
- *Third-level headings.* Use bold and the same type size as the regular text (specifically, Times New Roman 12 point); make them "run into" the paragraph.

Common Design for Headings

Level	Font & size	Face	Cap style	Position	Graphic
1	Arial 14 pt	Bold	Uppercase	Centered	—
2	Arial 12 pt	Bold-italic	Title case	Left margin	Ruled line above
3	Times New Roman,12 pt	Bold	Sentence case	Run in to paragraph	—
Body text	Times New Roman, 12 pt	—	Sentence case	Indented 1.0 inch from left margin.	—

This heading design will work for most of your technical documents. Notice that in shorter documents, such as in the end-of-chapter examples, the first-level heading is not used at all. However, in longer reports with separate "chapters," the first-level heading is a useful tool. The headings in Figure 7-1 use the specifications shown in the table above. Use these in your technical documents if you have no other preferences or requirements.

Font types for headings.   The preceding design uses Arial, a *sans serif* font, for headings and Times New Roman, a *serif* font, for regular body text. Serifs are the little curlicues that guide the eyes from letter to letter in fonts like Times New Roman. Sans serif fonts don't use those curlicues. In publishing, sans serif fonts are commonly used for headings, and serif fonts for body text. Times New Roman is commonly preferred for body text, while Arial is commonly preferred for headings.

Hanging-head design.   Notice also in the preceding design that body text is indented 1 inch while the first- and second-level headings are not indented. This creates the "hanging-head" design such as you see used in Figure 7-1. The hanging-head design makes headings stand out even more and shortens the line length of body text. Overly long lines of regular text are not comfortable to read.

HOW DO YOU USE HEADINGS?

Once you've designed a set of headings, you can start using them. There are two issues here. One involves your word-processing software and the mechanics of getting those headings into your text; that's covered in the next section. Just as important is the issue of using those headings in a standard way. This section covers some basic guidelines you need to know to use headings effectively:

- *Use a heading design consistently.* This guideline may seem obvious; but, just in case, don't vary the type styles, caps styles, font, or other characteristics you chose when you initially designed your headings. Don't create headings "on the fly."

Activity: Make a mock doc page that breaks these + see what it looks like (handwritten note)

2 ■ *Use subordinate headings.* If a section is "subordinate" to some other section—that is, at a lower level—use a lower-level heading. For example, if you have a report on fruits and vegetables, fruits and vegetables will be the first-level headings and things like apples, oranges, bananas, squash, and potatoes will be second-level headings. It wouldn't make sense for both vegetables and potatoes to be first-level headings any more than it would be for them to be I and II in an outline.

use logic (handwritten note)

3 ■ *Make the phrasing of headings accurately and adequately descriptive.* Avoid headings like "Background" or "Technical Information." Find the right set of words to indicate the subject matter of the section and build that into the heading. Remember that readers need your headings to give them a quick thumbnail idea of what the upcoming section is about.

4. ■ *Make headings parallel in phrasing.* Use the same style of phrasing for headings at the same level within the same section. Picture a traditional outline: the roman-numeral sections might use *how/when/where/what/why* phrasing, while the alpha items under II might use gerund phrasing (*-ing*), and the alpha items under III, simple noun phrases. Parallelism of phrasing in headings gives readers important clues as to the content of sections within a document. (See Appendix C for more on parallelism.)

5. ■ *Use task-oriented headings in instructions.* When you write procedures in which readers must perform the steps you present, use task-oriented phrasing: for example, "How to Set the Timer" (*how/when/where/what/why* phrasing) or "Setting the Timer" (gerund phrasing).

followed by imperative (handwritten note)

6. ■ *Avoid lone headings.* Avoid situations in which you have a single second-, third-, or fourth-level heading all by itself within a section—a problem known as a "lone heading." This problem is exactly analogous to an A without a B or a 1 without a 2 in outlines. Either delete the lone heading or find a way to create another companion heading within the same section.

7. ■ *Avoid stacked headings.* Avoid situations in which two or more headings occur without regular text between them—a problem known as "stacked headings." Ordinarily, you can insert useful introductory or overview material between headings to eliminate the problem.

8. ■ *Don't use headings as lead-ins to lists.* Avoid using headings as introductions to lists; instead use a sentence, clause, or phrase lead-in. Using headings as lead-ins to lists simply muddies the distinction between headings and regular text. (Chapter 8 on lists presents this same guideline with illustrations.)

9. ■ *Don't use headings as figure or table titles.* Figures and tables have their own title mechanism; don't confuse that with headings. Figure titles are typically located *below* figures (see Chapter 11 for details). Table titles are typically located *above* tables (see Chapter 10 for details).

*Figure titles above
Table titles below* (handwritten note)

10. ■ *Don't refer to headings with pronouns.* Avoid referring to headings with *this* or *it.* For example, if the heading "Lone Headings" were followed by the sentence "This problem occurs when . . .," then the phrase "This problem" would be using the pronoun "this" to refer to the heading. Because readers read and process headings differently than they do regular text,

they must pause for a fraction of a second to confirm what "this" refers to. Write the text following headings as if the headings were not there at all.

■ *Use the right number of headings.* It's just as easy to use too many headings as it is to use too few. There are no ratios for the right balance of headings and text, but, in a standard, single-spaced, 8.5 x 11-inch page, try for two to four headings. *per page*

HOW DO YOU CREATE HEADINGS?

Once you've designed headings, you're ready to use them in a document. When you first start using headings, you'll probably add them after you've written the draft. But as you become accustomed to using them, you'll find that you add them as you write. In fact, you may even prefer to create the headings in advance before you start writing any body text. These latter methods are preferable: they keep you organized and focused.

At whatever draft stage you create headings, you'll want to use software tools called *styles* to make your headings consistent and to make creating them easy and efficient. In the following sections, you'll see how to create and use styles in Microsoft Word and in HTML.

Creating Headings: Common Word-Processing Software

In Corel WordPerfect, Lotus Word Pro, and Microsoft Word, you can design headings manually by specifying font, face, size, and position each time you create a heading. Or, you can use your software system of styles to speed up the process and make it easier.

Manual approach.   You can certainly create headings the slow and tedious way. Here's an example of how you'd do that in Corel WordPerfect, Lotus Word Pro, and Microsoft Word (and the steps are much the same in other software). See the illustrations in Figures 7-2 through 7-4 for locations of the various menu options mentioned in this next section.

1. Type the text for a heading and keep it highlighted for the next steps.
2. In the Fonts menu option, change the font to Arial (or some other distinctive font).
3. In the Type Size menu option, make the type size 14 points.
4. Bold the text by pressing Ctrl+B.
5. To define the space below this heading, use the following steps:
   ■ In Corel WordPerfect, choose **Format→Paragraph→Format**, and change Distance in points to 18.
   ■ In Lotus Word Pro, choose **Text→Lines**. In the Properties for Text dialog box select the Alignment tab; in the Paragraph spacing Below field click **Custom**, and enter 18 (making sure to select **points**).
   ■ In Microsoft Word, choose **Format→Paragraph**. In the Indents and Spacing dialog, change Spacing After to 18 points.

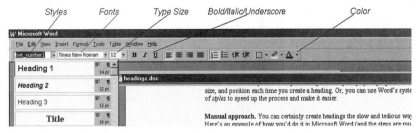

FIGURE 7-2

Menu options for typography and style options in MS Word. In Word, the Formatting toolbar contains most of options you need to change fonts and other typographical features (choose **View→Toolbars** to access it).

Software-supplied styles. One shortcut to the preceding approach is to use the default heading styles supplied with most software applications. See Figure 7-2 for the Styles menu option, where numerous levels of headings are available. To use these headings follow these steps:

1. Position your text cursor on the line that you want to change into a heading.
2. To select a software-supplied style, follow these steps:
   - In Corel WordPerfect and Microsoft Word, click the drop-down menu in the Styles box to see a list of the available styles.
   - In Lotus Word Pro, choose **Text→Text Properties** (or just press Alt + Enter) and click on the Named Styles tab in the properties dialog.
3. Click on Heading 1, Heading 2, or Heading 3 to apply it to the line on which your cursor is located. The text will change to the characteristics of the heading style you selected.

Styles approach. What if you don't want to use the styles that Corel, Lotus, or Microsoft have decreed? You can create your own styles. For

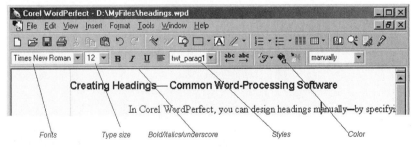

FIGURE 7-3

Menu options for typography and style options in Corel WordPerfect. In WordPerfect, the Property toolbar contains most of the options you need to change fonts and other typographical features. (Choose **View→Toolbars** to access it.)

advanced or professional work, styles are a great help. But for simple or brief documents, just use the styles supplied by your software, as explained in the preceding. Imagine that you want a heading style that uses a nice informal font such as Lucida Sans:

1. Move to a blank line in your document, type a few words, and highlight them.
2. Change the font to Lucida Sans (or some other distinctive font).
3. Make the type size 14 points, and make the text bold (press Ctrl+B).
4. Using the steps in "Manual approach," define the space above to be 18 points and the space below to be 9 points.
5. To record these settings as a style, follow these steps:
   - In Corel WordPerfect, choose **Format→Styles→QuickStyle**. In the QuickStyle dialog, give the style a distinctive name, such as my_head1.
   - In Lotus Word Pro, choose **Text→Named Styles→Create** (or just press Alt+Enter), click **Create Style** in the Text Properties dialog box, and give this style a distinctive name, such as my_head1.
   - In Microsoft Word, choose **Format→Style**, select **New**, and give this style a distinctive name, such as my_head1.
6. To confirm that your new style is available, click on the style menu and scroll until you find it. To confirm that it does what you want, move to some new line of text in your document, and then click on your new style. The text should change accordingly in only one step instead of five!

Great, isn't it? By default, your styles may be available only to your current document. To make them available to other documents, copy them to

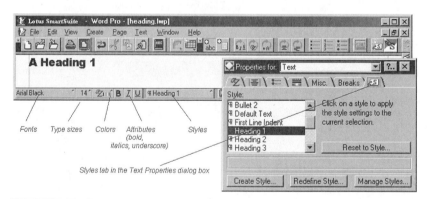

Fonts   Type sizes   Colors   Attributes (bold, italics, underscore)   Styles

Styles tab in the Text Properties dialog box

FIGURE 7-4

Menu options for typography and style options in Lotus Word Pro. In Word Pro, look to the bottom edge of the window for the options you need to change fonts and other typographical features. (Choose **Text→Text Properties** or press Alt + Enter to create or edit styles.)

a template of your own. Most word-processing software stores things like styles in *templates*. Procedures for adding styles to templates vary according to the software you use. Creating templates is covered in Chapter 13 on business communications.

Creating Headings for Web Pages

When you create headings with HTML tags, you have the same manual and styles-based approaches that you do with word-processing software. To understand the following, you'll need to know how to create a simple Web page, which is covered in Chapter 17.

Manual approach. To create headings with HTML tags, follow these steps:

1. Find the text you want to convert into a heading.
2. For a first-level heading, enclose the heading text with <H1> and </H1> tags: for example, <H1>First-Level Heading</H1>.
3. For a second-level heading, enclose the heading text with <H2> and </H2> tags: for example, <H2>My Second-Level Heading</H2>. (HTML provides more heading levels, but three or four are sufficient.)
4. View these headings through a Web browser to see how they look. Add some text before and after these headings to see how they look in context.
5. For the hanging-head format, add one or more </BLOCKQUOTE> tags before each heading and the same number of <BLOCKQUOTE> tags after each heading.

Most Web browsers use Times New Roman as the default font and black as the default color. What if you don't want to use the specifications

First-Level He

Some introductory text here.

Second-Level Heading

Add some text here. Lotsa text!

Second-Level Heading

More text here too.

```
<HTML>
<HEAD>
<TITLE>Web Page with Headings</TITLE>
</HEAD>
<BODY>
<CENTER>
<H1>First-Level Heading</H1>
</CENTER>
<BLOCKQUOTE><BLOCKQUOTE>
Some introductory text here.
</BLOCKQUOTE></BLOCKQUOTE>
<H2>Second-Level Heading</H2>
<BLOCKQUOTE><BLOCKQUOTE>
Add some text here. Lotsa text!
</BLOCKQUOTE></BLOCKQUOTE>
<H3>Second-Level Heading</H3>
<BLOCKQUOTE><BLOCKQUOTE>
More text here too.
</BODY>
</HTML>
```

FIGURE 7-5

HTML tags to create three levels of headings. Notice how the <BLOCKQUOTE> tags indent the left margins of the paragraph text.

decreed by the browser? You can specify fonts and colors, among other things. To force the <H1> heading in the preceding to use Arial and blue, use this tag: <H1><FONT FACE="Arial" COLOR="blue">My Heading</FONT></H1>. Using color in Web pages is a good idea; however, keep it under control. For example, make all your headings one color (not multiple colors) and your text black.

Styles approach.   You may not like the idea of entering all those extra tags just to get the fonts and colors you want. HTML offers a system of styles called cascading style sheets (CSS). Imagine that you want all your first-level headings to use italicized Lucida Sans font and the color teal. Without CSS, you must tag each of your first-level headings this way:

> <H1><FONT FACE="Arial" COLOR="teal"><I>*heading*</I> </FONT> </H1>.

Using CSS, all you have to do is to insert the following style definition within the HEAD tags:

```
<HTML>
<HEAD>
<STYLE type="text/css">
<!-- H1 {font-family: Arial; font-style: italic; color: teal} -->
</STYLE>
</HEAD>
<BODY>
```

Every time you use the <H1> tags, the result will be an Arial, teal-colored italicized heading. And, if you ever want to change to some other font, face, or color, you just change the style definition once, instead of in each instance.

WORKSHOP: HEADINGS

Here are some additional ideas for practicing the concepts, tools, and strategies in this chapter:

1. *Review of heading designs.* Find a sampling of technical documents (books, reports, articles, online materials) and analyze the heading designs you see in them. Use a grid like the following to record your observations:

Level	Font & size	Face	Cap style	Position	Graphic
1					
2					
3					

If you are not sure of fonts, just indicate whether the font is serif or sans serif. If you are not sure of size, just indicate whether a heading is larger or smaller in relation to others. ("Face" refers to bold, italics, and other such effects.)

2. *Simple headings for print text.* Using your preferred writing software (Word, WordPerfect, etc.), manually add the supplied headings with the specified characteristics to the text provided in the Instructor's Resource or available at **www.io.com/~hcexres/power_tools/ headings/exer2.html.**

3. *Simple headings with styles for print text.* Using the same headings and text in the previous exercise, create *styles* for the different heading levels in your preferred writing software.

4. *Simple headings for Web pages.* Using the same headings and text in the previous exercise, create a Web page with heading levels corresponding to the appropriate HTML tags. Manually tag each instance of the headings.

5. *Simple headings with styles for Web pages.* Using the same headings and text in the previous exercise, create HTML cascading style sheet styles for those same heading levels.

6. *Custom heading design for print or Web pages.* Using your preferred writing software or HTML tags or both, insert the headings into the text available at **www.io.com/~hcexres/power_tools/headings/exer2 .html.** In this exercise, you decide on the placement and design of the headings. When you've finished, compare your results to those of others— the headings can be handled in a variety of ways.

7. *Common heading-design problems.* In the excerpts in the Instructor's Resource or at **www.io.com/~hcexres/power_tools/headings/ exer3.html,** identify the problem or problems that occur in each one (such as stacked or lone headings, lack of parallelism, and so on).

8. *Custom heading composition and design for print or Web pages.* Using either your preferred writing software or HTML tags (or both), compose and design the headings for the text provided in the Instructor's Resource or available at **www.io.com/~hcexres/power_ tools/headings/exer4.html.** In this last exercise, you have to write the heading text, design the heading levels, place them in the text, and do any necessary rewriting of surrounding text as necessary.

CHAPTER 8

Lists: Bulleted, Numbered, and Others

HUMAN GENOME PROJECT

As you move into this chapter on lists, consider the ongoing international effort to list the more than 80,000 human genes and interpret their function:

National Institutes of Health. National Human Genome Research Institute. **www.nhgri.nih.gov**

Stanford Human Genome Center. **www-shgc.stanford.edu**

UK Human Genome Mapping Project Resource Centre. **www.hgmp.mrc.ac.uk**

Human Genome Project Information. U.S. Department of Energy. **www.ornl.gov/TechResources/Human_Genome**

About.com. Genetics (see the link for Human Genome Projects). **genetics.about.com/education/scilife/genetics**

University of Kansas Medical Center. Ethical, Legal, Social, Implications of Human Genome Project. **www.kumc.edu/gec/prof/geneelsi.html**

Accessed January 16, 2001.

For almost as long as you've been reading, you've been looking at bulleted and numbered lists; but you've probably never stopped and thought about them. Lists can be a big help to your readers, enabling them to skim your text faster, see the important points, and follow sequential material more easily. They also add white space, cutting down on big, thick, dense paragraphs.

In this chapter, you learn about the different types of lists, their design and format, standard list guidelines, and some basic techniques for creating lists with your software and for Web pages.

WHAT ARE LISTS?

Before getting into guidelines for lists, take a moment to review the various types that you can use in your writing, all of which are illustrated in Figures 8-1 through 8-3.

- *Bulleted lists.* Use bulleted lists for situations in which you want to emphasize two or more items. The bullet says, "Hey, I'm important!" Use bullets for items that are not in any required order and that will not be referred to by number. Avoid creating bulleted lists over 7 items[1] but if you do, consider using bullets with introductory labels, also discussed in the following. (See Figure 8-1 for an example of a bulleted list.)
- *Numbered lists.* Use numbered lists for items that are in a required order or that must be referred to by number. The most common use for numbered lists is for instructions in which you must help readers follow a sequence of steps. The numbers say, "Hey, follow this sequence!" If a numbered list goes over 7 items, start looking for ways to consolidate shorter numbered items; if it goes way over 7 items, look for ways to break up the list, insert additional lead-ins, and renumber. (See Figure 8-1 for an example of a numbered list.)
- *In-sentence lists.* In an in-sentence list, the items are in standard paragraph format and use either numbers or lowercase letters enclosed in

---

[1] George A. Miller. "The Magical Number Seven, Plus or Minus Two: Some Limits on Our Capacity for Processing Information." In *The Psychology of Communication* (New York: Basic Books, 1967).

Mitosis is the process of cell duplication, during which one cell produces two identical daughter cells. The process consists of four phases: prophase, metaphase, anaphase, and interphase:

1. In prophase, the genetic material thickens and coils in chromosomes, the nucleolus disappears, and a group of fibers begins to form a spindle.
2. In metaphase, the chromosomes duplicate themselves and line up along the midline of the cell. The halves are known as chromatids.
3. In anaphase, the chromatids are pulled at opposite ends of the cell by the spindle fibers. At this point, the cytoplasm of the mother cell divides to form two daughter cells, each with the number and kind of chromosomes the mother cell possessed.
4. In interphase, the daughter cells begin to function on their own, once their nucleus membranes and nuclei form.

Unprecedented progress in identifying and understanding the 50,000 to 100,000 or so genes that make up the human genome provides an opportunity for scientists to develop strategies to prevent or reduce the effects of genetic disease. Scientists have shown that straight-forward inherited errors in our genes are responsible for an estimated 3,000 to 4,000 diseases, including the following:

- Huntington's disease
- Cystic fibrosis
- Neurofibromatosis
- Duchenne muscular dystrophy.

More complex inheritance of multiple genetic errors also can increase an individual's risk of developing common disorders such as cancer, heart disease, and diabetes.

FIGURE 8-1

Numbered and bulleted lists. Use numbers for list items that occur in a required sequence. Use bullets for items in no necessary sequence.

parentheses. In-sentence lists could be called "horizontal" lists in contrast to the "vertical" format used in bulleted and numbered lists. (See Figure 8-2 for an example of an in-sentence list.)

- *Labeled lists.* A nice touch you can apply to lists, particularly long or complex ones, is to add a brief identifying label at the beginning of each item, which you bold or italicize. (See Figure 8-2 for an example of a labeled list.)
- *Nested lists.* Occasionally, you'll create lists within lists—in other words, sublist items. For example, for a complex numbered-list item, create subitems with lowercase letters. In Figure 8-3, notice how the subitems align to the text of the higher-level items.
- *Two-column lists.* Some lists contain paired items, for example, a technical term and its definition. You can use the labeled-list style just discussed, or you can use the two-column style. Actually, the two-column list is a table in disguise, without the grid lines showing. Use tables rather than tabs or spaces to create two-column lists. See Chapter 10 for details on tables.
- *Simple lists.* A simple list is a vertical list in which the items are not numbered or bulleted. This type is often used for equipment or supply lists, in which the emphasis created by the bullet or number is just not needed.

Deoxyribonucleic acid (DNA) carries the genetic information that is in a cell. DNA makes up chromosomes, of which humans possess forty-six. The DNA helix resembles two snakes intertwining and is made up of bases called nucleotides. There are four of these nucleotides: (a) adenine (b) thymidine, (c) guanine, and (d) cytosine.

Two types of genetic testing can occur in the workplace, both of which can be used unfairly to discriminate against or stigmatize individuals on the job:

- *Genetic screening*. Genetic screening examines the genetic makeup of employees or job applicants for specific inherited characteristics. It may be used to detect general heritable conditions that are not associated with workplace exposures in employees or applicants.
- *Genetic monitoring*. Genetic monitoring ascertains whether an individual's genetic material has changed over time due to workplace exposure to hazardous substances.

FIGURE 8-2

In-sentence and label lists. For in-sentence lists, be sure to use both parentheses.

Resources for human chromosome maps include the following:

GeneMap'98
Science/NCBI Human Transcript Map
IMAGE Consortium
NHGRI Human Chromosome 7 Mapping and
   Sequencing

Chromosome maps of other organisms include the following:

- *Arabidopsis*
  – AtDB (Stanford)
  – European Union Arabidopsis Genome Project
- *C. elegans*
  – University of Texas Southwestern Medical Center at Dallas
  – Sanger Center
- Dog Genome Project
- FlyBase
- Fungal Genome Resource (University of Georgia)
- Mouse Genome Database

FIGURE 8-3

Simple and nested lists. Use an en dash for second-level bullets. For a subnumbered list, use lowercase letters. For a bulleted list that is subordinate to a numbered list, use the regular solid-disk bullet. Similarly, for a numbered list subordinate to a bulleted list, use regular arabic numerals.

WHAT ARE LISTS GOOD FOR?

Why bother with lists in the first place? For one thing, lists increase the readability of your text. Lists enable readers to scan your text more readily, see the important points, and follow stepwise instructions more easily. Lists also increase the "white space" in text, reducing those long deadly paragraphs and the overall density of the text.

- *Emphasis.* The primary goal in creating lists should be to add emphasis. A bulleted list of three items emphasizes those three items.
- *Readability.* Another primary goal is to increase readability. The numbered-list format used in instructional steps makes it easier to follow those steps.
- *White space.* An important side effect of lists is that they create white space, which in turn increases readability. However, don't create lists just to increase white space. Using too many lists, as well as lists with too many items, loses the advantage of the list format altogether.

The content of the text must support the list. There must be something "bullet-able" or "number-able" in the text; and even if there is, it may not automatically warrant creating lists.

WHERE SHOULD YOU USE LISTS?

If you've never used lists in any systematic way, you'll probably start by going back and searching for ways to reformat your text to incorporate lists. After awhile, your sense of when to use lists will catch up with your composing practices. You'll anticipate lists and create them as you compose, or you'll reformat paragraphs into lists almost as soon as you've written them. Here are some ideas on how to recognize opportunities for working lists into your technical and business writing:

- *Sequenced items.* Whenever your text contains segments of information that are in a required order (typically, chronological order), consider using a numbered vertical list.
- *Overview list.* The individual sections of technical reports often contain overviews of the subtopics to be covered; these are good spots for in-sentence lists (using either numbers or lowercase letters).
- *Important points.* Text containing three or four key points about a topic is a good candidate for a bulleted list. If your discussion focuses on features, characteristics, elements, factors, guidelines, issues, or other such elements, that's a tip-off that you may want to reformat using bullets.
- *Paired items.* If your text contains pairs of items (for example, a term followed by its definition), try reformatting the text with a two-column list in which the terms are in the left column and their definitions are in the right column.

WHAT ARE THE GUIDELINES FOR LISTS?

Figure 8-4 summarizes key guidelines involving lists. Most importantly, use the right types of lists. In the technical world, using a numbered list for items not in a required order can cause serious confusion, as can using

Use

Guidelines for Lists

Follow standard guidelines for lists. Regardless of which type of list you create, you must keep some general guidelines in mind. These are standard guidelines for style and format of lists that you will see observed in most published information.

- *Use the right type of list.* Use bullets for items in no necessary order and numbers for items in some required order.
- *Include a lead-in.* Introduce all lists with a lead-in phrase, clause, or sentence, which you may punctuate with a colon. (Some styles specify that when the list items complete the sentence started by the lead-in, no colon should be used.) Don't use headings as list lead-ins.
- *Avoid using too many lists or creating lists with too many items.* Don't crowd too many lists on a page. For a standard single-spaced page, two lists is enough. If everything on a page is vertical lists, then the effect of lists is lost. Keep numbered or bulleted lists below seven items. (Researchers have found that seven is the maximum number that most people can manage cognitively.) Again, the effect of listing is lost when nearly everything is a list.
- *Avoid lists with only one item.* Avoid lists with only one bullet or only one number. Figure out how to create a second item, or don't use the list format at all.
- *Use standard punctuation and capitalization on list items.* Practice varies on how to punctuate list items. The easiest method is not to use any end punctuation except for periods on list items that are complete sentences. Practice also varies on capitalizing the first word of list items. An easy solution is always to use either upper or lowercase on the first letter of the first word of list items and not to sweat the fine distinctions.
- *Adjust spacing between list item for readability.* For short items of only a few words, use the normal spacing for body text (single-spacing). For items two lines or longer, put some space (half a line or even a full line) between the items for better readability.
- *Make the phrasing of list items parallel.* See Appendix C for details on parallelism. Parallelism is another way to increase the readability and comprehension of lists.
- *Use the lead-in to eliminate repetition,* but check the grammatical connection between list items and their lead-ins. In some lists, you can transfer repetitive words from the list items into the lead-in and cut overall word count. Each list item should read grammatically with its lead-in. This can become a problem if the list items actually complete the grammar of the lead-in—make sure each one does.
- *Avoid lead articles on list items.* Whenever possible, eliminate articles at the beginning of list items; doing so decreases verbal clutter around the item.
- *Correctly align list items and nested list items.* Carefully study how list items are aligned with nested list items.

Consistency

A or The

FIGURE 8-4

Guidelines for lists. The guidelines explained in the preceding are general standards used in the technical publishing industry. However, practice does vary. Take a look at the design of lists in a sampling of technical publications to study variations.

a bulleted list for items in a required order. Avoid overusing lists. Because they contrast with normal paragraphs, lists convey emphasis. If everything is a list, then that emphasis is lost. The same holds true for lists with too many items. Most of the other list guidelines you see in Figure 8-4 have to do with readability and consistency.

HOW DO YOU CREATE LISTS?

Take the time to learn how to create lists using your preferred software, such as Corel WordPerfect, Lotus Word Pro, or Microsoft Word. The same goes for lists in Web pages. Merely typing the number and then spacing or tabbing to enter the text is tedious, inefficient, and unprofessional.

Creating Lists: Common Word-Processing Software.   Here's a mini tutorial on creating lists with WordPerfect, Word Pro, and Word. (See Figures 8-5 through 8-7 for references to menu options.)

Numbered lists. To start a new numbered list or to change ordinary text to a numbered list:

1. Type several lines of text, separating each one by pressing the Enter key.
2. Highlight all three lines.
3. Click on the numbered-list icon ⊞ or,
   - In Corel WordPerfect, choose **Format→Outline/Bulleted & Numbering** and then click the **Numbers** tab.
   - In Lotus Word Pro, choose **Text→Bullets & Numbers,** and if necessary select the **Bullets/Numbers** tab.
   - In Microsoft Word, choose **Format→Bullets and Numbering.** Click on the **Numbered** tab, and select the simple Arabic numeral format followed by a period (Figure 8-5).
4. Each time you want to create a new numbered-list item, press the Enter key.
5. When you are ready to end the numbered list, press the Enter key twice, or click on the numbered-list icon.

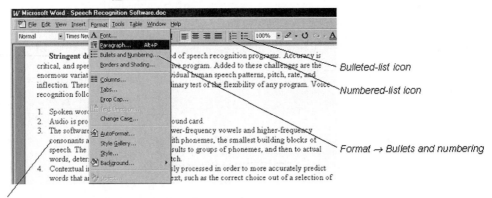

Use your word-processing application's list-formatting styles: notice how the "run-over" lines are nicely formatted.

FIGURE 8-5

Creating numbered and bulleted lists in Microsoft Word. Don't create lists manually—they look tacky. Use the tools that software applications give you, such as these in Microsoft Word. Either click on the bulleted-list icon or the numbered-list icon, or use the Format menu option.

auto format
Use Edit to fix

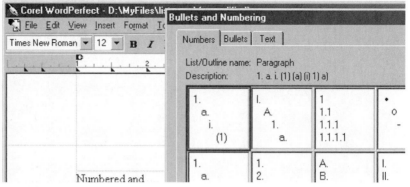

FIGURE 8-6
Creating lists in Corel WordPerfect. You can click the numbered-list icon, or choose **Format→Outline/Bulleted & Numbering**, and select the **Numbers** tab.

Cut + will paste will continue the numbering

6. If you use more than one numbered list, you must reset the numbering to 1:
   - In Corel WordPerfect, choose **Insert→Outline/Bullets & Numbering**, and at the **Numbers** tab click **Resume outline or list** (Figure 8-6).
   - In Lotus Word Pro, numbered lists restart at 1 if there is a break.
   - In Microsoft Word, choose **Format→Bullets and Numbering**, and click **Restart numbering**.
7. If you want to interrupt a numbered list with a paragraph, press Enter to create the paragraph and then click on the numbered-bullet icon.

Bulleted lists. To start a new bulleted list or to change ordinary text to a bulleted list, follow these steps:

1. Type several lines of text, separating each one by pressing the Enter key.
2. Highlight all three lines.
3. Click on the bulleted-list icon or:
   - In Corel WordPerfect, choose **Format→Outline/Bulleted & Numbering** and then click the **Bullets** tab.
   - In Lotus Word Pro, choose **Text→Bullets & Numbers** and if necessary select the **Bullets/Numbers** tab (Figure 8-7).
   - In Microsoft Word, choose **Format→Bullets and Numbering**. Click on the **Bulleted** tab, and select the black dots.
4. Each time you are ready to create the next bulleted-list item, press the Enter key.
5. When you are ready to end the bulleted list, press the Enter key twice, or click on the bulleted-list icon.

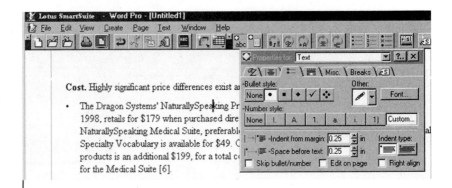

FIGURE 8-7
Creating bulleted lists with Lotus Word Pro. Click **TextBullets & Numbers** and **Bullets/Numbers** (as shown) if necessary.

Creating Lists: Web Pages. If you are creating Web pages, make sure that you use the correct HTML tags for lists. As of the year 2000, some HTML editors and converters do not use the correct list tags and produce very unprofessional-looking results. Use the following mini tutorial on Web-page lists for the basics. (For an introduction to creating Web pages, see Chapter 17.)

■ To begin a numbered list, start with the <OL> tag; for a bulleted list, use the <UL> tag. Just type the tag on a line by itself where you want the list to start.
■ For each list item, either numbered or bulleted, use the <LI> tag. Begin each list item on its own line, with the <LI> tag at the beginning and </LI> at the end of the item.
■ To end a numbered list, use the </OL> tag; for a bulleted list, use the </UL> tag. Just type this tag on a line by itself after the final list item.
■ To add space between list items to increase readability, use the <P> tag. Just type this tag at the end of each list item.
■ To create a nested list, type <OL> or <UL> on the line *within an existing list* where you want the sublist to start. If you wanted a sublist using lowercase letters within a numbered list, type <OL TYPE="a">. Begin each sublist item with <LI>. When you've completed the sublist, type </OL> or </UL> and resume your original list.

See Figure 8-8 for the HTML tagging you would use to create a numbered list. (How would you change the numbered list in the same figure to a bulleted list?)

Stringent dema | **The <B> and the </B>** | <B>Stringent demands</B>. For speech-recognition
essential. Howe | tags bold the text | programs, accuracy is critical, and speed is
enormously. In | contained between | essential. However, individual human speech
follows these st | them. | patterns, pitch, rate, and inflection vary
| | enormously. In an attempt to account for this
1. Spoken | The <OL> tag begins | variability, voice-recognition software follows
| the numbered list. (A | these steps:
2. The co | <UL> tag would have | <P>
| started a bulleted list.) | <OL>
3. To dete | | <LI>Spoken words enter a microphone.
low-freq | The <LI> tag creates a | <P>
with ph | numbered-list item. (If a | <LI>The computer's sound card processes the audio
| <UL> tags had been | stream.
4. Context | used, <LI> tags would | <P>
most lik | create bulleted items.) | <LI>To determine the most likely match, the
Mary. | | software distinguishes between low-frequency vowels
| | and higher-frequency consonants, compares the
5. Selected | The <P> tags add | results with phonemes, then to groups of phonemes,
sentenc | space between the | and then to actual words.
| numbered-list items as | <P>
| well as before and after | <LI>Contextual information is simultaneously
| the entire numbered list | processed in order to predict words most likely to
| | be used next or to distinguish homonyms such as
| | <I>merry</I>, <I>marry</I> and <I>Mary</I>.
| The <I> and </I> tags | <P>
| italicize the text con- | <LI>Selected words are arranged in the most
| tained between them. | probable sentence combinations. The sentence is
| The </OL> tag ends | then transferred to a word processing application
| the numbered list. | [11].
| | </OL>

FIGURE 8-8

Creating lists with HTML. Open a simple editor like Macintosh's SimpleEdit or Microsoft Notepad, and enter the text and HTML tags shown in this figure. Also, add <HTML><HEAD><TITLE>Lists</TITLE></HEAD><BODY> to the very top of this text and then </BODY></HTML> to the very bottom. Save this file as "lists.html" and then view it through Netscape or Internet Explorer. (For an introduction to creating Web pages, see Chapter 17.)

WORKSHOP: LISTS

Here are some additional ideas for practicing the concepts, tools, and strategies in this chapter:

1. *Analyzing style and format of lists.* Photocopy a half-dozen pages from various technical documents in which different types of lists are used. Compare the style and format you see used in these examples to what is presented in this chapter. In particular, look at the following:
   a. Type of list used: in-sentence, bulleted, numbered
   b. Punctuation of the lead-in to the list
   c. Capitalization and punctuation of the items
   d. Indentation of the items
   e. Apparent reasons for the list; its effectiveness

2. *Creating lists.* Convert the following text to the appropriate kinds of lists. Use your preferred word-processing software:

a. To request a background report on a new employee, you will need the following information: name, date of birth, social security number, state, and county.
b. There are three main types of faults. A divergent fault occurs when two plates are moving away from each other. When two plates come together, the result is a convergent fault. A fault that occurs when two plates slide past each other is known as a transform fault.
c. When constructing a pond in your backyard, you will need to determine which size pond liner you will need. First, dig out the pond. Next, measure the length, width, and depth of your pond. Then use the following formula to determine the pond liner size you need:
Length + twice the depth + 2 extra feet = length of pond liner needed
Width + twice the depth + 2 extra feet = width of pond liner needed

3. *Creating lists for Web pages.* Reformat the lists you created in the preceding workshop for presentation on the World Wide Web.

CHAPTER 9

Notices: Dangers, Warnings, and Cautions

EL NIÑO AND LA NIÑA

Some are warning us that the weather patterns in the Pacific known as El Niño and La Niña will cause major disruptions in the Western Hemisphere, particularly the southwestern United States.

Matt Rosenberg's Geography Links.
geography.about.com/education/scilife/geography/msubnino.htm

U.S. Geological Survey. Effects of El Niño on Streamflow, Lake Level, and Landslide Potential.
geochange.er.usgs.gov/sw/changes/natural/elnino

U.S. Department of Commerce National Oceanic and Atmospheric Administration (NOAA). El Niño Theme Page.
www.pmel.noaa.gov/toga-tao/el-nino/nino-home.html

NOAA. La Niña Page. **www.elnino.noaa.gov/lanina.html**

PBS Online. Tracking El Niño.
www.pbs.org/wgbh/nova/elnino/textindex.html

The Why Files. El Niño Rules.
whyfiles.news.wisc.edu/050el_nino/index.html

Accessed January 17, 2001.

If you've ever used anything that had the remotest chance of hurting you, you've seen *notices*—specially formatted text alerting you that you could hurt yourself or others, damage property or equipment, ruin the outcome of the procedure, or just generally increase your frustration level. And if you've ever used poorly written instructions, you have probably seen monstrosities like the one shown in Figure 12-1 in Chapter 12—the very thing that notices are designed to prevent.

This chapter shows you the strategies for creating, formatting, and using these important elements of the technical-writing trade. In addition, you'll see how to create notices in word-processing software and in Web pages using HTML tags.

Note: Study this chapter when you are preparing to write instructions (Chapter 2). Notices are essential in instructions.

WHAT ARE NOTICES?

Notices are special emphasis techniques for extended text. They warn readers of the possibility of injuring themselves, damaging equipment, or ruining the outcome of a procedure. They also provide readers with tips, hints, and so on. Notices accomplish this by using special format; for example, the text of a caution notice may be formatted with the word **CAUTION**, with a border around it, calling attention to itself. (For individual words or brief phrases, you can use the highlighting and emphasis techniques such a bold or italics, as presented in Chapter 12.)

Each industry—and sometimes almost every organization within an industry—has its own standards for notices. For example, one corporation may use warning notices for situations involving potential damage to equipment or data while another corporation uses caution notices for the same situation. Although corporations work together to create and maintain industry standards, such as those offered by American National Standards Institutes, individual corporations typically find these standards inadequate for their specific products.

For example, semiconductor, medical-equipment, and heavy-machinery industries must use much higher powered notices than the software industry. Fabrication (fab) workers are surrounded by extremely high voltages, toxic gases, and blinding lasers. Figure 9-1 illustrates a fairly common format for notices. It is by no means universal, but you'll see this design used often in technical publications.[1]

The types of notices are defined as follows, and are illustrated in Figure 9-1:

---

[1] Christopher Velotta, "Safety Labels: What to Put in Them, How to Write Them, and Where to Put Them." *IEEE Transactions on Professional Communication.* 30 (1987): 121–136.

Box

Simple note. Use this note to point out special details or exceptions.

El Niño refers to the irregular increase in sea surface temperatures from the coasts of Peru and Ecuador to the equatorial central Pacific. This phenomenon is not totally predictable but on average occurs once every four years. It usually lasts for about 18 months after it begins.

Note: El Niño is Spanish for "Christ Child." Historically, the term was used by the fisherman along the coasts of Ecuador and Peru to refer to a warm, nutrient-poor ocean current that typically appears around Christmastime and lasts several months.

Recent years in which El Niño events have occurred are 1951, 1953, 1957–1958, 1965, 1969, 1972–1973, 1976, 1982–1983, 1986–1987, 1991–1992, 1994, and 1997.

Caution: Use this note to alert people to the possibility of damage or failure. This example warns you not to plan a picnic or sink all your savings into soybean futures based on weather projections.

shading

Caution: These climate projections are intended to provide emergency managers, planners, forecasters, and the public advance notice of potential threats related to weather conditions. Although the best-known projection models are used, there is no guarantee of their accuracy.

Warning: Use warnings to alert people to possible injury—but not serious or fatal injury. Should a high-winds warning be upgraded to a danger notice?

weather report

A mostly zonal storm track with fast-moving storms and a fairly strong north to south temperature gradient should prevail across the lower 48 states from Friday, Jan 14 through Sunday, Jan 16, 2000. Although the overall pattern is expected to remain fairly stable, weather models are showing an amplification of the wave pattern over the U.S. during the week of Jan 16, which could produce a deep enough trough over the Northeastern states to bring some real winter weather into that region toward the middle of the week.

Warning: High winds are expected to accompany a storm coming ashore in the Pacific Northwest on Friday Jan 14.

Danger: Use this one to warn of possible serious or fatal injury. We definitely need danger notices for tornado information.

A tornado watch is issued by the National Weather Service when tornadoes are possible in your area. Remain alert for approaching storms. This is the time to remind family members where the safest places within your home are located and to listen to the radio or television for further developments. A tornado warning is issued when a tornado has been sighted or indicated by weather radar.

DANGER!
Never try to outdrive a tornado in a car or truck. Tornadoes can change direction quickly and can lift up a car or truck and toss it through the air.

FIGURE 9-1
Common design for notices. If you have no preferences or requirements concerning notices, use the designs illustrated here. See additional examples later in this chapter.

- *Danger:* For situations in which serious injury or even fatality could occur.
- *Warning:* For situations in which minor injury could occur.
- *Caution:* For situations in which damage to equipment or data could occur, or for problems that could cause the entire procedure to fail.
- *Note:* For situations where information needs to be emphasized, for exceptions, special points, hints, and tips—anything deserving special emphasis that does not match the criteria for danger, warning, or caution notices.

Don't alarm reader

Underwater characteristics such as temperature, visibility, marine life, and other factors vary from region to region and can influence the amount and type of work that divers can carry out underwater.

The following describes the diving conditions most likely to be encountered in various regions around the United States and in other parts of the world. **WHEN DIVING IN AN UNFAMILIAR REGION, INFORMATION ABOUT LOCAL CONDITIONS SHOULD BE OBTAINED FROM DIVERS WHO ARE FAMILIAR WITH THE WATERS. A CHECKOUT DIVE SHOULD BE MADE WITH A DIVER FAMILIAR WITH THE AREA.**

Northeast
Diving in northeastern waters can be described as an exciting and chilling experience.

Who wants to read text like this that seems to be screaming at you?

In this version, the word "Note:" is bold; the text of the note uses regular font for readability.

(Notice that the passive-voice constructions in the original have been changed to active.)

Underwater characteristics such as temperature, visibility, marine life, and other factors vary from region to region and can influence the amount and type of work that divers can carry out underwater.

The following describes the diving conditions most likely to be encountered in various regions around the United States and in other parts of the world.

Note: When diving in an unfamiliar region, get information about local conditions from divers who are familiar with the waters. Make a checkout dive with a diver familiar with the area.

Northeast
Diving in northeastern waters can be described as an exciting and chilling experience.

imperative

FIGURE 9-2

Using notices to emphasize. Few readers care to read text that seems to be screaming at them. The notice format enables you to call attention to the important information without, at the same time, creating unreadable text.

Notices solve a major problem in technical writing. To emphasize a chunk of text, inexperienced writers often use motley combinations of bold, italics, all-caps, and larger type size right in the middle of the paragraph. The result is the exact opposite of what is intended: most readers avoid screaming, hyperactively busy text. Notices solve this problem by yanking the important text out of regular paragraphs and putting it in a special format. While the notice *label* (the word "warning," "caution," "danger") may use bold, italics, all-caps, or larger type, the actual text of the notice regular uses the regular body font. (See Figure 9-2.)

HOW DO YOU USE NOTICES?

Imagine that you've developed a terrific industrial-strength set of notices. How do you use them?

- *Search your text for situations that match the situations for which you have defined your notices.* When you first start using notices, you'll probably have to go back and study your rough drafts to find text to reformat as notices. As you become accustomed to using notices, you'll find that you add them as you write.
- *Place notices with the text to which they apply.* The standard rule is to place notices before the point at which the potential for damage, failure, or injury exists. In actual practice, however, simple notes and cautions typically follow the step to which they apply. High-severity notices are placed at the beginning of the section, chapter, or document and then repeated after the step to which they apply.
- *Present high-severity notices at the beginning of a document.* Take a look at a few operator guides. In a section at the beginning, typically entitled "Safety Notices," they repeat all the warning, caution, and danger notices occurring anywhere in the rest of the guide.
- *Align notices with the text to which they apply.* If, for example, a note refers to a numbered-list item, that note should align to the text of the numbered-list item (not the numeral). The same goes for items in bulleted lists. If the notice applies to the entire numbered or bulleted list, don't indent the notice at all.
- *Consolidate multiple notices.* If multiple warnings and cautions occur close together, combine and use a label such as "Cautions and Warnings."
- *Use notice types consistently.* Plan how you will use notices; don't use them inconsistently and thus confuse readers. Don't dilute the impact of your notice design by creating new notice types on the fly—for example, "Important!" or "Read This!"

HOW DO YOU WRITE NOTICES?

Writing the text of notices is a good challenge of your skills as a technical communicator. You must pay particular attention to the kinds of information you put in notices, the style of writing you use, and the number of words you use.

Elements of notices. When you write the actual text of notices—especially higher severity notices like warnings and dangers—consider including the following kinds of information as needed (see Figure 9-3 for a labeled example):

- *Conditions.* Describe the conditions in which readers should avoid or take the action. For example, "Before rewiring the lamp, be sure to unplug it." Place the conditional information before the action statement.
- *Actions to avoid or to take.* State clearly and firmly what readers should do or not do; for example, "Do not push the red button!" or "Be sure to unplug the lamp."
- *Consequences.* Of course, most of us want to know why we can't push the red button. Why must we avoid the action or be sure to perform the action? After stating what to do or what to avoid (and the conditions), explain what might happen if the action statement is ignored. *Why*
- *Recovery.* Of course our best warning, caution, and danger notices will occasionally go unheeded, and people will push the red button. In some notices, you must include recovery directions—what to do in case they ignored you!

Writing style in notices. If you put all the information just described into one notice, you risk creating an overly long paragraph no one will

---

This example has all but one of these elements:

Conditions: The situation here is lack of use.

Actions: Charge, drain, and recharge up to six times if the battery has not been used recently.

Consequences: The battery will not recharge fully if it hasn't been used recently.

Recovery: This example does not involve an action to avoid; therefore, there is no recovery.

Charging the Battery Pack

You can charge the battery pack when the AC adapter is connected to the computer and the battery pack is installed. You need to charge the battery pack in any of the following conditions:

- When you purchase a new battery pack
- If the battery status indicator starts blinking
- If the battery pack has not been used for a long time

Note: If the battery pack has not been used for a long time, it cannot be fully charged with only a single charging. You will have to completely discharge it; then recharge it three to six times to maximize battery operating time.

FIGURE 9-3

Types of information included in notices. Consider including information as to actions, conditions, consequences, and recovery in the text of notices. At the same time, keep the notice as succinct as possible, but without resorting to "telegraphic writing" style.

Take battery .. Put in box.

Telegraphic style:

Danger! Never try to outdrive tornado in car or truck. Tornadoes can change direction quickly and can lift up car or truck and toss in air.

Caution! Never open back of camera before film is rewound back into cassette. Doing so will expose entire roll to light thus ruining all pictures.

Revisions:

Danger! Never try to outdrive a tornado in a car or truck. Tornadoes can change direction quickly and can lift up a car or truck and toss it in the air.

Caution! Never open the back of a camera before the film is rewound back into the cassette. Doing so will expose the entire roll to light, thus ruining all your pictures.

[handwritten: Too to speak]

[handwritten: Complete sentences]

read. Of course, not every notice needs all the material just described, and much of it can be combined. Keep notice text as succinct as possible, especially in high-severity notices. At the same time, avoid the extremes of the *telegraphic style*—omitting "understood" words like articles and verbs. Refer to the table shown above for examples of telegraphic style.

HOW DO YOU DESIGN AND CREATE NOTICES?

If your writing project requires notices, spend some time planning and designing them first. Decide which types of notices you'll use and for what situations.

Creating Notices: Common Word-Processing Software

Unfortunately, software applications like Corel WordPerfect, Lotus Word Pro, and Microsoft Word do not enable you to design styles for notices easily. You can specify fonts, size, margins, and borders; but it's hard to specify the actual text for the notice label—the actual word "note," "warning," "caution," "danger," and so on. On the other hand, true desktop-publishing tools like Adobe FrameMaker and Pagemaker, Quark Xpress, and Interleaf enable you to build these labels right into the style, along with graphic elements such as boxes or icons.

The following guides you through the design of notices in common word-processing. You don't have to use these exact designs, but these procedures will give you the tools to design your own.

Simple Notice

An excess of carbon dioxide in the tissues can be caused by interference with the process of carbon-dioxide transport and elimination. In diving, carbon-dioxide excess occurs either because of an excess of the gas in the breathing medium or because of interference with eliminating the carbon dioxide produced.

Note: There is only about 0.033 percent carbon dioxide in clean fresh air.

FIGURE 9-4

Caution Notice

Scuba regulators should be functionally tested on a regular basis; every six months is recommended.

Caution: Hoses for double-hose regulators must be washed with soap and water and thoroughly rinsed and dried after each use to prevent rapid buildup of bacteria.

FIGURE 9-5

Simple notices.   Here is the simplest method (Figure 9-4):

1. Move to a line where you want the notice to begin.
2. Type the notice label—for example, type "Note," highlight it, and press Ctrl+I (on a PC) to make it italics.
3. Type the note text in the same font as your body text (not in italics).
4. Optionally, indent the right and left margins, using the following steps:
   - In Corel WordPerfect, choose **Format→Margins**, and add **0.5** to the current margin settings.
   - In Lotus Word Pro, choose **Text→Text Properties** (or just press Alt+Enter), click **Options**, and then set All lines from left and All lines from right to **0.5**.
   - In Microsoft Word, choose **Format→Paragraph**, and change Left and Right to **0.5** inches under Indentation.

Caution notices.   Try the "hanging-indent" style for a caution-notice design (Figure 9-5):

1. Move the text cursor to a new line where you want the notice to begin.

2. Type the notice label; for example, type "Caution," highlight it, and press Ctrl+I to italicize it. Next, use the following steps to make the label stand out more:
   - In Corel WordPerfect, choose **Format→Font** and select **Arial** in the Font face field.
   - In Lotus SmartSuite, choose **Text→Text Properties** (or just press Alt+Enter); click the Fonts, attributes, and color tab; and select **Arial** in the Font name field.
   - In Microsoft Word, choose **Format→Font** and select **Arial** in the Font field.
3. Press Tab, and then type the note text in the same font as the body text. (You may not see any effect when you press Tab.)
4. Use the following steps to set the hanging indent:
   - In Corel WordPerfect, choose **Format→Paragraph→Format**, and set First line indent to –0.75 and Left margin adjustment to 0.75. Also, clear all existing tabs and set one tab at 0.75.
   - In Lotus SmartSuite, choose **Text→Text Properties** (or just press Alt+Enter), click **Options**, and change Rest of paragraph to 0.75 inches. Also, clear all existing tabs and set one tab at 0.75.
   - In Microsoft Word, choose **Format→Paragraph**. Under Special, select **Hanging** and set the hanging indent at 0.75 inches. Also, clear all existing tabs and set one tab at 0.75.
5. If the notice doesn't look like Figure 9-5, keep changing the tab and hanging-indent values until the spacing looks right (but keep the tab and hanging-indent values the same numerical value). While this caution notice alerts you to potential damage to hoses, you could certainly argue that it should be a warning or danger if physical injury is involved.

Warning notices. The warning notice needs to be more immediately noticeable and indicate a higher level of severity than the caution notice. For the warning notice, bold the label "Warning" and use the steps and format shown previously for the caution notice. The warning in Figure 9-6

Warning Notice

The term *hypoxia*, or oxygen shortage, is used to refer to any situation in which tissue cells fail to receive or are unable to obtain enough oxygen to maintain their normal function.

Warning: There is no natural warning that alerts the diver to the onset of hypoxia.

FIGURE 9-6

alerts readers to a situation that could cause injury, but not immediate, serious, or fatal injury.

Danger notices.   The danger notice is a good spot for borders. As you can see in Figure 9-7, the border and the all-bold text make it the most visually prominent. Normally, avoid using special effects such as italics, bold, all-caps, or color for extended text like this. Because it alerts readers to the potential for serious injury, however, the danger notice must be immediately and unavoidably noticeable. Use the following steps to create a border:

1. Type the label and text of the notice, highlight it, and then bold it.
2. With the text still highlighted, add the border using the following steps:
   - In Corel WordPerfect, choose **Paragraph→Border/Fill**, choose the style of border you want, and then click the Advanced tab to adjust the spacing.
   - In Lotus Word Pro, choose **Text→Text Properties**, select the Color and line style tab, select the type of border you want, and click Distance from text to adjust the spacing.
   - In Microsoft Word, choose **Format→Borders and Shading**. Under Settings, click **Box**. To widen the distance between the borders and the text, click **Options** and then set the margins to around 18 points.

Bold, italics, alternate fonts, hanging indents, and borders enable you to create visually prominent notices that indicate increasing levels of severity. When you design your own notices, there are some design problems to avoid:

Danger Notice
The most widely used underwater welding process is shielded metal-arc welding. The weld is produced by creating an electric arc between a flux-covered metal electrode and the work piece.

> **DANGER**
> **Take the required precautions when using underwater cutting or welding tools. Failure to do so may cause serious injury or death.**

Explosives
A variety of explosives are used for the removal of subsurface structures, stumps, or wrecks.

FIGURE 9-7

- Avoid using all-bold, all-italics, all-underscore, all-caps, or other such effects for the text. People don't want to read something that is screaming at them!
- For the text of notices, use a type size no larger than the body font. The special format is enough—the larger type size is overkill.
- Use larger type sizes for notice labels, but make it no larger than the type size of the smallest heading in your document.

Creating Notices: Web Pages

To design notices for Web pages, use HTML tags carefully so that your notices are increasingly *noticeable* from less to more critical ones.

Simple notes.   Figure 9-8 shows you the HTML for a simple *note*. If you have warning, caution, and danger notices in the same document, it is *not* a good idea to put a border around a simple note. However, this technique is shown in the following sections.

Caution notices.   If you use the simple or indented designs for the note-type notice, illustrated in Figure 9-8, you may want to use the design found in Figure 9-9 for the caution notice. As you can see, this HTML tagging creates a two-cell table in which the border is hidden. If you want the

Simple Notes

If the numeric keypad is enabled, press and hold **Shift** to temporarily use the cursor- and screen-control keys.

Note: The functions of the cursor- and screen-control keys the keys.

If the numeric keypad is enabled, press and hold **Shift** cursor- and screen-control keys.

Note: The functions of the cursor- and screen-c printed on the keys.

```
Simple Notes
If the numeric keypad is enabled, press and hold
<B>Shift</B> to temporarily use the cursor- and
screen-control keys.
<P>
<I>Note:</I> The functions of the cursor- and
screen-control keys are not printed on the keys.
<P>
<HR>
<P>
If the numeric keypad is enabled, press and hold
<B>Shift</B> to temporarily use the cursor- and
screen-control keys.
<P>
<BLOCKQUOTE>
<I>Note:</I> The functions of the cursor- and
screen-control keys are not printed on the keys.
</BLOCKQUOTE>
<P>
```

FIGURE 9-8
Creating simple notes in HTML.

Caution Notices

Begin the installation process by removing the cover from your computer.

Caution:

The discharge of static electricity can damage elec discharge by touching a grounded metal object suc before and during installation of any hardware ins wearing a grounding strap connected to ground.

```
Caution Notices
Begin the installation process by removing the
cover from your computer.
<P>
<TABLE BORDER=0 CELLPADDING=5 WIDTH="70%">
<TR>
<TD VALIGN="top"><B>Caution:</B></TD></TR>
<TR>
<TD>The discharge of static electricity can damage
electronic circuits. Avoid static discharge by
touching a grounded metal object such as your
computer's casing before and during installation of
any hardware inside your computer or by wearing
a grounding strap connected to ground.</TD>
</TR>
</TABLE>
```

FIGURE 9-9
Creating caution notices in HTML.

border to show, just change BORDER=0 to BORDER=1. However, to keep your notices visually distinct, you may want to reserve borders for a higher level of severity.

Warning notices. For a notice that is still more severe, such as a warning, you might want to use the design in Figure 9-10. There are two important differences in this warning-notice design compared to the caution-notice design: the borders show, and the hanging-indent format is used. Notice how a table within a table is used to force the warning label to the left and the warning text to the right without displaying the vertical grid line. This makes the warning notice visually more prominent than the caution notice.

Danger notices. Because it is the most severe, the danger notice requires the highest visual prominence. Even so, avoid using bold, italics, underscores, all caps, or color for the entire text of *any* notice—danger or otherwise. The danger-notice design shown in Figure 9-11, however, breaks this rule. It does so because the other notice designs have used up the other formats and because the text of the danger notice is not lengthy. With Web pages, however, you can readily use color to differentiate between types of notices.

Actually, the danger notice illustrated here uses several tricks to make it the most visually prominent. Not only is a border used, but a thicker border style is specified by BORDER=2. Greater spacing between the border and the text is specified by CELLPADDING=10. Different font, size,

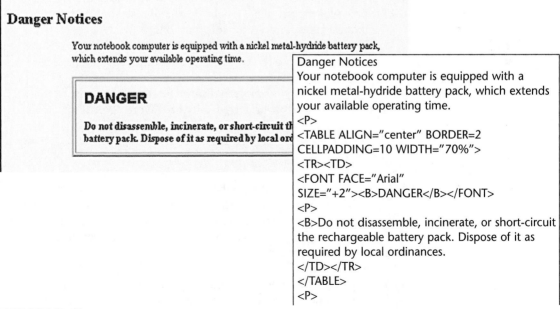

Warning Notices

Begin the installation process by removing the cover from your computer.

Warning	When you open your computer, be careful of any sharp object that may be inside.

Warning Notices
Begin the installation process by removing the cover from your computer.
<P>
<TABLE BORDER=1 CELLPADDING=0 WIDTH="70%">
<TR><TD>
<TABLE ALIGN="center" BORDER=0 CELLPADDING=5>
<TR>
<TD VALIGN="top"
WIDTH="20%"><B>Warning</B></TD>
<TD>When you open your computer, be careful of any sharp object that may be inside.</TD>
</TR>
</TABLE>
</TD></TR>
</TABLE>
<P>

FIGURE 9-10
Creating warning notices in HTML.

Danger Notices

Your notebook computer is equipped with a nickel metal-hydride battery pack, which extends your available operating time.

DANGER

Do not disassemble, incinerate, or short-circuit the battery pack. Dispose of it as required by local ordinances.

Danger Notices
Your notebook computer is equipped with a nickel metal-hydride battery pack, which extends your available operating time.
<P>
<TABLE ALIGN="center" BORDER=2 CELLPADDING=10 WIDTH="70%">
<TR><TD>
<FONT FACE="Arial"
SIZE="+2"><B>DANGER</B></FONT>
<P>
<B>Do not disassemble, incinerate, or short-circuit the rechargeable battery pack. Dispose of it as required by local ordinances.
</TD></TR>
</TABLE>
<P>

FIGURE 9-11
Creating danger notices in HTML.

and color are specified for the danger label by <FONT FACE="Arial" SIZE="+2" COLOR="red">.

WORKSHOP: NOTICES

Here are some additional ideas for practicing the concepts, tools, and strategies in this chapter.

1. *Make an inventory of notices.* Explore as many examples of instructions as you can, and catalog the types of notices you see. For each type you find (note, warning, caution, danger, etc.), describe the situation for which it is used and the format that it uses. Photocopy one good example of each, label the types of information it includes (action, conditions, consequences, and recovery), and identify it according to type and situation.

2. *Create notices.* Using the guidelines in this chapter, write and format a notice for each of the following descriptions.
   a. Many of the operations described in this section have the potential to severely damage or permanently alter your musical instrument. Do not attempt these repairs if you have any doubt about your ability to perform a particular operation.
   b. The Overlook Cliff Trail is a wonderful place to hike and camp, but there are places and things on the trail that can be dangerous to visitors. Do not let your guard down. The trail runs through undeveloped wilderness. Please contact the forest service for the latest updates, rules, and visitor information.
   c. This script erases the partition on which it runs the test. It is used for testing purposes only. Use with great caution.

3. *Format notices in your preferred software.* Use the text in Exercise 2 to create notices in your preferred software (Word, WordPerfect, etc.).

4. *Create notices using HTML tags.* Use the text in Exercise 2 to set up notices for Web pages.

5. *Anticipate notices.* Consider the following descriptions of instructions. Using the types of notices recommended in Figure 9-1, make a list of the notices that you think these instructions would need. Identify not only the type, but also make notes on the actions, conditions, consequences, and recovery.
   a. How to change a baby's diaper
   b. How to unload and load film into a camera
   c. How to open a bottle of champagne
   d. How to install a new light switch
   e. How to unstop the kitchen sink

CHAPTER 10

Tables, Graphs, and Charts

EARTHQUAKES AND PLATE TECTONICS

On the World Wide Web, you'll find plenty of fine, beautifully illustrated information about earthquakes and plate tectonics:

About.com. Earthquakes and Plate Tectonics.
geography.about.com/education/geography/msub27.htm

University of Nevada–Reno. "About Earthquakes."
www.seismo.unr.edu/htdocs/abouteq.html

Rosanna L. Hamilton. "Earth's Interior & Plate Tectonics."
www.netvigator.tw/~geology/earth5/Earthint.htm

Donald L. Blanchard. "ABC's of Plate Tectonics."
webspinners.com/dlblanc/tectonic/ptABCs.shtml

U.S. Geological Survey. "This Dynamic Earth."
pubs.usgs.gov/publications/text/dynamic.html

Hawaii Natural History Association. "Plate Tectonics."
volcano.und.nodak.edu/vwdocs/vwlessons/plate_tectonics/introduction.html

Accessed January 19, 2001.

No doubt you've seen plenty of tables, graphs, and charts, but you may not have paid much attention to their design. This chapter provides you with some strategies for when to use these communication tools and how to design them. In addition, you will learn how to use common word-processing software to design tables, graphs, and charts and how to create these elements in HTML (for World Wide Web pages). You will also learn how to generate graphs and charts in Lotus 1-2-3 and Microsoft Excel and then paste them into documents or Web pages.

Note: A good writing project with which to combine tables, charts, and graphs is the recommendation report (Chapter 4). This type of report compares options, the key comparative details of which can be presented with tables, graphs, and charts.

WHAT ARE THEY?

Before getting into the strategies for when to use these tools and how to design them, make sure you know what they are:

- *Tables.* Tables are rows and columns of numbers, words, or symbols. They provide an efficient means of presenting comparative information about similar things—for example, cost, miles per gallon, horsepower, and other such details about three or four makes of automobiles. Readers can see the key comparisons more readily in tables than in paragraphs.
- *Graphs.* A graph shows changes in data over time. For example, in a graph showing variations in high temperature over the month, you'd see a line snaking up and down accordingly. You could use multiple lines to show temperature variations in different years for the same month.
- *Charts.* The most common types of charts are pie charts and bar charts. Others exist but you need a commercial arts degree to create them. A pie chart shows percentages of a whole: for example, who the leaders are in the market for minivan automobiles and how big each one's slice of pie is. A bar chart could show the same thing, with the length of each bar representing total sales.

WHEN TO USE WHICH?

Often, you can present the same information in a table, in a graph, and in a chart. Tables show the greatest amount of detail but require readers to study carefully to pick out the key trends or contrasts. Graphs and charts illustrate key trends or contrasts more dramatically, but sacrifice detail. To show the declining market share of Company A to the penny as opposed to the rising market share of Company B, use a table. Use a graph or chart to convey the magnitude of these declines and rises, although at the loss of the down-to-the-penny detail.

It's startling how many earthquakes are located worldwide per year—between 12,000 and 14,000. However, the magnitude and intensity, as measured on the Richter scale, is such that most don't make the front page of your local newspaper. The monster earthquakes, those 8.5 and higher, occur only 0.3 times per year—but that's certainly more than enough! Earthquakes measuring 8.0 to 8.4 are slightly more frequent at 1.1 occurrences per year. Any earthquake 8.0 or over is considered a "great" earthquake. "Major" earthquakes are those between 7.0 and 7.9. In the upper half of that range, 3.1 occur per year, while 15 occur in the 7.0 to 7.4 range. The frequency is considerably higher in the 6.5 to 6.9 range: an average of 56 per year, while 210 occur in the 6.0-6.4 range per year. See **www neic.cr.usgs.gov/neis/general/handouts/mag_ vs_int.html**, the U.S. Geological Survey's Web page on magnitude and intensity comparisons.

Notice how much text is needed to explain how many earthquakes occur on average per year in the different magnitude ranges.

In the tables version, the writer can provide more explanation. Notice that the writer refers readers to the table and gives them a start interpreting it. Because the writer doesn't refer to this table elsewhere in the document, numbering it is unnecessary.

It's startling how many earthquakes are located worldwide per year—between 12,000 and 14,000. However, the magnitude and intensity, as measured on the Richter scale, is such that most don't make the front page of your local newspaper. As the following table shows, the monster earthquakes, those 8.5 and higher, occur only 0.3 times per year—but that's certainly more than enough! As the magnitude decreases, the average per year increases. Earthquakes 8.0 and above are referred to as "great" earthquakes; those in the 7.0-7.9 range are referred to as "major" earthquakes. See the U.S. Geological Survey's Web page on magnitude and intensity comparisons at: **wwwneic.cr.usgs.gov/ neis/general/handouts/mag_vs_int.html**.

Earthquakes Worldwide per Year

Magnitude	EQ/year
8.5 – 8.9	0.3
8.0 – 8.4	1.1
7.5 – 7.9	3.1
7.0 – 7.4	15
6.5 – 6.9	56
6.0 – 6.4	210

FIGURE 10-1
Converting text to tables. Readers can see the details much faster; the writer spends less time tediously explaining statistics.

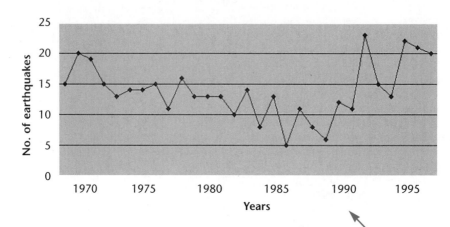

Major Earthquakes: 1969–1997

Major Earthquakes: 1969–1997

Year	EQs	Year	EQs
1969	15	1984	08
1970	20	1985	13
1971	19	1986	05
1972	15	1987	11
1973	13	1988	08
1974	14	1989	06
1975	14	1990	12
1976	15	1991	11
1977	11	1992	23
1978	16	1993	15
1979	13	1994	13
1980	13	1995	22
1981	13	1996	21
1982	10	1997	20
1983	14		

Create this line graph by copying the column for the earthquake totals into a spreadsheet like Lotus 123 or Microsoft Excel. In Excel, select the column of numbers, click **Insert→Chart**, select **Line** as the chart type then **Columns**, fill in the title for the chart and the labels for X- and Y-axes, and then click **Finish**. (Excel is not cooperative in modifying the numbers on the axes; the 5-year intervals on the X-axis above are a textbox overlaid on the graph.)

FIGURE 10-2

Converting a table to graph. It's easier for readers to get the exact numbers from a table, but easier to spot highs, lows, and trends in a line graph. (Note how the definition of "major" earthquake is included in the title for the graph.)

- *Text as opposed to a table?* Writers pass up many good opportunities to use tables. Instead, the information, which could be presented in a table, remains in a dense paragraph that some readers are reluctant to read. See the example in Figure 10-1.
- *Table as opposed to a chart or graph?* Just as commonly, data remains locked in dense tables when it could be more dramatically presented in graphs or charts. Figure 10-2 shows how a table can be converted to graph.

HOW DO YOU DESIGN TABLES, GRAPHS, AND CHARTS?

If you've read the preceding sections on when to use tables, graphs, and charts, consider now how to design them. The following gives you the basic terminology to refer to the different parts of tables, graphs, and charts as well as the basic design requirements, irrespective of the tools you use to create them.

Designing Tables

Here are some of the common guidelines to keep in mind as you create and edit tables (see Figure 10-3 for definitions of the parts of a table):

- *Double-check your text for information that could be presented as tables.* If you haven't used tables before, watch for instances where you can either convert the presentation into a table or represent the information as a table.

Table title: The title is the first row of the table and "spans" all four columns.

Column subheadings: The main column, "Estimated Annual Rate of Earthquakes," is divided into three subcolumns, one each of the three Richter-scale ranges.

Row subheadings: "Bakun" and "HERP+CNSS" are the two sources used to calculate the average annual rates here.

Historical Rates of Earthquakes			
Catalog Data and Time Interval	*Estimated Annual Rate of Earthquakes*		
	M>=6.7	**M**>=7	6<=**M**<=6.7p
Bakun, 1999			
1850–1905	0.060	0.032	0.195
1850–1877	0.040	0.021	0.13
1878–1905	0.080	0.043	0.26
HERP + CNSS Declustered Catalog			
1942–1949	0.015	0.0083	0.044
1950–1959	0.013	0.0073	0.039
1960–1969	0.011	0.0059	0.031
1970–1979	0.013	0.007	0.037
1980–1989	0.017	0.0093	0.049
1990–1998	0.016	0.0087	0.046

Alignment: Right-, or decimal-aligned numerical data. Notice the items are not centered in relation to each other.

FIGURE 10-3

Components of a table. This complex table shows you almost all of the components—title, column and row headings, column and row subheadings, and of course the actual columns and rows of data. *Source:* U.S. Geological Survey. "Earthquake Probabilities in the San Francisco Bay Region: 2000 to 2030—A Summary of Findings." geopubs.wr.usgs.gov/open-file/of99-517. Accessed January 18, 2001.

■ *Include titles for tables.* For all but the simplest tables, create a title. Center the title either in the first row of the table or just above the first row. Cite the source of any information you borrow to create the table.

■ *Use bold or italics for the title, column headings, and row headings.* Highlighting for table titles, column headings, and row headings varies widely. In a small table, using bold for all three elements is too much. Instead, try bold for the table title and italics for the column and row headings.

■ *Design for horizontal comparison.* Imagine that you have three products to compare in three categories (cost, reliability, and ease of use). Standard table-design wisdom says to make the products the row headings and the categories of comparison the column headings. That way, to compare costs of the three products, readers look down rather than across.

■ *Align columns according to the material in the cells.* Left-align columns containing text material; right-align columns containing numerical materials; left-align cells containing a mix of textual and numerical material.

■ *Left-align or center columns with column headings.* Center column headings within their cells. If the column heading is roughly the length of the material in the column, left-align the column heading with the column. If the column heading is significantly longer than the items in the column, center the items in the column in relation to the column heading.

■ *Specify measurements in the column or row headings.* Instead of specifying a measurement (inches, pounds, millimeters) in each cell, put the measurement or its abbreviation in the column heading. (Figure 10-3 puts "M" for magnitude in the column headings rather than in each data cell.)

■ *Explain key points of the table in Figure 10-3.* Refer to tables in nearby text and give readers some idea as to their significance. For example, say something like, "As you can see in Table 4, Product A is less expensive but is also less reliable."

■ *Create subcolumns and subrows as needed.* If Company A has Models 1, 2, and 3 and Company B has Models X, Y, and Z, create two main rows for the companies and subrows for their respective products. Similarly, for a main category called Performance and two subcategories called City and Highway, create columns and subcolumns. See Figure 10-3 for illustrations of the format of subcolumns and subrows.

Designing Graphs and Charts

Here are some of the common guidelines to keep in mind as you create and edit graphs and charts:

■ *Double-check text and tables for possibilities to represent them as graphs.* Check the tables you include in your technical documents:

would the dramatic effect of a graph or chart be better than the detail of a table?

■ *Include titles for graphs.* Create a descriptive title for your graph or chart, and position it just below the graph or chart. Remember to cite the source of the information you borrow for graphs and charts.

■ *Label the axes of graphs.* For the typical graph, the left edge is one axis and the bottom edge is the other axis. For a graph of sales over a five-year period, you'd label the vertical axis something like "Total Sales (millions U.S. dollars)." For the horizontal axis, you'd mark off each of the years and label each mark with the appropriate year. No need to label for this axis—the year numbers make that obvious.

■ *Label the graph lines or provide a legend.* For the sales graph, you could label the individual graph lines, or you could include a legend. In a graph, a *legend* is a key telling readers what the different color, textures, or shadings represent.

■ *Discuss the key points in the graph in Figure 10-4.* Refer to graphs and charts in text just preceding them, and comment on the key points in those graphs.

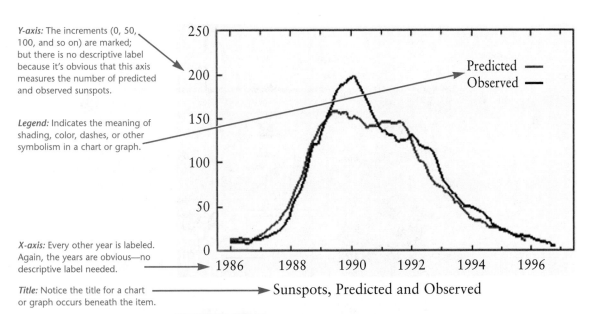

FIGURE 10-4

Components of a graph or chart. In this example, you see the X-axis label, Y-axis label, legend, and title. If the meanings of the two axes were not obvious, descriptive labels would be included (for example, "No. of sunspots" and "Year"). *Source:* National Oceanic and Atmospheric, "Geosynchronous Operational Environmental Satellites (GOES) Stuff to Look For." spidr.ngdc.noaa.gov:8080/production/html/GOES/goeslook.html

HOW DO YOU CREATE TABLES, GRAPHS, AND CHARTS?

The following shows you some techniques for creating tables, graphs, and charts in common word-processing and spreadsheet software as well as in HTML.

Creating Tables

Here's a quick introduction to creating tables in Corel WordPerfect, Lotus Word Pro, and Microsoft Word.

Creating Tables: Common Word-Processing Software. To create a table, follow these steps:

1. To start a table:
   - In Corel WordPerfect, choose **Insert→Tables**.
   - In Lotus Word Pro 9 (see Figure 10-5), choose **Create→Table**.
   - In Microsoft Word, choose **Table→Insert Table**.
2. Specify the number of rows and columns you need, and then press Enter or **OK**. (No need to be exact; you can modify later.)
3. Enter your information into the cells of the table, using the suggestions discussed previously. In particular, consider using bold or italics for the column and row headings.

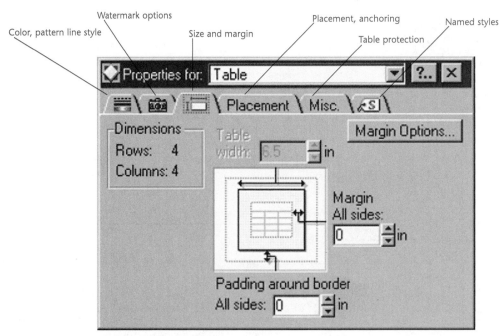

FIGURE 10-5
Table formatting in Lotus Word Pro. Click **Table→Table Properties** to get to this dialog.

4. Most tables require some fine-tuning; here are some of the most common:

- *Resizing columns or the entire table.* To change the size of certain columns or the entire table, move the mouse pointer over one of the vertical grid lines of the column you want to change, and then drag it to the position you want.
- *Changing the alignment of the table with nearby text.* To align the table to a preceding paragraph:
  - In Corel WordPerfect, move the cursor inside the table, right-click the mouse, select **Table Tools→Format**, and use the Column and Row tabs.
  - In Lotus Word Pro, choose **Tables→Table Properties**. Select the Size and margin tabs, click **Margin Options**, and make the changes you want.
  - In Microsoft Word, choose **Tables→Select Table**, then choose **Tables→Cell Height and Width**, select the Row tab, and change Indent from left.
    - *Aligning columns.* By default, text is usually jammed to the left edge of cells. Remember that *text* columns should be left-aligned, and *numerical* columns should be right-aligned. To right-align items in a column:
      — In Corel WordPerfect (see Figure 10-6), select the column, right-click the mouse, select **Table Tools→Format**, select the

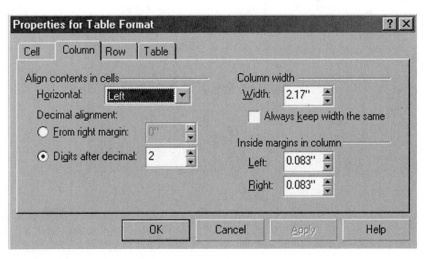

FIGURE 10-6

Table tools in Corel WordPerfect. To access the Tools dialog box, start a table, right-click, and select **Table Tools**. To access the Properties dialog box, click **Format**.

FIGURE 10-7

Table control tools in Microsoft Word. These options become available when the cursor is located in a table.

Column tab and select **Center** in the Align contents in cells field. To move items in a column more to the middle of the column, select **Table Tools→Format**, select the Column tab, and then change the Inside margins in column field as necessary.

— In Lotus Word Pro, move the mouse pointer into the column, select **Table→Select→Column Contents**. Then select **Text→Alignment→Center**. To move items in a column more to the middle of the column, select the column, select **Table→Size Row/Column**, and then change the left margin as necessary.

— In Microsoft Word, move the mouse pointer into the column, choose **Tables→Select Column**, choose **Format→ Paragraph**, and then change Indentation to **Right.** To move items in a column more to the middle of the column, select the column, select **Format→Paragraph**, and then change the left or right margin (for example, to 0.25 inches).

▪ *Adding rows and columns.* If you must insert a row or column:

— In Corel WordPerfect, right-click inside the table, select **Insert,** and fill out the Insert Columns/Rows dialog. To add a row at the bottom, move the cursor to the last cell and press the Tab key.

— In Lotus Word Pro, click **Table→Insert→Row** or **Column**. To add a row at the bottom, move the cursor to the last cell and press the Tab key.

— In Microsoft Word (see Figure 10-7), click **Table→Insert Row** to insert a blank row *above* your cursor location. To add a row at the bottom, move the cursor to the last cell and press the Tab key. To add a column, select the column at which you want the new column to occur and then click **Tables→Split Cells**.

■ *Joining and splitting cells.* To create a title for a table, use one row that spans all the columns. To create such a row, you combine all the cells of that row:

— In Corel WordPerfect, select the entire row, right-click the mouse, and select **Join Cells**.

— In Lotus Word Pro, select the entire row, and click **Table→ Connect Rows**.

— In Microsoft Word, select the entire row, and click **Tables→ Merge Cells**.

To split one or more cells:

— In Corel WordPerfect, right-click the mouse, and select **Split Cell**.

— In Lotus Word Pro, select each cell you want to split and click **Table→Split Cell**.

— In Microsoft Word, select each cell to split and click **Tables→Split Cells**.

■ *Formatting text within cells.* You can change font, type sizes, bold, italics, and other such features within cells just as you would any other text. For example, to change the type size to 9, select the entire table, click **Font Size** in Microsoft Word, and select **9**.

Creating Tables: Spreadsheet Software. While some word-processing software like WordPerfect, Word Pro, and Word enable you to perform calculations within tables, spreadsheet software like Lotus 1-2-3 and Microsoft Excel is much better suited. Enter data, calculate, and then copy or link the table into a document:

1. Open 1-2-3 or Excel, and enter the data shown in Figure 10-8. (See the Help functions in Lotus or Excel for how to calculate the totals column and row.) Select it all by holding down the Shift key and using the arrow keys.

2. Copy the range by pressing Ctrl+Insert (or select **Edit→Copy**; or press the right mouse button and click **Copy**).

3. Move to the line in the document into which you want to insert the data, and press **Edit→Paste**. If you are inserting the cells from 1-2-3 or Excel into Word, you will probably have a table whose grid lines are hidden.

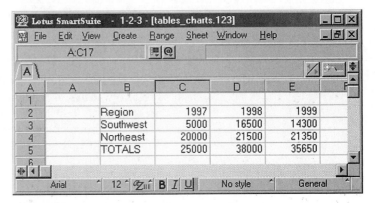

FIGURE 10-8
Data for Spreadsheet.

Creating Tables: Web Pages. Creating tables with HTML may seem like a nightmare at first. The following explanations show you how to create a table in a Web page:

- *Setting up a table (Figure 10-9).* Put <TABLE BORDER="1" WIDTH= "80%" ALIGN="center"> at the very top of the table and </TABLE> at the very bottom. If you specify 0 as the table border, the grid lines will not show. WIDTH specifies that the table uses 80% of the horizontal browser space; ALIGN specifies that the table will occur in the center of that space.
- *Specifying rows and cells.* Each row of a table starts with <TR> and ends with </TR>. Each cell in a table begins with <TD> and ends with </TD>. You build tables row by row. Don't forget: you must have the same number of cells for each table row!
- *Adjusting column widths.* Adjust the width of a column by specifying the width for *each* cell in that column: for example, <TD WIDTH= "15%">. (Otherwise, the Web browser tries to even out the column widths.)
- *Aligning text within columns.* To right-align text, specify <TD ALIGN= "right"> in each cell of that column ("center" is another option). To force text to the top of a cell, specify <TD VALIGN="top">, with "middle" and "bottom" being the other options.
- *Spanning columns and rows.* To create a table title cell, use the COLSPAN tag. For a four-column table, you'd specify <TD COLSPAN="4"> Table 1: Regional Sales</TD>. The ROWSPAN tag works the same way for rows.
- *Formatting text within cells.* Make text bold, italics, different colors, or different fonts just as you would any regular text.

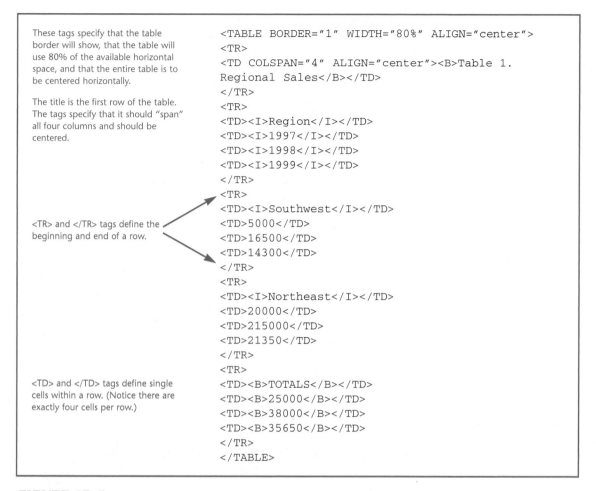

These tags specify that the table border will show, that the table will use 80% of the available horizontal space, and that the entire table is to be centered horizontally.

The title is the first row of the table. The tags specify that it should "span" all four columns and should be centered.

<TR> and </TR> tags define the beginning and end of a row.

<TD> and </TD> tags define single cells within a row. (Notice there are exactly four cells per row.)

```
<TABLE BORDER="1" WIDTH="80%" ALIGN="center">
<TR>
<TD COLSPAN="4" ALIGN="center"><B>Table 1.
Regional Sales</B></TD>
</TR>
<TR>
<TD><I>Region</I></TD>
<TD><I>1997</I></TD>
<TD><I>1998</I></TD>
<TD><I>1999</I></TD>
</TR>
<TR>
<TD><I>Southwest</I></TD>
<TD>5000</TD>
<TD>16500</TD>
<TD>14300</TD>
</TR>
<TR>
<TD><I>Northeast</I></TD>
<TD>20000</TD>
<TD>215000</TD>
<TD>21350</TD>
</TR>
<TR>
<TD><B>TOTALS</B></TD>
<TD><B>25000</B></TD>
<TD><B>38000</B></TD>
<TD><B>35650</B></TD>
</TR>
</TABLE>
```

FIGURE 10-9

Complete HTML tagging for the regional sales table. The <B> and </B> tags bold the text they enclose; the <I> and </I> tags italicize the text they enclose.

There are plenty of other table-formatting techniques that are not covered here. On the World Wide Web, you can find some excellent resources for designing tables, such as the following:

■ Tech Corps. "webTeacher." **www.webteacher.org/winnet/indextc.html**
■ Webmonkeys. "Tables." **hotwired.lycos.com/webmonkey/authoring/tables**
■ Web Developer's Virtual Library: **www.wdvl.com/Authoring/HTML/ Tutorial/basic_tables.html**
■ Gorin & Cook, Inc. "HTML Table Tags." **www.gorin.com/class/ classtable.html**

Creating Graphs and Charts

The following shows how to create graphs and charts in Lotus 1-2-3 and Microsoft Excel and how to copy them into print documents or convert them for Web pages.

Creating Graphs and Charts: Common Spreadsheet Software. Graphs provide a more visually dramatic view of changes in data over time. If you want to show how Company B is taking a nosedive compared to Company A, a graph will show that comparison far more dramatically.

1. Open Lotus 1-2-3 or Microsoft Excel and enter the data shown in Figure 10-10. Entering data into a spreadsheet is fairly easy: use arrow keys, the Tab key, or the mouse to move to the cell and enter data.
2. When you've entered this data, select it and then click **Create→Chart** in 1-2-3 or **Insert→Chart** in Excel. Both applications provide an "assistant" or "wizard" to guide you (see Figure 10-11). In Lotus 1-2-3, insert the chart and then right-click within it to change the type, format, or other properties. In Excel, take a look at all the types you have to choose from. Select **Column** and the chart sub-type as shown in Figure 10-11, and then click **Next**.
3. In Lotus 1-2-3, you can click on items like **Title**, and enter the titles and labels you want (see Figure 10-12). In Excel, the wizard prompts you for these items.
4. To copy this chart into a document, make sure the chart is selected, and then choose **Edit→Select** (or click the right mouse button and click **Copy**).

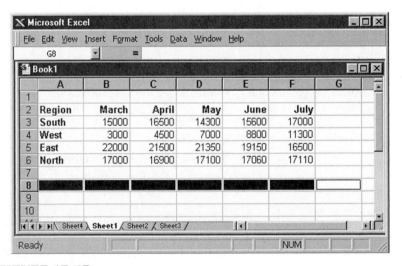

FIGURE 10-10

Entering data in Microsoft Excel for a graph or chart.

5. Move to the document into which you want to place the chart, position the cursor at the point in the text where you want the chart, and choose **Edit→Paste**.

With this introduction, you'll be able to figure out how to create other charts. But just to be sure, use the same data to create these charts:

- *Line graph* (Figure 10-13): In 1-2-3, right-click in the chart and select **Chart Type** and select **Line**. In Excel, click **Insert→Chart** and select **Line**. From this point, the process is the same as when you created the column chart.
- *Pie charts* (Figure 10-14): In pie charts, percentages of a whole are expressed in wedges of a circle. To create a pie chart for the month of March in 1-2-3, select the March column; click **Create→Chart**; paste the initial chart; right-click within it and select **Chart Type→Pie**. In Excel, click **Insert→Chart** and select **Pie**.

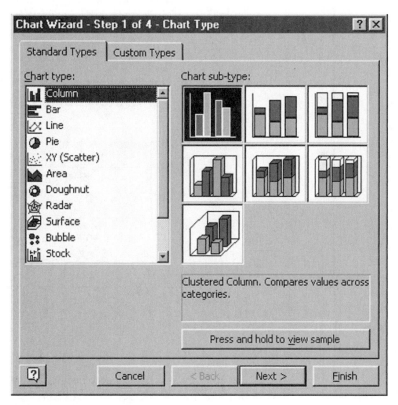

FIGURE 10-11
Microsoft Excel Chart Wizard.

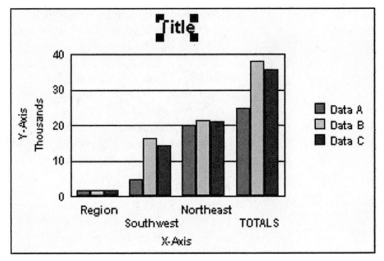

FIGURE 10-12

Lotus 1-2-3 enables you to click on any text item and change it. In this illustration, "Title" is selected; all you have to do is type the text you want in its place.

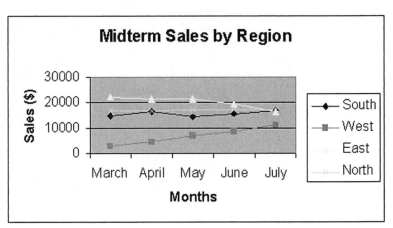

FIGURE 10-13

Line graph.

Although you may need plenty of refinements and special features, this introduction should get you started.

Creating Charts and Graphs: Web Pages.   As of the year 2000, Web page development tools lack "wizards" for creating charts and graphs. Try these steps, though:

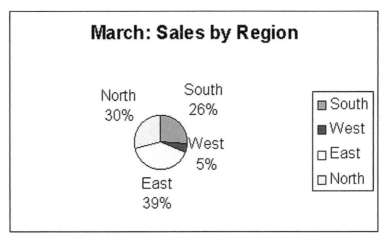

FIGURE 10-14
Pie chart.

1. Create the graph or chart in a software application like Lotus or Excel. While still in the software application, select the graph or chart and then copy it. (Or make a screen capture—in Windows, press Alt+PrtScr.)
2. Paste the copied graph or chart into an application like PaintShop Pro. Size or crop the image as necessary, and save the image as a GIF or JPG file. (For further details, see Chapter 11.)
3. To display the graph on a Web page, use `<IMG SRC="image.gif">` (replacing `image` with the name of your graph or chart file). For more on Web pages, see Chapter 17.

WORKSHOP: TABLES, GRAPHS, AND CHARTS

Here are some additional ideas for practicing the concepts, tools, and strategies in this chapter:

1. *Simple table.* Using your preferred software, create a simple, informal table (with table title, source, and column headings) from the following data:

```
Column headings should be year, month, day, time (GMT),
latitude (north), longitude (west), magnitude, loca-
tion. 1995, 2, 19, 403, 40 37.00, 125 54.00, 6.6, W.
of Eureka; 1995, 9, 20, 2327, 35 46.00, 117 38.00, 5.5,
Ridgecrest; 1996, 7, 24, 2016, 41 47.04, 125 54.66,
5.7, W. of Eureka; 1997, 1, 22, 717, 40 16.32, 124
23.64, 5.7, Punta Gorda; 1999, 8, 1, 1606, 37 23.40,
117 4.80, 5.7, Scotty's Junction, Nevada; 1999, 10, 16,
```

947, 34 35.64, 116 16.26, 7.1, Hector Mine; 2000, 3, 16, 1520, 40 23.16, 125 16.74, 5.9, Mendocino Fracture Zone. (Title "California Earthquake History 1769 Present." URL: **pasadena.wr.usgs.gov**; last updated 05/04/00; visited 05/31/00; source: Ellsworth, William L., "Earthquake History, 1769-1989" in USGS Professional Paper 1515, Robert E. Wallace, ed.,1990; William Ellsworth, personal communication; and USGS earthquake catalogs; maintained by Lisa Wald.)

2. *Text to table.* Study the following text and convert the comparative data to a table; use other text as introduction to the table. Include table title and column headings, as well as a source citation:

Magnitude measures the energy released at the source of the earthquake. Magnitude is determined from measurements on seismographs. The following table gives intensities that are typically observed at locations near the epicenter of earthquakes of different magnitudes. Earthquakes with a magnitude ranging from 1.0 - 3.0 are generally not felt except by a very few under especially favorable conditions. Earthquakes with a magnitude ranging from 3.0 - 3.9 are felt only by a few persons at rest, in a few cases quite noticeably, especially on upper floors of buildings. Many people do not recognize it as an earthquake. Standing motor cars may rock slightly. Vibrations are similar to those of passing a truck. Earthquakes with a magnitude ranging from 4.0 - 4.9 are felt indoors by many, outdoors only by few during the day. At night, some are awakened. Dishes, windows, and doors are disturbed; walls make cracking sounds. Standing motor cars rock noticeably. Closer to 4.9, earthquakes are felt by nearly everyone; many are awakened; some dishes and windows are broken; unstable objects are overturned. Earthquakes with a magnitude ranging from 5.0 - 5.9 are felt by all; many are frightened. Some heavy furniture is moved, but damage is slight. Closer to 5.9, damage is negligible in buildings of good design and construction; slight to moderate in well-built ordinary structures; considerable in poorly built or badly designed structures. Earthquakes with a magnitude ranging from 6.0 - 6.9 result in slight damage to specially designed structures; considerable damage in ordinary substantial buildings with partial collapse; and great damage in poorly built structures. Chimneys, factory stacks, columns, monuments, and walls collapse. Heavy furniture overturned. Closer to 6.9, damage is considerable even in specially designed structures; well-designed frame structures thrown out of plumb. Damage great in substantial buildings, with partial collapse and buildings shifted off foundations. In earthquakes with a magnitude of 7.0 and higher, even well-built wooden structures are destroyed; most masonry and frame structures are destroyed with foundations; few if any structures remain standing. Bridges are destroyed; rails bent greatly. Damage is total; objects thrown into the air. ("Magnitude/Intensity Comparison." URL: **wwwneic.cr.usgs.gov**. Last updated: May 12, 2000; visited: May 31, 2000. Maintained by M. Zirbes.)

3. *Simple Web-page tables.* Using the data in exercise 1, create a table for a Web page with HTML tags.

4. *Complex Web-page tables.* Using the data in exercise 2, create a table for a Web page with HTML tags.

5. *Graphs.* Using your preferred software, create a line graph from the following data and paste it into a document (such as a report):

Major earthquakes (7.0-7.9 on the Richter scale) by year: 1969 – 15; 1970 – 20; 1971 – 19; 1972 – 15; 1973 – 13; 1974 – 14; 1975 – 14; 1976 – 15; 1977 – 11; 1978 – 16; 1979 – 13; 1980 – 13; 1981 – 13; 1982 – 10; 1983 – 14; 1984 – 08; 1985 – 13; 1986 – 05; 1987 – 11; 1988 – 08; 1989 – 06; 1990 – 12; 1991 – 11; 1992 – 23; 1993 – 15; 1994 – 13; 1995 – 22; 1996 – 21; 1997 – 20. (Title: "Are Earthquakes Really on the Increase?" URL: **wwwneic. cr.usgs.gov/neis/general/handouts/increase_in_earthquakes.html**; visited May 31, 2000; last updated May 12, 2000. Maintained by M. Zirbes.)

6. *Bar charts.* Using your preferred software, create a bar chart from the following data and paste it into a document (such as a report):

Estimated deaths per year worldwide from earthquakes 6.0 to 9.9 (Richter scale): 1980 – 8620; 1981 – 5223; 1982 – 3328; 1983 – 2372; 1984 – 174; 1985 – 9846; 1986 – 1068; 1987 – 1080; 1988 – 26552; 1989 – 617. Try including the total number of 6.0-9.9 earthquakes for the same 1980 to 1989 period, respectively: 119, 103, 95, 140, 99, 124, 94, 123, 101, 86. (Title: "Earthquake

Facts and Statistics." URL: **wwwneic.cr.usgs.gov/neis/eqlists/ graphs.html**; updated May 12, 2000; visited May 31, 2000. Maintained by M. Zirbes.)

7. *Pie charts.* Using your preferred software, create pie charts from the following data and paste it into a document (such as a report).

This series of three pie charts will show distribution of water on our planet Earth: 97% is in the oceans, while 3% is classified as "other." Of that 3% described as "other," 22% is ground water, 77% is in glaciers, icecaps, and inland seas, while 1% is classified as "other." Of that 1%, 61% is in lakes, 39% in atmospheric and soil moisture, while 0.4% is in rivers. Title of this pie chart is "Distribution of Water on Earth." (Title: "Earth's Water Distribution." URL: **ga.water.usgs.gov**. Last updated: February 3, 2000. Visited May 31, 2000.)

8. *Web-page graphs and charts.* Copy the bar chart, line graph, or pie chart that you created in one of the preceding exercises into a Web page. Using your preferred software, copy the chart or graph into a graphics application, or get a screen capture of it and then crop it with your preferred graphics application.

CHAPTER 11

Illustrative Graphics

FRACTALS: THE ULTIMATE GRAPHICS

However hard they are to define, fractals are graphics. (See an example of a fractal in Figure 11-1.) Here are some Web sites that focus on the nature and applications of fractals:

Fractal Microscope. Interactive tool designed by the Education Group at the National Center for Supercomputing Applications for exploring the Mandelbrot set and other fractal patterns:
www.ncsa.uiuc.edu/Edu/Fractal/Fractal_Home.html

About.com—Fractal Design & Metacreations. Judy Litt, guide.
graphicdesign.about.com/arts/graphicdesign/msubfd.htm

Noel Giffin. Fractint: fractal software and tutorials.
spanky.triumf.ca/www/fractint/fractint.html

Fractals As Art. Melisa Binde.
www.cs.swarthmore.edu/~binde/fractals/index.html

Yahoo! Fractals.
dir.yahoo.com/Arts/Visual_Arts/Computer_Generated/Fractals

Chaos and Fractals. Joakim Linde.
www.dd.chalmers.se/~gu94joli/caf.html

Fractal Bibliography. **www.ncsa.uiuc.edu/Edu/Fractal/Fbiblio.html**

Accessed January 19, 2001.

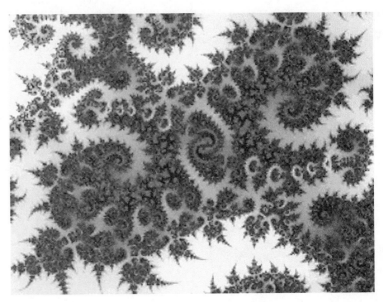

FIGURE 11-1

Fractal created by Noel Giffin. Located at **spanky.triumf.ca/www/fractint/ NOEL/NOEL.HTML**. Reprinted here with the author's permission.

This chapter shows you some techniques for finding or creating illustrative graphics and getting them into your technical documents. *Illustrative graphics* include things like drawings, photos, diagrams, schematics, flowcharts, and so on.

Note: Tables, bar and pie charts, and line graphs, which illustrate concepts and data rather than objects, are discussed in Chapter 10.

WHAT SHOULD BE ILLUSTRATED?

Before getting into details about creating and using graphics, stop a moment to think about what can be illustrated in technical documents:

- *Instructions:* Imagine providing instructions on grafting a fruit tree, performing CPR, setting up a VCR, or installing a ceiling fan. Illustrations are needed for the various components of the objects involved, the tools used to work on those objects, and the orientations between the objects and tools in the procedure. Locations of certain features on the objects—for example, the MIDI plug on the VCR—must be shown. Actions must also be illustrated; for example, VCR instructions may include an illustration of someone pushing a videocassette into the VCR.

■ *Technical background reports:* Imagine the illustrative graphics for reports on the Exxon Valdez oil spill, the causes and effects of El Niño, or new developments in solar automobiles. Maps combined with diagrams and drawings could show the flow of the oil spill or the formation of El Niño. Photographs of oil-spill effects on shorelines or photographs of several solar cars could be used. Drawings and diagrams could be used to illustrate the design of solar cars. Conceptual drawings combining maps, illustrative details such as clouds, rain, and sunshine, and indications of movement and cycle could be used to illustrate the process involved in El Niño or La Niña.

Certain key elements in technical documents need to be illustrated:

■ *Objects, parts and features of objects:* Obviously, objects (mechanisms, places, areas, things, stuff!) central to the discussion must be illustrated. In instructions for grafting, readers need to see the graft and the root stock. To make readers fully aware of the horror of an oil spill, include some photographs of the Valdez spill. To refer to the components of the VCR, include an illustration with each of those components labeled.
■ *Orientations, relationships:* Some illustrations, particularly for instructions, must show the position of things or people in relation to each other. In CPR instructions, show how to position your body in relation to the victim's body, where to apply pressure on the victim's chest, and so on.
■ *Actions, movements:* Some illustrations must also convey a sense of movement and direction. For example, an arrow indicating the direction that pressure needs to be applied or an arrow indicating the direction one object needs to be inserted into another may be part of your illustration.
■ *Concepts, ideas:* Graphics can also be used to illustrate concepts. For example, a company's organizational chart doesn't depict anything in the physical world; instead, it shows interrelationships of individuals and groups within the organization. The same is true of flowcharts, which can be used for a manufacturing process for example. When you explain a complex idea, look for ways to illustrate that idea conceptually or symbolically.

As you plan, write, and revise technical documents, look for opportunities to illustrate important objects, parts or features of objects, orientations and relationships, actions and movements, and concepts and ideas.

WHAT ARE THE TYPES OF ILLUSTRATIONS?

To keep it simple, let's define four types of illustrations (illustrated in Figures 11-2 through 11-5) based on the amount and kind of detail they contain:

FIGURE 11-2

Photographs. Homeowners considering "going solar" will want to know what those photovoltaic panels will look like on their roofs and what those batteries will look like on the side of their houses. (Pictured here are 32 Siemens SM55 solar panels and 24 Trojan L16 batteries.) *Source:* Texas Solar Power Company.

■ *Photographs (Figure 11-2):* Photographs contain the most illustrative detail, although for some technical contexts they have too much detail. For an oil spill report, photographs of wildlife victims along the shoreline are painfully dramatic. However, if you want to orient readers to the components of a photovoltaic system (shown in Figure 11-2), photographs provide too much detail, and the detail is often obscured by lack of contrast. Still, the photographs in Figure 11-2 give readers a nice visual sense of what a system would look like installed at their homes.

■ *Drawings (Figure 11-3):* For many technical contexts, drawings are the ideal type of illustration. Drawings suppress unnecessary detail and allow readers to focus on the important objects, tools, and actions. Drawings illustrate relationships and concepts that photographs simply cannot. For example, you've probably seen exploded and cutaway illustrations. You can also use drawings to show, for example, a cross-sectional view of a volcano or the movement of an oil spill.

■ *Flowcharts and other conceptual drawings (Figure 11-4):* Consider the classic organization chart: it illustrates relationships between people and subgroups within the organization; it also depicts the flow of information within the organization. Consider conceptual drawings: the classic illustration of hypertext shows squares ("nodes") with arrows connecting them in a spiderweb-like manner, introducing us to the concept of hypertext.

■ *Diagrams and schematics (Figure 11-5):* This final type of illustration removes so much detail that the object being illustrated is no longer recognizable. The classic example is the wiring schematic for an electronic appliance. Is that really your microwave oven?

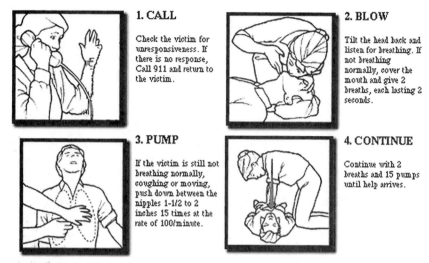

FIGURE 11-3

Examples of drawings. Simplified drawings in this case are better than fully detailed photographs. They clarify the critical actions, positions, and orientations. *Source:* Learn CPR: **www.learncpr.org**

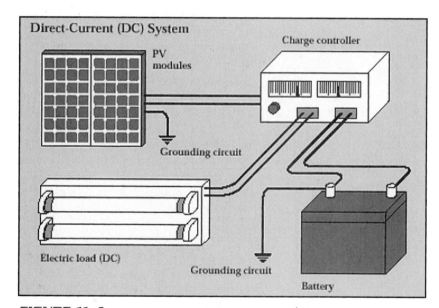

FIGURE 11-4

Example of a flowchart. This flowchart depicts the flow of solar energy and electricity through a photovoltaic system. The PV modules are typically located on a roof to gather solar energy. *Source:* U.S. Department of Energy. *Photovoltaics: Basic Design and Components*, DOE/GO-10097-377.

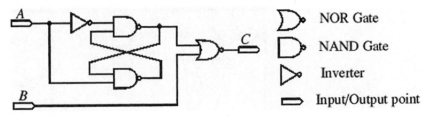

FIGURE 11-5

Example of a diagram. Notice how the graphic artist provides a "legend" here to define the meanings of the symbols used in the diagram.

HOW DO YOU FIND OR CREATE ILLUSTRATIONS?

You've seen some nice, professionally done illustrations in this chapter so far. But you are right to wonder: "How can I get such illustrations without hiring a commercial artist?" One solution is to get electronic copies of the illustrations you want. You can embed them electronically right into your documents rather than manually taping them into printouts. However, the old-fashioned cut-and-paste method is an option. This method is presented later in this chapter.

Finding illustrations. Search for your topic, just as you would search for textual information on that topic. (See Chapter 20 for strategies for information searching.)

Copying images from Web pages. When you find graphics on Web pages, you can copy them. Try this out:

1. To get a great picture of some potatoes, go to this Web page: **www.io. com/~hcexres/tcm1603/acchtml/instrxx4c.html**
2. Move your cursor on top of the image, press the right mouse button, and click **Save Image As** (in Netscape) or **Save Picture As** (Internet Explorer).
3. In the dialog box, rename the graphics file however you wish, and store it in a folder with a name you'll remember.
4. Make a note of the full Web address (URL), title, date of the Web page, author name (either individual or corporate), and date you copied the image. You'll need this for the source citation.

Skip to the section on formatting to see how to bring illustrations into a document.

Making screen captures. Another way to get illustrations into documents electronically is to make screen captures directly from your computer screen. Try this example:

1. Select a software application you often use, and open it to an area that might require some illustration—for example, the dialog box for a macro editor.

2. When you have the screen set up just the way you want it, you can do one of two things using the standard personal computer keyboard:
   - Press the Print Screen key on your keyboard. This captures what's displaying on the entire computer screen.
   - Press and hold the Alt key and press the Print Screen key. This captures the "active" window (the window in which your application is running).
3. You can now paste this captured image into a document or into a graphic application such as Jasc's PaintShop Pro (**www.jasc.com**) or Microsoft's Paint (available through **Start→Programs→Accessories→ Paint**).

You will probably want to crop (select a portion of) or size (reduce or enlarge) the image. These techniques are explained later in this chapter.

Using clip art. The Internet contains a wealth of clip art resources. Here are a few addresses of the many Web sites available:

- *Resources for Icons, Images, and Graphics.* Go to the site provided by Aphids Communications—**www.aphids.com/susan/imres**—for resources on finding or learning how to use graphics on Web pages, along with links to references, tools, and other image indexes.
- *Clipart.com.* Categorized site for links to clip art, fonts, photos, and Web graphics: **www.clipart.com**
- *Web Developer's Virtual Library. VL-WWW: Images_and_Icons:* **www. stars.com/Vlib/Providers/Images_and_Icons.htm**
- *Clip art Sources.* Go to **pauillac.inria.fr/~lang/hotlist/clipart** for links to dozens of clip art and icon resources, including tools to create or edit graphics.

These will get you started and will lead to many more. When you borrow clip art from the Internet, be sure to cite the source properly. You must cite the source of *any* borrowed information, including graphics.

Drawing your own illustrations. Although you may not be ready to draw complex images such as people, animals, vegetation, or machinery, you can indeed draw some things right now. Notice the hand-drawn illustration of the flashlight in the example at the end of Chapter 1.

HOW DO YOU FORMAT ILLUSTRATIONS?

Once you have an electronic copy of the illustration you want, the next steps involve editing and inserting it into a document and adding cross-references, titles, and source citations.

Cropping illustrations. When you *crop* an image, you select just a portion of it to show in your document. There are several ways to crop images. Follow these steps using Corel WordPerfect, Lotus WordPro, and Microsoft Word or a similar application:

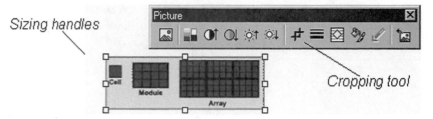

FIGURE 11-6

Cropping and sizing tools. Click on the cropping tool and then move the mouse pointer to one of the handles and crop.

1. Paste the image you want at the point in the text where you want it. (If you are using Paintshop Pro, paste the image into the workspace.)
2. With the image selected:
   - In Corel WordPerfect, see the helps for cropping images.
   - In Lotus Word Pro, click the right mouse button over the image, select **Bitmap Object→Crop**, and use the sizing handles to drag the edges of the image inward as necessary.
   - In Microsoft Word, click the right mouse button over the image, select **Show Picture Toolbar**. Select the cropping tool (shown in Figure 11-6), position the mouse pointer over any of the sizing handles on the image to drag the edges inward as necessary.
   - In Paintshop Pro, select the cropping tool (which looks the same as the one shown in Figure 11-6) and position the mouse pointer over any of the sizing handles on the image to drag the edges inward as necessary.

Sizing illustrations.   Sometimes, you may also need to size illustrations. *Sizing* an image means reducing or enlarging it. Changing the size of graphics can be a problem though. Bit-mapped images, which end with **.bmp,** cannot be sized: when you try to resize them, they blur and distort. You must convert these images to vector graphics. Select an image and then drag the sizing handles (see Figure 11-6) to get the image the size you want it

Labeling illustrations.   As with cropping images, you can either add labels to images within your word-processing software or add the labels separately in a graphics application such as PaintShop Pro. To add labels to a graphic in Corel WordPerfect, Lotus Word Pro, or Microsoft Word, follow these steps:

1. Scroll to the area in which you've displayed the graphic you want to label and then:
   - In Corel WordPerfect, select **Insert→Text Box**. Drag the text box to position it in relation to the graphic.
   - In Lotus Word Pro, select **Create→Frame** and position the frame (text box) where you want it.

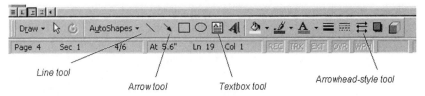

FIGURE 11-7

Drawing toolbar in Microsoft Word. When you are formatting and labelling graphics, display this toolbar to make your work easier.

- In Microsoft Word, display the Drawing toolbar by selecting **View→Toolbars→Drawing**. Click the textbox icon, and then create a textbox by dragging the mouse with the left mouse button held down. (See Figure 11-7 for locations of the icons and tools.)
2. Type some words in the textbox. For labels, try a type size 1 or 2 points smaller than regular body text (but *never* larger than body text). A nice design is to make labels the same font you use for headings. For example, if you use Arial for headings and 12-point Times New Roman for regular text, try 9- or 10-point Arial for labels.
3. To hide the border of the textbox, select the textbox, click the right mouse button, and then:
   - In Corel WordPerfect, select **Border/Fill** and select the appropriate icons.
   - In Lotus Word Pro, select **Frame Properties**, select the Color, select pattern line style tab, and select the appropriate icons.
   - In Microsoft Word, select **Format Text Box**. For Fill and Line, select **No Fill** and **No Line**, respectively.
4. To resize the textbox, select it and then move the cursor over the sizing handles. Hold down the left mouse button and drag the textbox until it is the size you want.
5. To move the textbox into a position where you want it, select the textbox and drag it to the correct location.
6. If you want to add a line or arrow pointing from the label to a specific area in the image:
   - In Corel WordPerfect, select **Insert→Shape→Draw line** (or **Arrow**).
   - In Lotus Word Pro, put everything into a "drawing" and select the polyline icon.
   - In Microsoft Word, click on the line tool in the drawing toolbar. (Use the arrow-style tool to specify which end of the line is used for the arrowhead.)
7. Once you've created all the labels and arrows you want and have positioned them where you want, you must *group* them. That way, all the parts of the graphic move as one piece. To group the graphic, labels, and arrows:

- In Corel WordPerfect, select all objects by holding down the Shift key and click each one; then press the right mouse button and select **Group**.
- In Lotus Word Pro, select all objects by holding down the Shift key and click each one; then select **Draw→Group**.
- In Microsoft Word, hold down both the Ctrl and Shift keys and left-click each element until you have selected all of them. With the cursor appearing as a four-pointed crosshair, right-click the mouse and select **Grouping→Group**.

Adding figure titles and indicating sources. Place figure titles below graphics, and make them descriptive. Readers who skim through your text will appreciate these identifiers. Use a figure number if you cross-reference graphics from other pages. To format figure titles, use the same font that you use for headings but one or two point sizes smaller than regular body text. For example, if you use Arial for headings and 12-point Times New Roman for regular text, try 10-point Arial for figure titles. Identify the source of your borrowed graphics in the figure title.

Cross-referencing illustrations. Don't just toss graphics into documents without alerting readers to them and helping them to understand those graphics. Cross-reference each graphic before it appears in the text. For example, this chapter refers to tools for creating graphics, and cross-references have alerted you to illustrations of those tools; otherwise, you might have been unaware of them. In cross-references, include as many of the following elements as you think readers will need:

- *Title.* You can refer to the graphic merely as "Figure 3," or go a bit further and refer to it as "Figure 3, Drawing Toolbar." Citing the exact title of the figure helps indicate its subject matter.
- *Page number.* If your graphics are numbered, if the cross-referenced graphic is nearby, and if the document is not overly long, readers can find the graphic *without* a page reference. Keep it simple!
- *Subject matter and relevance.* Briefly indicate the subject matter of the graphic—this helps readers decide whether to go look at it. Explain how the graphic is related to your discussion; otherwise readers may not bother.
- *Description or interpretation.* Provide brief explanations of your graphics; don't force readers to interpret them on their own.

You'll find all these elements in Figure 11-8.

HOW DO YOU INCORPORATE GRAPHICS INTO DOCUMENTS?

Let's imagine that you have a nice graphic out there just waiting to be added into your technical document. How do you get it into your file where you want it?

From 1995 through 1996, the Hubble Space Telescope (HST) was able to resolve Cepheid variable stars in galaxies in the Virgo cluster (which includes the M100 galaxy as shown in Figure 5). This ensured a much better calibration of distance measures. This has allowed more accurate estimates to be made of Hubble's constant H. Early galaxies and quasars have also been observed by the HST, raising serious doubts about current structure formation models.

Cross-reference

Illustration

Figure title

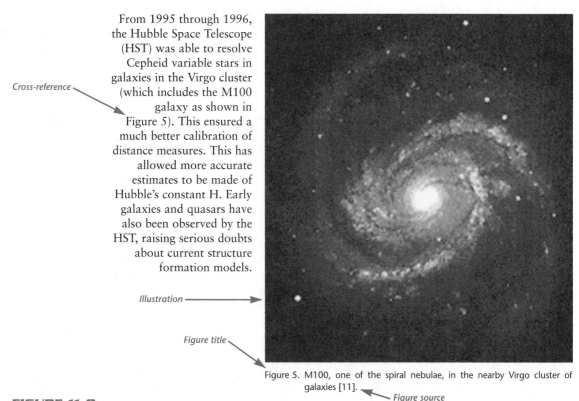

Figure 5. M100, one of the spiral nebulae, in the nearby Virgo cluster of galaxies [11].

Figure source

FIGURE 11-8

Key elements of a graphic in text. Make sure to cross-reference each graphic from nearby text, include a descriptive figure title, and indicate the source (if you borrowed it).

Inserting and positioning illustrations.   Once you've copied a graphic from another application (such as PaintShop Pro or MS Paint) or have made a screen capture, you can paste it into a document:

1. Move to the spot in the document where you want to insert the graphic. Press Enter to create a blank line, and move your cursor to that blank line. Then in Corel WordPerfect, Lotus Word Pro, or Microsoft Word, choose **Edit→Paste** (in some instances, it may be **Edit→Paste Special**).

2. To force text out from under the graphic and to force text to appear above and below the graphic only, select the graphic and then:

   ■ In Corel WordPerfect, right-click the mouse and select **Wrap→ Neither side.**

   ■ In Lotus Word Pro, select **Frame Properties→Placement.**

   ■ In Microsoft Word, with the cursor in the shape of a four-pointed arrow icon, click the right mouse button. Select **Format Picture→ Wrapping→Top & bottom.**

3. To "lock" the graphic into place between the text elements above and below it, select the graphic, click the right mouse button, and then:

   ■ In Corel WordPerfect, select **Position**, then **Paragraph** in Attach Box To, and then drag the box to the paragraph you want to attach it to.

   ■ In Lotus Word Pro, select **Frame Properties→Placement**. Select **With paragraph above** in the Place frame field.

   ■ In Microsoft Word, when the cursor appears as a four-pointed crosshair, click **Format Object→Position** and then check both **Move object with text** and **Lock anchor**.

4. To set a standard distance between preceding text and the graphic as well as between the graphic and following text, select the graphic, right-click the mouse, and then:

   ■ In Corel WordPerfect, select **Position** and try 0.2 inches for Vertical.

   ■ In Lotus Word Pro, select **Frame Properties** and click the Size and margin tab. (Click **Margin Options** to set individual margins.)

   ■ In Microsoft Word, select **Format Picture→Wrapping**. For starters, try 0.2 (inches) for both top and bottom under Distance from text.

5. To fine-adjust the location of the graphic, select it and then use the arrow keys to move it in small increments.

HOW ABOUT THE OLD-FASHIONED WAY?

If you simply refuse to use computers to incorporate graphics into your technical documents, you can do it the old-fashioned way—with real scissors, real tape, and photocopy machines (as shown in Figure 11-9).

1. Collect the illustrations you need from books, magazines, reports, the Internet, and other such sources. See the preceding pages of this chapter for strategies.

2. When you have the illustrations you need and a draft of the text you want them in, photocopy those illustrations or print them out. Reduce

FIGURE 11-9

Taping illustrations into technical documents. The old-fashioned way still works! Follow the suggestions in this section to make the results look neat and professional.

or enlarge them so that they fit neatly within the normal margins of your document.

3. Just after those points where you mention the illustrations, add space so that the illustrations fits, with about a half-inch white space above and below. If space is lacking, push the graphic to the top of the next page, and fill the remaining open space with text.

4. In the open space you've created for the illustration, type the figure title, including source information if you borrowed the graphic. Don't forget to add a cross-reference to your graphic in nearby text.

5. Tape in your illustrations carefully, making sure they are right in the middle of that open space both horizontally and vertically.

6. If your illustrations need labels, print them separately and tape them in (unless you have very neat handwriting). Don't draw or color directly on final pages.

7. When you have done all this, get a sharp photocopy of the entire report, bind it, and hand it off to your instructor or client. Test a few of your pages with taped-in illustrations first. If the edges of the taped-in material show, see if making the copy lighter will make them go away.

HOW DO YOU ADD GRAPHICS TO WEB PAGES?

As of the year 2000, Web browsers display only GIF, JPG, and PNG graphics. You may be familiar with bitmap (BMP) files. If you make a screen capture on a PC using Microsoft products and save it, it will probably be a BMP file. Thus the first step in getting it ready for Web pages is to convert it to GIF, JPG, or PNG. Use the GIF format for simple graphics and JPG for photographic-quality graphics.

Converting graphic file formats.   Here is how to convert a graphic to GIF or JPG format:

1. Open a graphics application such as JASC's PaintShop Pro (available at **www.jasc.com**) or Microsoft's Paint (available through **Start→Programs→Accessories→Paint**).

2. In the graphic application, open the graphic you want to convert (usually through **File→Open**). If you can't find it, make sure the file type indicator shows *.*.

3. Click **File→Save As** and select either GIF (where photograph-quality detail is not essential) or JPG (for photographic files). Change the file name extension to .gif or .jpg, respectively.

Linking Web pages to graphic files.   Now you have a graphic file that you can use in your Web pages. Graphic files are always separate from (not embedded into) Web pages. Here is how to link from a Web page to a graphic:

1. Move to the point in your HTML file where you want the graphic. (If you've not learned the basics of creating Web pages, see Chapter 17.)
2. At that point, enter the following tags (substitute the name of your graphic for *filename* and some description or commentary for *description_comment*):

   ```
   <P>
   <IMG SRC="filename" ALT="description_comment.">
   <P>
   ```
3. Remember those potatoes you copied from the Internet earlier in this chapter? You'd show them like this: `<IMG SRC="potatoes.gif" ALT="Some nice potatoes">`. The paragraph tags, `<P>`, simply create some white space above and below the graphic.
4. To align the graphic:

   `<IMG SRC="filename.gif" ALIGN="top">` Text following the graphic aligns to the top of the graphic.

   `<IMG SRC="filename.gif" ALIGN="middle">` Text following the graphic aligns to the middle of the graphic.

Otherwise, by default, text aligns at the bottom of a graphic. For more complex alignment of graphics, use a table in which the borders do not show. (See Chapter 10 on creating tables for Web pages.)

WORKSHOP: GRAPHICS

Here are some additional ideas for practicing the concepts, tools, and strategies in this chapter:

1. *Creating old-fashioned graphics:* Paste in a graphic the old-fashioned way, using the directions provided in this chapter:
   a. Go to **www.io.com/~hcexres/power_tools/graphics/exer1.html** for the text and the graphic.
   b. Print out the graphic, and then copy the text into a word-processing document with software such as Word or WordPerfect, leaving enough room for the graphic.
   c. Just below the open space, use the notes available with the text to create a figure title.
   d. Print out this document, trim the graphic you printed, and then tape it into the open space in the text.
   e. Finally, photocopy this page and see how good it looks!

2. *Making screen captures:* Imagine that you are writing instructions that will enable people to perform some task on your computer and that you need screen captures:
   a. Set up your computer screen so that it displays the application for which you are providing instructions, and make the screen capture.

b. Bring the screen capture into a graphics program and crop it to an appropriate portion.

c. Use any of the methods suggested in this chapter to add labels to the graphic. When you are done, group all the labels and the graphic into one unified graphic.

d. Import the graphic into a text file, and add a figure title just beneath, including information on its source.

3. *Cropping, sizing, and changing file format.* Using the screen capture you made in the preceding exercise, trim away the unnecessary parts of the image (cropping), adjust the overall height and width of the image (sizing), and convert it to a GIF image (changing file format). For these tasks, use your preferred word-processing software or graphics application such Adobe Photoshop, Jasc Paint Shop Pro, or Microsoft Paint.

4. *Adding labels and figure titles with source.* Add at least three labels to the screen capture you made in the preceding exercise. Make sure that the textbox for each label is transparent and that the lines do not show. Draw arrows from each textbox to the related part of the image. Create a figure title as a text box and attach it to the bottom edge of the image. In it, Use the label "Figure" followed by a number and period, followed by a descriptive title, followed by the label "Source:" in italics followed by the manufacturer, name, and version number of the software. Group all of these image elements together.

5. *Adding images to documents.* Use the instructions, text, and graphics available at **www.io.com/~hcexres/power_tools/graphics/exer5.html** to create a document in your preferred word-processing software and add graphics with labels and figure titles to it.

6. *Adding graphics to Web pages.* Use the instructions, text, and graphics available at **www.io.com/~hcexres/power_tools/graphics/exer6.html** to create a Web page and add graphics with labels and figure titles to it.

CHAPTER 12

Highlighting and Emphasis

PHOTOVOLTAICS: ELECTRICITY FROM THE SUN

On the Web, you'll find all the information you need to light your house using electricity that you generate directly from the sun:

Solar Electric Light Fund (SELF): non-profit organization promoting solar rural electrification in developing countries. **www.self.org**

Mark Fitzgerald, Science Communications, Inc., PV Power Resource Site. **www.pvpower.com**

Office of Energy Efficiency and Renewable Energy Network (DOE). Million Solar Roofs Initiative. **www.eren.doe.gov/millionroofs**

Home Power: Hands-On Journal of Home-Made Power. **www.homepower.com**

U.S. Department of Energy. National Center for Photovoltaics. **www.nrel.gov/ncpv**

Mr. Solar. Design Your Preferred Energy System. **www.ases.org**

Accessed January 21, 2001.

Now that just about everyone has powerful desktop-publishing software, we can all go wild with special typographical effects such as bold, italics, underscores, small caps, larger or smaller type sizes, different fonts, and even colors. It's irresistibly fun to play with these tools, but not so much fun for readers. Overdoing it with highlighting creates a busy, uncomfortable, hyperactive-looking text that readers prefer to avoid.

This chapter focuses on gaining control over highlighting and emphasis, developing a logical plan for using these techniques, and avoiding the common problems associated with them. You'll also see how to add highlighting and emphasis to your text using character styles in Corel WordPerfect, Lotus Word Pro, and Microsoft Word and how to use HTML tags to create these same effects in your Web documents.

Note: See the recommended guidelines and specifications for highlighting at the end of this chapter.

WHAT IS HIGHLIGHTING AND EMPHASIS?

The terms "highlighting" and "emphasis" are almost synonymous. *Emphasis,* in this case, refers to typographical effects such as bold or italics that make text more noticeable. *Highlighting* refers to typographical effects that enable readers to anticipate the meaning of text. Used properly, highlighting and emphasis can help readers understand text more readily. For example, computer documents often use Courier for text that readers must type in verbatim. Once readers get used to this idea, they think, "Oh yes, here's that funny-looking font—I've got to type this stuff in!" In computer documents, highlighting eliminates the need for quotation marks, which readers might otherwise think they must type in as well.

However, highlighting and emphasis are easy to overuse. Typographical effects such as bold, italics, and different type sizes or fonts should *not* be used for more than a few words—at most, no more than a sentence. Beyond that, text becomes too busy, and readers are less likely to read it (see Figure 12-1). Instead of bolding or italicizing an entire paragraph, use

JER OPEN CALL PROCEDURES

1) The **Help Desk Technician** is to answer the phone by stating "**JER HelpDesk**" and his or her first name. The **Help Desk Technician** should immediately ask for the *customer's name, site, area code*, and *phone number*, what *credit-card company* he or she is with (American Express, MasterCard, Visa, etc. . . .) followed by "*How may I help you?*" {JER Help Desk. This is [STATE YOUR NAME], **may I please have your name, area code, and phone number? Thank you. [STATING CALLER'S FIRST NAME], which credit-card company are you with?** (American Express, MasterCard, Visa, etc. . . .) **How may I help you, please?"}**

2) Enter the station's area code and phone number on the "*Open Call Screen*" next to "**PHONE NUMBER:** " Don't worry about the ( ) or -, just type in the n[umber] and press the **<enter>** key once.

3) Make sure the flashing cursor is next to "[PHONE] NUMBER:" prompt and press the **<insert>** ke[y.] (This is a macro key set for the **Find** function.) Next, ch[eck] the "*Site Search Screen*" and the flashing curso[r is] on "**KEY:**" prompt. Press the **C** key once for [city.] The flashing cursor will automatically move to [the] prompt, just below the "**Y**" field just bel[ow] "**ACTIVE SITES ONLY:**" prompt. Type in the [name of] the *city* that the station is located in and p[ress the] **<enter>** key once. Read down the list of sites [looking] for the *street number* and the *name of the stat[ion]* you are looking for. If you see "**PRESS PRE[VIOUS]** {PREV}, {NEXT} or {RETURN} FOR MOR[E**]"**" at the bottom of the screen, there are more [sites to] check. Press the **<page down>** key once.

← Frightening, isn't it?

JER OPEN CALL PROCEDURES

1. As the help desk technician, answer the phone by stating that the customer has reached the JER HelpDesk and then state your first name.

2. Immediately ask for the customer's name, area code, phone number, and credit card company.

3. Then ask how you can help this customer. For example:

> JER Help Desk. This is *YourName*. May I please have your name, area code, and phone number? Thank you, *CallerName*, what credit card company are you with? . . . How may I help you, please?

4. Enter the area code and phone number on the Open Call Screen, and press Enter once.
    Note: Don't worry about the ( ) (parentheses) or – (dash). Just type in the numbers without spaces.

5. Make sure the cursor is next to the phone field, and press Insert once. (This starts the search process.)

6. With the cursor on the key prompt in the Site Search Screen, press C once for city.

7. Type in the name of the city and press Enter once.

8. Search the list of sites for the customer's street number and the name of the station. If more sites are listed, press PageDown once.

Better? →

FIGURE 12-1

Highlighting out of control. How happy would you be about reading the version on the left? Notice how much calmer and simpler the version on the right is. The bold, the italics, the curly braces, the square and angle brackets, the capital letters, the quotation marks, the thick paragraphs—the crazy mixture of all these devices creates a typographical nightmare!

the notice format as presented in Chapter 9. Notices provide extended emphasis in a way that remains readable.

WHAT CAN BE HIGHLIGHTED, AND HOW?

If you browse a selection of technical documents, you'll see some common patterns of highlighting. Here are some common uses:

- **Emphasis words.** Most commonly, words like "not," "must," "never," and "always" are emphasized. Italics has been the standard way of emphasizing such words. However, in technical text that uses lots of bold and other fonts, italics is easy to overlook. That's why you'll often see bold used for emphasis. Whichever you use—italics or bold—be consistent with it. And, *under no circumstances*, should you use all caps.
- **Words used in an unusual way.** Technical subjects often force us to use words in unusual ways. For example, the help pop-up "hovers" over the button it describes; the computer "crashes"; the stock market experiences a "hiccup." Until these words become generally accepted, we use quotation marks around them. If you use a word in a new or unusual way to convey a technical idea, put it in quotation marks—but on the first occurrence only!
- **Words, letters, numbers, or symbols discussed as such.** It's standard to use italics for words, letters, numbers, and symbols that you refer to as such. For example, you may have seen, "If the information is not available, enter *NA* in the blank."
- **Commands.** In computer documents involving procedures where you enter commands at a command line, such as in DOS or UNIX, the typical practice is to bold the command. For example, a computer document may say, "To delete the directory, type **rmdir** followed by the name of the directory you want to delete."
- **Variables.** In command-line procedures, variables are those placeholder words for which you are to substitute your own words. The common practice is to use italics. For example, variables may appear like the following: "To delete the file, enter **rm** *filename*, where *filename* is the name of the file you want to delete."
- **Text displayed on screen.** With any equipment that uses monitors or displays, such as LCD panels, it's a common practice in technical documentation to use a contrastive font. Typically, when a serif font such as Times New Roman is used as the regular body font, a sans serif font or typewriter-style font such as Arial or Courier is used for warnings and messages that display on screen. Using a contrastive font eliminates the need for quotation marks.
- **Examples and user-entered text.** Technical documents commonly use a contrastive font such as Courier for examples. This "cues" readers that the text is an example only, not required. For example, a technical document may say, "To delete letter.doc, type `rm letter.doc`." This same

technique is used for extended examples of code; in most programming books, lines of code are in another font, typically Courier.

- **Hardware button names.** References to buttons on equipment are handled in a variety of ways (but *not* with quotation marks): all caps, small caps, initial caps, bold, contrastive font, or some combination. Highlighting the button name cues readers to press the button. Notice the small-caps Arial in this example: "To shut down the engine, press the **POWER OFF** button." If the button uses a symbol rather than a word, use a standard name for the button and show the symbol in parentheses: "Press the **POWER ON** (|) button."

- **Buttons and icons on screen.** In graphical interfaces (like Macintosh or Windows), you click on buttons or icons to make things happen. Technical communicators often treat these elements like commands and bold them. For example, a technical communicator may write, "Press **Cancel** to return to the main menu."

- **Keyboard key names.** Like hardware button names, keyboard key names are handled many different ways. The insert key on your keyboard can be shown as INS, Insert, INS, Insert, **INS**, **Insert**, INS, and so on. To decide on which to use, consider the other highlighting in your document and do something functionally similar.

- **Window and screen names.** When you work in graphical interfaces (like Macintosh or Windows), screens and windows are constantly popping up at you, each with its own name. Typically, technical communicators do *not* use any special highlighting in this case, other than initial caps for the name of the window or screen. For example, a technical communicator may write, "Fill out the fields in the New Customer Order screen."

- **Menu and menu-option names.** With menus and menu options, however, some form of highlighting is often used. For example, you click on a menu name such as **File** and then on an option such as **Open**. To reduce the number of words needed to explain such maneuverings, writers often use arrows: **File→Open**. This means click **File** and then click **Open**.

- **Field names.** Online, "field" names are the text labels beside entry areas. For example, you may see, "Type the name of the customer in the Customer Name field." If plenty of highlighting is already in use, writers just use initial caps.

- **Web addresses (URLs).** Practice is mixed as to whether Web addresses should be highlighted and which style of highlighting should be used. In plenty of instances, no highlighting is used; but in plenty of others, a "monospaced" font like Courier is used: `www.io.com/~hcexres`. In monospaced fonts, each letter takes up exactly the same amount of space: the i's, l's, and j's are not "scrunched."

The preceding discussion doesn't prescribe a system of highlighting. Practice varies widely in technical documents. Although most of the preceding examples involve computers, the same concepts apply to any equipment.

HOW DO YOU PLAN A HIGHLIGHTING SCHEME?

A *highlighting scheme* is a plan for the kinds of highlighting you'll use and the situations in which you'll use them. The preceding sections presented the different tools you can use for highlighting and emphasis as well as the different textual elements you can highlight. This section puts it all together into a plan that ensures a functional and consistent usage of highlighting.

- *Functional* means that the highlighting somehow reinforces or combines with the purpose and content of the text.
- *Consistent* means that things like bold, italics, or other fonts are used the same way in the same situations throughout the document.

Remember that there is no one right way to highlight a text unless you are writing within a company, organization, industry, or profession that expressly requires a certain highlighting style. For example, if you are a technical writer for Dell, IBM, or Hewlett-Packard, you probably have a corporate style guide that tells you exactly when to use bold, italics, alternate fonts, and so on.

Once you've planned a highlighting scheme, you must create a *style guide* in which you provide a quick reference for the rules you have decided on. And of course another way of ensuring that you use your highlighting scheme is to have your drafts reviewed or edited by someone who knows that style guide.

Here's a simple scenario of how you might develop a highlighting scheme. Imagine that you are writing a set of instructions for one of those inexpensive toy watches featuring the latest Disney cartoon character. There is an LED display and three buttons labeled Mode, Set, and Select. The watch enables you to see the time, the date, or both, alternating back and forth every 5 seconds. (Parents, are you familiar with the item?) In terms of highlighting, you know you may want to do something to emphasize the button labels, the information displayed in the LCD, and the emphasis words (**not! never! always!**). Here are some suggestions:

Simple Highlighting Scheme

Text or element	Highlighting style
Regular body font	Times New Roman.
Button names	Arial small caps. (In MS Word, press Ctrl-D and select Small caps.)
LCD display	Courier (or Line Printer, System, or Terminal for a "techie" look).
Emphasis	Bold, regular body font.

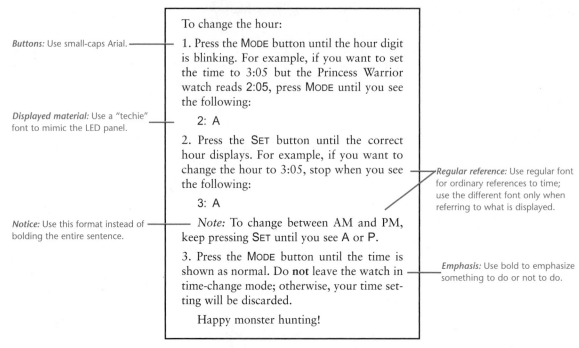

Buttons: Use small-caps Arial.

Displayed material: Use a "techie" font to mimic the LED panel.

Notice: Use this format instead of bolding the entire sentence.

To change the hour:

1. Press the MODE button until the hour digit is blinking. For example, if you want to set the time to 3:05 but the Princess Warrior watch reads 2:05, press MODE until you see the following:

2: A

2. Press the SET button until the correct hour displays. For example, if you want to change the hour to 3:05, stop when you see the following:

3: A

Note: To change between AM and PM, keep pressing SET until you see A or P.

3. Press the MODE button until the time is shown as normal. Do **not** leave the watch in time-change mode; otherwise, your time setting will be discarded.

Happy monster hunting!

Regular reference: Use regular font for ordinary references to time; use the different font only when referring to what is displayed.

Emphasis: Use bold to emphasize something to do or not to do.

FIGURE 12-2

Simple highlighting scheme in action. If the Arial small-caps is too "busy" for you, consider using small caps and regular body font. Notice that "AM" and "PM" are not highlighted if they refer to actual time, whereas "A" or "P" use a "techie" font to refer to what is displayed in the LED panel of the watch.

If you were to write the instructions for the toy watch using the highlighting scheme in the preceding table, you might decide that the Arial font makes the text look too busy. After all, one of the standard page-design rules is not to use more than one font; we've got three: Times New Roman, Courier, and Arial. A good idea might be to use small caps on the button names and not use Arial at all. Take a look at the highlighting in the instructions for the toy watch in Figure 12-2.

Now consider a more complex situation. Imagine that you are writing procedures for using a Web page editor. Think of all the possibilities for highlighting! But control yourself—too much highlighting will send readers diving for their barf bags. Consider the candidates for highlighting: text you type in the editor, button and icon names, menu names, option names, screen names, file and directory names, field names, and simple emphasis. But few people would want to read text with all of those elements highlighted. The following table shows a highlighting scheme you could use. It's typical of computer documents and, while rather heavy on highlighting, does not overdo it:

Take a look at the excerpt in Figure 12-3, which uses these guidelines.

Complex Highlighting Scheme

Text or element	Highlighting	Example
Regular body font	Times New Roman	To run Arachnophilia from the DOS command line . . .
Text you must type	Courier New	`c:\arach\arachno.exe\`
Simple emphasis	Italic, regular font	Do *not* edit binary files in Arachnophilia.
Terms at point of definition	Italic, regular font	A *macro* is a recorded set of keystrokes you can replay again. . . .
Text displayed on screen (warnings, messages)	Courier New	`The file already exists. Are you sure you want to replace it?`
File and directory names	Bold, regular font	**arachnophilia.exe** **c:\arach**
Button and icon names	Bold, regular font	**OK, Help, Cancel**
Menu names	Bold, regular font	**File, Edit, Insert**
Menu-option selections	Bold, regular font	**File→Open→HTML**
Screen names	Initial cap, regular font	Arachnophilia Macro Editor
Field names	Initial cap, regular font (but omit the colons)	Name:, SSN:, E-mail address:
Keyboard key names	Initial cap, regular font	Ctrl, Shift, Enter
Web addresses (URLs)	Courier New	`www.io.com/~hcexres/doc1`

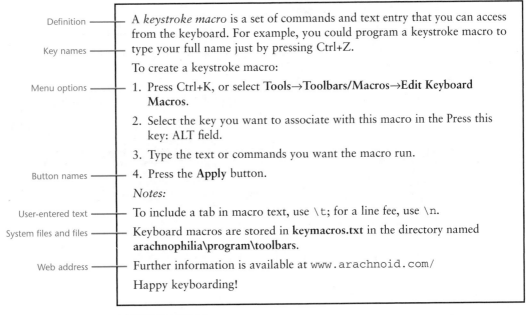

Definition —— A *keystroke macro* is a set of commands and text entry that you can access from the keyboard. For example, you could program a keystroke macro to

Key names —— type your full name just by pressing Ctrl+Z.

To create a keystroke macro:

Menu options —— 1. Press Ctrl+K, or select **Tools→Toolbars/Macros→Edit Keyboard Macros**.

2. Select the key you want to associate with this macro in the Press this key: ALT field.

3. Type the text or commands you want the macro run.

Button names —— 4. Press the **Apply** button.

Notes:

User-entered text —— To include a tab in macro text, use \t; for a line fee, use \n.

System files and files —— Keyboard macros are stored in **keymacros.txt** in the directory named **arachnophilia\program\toolbars**.

Web address —— Further information is available at www.arachnoid.com/

Happy keyboarding!

FIGURE 12-3

A more complex highlighting scheme in action. The highlighting used in this excerpt is rather typical of what you see in computer publications.

HOW DO YOU ADD HIGHLIGHTING AND EMPHASIS?

Word-processing and desktop-publishing software makes it easy and fun to add highlighting and emphasis to technical documents—in fact, way too easy. The following sections review the basics of highlighting in Microsoft Word and in Web pages. If you find yourself bolding and italicizing everything in sight, go back and reread the preceding sections!

Highlighting with Common Word-Processing Software

You're probably familiar with making text bold or italics or with changing fonts or font sizes in Word, WordPerfect, or Word Pro. However, you may not be familiar with using character styles to achieve a well-planned and consistent highlighting scheme.

Manual highlighting.   If you've never used bold, italics, different fonts, or different type sizes before, try out the following in Corel WordPerfect, Lotus Word Pro, or Microsoft Word (see Figures 12-4, 12-5, and 12-6):

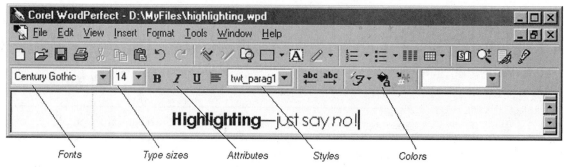

FIGURE 12-4

Basic formatting controls in Corel WordPerfect. Fonts, type sizes, attributes (bold, italics, underscore), styles, and other options are available in the Property toolbar (choose **View→Toolbars** to access it).

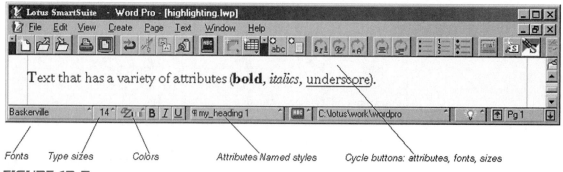

FIGURE 12-5

Basic formatting controls in Lotus Word Pro. Look to the bottom of the Word Pro window for style, font, type size, bold, italics, and other options.

Style menu   Font menu   Type-size menu   Bold and italics icons

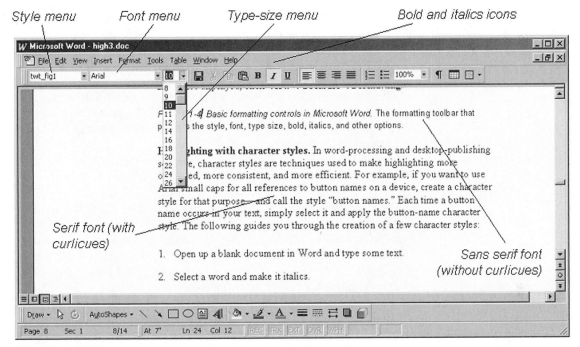

Serif font (with curlicues)

Sans serif font (without curlicues)

FIGURE 12-6

Basic formatting controls in Microsoft Word. Here is the formatting toolbar that provides the style, font, type size, bold, italics, and other options.

1. Open up a blank document in Word, WordPerfect, or Word Pro and type some text.
2. Select a word and make it italics by clicking the italics button (*I*) in the formatting toolbar or by pressing Ctrl+I.
3. Select another word and make it bold by clicking the bold button (**B**) in the formatting bar or by pressing Ctrl+B.
4. Select another word and change the font it uses by clicking the down-pointing arrow next to the font menu and selecting some other font, such as Arial Narrow.
5. Select another word and change its type size by clicking the arrow next to the type-size menu and selecting a number.

Highlighting with character styles. In word-processing and desktop-publishing software, character styles are advanced techniques that make highlighting more organized, more consistent, and more efficient. For example, to ensure that all device button names use Arial small caps, create a character style and call it "button names." Each time a device button name occurs, select it and apply the button-name character style. For simple or brief documents, there's no need to develop character styles. However, if you are doing a complex project, they are a great help. The following guides you through the creation of a few character styles:

1. Open up a blank document in Corel WordPerfect, Lotus Word Pro, or Microsoft Word and type some text.
2. Select a word and make it italics.
3. With the italicized word still selected, create the character style:
   - In Corel WordPerfect, click **Format→QuickStyle**, in the Style name field type `variable`, and click the **Character** radio button.
   - In Lotus Word Pro, click **Text→Text Properties** (or just press Alt+Enter), click **Create Style**, in the Style name box type `variable`, and in the Style type box select **Character**.
   - In Microsoft Word, click **Format→Style→New**. Under Style, select **Character**. Under Name, type `variable`.
4. Click **OK** or **Apply** as necessary to complete this character style.
5. Move somewhere else in the regular text, select a word, and apply the variable character style you just created.

   We named this character style "variable" because in technical documentation variables are commonly italicized. For example, if you tell your reader "delete *filename*" you're telling them to substitute their own file name for the variable *filename*.
6. Create the following additional character styles for commonly used highlighting in technical documentation. (These character styles assume that you are using 12-point Times New Roman as the regular body text. However, 11-point Courier New is used because 12-point Courier New looks too big in the same text with 12-point Times New Roman.)

Character and Paragraph Styles

Text or element	Technique	Usage
Regular text	12-point Times New Roman	For text in which special highlighting rules do not apply.
Command	Bold	For references to command names.
User text	11-point Courier	For text users must type.
Screen text	11-point Courier	For text displayed on the computer screen.
Example text	11-point Courier	For example text, such as programming code.
Menu names	Arial	For references to the names of screens, windows, or menus.

Highlighting in Web Pages

Use the following mini-tutorial to learn how to use text elements such as bold, italics, underscore, alternate fonts, alternate colors, and different type sizes. (For an introduction to creating Web pages, see Chapter 17.)

1. To begin, use a simple text editor like Macintosh Simple Edit or Windows Notepad to open a file. Save it with the name `high.html`.

2. In this file, type the following text and HTML tags. (See Figure 12-7 for the finished product as displayed in Netscape.)

```
<HTML>
<HEAD>
<TITLE>Fun with Fonts!</TITLE>
</HEAD>
</BODY>
<H1>Fun with Fonts!</H1>
Never let anyone make you think creating Web pages
by typing in the HTML tags is too hard!
<P>
It's easy and you don't have to buy any software!
<P>
Creating Web pages is also fun. You can make words
different colors (for example, red), different sizes
(such as smaller), and different fonts (such as Courier
New).
<P>
You can really go big time!
</BODY>
</HTML>
```

3. Save this file. To look at it through Netscape or Internet Explorer, open your browser, choose **File→Open Page** in Netscape or **File→Open** in Internet Explorer, and then select high.html in whichever folder you saved the file.

4. Return to your text-editor version of this Web page, and find the word *Never* and put <B> just in front of it and </B> just after. Find the word *any* and enclose it between <U> and </U>. These tags create bold and underscore, respectively.

5. To view this page, return to your browser and reload (or refresh) this file: choose **View→Reload** in Netscape or **View→Refresh** in Internet Explorer. You should see the word *Never* in bold and the word *any* underscored.

6. In the simple text file version of high.html, find the word *fun*, and enclose it between <I> and </I>. Return to your Web browser and reload. You'll now see the word *fun* in italics.

7. Now, add a number of highlighting changes, and then return to your browser and reload or refresh the page to see all these interesting effects!

   a. Enclose the word *red* between <FONT COLOR="red"> and </FONT>.

   b. Enclose the word *smaller* between <FONT SIZE="-1"> and </FONT>.

   c. Enclose the words *Courier New* between <FONT FACE="Courier New"> and </FONT>. (Other interesting fonts to try are Comic Sans MS, Century Gothic, and Lucida Sans.)

   d. And just to show you how these HTML tags can be used together, enclose the words *big time* between <FONT FACE="Arial" COLOR= "blue" SIZE="+2"><B><U> and </U></B></FONT>.

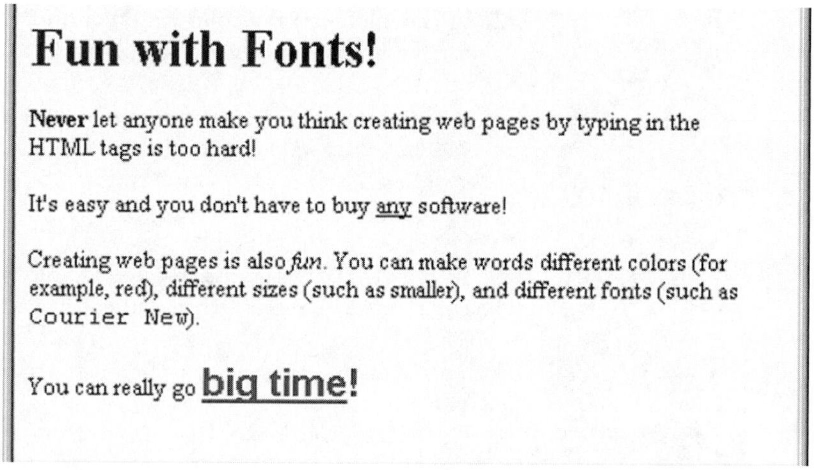

Fun with Fonts!

Never let anyone make you think creating web pages by typing in the HTML tags is too hard!

It's easy and you don't have to buy <u>any</u> software!

Creating web pages is also *fun*. You can make words different colors (for example, red), different sizes (such as smaller), and different fonts (such as `Courier New`).

You can really go **big time!**

FIGURE 12-7

Using HTML to highlight Web pages. Follow the steps in this chapter to create a Web page that looks like this. For more about creating Web pages with HTML tags, see Chapter 17.

Notes:

■ *Other colors.* As of 2000, you could enter the names of most basic colors—blue, green, purple, and so on—using their English name. For less common colors, you must enter a 6-digit code number. For example, `<FONT COLOR="#800000">` creates a nice reddish-brown color. For a listing of color names and codes, see Lynda Weinman's "Browser-Safe Color Palette" at **www.lynda.com/hex.html**.

■ *Other fonts.* You can use any of the fonts that your browser indicates are available. In Netscape, click **Edit→Preferences→Font** and look at the choices under Variable Width Fonts as well as those under Fixed Width Fonts. Keep in mind that if visitors to your Web pages don't have the fonts you choose, their Web browsers will use a default font.

WORKSHOP: HIGHLIGHTING

Here are some additional ideas for practicing the concepts, tools, and strategies in this chapter:

1. *Highlighting survey.* Find a technical document—preferably one that provides instructions—and make a list of the highlighting techniques that you see used there. Also, determine how the techniques are used in the document, using a table like the following:

Text or element	Highlighting style	Example

Note: See Chapter 10 for help on creating tables.

2. *Highlighting print documents.* Use the text and instructions available at **www.io.com/~hcexres/power_tools/highlighting/exer2.html** to get some practice creating character styles in Word, WordPerfect, or whatever word-processing or desktop-publishing software application you use.

3. *Highlighting Web pages.* Use the text and instructions available at **www.io.com/~hcexres/power_tools/highlighting/exer3.html** to get some practice using bold, italics, different colors, different fonts, and different type sizes in Web pages.

HIGHLIGHTING: GUIDELINES AND SPECIFICATIONS

General guidelines. Here are some general guidelines to keep in mind when you design and use headings:

- Use highlighting (bold, italics, alternate fonts, or alternate color) for emphasis or to cue readers to meaning of text (such as a button to be clicked).
- Avoid using highlighting techniques for more than a few words—and never for more than a sentence. For extended highlighting or emphasis, use notices (see Chapter 9).
- Develop a highlighting scheme for documents and use it consistently.
- When possible, use the highlighting style commonly used in your organization, field, or profession.
- Avoid redundant highlighting techniques—for example, using both bold and italics for a word or phrase.
- Never use caps or quotations as highlighting techniques. Techniques using bold, italics, and alternate fonts are developed specifically to eliminate the need for caps and quotation marks.
- Avoid over-highlighting documents. While keeping your highlighting consistent and functional, find reasons *not* to highlight certain elements (for example, keyboard key names, titles of menus, or field names).
- Have functional reasons for your highlighting techniques—for example, bold cues readers that they must press or select something; Courier New indicates that they must type something in.
- If you use color as a highlighting technique, limit yourself to one color in addition to black (for example, blue or teal). Readers will probably not understand the function of any additional colors.
- Avoid decorative highlighting. Avoid nonfunctional highlighting; for example, why highlight every instance of a product name? Avoid nonfunctional use of additional color.
- Never use a larger type size to emphasize regular text.

Specifications. Here are some suggested specifications for highlighting (but keep in mind that practice in the technical-publishing industry varies widely):

- Use italics for simple emphasis (for example, *not, never,* or *only*).
- Use bold for button names and menu options—anything that readers press or select to cause something to happen.
- Use initial caps for computer-keyboard key names, but no other highlighting.
- Use italics for variable names for which users must substitute their own items. For example, use *filename* to indicate that users must use their own file name.
- For titles, screens, or menus use initials caps but not other highlighting.
- For field names (as in forms, for example), use the cap style shown, but no other highlighting.
- For examples that users must type or for code excerpts, use Courier New.
- For names of buttons, knobs, and switches on hardware, use bold for the name as it is inscribed on the hardware. If no name is inscribed, use the conventional name and bold it as well, and put the symbol in parentheses( ).
- Limit your fonts to three; for example, use Times New Roman for regular text, Arial for headings, and Courier New for example text.
- Never highlight more than a sentence. For extended highlighting or emphasis, use the notice format (see Chapter 9).

PART III

Document-Delivery Tools

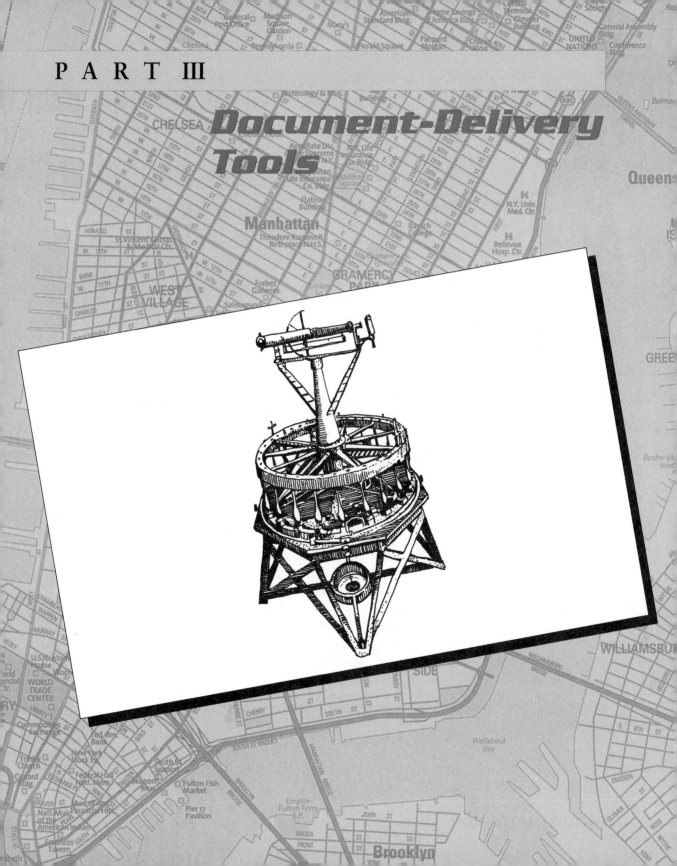

CHAPTER 13

Business Communications: Letters, Memos, and E-Mail

COMMUNICATION STYLES: INTERNATIONAL BUSINESS

If you wanted to send an inquiry from the U.S. to an expert living in Japan, India, Brazil, or Saudi Arabia, how would you write that inquiry? Would you modify the communication in consideration of the different culture and communication style of the recipient? An interesting and growing body of knowledge is available on international communication styles:

Nancy L. Hoft. *International Technical Communication: How to Export Information About High Technology* (New York: Wiley, 1995).

Saburo Haneda and Shima Hirosuke. "Japanese Communication Behavior as Reflected in Letter Writing." *Journal of Business Communication* 19 (1983): 19–32.

National Y Forum on People's Differences.
www.yforum.com/index.html

Career Magazine's Focus on Diversity.
www.careermag.com/db/cmag_diversity_index

Café Progressive. Many links on diversity, multiculturalism.
www.cafeprogressive.com

The United States vs. The World: A Theoretical Look at Cultural Imperialism.
www.utexas.edu/ftp/depts/eems/cultimp.387._.html

About.com Global Business page. International etiquette, business cultures, and country-by-country links.
globalbusiness.about.com/finance/globalbusiness

Working Globally—provided by the *Wall Street Interactive Edition*.
careers.wsj.com

Accessed January 23, 2001.

Business communications—letters, memos, and e-mail—often must convey technical information just like other sorts of documents. In fact, business letters and memos are often the "wrapper" for brief technical reports. This chapter provides tips on writing effective business communications, no matter what the medium; how to format letters and memos; and finally, how to write effective e-mail. Also included in this chapter is a step-by-step explanation of how to create a template. Of course, you can use templates for any document that has a standard format and layout, not just a letter or memo.

Note: For additional examples of the documents discussed in this chapter, see **www.io.com/~hcexres/power_tools/examples**.

HOW DO YOU WRITE EFFECTIVE LETTERS, MEMOS, AND E-MAIL?

This chapter covers format and style for the types of business communications. However, more important are the strategies you need to write *effective* letters, memos, and e-mail.

Tone.   Think of tone as the personality, attitude, or mood of a document. You can define tone in terms of a range. For example, business letter can range from formal to informal, impersonal to personal, and so on. In an e-mail inquiry to an expert, you want the tone to be respectful, friendly, but somewhat formal. In a complaint letter concerning a faulty product, you want the tone to be firm, formal, demanding, but not threatening.

Brief, state-your-purpose introduction.   The first lines of any business communication—letter, memo, or e-mail—should clarify topic and purpose. Keep it brief—no more than four or five lines. Our tendency is to dive into details, leaving readers to figure the point of the communication for themselves.

Review the context.   If your communication is in response to some other communication, repeat the details of the context. For example, to reply to a customer's complaint letter, the first paragraph can say something like "in reference to your June 15 letter concerning the problem you had with . . ." Context is particularly important in e-mail. If you write and read lots of e-mail everyday, it's hard to remember what you are discussing with whom.

Good-news-first, bad-news-last strategy.   A common strategy in business correspondence is to state good news—or at least neutral news—first and then bad news. For example, if you have lots of good qualifications for a job, except for one detail, state the positive first. Save the not-so-good for later, or don't even mention it at all! In a response to a complaint letter, don't state the rejection of the customer's request until after you've explained the reasons for rejecting it.

Reader-first strategy.   Business communications are typically efforts to achieve a transaction with the recipient. For example, you want to get information, a job interview, or compensation for a faulty product. In such transactions, both parties need to feel as though they have gained something. In an employment situation, the employer gets someone to handle important tasks and you get a salary! In a customer-complaint situation, the customer gets her money back and the company retains that customer's business and good will. Thus, business correspondence must focus on the needs and interests of the recipient.

Organization-based paragraphing.   Make the paragraphs of your business communications indicate the logic and topics of your message. Always reserve the first paragraph for the introduction, in which you indicate the topic, purpose, and context of the communication (and provide an overview of what follows if your communication is longer than a page). Make sure that each paragraph has an obvious purpose and topic. For example, after the introduction in a complaint letter, use a paragraph to narrate and describe the problem; use the next paragraph to state the compensation you are requesting; then use still another paragraph to explain why your request is justified. Don't let these three basic functions overlap paragraphs.

Short-paragraphs strategy.   Keep the paragraphs of business communications short—for example, fewer than eight lines. People can read and scan short paragraphs faster. They are less likely to read long, dense paragraphs. To achieve such scannability, you may also need to reduce line length and use a type size of 12 points. (While you can't control these variables in e-mail, you can certainly keep the paragraphs short.) Even so, don't break paragraphs just anywhere. Break paragraphs at those points where you shift from one topic to another.

Headings, lists, tables.   Just because it is a business letter, memo, or e-mail doesn't mean you can't use headings, lists, tables, and other page-design tools such as those covered in Part II of this book. In fact, look at the memo report on the Ann Arbor energy-efficient housing study at the end of Chapter 1. Except for short communications under a page or two, use headings to mark off main sections, use bulleted lists for key points, use numbered lists for sequential items, and use tables to enable comparison of information.

Action conclusion. Because most business communications attempt to transact something, the final paragraph should make clear what you expect the recipient to do. Avoid limp-noodle endings such as "Hoping to hear from you soon" or "Let me know if you have any questions." In a job-application letter, end by telling the potential employer that you hope to hear from him in the next two weeks and will call if you have not. Gently and politely force the reader to do something.

HOW DO YOU FORMAT A BUSINESS LETTER?

The following shows you formatting details such as margins, indentation, and type style for different types of business letters. For details on using business letters or memos for technical reports, see Chapter 15.

Types of business letters. Traditionally, these are the common business-letter formats, which are illustrated in Figure 13-1.

- *Block letter.* The block format is nearly the only style used in business letters. It's certainly the easiest, requiring no indentation of any of its parts. The date, heading, inside address, salutation, body paragraphs, and signature block (containing the complimentary close, signature, typed name, initials, and enclosures) all start on the standard left margin.
- *Modified block letter.* In this format, the date, complimentary close, signature, and typed name are indented as far to the right as possible. These elements are not right-aligned; they are just indented such that the longest element still fits on the same line.
- *Simplified letter.* The simplified format omits the salutation, and thus the problem of deciding whether to write "Dear Sir" or "To Whom It May Concern." Be careful about using this format. In letters in which personal relations are important, use the block or modified block style—for example, in a job application letter.

Format of business letters. Whichever type of business letter you write, follow these guidelines:

- *Salutation.* Punctuate the salutation with a colon, not a comma. The comma is for personal letters. (It's easy to forget this detail; Microsoft Word's letter template insists on a comma.) In the salutation, use the name of the person to whom you are sending the communication. If you don't know the name, use the title of the position or the department name. Avoid "Dear Sir" (sexist), "Dear Sir/Madame" (clumsy), "Dear People" (stupid), and "To Whom It May Concern" (trite).
- *Complimentary close.* Phrases like "Sincerely" and "Regards" are common for the complimentary close. Punctuate the complimentary close with a comma and capitalize only the first word, as in "Best wishes," for example.

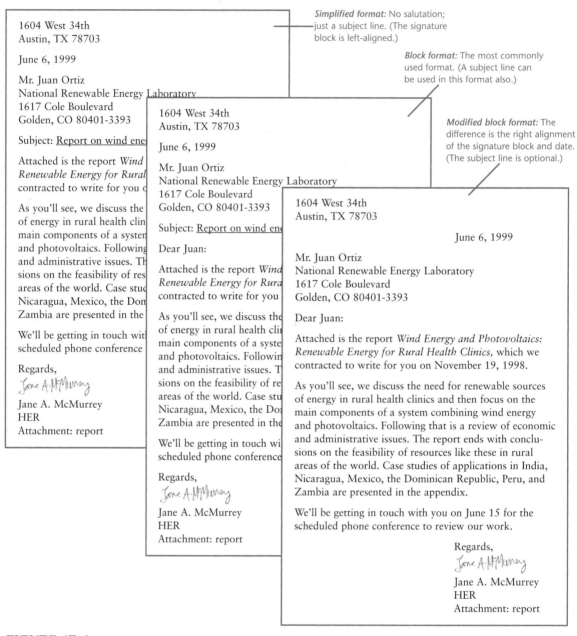

FIGURE 13-1
Business letter format. The simplified, the block, and the modified block letter formats.

- *Signature block.* Skip four lines between the complimentary close and your typed name. Single-space the lines for your typed name, the initials (yours and the typist's), and the enclosure.
- *Continuation pages.* If your letter goes over one page, use one of the formats shown in Figure 13-2 for the header on all following pages.
- *Margins.* Left, right, top, and bottom margins for business letters are variable. Notice that some software has a default left margin of 1.25 inches and default margins of 1.0 inch for the others. You can "fudge" these margins up to a half-inch to make the contents of a business letter fit the page better.
- *Alignment, justification.* Keep everything left-aligned in your business letters, unless you use the modified block format. Don't use full justification (where the right margin is also aligned). "Ragged" right margins actually help readers get through your letter faster.
- *Paragraph indentation.* The first line of paragraphs in business letters is typically not indented.
- *Line spacing.* Single-space *within* the paragraphs of business letters; skip a line *between* paragraphs of business letters. (Use the default line spacing of 13.95 for 12-point type as commonly offered by word-processing software.)
- *Type style.* Use a standard type style such as Times New Roman, Arial, Garamond, or Century Gothic. Unusual fonts may be fun for you, but they are not fun for your readers. Don't use all bold, all caps, all italic, or other such special effects for any extended segment of your letter. (See Chapter 12 on highlighting.)
- *Type size.* Standard 12-point type size works for most type styles, such as Times New Roman. You can vary type size to fit the contents of a letter to a page. However, don't go smaller than 9 points or larger than 14 points. Also, notice how much smaller or larger some type styles look in the same type size. For example, take a look at the difference between 12-point Times New Roman and 12-point Arial.

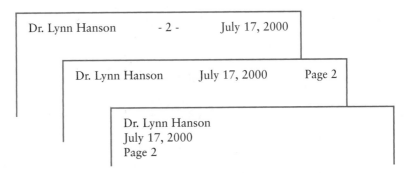

FIGURE 13-2

Continuation headers for letters and memos. Use any of these three formats at the top of following pages of your letters or memos.

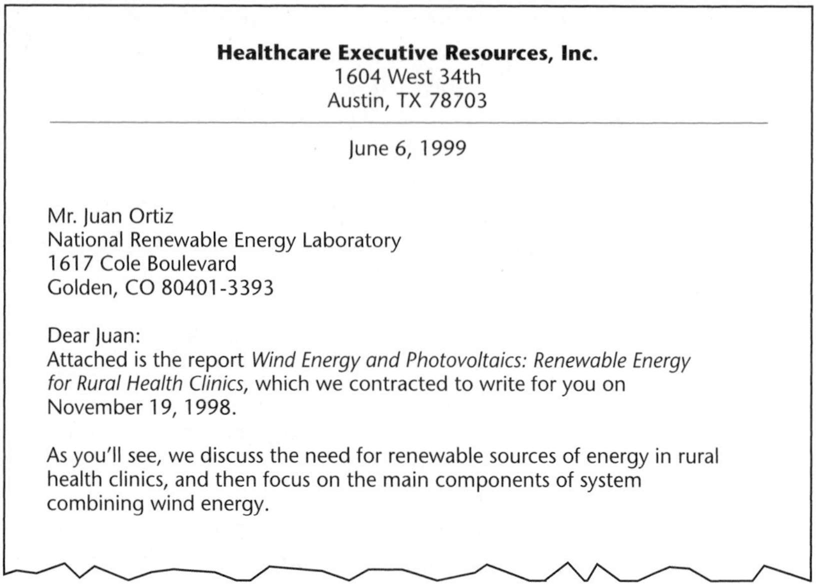

Healthcare Executive Resources, Inc.
1604 West 34th
Austin, TX 78703

June 6, 1999

Mr. Juan Ortiz
National Renewable Energy Laboratory
1617 Cole Boulevard
Golden, CO 80401-3393

Dear Juan:
Attached is the report *Wind Energy and Photovoltaics: Renewable Energy for Rural Health Clinics*, which we contracted to write for you on November 19, 1998.

As you'll see, we discuss the need for renewable sources of energy in rural health clinics, and then focus on the main components of system combining wind energy.

FIGURE 13-3

Letterhead business letters. You can create nice, attractive letterheads for your business letters, such as this example. It uses Arial italics. In MS Word, create the separator line by selecting **Format→Borders and Shading** and selecting the lower border icon:

- *Paper.* Use standard white 8.5 × 11 paper. Odd shapes or sizes of paper, colors, and other such departures are not a good idea in most business contexts.
- *Letterhead.* Use letterhead stationery for the first page only. For following pages, use the same quality of paper as is used for the letterhead page. If you are writing as an individual, unassociated with an organization, consider making up your own letterhead. See the example in Figure 13-3. And while you're at it, create a template with your letterhead in it, as explained later in this chapter. That way, it's ready whenever you need it.

HOW DO YOU FORMAT A MEMO?

Memos are business communications that stay "in house" within an organization. However, they are not necessarily less formal than business letters. Imagine a department manager sending a memo to tell everyone to stop surfing the World Wide Web for entertainment and get back to work. Just about any purpose or content in a business letter has its equivalent in the memo: job applications, complaints, refunds, inquiries, bad news, and good news of practically any kind. Also, plenty of reports are also formatted as memos. For details, see Chapter 15.

```
DATE:      June 15, 2000
TO:        Maury Hughes, Jr., Principal
           Hughes Energy Consultants
FROM:      Carrie Hughes Brown, HVAC Specialist
SUBJ:      Report on my trip to the Ann Arbor energy-efficient
           housing study

Maury, I have just returned from the second trip you requested I make to
```

FIGURE 13-4

Header alignment in memos. Set tabs so that text left-aligns after DATE:, TO:, and the other memo header elements.

■ *Memo header.* Standard format for a memo includes DATE:, TO:, FROM:, and SUBJECT: at the top. These labels are typically bold. A nice touch is to set margins about a quarter-inch past the longest label (in this case, SUBJECT:) so that all the text items following these labels left-align. (See Figure 13-4 for an illustration.)

■ *Margins.* Left, right, top, and bottom margins for memos are variable. Some software has a default left margin of 1.25 inches and default margins of 1.0 inch for the others. You can "fudge" these margins up to a half-inch to make the contents of a memo fit the page better.

■ *Alignment, justification.* Keep everything left-aligned in your memos. Don't use full justification (where the right margin is aligned also). "Ragged" right margins actually help readers get through your memo faster.

■ *Paragraph indentation.* The first line of paragraphs in memos is typically not indented.

■ *Line spacing.* Single-space *within* the paragraphs of memos; skip a line *between* paragraphs of memos. (Use the default line spacing of 13.95 for 12-point type as commonly offered by word-processing software.)

■ *Type style.* Use a standard type style such as Times New Roman, Arial, Garamond, or Century Gothic. Unusual fonts may be fun for you, but they are not fun for your readers. Don't use all bold, all caps, all italic or other such special effects for any extended segment of your memo. (See Chapter 12 on highlighting.)

■ *Type size.* Standard 12-point type size works for most type styles, such as Times New Roman. You can vary type size to fit the contents of a memo to a page. However, don't go smaller than 9 points or larger than 14 points. Also, notice how much smaller or larger some type styles look in the same type size. For example, take a look at the difference between 12-point Times New Roman and 12-point Arial.

■ *Paper.* Use standard white 8.5 × 11 paper. Odd shapes or sizes of paper, colors, and other such departures are not a good idea in most business contexts.

■ *Continuation pages.* If your memo goes over one page, use any of the same formats for business letters shown in Figure 13-2.

HOW DO YOU CREATE A LETTER OR MEMO TEMPLATE?

Templates are handy tools to make your professional writing more efficient and consistent. You can use the templates supplied by your software, or you can create your own. And you can create templates for any type of document you use often, not just letters and memos. Here's how to create and use a template:

1. To start a template file:
   - In Corel WordPerfect, click **File→New→Options→Create WP Template**.
   - In Lotus Word Pro, click **File→New** and select plain document. (You designate this file as a template file when you save it.)
   - In Microsoft Word, click **File→New** in the menu bar. Click the **Template** radio button in the Create New section, and click **OK** (see Figure 13-5).
2. Change all margins to 1.5 inches:
   - In Corel WordPerfect, click **Format→Page→Page Setup**, select the Page Margins tab, and change Left, Right, Top, and Bottom to **1.5**.
   - In Lotus Word Pro, click **Text→Text Properties** or press Alt+Enter, select **Page layout – All Pages** in the Properties for field, and change Top, Bottom, Right, and Left to **1.5**.
   - In Microsoft Word, press **File→Page Setup**, and under the Margins tab change Top, Bottom, Right, and Left to **1.5**.
3. To create a logo in the header portion of this template:
   - In Corel WordPerfect, click **Insert→Header/Footer**, click **Header A**, and type your name and address in italic 10-point Arial and center it.

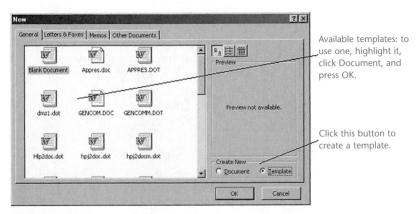

Available templates: to use one, highlight it, click Document, and press OK.

Click this button to create a template.

FIGURE 13-5

Templates in MS Word. From this same dialog you can create a new template or select an existing template.

- In Lotus Word Pro, click **View→Page Layout**, move into the header area, and type your name and address in italic 10-point Arial and center it.
- In Microsoft Word, click **View→Header and Footer**. In the header box, type your name and address in italic 10-point Arial and center it.

4. To save this template:
   - In Corel WordPerfect, click **File→Save**, give your template some distinctive name, select **Custom WP Templates,** and save your template. Notice that WordPerfect gives the template a **.wpt** extension and stores it a templates directory.
   - In Lotus Word Pro, click **File→Save**, give your template some distinctive name, and in the Save as file type field select **Lotus Word Pro Smartmaster (*.MWP)**.
   - In Microsoft Word, click **File→Save** and give your template some distinctive name. Notice that MS Word gives your template the **.dot** extension and stores it in a templates directory.

5. To use the template you just created:
   - In Corel WordPerfect, click **File→New**, select **Custom WP Templates,** select the template you want, and click **Create.**
   - In Lotus Word Pro, click **File→New**, and select the template you want, and click **OK.** If you have already started a document and want to change templates, click **File→Choose Another Smartmaster.**
   - In Microsoft Word, click **File→New** again. Highlight your template file (for example, mine is dmz1.dot in Figure 13-5), click **Document** in the Create New section, and press **OK.** If you have already started a document, you can import your template: click **Tools→Templates and Add-Ins,** then click the **Attach** button as shown in the following illustration, and select your template (see Figure 13-6 where my template is again dmz1.dot).

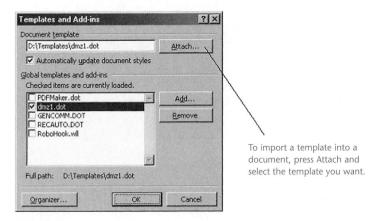

To import a template into a document, press Attach and select the template you want.

FIGURE 13-6

Importing a template in MS Word. To use a template you've created, you must "import" it into the document on which you are working.

WHAT ABOUT E-MAIL?

In scarcely more than five years, e-mail has become an essential business-communication tool. It's faster and easier than print communications and has more permanence than a telephone call. Still, e-mail has distinct limitations—not to mention some distinct risks.

E-mail lacks the reputation for permanence that printed letters and memos have. It's easy to delete or misplace e-mail. E-mail also lacks the formality of printed letters and memos. Would you send a job application to a potential employer by e-mail? Would you announce your resignation by e-mail? If you would hesitate, you understand the limitations of e-mail. Here are some guidelines for e-mail:

- Decide whether e-mail is the best method for the communication. Maybe your message would be more appropriate as a letter or memo?
- Compose an adequately descriptive subject line. E-mail in-boxes only give you about 8 to 10 words. To ensure that the recipient doesn't ignore your e-mail, make those words indicate your subject or purpose.
- Keep a copy of all e-mail you send; make sure your e-mail software does so. (For example, Eudora keeps all sent e-mail in the "out" box.) Use folders to keep your e-mail organized by subject matter or recipient.
- If you are responding to e-mail, be sure to indicate the context at the very beginning. If you handle lots of e-mail, you may forget what you are discussing with whom. If someone writes you, "I don't agree with you on that," without explaining the context, you're lost! If you are replying to someone else's e-mail, attach the original at the bottom. (Most e-mail software prompts for this.)
- Keep the paragraphs of e-mail messages short—even shorter than in business letters and memos. Avoid going over 5 lines.
- If your message is long and detailed, make it a separate document in your word-processing software and attach it to the e-mail. That way, the recipient can download and print it for easier reading.
- Be careful about sending e-mail abruptly. Ensure that it's addressed to the correct recipient and reread your message. Typos are rather common in e-mail—clean them up. Look for missing words such as *no* or *not*! If you are angry, don't send the e-mail right away. Reread it an hour or two later.
- Make sure you know who will be receiving your e-mail. Double-check that e-mail address to make sure other recipients will not mistakenly receive your e-mail.

HOW DO YOU WRITE PROBLEM COMMUNICATIONS?

In business and professional life, you face all kinds of problems, many of which require written documents. The three kinds discussed here are the following:

- *Complaint communications:* For complaints about a bad product or service and requests for appropriate compensation.
- *Adjustment communications:* For responses to complaint communications, granting or denying the requested compensation.
- *Inquiry communications:* For requests for information and other sorts of help.

These are "communications": they can be sent not only as conventional printed business letters or memos, but also as e-mail.

Complaint Communications

If you experience a problem with a product or service, sometimes you can't resolve it over the phone. Instead, you must put your complaint in writing, along with your request for compensation. The complaint communication describes the problem, requests compensation, and justifies the request. It's an interesting exercise in persuasion. See Chapter 6 for a review of persuasive strategies.

1. **Find a problem with a product or service you've experienced.** That's probably not so hard for most of us. Ideally, find a problem that has a technical aspect to it. Give your technical-writing skills a workout.

   Imagine that you were recently in a stage production of *King Lear* in which you had to wear heavy stage makeup. During that time, you experienced a problem with the mascara. After using it for several days, you noticed that your eyelids were itching and inflamed, and then your eyelashes began falling out. You stopped using the mascara, but the itchiness and inflammation continued, and almost all your eyelashes fell out. (This is taking *King Lear* way too far.)

2. **Describe or narrate the problem (or both).** Write a detailed narration and description of the problem you experienced. Supply specifics such as times, dates, individual or company names, addresses, and brand and model names. If you find yourself gleefully blowing off steam, get over it. Then rewrite the account of the problem neutrally. This information supports your logical appeal (but it brings in the emotional appeal through the back door).

   In one or more paragraphs, narrate and describe the mascara problem. Cite the exact name of the mascara, any identifying batch numbers on the package, the date of purchase, as well as the name and address of the store from which you bought it. Provide exact dates on which you started using the mascara, how much you used, how often, and when you discontinued it. Explain when you went to the doctor, who the doctor was, and how much the visit cost you. Describe your symptoms—if you can get your doctor's medical-style description, even better. Make this discussion as objective as you can. You'll get to blow off steam in the next paragraph.

3. **Describe the compensation you are requesting and the reasons why that request is justified.** Keep your complaint neatly compartmentalized. In one (or more) paragraphs, tell the story and describe the problem. Save the request for compensation and its justification for the next paragraph.

Practical Ethics: Murky Waters

 Some ethical dilemmas don't really feel like dilemmas. Should you blow the whistle on a company that is knowingly polluting a river? The answer seems to be a resounding "Yes!" Yet, as with many ethical dilemmas, the deeper you dig, the murkier the water and the harder it is to figure out what to do.

Imagine you are the public relations representative for a paper mill that is polluting a river. What should you do? Mike Markel says in his book *Technical Communication* that you have three obligations: to your employer, to the public, and to the environment.[1] A fourth obligation is to yourself.

Like most people in America, you are environmentally conscious. It is disturbing that a river is being polluted. Pollution affects fish, birds, and any other animals that use the river as a source of food or water. You suspect the pollution is making its way into the soil where it will affect plants and may damage entire ecosystems. If this is true, your obligation to the environment says the pollution must stop, whatever the cost.

On the other hand, your obligation to your employer tells you that news of the pollution could have an adverse effect on the company image and sales. Large fees could be imposed and cleanup would be costly. The possibility exists that the company would be forced to go under.

Your obligation to the public says that you need to inform them of safety risks. In this case, they would need to know if their health is being compromised. However, the paper mill is the largest employer in the county and if it went out of business, thousands of people would be out of work without much possibility of finding employment. Large-scale unemployment would have a detrimental effect on the economy. Which is worse? Living with pollution or being unemployed? It's a difficult question (and who are you to decide this for thousands of other people?).

You also have obligations to yourself. Even though it is your job to keep the public informed, letting this information out could bring you under fire from your supervisors. People have been fired for less. Is losing your job a price you're willing to pay? Your conscience says yes, but the financial and emotional strain it would put your family under says no.

In the process of considering all these angles, you have come up with competing answers to a dilemma that once didn't seem so complicated. In your mind, which obligations hold the most weight? Why? What would you do in this situation?

What if you talked to your supervisors and were told that they knew of the pollution and "had it under control." A little investigating on your part revealed that the Environmental Protection Agency also knew of the problem and assessed your company a yearly fine of a few hundred dollars, but hadn't demanded the pollution stop or be cleaned up. What would you do then?

[1] Markel, Mike. *Technical Communication: Situations and Strategies*, 4th edition. St. Martin's Press: New York, 1996, pp 24–28.

Now comes the fun part—but the challenging part as well. What do you want to request as compensation? Your drama group probably spent no piddly sum on the mascara. The doctor bill is not cheap either. More importantly, you'd like the manufacturer to know about this problem to prevent others from experiencing it. Thus you may be asking for both monetary compensation and reassurances, not to mention some abject apologies.

4. **Write a firm but civil conclusion.** You'll get nowhere by threatening or name-calling in a complaint. In the conclusion, say that you are confident that the recipient will grant your request and that you can continue doing business together. Obviously, that's a veiled threat, but it's civil and controlled. Keeping the lid on throughout this complaint creates a personal appeal: it establishes you as a calm, level-headed, fair-minded person.

In the final paragraph, you can express confidence that the manufacturer of the mascara will grant your requested compensation and investigate the problem. You might also express hope that your drama group can continue using the mascara and not be forced to warn other college drama groups with which you compete.

5. **Write the introduction.** To counteract the tendency to start blasting away from the very start, it's wise to write the introduction last. Indicate the purpose of this communication and provide an overview of what it contains. As with any persuasive effort, you don't necessarily state your main argumentative point in the introduction: some readers might just stop reading. Instead, you can say that you are writing about a problem you've had with the recipient's product or service. And don't forget to keep paragraphs of business communications short, especially the introduction!

Start this way: say that you are writing about a serious problem you had with the mascara—that indicates the topic and purpose of the letter. For the overview, you can state that you want to explain what happened and request that something be done about the problem. Having said this in 4 or 5 lines, you have avoided diving headlong into the gory details. Obviously, anybody can read between the lines, but you stand a better chance of having the entire letter read.

6. **Review and revise your rough draft.** Use the strategies in Chapter 18 to systematically review and revise your communication. Use the top-down approach described in Chapter 18: start by reviewing for audience, purpose, and situation; then move on to content, organization, and transitions; then headings, lists, tables, and graphics; then on to sentence-style revision and technical style; and finally grammar, usage, spelling, and punctuation problems.

Adjustment Communications

An adjustment letter, memo, or e-mail is a reply to a complaint. Its job is either to grant or to deny the requested compensation, explain why, find some way to placate the customer and thus keep that customer's business, and defend the company's concern for quality and for its customers. Whether denying or granting a request, the adjustment communication is a challenging exercise in persuasion.

1. **Find a situation involving a problem with a product or service.** The ideal situation is a problem occurring in your own workplace. If you can't find such, think of a problem you experienced, and put yourself in the position of the poor customer-relations employee who must answer your complaint.

    Imagine that you work for the admissions and records department of your college. Today, you were given a student complaint letter to answer. A student has received an F for a course in which she actually made an A. She has made several prior requests for the grade change, but somehow her requests have been lost in your office. While this grade remained unchanged and her grade point unrealistically low, she missed an opportunity to get a scholarship. She is requesting not merely the grade change, but monetary compensation equaling the amount of the scholarship she lost.

2. **Decide whether you can grant the requested compensation or some portion of it.** If you write a reply to your very own complaint letter, don't get greedy. Perhaps you can write *two* adjustment communications—one granting the request and one denying it. Also consider the idea of some partial compensation or some good-will gesture—for example, a discount on future purchases.

    Certainly the grade can be changed, but the college cannot reimburse the full scholarship amount. Even though the student's request is unrealistic, there is the concern that she might bring a lawsuit against the college. What to do? Knowing that you cannot grant her monetary request, what can you do to placate this individual?

3. **Define the reasons for your decision.** If the request is totally outrageous, you may have to invent diplomatic reasons for the denial. The problem may have occurred because of the customer's clumsiness. Or, the customer may be acting unscrupulously. You still must find diplomatic ways to state your reasons for denial. Doing so establishes your personal appeal as a calm, level-headed, fair-minded, and caring person.

    What are your reasons for denying the student's request? First, it isn't certain that the student would have won the scholarship anyway.

Second, the student cannot expect such a large compensation for an honest mistake. Can you think of others?

4. **If you deny the request, find a way to placate the customer.** What can you do to soften the blow of the denial? Some companies offer coupons, discounts, and other things. Perhaps you can offer partial compensation. In some cases, the best option may be to express your regrets and your hopes that business relations can continue and just be done with it.

   There are various possibilities: you could offer the student a discount on her next registration or reimburse her expenses for the course in question. If these seem like blatant attempts to buy her off, then let's just say we are truly sorry and sign off.

5. **If you grant the request (or even deny it), find a way to defend your organization.** In an adjustment letter, your job is to defend the reputation of your organization. If your organization made a mistake, acknowledge it but insist that it doesn't reflect on your organization's concern for quality.

   Privately, you are all too aware that your department is understaffed. You stay too busy to overhaul your process. Everybody certainly tries hard and cares about students. In defense of your department, you might want to mention these things—but no whining!

6. **Write the introduction.** Now, at long last, you are ready to write an introduction. Start by indicating that your letter is in response to the complaint—that's the topic and purpose. Explain that your letter reviews the problem and addresses the writer's concerns—that's the overview. But don't blurt out the denial. Doing so might upset readers and prevent them from reading the rest of what you have to say.

   Begin by expressing your thanks that the student took the time to write. Express concern over the problem, and indicate that you'll address that problem as well as her request. This indicates topic and purpose, provides an overview of what the rest of the letter contains, but does not blurt out your outright refusal of her request.

7. **Review and revise your rough draft.** Use the strategies in Chapter 18 to systematically review and revise this letter. Use the top-down approach described in Chapter 18: start by reviewing for audience, purpose, and situation; then move on to content, organization, and transitions; then headings, lists, tables, and graphics; then on to sentence-style revision and technical style; and finally grammar, usage, spelling, and punctuation problems.

Inquiry Communications

In an inquiry communication, you ask someone for information, such as a favor. If you address an organization that advertises its products or services, it's a "solicited" inquiry. If you address the inquiry to a researcher who is quietly working away in her field and has done nothing to invite your inquiry, it's "unsolicited." In unsolicited inquiries, you must use some quiet persuasion to convince the recipient to help you. Here are some steps for writing this kind of communication.

> For an inquiry communication, imagine you are working on that recycling project discussed in Chapter 6. Your job is to contact cities and ask specific questions about their recycling programs. For this communication, e-mail might be the best approach.

1. **Make a list of exactly what information you want.** If it's a series of questions, make those questions pinpoint precise. Throw out general questions that would require writing a textbook to answer. Whenever possible, seek local experience. For example, if you inquire about a new insulin system for diabetics, ask about the experience of patients at the recipient's clinic.

> Imagine that you want statistics on participation in recycling programs. If there have been increases, you want to know why they happened. You also want to know about the volumes of recycled materials handled, variations in prices, and problems experienced with suppliers and vendors. Avoid asking general questions such as "What problems have you experienced" or "How's it going."

2. **Ensure that the information you are requesting is not easily available elsewhere.** What could be more aggravating than to be asked for information easily found in general textbooks and encyclopedias?

> You've checked to see if any municipal reports are available for the city's recycling project—none are. The information is safely tucked away in electronic databases in various computers in municipal offices. This is legitimate information to request.

3. **Explain why you need the information and how you've tried to get it elsewhere.** In an unsolicited inquiry, your inquiree will be more cooperative if you explain why you need the information. People are receptive to students working on technical reports. To reassure them that you're not lazy, explain the efforts you made to get his information by other means.

> You are working on this project for your city. Thus, you can hope for some comradeship with the recipient of your inquiry. Mention that

you've made several phone calls and e-mail inquiries trying to find out if any reports exist.

4. **Find ways to make replying easier.** In the actual request, try to ease the recipient's job of replying. For example, number the questions; create a form to fill out; include self-addressed stamped envelopes; offer to come copy materials; or ask for information sources, Web sites, or contacts.

   You're asking mostly for numbers. Therefore, you might be able to set up a fill-in-the-blank questionnaire. Or the recipient of this inquiry might be able to send you electronic files containing the data you need.

5. **Write a closing paragraph indicating how the recipient of this inquiry might benefit.** Try to find some way to return the favor— some gesture of gratitude and good will. Offer to send your completed project, with the recipient's contributions gratefully acknowledged.

   In this inquiry, express sincere appreciation for the recipient's efforts in helping you. As a gesture of gratitude, perhaps you can promise to send a copy of the report or pass along cost-saving techniques if you stumble across any. Otherwise, you can appeal to the recipient's general sense of comradeship regarding recycling programs.

6. **Review and revise your rough draft.** Use the strategies in Chapter 18 to systematically review and revise your letter. Use the top-down approach described in Chapter 18: start by reviewing for audience, purpose, and situation; then move on to content, organization, and transitions; then headings, lists, tables, and graphics; then on to sentence-style revision and technical style; and finally grammar, usage, spelling, and punctuation problems.

WORKSHOP: BUSINESS LETTERS, MEMOS, E-MAIL

Here are some additional ideas for practicing the concepts, tools, and strategies in this chapter:

1. *Choose a type of communication.* Consider the following situations. Which forms of communication discussed in this chapter (in-person conversation, phone, e-mail, memo, letter, or other) would be the best to use, the worst to use, and why?
   a. You want to request an extension of the due date on your report project from your instructor.

b. You want to complain about the rudeness and lack of responsiveness of the Human Resources Department in handling your questions concerning your health benefits.

c. You want to ask your manager for a raise.

d. You want to see if a certain business might be interested in your services (courier, computer maintenance, janitorial service, etc.)

e. You want to request that your fellow employees format their monthly status reports a certain way before they give them to you (you integrate them into one comprehensive department report).

f. You want to make sure your client understands that the technical staff of that client has not provided you with any reviews or other input on the project you are doing for that client.

g. You want to wish your manager a happy birthday.

2. *Get the tone right.* Consider the following situations. Describe the tone that you would try for in each and explain why.

a. You signed up for a cruise and put down a deposit. Now you read on an Internet travel discussion list that the company is no longer using the ship you signed up to travel on—it is using a smaller, older ship. Customers are returning from their cruises complaining about safety, service, and quality of the food on the cruise. There's a rumor the company is going into bankruptcy. You write a letter canceling your trip and requesting a refund of your deposit.

b. Your child's high school always has a prayer at its commencement. You don't mind the prayer, but because a large minority of the students belong to other religions, you write the administrators requesting that any prayer be nonsectarian.

c. You've been the principal of a small private school for 12 years and every year you have to nag the parents to follow the designated traffic pattern when they pick up or drop off their children. Some of the parents ignore the rules, and yesterday one of the teachers was almost run over. If parents don't cooperate, you feel that you must hire officers to direct traffic every day, and this cost will have to be passed on in the cost of tuition. Write a letter to all the parents.

3. *Survey international communication styles.* Select any of the example letters, memos, or e-mail messages in this book and do a survey on how people from other cultures would respond to them. Find out not only whether the language is understandable but also whether the style strikes your international readers as blunt, rude, impersonal, or impolite.

4. *Create personalized templates for your letters and memos.* Use the steps discussed in this chapter to design your own templates for business letters and memos. For the letter template, put your name, address, phone number, and e-mail address in the header. Try putting a solid ruled line at the bottom of the header area, and another such line

at the top of the footer area. Also, try changing the margins. Do the same with the memo, but be sure to include the DATE:, TO:, FROM:, and SUBJECT: lines. See if you can automate the date in both the letter and memo templates. And, if you're really adventurous, try including a graphic logo in the header of either or both templates.

<table>
<tr><td>

Letter format: This complaint letter uses the block format, in which all letter components start at the left margin.

</td><td>

COMPLAINT LETTER[2]

1313 Horse Trail Rd.
Buda, Texas 78610
6 June, 1996

</td></tr>
<tr><td>

Heading and inside address: When you use the traditional business-letter format, put your address and the date at the top, followed by the full name and address of the recipient of the letter.

</td><td>

Customer Relations/Claims Company
John Duke Manufacturing Company
1104 Sutton Drive Suite #112
Cairo, MI 45006

</td></tr>
<tr><td>

Salutation: Notice this writer's solution to the problem of what to put after "Dear." This works for a complaint letter but not other types of communication, such as the application letter.

</td><td>

Dear Representative:

</td></tr>
<tr><td>

Introduction: Notice how short this first paragraph is, how it announces the purpose of the letter, and how it does not get into the details of the problem.

</td><td>

I am writing in regards to a digital multimeter (DMM) that I recently purchased by mail-order from your company. Because the DMM only functions partially, I am requesting repairs, another DMM with comparable features, or a refund of the purchase price plus C.O.D. charges, and shipping and handling.

</td></tr>
<tr><td>

Problem description: Notice that the writer calmly and objectively describes the details of the purchase and then the details of the problem, providing dollar amounts, dates, and other such specifics.

</td><td>

I purchased the meter for $250.00 by calling the 1-800 number listed in an advertisement. My phone order occurred on August 20th. The meter was delivered on August 23rd via UPX C.O.D. The total purchase price was $282.50. The following items were included with the DMM: one set of meter leads, one power supply cord, and one black nylon-fiber carrying case.

The DMM (Duke Model 8012A) will not register an accurate voltage or current reading. The other features function as intended, and the fuse that protects the AC circuitry is in good operating condition. However, when a regulated AC voltage or current is applied to the meter leads, the only reading displayed is a low negative value. This is true whether the function switch is set to measure either AC voltage or current.

</td></tr>
</table>

[2] Many thanks to Robert Hutchison, Austin Community College technical writing student, for this complaint letter and permission to adapt it here.

Justification: In this fourth paragraph, the writer explains why he believes he should be reimbursed. Notice the diplomatic assumption that this was a "temporary" problem that can "easily" be fixed.

When I received the DMM, I inspected the packaging in which the meter was shipped, and there was no evidence of damage. Styrofoam inserts were used to protect the meter from any shock during the shipping process. Because I saw no loose components when inspecting the primary fuse, I am led to believe the problem somehow occurred during manufacture. No doubt, there is a temporary malfunction that can easily be fixed.

Compensation request: Notice that this writer chooses to state his request for compensation in the very first paragraph rather than toward the end of the letter. Not one to beat around the bush, he probably assumes that his situation is so obvious no rhetorical finesse is needed.

Your prompt attention and response would be greatly appreciated as I intend to use the meter in conjunction with my job.

Sincerely,

Terry Ward

Terry Ward

Enclosures: This writer is sending everything back including a copy of the receipt. This will act as evidence supporting his request.

Enclosed: 1 Duke 8012A DMM, Lot #3308-WIC4
1 set of meter Leads, 1 power supply cord
1 black nylon-fiber carrying case,
Copy of purchase receipt

INQUIRY LETTER[3]

0000 Paul's Path

Austin, TX 78700

July 12, 1998

Technical Support

Red Hat Software, Inc.

4201 Research Commons, Suite 100

Research Triangle Park, NC 27709

Dear Technical Support Department:

I am writing to ask you some technical questions about hardware support for Red Hat Linux version 5.1. I saw Red Hat Software's advertisement for version 5.1 of Linux in the August, 1998 issue of *Linux Journal.* I was quite impressed with the capabilities as listed in the advertisement and would like to learn more about the product. Before I make the decision to purchase the software, I need to be certain that it will work properly on my computer.

I have three hardware support questions that I would like you to answer. I have reviewed the technical support information at Red Hat Software's home page (www.redhat.com), but I have not been able to find answers to my questions. The three hardware-related questions that I have are as follows:

1. Does the latest release of Red Hat Linux support the Diamond Viper 330 PCI video card? This card uses the Riva chipset released by NVIDIA Corporation.

2. If Red Hat Linux does not currently have a driver for this card, is there a timetable for when the card will be supported?

[3] Thanks to Gary Ninn, former technical writing student at Austin Community College for this inquiry letter and permission to adapt it here.

3. Is there an online site for the latest list of supported hardware? This would be a great aid to me in the future, as I often upgrade my machine.

I am aware that some of the early versions of Red Hat Linux were not able to support some of Diamond Multimedia's products. I hope that new drivers are available in this latest software release. If the latest release of Red Hat Linux can support my video hardware, I will definitely purchase the product. The price is exceptional, and the range of features is outstanding.

For your convenience, you can respond to me by e-mail. My e-mail address is garyc@nnn.com. If you prefer to respond by telephone, you can reach me at (512) 000-0000. I appreciate any assistance that you are able to provide me.

Sincerely,

W. Gary Ninn

W. Gary Ninn

Rationale and benefit: This writer explains why he needs this information, even though this is a "solicited" inquiry. This writer also suggests why it is in the interests of the recipient to help him—he's a potential customer!

CHAPTER 14

Employment-Search Tools: Application Letters, Resumes

EMPLOYMENT TRENDS AND PROJECTIONS

The World Wide Web is loaded with interesting information about the contemporary and evolving workplace, trends in employment, and projections about upcoming occupations, not to mention job-hunting, resume-writing, and interviewing tips:

Bureau of Labor Statistics. Go to Publications and look at the *Occupational Outlook* publications. **www.bls.gov**

About.com Telecommuting Guide. How about working at home? **telecommuting.miningco.com/business/business/telecommuting/mbody.htm**

Thirty-Hour Work Week. **lamar.colostate.edu/~terrel**

"Affluenza—Epidemic of Overconsumption." A National Public Radio special. **www.pbs.org/kcts/affluenza**

Vault.com—about today's workplace including information about schmoozing, office politics, and other subjects. **www.vaultreports.com**

Provided by the *Wall Street Interactive Edition*, this Web site includes interesting articles on careers, jobs, job-hunting and interviewing advice, and trends. **careers.wsj.com**

A Career and Job-Hunting Resources Guide, from Quintessential Careers. **www.quintcareers.com**

JobWeb from the National Association of Colleges and Employers. **www.jobweb.org/**

Accessed January 23, 2001.

This chapter focuses on two important job-getting tools—application letters and resumes. Although other aspects of the job hunt, such as finding jobs, researching companies, developing a portfolio, interviewing, and negotiating are not covered in detail here, you will find links to Web sites and references to printed resources that will help.

Resumes and especially application letters are essentially efforts to persuade people to interview you for a job or to hire you. Thus persuasion is the key infrastructure of these two employment-search tools. If you understand the concepts and strategies associated with persuasion as they are discussed in Chapter 6, you've got a fighting chance to write more effective application letters and resumes.

This chapter focuses briefly on things you can do to gear up for a job search, then discusses planning and designing resumes and application letters. The resume section provides suggestions on designing scannable and online resumes.

Note: For additional examples of application letters and resumes, as well as the documents discussed in this chapter, see **www.io.com/~hcexres/ power_tools/examples**.

HOW DO YOU GET STARTED ON A JOB SEARCH?

Here are some things you can do to begin a job search:

- **Find jobs you are interested in.** In addition to bulletin boards at school or work and the classified sections of newspapers, look at job announcements in professional journals. Watch for "job fairs" and "career days" held locally. Check the local chapters of professional organizations in your field: they often maintain "job banks." Don't forget the World Wide Web, where you can search nationally and internationally. Job-search Web sites are easy to find; consider these for starters:

Yahoo! Classifieds—**classifieds.yahoo.com/employment.html**

Monster.com—**campus.monster.com**

Intern Center at Monster.com—**new.interncenter.com/new**

JobDirect.com—**www.jobdirect.com**

NationJob Network—**www.nationjob.com**

InternshipPrograms.com—**www.internshipprograms.com**

- **Research the company, organization, or industry.** When you've found a job or two, research the industry those companies operate within and the companies themselves. Here are just a few of the resources on the Web:

SuperPages.com's BigBook—**www.bigbook.com**

BizWeb Business Guide to the Web—**www.bizweb.com**

Monster.com—**company.monster.com**

Yahoo! Careers: Company Research—
   careers.yahoo.com/employment/company_research

Yahoo! Careers: Industry Research—
   careers.yahoo.com/employment/industry_research

- **Conduct information interviews.** In an information interview, you gather information about the company, its products or services, and possible employment opportunities. Don't ask for information that is readily available in a library or on the Internet. Information interviews give you contacts, get your name "out there," and enable you to know what's going on in your field. However, don't expect to walk in unannounced for an information interview. Make a formal appointment, and prepare your questions ahead of time.
- **Start a job-search database, log, and timeline.** In the thick of a job hunt, it's easy to get confused and forget. Start a database in which you list every contact with a potential employer you've had, including dates, names (especially the names of secretaries and receptionists), addresses, phone numbers, and so on. Also, start a combination log, timeline, and to-do list. After sending an application letter, make a note of that on a timeline. Make another note about two weeks to the right on that timeline as a reminder to send a follow-up letter if you've not heard from the potential employer.
- **Check with placement agencies.** Since the 1990s, employers have increasingly relied on placement agencies for temporary workers. Employers sometimes use a "try-and-buy" approach: if they like a particular contract worker, they hire that individual full time. Find one or two placement agencies that handle your kind of work, schedule an information interview, and bring along your resume. Have a placement specialist assess your qualifications and tell you what you'll need to do to become more employable.

- **Visit with local professional organizations.** One of the best ways to get started is to join or attend the meetings of a professional society related to your career. One of their important functions is to enable people to network. Often these groups have job banks (listings of open jobs) and resume-posting services. Go to these meetings, get to know a few people, and get some advice.
- **Rehearse for interviews.** It's not a bad idea to practice answering some of the common interview questions such as the following:

Can you tell us about your previous work experience in relation to this job?

How has your education gotten you ready for this job?

Do you like working on your own or as part of a team?

What do you know about our corporation? Why do you want to work here?

Explain how your background has prepared you for this position.

Tell us about a difficult situation you faced and how you dealt with it.

Do you have any questions for us about this job or our corporation?

Quite a few of the employment Web sites have tips on interviewing, proper attire of interviews, and much more. As of the year 2000, for example, you could visit the following Web sites:

WetFeet.com—**www.wetfeet.com/asp/home.asp**

Yahoo—**careers.yahoo.com/employment/advice/interviewing_guidance**

JobsSmart: Advice on resumes, samples and cover letters, electronic resumes—**www.jobsmart.org/tools/resume**

Monster.com—**content.monster.com/jobinfo**

Rebecca Smith's eResumes & Resources: good info on electronic resumes plus jobs and job searching in general—**www.eresumes.com**

How to Create an Online Resume (from Illinois Wesleyan University)—**titan.iwu.edu/~ccenter/resume**

Career City—**www.careercity.com/content/interview/index.asp**

Help for the job hunt, including tips and samples for letters and resumes—**www.rileyguide.com**

HOW DO YOU WRITE A RESUME?

A resume is a summary of your work experience, education, training, and anything else that supports your efforts to get employment.

Plan a Resume

To get a sense of the planning process for a resume, follow these planning steps of the job announcement shown in Figure 14-1:

1. **Find a job to apply for.** Use the suggestions in the preceding sections to find a job.

   > Imagine that you are interested in getting an entry-level job as a "web-master"—Web designer, programmer, manager, and other such. In the local newspaper, you find six local webmaster or internet-technical jobs under Employment–Internet. Calling some placement agencies, you find out that they also have jobs for webmasters, Web technicians, and other such jobs. At yahoo.com, your search on "webmaster" delivers 431 hits. You see rates ranging from $15.00 to $135.00 per hour and salaries ranging from $20,000 to $85,000 per year. You see a wide variety of requirements and a dizzying array of acronyms: HTML, DHTML, XML, Perl, CGI, ASP, Java, IIS, TCP/IP, UNIX, NT, PHP, and more.

Title:	Webmaster
Skills:	HTML, Perl, Web Development
Posted:	09/12/01
Location:	Austin, TX
Area code:	512
Start:	11/15/01
Type:	Full-time
Pay:	$25K - $40K
Length:	Permanent
E-mail:	resumes@web_brokers.com
Web:	www.web_brokers.com

Job Description:
Experienced webmaster and Web designer with at least two years experience working on such projects. Should have strong HTML, Javascript, and Perl skills, along with good aesthetic sense.

This is for a young company involved with online brokerage transactions, and is an excellent opportunity for anyone with the above skills.

Interested parties should reply by e-mail to:

Dingglas Smoss
Web Brokers, Inc.
Dingglas.Smoss@web_brokers.com

FIGURE 14-1
Example job announcement.

2. **Analyze the job announcement carefully for the stated job requirements and any underlying assumptions.** Make sure you understand exactly what the potential employer is looking for.

   While these jobs look rather intimidating, you find several that you may be able to talk your way into. After all, job requirements are sometimes more like wish lists. The job announcement shown in Figure 14-1 requires creating and editing Web pages (HTML), programming in Perl and JavaScript, and using your aesthetic sense to create attractive Web sites. You get the feeling that this is a young company. That, and the mere two years of experience required, lead you to believe you might have a chance.

3. **Find out what you can about the company, its operations, and the job.** See the preceding suggestions on researching companies and industries.

   You try some of the company-research tools listed in the preceding, but to no avail. This company is too new, too small, and too local. You go to the company's current Web site and get a sense of the company's business—investment brokering—but not much else. You get a friend to check out the company in person: only seven people in the office suite, very casual, very young.

4. **Make a list of your work experience.** For each of your work-experience items, take notes on the beginning and ending dates, the full name and address of the organization you worked for, your primary duties, the names of projects you worked on, the departments or areas you worked in, the names of the equipment you used, awards you received, and any other quantifiable information such as employees supervised, throughputs (such as calls answered, problems resolved, product manufactured), savings you were able to accomplish for your employers, and so on.

   As a graduating college student, you have little work experience. You've created basic Web sites for several churches and worked in the college bookstore and a nearby coffee shop. You take notes on the two church jobs: the dates you did the work; names and addresses of contacts at those churches; URLs for the Web sites you designed; descriptions of those Web sites; and details on the JavaScript and Perl scripts you used to create guest books, chat rooms, and popup information. For the other jobs, you list names, addresses, supervisors, beginning and ending dates, your hours, and your primary responsibilities. Knowing that the potential employer is involved in financial matters, you plan to emphasize the bookkeeping work you did using various software applications.

5. Make a list of your education. For each education item, take notes on beginning and ending dates, degrees or certificates received, important courses and projects, grade point average, major topics covered, instructor names, awards or scholarships, organizations you belonged to, and so on.

> You write down as many potentially helpful details as you can think of relating to your education: your business administration degree, the dates started and completed, important courses (including the course on e-commerce and marketing on the Web), your GPA, instructor's names that may be recognized in the community, and your research project about the potential impact of the Web on telecommuting. You also list the special seminars you attended on creating Web pages with HTML and that introduction to CGI and Perl you took (offered free by the college). To connect with the "aesthetic" requirement, mention that History of Art course you took. Unfortunately, you never received any awards or scholarships. Also, you decide to become a member of a national professional web-master society—and quick!

6. Make a list of your military training and experience. Take the same kinds of notes for your military service. Merge your military training into your education section and your military work into your work experience, or present this information in a separate section of your resume.

> Unfortunately, you don't have any military experience to cite. If you did, it might be something like systems management, security, and networking. These Internet-related technical skills might appeal to your potential employers.

7. List other related activities and experience. You can include hobbies, organizations you belong to, and other skills you possess in a resume. They "round you out" as a real person, and can help you fill up the rest of a resume page if you are at the beginning of a career.

> What makes you a real person, not a work-obsessed robot? You might be a great lover of jazz or classical music, an avid backyard gardener, an amateur gourmet chef, or a connoisseur of the detective fiction of certain choice authors. Maybe you like hanging out in all-night coffee shops with friends—oops, better leave that one out. At the beginning of a career, details like these can help fill resumes and prevent them from looking skimpy.

8. Develop an organizational strategy for the resume contents. Resume writers typically use one of three strategies to organize and present information about their work experience, education, training, military experience, and other such qualifications:

- *Reverse-chronological strategy.* Divide your background into areas such as work experience, training, military experience, and education, and then list related items for each in reverse-chronological order.
- *Functional strategy.* Find the "themes" or "functions" in your career (such as computer networks, bookkeeping, supervision, recruitment, project management, programming, intensive-care nursing, and so on). For each, list work experience, training, education, or anything else that relates.
- *Combined strategy.* Some employers dislike the functional strategy because it does not show the chronology of a career. Others dislike the reverse-chronological strategy because it does not adequately show your qualifications in each area. You can combine the two strategies to get the best of both. Present the functional sections first, then present your career chronology under a heading like "Work History" toward the bottom.

Which to use? Standard wisdom says to use the reverse-chronological strategy if you are at the beginning of your career. But experiment with both. (See Figure 14-2 for an example in which the same information is organized in these two contrasting ways.)

You consider the functional approach. You could have headings such as Web Page Design, Web Programming with Perl and JavaScript, Business Experience, and so on. Under each of these headings, list your jobs, course work, seminars, and any related self-teaching you've done. But that may look skimpy. Instead, you decide on the reverse-chronological approach: a straight listing of your education and training with *lots* of detail on each item, and a following section listing your work experience—again, with *lots* of detail.

9. **Plan to include lots of detail.** Pump in as much detail as you can for each experience, education, training, or service item. Cite specific product names, specific industry-standard names, and specific statistical detail (number of employees, average calls handled per month). Details like these with capital letters and numbers force potential employers to slow down and read carefully—which is exactly what you want them to do. Don't say "Familiar with many software applications"; list the ones you know. Don't say that you work in a "fast-paced, high-throughput office." Put some actual numbers with those statements: "fast-paced" in terms of what and how many? What was being "through-put" and how much? Where was the office? What do they do there?

In this resume, you want to emphasize that you entered HTML directly into plain-text files using MS Notepad and Paul Lutus's

Reverse-Chronological Approach	Functional ("Thematic") Approach

Education

Southwest Texas State University, San Marcos, TX

Bachelor of Business Administration (AASCB accredited) in Computer Information Systems (1995–2000)

Member of Association of Information Technology Professionals and World Organization of Webmasters.

Computer skills include HTML, Perl/CGI, JavaScript, Visual Basic, COBOL, SQL, Windows 95/98/2000, MS Access and Excel, Intuit Quicken, Lotus 1-2-3.

Related course work includes e-commerce, Web marketing, finance, accounting, systems analysis, COBOL, Visual Basic, database design, management information systems, data communications, Web databases, client/server applications, art history.

Continuing education credits in Perl/CGI, HTML, JavaScript.

Austin Community College, Austin, TX

Webmaster Certification Program (1999–2001)

Pursuing ACC Webmaster Certificate with specialization in System/Application Programming. Courses in JavaScript, Java, Perl, CGI, Web database applications, ASP, TCP/IP, UNIX and Windows NT. Expected completion December 2001.

Experience

St. Ignacius Episcopal Church, 16 Exposition, San Marcos, TX 78700

Web designer. Developed and maintain church Web site: Web pages developed in direct HTML coding, with tables, frames, graphics, and forms. Interactive forms developed using Perl/CGI and JavaScript (1999–present).

Java Place, 1703 University Blvd., San Marcos, TX 78700

Store assistant manager. Designed menus and ads for local newspapers, kept books in Intuit Quicken, interviewed and trained new employees, managed store during weekends, waited tables (1998–present).

St. Martin's Lutheran Church, 1000 Ranch Rd., Wimberly, TX 78700

Web designer. Developed and maintain church Web site: Web pages developed in direct HTML coding, with tables, frames, graphics, and forms. Interactive facilities developed using Perl/CGI and JavaScript (1998–present).

University Bookstore, 1200 University Blvd., San Marcos, TX 78700

Clerk. Designed advertisements for student newspaper, stocked shelves, did inventory, ran cash register (1997–1998).

Website Development

Developed and maintain church Web sites: Web pages developed in direct HTML coding, with tables, frames, graphics. St. Ignacius Episcopal (1999–present); St. Martin's Lutheran (1998–present).

Pursuing Webmaster Certificate at Austin Community College with specialization in System/Application Programming. Courses in JavaScript, Java, Perl, CGI, Web database applications, ASP, TCP/IP, UNIX and Windows NT. Expected completion December 2001.

Member of Association of Information Technology Professionals and World Organization of Webmasters.

Web Programming

Interactive forms (guestbooks, congregation databases, announcement bulletin boards) developed using Perl/CGI and JavaScript. St. Ignacius Episcopal (1999–present); St. Martin's Lutheran (1998–present).

Course work includes COBOL, Visual Basic, database design, management information systems, data communications, Web databases, client/server applications.

Continuing education credits in Austin Community College Webmaster Certification Program JavaScript, Java, Perl, CGI, Web database applications, ASP, TCP/IP, UNIX and Windows NT.

Design Experience

Designed menus and ads for local newspapers. Java Place, 1703 University Blvd., San Marcos, TX 78700.

Developed and maintain church Web site: Web pages developed in direct HTML coding, with tables, frames, graphics, and forms. Interactive facilities developed using Perl/CGI and JavaScript (1998–present). St. Martin's Lutheran Church, 1000 Ranch Rd., Wimberly, TX 78700.

Courses in art history: ArtH 3313 Introduction to Fine Arts, ArtT 2371 Fundamentals of Art Theory and Practice

Member of Amon Carter Museum and Kimbell Art Museum (Fort Worth, TX)

General Business

Designed advertisements for student newspaper, stocked shelves, did inventory, ran cash register (1997–1998). University Bookstore, 1200 University Blvd., San Marcos, TX 78700.

Related course work includes e-commerce, Web marketing, finance, accounting, management information systems.

Kept books in Intuit Quicken, interviewed and trained new employees, managed store during weekends, waited tables (1998–present). Java Place, 1703 University Blvd., San Marcos, TX 78700.

FIGURE 14-2

Two approaches to experience–education sections of resumes. The reverse-chronological approach, shown on the left, is more often used by students and recent graduates. The functional, or "thematic," approach, shown on the right, is more often used by people with several years of professional experience.

Arachnophilia. You want to mention that your Web pages made extensive use of tables and frames. Also mention that you used Paint Shop Pro to create or edit graphics and add text labels to them. Describe the Perl and JavaScript applications—guest books, "post it" boards, questionnaires, quizzes, and so on. You don't have a lot to put in your resume, so push details like these extra hard—they help fill a resume with legitimate "stuff."

10. Plan the resume heading section. Think about what to include at the very top of your resume: name, addresses, phone numbers, mailing addresses, e-mail addresses, your home Web page, professional or occupational title, key certifications, name and number of the job you are seeking, and so on.

In the resume heading, you decide to include your name (using the same style you use in your major headings). Beneath that will be your apartment and parents' addresses. Associated with these will be phone numbers. The heading will include your e-mail address and the URL of your personal home page. Anything else?

11. Consider an objectives section. An objective section states your career goals or objectives in two or three lines. However, some believe that such a section limits your opportunities. For example, you may have done design, training, and supervision in your field. If your objective mentions only design, you may not make the cut for training and supervision jobs. Also, these sections are sometimes embarrassingly general and self-congratulatory. Still, an objectives section can define your professional focus sharply.

An objectives section may help—it will certainly help fill out the resume page, which is something you're worried about. You want to spotlight your business administration education, your experience with Web site development, and your interest in business possibilities on the Web. Find a statement general enough not to lock you into one area or to exclude you from others. Still, it must be specific enough so that potential employers understand what you are about.

12. Consider a highlights section. Many resumes include a highlights section. Typically, it is a bulleted list just below the resume heading. Listing a half-dozen or so of your best qualifications, it provides a quick-reference to the rest of your resume, a kind of resume-at-a-glance to draw employers in.

You could create a highlights section, although it would be a stretch considering your lack of experience. The bullets might include the following: direct, manual work in HTML, with thorough knowledge of HTML tags; programming in Perl to create guestbooks, chatrooms,

and online questionnaires; skills with UNIX systems and Internet con-
nectivity; basic JavaScript abilities for creating banners, quizzes and
popups; or knowledge of business software such as spreadsheets
and databases. Knowing that an online brokerage firm must post
tables, graphs, and charts, you claim the ability to dynamically link
such material to Web pages. Of course, at the moment you write the
resume, it's not technically true that you know how to do these
things—but it will be true tomorrow!

Okay! You've developed a rather detailed idea of the contents, organization, and even the format for a resume. Now start thinking about putting
this material into different delivery media—specifically, the conventional
printed resume, the scannable resume, and the Web-based resume.

Design a Standard Print Resume

For the print version of a resume, decide on margins, type style (font), type
size, heading styles, body text styles, use of bold and italics (highlighting),
special indentation, bulleted and numbered lists, multicolumn text or
tables, and so on.

For the print version of your resume, you decide to try these specifications (the results of which are shown in the resume at the end of this
chapter):

- *Margins:* 1.5-inch margins to ensure that the resume fills the page;
  "hanging-head" style (body text indented a half or full inch in relation
  to headings).
- *Body type:* 12-point Arial for body text, including address, phone,
  and Internet information; the objective statement; the bulleted items in
  the highlights section; the text in the work-experience and education
  sections; and the text under the technical-skills and personal-details
  sections.
- *Headings:* 14-point bold Arial for your name and for the major headings (Highlights, Education, Experience, Technical Skills, and Personal
  Details).
- *Other format:* Bulleted lists to itemize the details of your education,
  training, work experience, projects, technical skills, and personal information (which will also help extend the resume farther down the page.)
  Bold for the names of the educational institutions you've attended and
  organizations you've worked for.

Design a Scannable Resume

In the 1990s, organizations began scanning resumes into databases so
that they could do electronic searches. For example, a company looking
for medical-technical professionals experienced with certain MRI equipment could search an applicant database for a specific manufacturer, or a

specific MRI model name, as well as "MRI" and "magnetic resonance imaging." The recruiters would then review only those resumes retrieved from the search.

Considering this scenario, you can see why it is of the utmost importance to include specific manufacturer names, model names and numbers, version and release numbers, and other such specifics in any resume, especially scannable ones.

However, you must avoid fancy formatting such as that discussed in preceding chapters. Instead, use a common type style and size (for example, 12-point Times New Roman) throughout the scannable resume, including headings. Avoid using bold, italics, different type sizes or fonts, or indented text. Instead of bullets, use asterisks. Separate the asterisk and the text following it with a single space, and let following lines of bulleted items wrap back to the left margin. (See the scannable version of the resume at the end of this chapter.)

Obviously, this feels like a retreat into the dark ages! However, software applications and scanning equipment are likely to evolve to the point that your beautifully formatted print resume will scan nicely and will convert to HTML at the touch of a button—some day.

Design a Web Resume

Now that the World Wide Web has moved onto center stage of professional life, you need a resume in every conceivable format: standard print format, scannable, and online. Posting your resume on the Web gives you a number of opportunities to provide more detail, make it more rapidly accessible, and of course more easily updatable and more readily available. You can cite the URL (Web address) of your Web resume on your business card or in your letters and e-mail and link to it from your home page.

Examples of Web resumes. To get an idea of what's possible with a Web resume, explore the resumes at some of these resume-posting sites, or just do a search on "resumes" at **monster.com, careers.yahoo.com/ employment**, or **www.jobsmart.org/tools/resume**.

Advantages of Web resumes. Notice some of the techniques that these Web-resume writers use:

- *Centralized menu of links and use of color.* Place links to all the main sections of your resume at the top of the page. That way, readers can go directly to highlights, work experience, education, or technical skills as they wish. Web pages make it easy to use color—discretely, of course— to brighten up the overall appearance. Don't overdo it: use a different color only for headings, and stick with black text on white background for the body of the resume.
- *Links to home pages of other employers.* Adding links to your previous employers enables the prospective employer to find out where you previously worked and what sort of organization it is. Obviously, this capability is special to the Web resume.

- *More extensive detail, if desired.* As you gain experience, you run into problems keeping everything on a single resume page. Using links, you can provide as much detail as you want: readers can link to it if they want, but the main page of your resume stays neat and concise.
- *Links to projects and other examples of work.* A Web resume also enables you to link to examples of your work. You can show off documents you developed by converting them to Web pages or portable document files (PDFs). If you've developed Web sites, set links to them. If you've done construction work—decks, pools, landscaping, renovations, restorations, or artwork—you can set links to pictures of this work.
- *Different versions of the resume.* As you know from earlier in this chapter, you can arrange resume details several ways—namely, the functional, the reverse-chronological, and combinations. Instead of fretting over which to use, you can provide both and readers can link to the one they prefer.
- *Links to printable and scannable versions.* To enable potential employers to print out or scan your resume, provide links from your Web resume to these versions of your resume, as well.

Problems to avoid.   Web resumes enable you to provide much more information about your qualifications, experience, and education than conventional print media normally could. However, it's easy to overdo it:

- *Don't include personal details unrelated to employment.* Don't include pictures of yourself, your family, your pets, or other unrelated items in an online resume any more than you would in a conventional print resume.
- *Avoid garish multi-color, multi-font combinations.* Keep the use of color under control. Avoid hard-to-read color combinations, for example, blue letters on a red background. Conventional black text on white background is okay.
- *Avoid creating a jumbled, cramped-looking resume.* Design your Web resume so that it feels neat, clean, simple, roomy, and well-organized.

Steps for creating a Web resume.   How do you create a Web resume? Try converting your current resume to HTML. All major word-processing applications claim this ability. In Microsoft Word, for example, open your resume file, click **File**, then **Save As**, and then, in the Save as type field, select **HTML Document**. (Typically, the results are appalling. You might as well enter the HTML tags directly.)

1. To learn how to design your own Web resume, find a Web resume that you like and take a look at its "source"—its HTML tagging—to see how the page is designed. (In Netscape, click **View** and then **Reload**.)
2. Read "How Do You Create a Web Page?" in Chapter 17. There, you'll find the basics of creating and designing Web pages. Then consider starting with an HTML resume template, such as the one shown in Figure 14-3.

| Replace all the italicized text with your information. | ```
<HTML><HEAD><TITLE>Resume of YourName</TITLE></HEAD>
<BODY BGCOLOR=color TEXT=color>
<CENTER>
<FONT COLOR=color><H1>YourName</H1></FONT>
<B>YourAddress<BR>
YourPhone &210; A HREF="mailto: YourEmail">YourEmail<A></B>
</CENTER>
<HR>
``` |
| Replace "Color" with "blue," for example, or with the names of any of the basic colors.<br><br>The <LI> tag creates a bullet (when it is inside the <UL> and </UL> tags). Use an <LI> tag for each additional highlight you want to include. | ```
<FONT COLOR=Color><H1>Highlights</H1></FONT>
<UL>
<LI>BestHighlight
<LI>NextBestHighlight
</UL>
<HR>
<FONT COLOR=color><H1>Work Experience</H1></FONT>
<A HREF="CompanyURL">CompanyName</A><BR>
<B>JobTitle</B>, StartDate-EndDate
<UL>
<LI>FirstHighlight
<LI>SecondHighlight
</UL>
``` |
| The <BR> tag creates a line break.<br><br>The <UL> tells the browser to create a bulleted-list item each time it sees an <LI> tag. The </UL> tag ends the bulleted list. | ```
<HR>
<FONT COLOR=color><H1>Education and Training</H1></FONT>
<A HREF="CollegeURL">InstitutionName</A><BR>
<B>Major</B>, StartDate-EndDate
<UL>
<LI>FirstHighlight
<LI>SecondHighlight
</UL>
``` |
| The <HR> tag creates a solid line across the page. | ```
<HR>
<FONT COLOR=color><H1>Technical Skills</H1></FONT>
<UL>
<LI>FirstSkill
<LI>SecondSkill
</UL>
``` |
| Used inside the <A HREF> tag, "mailto" opens an e-mail box with the indicated address in the TO: field.<br><br>The <P> tag creates a paragraph break—in other words, a blank line. | ```
<HR>
<FONT COLOR=color><H1>References</H1></FONT>
<UL>
<LI><A HREF="mailto:EmailAddress">ReferenceName</A><BR>
Address<BR>
Phone
<P>
<LI>(repeat above tagging for each reference)
</UL>

<CENTER>References provided on request</CENTER>
</BODY></HTML>
``` |

FIGURE 14-3

HTML tagging for a simple Web resume. Replace the italicized material with your own text. Create additional items with <LI> tags under Highlights, Work Experience, Education and Training, and Technical Skills as needed. Enter this text into a plain text file (using BBedit or MS Notepad, for example), name it `resume.html`, and then view it through Netscape or Internet Explorer.
```

3. For other formatting:

Hypertext	Use the hypertext concepts and design in Chapter 17.
Headings	Follow the steps in the HTML section of Chapter 7 to create the main headings of your resume.
Lists	Follow the steps in the HTML section of Chapter 8 to create bulleted and numbered lists detailing your experience and education.
Highlighting	Follow the steps in the HTML section of Chapter 12 to make text bold, italic, and larger or smaller, and to use different colors or fonts.
Tables	Follow the steps in the HTML section of Chapter 10 for using tables to better control the format of your Web resume.

HOW DO YOU WRITE AN APPLICATION LETTER?

Addressed to a specific employer, an *application letter* highlights your best qualifications for a specific position. Sometimes, the application letter is called a "cover letter." Strictly speaking, a cover letter just identifies the job and introduces the resume. A real application letter has a lot more work to do.

Think of the application letter as an intermediary between the job announcement and your resume. The letter helps employers see the match between your qualifications and the job requirements. In a resume, employers have to dig for these details; they are showcased in an application letter. The letter is not a qualifications summary. It is a careful selection of details that make you right for the job along with careful, low-keyed self-promotion (not the shameless kind).

Strategies for Application Letters

Think carefully about the contents and organization of an application letter, particularly the introduction, as well as the tone.

Organizational strategies. To achieve this selective showcasing of your qualifications for a particular job, consider using one of the following organizational strategies:

■ *Education–experience approach.* Particularly for people just beginning a career, a common strategy is to have an education section followed by work-experience section. You're not limited to these two. For example, you could have separate sections for your military experience, volunteer work, or special projects you've done.

■ *Functional approach.* If you're further along in your career, another approach is to create sections for each area of your qualifications to match the job requirements. For example, for a job as a Web designer, the requirements might include graphic design using specific software tools, HTML work, and experience with adapting audio and video to Web pages. Three of the main paragraphs of your application letter could focus on those three areas. Each paragraph would summarize work experience, training, or education related to that job requirement.

Strategies for the introduction. The first paragraph of the application letter is critical—it must use just a few lines to do the following:

- *Indicate the purpose of the letter.* You don't have to make it sleep-inducing (for example, "The purpose of the following letter is to apply for . . ."), but indicate that the purpose of the letter is to apply for a job.
- *Identify the job you're applying for.* Cite the specific job title, job number, and your source for finding out about the job.
- *Draw readers in and make them read further.* Classic strategies include naming your best qualification or mentioning the name of someone with whom you've worked that readers will recognize. If none of these strategies work, try sounding enthusiastic about the job or the company.

Content strategies. Regardless of the organizational approach you use, keep the following in mind as you write and revise the application letter:

- *Address readers' needs rather than your own.* Explain how you can help the potential employer and how your background enables you to do the work. It won't help to rave about how much the job fits into your career plans, how convenient the location is, or how much you like the dental plan.
- *Provide specifics, details, and examples.* Include the full names of companies, departments, product names and numbers, years and dates, people's names and titles, dollar amounts, and other directly relevant numerical information. Your letter should contain lots of capital letters and numbers, which slows readers down and makes them read more carefully. Take a look at the contrastive examples in Figure 14-4 to see the effect that specifics have.
- *Avoid self-congratulatory statements.* Saying that you are a "quick learner," that you "work well under pressure," or that you are "people oriented" just doesn't help. In fact, some readers may mutter, "Oh yeah, sez who?" Let the details, the specifics, and the examples in your application letter *show* that you are these things. Let readers make these judgments for themselves.
- *Sound interested.* Ideally, your application letter should have some energy and sparkle to it, without sounding phony. An application letter should be direct, energetic, and positive while remaining an expression of your essential personality. If you are excited about this line of work, if you admire the company, if you like its products—say so!

As for my work experience, I have been employed with organizations that have drawn on my computer-programming skills. At one organization, I was involved in setting up new software, training personnel, and managing networked users. In the other organization, I basically did various aspects of programming. I work well under pressure and am team oriented.

I will soon graduate with a computer degree. In my degree program, I have studied numerous programming languages and have developed an excellent grasp of them.

How can anyone get interested in this blah individual? Can you find a single specific detail? There's not much here to support this individual's claims.

Notice how many specifics in which this version works: specific organization names, months there, employees trained, network size, university name, degree name, expected graduation date, GPA, and specific programming languages.

As for my work experience, I have been employed with two organizations over the past three years that have drawn on my computer-programming skills. In my eighteen months with CMB*LIC Mortgage Corporation, I was involved in setting up new accounting and management software, training groups of ten employees on a monthly basis, and managing users of AutoCAD on a 10-user LAN. In my ten months with Hydronic Corporation as an assistant programmer, I did much of the same design, code, and test work as the regular programmer/analysts.

In December, I will graduate with a Bachelor of Science from Southwest Texas State University. My overall grade point average is 3.125. In my degree program, I have studied and developed a portfolio of applications in the following programming languages: Pascal, Assembler, COBOL, RPG, and C.

FIGURE 14-4

Power of details in application letters. Don't just summarize your resume; highlight key details that make you right for the job. Notice how the revised version drops the annoying self-praise ("work well under pressure" and "team oriented"), but the details create a stronger sense that this individual really does have these qualities.

■ *Avoid negatives such as salary requirements or complaints about former employers.* Imagine how complaints about other employers sound to a potential employer. By including complaints, you may label yourself as a malcontent and a whiner. Similarly, don't mention salary requirements unless directed to do so by the job announcement.

Plan an Application Letter

To get an idea of how to develop an application letter, follow the process through these common stages. Use the job announcement shown in Figure 14-1.

1. **Analyze the job announcement.** Look carefully for the stated job requirements and try to uncover any underlying assumptions. Ordinarily, it's best to develop the application letter after the resume. The resume is like an inventory of your professional background and skills. Select from that inventory to write the application letter.

   Study that job announcement in Figure 14-1 carefully. For skills, it lists HTML, Perl, and something called "Web development." That phrase is probably a scattershot—the potential employers may lack the technical background necessary to understand the term. Notice, however, in the descriptive paragraph, two requirements are added: JavaScript and aesthetic sense. Does that suggest that these additional requirements are less important? And what does it say about these people that they would use the term "aesthetic"? You know that this is a new company; its owners and staff are young. The salary range is rather low. A "real" webmaster, bristling with experience could expect double that. Thus it's clear that this is an entry-level job—just right for you to talk your way into.

2. **Find out what you can about the company.** Research the company (or its local site), its operations, and this particular industry or area of work.

   You've visited the company's Web site and read everything there. You make note of unfamiliar terms and look them up. You get a friend to visit the company in person to pick up brochures, look around, and check out the staff and office. You check the local Better Business Bureau to see if anyone has complained about this company. You ask around—*network*—to see if you can find business people who might know this company or its principals.

3. **Make a list of your strongest qualifications.** List what makes you right for this position, as well as areas where you lack qualifications.

   What about you will get you employed at this place? The two Web sites you did for those churches were easy and fun but only add up to a year's worth of experience. You can honestly claim to know HTML rather than relying on Web-page editors. You are good with graphics—scanning, creating, editing, adding text labels—even though the job ad merely states something about an "aesthetic sense." You are still learning Perl and JavaScript, but you can modify and adapt existing code for most of the basic interactive facilities: chat rooms, bulletin boards, fill-in-the-blank forms, questionnaires, quizzes, and simple databases. As for aesthetic sense, the Web sites you designed for yourself and the two churches are attractive. Also, you designed advertisements and menus for the bookstore and coffeeshop, not to mention all those museums you visit regularly.

4. Plan the strategy for the main paragraphs of your application letter. Decide whether you want to use a functional or an education–experience approach (as discussed earlier).

You have two choices in terms of organization and content for this letter:

■ *Education–experience approach.* You can have separate paragraphs about your work experience and about your education. In the experience paragraph (or paragraphs), discuss those church Web sites, making sure to say "HTML," "Perl," "CGI," and "JavaScript" often. In the education paragraph, mention your Bachelor of Business Administration degree and your special project involving e-commerce. Say something about that art history course and your museum habit. As for your work at the bookstore and the coffeeshop, you developed skills with business software like Quicken, Excel, and Lotus 1-2-3, and you exercised your aesthetic sense by designing advertisements and menus. Mention the business-graphics software you know—the potential employers will want to show graphics, charts and tables "dynamically" on their Web pages, even if they don't realize it yet.

■ *Functional approach.* Instead of the education-experience approach, you can include a paragraph about your Web page work using HTML, a paragraph about your Perl and JavaScript programming work, a paragraph about your business-administration studies with references to business software tools you learned, and perhaps a final paragraph about your "aesthetic sense."

In general, you want this letter to have a youthful, energetic, perky, good-natured feel to it—just like you in person. You want the potential employer to get the sense that you'd be fun to work with, a dependable and reliable worker, a flexible and adaptable person, and a quick learner.

5. Select the details for each of the main sections. When you write the actual draft of these sections, remember to use specific details— specific company names, dates, product names, dollar amounts, and so on. (See Figure 14-4 for an example.)

This is easy. You'll cite the full names of the two churches and the names of the individuals with whom you worked closely at each church. You'll mention that you used HTML 3.2 and Arachnophilia as your design tools. You used Paint Shop Pro 6.0 for graphics work and Netscape 5.6 as the browser, although you tested your pages in MS Internet Explorer 4.7 as well. You've used Intuit Quicken version 6.3, Lotus 1-2-3 version 7, Harvard Graphics 3.07 and CorelDRAW 9. Your advertisements for the University Bookstore in San Marcos, TX, appeared throughout the spring 1999 semester in the *Daily Bearcat*. The menus you designed for the Java Shop in 2000 are still being used, although a few items and some prices have changed. You'll mention that research paper you wrote in the spring semester of 1999,

"E-commerce Potential for Small Rural Businesses." You can cite *by full name* those e-commerce and Web marketing courses you took. This is the kind of detail you want in the letter (although the swarm of software version or release numbers might be overwhelming).

6. **Plan the introduction to this application letter.** Remember that, while it must be brief, the introduction must indicate that an application letter follows, provide some reference to the job you are applying for, capture readers' attention, and make them want to continue reading.

> Remembering that the introduction paragraph must be brief but compelling, you decide to begin with a simple statement saying that this is an application for the company's webmaster position, which you found on the Web site of the local newspaper. Also, you'll state that you have a good combination of Web-development skills, business background, and aesthetic sense that will enable you to do a great job. You hope these statements will get these employers curious enough to read the rest of the letter to find out just what that "combination" is and how you acquired it.

7. **Plan the conclusion to this application letter.** The main jobs of the conclusion are to press readers for an interview and to facilitate readers in getting in touch with you.

> You decide to finish off this letter quickly, mentioning your phone number, e-mail address, and times when you'll be available to interview. You also invite them for a cup of coffee at the JavaShop. To ensure that this process moves forward, you state that you'll call in 10 days if you've not heard from them.

8. **Plan the delivery mode.** In this new world of fax machines, e-mail, and the World Wide Web, how should you send a job application or make it available? Study the job advertisement; do what it says. If you are uncertain, contact the employer and find out what's preferred.

> The job ad (in Figure 14-1) says to reply by e-mail—rather vague and unhelpful instructions. You decide to call, which will also give you more of a sense about the company. The phone call leaves you with a vague, informal sense, as if these people aren't used to the hiring process. So! You decide to write a smaller version of your application letter to put in e-mail that you send to these employers. You'll also attach a full version of the letter and resume to this same e-mail. You'll give these two attachments identifiable names—ennderson_let ter.doc and ennderson_resume.doc. Your e-mail, your attached letter, and your attached resume will all cite the Web version of your resume where you provide links to more detail about your work, studies, and

projects. (You decide to dust off that e-commerce report you wrote and put it on the Web. You also decide to scan those advertisements and menus you designed and link them to your Web resume as well.)

Design and Format the Application Letter

Chapter 13 covers the essentials for formatting business letters. Here are some reminders:

■ Remember that you can adjust page margins so that the letter fits nicely on the page. You don't want just a few lines falling over to a second page, nor do you want the letter huddled at the top of one page, making it look skimpy.

■ Use a standard font and type size—avoid the unusual or strange (unless that's just you). Text using 12-point Times New Roman and Arial works fine.

■ Use a "block" format as shown in the examples at the end of this chapter. Left-align all the elements of the application letter. (Don't forget to sign your name between the complimentary close and your typed name.)

■ A nice professional touch is to design your own letterhead like the ones shown in the examples. Doing so also gets your name at the top of the letter.

WORKSHOP: APPLICATION LETTERS AND RESUMES

Here are some additional ideas for practicing the concepts, tools, and strategies in this chapter:

1. *Search for jobs.* Using any of the tools mentioned earlier for finding jobs, list a half-dozen jobs that fit your current qualifications (or those you will have upon graduation).

2. *Define job qualifications.* For several of the jobs you found, make a list of the qualifications you'd need to be seriously considered. Don't just repeat the qualifications stated in the job—include the unstated ones as well.

3. *Research a company.* For one of the jobs you found in the preceding, use the tools discussed earlier in this chapter to find pertinent information about the company. Don't just grasp at any information—find information that you could actually use in an interview in some way. For each item of information, jot some notes as to how you would use that item.

4. *Design a "perfect" resume.* Imagine that you are a perfect fit for one of the job descriptions in the preceding. Sketch the corresponding resume, making up the appropriate details.

5. *Design a "first-job" resume.* Imagine that you want to apply for one of the jobs you located in the preceding, but are just out of college with no formal work experience in the field. Sketch a resume in which you include every conceivably related bit of experience (internships, volunteer work, semester projects, and so on).

6. *Design a resume from raw materials.* Select one of the sets of raw materials available at **www.io.com/~hcexres/power_tools/resumes**, and design a resume from that material. Try designing one version that uses the reverse-chronological approach and another that uses the functional approach.

7. *Anticipate interview questions.* For one of the jobs you found in the preceding, write a script, complete with the questions the interviewers would ask you and your answers. For ideas, see some of the employment sites on the World Wide Web such as **www.wetfeet.com/asp/home.asp**.

Application Letter

3010 Norwood Hills
Austin, Texas 78723
June 3, 2000

Sulzer Orthopedics Inc.
9900 Spectrum Dr.
Austin, Tx 78717
Subj.: Application for full-time position as System Support Specialist

Please consider me for the full-time position of System Support Specialist. I found out about this position from Adrian Dupre who currently works for Sulzer Orthopedics in the IS Department as the Help Desk Supervisor. My work in the IS Department as a part-time temporary employee for the last 10 months will enable me to begin contributing immediately with little or no transition time.

I have extensive experience in configuring, installing, and troubleshooting PCs, laptops, servers, and Palm Pilots. I have personally set up over 50 desktop PCs including hardware, operating system, and application installation. I have also provided technical support to the Help Desk in troubleshooting hardware and application failures in the DOS, Windows 95/98, Windows NT, Novell, and UNIX environments. Typical hardware support included troubleshooting motherboards, CD-ROMS, hard drives, floppy drives, video cards, modems, and network cards. Typical application support included Microsoft Word, Excel, Powerpoint, Access, Internet Explorer, Outlook, Netscape Navigator, and Oracle applications. In the IS department, I have also done customer-service work, for which I have received several recognition awards.

While pursuing my AAS in Electronic Technology with a minor in Computer Science, I have also taken numerous programming classes, which gave me some proficiency in Pascal, C++, and assembly language. One of my projects involved creating a front-end prototype in C++ for a system-support database, which enables rapid documenting, searching and tracking of customer problems.

I looking forward to meeting with you at your convenience. I can be reached at any time at (512) 926-6266 or at msalinas@austin.org

Sincerely,

Michael Salinas

Michael Salinas
Encl: resume

Print Resume

Kaharen Ennderson

1307 Mirsall Lane #72	1801 Oak Path
San Marcos, TX 78000	Baytown, TX 77000
(512) 000-0000	(281) 000-0000

kah_ennder@swt.edu—www.swt.edu/~kah_ennder

Objective

To obtain an entry-level position with a company needing my abilities in World Wide Web development and business administration.

Summary

- Proficient at developing, maintaining, and using direct HTML coding with graphics, tables, frames, and forms.
- Customized and maintain guestbooks, listservs, questionnaire databases, and other interactive facilities, using Perl/CGI and JavaScript.
- Proficient with Web graphics using tools such as Paint Shop Pro.
- Completed Bachelor of Business Administration with special courses in finance, marketing, and e-commerce.
- Proficient with business-related software such as Microsoft Access and Excel, Lotus 1-2-3, Intuit Quicken, Harvard Graphics, and CorelDRAW.
- Life-long interest in the arts, particularly painting, art courses, and museums.

Education

Southwest Texas State University, San Marcos, TX
Bachelor of Business Administration (AASCB accredited) in Computer Information Systems (1995–2000)

- Member of Association of Information Technology Professionals and World Organization of Webmasters.
- Computer skills include HTML, Perl/CGI, JavaScript, Visual Basic, COBOL, SQL, Windows 95/98/2000, MS Access and Excel, Intuit Quicken, Lotus 1-2-3.
- Related course work includes e-commerce, Web marketing, finance, accounting, systems analysis, COBOL, Visual Basic, database design, management information systems, data communications, Web databases, client/server applications, art history.
- Continuing education credits in Perl/CGI, HTML, JavaScript.

Austin Community College, Austin, TX
Webmaster Certification Program (1999–2001)
Pursuing ACC Webmaster Certificate with specialization in System/Application Programming. Courses in JavaScript, Java,

Note: Using standard page margins and type sizes, this resume would fit on one page. For presentation in this book with annotation, it runs over to two pages.

The entire resume is done in Arial font. The heading uses bold 11-point Arial; the address area uses 9.5-point Arial; the main headings (Objective, Summary, etc.) use 9.5-point bold Arial; and the main text uses 9-point Arial.

The address area uses a two-column table so that the current and parents' address information aligns nicely.

Notice how this resume writer attempts to highlight her Web-design experience, her experience with the worlds of business and investment, and her graphic design experience.

This writer uses the "reverse-chronological" strategy, presenting education first, then work experience.

Notice that this resume writer bolds the name of the organization and italicizes her job title, major, or degree name. Doing so provides a consistent overall design across the education and employment sections.

Notice how this writer gives herself a job title even though she probably did not have an official title in these rather informal jobs.

Notice how she accentuates Perl, CGI, HTML, Web page, and JavaScript every chance she gets—these are the buzzwords the potential employer is looking for.

Notice how this writer "plays up" her graphic design experience by emphasizing her design work on advertisements and on Web sites. At the time, this work might have seemed no more glamorous than sweeping the floor, but now it counts!

She uses this final section to "round" herself out as a human being with her own personality and interests. But notice that even in a section like this she has an agenda: professional interests and activities involving computers and the World Wide Web, team activities and leadership, and aesthetics (cuisine, jazz, and art museums).

Perl, CGI, Web database aplications, ASP, TCP/IP, UNIX, and Windows NT. Expected completion December 2001.

Employment

St. Ignacius Episcopal Church, 16 Exposition, San Marcos, TX 78700
Web designer. Developed and maintain church Web site: Web pages developed in direct HTML coding, with tables, frames, graphics, and forms. Interactive forms developed using Perl/CGI and JavaScript (1999–present).

Java Place, 1703 University Blvd., San Marcos, TX 78700
Store assistant manager. Designed menus and ads for local newspapers, kept books in Intuit Quicken, interviewed and trained new employees, managed store during weekends, waited tables (1998–present).

St. Martin's Lutheran Church, 1000 Ranch Rd., Wimberly, TX 78700
Web designer. Developed and maintain church Web site: Web pages developed in direct HTML coding, with tables, frames, graphics, and forms. Interactive facilities developed using Perl/CGI and JavaScript (1998–present).

University Bookstore, 1200 University Blvd., San Marcos, TX 78700
Clerk. Designed advertisements for student newspaper, stocked shelves, did inventory, ran cash register (1997–1998).

Personal Interest and Activities

- Active member of the World Organization of Webmasters and Association of Information Technology Professionals.
- Computer-game design hobbyist using Java and Visual Basic.
- Chinese cuisine efforts (weekends only!)
- Jazz piano work of Red Garland, Thelonious Monk, Kenny Barron.
- Mystery and detective fiction, especially Georges Simenon and Jonathan Kellerman.
- SWT Sport Cycling Team (past vice-president)
- Texas Eagles Cycling Team (co-founder, secretary)
- Frequent visitor to the fine arts museums in Austin, San Antonio, Dallas, Fort Worth, and Houston.

Scannable Resume

KAHAREN ENNDERSON

Current address & phone:
1307 Mirsall Lane #72
San Marcos, TX 78000
(512)000-0000

E-mail: kah_ennder@swt.edu
Home page: www.swt.edu/~kah_ennder

OBJECTIVE
To obtain an entry-level position with a company needing my abilities in World Wide Web development and business administration.

SUMMARY
* Developed and maintain Web sites for St. Ignacius Episcopal Church and St. Martin's Lutheran Church, using HTML coding.
* Customized and maintain guestbooks, listservs, questionnaire databases, using Perl/CGI and JavaScript.
* Proficient with Web graphics using tools such as Paint Shop Pro.
* Completed Bachelor of Business Administration with special courses in finance, marketing, and e-commerce.
* Proficient with business-related software such as Microsoft Access and Excel, Lotus 1-2-3, Intuit Quicken, Harvard Graphics, and CorelDRAW.
* Life-long interest in the arts, particularly painting, art courses, and museums.

EDUCATION
Southwest Texas State University, San Marcos, TX
Bachelor of Business Administration (AASCB accredited) in Computer Information Systems (1995–2000)
Member of Association of Information Technology Professionals, World Organization of Webmasters.
Computer skills include HTML, Perl/CGI, JavaScript, Visual Basic, COBOL, SQL, Windows 95/98/2000, MS Access and Excel, Intuit Quicken, Lotus 1-2-3.

Related course work includes e-commerce, Web marketing, finance, accounting, systems analysis, COBOL, Visual Basic, database design, management information systems, data communications, Web databases, client/server applications, art history.
Continuing education credits in Perl/CGI, HTML, JavaScript.

Austin Community College, Austin, TX
Webmaster Certification Program (1999–2001)

Parents' address & phone:
1801 Oak Path
Baytown, TX 77000
(281) 000-0000

Pursuing ACC Webmaster Certificate with specialization in System/Application Programming. Courses in JavaScript, Java, Perl, CGI, Web database applications, ASP, TCP/IP, UNIX, and Windows NT. Expected completion December 2001.

EMPLOYMENT
St. Ignacius Episcopal Church, 16 Exposition, San Marcos, TX 78700
Developed and maintain church Web site: Web pages developed in direct HTML coding, with tables, frames, graphics, and forms. Interactive facilities developed using Perl/CGI and JavaScript (1999–present).

Java Place, 1703 University Blvd., San Marcos, TX 78700
Designed menus and ads for local newspapers, kept books in Intuit Quicken, interviewed and trained new employees, managed store during weekends, waited tables (1998–present).

St. Martin's Lutheran Church, 1000 Ranch Rd., Wimberly, TX 78700
Developed and maintain church Web site: Web pages developed in direct HTML coding, with tables, frames, graphics, and forms. Interactive forms developed using Perl/CGI and JavaScript (1999–present).

University Bookstore, 1200 University Blvd., San Marcos, TX 78700
Designed advertisements for student newspaper, stocked shelves, did inventory, ran cash register (1997–1998).

PERSONAL INTERESTS AND ACTIVITIES
* Computer-game design hobbyist using Java and Visual Basic.
* Chinese cuisine efforts (weekends only!)
* Jazz piano work of Red Garland, Thelonious Monk, Kenny Barron.
* Mystery and detective fiction, especially Georges Simenon and Jonathan Kellerman.
* SWT Sport Cycling Team (past vice-president)
* Texas Eagles Cycling Team (co-founder, secretary)

HTML Code for Web Resume

The "frameset" file: you provide a link to this file, not to either of the other two. You might name this file "resume0.html."

```
<HTML>
<HEAD>
<TITLE>Kaharen Ennderson: Resume</TITLE>
</HEAD>

<FRAMESET COLS="35%,*">
    <FRAME NAME="menu_frame" SRC="resume1.html">
        <FRAME NAME="reading_frame" SRC="resume2.html">
</FRAMESET>

<NOFRAMES>
        Go to <A HREF="resume2.html">
</NOFRAMES>

</HTML>
```

The "menu" file: this is the material that appears in the left frame. Its file name is "resume1.html."

```
<HTML>
<HEAD>
<TITLE></TITLE>
</HEAD>

<BODY BGCOLOR="white" link="teal" alink="#008080"
vlink="#800000">
<FONT COLOR="#8000000" FACE="Arial">
<CENTER><H3><FONT SIZE="-2">Resume of</FONT><BR>
Kaharen Ennderson</H3></CENTER></FONT>
<FONT FACE="Arial" SIZE="-2">
<BR><BR>
<UL>
<LI><A HREF="resume2.html#contact">Contact information</A>
<LI><A HREF="resume2.html#objective">Objective</A>
<LI><A HREF="resume2.html#summary">Summary</A>
<LI><A HREF="resume2.html#education">Education</A>
<LI><A HREF="resume2.html#employment">Employment</A>
<LI><A HREF="resume2.html#personal">Personal Interest and
Activities</A>
</UL>

</BODY>
</HTML>
```

The "reading" file: this is the material that appears in the right frame. Notice how the A NAME tags provide a "target" for A HREF tags.

```
<HTML><HEAD><TITLE></TITLE></HEAD><BODY>
<FONT FACE="Arial" SIZE="-2"><CENTER>
<A NAME="contact"> </A>
<TABLE><TR><TD ALIGN="center" COLSPAN="2"><FONT
FACE="Arial">
<H3><FONT SIZE="-2">Resume of</FONT><BR>Kaharen
Ennderson</H3></TD>
</TR><TR>
<TD WIDTH="75%"><FONT FACE="Arial" SIZE="-2">1307 Mirsall
Lane #72</TD>
<TD><FONT FACE="Arial" SIZE="-2">1801 Oak Path</TD>
</TR><TR>
<TD WIDTH="75%"><FONT FACE="Arial" SIZE="-2">San Marcos,
TX 78000</TD>
<TD><FONT FACE="Arial" SIZE="-2">Baytown, TX 77000</TD>
</TR><TR>
<TD WIDTH="75%"><FONT FACE="Arial" SIZE="-2">(512) 000-
0000</TD>
<TD><FONT FACE="Arial" SIZE="-2">(281) 000-0000</TD>
</TR><TR>
<TD COLSPAN="2" ALIGN="center"><FONT FACE="Arial" SIZE=
"-2">
<A HREF="mailto:kah_ennder@swt.edu">kah_ennder@swt.edu</A>—
<A HREF="www.swt.edu/~kah_ennder">www.swt.edu/~kah_ennder
</A></TD>
</TR></TABLE></CENTER>
<H3>Objective</H3>
To obtain an entry-level position with a company needing my abilities in
World Wide Web development and business administration.

<A NAME="summary"><H3>Summary</H3></A>

<UL>
<LI>Developed and maintain Web sites for St. Ignacius Episcopal
Church and St. Martin's Lutheran Church, using direct HTML coding.
<LI>Customized and maintain guestbooks, listservs, questionnaire
databases, and interactive facilities, using Perl/CGI and JavaScript.
<LI>Proficient with Web graphics using tools such as Paint Shop Pro.
<LI>Completed Bachelor of Business Administration with special
courses in finance, marketing, and e-commerce.
<LI>Proficient with business-related software such as Microsoft Access
and Excel, Lotus 1-2-3, Intuit Quicken, Harvard Graphics, and
CorelDRAW.
```

In the left frame (menu frame), the reader can click on underlined items and see the related text in the right frame (reading frame). For example, you can click on Employment in the menu frame and the reading frame will scroll to the employment section and display it.

```
<LI>Life-long interest in the arts, particularly painting, art courses, and
museums.
</UL>


<A NAME="education"><H3>Education</H3></A>
<B><A HREF="www.swtsu.edu">Southwest Texas State
University</A></B>, San Marcos, TX<BR>
<I>Bachelor of Business Administration</I> (AASCB accredited) in
Computer Information Systems (1995–2000)
<UL>
<LI>Member of Association of <A HREF="www.aip.org">Information
Technology Professionals</A>, <A HREF="www.wow.org">World
Organization of Webmasters</A>.
<LI>Computer skills include HTML, Perl/CGI, JavaScript, Visual Basic,
COBOL, SQL, Windows 95/98/2000, MS Access and Excel, Intuit
Quicken, Lotus 1-2-3.
<LI>Related course work includes e-commerce, Web marketing, finance,
accounting, systems analysis, COBOL, Visual Basic, database design,
management information systems, data communications, Web
databases, client/server applications, art history.
<LI>Continuing education credits in Perl/CGI, HTML, JavaScript.
</UL>
```

Resume of
Kaharen Ennderson

- Contact information
- Objective
- Summary
- Education
- Employment
- Personal Interest and Activities

Opens an e-mail box so that the reader can send e-mail.

Links to the resume writer's Web page.

Links to the home page of her college.

Links to Web pages of the professional associations to which she belongs.

Resume of
Kaharen Ennderson

Mirsall Lane #72
San Marcos, TX 78000
(512) 000-000

1801 Oak Path
Baytown, TX 77000
(281) 000-000

kah_ennder@swt.edu — www.swt.edu/~kah_ennder

Objective

To obtain an entry-level position with a company needing my abilities in World Wide Web development and business administration.

Summary

- Developed and maintain websites for St. Ignacius Episcopal Church and St. Martin's Lutheran Church, using direct HTML coding.
- Customized and maintain guestbooks, listservs, questionnaire databases, and interactive facilities, using Perl/CGI and JavaScript.
- Proficient with web graphics using tools such as Paint Shop Pro.
- Completed Bachelor of Business Administration with special courses in finance, marketing, and ecommerce.
- Proficient with business-related software such as Microsoft Access and Excel, Lotus 123, Intuit Quicken, Harvard Graphics, and CorelDRAW.
- Life-long interest in the arts, particularly painting, art courses, museums.

Education

Southwest Texas State University, San Marcos, TX
Bachelor of Business Administration (AASCB accredite4d) in Computer Information Systems (1995-2000)

- Member of Association of Information Technology Professionals, World Organization of Webmasters.
- Computer skills include HTML, Perl/CGI, JavaScript, Visual Basic, COBOL, SQL, Windows 95/98/2000, MS Access and Excel, Intuit Quicken, Lotus 123.
- Related course work includes ecommerce, web marketing, finance, accounting, systems analysis, COBOL, Visual Basic, database design, management information systems, data communications, web databases, client/server applications, art history.
- Continuing education credits in Perl/CGI, HTML, JavaScript.

CHAPTER 15

Formal Reports: Design, Format, Abstracts

WIND ENERGY

The advance of this important technology, like many others mentioned in this book, depends on technical reports—information about new techniques and materials that squeeze every last watt out of even the mildest breeze:

American Association for Wind Engineering. **www.aawe.org**

American Wind Energy Association. **www.awea.org**

DOE Wind Energy Program. **www.eren.doe.gov/wind**

Center for Renewable Energy Systems Technology. **solstice.crest.org/index.shtml**

About.com. Wind Energy—General. **energyindustry.about.com/business/energyindustry/msub21.htm**

Sandia National Laboratories: Wind Energy Technology. **www.sandia.gov/wind**

Guided Tour on Wind Energy. From the Danish Wind Turbine Manufacturers Association. **www.windpower.dk/tour**

Accessed January 25, 2001.

This chapter focuses on design and format for various types of technical documents. You'll see common designs for the following:

■ *Business-letter reports.* Used for relatively short documents sent to a client or customer (external to your organization).
■ *Memo reports.* Used for relatively short documents that stay "in house" within your organization.
■ *Formal reports.* Used for longer documents (more than 4 pages, for example). Use a cover letter or cover memo, depending on whether the document goes external or stays internal to your organization.

This chapter also covers strategies for writing executive summaries (also called abstracts), an important component of longer technical reports.

Note: For additional examples of the documents discussed in this chapter, see **www.io.com/~hcexres/power_tools/examples**.

Technical Documents: Design and Delivery Options

Self-contained business letter	Put a short document (for example, under 4 pages) that goes to an external audience in a business letter. You still use headings, lists, tables, and graphics.
Self-contained memo	Use the memo format (TO, FROM, SUBJ) if the document stays "in house." Take a look at the example memo report at the end of Chapter 1.
Self-contained e-mail	Brief reports can be sent through e-mail. The entire document occurs within the body of the e-mail, which limits how much fancy formatting you can do.
Formal document with transmittal letter	Put longer documents (for example, over 4 pages) in their own separate bindings with formal elements such as identifying cover labels, title pages, and tables of contents. Paper-clip the transmittal letter (cover letter) to the front of the bound document. This design is discussed later in this chapter; see the example at the end of this chapter as well as the progress report at the end of Chapter 6.
Formal document with transmittal memo	Instead of a transmittal letter, attach a transmittal memo if the document stays in house.
Formal document as attachment to e-mail	If you ship a document attached to e-mail, your e-mail can serve as the transmittal. However, because your e-mail may not stay with the printed document, create a transmittal letter or memo as the first page of the printed document.
Web-page document	To deliver technical documents over the World Wide Web, know something about hypertext and HTML (presented in Chapter 17). Take a look at the example of the main-menu page in that chapter designed for the recommendation report in Chapter 17.
Oral presentation	You can also deliver a report orally. See Chapter 16 for strategies on delivering oral presentations.

DESIGNING TECHNICAL DOCUMENTS

You have a number of possibilities for the design and delivery of a technical document, depending on how formal the situation is, whether the document is for external or internal readers, how long the document is, and how it will be used (see table opposite).

Regardless of which design and delivery method you choose (except for oral presentations), use headings, lists, tables, and graphics just as you would in any other technical document.

FORMAL REPORTS AND OTHER TECHNICAL DOCUMENTS

Formal reports are "formal" because they have special covers, are bound, and contain front- and back-matter elements such as title pages, tables of contents, lists of figures, abstracts, and so on. Formal reports are used more like books: people read and reread them, pass them around, and store them on shelves. They are not necessarily for readers external to the organization. Plenty of formal reports stay "in-house" in organizations like IBM, Hewlett-Packard, and Dell.

General Layout

For most formal documents, consider using the following specifications:

- Use standard 8.5- by 11-inch paper, and use only one side of the paper.
- Use 1, 1.25, or 1.5 inches for the top, bottom, left, and right margins. In some documents, the left margin is a half-inch larger than the right in order to accommodate the binding.
- Use a standard *serif* font such as Times New Roman, Garamond, or Century for the body text. Use 9-, 10-, 11-, or 12-point type size for body text.
- Use a *sans serif* font such as Arial or Helvetica for headings. Type size, of course, varies according to the level of the heading but ranges from 24 points down to the same point size as the body text.
- Choose a line spacing according to local requirements or your preferences. In the days of the typewriter, body text was double-spaced. With word-processing and desktop-publishing software, double-spacing is unnecessary. For readability, however, use a line-spacing value that equals 1.5 to 2.0 points plus the point size of the font. Notice in Figure 15-1, for example, that Microsoft Word defaults to 13.95 points for 12-point text.
- Keep lines from becoming too long: for example, 6.5-inch lines of 10-point type is no fun to read! Try increasing the type size to 12 and adjusting margins to 1.0 inches. Or try the "hanging-head" format discussed in Chapter 7 for headings. In the hanging-head format, main headings have a left margin of 0; body text has a left margin of 1.0 to 1.5 inches.

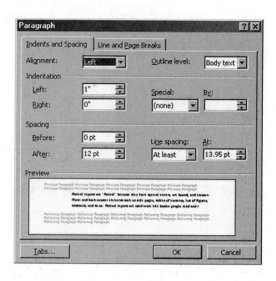

Indentation: This paragraph is indented 1 inch.

Bottom margin: This paragraph has 12 points of space below it.

Line spacing: The text for this paragraph is 12-point Times New Roman. The line spacing is nearly 2 points greater (creating roomier, more readable lines).

FIGURE 15-1

Controls for paragraph format. In Microsoft Word, access this dialog box by clicking **Format→Paragraph**.

Covers, Labels, and Binding

A formal report needs sturdy covers, a label, and binding because it gets read, reread, and passed around. For report covers, pick a simple card stock (like a thicker paper). For the binding, pick something that will enable the report to lie flat when open. (Simple brad-type folders prevent pages from lying flat and force readers to hold pages down.) Avoid the clear plastic covers with the plastic sleeves.

Use ring binders if the actual use of the report necessitates doing so. Ring binders are particularly useful if readers will need to add or substitute pages periodically.

Often, the best bindings for reports produced in technical-writing courses are the plastic-spiral, wire-spiral, or "perfect-bound" styles (see Figure 15-2). Spiral bindings enable the report to lie flat without forcing the reader to pry it open or struggle to keep the pages down. The perfect-bound style looks like thick tape has been applied to the inner half-inch edge of the report. It also enables a report to lie flat easily when open.

Transmittal Letter or Memo

The transmittal letter or memo is essentially a "cover" letter or memo. It tells the reader, "Here it is!" Although quite brief, its contents include the following:

- Reference to some initial agreement between the recipient and you as to the production of the report and its due date.
- Brief review of the report's purpose and overview of its contents.
- A closing that urges the recipient to review the report and to get in touch with questions or concerns.

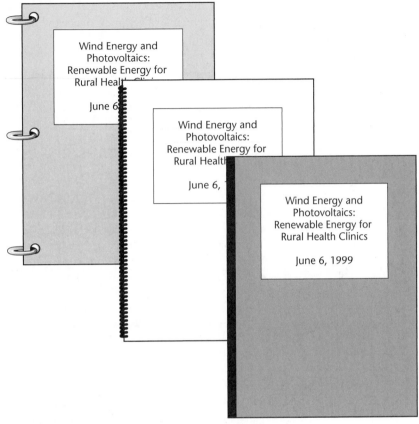

FIGURE 15-2

Different possibilities for report bindings. Avoid the clear-plastic covers with the plastic sleeve! Spiral or perfect bindings are the best.

Don't forget: if your document is for an external audience (an individual or organization external to you or your organization), use a business-letter format such as in the example report at the end of this chapter and the progress report and proposal at the end of the Chapter 6. If the report stays "in house," use a cover memo. Unless you have local requirements, paper-clip the transmittal letter or memo to the front of the document. See Figure 15-4A at the end of the chapter for an example of a transmittal letter.

Title Page

Although the contents of the title page can vary, the following are the minimum requirements:

- Full title of the report
- Name, title, and organization for whom the report was prepared
- Name, title, and organization of the preparer of the report

- Date of the report
- Descriptive abstract (quick overview of the report's purpose and contents)

If you browse a sampling of formal reports, you'll find other elements, such as report tracking numbers (for in-house storage), contract numbers, and logos, as well as copyright and trademark symbols. If you are preparing a report in-house for an organization, be sure to find out the preferred format and use it.

Notice these details about the design of the title page in Figure 15-4B at the end of this chapter:

- All of the material on the title page, except for the descriptive abstract, is centered.
- Notice that the same font type and size is used for the title of the report as for the main headings within the body of the report. Specifically, a 14-point, bold, sans serif font is used for the title.
- Notice that the identifying labels, names, titles, and organizations of the preparer of the report and its recipient use a smaller, nonbold type style, but that it is sans serif as well. Notice that italics are used to provide contrast.
- Notice finally that regular body text font (specifically, 12-point Times New Roman) is used for the descriptive abstract.

Table of Contents

The table of contents (TOC) is typically the next component after the title page. In the example TOC shown in Figure 15-4C at the end of this chapter, notice the following details:

- The title, "Table of Contents," is centered and uses a sans serif font, bold, and all caps.
- All first-level items are on the left margin, use the sans serif font but without bold, and all caps.
- Second-level items are indented to the *text* of the first-level items, and use the same but smaller sans serif font. Headline-style caps are used for these items.
- If third-level items were needed, they would be indented to the *text* of the second-level items. They would use the same font and type size as the second-level items, but sentence-style caps instead.
- "Leader dots" guide the eye to the page number corresponding to each item. The page numbers indicate the page on which the section *starts* and are right-aligned (for example, the number 9 aligns to the 0 in the number 10).
- The list of figures and the executive summary are listed at the top of the TOC. The heading "Appendixes" followed by an indented list of the individual appendixes is at the bottom of the TOC.

- Vertical spacing in a TOC can vary as long as it is consistent. If you have relatively few items in a TOC, you can double-space everything. If you have many items, you can single-space between lower-level items.

Some documents may have so many headings and so many levels of headings that you can use only two of those levels. An overly long, overly detailed TOC is unusable.

List of Figures and Tables

For documents containing graphics, tables, or both that are numbered and labeled, include a figure list just after the TOC. Remember that, except for tables, everything is a figure—illustrations, photographs, drawings, diagrams, charts, and graphs. If you have six or less figures and tables total, put them on the same page. Notice the following details about the figure list in Figure 15-4D at the end of this chapter. *fewer?*

- The title, "List of Figures," uses the same style and format as the TOC.
- Notice that two column headings are used, one over the figure and table numbers and one over the page numbers. Notice that these column headings use the same style as the second-level headings in the TOC.
- Notice that the figure and table titles use the same style and size as the body-text font (a serif font) and that they use sentence-style caps. (If you look at the figure title as it occurs in the actual text, notice the title is considerably longer than it is in the figure list. In the figure list, you can trim it to something brief but meaningful.)
- Leader dots guide the eye to the page number on which the figure or table occurs; the page numbers are right-aligned just as they are in the TOC.
- Spacing between the column headings and the figure- or table-list items and between the figure- or table-list items themselves is variable. In Figure 15-4D, the vertical distance between the title and the column headings is the same as it is between the title and the first TOC item in the table of contents. The vertical distance between the figure- and table-list items resembles double-spacing.

Executive Summary (Informative Abstract)

See "Summaries and Abstracts" in the following for details on these parts of technical reports.

Body

At long last, we get to the actual text! The body text uses all the standard characteristics discussed throughout this book, such as headings, lists, notices, tables, figures, and highlighting. The body uses the same margins, type style, and vertical spacing as in the title page, table of contents, executive summary, and so on.

Practical Ethics: Association Guidelines

Many professional associations and employers have established ethical guidelines for their members or employees. The Society for Technical Communication (STC) is an association of technical writers in a variety of different fields that provides opportunities for education and networking. The following ethical guidelines can be found on the STC Web site (*www.stc-va.org/*)[1]:

Legality: We observe the laws and regulations governing our profession. We meet the terms of contracts we undertake. We ensure that all terms are consistent with laws and regulations locally and globally, as applicable, and with STC ethical principles.

Honesty: We seek to promote the public good in our activities. To the best of our ability, we provide truthful and accurate communications. We also dedicate ourselves to conciseness, clarity, coherence, and creativity, striving to meet the needs of those who use our products and services. We alert our clients and employers when we believe that material is ambiguous. Before using another person's work, we obtain permission. We attribute authorship of material and ideas only to those who make an original and substantive contribution. We do not perform work outside our job scope during hours compensated by clients or employers, except with their permission; nor do we use their facilities, equipment, or supplies without their approval. When we advertise our services, we do so truthfully.

Confidentiality: We respect the confidentiality of our clients, employers, and professional organizations. We disclose business-sensitive information only with their consent or when legally required to do so. We obtain releases from clients and employers before including any business-sensitive materials in our portfolios or commercial demonstrations or before using such materials for another client or employer.

Quality: We endeavor to produce excellence in our communication products. We negotiate realistic agreements with clients and employers on schedules, budgets, and deliverables during project planning. Then we strive to fulfill our obligations in a timely, responsible manner.

Fairness: We respect cultural variety and other aspects of diversity in our clients, employers, development teams, and audiences. We serve the business interests of our clients and employers as long as they are consistent with the public good. Whenever possible, we avoid conflicts of interest in fulfilling our professional responsibilities and activities. If we discern a conflict of interest, we disclose it to those concerned and obtain their approval before proceeding.

Professionalism: We evaluate communication products and services constructively and tactfully, and seek definitive assessments of our own professional performance. We advance technical communication through our integrity and excellence in performing each task we undertake. Additionally, we assist other persons in our profession through mentoring, networking, and instruction. We also pursue professional self-improvement, especially through courses and conferences.

[1] Reprinted with permission from the Society for Technical Communication, Arlington, VA.

Keeping margins, fonts, vertical spacing, and other such details consistent throughout will give your document a clean, simple, inviting look. Readers won't notice your careful attention to fonts, type sizes, type faces, margins, and vertical spacing, but they will be put off by variation in these elements. Such variation creates a busy, complicated, uninviting text that readers would prefer not to read. See Figure 15-4I through 15-4K at the end of the chapter.

Appendixes

Appendixes are good places to stash material that just doesn't fit in the regular text. Full-page maps, multipage tables, detailed specifications, forms used for questionnaires, and names and addresses of companies or individuals just get in the way in the regular body text:

- The appendix title uses the same style and format as first-level headings in the body of the report.
- Each appendix title begins with "Appendix," followed by a letter, ending with a descriptive title.
- Otherwise, all other style and format details are the same as in the body of the report—headings, lists, tables, figures, highlighting, font types, margins, vertical spacing, and so on.

Information Sources

For some technical documents, the only appendix you may have is the list of the information sources. Here are essential details on the information-sources list:

- Lists all books, articles, encyclopedias, reference works, government documents, online resources, and experts used to research and write the report (see Figure 15-4L at the end of the chapter).
- If there are no other appendixes, omit "Appendix A" from the title of the information-sources section and just center the title ("References" or "Works Cited") at the top.
- There are numerous styles for indicating the sources from which you borrowed information. Use your local requirements (those of your instructor or organization) or the style used by your field or profession.

Page Numbering

If you have a choice, use sequential page numbering from beginning to end of your report; center page numbers at the bottom of pages; don't display page numbers on the title page and the appendix divider page. Otherwise, follow your local requirements (those of your instructor or organization).

Positioning.   Formal reports use various styles for page numbering:

- *Alternating bottom left and right corners.* Standard book styles use "alternating-page" format: typically, the odd-page page number appears on the outer right edge of the odd page (usually the right-hand page); the even-page page number, on the outer left edge of the even page (usually the left-hand page).
- *Alternating top left and right corners.* This style is similar to the previous except that the page numbers appear on the outer *top* corners of the pages. These are even more complicated than the previous style because you must keep page numbers from showing on the first page of any major section.
- *Bottom center.* By far, the easiest solution is to show page numbers at the bottom center of each page.

Numbering styles.   You have just a few choices on page-numbering styles:

- *Sequential page numbering.* You can number each page sequentially from beginning to end of the report. (If you use the sequential style without front-matter page numbering, the first piece of paper within the report covers would be page 1—although the number is not actually displayed.)
- *By-section numbering.* You can restart page numbering at each section or chapter: for example, page numbers for Chapter 2 would be 2–1, 2–2, and so on; for Chapter 3, 3–1, 3–2, and so on.
- *Numbering for front-matter pages.* You may be expected to use lower-case roman numerals: i, ii, iii, iv, and so on. These page numbers would be positioned the same way they are in the body of the format. In this style, the first piece of paper after the front cover is page i, even though the number is not actually displayed.
- *Numbering for back-matter pages.* If you use by-section page numbering for the body of your report, use the same style in the back matter of your report as well. For example, page numbering for Appendix A would be A–1, A–2, and so on; for Appendix B, B–1, B–2, and so on.

Displayed page numbers. Regardless of which page-numbering style you use, page numbers are *not* displayed on certain pages, such as the title page or the appendix divider page. If you can't figure how to suppress the display of page numbers on certain pages, make those pages separate files.

To create page numbers, use the following steps:

- In Corel WordPerfect, choose **Format→Page→Numbering** and select the position and alignment you want. On the same dialog box, use the Position and Page numbering format fields or click **Set Value** to change the format or style of the page number (for lowercase roman numerals, for example).
- In Lotus Word Pro, choose **Page→Insert Page Number** and select the style (lowercase roman numerals, for example), position, and alignment you want.
- In Microsoft Word, choose **Insert→Page Numbers** and select the position and alignment you want. On the same dialog box, click **Format** to change the starting number or the number style (lowercase roman numerals, for example).

SUMMARIES AND ABSTRACTS

Different types of abstracts, also called summaries, accompany most formal reports. They summarize the key ideas and facts, the important findings and conclusions, main contents, or some combination. Abstracts and summaries enable readers to get a quick overview of the full report, as if someone had highlighted the key material in the report for them. Abstracts and summaries help readers decide if they should read the full report.

Introduction and background: This first part of the abstract summarizes key material from the introduction, including background on the research.

Methods: The next segment summarizes the methods used in the research.

Results: This segment discusses the results of these observations.

Discussion: The final segment of this abstract discusses and interprets the findings.

Abstract.[2]—Recent technological advances have made wind power a viable source of alternative energy production, and the number of windplant facilities has increased in the United States. Construction was completed on a 73-turbine, 25-megawatt windplant on Buffalo Ridge near Lake Benton, Minnesota in spring 1994. The number of birds killed at existing windplants in California caused concern about the potential impacts of the Buffalo Ridge facility on the avian community. From April 1994 through Dec. 1995 we searched the Buffalo Ridge windplant site for dead birds. Additionally, we evaluated search efficiency, predator scavenging rates, and rate of carcass decomposition. During 20 mo of monitoring we found 12 dead birds. Collisions with wind turbines were suspected for 8 of the 12 birds. During observer efficiency trials, searchers found 78.8% of carcasses. Scavengers removed 39.5% of carcasses during scavenging trials. All carcasses remained recognizable during 7 d decomposition trials. After correction for biases, we estimated that approximately 36 ± 12 birds (<1 dead bird per turbine) were killed at the Buffalo Ridge windplant in 1 y. Although windplants do not appear to be more detrimental to birds than other man-made structures, proper facility siting is an important first consideration in order to avoid unnecessary fatalities.

[2] *Source*: Robert G. Osborn, et al, "Bird Mortality Associated with Wind Turbines at the Buffalo Ridge Wind Resource Area, Minnesota." *American Midland Naturalist*, 143:41–52, 2000.

FIGURE 15-3

Abstract from a research journal. This type of abstract appears just after the title of the article and before the main text. It summarizes key concepts and facts from each of the main sections: introduction (which includes background on the study), methods, results, and discussion.

■ *Abstract.* Illustrated in Figure 15-3, the traditional research abstract (also called an informative abstract) summarizes the background, the research methods, the findings, and the discussion of those findings. For a background report, this type of abstract summarizes key points in each of the main sections of that report, including the introduction and conclusion.

■ *Descriptive abstract.* Also called a descriptive summary, this type is short—three to four sentences at most, regardless the length of the full report. It states the purpose of the report and provides an overview of the report's contents. It does not reveal any of the actual information presented in the body of the report; it just tells readers what topics the report covers. You can see an example of a descriptive summary in Figure 15-4B at the end of this chapter.

■ *Executive summary.* The executive summary is a hybrid of the descriptive and informative summaries. Written for "executives" whose focus is business decisions and whose background is not necessarily technical, it focuses on conclusions and recommendations but provides little background, theory, results, or other such detail. It doesn't summarize research theory or method; it makes descriptive-summary statements like, "theory of heat gain, loss, and storage is also discussed," for example. You can see an example of an executive summary in Figure 15-4E through 15-4G following this chapter.

To get a sense of how to develop an executive summary or informative abstract, use the process shown in the following examples. It is based on the recommendation report shown at the end of Chapter 4 and the primary research report show at the end of Chapter 3.

1. Review the text carefully, referring to its table of contents, if available. Identify the type of readers who would be reading the document and the type of abstract required.
   - *Recommendation report.* The recommendation report at the end of Chapter 4 is clearly to help executives make decisions about purchasing and implementing voice-recognition software. This report needs an executive summary.
   - *Research report.* The research report at the end of Chapter 3 is clearly for bat researchers who are interested in acquiring and advancing their knowledge about their favorite *Chiroptera.* This report needs an informative abstract.
2. Identify the major sections of the report. You must decide which of these sections to summarize and how much.
   - *Recommendation report.* The recommendation report at the end of Chapter 4 contains background on voice-recognition software, how it works, and what its memory requirements are. It moves on to a point-by-point comparison of four software packages, followed by a summary of conclusions, ending with a recommendation. For an executive summary, summarize the conclusions and recommendations and leave out the technical background.
   - *Research report.* The research report at the end of Chapter 3 contains the standard sections for the research question and background, research methods, findings, and discussion. For an informative abstract, summarize key details out of *each* of these sections.
3. When you write these abstracts and summaries, use good English; don't write telegraphically. but pack as much detail as you can in sentences to keep the abstract or summary as short as possible. You don't need to define key terms or cite sources: that's done in the body of the report.

WORKSHOP: DOCUMENT DESIGN AND FORMAT

Here are some additional ideas for practicing the concepts, tools, and strategies in this chapter:

1. *Report-formatting review.* Find a sampling of technical reports—produced either by governmental or corporate organizations—and compare their design and format to what you've read in this chapter. Make notes on any differences you find in the sequence of components (such as title pages, tables of contents, and abstracts), different components, or different contents or format of those components.

2. *Business-letter report formatting.* Use the instructions and unformatted text at **www.io.com/~hcexres/power_tools/report_format/report1.html** to create a short, business-letter report.

3. *Memo-report formatting.* Use the instructions and unformatted text available at **www.io.com/~hcexres/power_tools/report_format/report2 .html** to create a short, memo report.

4. *Formal-report formatting.* Use the instructions and unformatted text available at **www.io.com/~hcexres/power_tools/report_format/report3 .html** to create a formal report.

The transmittal letter identifies the report—what it is for, for whom it is written, what situation it addresses, and so on. The transmittal letter is typically paper-clipped to the front cover of the report. Imagine a report landing on your desk with no such identifying information!

Notice the letterhead: in your report, try creating your own letterhead design. Make up your own company name and address.

Notice the short introductory paragraph: it identifies the purpose of the letter and the attached report (notice that the report title is in italics, like a book).

The middle paragraph of the letter reviews the purpose and contents of the report.

The concluding paragraph has an "action" focus: it encourages the recipients to review the report and to be ready for the telephone conference.

Healthcare Executive Resources, Inc.[3]
1604 West 34th
Austin, TX 78703

June 6, 1999

Mr. Juan Ortiz
National Renewable Energy Laboratory
1617 Cole Boulevard
Golden, CO 80401-3393

Dear Juan:
Attached is the report *Wind Energy and Photovoltaics: Renewable Energy for Rural Health Clinics* we contracted to write for your November 19, 1998.

As you'll see, we discuss the need for renewable sources of energy in rural health clinics and then focus on the main components of a system combining wind energy and photovoltaics. Following that is a review of economic and administrative issues. The report ends with conclusions on the feasibility of resources like these in rural areas of the world. Case studies of applications in India, Nicaragua, Mexico, the Dominican Republic, Peru, and Zambia are presented in the appendix.

We'll be getting in touch with you on June 15 for the scheduled phone conference to review our work.

Regards,

Jane A. McMurrey

Jane A. McMurrey
HER
Attachment: report

FIGURE 15-4A

Sample report pages—transmittal letter. Don't forget to use the memo format if the report stays "in house." (This letter is typically clipped to the report front cover.)

---

[3] The following report samples were adapted with permission from National Renewable Energy Laboratory. Some details have been changed to fit this context.

The title page can be designed many different ways and contain a wide variety of information. This one has the standard minimal elements: title, recipients, authors, date, and descriptive abstract.

The writer of this report has created a realistic situation and audience for her report: NREL has contracted with her to report on the use of wind energy and photovoltaics in rural health clinics. She has made herself a partner in a healthcare management firm.

The descriptive summary: notice that it is very similar to the middle paragraph of the transmittal letter. That's because you cannot expect the transmittal letter to remain attached to this report and because, in any case, you want readers to have multiple opportunities to understand the purpose and contents of the report.

**Wind Energy and Photovoltaics:
Renewable Energy for
Rural Health Clinics**

for
National Renewable Energy Laboratory

prepared by
Jane A. McMurrey
Healthcare Executive Resources, Inc.

June 6, 1999

This report reviews renewable energy resources used in rural health clinics in India, Nicaragua, Mexico, the Dominican Republic, Peru, and Zambia. Topics include the need for renewable energy sources, components, system selection economics, and case studies.

FIGURE 15-4B

Sample report pages—title page with descriptive summary. The first page inside the report, or the first piece of paper you see when you open the report.

not the only way but clear

Notice the items included in this table of contents (TOC): the title page is excluded, as is the TOC itself. The list of figures, which occurs directly after the TOC, is the first item, followed by the executive summary.

In that it is the third page (third actual piece of paper) within the report covers, the list of figures is page iii. The traditional lowercase roman numerals are used for all pages before the first page of the introduction.

Notice that all top-level items in this TOC are uppercase. The next-level items use headline-style caps (initial caps on the main words.)

Check the sample pages in the following: you'll see that the body of the report has third-level headings, even though they are not shown in this TOC. That's your call as a writer. Including too many headings in a TOC can create clutter and reduce its effectiveness.

This report summarizes "case studies" in the appendix. Notice that each appendix uses a capital letter.

The list of information sources is the last appendix here. In your report, if the reference list is the only appendix, just title the section "Appendix" and indent "References" beneath it—without the capital letter "A."

The page number for the TOC is traditionally not displayed, even though it is page ii.

TABLE OF CONTENTS

FIGURE 15-4C
Sample report pages—table of contents.

The list of figures and tables shows readers the titles of figures and tables and the page number on which they occur in the report. You don't have to include the complete figure or table title, just the first few words that convey a full, grammatically complete idea of the figure or table contents.

You may be used to textbooks and reports numbering figures and tables according to chapter or section numbers. For example, figures in Chapter 3 would be numbered 3-1, 3-2, and so on. For a report under 30 to 40 pages, that's not necessary.

Notice that this page is numbered iii. This is a traditional report (and book) design. In traditional report design, all pages before page 1 of the introduction are numbered with lowercase roman numerals. You may have noticed that no page number appeared on either the title page or the table of contents page, even though they are i and ii, respectively. Again, that's traditional.

LIST OF FIGURES

LIST OF TABLES

iii

FIGURE 15-4D
Sample report pages—list of figures and tables.

The executive summary provides a summary of the important facts, conclusions, and recommendations contained in the body of the report. It is a summary written specifically for executive readers, focusing on their typical needs and interests. (See Chapter 19 for more on executive audiences.)

Not only does the executive summary condense this essential information in as few words as possible, it also selects the kinds of information an executive reader wants to see. In this example, the executive would be a planner who needs to know what works, what doesn't work, what are the installation and operating costs, and what are the best systems. This individual does not need summaries of how photovoltaic or wind-turbine systems actually operate.

Notice the format of this executive summary: it uses headings, subheadings, and bulleted lists to make the information more scannable. If executive readers want to go directly to information on photovoltaics, they don't have to struggle; they can find the related heading and go straight to it.

EXECUTIVE SUMMARY

Rural Health Clinics: Requirements

The most important needs of rural health clinics, which require energy resources, are as follows:

Refrigeration. Absorption refrigeration, fueled by propane or kerosene and common at nonelectric health clinics, is vulnerable to interruption and is thus inadequate for the vaccines needed in immunization programs for dangerous diseases including polio, diptheria, tetanus, pertussis, tuberculosis, measles, yellow fever, and Hepatitis B. Instead, compression-type refrigerators powered by 12- or 24-volt storage batteries and recharged by photovoltaic panels or a small wind turbine can meet these needs.

Lighting. Instead of kerosene lighting, common in nonelectric communities and a known safety hazard and contributor to poor indoor air quality, renewable energy technologies can improve lighting in rural health clinics for such important functions as emergency treatment, birthing, maternity care, surgery, and administrative tasks.

Communications. Health care services and emergency medical treatment, in particular, are greatly facilitated with reliable radio and radio-telephone communications to other health clinics and facilities in the region. Rural health clinics can have reliable two-way regional communication via VHF radio with electricity provided by a single 30-W PV module.

Medical appliances. Small medical appliances that operate on 120-volt AC electricity require an inverter, which is easily incorporated into wind- or solar-based systems. Although photovoltaic systems can provide the electricity needed for the high temperatures, approximately 120°C (250°F), needed in sterilization, solar thermal collector systems can produce high temperatures at a lower cost, especially in areas with good solar insolation.

Water. Solar and wind power can be used to generate high volumes of potable water in tandem with techniques such as ozone treatment, reverse osmosis, photochemical, also known as ultraviolet or UV, disinfection, and carbon filters. Ozone treatment is very suitable to solar- or wind-generated power requiring only 0.3 watt-hours per liter. Clean water can also be provided from deep wells but require an energy source for pumping significant volumes. Solar or wind power (or both) generated on site can economically meet the broad range of these needs.

iv

FIGURE 15-4E

Sample report pages—executive summary.

Informative summaries provide the highlights of each major section in the report. However, executive summaries provide highlights from only those sections that meet the needs of executive readers. Remember that executives read for administrative issues: costs, operation, maintenance, and outputs.

You can see that the section on health clinic applications is not summarized—the writer must believe that this is information that the executive reader already knows or does not need here. Otherwise, notice how closely the sections of this executive summary parallel the items in the table of contents for this report.

Too much detail? Consider this section on batteries. Is there material not needed by the executive reader that could be cut? Perhaps this reader doesn't need all the detail on charging and life-cycle characteristics of batteries. Perhaps the writer should simply state which battery type is recommended, why, and at what cost.

Notice that the pages of the executive summary are the last pages of the front matter before the introduction (which is arabic page 1). In traditional report design (and book design as well), all pages before page 1 of the introduction are lowercase roman numerals, as you see here.

modular and can be reconfigured easily to meet required load. The main disadvantage of PV is its high capital cost, although the savings from PV usage pays back the initial cost within a few years. The prices for bulk purchases of PV panels can go below $4,000 per kWp with warranties from 10 to 20 years. Additional costs (mounts, wiring, and installation) are typically $1,000–$1,500 per kWp. Current panels can be expected to last in excess of 20 years and are almost maintenance free.

Wind-turbine generators. For small turbines, the cut-in speed typically ranges from 3 to 4 m/s. After cut-in, wind turbine power increases may also depend on the application for which it is used. Most small turbines produce peak power at about 12–15 m/s. The turbine will produce at peak power until the wind speed reaches the turbine's "cut-out" speed. Cut-out speeds usually range from 14 to 18 m/s. Cut-out occurs to protect the turbine from over spinning in high winds. Similar-sized turbines can differ significantly in price, with installed costs generally varying from $2,000 to $6,000 per rated kW. However, wind turbines offer economies of scale, with larger wind turbines costing less per kW than smaller wind turbines. Maintenance costs for wind turbines are variable and greater than those for PV systems.

Batteries. For remote power applications, deep-cycle batteries are generally recommended. They are designed to be discharged down to a 20%–50% state of charge without damage. Shallow-cycle batteries, such as car batteries, are generally not recommended, though they are often used in small PV systems because of the lack of any alternatives. They can be prudently discharged only to an 80%–90% state of charge and will often be destroyed by only a handful of deeper discharges. Depending on the brand and model, battery lifetimes vary widely, ranging from less than 100 full cycles to more than 1500 full cycles. Typical float lives for good quality lead-acid batteries range between 3 and 8 years at 20°C (68°F). High ambient temperatures will severely shorten a battery's float life. A rule of thumb is that every 10°C (18°F) increase in average ambient temperature will halve the battery float life. The variations in cycle and float life, described earlier, make comparison of the cost-effectiveness of different batteries somewhat problematical. As a general starting point, costs are on the order of $70–$100 per kWh of storage for batteries with lifetimes of 250 to 500 cycles and float lives in the range of 3 to 8 years. There will be additional one-time costs for a shed, racks, and connection wiring.

Inverters. Inverters convert DC to AC power. This capability is needed because PV panels, batteries, and most small wind turbines produce DC power. Most common electrical applications and devices require AC power. Inverter costs are roughly $600–$1,000 per kW for good quality modified sine wave inverters. The technology for inverters larger than 5 kW is not as mature as for smaller inverters and costs may be somewhat higher.

v

FIGURE 15-4F
Sample report pages—executive summary, continued.

Notice that this executive summary does not provide basic definitions; the reader can consult the main report text for that. Notice too that sentences are long and densely packed with information. Keep summaries like this as short as possible, while retaining good, clear, readable English.

System Selection and Costs

While renewable-energy options tend to have high initial costs and low operating costs, nonrenewable options such as generators have low initial costs but high operating costs. The important variables are as follows:

Peak load. System components, especially wiring and power electronics, must be sized so that the system can deliver the peak load. The average load determines the size of the energy producing components and the components selected. PV systems are most competitive for very small loads such as those at smaller health clinics. Wind turbines and generators are competitive with the larger loads found at the larger clinics.

Load variations. Diurnal and seasonal load variations must be considered and may influence component selection. Summer and daytime loads favor PV. Winter loads are more suited for generators and, if winter is the windy season, wind turbines are a good choice. If the wind and solar resource are seasonally complementary (i.e., the wind resource is good during the low-insolation season) then a wind-PV hybrid system may be more appropriate.

Level of service. Level of service required and lulls in sun and wind have a major impact on system cost. For example, a PV system capable of handling an average daily load of 0.5 kWh, in a locale with the worst month insolation (3.0 sun hours/day), is expected to have a 25-year net present cost of between $2,500 and $5,000. A wind-turbine system that meets an average daily load of 1.0 kWh costs between $4,000 and $8,000 in a location with a worst month average wind speed of 5.0 m/s.

This executive summary may seem too long. However, it is the equivalent of 3 pages. With the body of the report about 30 pages, that makes it a ratio of 10 to 1, which is about right for this length of report. If the report were longer, you'd want to keep the executive summary or informative summary at 3 pages. Beyond that, it no longer serves its intended purpose, which is to provide a quick overview or summary of a large report.

Generator requirements. In system selection, a big decision is whether or not to use a generator. While the advantage of generators is their ability to provide power on demand, they have high operating costs because of fuel and maintenance, not to mention the problem of getting fuel and maintenance to remote sites. The number of operating hours drives the cost of using a generator:

- If the number of operating hours is low, generators can be competitive; but as the operating hours increase, costs escalate.
- If the loads consist of things such as lights and water pumps that are only on a few hours per day, then an all-diesel system may be cost competitive.
- If the generator must be run more than a few hours per day, another solution is needed: for example, a generator-battery system or a combination of a generator with PV panels, wind turbines, or both, to minimize the generator runtime.

vi

FIGURE 15-4G
Sample report pages—executive summary, continued.

Notice the format of this introduction. It repeats the full title of the report at the top of the page. Below that is the section number and section title.

Remember that the primary responsibilities of an introduction are to get readers ready to read the report—to indicate the topic, purpose, situation, and appropriate audience and to provide an overview of the contents of the report.

Providing background on the topic of the report is only a secondary responsibility for an introduction. For a report and introduction of these lengths, only a few sentences of background (history, conceptions, definitions) are necessary. If you have more background than that, put it in a section of its own following the introduction.

Notice the use of the bulleted list for the overview of contents. This format makes this material much more readable. (See Chapter 8 for more on lists.)

Notice that no page number is displayed here, even though it is arabic number 1. (Again, this is traditional report and book design.) Even though this section does not fill the page, the next section begins on a new page.

Wind Energy and Photovoltaics: Renewable Energy for Rural Health Clinics

I. INTRODUCTION

The following report, prepared for National Renewable Energy Laboratory, is intended primarily for decision-makers in government ministries and private agencies involved in health clinic electrification using renewable energy technologies. The purpose of this report is to help these readers assess their health clinics' electrical needs and select appropriate and cost-effective technologies to meet those needs.

This report gives a broad overview of health clinic electrification with an emphasis on the use of renewable energy technologies. The use of solar thermal technologies to meet various heating applications is briefly discussed.

- Section 2 reviews typical health clinic electrical applications, such as refrigeration, lighting, and communications. Information on typical power draws and duty cycles for each type of equipment is included.
- Section 3 discusses the components of stand-alone power systems. For each component there is a description of how it works, its cost, lifetime, proper operation and maintenance, and limitations.
- Sections 4 and 5 give an overview of life-cycle cost analysis and related local factors that can influence the design of stand-alone renewable energy technologies systems.
- Section 6 explores the various social and institutional issues that need to be addressed in order to have a successful health clinic electrification program.
- The appendixes include case studies of four health clinic electrification projects.

It is our sincere hope that this report meets the needs of planners in rural clinics in their attempts to achieve low-cost, reliable electrification using renewable energy technologies.

FIGURE 15-4H
Sample report pages—introduction.

Here's a typical page from the body of a formal report. Notice that the first-level heading ("III. Electrical System Components") always begins a new page, no matter where the previous section ended on the preceding page.

A typical report section is made up of multiple second-level headings such as the one shown here ("System Overview"). (For more on headings, see Chapter 7.)

This report uses third-level headings like the one shown here ("Photovoltaics"). See Chapter 7 for details on levels and format of headings.

When your report contains illustrations, attempt to place them on the pages where they are referenced, as is done here. Don't just stuff them at the end of the section or report. Be sure to use a descriptive figure title—not just "Figure 5." (For more on illustrations, see Chapter 11.)

III. ELECTRICAL SYSTEM COMPONENTS

This chapter gives an overview of the main components typically used in renewable energy systems. Diesel and gasoline engine generators are also discussed. For each item, the discussion includes how its operation, proper use, cost, lifetime, and limitations.

System Overview

A hybrid system comprises components that produce, store, and deliver electricity to the application. Figure 5 shows a schematic of a hybrid system. Not all systems have all the components shown. In general, PV panels, small wind turbines, and batteries are all DC devices.

If AC power is desired, the DC power must be converted to AC. Generators normally produce AC power, but some models also produce DC power. The components of a hybrid system fall into one of four categories.

Photovoltaics. Wind turbines and engines use generators to convert mechanical motion into electricity. PV panels convert sunlight directly into electricity.

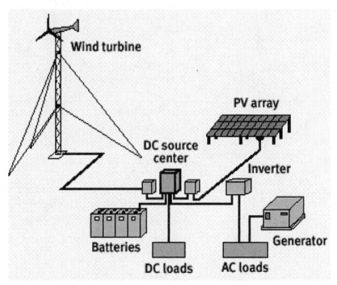

Figure 5. Hybrid System Configuration: Generalized hybrid system configuration showing energy storage components (photovoltaic, wind turbine, and generator), energy storage components (batteries), energy conversion components (inverter), and balance of system components (direct current source center and charge controller).

13

FIGURE 15-41
Sample report pages—body pages from the body of a formal report.

Another page from the body of this report, in this case, a page that does not begin with a first-level heading.

In order to maximize energy production, PV panels need to be mounted so as to be oriented towards the sun. To do this, the panels are mounted on either fixed or tracking mounts. Because of their low cost and simplicity, fixed mounts are most commonly used. These type of mounts can be made of wood or metal, and can be purchased or fabricated almost anywhere.

Tracking mounts (either single or dual axis) increase the energy production of the panels, particularly at low latitudes, but at the price of additional cost and complexity. The relative cost effectiveness of tracking mounts versus additional panels will vary from project to project.

Capital and operating costs. PV panels are available in a wide variety of ratings up to 100 Wp and panels rated as high as 300 Wp are manufactured. Individual PV panels can be connected to form arrays of any size. Panels may be connected in series to increase the array voltage, and can be connected in parallel to increase the array current. This modularity makes it easy to start out with a small array and add additional panels later.

Wind Turbine Generators

Wind turbines convert the energy of moving air into useful mechanical or electrical energy. Wind turbines need somewhat more maintenance than a PV array but with moderate winds, >4.5 meters per second (m/s), will often produce more energy than a similarly priced array of PV panels (Gipe, 1993). Like PV panels, multiple wind turbines can be used together to produce more energy.

APA-style citation of borrowed information. See the References page for details on the Gipe source.

Figure 6. Typical wind turbine components

15

FIGURE 15-4J

Sample report pages—body pages from the body of a formal report.

Notice the design of this table: the title is the first row; the numerical material is centered beneath the column headings and right-aligned; the table title uses bold; the column headings use italics. For more on table design, see Chapter 10.

Table 2. Power and Energy Consumption for Medical Appliances

Appliance	Power (watts)	On-time (hours/day)	Energy/day (watt-hours)
Vaccine refrigerator	60	5-10	300-600
Vaccine refrigerator/freezer	60	6-12	410-720
Lights (each)	20	2-12	40-240
VHF radio			
Stand-by	2	12	24
Transmitting	30	1	30
Microscope	15	1.0	15
Centrifuge nebulizer	150	0.3-2.0	50-300
Vaporizer	40	1.0-4.0	40-160
Oxygen concentrator	300	1.0-4.0	300-1200
Electric sterilizer	1500	0.5-2.0	750-3000

Another second-level heading, which is shown in the table of contents.

Notice the APA-style citation of information that this author has borrowed. See the References page at the end of the report for details on Fowler.

Batteries

Batteries are electrochemical devices that store energy in chemical form. They are used to store excess energy for later use. By far the most common type of battery is the lead-acid type. A distant second are the nickel-cadmium types. The remainder of this section discusses the lead-acid battery (Fowler, 1991).

Deep-cycle versus shallow-cycle. While batteries are sized according to how much energy they can store, in most cases a lead-acid battery cannot be discharged all the way to a zero state of charge without suffering damage in the process. For remote power applications, deep-cycle batteries are generally recommended. They are designed to be discharged down to a 20%–50% state of charge. Shallow-cycle batteries, such as car batteries, are generally not recommended, though they are often used in small PV systems because of the lack of any alternatives. They can be prudently discharged only to an 80%–90% state of charge and will often be destroyed by only a handful of deeper discharges.

Two third-level headings, which are not shown in the TOC.

Flooded versus valve regulated. Flooded batteries have their plates immersed in a liquid electrolyte and need periodic rewatering.

18

FIGURE 15-4K
Sample report pages—body pages with a table.

APA-style list of references, occurring at the end of a report.

Notice the inverted-indentation format of items in this list. It enables you to see the author (individual or corporate) and the year of publication more readily.

REFERENCES

World Health Organization. (1996). "Solar Energy and Rural Health Care." WHO Fact Sheet N132. Geneva, Switzerland. Available at www.who.int/inf-fs/en/fact132.html.

Fowler Solar Electric Inc. (1991). *Battery Book for Your PV Home.* Worthington, Massachusetts.

Werner, D.; Sanders, D.; et al. (1997). *The Politics of Primary Health Care and Child Survival.* HealthWrights, 946 Hamilton Ave., Palo Alto, CA, 94301.

World Health Organization. (1997). *World Health Report 1997.* Geneva, Switzerland. Available at www.who.int/whr/1997/whr-e.htm.

World Health Organization. (1980). *The Primary Health Care Worker,* Rev. Ed. Geneva, Switzerland.

Gipe, P. (1993). *Wind Power for Home and Business.* Chelsea Green Publishing Co., White River Junction, Vermont.

Cowen, W.D.; Borchers, M.L.; Eberhard, A.A.; Morris, G.J.; and Purcell, C. de V. (1992). *Remote Area Power Supply Design Manual.* 2 vols, Energy for Development Research Center, University of Cape Town, Cape Town, South Africa.

World Health Organization. (1997). *Product Information Sheets.* Order no. WHO/EPI/ LHIS/97.01. Geneva, Switzerland.

39

FIGURE 15-4L
Sample report pages—references list. This lists the information sources from which the author borrowed directly to write this report.

Oral Presentations: Preparation, Visuals, and Delivery

YEAR 2000 PROBLEM

By the time you read this book, we will be well past January 1, 2000, and we'll have seen just how many of the worst Y2K fears were realized. Even though the event is over now, it's still a fascinating topic. It illustrates our society's deep dependence on computers:

The Y2K Problem Links. **y2k2000.org/defining.htm**

Y2K for the Perplexed. From About.com.
websearch.about.com/library/weekly/aa091299.htm

Y2K: Research Help (For Business Majors). From About.com.
**businessmajors.about.com/education/businessmajors/library/
weekly/aa030999.htm**

The Year 2000 Problem: The Year the Earth Stands Still.
www.garynorth.com

Eight Myths about the Millennium Bug—from CNET.
www.cnet.com/Content/Features/Dlife/Millbug

Accessed January 29, 2001.

If you have ever spent any time in the corporate or governmental worlds, you have probably experienced painfully disorganized, time-wasting oral presentations. Just as the working world needs good technical-writing skills, it needs good oral-presentation skills. That's why many technical-writing courses include oral presentations. The classroom becomes the conference room, and the other students in the class become your work colleagues.

This chapter shows you some strategies for getting ready for and delivering oral presentations, for developing visuals and for using presentation software such as Microsoft PowerPoint or Lotus Freelance Graphics.

Note: For an example of the script of an oral report, see **www.io.com/~hcexres/power_tools/examples**.

HOW DO YOU PLAN AN ORAL PRESENTATION?

In corporations and governmental agencies, groups of employees—departments, areas, sections—often get together once a week for announcements, status reports, and other sorts of presentations. These presentations must be pertinent, focused, organized, and succinct.

1. Find a situation requiring an oral presentation. Try to find a real or realistic situation in which a specific group of listeners wants to hear your presentation. In the oral-presentation script at the end of this chapter, employees need training to test whether their office computers are Y2K ready.

   If you can't find a situation, try these ideas:

   ■ *Start with a report type.* Practically any of the types of technical documents in Part I can be developed for oral presentation, only in a shorter, less detail-dense form. For example, a progress report can work well as an in-person presentation. In fact, status reports, a near-cousin of the progress report, are often presented orally rather than in writing.

■ *Use an existing report.* You can rework a technical document you've already written. If you had written a technical background report on Y2K anxieties, you could present the highlights of that report orally.

■ *Do some brainstorming.* And of course you can use the project-finding ideas presented at **www.io.com/~hcexres/power_tools/topics .html**. Find a topic that is of interest to you, and then work "backwards" to a real or realistic workplace situation.

For the example oral-report project, assume we start with a topic, in this case the year 2000 problem. At the end of this chapter, there is an oral presentation that provides instructions on testing a computer to see if it is Y2K-compliant. But let's plan something different here.

2. **Define an audience and a purpose.** In a technical-writing course, the audience is obviously your instructor and the people in your class. If possible, invent a realistic audience and situation. At the beginning of your oral presentation, describe that audience and that situation to the class, and ask people to pretend that they are those listeners in that situation. For more audiences, see Chapter 19.

For this oral presentation, imagine the possibilities. You could provide a background report on some aspect of Y2K, instructions on checking your computers, stocking up and getting ready for the "Down Time," a recommendation report on different methods of testing and resolving the problem, or perhaps even a survey on people's understanding of Y2K—their level of concern and preparedness.

3. **Define a purpose.** Technical presentations in any medium have informative, instructional, recommendational, evaluative, or persuasive purposes. Are you going to show people how to perform a procedure, persuade them to approve a project, explain the status of an ongoing project, recommend one product over others, discuss a new technology, or argue for the feasibility and necessity of a plan or program?

For this example oral presentation, imagine you want to talk about the hysteria surrounding the Y2K problem. Sampling the crazy fears that have possessed people will be fun for listeners. But what would be a likely context? Who would attend? Here's an idea: you work in computer systems for a big state agency. You've been asked to present something about Y2K at a weekly brown-bag seminar series. Focusing on Y2K hysterics will be ghoulish fun for listeners (maybe it's close to Halloween). As a part of this presentation, you'll provide your viewpoint on Y2K and practical steps listeners should take, if any, to get ready.

4. **Research the topic.**

For the year 2000 problem, you'd find an extraordinary volume and range of information (such as the links listed at the beginning of this chapter). You'd want to collect and discuss the most lurid examples of Y2K hysteria at the beginning of your talk—that'll get their attention! But also find some reliable perspectives that are calm and reasonable; summarize their ideas about what is likely to happen (if anything) and what to do to get ready (if anything).

5. **Find the infrastructure.** Despite the differences between oral and written presentations, the infrastructure should be the same. For example, to show listeners how to perform a procedure, use the step-by-step process pattern. To present recommendations, use the point-by-point comparative pattern. The following table reviews the infrastructures presented in Part I.

In this Y2K presentation, let's start with a lively summary of Y2K hysterics, then discuss what is more likely to happen and how to prepare for it. This presentation will be primarily informative, with secondary persuasive and instructional purposes. We'll persuade people not to panic over Y2K and provide instructions on simple preparations. In the Y2K-hysterics section, we'll debunk examples of the hysterics.

Infrastructure	Description
Description	Part-by-part or characteristic-by-characteristic discussion of objects, mechanisms, places, organisms, even people. (See Chapter 1.)
Process	Step-by-step, event-by-event discussion of natural, mechanical, or human events, including historical events. (See Chapter 2.)
Causes and effects (problem-solution)	Cause-by-cause or effect-by-effect discussion of a situation, existing or potential. (See Chapter 3.)
Comparison	Point-by-point comparison of two or more products, plans, programs, places, even people, with a goal of recommending one. (See Chapter 4.)
Definition	Selection of infrastructures best amplifying a potentially unfamiliar term. (See Chapter 5.)
Classification	Category-by-category discussion of a topic, using definition to discuss each category. Also the attempt to place a topic into one of several categories (to categorize the topic)—an effort that relies on comparison. (See Chapter 5.)
Persuasion	An effort to persuade readers to adopt a certain point of view or to take a certain action. Relies on logical arguments, sometimes personal and emotional appeals, as well as rebuttals and concessions. (See Chapter 6.)

6. **Plan and develop the main content.** With the infrastructure identified, it's easier to define the content of the main sections. For example, to demonstrate a procedure, your main sections will be explanations of procedural steps. However, listeners may need more than just the steps. They may need background—for example, a definition of the procedure, its importance, skills needed, equipment needed, or conceptual background. That's how you work "backward" to the introduction, identifying additional main content that listeners may need to be able to understand the main sections.

> In this oral presentation, we'll probably have the following sections: (1) an introduction; (2) a main section on the Y2K hysterics; (3) a main section on what one can reasonably expect; (4) a main section on reasonable preparation; and (5) a conclusion.

7. **Plan and prepare the visuals.** Whenever possible, use graphics in your oral presentations. Ideally, you can display graphics on an overhead projector but you can also show physical objects, use flipcharts, or provide handouts. If you want to get fancy, prepare a series of "slides" using presentation software such as Lotus Freelance Graphics or Microsoft PowerPoint. Strategies for visuals in oral presentations are discussed later in this chapter.

> For Y2K, visuals may not immediately come to mind. Tables showing our dependence on computers might work. Conceptual graphics, perhaps flowcharts, depicting interdependencies of financial and governmental organizations, municipal utilities, food industries, and so on might be effective. Include a title slide, similar to the title page of a written document, on which you put the title of your presentation, your name, and other essential information. Display this slide while your audience is gathering. Another possibility for visuals is a simple outline of the presentation (which may help you from getting lost).

8. **Plan the introduction.** The introduction to an oral presentation is almost as important as the rest of the presentation put together. Your listeners need to know the following (but not necessarily in this order):

   - Who you are, whom you represent
   - What the purpose of your presentation is (avoid clumsy mechanical openers like "The topic of my speech is. . . .")
   - What you are going to cover
   - Some brief, essential background to enable people to get interested and to understand the rest of your presentation

   Study the example oral presentation at the end of this chapter to see each of these elements in action.

> In the introduction to this presentation, start by explaining who you are. This will establish your qualifications as someone who ought to know. Next, explain the purpose: to sort out all the hysteria about Y2K and

to reach a calm, reasonable perspective. Stating the purpose this way also provides an overview of what you'll cover. Don't forget a brief definition of the Y2K problem in this introduction—in case some of your listeners have just arrived from another planet. And spice up this introduction with some samplings of the craziness surrounding this topic.

9. **Plan the conclusion.** The wrap-up section can summarize, conclude, provide some final thought, or do some combination of these. Avoid mechanical summaries—phrases like "In this presentation, we have seen that . . ." can be deadly.

   ■ *Summary:* For complex oral presentations, a summary can be useful: it refocuses listeners on the main points you've covered.
   ■ *Conclusion:* A conclusion is a logical thing: if you presented lots of conflicting interpretations, a conclusion states the right interpretation.
   ■ *Final thoughts:* Another way of wrapping up is to consider one final topic, but in a general way, not obligating yourself to go into details.
   ■ You can also combine these methods of concluding an oral presentation.

   In the Y2K conclusion, you may not need to summarize or conclude anything. You might end by stating that no one can really know for sure what's going to happen and suggest some ways to find out if something problematic is happening.

10. **Rehearse!** Unless you have lots of oral-presentation experience, do some rehearsal. Don't assume you'll know what to say when you are standing in front of everybody. Here are some ideas for rehearsing your presentation:

   ■ *Write a script.* One of the best ways to get ready for an oral presentation is to draft a script. It forces you to make sure of your facts and get the words and timing right. As you practice reading, look for areas to cut, problems to fix, discussion to make clearer, and topics to expand on. During your presentation, keep the script handy, but don't read from it verbatim. Instead, deliver your presentation so that it feels like an organized conversation to your listeners.
   ■ *Create an outline.* Outlines are another method some presenters use to stay organized during an oral presentation. Outlines are useful if you've rehearsed your script so much you don't need the script any longer.
   ■ *Cue cards.* Cue cards are one other familiar method. They are particularly useful if you have specific details that you might forget—for example, statistical information that you just can't memorize!

   In any case, don't assume the words will just come to you, smoothly and effortlessly, when you get in front of the group. We see so many glib, smooth performers on TV that it's easy to fall into the notion that we can be just like them. Oral-presentation day is a tough way to find out that's not the case!

HOW DO YOU PREPARE VISUALS FOR AN ORAL PRESENTATION?

Plan to use visuals in your oral presentation, unless it's a very brief, very informal one. Visuals give listeners another way of absorbing information.

Practical Ethics: Graphically Speaking

Several years ago a new manager was hired to turn around the poor performance of a satellite branch of the company you work for. You have been asked to do a financial analysis to help your boss determine whether the branch manager has adequately increased sales. Your analysis shows a series of ups and downs, but overall, a significant increase. As you're writing your report, you decide to use graphs to show the growth in sales.

Look at the line graphs in Figure 16-1. Which would you use, graph A or B? Why? Is one more accurate than the other? Alternately, you could use a three-dimensional bar graph. Which would you choose in Figure 16-1, C or D? What's the difference between the two?

A key to creating graphs is finding a balance between too much detail and not enough. The problem with graph B is that it doesn't present an accurate picture of the overall climb in sales. Quarterly figures, especially in the short term, would appear to contradict graph B because the actual numbers would show a series of downturns that the graph leaves out.

Graph D is inaccurate because the 2000 column is doubled in width as well as height. To the eye, this implies that the sales were higher than they actually were, especially because all of the other columns have a smaller width. You may want to emphasize the amazing growth, but you shouldn't over-emphasize it by playing with a graph's visual scale.

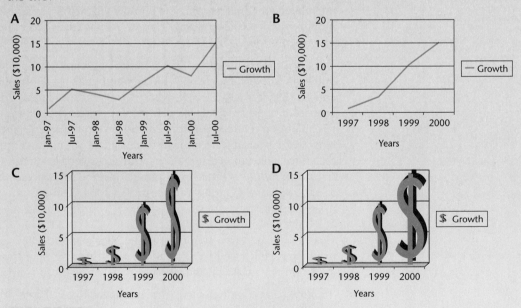

FIGURE 16-1
Which graph(s) accurately depicts growth in sales?

Some listeners may process detailed information better visually than aurally (by ear).

Media for Oral-Report Visuals

You have a lot of choices for visuals, but some, such as the following, take a lot of work to prepare and rely on specialized equipment:

■ **Transparencies for overhead projector.** For most presentations, an overhead projector is ideal. Create the items you want to show—such as a title page, outline, or list of terms and their definitions—and then print them out and photocopy them onto transparencies. You can also photocopy drawings or diagrams, and copy them onto transparencies (but don't forget to cite your sources on the transparencies just as you would for any written report).

Note: Whatever you do, don't overdo transparencies. Frantically shuffling through transparencies is distracting to you and your listeners. For a 7- to 10-minute talk, limit yourself to about 6 transparencies.

■ **Transparency handouts.** For longer, highly detailed presentations that use lots of transparencies, listeners appreciate a full set of the transparencies in printed form on which they can take notes.

■ **Flip charts.** If an overhead projector is not available, consider drawing your visuals on flipchart pages. Use good wide-tip markers and a straight edge to make your flipchart pages look neat and professional.

■ **Objects.** Some oral presentations necessitate having actual objects on hand. Do you dare demonstrate how to do an oil change in the classroom? If so, bring a can of oil, oil filter, and oil wrench. Do you dare demonstrate how to filet a fish? If so, bring the fish, a pan, filet knives, and some paper towels! Or else act out the tasks involving these objects with props or imaginary objects—and leave your fish at home.

■ **Handouts.** Some presenters hand out brochures, illustrations, and other such materials for listeners to look at during the presentation. However, handouts take away listeners' focus from you. Still, an occasional handout can be a nice change of pace. As with any visual, be sure to discuss your handouts, explain them, and walk your listeners through their most important details.

■ **Photographic slides.** Because they provide photographic detail and sharpness, slides can work well for an oral presentation. However, they require one more piece of equipment that may or may not work.

■ **Video clips.** If your presentation requires portrayal of action and movement, you may need video clips. Arrange for the equipment, and make sure that it is working and that you know how to operate it. Don't let the video take over your presentation though. Listeners should spend more time listening to you than viewing the video. Play a portion of the video, pause it, discuss that portion, introduce the next portion, and so on. That way, you are clearly in charge—not the video machine.

- **Presentation software.** Presentation software is the generic name for applications like Microsoft PowerPoint and Lotus Freelance Graphics. If you've watched a speaker fumble with a pile of transparencies, you know all too well what's great about using presentation software. Because applications like PowerPoint are rather complicated, they are discussed later.

Content for Oral-Report Visuals

To plan for graphics in an oral presentation, make sure what's available in the room where you'll present your report. An overhead projector is ideal. Don't plan to write your display material on a blackboard—at least, not the main parts of it. For whatever you think you might want to scribble on the board, type it up, print it out, and get a transparency of it. If an overhead projector is not available for the classroom, consider drawing your graphics on flipchart-size paper. Here are some additional ideas for visuals for your oral presentations:

- *Title page.* Prepare a title page with details about your presentation such as its title and your name. Display it when you first enter the room, while you are setting up, during your introduction, and during breaks.
- *Outline.* Give listeners a strong sense of an overview by showing an outline. As you move from section to section, show the outline again, reinforcing where you are in the presentation, what you've covered, and what's left. An outline may also save you, the presenter, if you get lost.
- *Key terms and definitions.* If your presentation contains specialized terms that you spend some time defining, have a visual for those terms and their definitions.
- *Actual physical objects.* See the discussion of this idea in the preceding section.
- *Drawings, diagrams, flowcharts, photos, animations, videos.* If you can't bring in the objects you refer to, show diagrams. Don't forget to create and show flowcharts relating to your presentation.
- *Tables: statistical detail, summaries.* Listeners can't absorb as much statistical detail through oral presentation as through print. For even simple statistics, display tables during your presentation. Put verbal summaries in tables as well: just list the key words and phrases associated with each topic.
- *Main conclusions.* A good way to summarize certain types of oral presentations is to review the main conclusions. For example, if you've compared several products, display a list of the main conclusions concerning which products were best in which categories.
- *Information sources.* In a "real" situation, your listeners would have attended your presentation out of a real need for your information or curiosity about your topic. If so, provide a listing of other sources of

information about your topic, particularly those you used to prepare your presentation.

HOW DO YOU USE PRESENTATION SOFTWARE?

With the rise of presentation software like Microsoft PowerPoint and Lotus Freelance Graphics, oral presenters have a powerful tool. You show a series of computer screens called *slides* that display words and graphics related to your presentation. Also, presentation software enables you to integrate photographic slides, video clips, and audio into one delivery medium. You don't have to roll in a fleet of overhead projectors, video players, and slide projectors and hope that they all work that particular day. And with the advent of "wizards," creating electronic presentations is surprisingly easy.

1. To begin developing an electronic presentation:
   - In Microsoft PowerPoint, click the icon on your desktop, or select **Start→Programs→Microsoft PowerPoint.**
   - In Lotus Freelance Graphics, click **Start→Programs→Lotus Smart Suite→Lotus Freelance Graphics.**
2. If you've never used an electronic presentation before, each of these applications has a "wizard" to guide you through the creation of your presentation. For example, in PowerPoint, select **AutoContent wizard.**
3. For the type of presentation, select **Generic.** Concerning how the presentation will be used, select **Presentations, informal meetings, handouts.**
4. For presentation output, select **On-screen presentation** and **Yes** for print output.

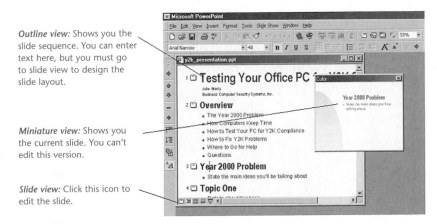

Outline view: Shows you the slide sequence. You can enter text here, but you must go to slide view to design the slide layout.

Miniature view: Shows you the current slide. You can't edit this version.

Slide view: Click this icon to edit the slide.

FIGURE 16-2

Outline view. This view gives you an overview of the text of each slide in your presentation. Click on any portion of the outline to see the layout of the slide in which that text occurs in the miniature view.

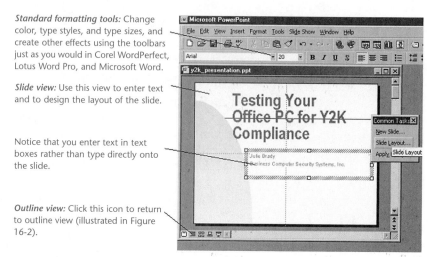

Standard formatting tools: Change color, type styles, and type sizes, and create other effects using the toolbars just as you would in Corel WordPerfect, Lotus Word Pro, and Microsoft Word.

Slide view: Use this view to enter text and to design the layout of the slide.

Notice that you enter text in text boxes rather than type directly onto the slide.

Outline view: Click this icon to return to outline view (illustrated in Figure 16-2).

FIGURE 16-3

Slide view. You can enter text in this view (by creating text boxes), but more importantly you can design the layout of the slide—colors, type styles and sizes, graphics, and so on.

5. In the fields for presentation title, name, and additional information, enter whatever you want to be displayed on the initial slide. (You can always go back and edit it.)

6. After you've done the preceding, go to "outline view," illustrated in Figure 16-2. While you can enter text here, the primary use for outline view is to get an overview of the text of all your slides. You can also get a miniature view of wherever your cursor is located. Try replacing some of the generic text supplied by PowerPoint or Freelance Graphics with your own. Also, try to change a bulleted item to regular text or a numbered-list item. Do this the same as you would in Corel WordPerfect, Lotus Word Pro, or Microsoft Word.

7. Click on the Slide View icon as illustrated in Figure 16-3. On that screen, try selecting some text, changing sizes, fonts, and color.

8. Make some other changes to your presentation, and then "run" it. When you run a presentation, you view it the same way your audience would view it, slide by slide. Click on the Slide Show icon in the bottom left of the window, or click on **Slide Show→View slide show** in the menu bar.

9. Press the spacebar to move from one slide to the next. Press Escape to go back to editing and designing the presentation.

HOW DO YOU DELIVER AN ORAL PRESENTATION?

The best way to deliver an oral presentation is to be well prepared. If you know your material and have rehearsed it, you'll do well no matter how nervous you are. Your first concern should be meeting the needs of your audience and accomplishing your purpose. Unless you are working for the wrong organization, substance ought to come first—way before showmanship. Here are some suggestions though for improving your delivery:

- *Control those nervous verbal mannerisms such as "uh," "you know," and "okay?"* If you practice from a script, develop an awareness of which of these annoying mannerisms you use and how often you use them. Practice just saying nothing instead.
- *Get in control of body language, eye contact, and gestures.* Although situations vary, normally you'll want to maintain a relaxed, confident, open demeanor during an oral presentation. Use gestures, move around, and perhaps even interject humor. But don't be so relaxed that you slouch over the lectern. Avoid the extremes of frenetic movement, on the one hand, and stone-like immobility, on the other. If your hands move everywhere when you speak, keep that under control, but don't get out the handcuffs. Occasional gestures are good; your listeners shouldn't think you are a statue.
- *Speak slowly.* It's just not as easy to hear an oral presentation as it is a face-to-face conversation. Also, because oral presentations don't permit the same give-and-take that conversation does, give listeners more time to get the gist of what you are saying. And finally, speak more slowly to counteract our natural tendency to speak more rapidly when we get excited or nervous.
- *Speak up.* Whether listeners will be able to hear you depends a great deal on the room in which you give your oral presentation. In some rooms, the acoustics are so good that you can practically whisper and still be understood. But don't count on it. To find out, start your presentation with the familiar "Can everybody hear me all right?" Be ready to speak up.
- *Don't be reluctant to summarize or repeat.* Effective oral presentations rely on more repetition than do written ones. You just can't expect to have your listeners' complete attention at every moment. You can't expect listeners to pop up and say, "Hey, will you repeat that?" The best kind of repetition in an oral presentation is not exact word-for-word repetition, but summaries that use slightly different words and connect to the preceding or upcoming topic. This kind of summarizing and linking creates a cumulative effect that will give listeners a sense of increasing understanding.
- *Use plenty of verbal headings.* This book emphasizes how important headings are to written technical documents. Oral presentations need something analogous to headings—some indication to listeners that you're finishing up one topic and moving on to another. See examples of verbal headings in the oral report at the end of this chapter.
- *Begin with a strong introduction.* As mentioned earlier in this chapter, a strong introduction is essential for a good oral presentation.

ORAL PRESENTATION EVALUATION

Using a 1 to 5 scale (with 5 the highest), evaluate the presenter in two ways: yes/no and a numeric rating. For example, if the presenter used verbal headings, answer yes; but if they were not particularly effective, rate the verbal headings 1 or 2.

Date:			
Start time:	**End time:**		**Total:**
Presenter's name:			
Presenter's topic:			

Evaluative category	Yes/No	Rating
Began with an explanation of audience, situation, topic (before starting the actual presentation)?		
Began the actual presentation with an introduction?		
Introduction indicated topic?		
Introduction indicated purpose?		
Introduction gave overview?		
Introduction attempted to motivate, interest?		
Used one or more visuals?		
Visuals were effective?		
Referred to, explained visuals?		
Used verbal headings?		
Presentation was organized?		
Explained technical information clearly?		
Speaking style/delivery was effective?		
Held my attention?		
Ended with a real conclusion?		
Presentation was the expected length?		
Presentation was adequate (overall rating)?		

Comments:

FIGURE 16-4

Oral-presentation evaluation form. This form enables you to answer yes or no, rate the category, or both.

- *Hammer home your main points.* A common guideline for oral presentations is that the typical 7- to 15-minute presentation can support more than three or four main points. That can mean three or four main subtopics, three or four main conclusions leading to a general conclusion, or three or four main sections (between the introduction and conclusion).
- *Emphasize the transitions.* As discussed in the section on transitions at **www.io.com/~hcexres/power_tools/transitions.html,** transitions show people how segments of information are connected. We use weak transitions without thinking, but strong transitions take some thought and practice. Look at the transitions in the example at the end of this chapter. While readers can go back and re-read a document, they can't go back and "re-hear" your presentation. That's why strong transitions are extremely important in oral presentations.
- *Walk listeners through your visuals.* Take time to show listeners the important details of your visuals. Don't just throw visuals out there, and never refer to them; introduce them, and explain their main points. And position yourself next to the screen so that people can see you—don't hide in the dark!
- *Only glance at a script—avoid reading it word for word.* Avoid monotone, head-down, line-by-line reading from a script. (When you look up, no one will be listening—some may even be asleep.) Instead, practice reading your script until you can look away from it without getting lost. During your presentation, know your script so well that you need only glance at it occasionally.
- *Don't get locked in to your script, outline, or plan.* Whichever method you use, be prepared to slow down when people don't seem to be getting it, speed up when they are looking bored, digress or add detail when they seem particularly interested, and be prepared to scrap segments of your presentation if people are clearly not interested or if you are running out of time.

HOW DO YOU EVALUATE ORAL PRESENTATIONS?

You can learn almost as much by listening to and evaluating oral presentations as you can by preparing and delivering them. If you deliver your presentation to the rest of your technical-writing class, your instructor may ask everyone to evaluate each presentation using a standard form, like the one shown in Figure 16-4.

WORKSHOP: ORAL PRESENTATIONS

Here are some additional ideas for practicing the concepts, tools, and strategies in this chapter:

1. *Evaluate a live oral report.* Try to find city-council, school-board, or regulatory-commission meetings on television, and evaluate one of the

presentations, which are usually brief. Use the evaluation form shown in Figure 16-4.

2. *Prepare an oral presentation of a written report.* Select a report you have written or one of the reports in this book, and plan how you'd rework it for oral presentation. Identify the audience and situation in which this oral presentation of the written report would realistically take place. Take notes on why you couldn't just read it verbatim to a group of listeners.

3. For the next three workshop items, choose from this list of oral-report projects (or use your own!):

Presentation to city council requesting more softball parks

Presentation to PTA concerning children's safety at school

Presentation to senior citizens concerning municipal recycling

Presentation to city gardening club concerning advantages of organic pest control methods

Presentation to parents concerning an initiative for all students to have notebook computers at school

Presentation to management requesting that employees be allowed to use the World Wide Web

a. *Audiences and situations for oral reports.* Take a look at the preceding list of oral-report projects, pick one, and write descriptions of one or more audiences and situations for that project.

b. *Infrastructures for oral reports.* Return to the list of oral-report projects, pick one, and identify the infrastructure you'd use for that report.

c. *Visuals for oral reports.* Return to the list of oral-report projects, and make a list of the visuals you might use in it.

Web Pages: HTML and Hypertext

[handwritten notes: hypertext — any text that contains links to other docs]

[handwritten notes: HyperText Markup Lang HTML — standard lang of web]

HYPERTEXT, THE INTERNET, AND THE WORLD WIDE WEB

The Internet and its gracious facilitator, the World Wide Web, have brought on a new era in information access. These new tools have added to the way we access information—and complicated matters considerably. Here are some links that explore the meaning of hypertext and take stock of the impact of the Internet and the Web:

Michael Lerner. "Birth of the Net."
www.learnthenet.com/english/html/01birth.htm *[handwritten: Read internet]*

PBS. "Life on the Internet." **www.pbs.org/internet**

About.com. "Internet for Beginners."
netforbeginners.about.com/internet/netforbeginners/msubhistory.htm

Web Developer's Virtual Library. "History of the Internet and the World Wide Web." **wdvl.internet.com/Internet/History**

Webmonkey Guides. "Who Runs the Internet."
www.hotwired.com/webmonkey/guides/net/runs.html

Vannevar Bush. "As We May Think." A pioneer whose ideas led to hypertext. Originally published in *The Atlantic Monthly*, July 1945.
www.isg.sfu.ca/~duchier/misc/vbush

Accessed January 29, 2001.

[handwritten notes: Internet (contd) → WWW (item in contd) single largest & most popular sub-network on the Internet]

[handwritten notes: Protocol = language]

[handwritten notes: hypertext transfer protocol = http language which allows us to jump to any other public web page 30 billion]

By the time you read this chapter, creating writing projects as Web pages may be as common as printing them out on paper. The 1980s and 1990s saw the move from traditional handwritten and typewritten text to "word-processed" text (created with software such as Corel WordPerfect, Lotus Word Pro, Microsoft Word, Claris Works, and Adobe Pagemaker). The first decade of the new millenium should see the addition of Web pages as another major, routinely used alternative to the methods we use to create and deliver documents.

This chapter does several things: it shows you how to create basic Web pages; it presents general strategies for structuring hypertexts; and it provides you with a strategy for developing a technical document as a Web site.

Note: If you've read much at all about hypertext, you'll find that the following takes a highly structured approach. That's intentional. The readers of most technical documents need and expect structure and guidance from writers.

HOW DO YOU CREATE WEB PAGES?

Before getting started, make sure you understand some basic terms (conceptually illustrated in Figure 17-1).

- *Web page.* A simple plain-text (ASCII) document—an electronic file— that uses special codes called HTML tags along with whatever information you want to provide.
- *HTML tags.* Codes that instruct the Web browser how to display the Web page—whether certain text should be bold or italics, red or blue, a numbered or bulleted list, a certain level of heading, and so on.

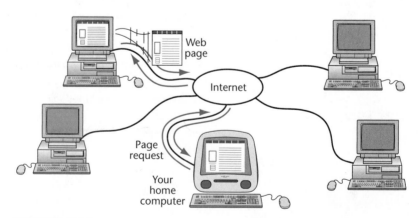

FIGURE 17-1

World Wide Web basics. When you click on a link on the Web, you are actually requesting that a Web page existing on some Internet-connected computer "out there" be downloaded to your own computer and displayed through your Web browser.

- *Web browser.* A software application installed on your computer that enables you to view the Web-page file in all its formatted glory. When you click on a link on a Web page (usually blue underlined text that turns your mouse pointer into a hand), you are requesting that a file be sent to your computer and then displayed by the Web-browser software on your computer.
- *Web site.* A term used here, along with "Web project," for a group of related Web pages. For example, if you wrote an online technical report on solar car designs, consisting of eight separate files all linked together hypertextually, that would be a Web site.
- *Internet computer.* A computer that is networked to the Internet; that is, "on the Web." When you put a Web-page file on a computer that is on the Internet and that has Web server software installed, that file is viewable by anybody in the world. To get our Web pages on the World Wide Web, most of us have to pay Internet service providers (ISPs) who own and maintain Internet computers.

Create Two Simple Web Pages

When you create two or more linked Web pages, you are actually creating a hypertext document. That concept is covered later in this chapter; for now the focus is creating simple Web pages like the ones you see in Figure 17-2. This chapter discusses how to create Web pages using HTML tags rather than a Web-page editor. Understandably, you may prefer Web-page software such as Macromedia's Dreamweaver, Microsoft's FrontPage, and shareware applications available on the Internet. Typing HTML tags can be tedious. However, if you have to do any extensive work, you'll appreciate knowing how the HTML tags work. If you run

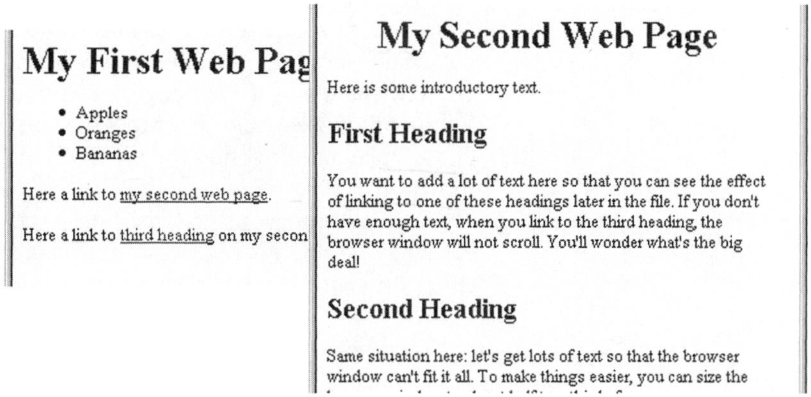

FIGURE 17-2

Simple Web pages. The steps explained in this chapter show you how to create these two Web pages, view them through a Web browser such as Netscape, change them, reload them, and then view your changes.

into a problem with a Web-page editor, it's usually difficult to resolve unless you know some HTML.

Create the first Web page.   You need to create *two* Web pages so that you can see how to link between them:

1. Start whichever text-editing or word-processing software you prefer, and create a file called first.html. Avoid software like Corel WordPerfect, Lotus Word Pro, and Microsoft Word: they try to force you into certain tagging styles you may not want. Instead, use something like Macintosh's BBedit or Microsoft's Notepad. To access Notepad, choose **Start→Programs→Accessories→Notepad**. Name the file .htm or .html—the Web browser (such as Netscape Navigator or Internet Explorer) will not recognize the file otherwise.

2. In this file, type the following at the very top:
   ```
   <HTML>
   <HEAD>
   <TITLE>My First Web Page</TITLE>
   </HEAD>
   <BODY>
   ```
   The text between the TITLE tags will appear in the bar at the top of the window in which your Web page is displayed.

3. At the very bottom of the file, type these lines:
   ```
   </BODY>
   </HTML>
   ```

4. Now, in between the <BODY> tags, enter the text that you want to show in the Web page. Typically, people start with <H1> tags and repeat the text between the <TITLE> tags. For example, you'd enter <CENTER><H1>My First Web Page</H1></CENTER>. Enter this just below the <BODY> tag. Type in regular text, inserting <P> every time you want a paragraph break (a blank line).

5. After you've typed some text and some additional headings, save the file. Make sure that you save it as a plain text file.

6. To view the file as a Web page, open your Web browser (Netscape or Internet Explorer), and select this file you just created and saved. Select **File→Open** and then find the file. It should look partially like the page shown in Figure 17-2.

7. Now, go back to your "source" file—the file in which you have been entering text and HTML tags—and make some changes. For example, enter a bulleted list and then resave the file:
   ```
   <UL>
   <LI>Apples
   <LI>Oranges
   <LI>Bananas
   </UL>
   ```

8. Return to the Web browser and reload (refresh). In Netscape, click **View→Reload** (or just press Ctrl+R). You'll see your most recent changes.

The preceding is how many people develop Web pages—entering text and tags in a plain text file, viewing it in the browser, then making changes in the text file, and then reloading the Web browser. True, you can use a Web page editor (such as Macromedia Dreamweaver) and avoid the HTML tags, but for simple pages or for special effects, knowing the HTML tags is so much better and easier.

Create the second Web page.   Now, create a second Web page, which you'll link to the first one:

1. Follow the same instructions as you did for the first Web page, except for this second page, put `My Second Web Page` between the `TITLE` and `H1` tags, and save it as `second.html`. (Make sure you save this second file in the same directory or folder as the first one.)
2. For the main heading of this page, use `<CENTER><H1>My Second Web Page</H1></CENTER>`.
3. Also, insert *lots* of text. Add 24 lines, and then insert this heading: `<H2>First Heading</H2>`. After the next 24 lines, insert this heading: `<H2>Second Heading</H2>`. After still another 24 lines, insert `<H2>Third Heading</H2>`. (This sets up this second file so that you can link to it in various ways from the first one.)
4. Return to your first Web page and add the following:
```
<P>
Here is a link to <A HREF="second.html">my second Web page</A>.
<P>
```
5. Now save this file and view it through a Web browser. The words "my second Web page" should be blue and underlined. You should be able to click on these words and go to your second file.
6. You can also link to specific points within a Web page—not just to the top. Return to your second Web page and change the third heading so that it looks like this:
```
<A NAME="third_spot"><H2>Third Heading</H2></A>
```
7. Return to the first Web page and enter these tags:
```
<P>
Here is a link to the <A
HREF="second.html#third_spot">third heading</A> on my
second Web page.
<P>
```
8. Save these files and test this link from the first Web page to the third heading on the second Web page. The A NAME tag is called an "anchor" tag; it creates an identifiable target for the browser.

Create Web Pages with Frames

A Web page using frames is divided into two or more sections or panels, which can display different files and can be independently scrollable. As illustrated in Figure 17-3, you can use frames to keep a main menu in the

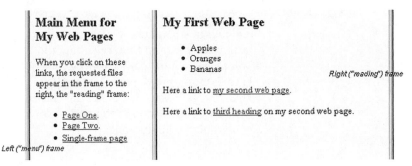

FIGURE 17-3

Web page with frames. In the Web page illustrated here, you can show one file in the left frame and another in the right frame. You can scroll around in either one without affecting the other. When you click on "Page Two" in the left (menu) frame, the page-two file will show in the right (reading) frame.

left frame and to display different text in the right frame. When readers click on a link in the left frame, the linked-to information appears in the right frame, while the left frame stays as it is. To design a frames-based Web project like the one in Figure 17-3, follow these steps:

1. Return to those two files, first.html and second.html, that you created in the preceding section. Create a "menu" file for these two files called menu.html and enter the following HTML tags into it:

```
<HTML>
<HEAD>
<TITLE></TITLE>
</HEAD>
<BODY>
<H1>Main Menu for My Web Pages</H1>
When you click on these links, the requested files
appear in the frame to the right, the "reading" frame:
<UL>
<LI><A HREF="first.html" TARGET="reading_frame">Page
One</A>.
<LI><A HREF="second.html" TARGET="reading_frame">Page
Two</A>.
<LI><A HREF="menu.html" TARGET="_top">Single-frame
page</A>.
</BODY>
</HTML>
```

Notice the TARGET tags: they specify the name of the frame in which to display the file—in this case, the "reading frame" on the right side of the browser window. Notice also TARGET="_top"; this tells the browser to get out of multiple-frame mode and display the file in a single-frame Web page.

2. Create another new Web page—let's call it the "frameset" file and name it `index.html`. Put the following tags in this file:

```
<HTML>
<HEAD>
<TITLE>My Main Frame Page</TITLE>
</HEAD>
<FRAMESET COLS="35%,*">
  <FRAME NAME="menu_frame" SRC="menu.html">
  <FRAME NAME="reading_frame" SRC="first.html">
</FRAMESET>
<NOFRAMES>
  Go to <A HREF="menu.html">
</NOFRAMES>
</HTML>
```

In this one, the `FRAMESET` tags create a left column, called `menu_frame`, covering 35% of the browser window; and another, called the `reading_frame`, covering the other 65%. The `SRC`, or "source" tag specifies which files to show in the two frames. `NOFRAMES` is for Web browsers that do not support frames (which should be very few by the time you read this book).

3. Once you've created and saved these additional files, open `index.html` in your Web browser and see how it works. (If your Web browser does not support frames, only `menu.html` will display.) You should be able to click on the Page Two link in the left (menu) frame and see the text change to that file in the right (reading) frame.

Here are some resources on the World Wide Web for further study of frames:

■ spunwebs.com. "Introduction to Frames."
   manda.com/frames
■ Web Developer's Virtual Library. "Frames—Multi-view Presentation of Documents." **wdvl.internet.com/Authoring/HTML/Frames**
■ WebTeacher Tutorials.
   www.webteacher.org/winnet/frames/framesintro.html
■ Selena Sol. "Basic Frames."
   wdvl.internet.com/Authoring/HTML/Tutorial/basic_frames.html
■ HTML Writers Guild. "Frames Frequently Asked Questions."
   www.hwg.org/resources/faqs/frameFAQ.html

Learn More about HTML

The preceding just gets you started creating Web pages. Use any of the following suggestions to continue learning HTML:

What's next? This book contains most of what you need to create functional Web pages. Most of the chapters, particularly those in Part II, show you how to use HTML tags to create the formatting under discussion there. Specifically:

To do this:	See:
Structure technical documents as Web pages	Chapter 17
Create headings for Web pages	Chapter 7
Create bulleted and numbered lists in Web pages	Chapter 8
Create warning, cautions, and danger notices for Web pages	Chapter 9
Create tables, graphs, and charts for Web pages	Chapter 10
Incorporate and align graphics in Web pages	Chapter 11
Use highlighting (bold, italics, color, other fonts) in Web pages	Chapter 12

Return to the Web-page sections of each of these chapters to see how to create these elements in your own creations.

Figure it out yourself.   Plenty of people just teach themselves. A useful trick for learning HTML tags is to view the "source" of the Web pages that you find on the World Wide Web. Imagine that you find a Web page that has some effects that you like. To view the HTML tags in Netscape, just choose **View→Page Source** once the page has finished loading. (In Internet Explorer, choose **View→Source**.)

Note: If the page uses frames, you'll have to be clever to view the complete source. View the source of the main frameset page, find the names of the files used in the frames (the file names are shown after the SRC tags), and then type them into the URL manually.

Buy some books.   As for learning the basic HTML tags, the various chapters of this book introduce you to them, in the context of the particular format or style discussed in that chapter. For additional detail, try these print resources:

- Castro, E. *HTML 4 for the World Wide Web, Fourth Edition: Visual QuickStart Guide.* Berkeley, CA: Peach Press, 1999.
- DiNucci, D. *et al. Elements of Web Design: The Designer's Guide to a New Medium,* 2nd ed. Berkeley, CA: Peach Press, 1998.
- Tittel, E., *et al. HTML for Dummies.* Indianapolis, IN: IDG Books, 1997.
- Tittel, E., *et al. More HTML for Dummies.* Indianapolis, IN: IDG Books, 1997.

Use online tutorials.   The World Wide Web itself is loaded with HTML-learning resources like the following:

- Webmonkey Tutorials. **www.hotwired.com/webmonkey**
- David McMurrey. HTML resources.
  www.io.com/~hcexres/doc1/html_resources.html

■ Web Developer's Virtual Library.
  wdvl.internet.com/Vlib/Authoring/Tutorials.html
■ Maricopa Community Colleges. Writing HTML–Guide to Creating
  Web Pages. **www.mcli.dist.maricopa.edu/tut**

Use Web-page software. HTML editors or Web editors supposedly make creating Web pages as easy as writing a document in Corel Word Perfect, Lotus Word Pro, or Microsoft Word. As of 2000, the best tools were Adobe PageMill, Claris Home Page, Macromedia Dreamweaver, Allaire's HomeSite, and a few others. Even so, these tools are expensive and complicated. It's worth the time to learn the HTML tags and to be able to create or edit your Web pages manually. Plenty of Web-page developers prefer simple text editors that have strong macro capabilities. They use tools like these to write text and pop in HTML tags with simple keystrokes. As of 2000, a wonderful tool of this sort is Paul Lutus' Arachnophilia, available as "careware" at **www.arachnoid.com**. It has numerous macros built in: for example, when you press Ctrl+I, you get <I> and </I> (HTML tags for italics) with the cursor right between the tags so that you can type the word you want to italicize. Arachnophilia also makes it easy to create your own macros.

WHAT IS HYPERTEXT?

If you have studied the preceding, you are now armed, dangerous, and ready to create Web sites. However, before you start creating great information labyrinths from which your visitors never return, learn something about the concept of hypertext. *Hypertext* is simply one or more documents stored electronically that use devices called *links* to permit rapid electronic cross-referencing and searching.

The idea of hypertext was first conceived in the 1940s by Vannevar Bush and was named in the 1960s by Ted Nelson, but it did not become practical until advances in computer speed, storage, and monitors came about in the 1980s. Before the World Wide Web, creating hypertext was difficult and expensive. Special tools for editing, building, and viewing hypertexts were necessary. The Web, however, brought forth a brilliant solution that made creating and viewing hypertexts practically free. All you need is an Internet-connected computer, a simple text editor, a Web browser, and some knowledge of HTML codes.

By whatever means it is delivered, a hypertext is characterized by several essential components (illustrated in Figure 17-4):

■ *Navigation.* A system that enables you to find your way around in the hypertext.
■ *Links.* "Hot" text on which you click to go to the cross-referenced information. A hypertext link consists of the *link* itself, where you

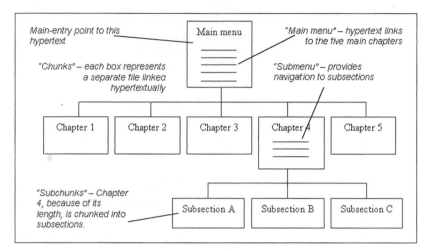

FIGURE 17-4

Hypertext concepts. A hypertext is made up of two or more electronic files ("chunks") connected by hypertext links. These links can be formatted as menus (like tables of contents in printed books), or they can occur right in the text. Hypertexts also include search mechanisms to enable readers to find information using "keywords." Links and search tools are the primary components of the "navigation" system—the way readers find their way around in the hypertext.

> start (the link-highlighted text you click on), and a *target*, where the link takes you.
> - *Menus and submenus.* Similar to tables of contents but with each item hypertext-linked to the related text.
> - *Search tools.* Devices that enable you to search for a keyword and then click on the links to the full-text occurrences of that keyword within the hypertext.

> If you've used the World Wide Web much at all, this is familiar ground. A hypertext can occur in any electronic delivery medium such as a CD-ROM, not just the Web. What may not be so familiar is how to structure a hypertext.

HOW DO YOU CREATE A HYPERTEXT TECHNICAL-WRITING PROJECT?

> This next section brings together everything in this chapter about hypertext and Web pages and explores how to structure a Web site for a writing project. We'll use the online report on voice-recognition software discussed in Chapter 4.

> **1. Analyze your audience's information needs.** As always, consider what your readers' information needs are and how they will use the information. Allow these perspectives to guide every decision as you

design the Web site. (See Chapter 19 on analyzing audiences and adapting writing projects to them.)

Imagine that you must put the recommendation report on voice-recognition software in Chapter 4 online for use by office managers. They know plenty about day-to-day office uses of computers but not much about technical aspects. They will use this report to determine whether voice-recognition software is right for their operations.

2. **Chunk the information into separate files.** If you've already written the text, segment it according to the major sections. Ideally, these "chunks" should be no more than three standard typewritten pages each (or four standard computer screens). Make each major section a separate file. Name each of these files with the .html extension and put them in the same directory (folder). See the illustration in Figure 17-5.

The printed version of the voice-recognition software report has a title page, a table of contents, a list of graphics, an executive summary, an introduction, a background chapter, a chapter on basic theory, an applications chapter, a chapter on various voice-recognition software products, a concluding chapter on the limitations and the future of this technology, and finally a list of information sources. The body sections average 6 pages each, making the entire printed report about 40 pages. Put each of these eleven "chunks" in a separate electronic file, each one ending with .html.

3. **Decide on a main-entry point.** For most Web sites, you can use the main menu as the main-entry point. A main menu offers links to all the major sections of the hypertext—it's just like opening a printed book to the table of contents. However, there are plenty of other ways to design the main-entry point.

For this example project, let's not delay in getting readers to the information they want: use the contents page as the main-entry point and link to each of the major sections (introduction, background, theory, applications, products, conclusion, and sources) from this main menu.

4. **Design the main menu.** If you have set up the main files for this project, or at least decided on their file names, create the main menu as a separate file. Name it index.html. To keep things simple, use bulleted lists for the links to the main sections, as illustrated in Figure 17-6. Consider adding some brief introductory information either before or after the menu—for example, a quick overview of the contents.

In this example, you'd have links to the individual files as shown in Figure 17-6. The link menu is formatted as a bulleted list using the <UL>, <LI>, and </UL> tags.

The complete printed document is just over 40 pages. Each of the "chunks" to the right begins a new page.

Some of these sections are only one page (like the title page); others are 4 to 6 pages (like the products section).

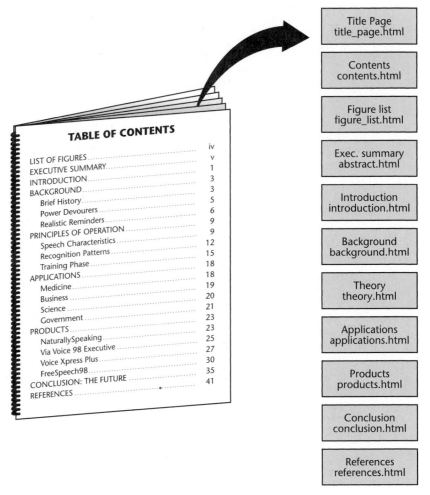

TABLE OF CONTENTS

Title Page
title_page.html

Contents
contents.html

Figure list
figure_list.html

Exec. summary
abstract.html

Introduction
introduction.html

Background
background.html

Theory
theory.html

Applications
applications.html

Products
products.html

Conclusion
conclusion.html

References
references.html

FIGURE 17-5

Chunking information for hypertext delivery. A first step in designing a hypertext is to segment information into usable "chunks." Illustrated above is the printed version of a technical report, opened to its table of contents. To its right are the individual electronic files into which it is segmented ("chunked") and their file names.

5. **Decide whether subitems are needed in the main menu.** Also, decide whether to link to subheadings. Adding the subitems gives readers a fuller sense of the contents of the hypertext.

Readers will probably want direct access to product information. Therefore, put links to those subsections in the main menu. To do so, change each heading in `products.html` to something similar to this: `<A NAME="naturally_speaking"><H2>NaturallySpeaking</H2></A>`. Make the main-menu links to the product subheadings look

```
<HTML>
<HEAD>
<TITLE>Voice-Recognition Software: Recommendation
Report</TITLE>
</HEAD>
<BODY BGCOLOR="white">
<CENTER><H1> Voice-Recognition Software: Recommendation
Report</H1></CENTER>
(Insert 4 to 5 lines of introductory text here.)
<UL>
<LI><A HREF="figures.html">List of Figures</A>
<LI><A HREF="abstract.html">Executive Summary</A>
<LI><A HREF="introduction.html">Introduction</A>
<LI><A HREF="background.html">Background on Voice-
Recognition Systems</A>
<LI><A HREF="theory.html">Human Speech Processing</A>
<LI><A HREF="applications.html">Uses for Voice-Recognition
Systems</A>
<LI><A HREF="products.html">Voice-Recognition Products</A>
<UL>
<LI><A HREF="products.html#naturally_speaking">Naturally
Speaking</A>
<LI><A HREF="products.html#via_voice">Via Voice</A>
<LI><A HREF="products.html#voice_express">Voice Express</A>
<LI><A HREF="products.html#free_speech98">FreeSpeech98</A>
</UL>
<LI><A HREF="problems.html">Limitations of Voice-Recognition
Systems</A>
<LI><A HREF="future.html">The Future of Voice Recognition</A>
<LI><A HREF="sources.html">Information Sources</A>
</UL>
</BODY>
</HTML>
```

Starts the main bulleted list.

Starts the sub-bulleted list.

Indicates that the link should go to the place marked `<A NAME="via_voice">` in the file named products.html.

FIGURE 17-6

HTML tagging for the main-menu page. This tagging creates a bulleted list that contains a sub-bulleted list. Each item is linked to the file specified by the A HREF tags.

similar to this: `<LI><A HREF="products.html#naturally_ speaking.html"> Naturally Speaking</A>`. The # (pound sign) tells the browser to go specifically to the section with the A NAME "target" labelled `naturally_speaking`. (See Figure 17-6 for the complete HTML.)

6. Create any necessary submenus. Submenus are menus occurring in an individual chapter. You'd need a submenu in a long chapter containing numerous headings and subheadings. The submenu enables

```
<HTML>                                          The # (pound sign) tells the
<HEAD>                                          browser to stay in this file and go
<TITLE>Voice-Recognition Software:                  to the point tagged
Product Survey</TITLE>                              <A NAME="via_voice">.
</HEAD>
<BODY BGCOLOR="white">

<H1> Voice-Recognition Software: Product Survey</H1>
<UL>

<LI><A HREF="#naturally_speaking">Naturally Speaking</A>
<LI><A HREF="#via_voice">Via Voice</A>
<LI><A HREF="#voice_express">Voice Express</A>
<LI><A HREF="#free_speech98">FreeSpeech98</A>
</UL>

<A NAME="naturally_speaking"><H2>Naturally
Speaking</H2></A>
```

Dragon Systems NaturallySpeaking offers a so-called Medical Suite targeted to medical professionals and specified as an alternative to transcription. Marketing materials state . . .

FIGURE 17-7

HTML tagging for a "submenu" page. To make navigation easier in products.html, offer a linked list at the top. Readers who want to go directly to FreeSpeech98, for example, can use the link to go directly to that point in the file.

readers to see what the chapter contains and to go directly to a specific section.

In the chapter on different manufacturers of voice-recognition software, create a submenu at the top—links to each of the software applications discussed within the chapter. This submenu along with its HTML tagging is shown in Figure 17-7.

7. **Ensure that all headings are fully descriptive.** In a hypertext, headings must be adequately descriptive of the sections they introduce. Picture each of your headings isolated from the text they introduce: are they descriptive enough to indicate the content of the section? Repeat keywords in headings and subheadings, even if they seem obvious.

In the online version of the report on voice-recognition software, expand a heading like "Software Applications" to "Voice-Recognition Software Applications"; "Limitations" to "Limitations of Voice-Recognition Software"; "Background" to "Background on Voice-Recognition Software." In fact, repeat the primary topic "voice-recognition software" in all related headings. Leave nothing for readers to guess.

1. The requirement for 256 of <u>L2 cache</u>, along with 40 MB of RAM and 180 MB for storage, makes Via Voice the most power-hungry of the applications compared.
2. Dragon Systems' NaturallySpeaking Medical Suite with Add-On Vocabularies is easily customizable for most practices' needs for specialized medical vocabularies and medical forms.
3. Dragon Systems' NaturallySpeaking technology is the most accurate of the four programs tested.

Spot link taking readers to the discussion of L2 cache in case they forgot what it is or didn't read that section.

FIGURE 17-8

Spot links. You can put hypertext links right into your main reading text, as shown here—but don't overdo it! Make sure the linked-to information is essential to readers' understanding.

8. Design standard ("generic") links. Standard links are the generic "next," "previous," and "main menu" links. Put these at the top or bottom of pages, in "menu" frames, or in imagemaps located somewhere on your pages. Design these links according to how you want readers to read your Web document. For sequential reading, use a "previous" and "next" links, and a "main menu" link to enable readers to return to the main menu. If your Web document doesn't read sequentially, just provide a "main menu" link in each file.

For the voice-recognition report, you can provide links to the preceding page, the main menu, and the next page. The report can be read sequentially, each section building on the preceding.

9. Decide on spot links. At this point, almost all of the "navigation" for your Web project is complete. However, you may need one more navigational tool: "spot links." These are links to related information occurring right in the paragraphs of your text (see Figure 17-8). Imagine that you explain an important concept in one section and discuss its applications in another. Readers can't understand the applications unless they understand the concept. That understanding is so vital that you set a hypertext link to the concept section—just in case certain readers skipped it. But remember that spot links are distracting. If it's a simple sentence-length definition, just repeat it on the spot—no need for the link.

10. Decide on related-information sections. To avoid littering a hypertext with numerous spot links that will drive readers crazy, you can use related-information sections. Collect all the "nice-to-have" links and put them there. Keep only the most critical or the most

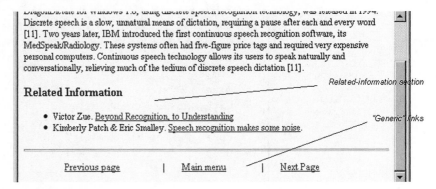

Discrete speech is a slow, unnatural means of dictation, requiring a pause after each and every word [11]. Two years later, IBM introduced the first continuous speech recognition software, its MedSpeak/Radiology. These systems often had five-figure price tags and required very expensive personal computers. Continuous speech technology allows its users to speak naturally and conversationally, relieving much of the tedium of discrete speech dictation [11].

Related Information   *Related-information section*

- Victor Zue. <u>Beyond Recognition, to Understanding</u>   *"Generic" links*
- Kimberly Patch & Eric Smalley. <u>Speech recognition makes some noise.</u>

<u>Previous page</u> | <u>Main menu</u> | <u>Next Page</u>

FIGURE 17-9

Related-information and "generic" links. Put "nice-to-know" links in related-information sections to avoid clutter. Use standard *(generic)* links to provide navigation to previous or next pages or to main menus or submenus.

essential—the "must-have"—links in the regular text. In the related-information section, you can indicate the topic and relevance of the linked-to items. (See the example in Figure 17-9.)

In the voice-recognition report, we needn't offer links in the related-information section to other parts of this same report. Instead, let's use related-information sections for outbound links to research and background material on voice-recognition technology and to the individual software makers' corporate Web sites.

If you've chunked your information, created menus and submenus, added related-information sections and spot links, and linked everything—you have yourself a basic hypertext. Readers can navigate around, find what they want to read, skip what they don't want to read, and recover when they get lost.

WORKSHOP: WEB PAGES AND HYPERTEXT

Here are some additional ideas for practicing the concepts, tools, and strategies in this chapter:

1. Find a Web site that has multiple "chunks" and other features as discussed in the section on hypertext in this chapter. Create a diagram of the hypertext of that Web site similar to the ones in Figures 17-4 and 17-5.

2. Find a report you have written, or photocopy one out of a technical journal, and create a paper mock-up of a hypertext. Chunk the report or article by cutting out the various sections. Create the main-entry point and main menu by writing the links and other information on

separate sheets of paper. Write the standard links at the bottom of each of the chunks. Write related-information sections at the bottom of any of the chunks as necessary. Find some place to tape these chunks up— for example, on a white board or on wrapping paper that you then tape onto a wall. Draw lines to connect all the links to their targets. Arrange the chunks similar to the ones in Figures 17-4 and 17-5.

3. Use the instructions and unformatted text available at **www.io.com/ ~hcexres/power_tools/hypertext** and transform them into a Web page with HTML tags.

PART IV

Tools for Project Development

Reviewing and Revising

ARTIFICIAL INTELLIGENCE, NEURAL NETWORKS

Some believe that one day software applications using some form of artificial intelligence will be able to proofread, copyedit, and even do high-level revision on our written work. Then all the writing teachers and editors will be replaced by software! Take a look at the some of the following links to see how soon that will be:

Neural Network Basics. Z Solutions. **www.zsolutions.com/neural.htm**

Eyal Reingold and Johnathan Nightingale. PSY371: Artificial Intelligence Tutorial Review. **psych.utoronto.ca/~reingold/courses/ai**

Kevin Gurney, University of Sheffield, UK. Neural Nets (introductory book available online). **www.shef.ac.uk/psychology/gurney/notes**

Denis Susac. "Artificial Intelligence." About.com. **ai.about.com/compute/ai**

Artificial Neural Networks Technology. Tutorial from U.S. Department of Defense, Data and Analysis Center for Software. **www.dacs.dtic.mil/techs/neural/neural_ToC.html**

Tim Beardsley. "Debunking the Digital Brain." *Scientific American.* **www.sciam.com/explorations/020397brain/020397explorations.html**

William H. Calvin. "The Emergence of Intelligence." *Scientific American.* 271(4):100-107, October 1994. **weber.u.washington.edu/~wcalvin/1990s/1994SciAmer.htm**

About AI. American Association for Artificial Intelligence (AAAI). **www.cs.pitt.edu/~peterson/**

Accessed January 30, 2001.

When you've written a rough draft, it's time to do some reviewing and revising. When you "review" a document, you study it to see if it meets its requirements—whether it works for the intended audience and purpose. When you revise a document, you make improvements that will enable it to meet those requirements and make it work for its intended audience and purpose.

Revising includes much more than fixing spelling errors and grammar mistakes. Most importantly, it includes making sure the document works for its intended readers. Among other things, that includes checking content, organization, transitions, format, and other "high-level" issues.

This chapter brings together the various concepts, strategies, and tools discussed throughout this book. It puts them into a unified overall strategy you can use when you are reviewing other people's written work as well when you are reviewing and revising your own.

To make this process less complex, divide your reviewing and revising into three stages: the first for the high-level issues such as audience, purpose, content, organization, and transitions; the second for format issues such as headings, lists, notices, highlighting, tables, and graphics; and the third for technical style, sentence style, grammar, usage, and punctuation.

FIRST PASS: AUDIENCE, PURPOSE, CONTENT

Read through your rough draft looking for problems involving audience, purpose, situation, content, organization, and transitions.

1. **Review your draft from the point of view of its intended readers, their situations, and their purposes.** See Chapter 19 for strategies for audience review.

   If readers are reading this document for a specific purpose, will they be satisfied?

   In what ways might readers be frustrated by this document?

   How might this document not meet their needs?

Does this document meet the needs of the situation in which it is required?

2. **Review your rough draft in terms of its content.** Check to see if you've provided too little information, too much information, information at the wrong level, or useless information. Use the brainstorming strategies provided in the section on content at **www.io.com/~hcexres/ power_tools/content.html** to help you identify additional content that might be needed. As you read a rough draft in this first pass, ask yourself questions like the following:

Do my readers really need this information?

Will readers understand this material? Is it way over their heads?

Is this material above, below, or just right for their level of understanding?

Is there anything left out—any important information vital to readers' understanding?

Are the sources of borrowed information indicated properly?

3. **Review your rough draft in terms of organization.** Consider the organization of the content of your draft—specifically, the sequencing of the major sections, the subsections, the paragraphs, and even sentences within individual paragraphs. See the section on organization at **www.io .com/~hcexres/power_tools/organization.html** for strategies for checking organization. As you review, ask yourself questions like the following:

Does the sequence of the main sections make sense?

Does the sequencing of segments within each main section make sense?

Are any paragraphs out of sequence within subsections?

Can you find any individual sentences out of sequence within paragraphs?

4. **Review your rough draft for transitions.** Do the same kind of phased review of transitions in your draft. Check transitions between major sections, between subsections, between paragraphs, and even major portions of paragraphs. See **www.io.com/~hcexres/power_tools/transitions .html** for strategies to use in checking transitions. As you review, ask yourself questions like the following:

Are there transition techniques at the beginning of each major section that indicate how it is related to the preceding?

Are transition sentences, complete with review and preview words as well as transition signals, used to link major sections and subsections?

Do transitions link one paragraph to the next, or groups of paragraphs to the next?

Are strong transitions—review words and preview words—used to link groups of related sentences to the following?

Practical Ethics: Universal Language

 Years after Shakespeare first penned his plays, people are still producing and going to see his dramas and comedies. Classics by Austen and Tolstoy are still being read. Shakespeare's bawdy humor still makes us laugh and we still fall in love and make tragic decisions. These are universal themes that can be found in the oldest and the most modern narratives.

While you might not write about such universal themes as love in technical projects, you can still increase your effectiveness by writing universally. This means being careful not to alienate readers by using language that makes them, in all their diversity, feel excluded.

In the past, "man" and "mankind" were frequently used to mean "all humans." The pronoun "he" was used similarly—not necessarily to mean a male person, but just a person in general. Today, however, it has been recognized that the use of these words has the potential to exclude and offend a percentage of your audience; in fact, careless use of these words is considered sexist. Communication is difficult enough without using words that turn off your listeners or readers.

The solutions are relatively easy. Just replace these nouns and pronouns with more universal ones. For instance:

1. **Problematic:** Man first encountered gorillas . . .
This excludes women. Don't give any of your readers reason to tune you out!
   Solution: Humans first encountered gorillas . . .

2. **Problematic:** When a surgeon washes his hands before surgery . . .
This implies that all doctors are male, which simply isn't true. Be careful not to stereotype any profession by gender.
   Solution A: When a surgeon washes his or her hands before surgery . . .
Constantly using "he or she" can be awkward. When appropriate, use plural nouns to eliminate the problem altogether:
   Solution B: When surgeons wash their hands before surgery . . .
   Solution C: When individual surgeons wash their hands . . .

3. **Problematic:** Chairman, delivery man, postman, etc.
Once again, these words are not universal. Find ways around this.
   Solution: Chairperson, delivery person, postal service worker, etc.

You may not feel like Tolstoy when you're working on a report or memo, but you can at least help your readers feel universally included.

SECOND PASS: DESIGN AND FORMAT

After reviewing high-level issues, consider design and format.

1. **Review the rough draft in terms of the document type and use.** Chapter 15 on format and the chapters of Part I provide strategies for deciding whether to use a formal report, business letter, or memo design.

   Are you using the right type of document in terms of content and purpose—background report, instructions, recommendation report, proposal, research report, or progress report?

   Are the right components included in the document according to its type?

Are you using the right type of document—memo report, business letter report, formal report (with cover memo or letter), or Web page report?

Have you used the right binding on this report—paper clip, spiral, or ring binder?

2. **Review the headings in your rough draft.** A good way to review the high-level organization of a rough draft is to review the headings in that draft. Chapter 7 provides strategies for designing and formatting headings. As you review, ask yourself questions like the following:

Are these headings explanatory and descriptive enough of the sections they introduce?

Are the headings designed to indicate levels?

Are there too few headings? Too many?

Are there lone headings or stacked headings?

Are certain headings not parallel in phrasing?

Are any pronouns used incorrectly to refer to headings?

Are headings used incorrectly as figure or table titles or as lead-ins to lists?

3. **Review your rough draft for its use of lists.** Chapter 8 presents strategies for designing various types of lists, which can increase the readability of a draft. As you review your rough draft for lists, ask yourself these questions:

Is there text you can reformat as in-sentence, bulleted, or numbered lists?

Are numbered lists used for list items in a required order?

For in-sentence lists, are list numbers or letters enclosed by both parentheses?   (i)   (a)

Are all lists introduced by a lead-in and punctuated by a colon?

Are list items parallel in phrasing?

Do you capitalize and punctuate list items consistently and according to some standard, such as those presented in this book?

4. **Review your rough draft for its use of tables, graphs, and charts.** Chapter 10 presents guidelines and strategies for tables, graphs, and charts. As you review a rough draft, consider these related questions:

Can you find text that can be presented more effectively as tables?

Are your tables designed for vertical comparison?

Are table titles centered at the top of tables?

Are measurement types (in., mm, $) kept in row or column headings when possible?

Are text columns left aligned with their headings?

Are "skinny" columns centered and numeric columns right or decimal aligned?

Is the source of information borrowed to create tables cited properly?

Are tables placed just after the point in the text where they are relevant?

Are there cross-references to tables, which discuss their main significance?

Could text or tables be presented more effectively as graphs or charts?

Do you include appropriate titles, axis labels, and legends in your graphs and charts?

5. **Review your rough draft for its use of graphics.** Technical documents typically include illustrations, drawings, diagrams, flowcharts, and so on. Review Chapter 11 for guidelines and strategies for the creation and use of graphics. When you review a rough draft, ask yourself these questions:

Are there areas where graphics are needed but not supplied?

Are the graphics in the draft right for the needs and level of the audience?

Are graphics placed near the point in the text where they are relevant?

Do cross-references briefly explain the important aspects of the graphics?

Are numbered, explanatory titles used for graphics as necessary?

Are the sources of any borrowed graphics indicated?

6. **Review your rough draft for its use of highlighting.** Chapter 12 covers guidelines and strategies for bold, italics, alternate fonts and color, and different type sizes. As you review your draft, ask questions like the following:

Is your use of bold and italics consistent and in keeping with a standard?

Do you avoid using capital letters and quotation marks for emphasis?

Do you limit the document to one alternate font (for example, Arial for headings, Times New Roman for body text, and Courier New for the alternate font)?

Except for headings, do you keep type size no larger than that for body text?

THIRD PASS: STYLE, GRAMMAR, MECHANICS

Once you've revised a rough draft for high-level issues and for design and format, you're ready to check for style, grammar, mechanics, and spelling problems.

Chak

1. **Review your rough draft for sentence problems.** Look for classic wordiness problems such as bad passive voice, weak *be* verbs, and redundant phrasing as covered at **www.io.com/~hcexres/power_tools/sentence_style.html**. Don't forget—as a technical writer, you are not being paid by the pound! Specifically, ask yourself questions like these:

   Can you find passive-voice sentences that would be clearer, more direct, and more succinct using active voice?

   Can you find complicated noun stacks that could be "unstacked," making your document more immediately understandable?

   Can you find unnecessary use of expletives (any variation of *there is* or *it is*)?

   Can you find redundant phrasing that could be cut?

2. **Review your rough draft for technical-style problems.** Technical documents typically contain vexing problems involving abbreviations, acronyms, numbers, hyphens, symbols, and the like. Use Appendix A to resolve them. As you review, ask yourself questions like these:

   Do you use digits for numbers as opposed to words for numbers consistently and according to a standard?

   Do you use symbols in your document consistently and according to a standard, defining the potentially unfamiliar ones on first use?

   Do you establish the meaning of acronyms and unfamiliar abbreviations on first use?

3. **Review your draft for grammar, usage, punctuation, and spelling problems.** Don't forget to review for the old favorites—fragments, run-ons, comma splices, agreement errors, parallelism problems, sexist language, and the like. Use Appendix C for help in these areas.

   Can you find any comma splices or fragments in your rough draft?

   Can you find verbs or pronouns not in agreement with their counterparts?

   Can you find series items (in headings, lists, or sentences) that are not parallel in phrasing?

   Can you find introductory elements, compound sentences, or series "and" elements not punctuated with a comma?

   Do you use hyphens for potentially confusing compound modifiers?

   Do you avoid using quotation marks for emphasis?

Do you avoid Latin abbreviations such as *e.g.*, *i.e.*, and *etc.*?

Have you run a spell-checker on your document?

Can you spot any problems with similar-sounding words, such as *affect/effect*, *principle/principal*, *to/too/two*, or *its/it's*?

4. **Check the readability statistics on your document.** Most word-processing software includes readability statistics. Readability formulas use syllables per word, words per sentence, and vocabulary ratings to calculate grade level. Although there is much skepticism about these formulas, some organizations use them, requiring a seventh- or eighth-grade reading level. To see readability statistics on your draft, open it and then use the following steps:

   ■ In Corel WordPerfect, choose **Tools→Grammatik**, and then on the Grammatik dialog choose **Options→Analysis→Readability**.
   ■ In Lotus Word Pro, choose **Edit→Proofing Tools→Check Grammar**. On the Grammar Check dialog, select **Done** to see readability statistics.
   ■ In Microsoft Word, choose **Tools→Options→Spelling & Grammar**. Check **Check spelling with grammar** and **Display readability statistics**, click **OK**, and choose **Tools→Spelling and Grammar**.

WORKSHOP: REVIEWING AND REVISING

Here are some exercises to give you some practice reviewing and revising. For additional practice, see **www.io.com/~hcexres/power_tools/reviewing_revising**.

1. *First-pass reviewing.* Use the strategies discussed in this chapter to review for audience, purpose, content, organization, and transitions in the excerpt at the end of this section.

2. *Second-pass reviewing.* Use the strategies discussed in this chapter to review for design and format in the same excerpt.

3. *Third-pass reviewing.* Use the strategies discussed in this chapter to review for style, grammar, and mechanics in the same excerpt at the end of this section.

4. *Revision.* Now, use your review notes to revise the excerpt.

PREPARING THE AQUARIUM

Make sure you take care of the following items before you begin draining your aquarium:

- Unplug all electrical accessories
- Remove hood from tank
- Spread out towels on floor around base of aquarium
- Set out buckets around the base of the aquarium

Equipment Check

Before you begin make sure you have all of the needed equipment and chemicals. It would not be a good idea to begin draining your aquarium and then realize you don't have the needed supplies. This would mean an emergency trip to the nearest pet store to obtain the missing items, and you are taking a chance of losing fish while your aquarium sits half empty at home. To avoid this, the equipment and supplies you will need are listed below.

1. Buckets
2. Towels
3. Water Conditioner
4. Clean filters
5. Pipe cleaner brushes
6. Soft cloth
7. Siphon Tube

DANGER: YOU MUST USE ITEMS THAT HAVE NEVER BEEN USED TO CONTAIN OR CLEAN UP CHEMICALS OR PAINT. ONCE YOU GET ALL OF THESE SUPPLIES GATHERED YOU WILL WANT TO USE THEM EXCLUSIVELY FOR YOUR AQUARIUM.

Text in need of revision. See the preceding workshop for suggestions to revise this text.

CHAPTER 19

Audience and Task Analysis

GENETIC ENGINEERING, GENE THERAPY, AND CLONING

One of the latest theories from academia is that you must construct a mental replica of your audience to write effectively—essentially, mental cloning! (For further details on this interesting idea, read this chapter):

About.com. Genetics→Cloning Human, Genetic Engineering, and Gene Therapy. **genetics.about.com/education/genetics/msubch.htm**

ReligiousToleration.org. Ethical Aspects of Human Cloning. **www.religioustolerance.org/cloning.htm**

New Scientist. Cloning Special Report. **www.nsplus.com/nsplus/insight/clone/clonelinks.html**

Pharmaceutical Research and Manufacturers of America. Cloning. **genomics.phrma.org/genomics/cloning.html**

Microarrays and "DNA Chips." **genomics.phrma.org/cloning.html**

Yahoo Full Coverage: Cloning. **headlines.yahoo.com/Full_Coverage/Tech/Cloning**

Human Cloning Foundation. **www.humancloning.org**

Accessed January 30, 2001.

Technical documents often fail because their writers lose sight of their readers' needs, interests, and knowledge—or they never understood their readers to begin with. One of the great paradoxes of technical writing—in fact, of all writing—is that the simplest, most fundamental of concepts is the most overlooked: What could be more obvious than not talking rocket science to your kindergartner? Closely related to audience analysis is task analysis—the business of determining the tasks about which readers want information.

This chapter explores just who the readers of technical documents are, how to identify characteristics affecting their ability to understand, what tasks they typically need explained in technical documents, and then how to plan, write, and revise with readers fully in mind.

Note: Audience and task analysis is the starting point for any study of technical communication as well as any technical-writing project. If you are not familiar with the organization of this book, see the Preface.

WHO READS TECHNICAL DOCUMENTS?

To begin with, readers of technical documents are not all rocket scientists. More commonly, readers of technical brochures, instructions, handbooks, and manuals are nonspecialists—entry-level people just breaking into the field, or just plain consumers.

One of the long-standing definitions of audiences for technical documents is the four-audience definition developed by Kenneth Houp and Thomas Pearsall. It defines technical audiences this way:

- *Laymen.* Nonspecialist readers who lack background (knowledge or experience) in the subject matter of the technical document.
- *Technicians.* Readers who have or need the sort of background required to assemble, operate, maintain, or repair equipment or to run complex processes.
- *Executives.* Readers who may not have much technical background but who use technical information to make decisions: to purchase, sell, implement, regulate, and so on.
- *Experts.* Readers who know everything about the technology—its design, construction, uses, operation, as well as the theory behind it.

If you've read Chapter 5 on classification, you'll recognize that *two* bases of classification are used here: how much technical knowledge the audience possesses and how the audience will use the technical information. This definition works because it matches what we often find in the real world.

What people do with technology is possibly the best approach to defining audience categories. Consider the uses of the technology—the way people associate themselves with it—and define the different types of readers accordingly. The computer industry is an interesting example. You'll typically find some combination of the following types of audiences for computer information:

- *System administrators.* Install, configure, customize, and manage computer hardware and software.
- *Programmers.* Develop new applications to be used on the computer, fix "bugs" in the existing applications, or both. Also known as "software engineers" or "developers."
- *Engineers.* Develop the computer hardware, the chips, the buses, the drives, the cases, and so on. Also known as "hardware engineers" or "developers."
- *Support technicians.* Provide help to customers who have problems with their computers.
- *Site planner/purchasers.* Plan the purchasing and implementation of computer installations. Although this role was much more important in the days of the big mainframes, people still play this role, which is largely an executive one.
- *End users.* Actually use computers to get work done—write documents, print them, create graphics, update spreadsheets, generate graphs, use the Internet, and so on.

Once you've defined the audience's relationship to the technology, you can then define that audience's background—knowledge, experience, even attitude—in relation to that technology. Background is typically defined this way:

- *Entry-level, novice users; nonspecialist, layman readers.* They know next to nothing; they need lots of hand-holding, tutorials, and reinforcement.
- *Intermediate, occasional users.* They've done this before but have forgotten some details. They don't want tutorials—just reminders or memory-joggers. These users present a special challenge for technical writers: their needs are right between those of the beginning and experienced user.
- *Expert, advanced, heavy users or readers.* They know the subject matter very well; they need to know the new stuff, the theory, and the latest research.

WHY DO THEY READ? WHAT ARE THEIR TASKS?

Readers of technical documents read to solve practical problems, accomplish important tasks, and gather information. While audience analysis focuses on the characteristics of your readers—their knowledge, experience, and skills—*task analysis* focuses on what kinds of information they need, which tasks they seek to accomplish, and which types of information they need to make decisions.

To get a sense of one common form of task analysis, consider that microwave oven in your house, apartment, or dorm room. What are the tasks you do with it?

Task Analysis—Instructions: Microwave Oven

Unpacking and setting up	You may need information on how to set up the microwave, or how to break it in.
Safety considerations	Although safety considerations are not really tasks, they are certainly important. Don't leave that metal spoon in your coffee cup when you reheat!
Simple cooking	You need quick information on how to heat up a cup of coffee or those leftovers!
Occasional cleaning	Your parents are paying a visit; you've got to get the place cleaned up, especially the microwave.
Cooking with different power levels	You also need to know how to use the power levels if you are trying to cook something fancy to impress your date.
Setting the time	When the power goes out, you need to reset the time on the microwave, along with dozens of other electronic devices.
Using the timer	You need to use the timer: it's finals week, and you're making brownies and don't want them to burn.
Packing and moving the microwave	When the semester is over and you're moving back home, you may need some tips on packing the microwave to keep from damaging it during transit.

Task analysis for instructions is straightforward as the microwave example shows. Define the common uses of the device and then write accordingly. If you don't have much experience with the equipment, go observe typical users—and even interview them as to the tasks they typically perform with that equipment.

However, consider a non-instructional project in terms of task analysis. It could be called a "topic analysis"—readers reading a background report are looking for certain topics to meet their needs. Consider a global warming report for coastal real-estate developers.

This task analysis addresses the readers' need to understand the theory, understand its worst implications, see the other side of the argument, see your balanced view of the matter, and get a better perspective from your

Task Analysis—Noninstructional Information: Global Warming Report

Global warming causes	Explain the standard model used by proponents of the global-warming theory; explain how radiation is trapped in the atmosphere. Discuss the sources of this trapping effect. Perhaps discuss the theory of "natural" warming and cooling trends in relation to the theory of a human-induced warming trend.
Global warming effects	Discuss predictions made by proponents of the theory, from the most dire to the most conservative. Discuss any scientific support that research has uncovered to support the predictions.
Arguments against the theory	Review the arguments against the global-warming theory.
Balanced view	Compare the arguments of the proponents of the theory against those of the critics, and state your own view.
Current research	Briefly survey the research being done on the theory; provide some ideas on how to stay current with developments relating to the global-warming theory.
Current efforts to combat global warming	Review what governments and other organizations are doing in relation to global warming and their chances for success.

report with which to make their own decisions. Using this report, they can make their own decisions on whether to hold onto their coastal real estate investments.

HOW DO YOU IDENTIFY TASKS?

In a technical-writing course, your audience is almost always your instructor. However, technical documents are written for real workplace situations. Find out how your technical-writing instructor wants to handle this problem.

■ *Real projects—real audiences—real feedback.* In some technical-writing courses, you must find real projects with real audiences. They will give you real feedback as to how well your technical document meets their needs. For example, a guide might be needed for the printers in the computer lab: the actual users of your guide (as well as your instructor) will let you know how successful you are in meeting their needs and solving their problems.

■ *Invented, "hypothetical" projects and audiences.* In other courses, you are invited to use your imagination and define a hypothetical audience. For the topic of global warming, you might invent an audience of coastal real-estate investors. Rising sea levels and increased storm activity would have a major impact on their investments.

With this background on audience, let's walk through an audience definition and analysis. We'll use two scenarios—one involving a printer guide for the school's computer lab, and the other a global-warming report.

Printer Guide for the Computer Lab

For this first scenario, imagine that you want to do a "real" project, one that will be used by real people to meet their needs, answer their questions, and help them solve technical problems.

1. First of all, you need a project, which includes a topic and purpose.

> Imagine you are writing a printer guide for one of the school's computer labs. The faculty sponsor has requested that you write this guide as a part of your work there.

2. Make a list of the people who will be using your technical document. Identify them by roles.

> The people who will use the printer guide will be both students and lab technicians. Students are "end users," as defined above. Lab technicians are "system administrators" or "technicians," as discussed above.

3. Make a list of the tasks these readers must perform—not just the most common ones, but also those infrequent but critical tasks.

> Students come to the lab to print their papers. Because the lab is busy and typically understaffed, they may have to fix a paper jam, add paper, turn on the printer, or determine on which machine their papers will be printed. Lab technicians, on the other hand, have standard system administrative and maintenance jobs: changing the destination of a printout, reestablishing network connection to a printer, and most likely adding paper and clearing paper jams (rather than students). As the technical writer, you need to determine who can or should do what.

4. Identify the amount of experience, knowledge, and skills these readers typically have in relation to the technology you are documenting.

In the typical school computer lab, some students have very little experience while others have enough to act as lab technicians. As the technical writer, you must decide "just how low you can go." Lab technicians can range from relatively experienced end users without system-administrative background to experienced lab technicians who don't need the printer guide at all. As a technical communicator, you realize that the printer guide will take the load off the experienced lab technicians and enable the entry-level lab technicians to find answers to their own questions—especially when there is no one to provide help.

5. **Observe your audience and identify the tasks for which they may need information. Interview them to ensure you get a complete list of tasks.**

Go to the computer lab and watch the students—see how they print out documents; see what problems or questions they have. Watch the lab technicians and make a list of the tasks they perform. Interview several lab technicians (both experienced and brand new ones). Add to your list of tasks. And finally interview the head administrator of the computer lab. Find out if you've missed any tasks; find out how that individual wants the printer guide to be used in the lab.

6. **Make a list of the concepts and terminology your readers must know.**

Students using the lab may need help with unfamiliar terms, for example, "print queue" or "network printer." If students can designate a different networked printer, you may want to explain the concept of computer networks. The lab technicians, on the other hand, will need discussions of networks, permissions, queues, and much more.

7. **Create an audience description in which you briefly describe the audience (or audiences), their uses for the information, and their background.**

The project will be a printer guide for use by students and lab technicians in the school computer lab. To enable students to print their documents, check printer queues for the status of their print jobs, and to determine to which printer their documents will print, the guide will provide step-by-step instructions and explain concepts and terms that must be used. To enable lab technicians to clear queues, restart printers, check networks, fix paper jams, and add paper, the guide will also offer step-by-step instructions as well as explanations of key terms and concepts. The guide will assume that students have general familiarity with the operating system and the applications but, in terms of printing, nothing more than the location of the print option in their application. The guide will assume that entry-level lab technicians have at least a student's level of understanding and the ability and intention to learn the rest.

The following is an example audience description like the type that your technical-writing instructor or your lead writer may ask you to prepare:

> *Audience description:* For a printer guide to be used in the computer lab in NRG 4209 by both lab assistants and students using the lab. The guide will be aimed at two audiences: lab assistants who have just started working in the lab who are not much more than well-experienced end users; and students who need to do certain tasks when a lab assistant is not available. The guide will be divided into two sections: one for lab assistants; the other for students using the lab. The guide will take the load off experienced lab assistants and help new assistants when they are on their own. It will also help students who are using the lab to accomplish simple tasks when a lab assistant is not available.

Global-Warming Report for Real Estate Investors

For this second scenario, imagine that you "invent" an audience with a direct, vital interest in a report on a technical topic (which just happens to be of great interest to you, the technical-writing student).

1. First of all, you need a project, which includes a topic and purpose.

For this noninstructional scenario, imagine you are writing a technical background report on global warming for real-estate investors.

2. Get exact information on the individual who is requesting the report.

For this report, imagine that the requestor is the head of an association of real-estate investors, or some deputized agent of it. This report is being commissioned and paid for by the association; any member who requests a copy will get one. Imagine that the hypothetical requestor is Mr. John Smith, President, Texas Coastal Real Estate Association. His hypothetical address is 300 West Padre, Suite 1000, Corpus Christi, Texas 78796.

3. Identify the readers' interests in or needs for the report. How are they going to use the report?

Having heard gloom-and-doom predictions of a ten-foot rise in sea level and dramatic increases in tropical-storm activity, these real-estate investors want balanced, objective information on the global-warming issue. They are not requesting a recommendation, just detailed information they can use to make their own decisions. They want to understand the basic theory and some essential terminology presented in nonspecialist terms—not in-depth scientific detail.

4. Identify the concepts and terminology your readers can be expected to know and those that your readers can't be expected to know.

Your readers are investors, businesspeople, and experts in real estate. As such, their backgrounds are business, marketing, real estate, and finance—not science. If you could interview them, they might prove to be political conservatives and thus skeptical of "environmentalists" (which they pronounce with a certain hissing noise).

5. Determine which topics you should discuss and which you should leave out of the report. Determine the level of detail and technical specifics you should discuss in the topics you do cover.

You know that you must discuss the basic cause-and-effect mechanism of the global-warming theory and present some statistical and theoretical support—in other words, why some people take the theory seriously. You must survey the dire predictions regarding the theory: this will enable your real-estate-investment audience to consider "worst-case" scenarios. You'll want to summarize the viewpoints of opponents of this theory. You can also discuss what governments are doing or proposing to do about the problem. You might even discuss current research and how to stay abreast of the issue. And finally and most importantly, your readers expect you (the expert whose professional services they are paying for) to provide your balanced, objective perspective on the matter.

6. Create an audience description in which you briefly describe the audience (or audiences), their uses for the information, and their background.

This report is being commissioned by Mr. John Smith, President, Texas Coastal Real Estate Association. You will address the report to his address: 300 West Padre, Suite 1000, Corpus Christi, Texas. Mr. Smith and his associates have business, real estate, marketing, and finance background and know little about environmental science. Using your report, they hope to gain a basic understanding of the theory of human-induced global warming, its causes and effects, the full range of predictions associated with the theory, arguments by critics of the theory, and your balanced or objective perspective. You will discuss only those scientific concepts necessary for these readers to meet their needs and will use specialized terminology only when absolutely necessary. Your readers are not looking for investment recommendations, but rather information they can use to make their own decisions.

> *Audience description:* For Mr. John Smith, President, Texas Coastal Real Estate Association (300 West Padre, Suite 1000, Corpus Christi, Texas); a technical-background report on global warming for the coastal real-estate association of which he is president. The report will summarize current scientific thinking on the possibilities of the worst predictions based on the theory of global warming, designed for nonscientific, executive readers. The client wants a balanced, objective summary of this issue, which his membership will use to make long-range investment plans. Association members can get copies of the report by sending a request to the association's main office.

HOW DO YOU WRITE FOR AN AUDIENCE?

If you have carefully analyzed your audience, you should be able to write for that audience, right? Not exactly. It's one thing to know your readers and quite another to write with them fully in mind at all times. Writing with an audience firmly in mind is not a step-by-step process like audience and task analysis. It's a frame of mind, a mental perspective, an attitude. To characterize this attitude, scholars have resorted to some interesting and occasionally amusing metaphors.

Old metaphors: passive one-way communication.   Since the 1980s, scholars of rhetoric have become increasingly uncomfortable with traditional communication metaphors. For example:

- *Toss and catch metaphor.* In one of the favorites, you (the writer) toss (the act of writing) the ball (the message) to the reader. If the reader drops the ball (doesn't catch the message), it's your fault—you (the writer) need to revise.
- *Target and arrow metaphor.* In another favorite, you (the writer), armed with your bow (your pen, pencil, typewriter, or computer), shoot the arrow (the message) in an attempt to hit the target (the audience). Just don't take this troubling metaphor any further.
- *Shovel and wheelbarrow metaphor.* This last metaphor varies; it involves filling the reader up with something. For example, you (the writer) shovel the dirt (your message) into the wheelbarrow (the reader).

Understandably, rhetoricians are uncomfortable with these metaphors—they imply total passivity on the part of readers. Readers do more than passively receive written messages.

A better model: in-person communication.   Think about how live, in-person communication works: the speaker and listener engage in a give-and-take process. The listener may look puzzled, exasperated, bored, and may even interrupt to ask questions; the speaker reacts accordingly, restating, clarifying, answering the listener's questions, or moving on to more interesting topics. When you write, the reader is not there to react and help you with clarity or interest level. Nor are you, the writer, likely to be there when the reader reads your document.

[handwritten margin note: What is the reader's responsibility]

FIGURE 19-1

Questions from your "inner audience." Know your audience so well and write with those readers' needs and interests so fully in your mind that questions like these pop up as you write or as you review.

Contemporary rhetoricians have theorized that as writers we construct an imaginary audience with whom we engage in a mentalistic give-and-take right inside our own brains. We mentally recreate the live, in-person situation. Although this may sound like a short path to therapy, the logical implications of this idea are as follows:

- Successful writers possess more detailed, more clearly defined understanding of their audiences.
- Those imaginary audiences somehow match more closely their real flesh-and-blood counterparts—actual readers.
- As they write and as they review and revise, successful writers carry on a much more active, more detailed dialog with those imaginary readers.

If you look at written documents in the right light, you'll see traces of this internal dialog with imaginary readers. The wisecrack in the preceding about a "short path to therapy" is an example. It directly addresses you, the reader, and attempts to provoke a little humor. If it had been face-to-face communication, you might have been glazing over or becoming impatient with this heavy philosophical digression. It also acknowledges what might be highly skeptical reactions on the part of some readers. Weird stuff, huh?

New metaphors for written communication.   How can you develop this ability to dialog internally with your imaginary readers? Obviously, new metaphors are needed—bows and arrows, dead readers, and wheelbarrows full of dirt will not do! The story of Pinocchio might work as an analogy.

Jiminy Cricket is Pinocchio's imaginary audience ("always let your readers be your guide"). When he stops listening to that pesky cricket, his nose grows (he has strayed from his audience). Find something to hang over your computer—a toy cricket, a fake Halloween skull, a spider, a Barbie doll, or a GI Joe doll. Regardless of which trick you use to stay "ever mindful" of your reader, that imaginary reader should occasionally scold you and pester you with annoying questions like those in Figure 19-1.

Can you stand hearing voices like those in Figure 19-1 in your head? Do those voices resemble those of your eventual flesh-and-blood readers? If so, your writing stands a better chance of connecting with its readers (but that's another metaphor).

HOW DO YOU REVISE FOR AN AUDIENCE?

No matter how detailed your image of your audience is, no matter how closely that image resembles your real audience, no matter how active your dialog with your imaginary audience is—you still lose them at times. That's

FIGURE 19-2

Reader-based questions and comments in the review process. The excerpt shown was obviously written for geneticists, but imagine the questions nongeneticists would have. When you review, pretend you are your intended readers and see what questions, frustrations, comments, and even wisecracks they are likely to have as they read. *Source:* Francis Collins and David Galas, "A New Five-Year Plan for the U.S. Human Genome Program." URL: <www.nhgri.nih.gov:80/HGP/HGP_goals/plan.html>. Visited February 1, 2001.

why the review and revision phase is so important. Just as you listen to that internal voice as you write, you need it again as you review. (See Figure 19-2 and Chapter 18 for reviewing strategies.) In fact, try to undergo a complete (though temporary) personality change and *become* your intended reader as you review your draft. (Just be able to snap out of it!)

If the internal-voice metaphor just does not work for you, you might try something a bit more mainstream. See Chapter 18 for a multi-phase method of reviewing: you start with high-level issues such as content, audience, and organization and work all the way down to grammar, usage, and punctuation.

WORKSHOP: AUDIENCES AND TASKS

Here are some additional ideas for practicing the concepts, tools, and strategies in this chapter:

1. *Defining audiences' needs and interests.* Take a look at the following pairs of technical topics and audiences. Make a list of the audiences' likely interests and needs in relation to those topics:

   Child abuse—New caseworker

   Internet privacy issues—New
     Internet user

   Internet privacy issues—
     E-commerce Web site developer

   Bioengineering—Student
     considering a career

   Lyme disease—Camping enthusiast

   Lyme disease—Family practice
     physician

   Wildlife rehabilitation—
     Veterinarian

   Food-borne pathogens—
     Restaurant worker

2. *Inventing audiences.* Consider the following technical-document projects, or topics, and invent audiences for them. Make sure your audiences are realistic and have a very definite need for the technical information.

Food-borne diseases	Accident prevention
Biodiversity	Big Bang Theory
Pesticides	Human Genome Project
Acoustics	Computer viruses
Math anxiety	Video game violence
Artificial intelligence	Fire ants

3. *Deciding what to include and what to leave out.* Choose one of the pair of technical topics and audiences in Exercise 1, and think of a writing project for it. Then, for the writing project, make a list of topics, concepts, and terminology you would include and those you would leave out.

4. *Listing tasks.* Consider the writing project in the following. Identify the tasks that the readers would expect information on.

Writing Project	Audience
Guide for above-ground pool maintenance	Ordinary home owners without chemistry background
Cable modems: installation and use	Purchasers for home installation and use
Report on super-string theory	High school physics instructors

5. *Listening to your "inner audience."* Take a look at the excerpt from a technical-writing project in the following table. Based on the audience described, what questions would pop up in your mind if you were reading from their point of view?

Audience & Purpose:	Information included in a CPR handbook for nonmedical people learning CPR.
Excerpt:	Cells in our bodies need energy to perform certain processes, such as contracting or producing chemicals such as insulin and adrenaline. They obtain this energy through *cellular respiration*—the conversion of nutrients and oxygen into carbon dioxide, water, and energy:
	nutrients + oxygen → carbon dioxide + water + energy
	The nutrients used are typically sugars stored in the cell—for example, glucose:
	$C_6H_{12}O_6$ (glucose) + 6 O_2 → 6 CO_2 + 6 H_2O + energy
	Therefore, for each oxygen molecule used, a molecule of carbon dioxide is produced as waste. This CO_2 molecule passes out of the cell, through the capillary wall and into a red blood cell.
	The transfer of gases between cells and the bloodstream is a two-way process—as oxygen is taken out of the red blood cells in the oxygenated blood, it is replaced with carbon dioxide to produce *deoxygenated blood.*
	As you exhale, air in the lungs is forced out of the body. This air contains about

Continued

15% oxygen, with about 4% carbon dioxide and an appreciable quantity of water vapor. The overall change in composition between air breathed in and out is summarized below:

Percentage compositions: air breathed in and out

	Air In	*Air Out*
Nitrogen	78	78
Oxygen	21	15
Carbon dioxide	0.03	4
Water vapor	<1	2
Others	**<1**	**<1**

As you would expect, there is a net input of oxygen into the body and a net output of carbon dioxide. The proportions of each in the air we exhale varies—when doing vigorous exercise, for instance, cells in our muscles would be working much harder and therefore using more energy. As a result, these cells convert oxygen to carbon dioxide much more quickly than when at rest, and therefore there is less oxygen and more carbon dioxide found in exhaled breath when exercising than when resting.

Finding Information:
Print, Internet,
Informal Sources

INTERNET 2

Research and development has been under way for some time to develop a bigger, better Internet—called Internet 2. When you read this, Internet 2 may already be a reality. Here are links that show how it was being discussed in the year 2001:

Internet 2 Project. From University Corporation for Advanced Internet Development. **www.internet2.edu**

Next Generation Internet (NGI) Initiative. **www.ngi.gov**

Yahoo! News—Internet 2.
headlines.yahoo.com/Full_Coverage/Tech/Internet_2

PC Week. "Building the Next Internet."
www.pcworld.com/pcwtoday/news/index.asp

Wired. "Internet Deux: Not Your Father's Net."
www.wired.com/news/technology/0,1282,4202,00.html

Accessed February 1, 2001.

This chapter provides strategies for finding information on the Internet, in libraries, and from other resources, such as informal, unpublished sources. You'll also see how to evaluate the information you find.† For full details on how to cite a wide range of borrowed information, see Chapter 21.

HOW DO YOU SEARCH FOR INFORMATION?

Before you go racing off to the library or spend all night surfing the Web, think about the kinds of information you need and where they might be located.

Find a Librarian

Experienced librarians know where to start looking, how to choose keywords to make a search more precise, how to choose another strategy if the first one doesn't work, and how to help you narrow and focus a topic so you can complete your project within a specified period of time. Explain your project to a librarian and you'll get valuable guidance as to which resources are likely to be the most useful. If an experienced librarian is not available, try asking yourself these questions about your project:

- *What am I really looking for?* Write your topic as one or more questions. Examine those questions to determine what kind of information you need: descriptions, technical information, history, analysis. What's your "take" on your topic? Which aspect of the topic do you want to focus on? If your topic is Internet 2, for example, do you want to focus on the new functions and power it will bring? Perhaps you are more interested in the administrative logistics and financing of Internet 2.
- *What are the key terms for my topic?* List *keywords* before you start searching; add to them as you find new ones. For example, you might start with global warming but then realize that greenhouse effect and global climate change are also useful.

---

†Many thanks to Teresa Ashley, MLS, Austin Community College Librarian, for her work on this chapter.

▪ *Do I need recent information, or is there a period of time when this topic was really "hot"?* As of year 2000, a topic like Internet 2 is absolutely "now," whereas Halley's Comet was in the news when it last visited us in 1986.

Find a Guide

Although an experienced librarian is the best guide you could ask for, certain Web sites and reference books act as "guides" to specific fields of knowledge and practice. See the examples of print and Web site guides in the following discussions.

Choose Your Resources

An experienced librarian can help you avoid wasting time searching information in the wrong resources. For example, a topic like Internet 2 is so

---

GUIDE BOOKS AND GUIDE WEB SITES FOR INFORMATION SEARCHES

Try to find a "guide" that will orient you to all the information resources in a particular field, like the following examples.

Dennis F. Shaw, ed. *Information Sources in Physics.* A guide to journals, reference materials, and books in the different fields of physics.

Michael R. Lavin, ed. *Business Information: How to Find It, How to Use It.* Descriptions of some 400 sources of print and nonprint business information with explanations of how to use them.

H. V. Wyatt, ed. *Information Sources in the Life Sciences.* 4th ed. New York: Saur, 1997.

Michele Shoebridge, ed. *Information Sources in Sport and Leisure.* New York: Bowker-Saur, 1992.

Stephen Goddard, ed. *A Guide to Information Sources in the Geographical Sciences.* Totwa, N.J.: Barnes & Noble, 1983.

Austin Community College—Web Links by Subject. This resources created by ACC librarians provides links to many subjects and reference topics as well: **library.austin.cc.tx.us/research/w3/w3_Links.html**

Internet Public Library: Reference Center. Take a look at the collection of links under Business & Economics, Computers & Internet, Health & Medical Sciences, Sciences & Technology: **www.ipl.org/ref**

Columbia University Libraries. Selected Subject Guides & Resources: **www.columbia.edu/cu/libraries/subjects**

About.com. A commercial enterprise that employs "guides"—human beings who are experts on their topics—who select and present Web resources. Click on the A-Z listings: **www.about.com**

Refdesk.com. Bob Drudge's wonderful collection of everything imaginable for a complete reference desk. In particular, see the section entitled "Refdesk's Categories": **www.refdesk.com**

new that newspaper and magazine articles may be the best, or only, resources rather than books. Here are strategies for choosing information resources. See also the following list for some suggestions for guide books and guide Web sites for information searching:

- *Internet.* The World Wide Web is a great starting point. However, information on the Web can change overnight. While most news sites constantly update their coverage of news topics, they do not archive them. Nor are you likely to find Internet versions of material that is expensive to produce or that dates from the 1980s or earlier. Often, you have to pay for the best information. After all, information is a commodity. Even if you find plenty of information on the Web, don't stop there. Get out of the apartment and go to the library.
- *Books.* Books usually represent stable, well-established knowledge. Because of the time and expense it takes to produce books, the information in them is not as up-to-date or "last minute" as the information in newspapers, magazines, and journals or on the Web. Although you may not find a reliable book on a new scientific discovery reported on the ten o'clock news, you will find books providing background to help you understand that discovery.
- *Encyclopedias and other reference books.* Reference books (encyclopedias, handbooks, and dictionaries) are even more settled, well-established resources. Information in these works has been accepted by many and is not likely to be challenged. These resources give you the "lay of the land" on a topic—basic theory, formulas, definitions, overviews, diagrams, history, and so on. For an unfamiliar topic, encyclopedia articles are good places to start, in particular, subject-specific encyclopedia articles written by experts.
- *Magazines and journals.* Use magazine and journal articles to "zoom in" on specific parts of a topic. Although magazines and journals contain information that is more up-to-date than books, you typically cannot expect the same depth of information that you can from a book. An article in a scholarly journal may be so specific that it's the only published material on a particular aspect of a topic.
- *Newspapers.* Articles published in newspapers often contain the most up-to-date information on a topic. If you had been researching advances in computer memory when Hewlett-Packard announced its nanotechnology-based computer-switching devices, news articles would have been the only place to find any information on that topic.
- *Government documents and reports.* The U.S. government commissions book-length reports as well as pamphlets that are so specialized that they are not commercially viable. Certain large university and public libraries act as "depository libraries" to store these publications. Government publications are increasingly available on the Internet. To find government documents, see "What About Government Documents?" later in this chapter.

- *Product literature*. Information published by makers of products can be very useful—so long as you keep in mind its natural tendency for bias. Not only might a manufacturer send you product specifications, you might also receive white papers and other general literature about the technology.
- *Informal, unpublished resources*. Don't forget, you can also interview local experts, send e-mail inquiries to knowledgeable individuals, investigate local facilities, as well as conduct surveys or send out questionnaires. (See the suggestions at the end of this chapter.)

Know How to Search Online

Whether you search the Internet, an online periodical index, a Web-based encyclopedia, or a library's computer catalog, you are doing online searches. Common to all of these resources is the electronic database, which provides some combination of the following search tools:

- *Boolean searches*. Boolean operators ("and," "or," and "not") define logical relationships between search terms. Different search engines perform searches differently. Read the "search hints" to see how your search engine works. For explanations of the Boolean operators, see:
  - Austin Community College's "Searching the World Wide Web" at **library.austin.cc.tx.us/research/engines.htm**
  - InfoPeople Project's "Search Engines Quick Guide" at **infopeople.org/ src/guide.html**
- *Proximity searches*. Proximity operators ("near," "with," "adjacent," and others) specify how close to each other your search terms should appear. For example, "global n2 warming" means that the word "global" should appear near "warming" with no more than two words between the two terms.
- *Phrase searches*. Phrase searching (two or more words commonly found together) is another way to limit your search results. In a search on global warming, you'd want to exclude global warfare, global travel, warming up leftovers, and so on. Different search engines perform phrase searching differently. In Excite, you type in global AND warming. In other search engines, you might type "global warming" (with the quotation marks) or "global+warming."
- *Searches using truncation*. Use truncation to search on a portion of a word to retrieve alternate forms: "politi*" may retrieve "political," "politics," "politician," and "politicians"—which is like doing four separate searches!

Start Collecting Keywords

When you start your information search, you need a good set of keywords:

- For a report on Internet 2, keywords like "Internet 2," "Internet2," "Internet II," and even "new Internet" might be useful.

- For global warming, you might use "global warming," "greenhouse effect," "global climate change," and even something as broad as "environment."

No one magical reference book contains all known keywords. Last updated in 1994, *Library of Congress Subject Heading* may help, but not for current technology topics. Instead, do some brainstorming, think of synonyms, use keywords you know, look in encyclopedias and other introductory resources, and keep a running list of additional synonyms you find.

WHAT ABOUT THE INTERNET?

The Internet has become quite the resource for technical-writing projects. Whatever you find on the Web, you must evaluate it carefully. Anyone can publish on the Web—Nobel prize winners, well-intentioned amateurs, and any fringe group. Imagine what you'd find on the Web about UFOs!

Searching for Information on the Internet

To start investigating Internet resources for a writing project, first learn something about how search engines work and what's "out there." The following lists some tutorials and information on searching the Web.

**TUTORIALS AND INFORMATION ON SEARCHING
THE WORLD WIDE WEB**

University of South Carolina. Bare Bones 101—A Basic Tutorial on Searching the Web: **www.sc.edu/beaufort/library/bones.html**

Cal Poly State University. Information Competency: **www.lib.calpoly.edu/infocomp/modules**

Austin Community College. Searching the World Wide Web: **library.austin.cc.tx.us/research/engines.htm**

Austin Community College. List of general search engines: **library.austin.cc.tx.us/research/w3/voc_tech/TCM/srch/websrch.htm**

Austin Community College. List of meta-search engines: **library.austin.cc.tx.us/research/w3/voc_tech/TCM/srch/meta.htm**

InfoPeople Project. Best Search Tools: **infopeople.org/src/srctools.html**

InfoPeople Project. Search Engines Quick Guide: **infopeople.org/src/guide.html**

InfoPeople Project. Search Tools Chart: **infopeople.org/src/chart.html**

Guide sites. A "guide" site contains links carefully selected and organized by real people—often by librarians, professors, and subject experts. To find subject-specific guide sites, try Google at **www.google.com**. Because Google ranks a page by how many other pages link to it, guide sites come to the top. They are valuable starting points in Internet searching.

General search engines. General search engines claim to search the entire Web. Actually, they search only that part of the Web that they have collected into a database. These search agents use "spiders" or "crawlers" that continuously search for Web sites to add to their databases. Most general search engines provide for a basic search or quick search, as well as for an advanced or power search. After you have run a basic search, read the search hints and make use of the advanced features for greater precision. General search engines include AltaVista at **www.altavista.com**, Excite at **www.excite.com**, Google at **www.google.com**, HotBot at **hotbot. lycos.com**, Infoseek at **infoseek.go.com**, and Lycos at **www.lycos.com**.

Meta-search engines. Meta-search engines let you run a search on several general search engines simultaneously, enabling you to scan what is available quickly. However, none of the special search features of general search engines are available. Meta-search engines are great for "quick and dirty" searches. Meta-search engines include Inference Find at **www. infind.com**, Dogpile at **www.dogpile.com**, MetaCrawler at **www.metacrawler.com**, and Savvy Search at **www.savvysearch.com**.

Specialized search engines. Specialized search engines focus on a particular type of site or query (for example, people, businesses, or Usenet newsgroups). Deja.com at **www.deja.com** provides different search methods, "Quick Search," "Power Search," and "Browse" to get to newsgroups, forums, and threads on the Internet, plus keyword searching for specific subjects. Reference.com at **www.reference.com** is very similar to Deja.com, except that you can search mailing lists as well as newsgroup postings.

Another specialized search tool is Northern Light at **www.northern light.com**. It can search more than one database simultaneously; it searches its own database along with a database of about 2,000 journal articles and other publications. Search results are placed in special folders to help you narrow a search and review results. You can purchase the journal articles (prices range from $1.00 to $4.00) or, better yet, check to see if a library near you subscribes to the publication. **SearchEdu.com** searches educational sites only, which is helpful when you are looking for reliable sites. **SearchGov.com** enables you to search for specific subjects in just about every area of U.S. federal and state governments.

Evaluating Internet Information

Be careful about Web sites you use to support a research project. Anyone can put Web pages out there for the whole world to read and believe. On the Internet, anyone can copy a Web site and pass it off as the original. **www.whitehouse.net** satirizes the official White House Web site at **www. whitehouse.gov**. How can you determine whether the information at a Web site is reliable, credible, and legitimate? Although there are no sure-fire answers, the following list provides some suggestions:

■ *Look for bias in the title.* Titles often indicate a friendly or hostile attitude toward the topic. The phrase "rising CO_2 content in the atmosphere"

**EVALUATING INFORMATION FROM
THE WORLD WIDE WEB**

Austin Community College, Learning Resource Services. "Finding and Evaluating Information on the Internet": **library.austin.cc.tx.us/research/ guides/findinternet/findeval.htm#evaluating**

University of South Carolina. Bare Bones 101—A Basic Tutorial on Searching the Web: **www.sc.edu/beaufort/library/bones.html**

Cal Poly State University. Information Competency: **www.lib.calpoly.edu/infocomp/modules**

Grassian, Esther. UCLA College Library. "Thinking Critically about World Wide Web Resources": **www.library.ucla.edu/libraries/college/help/critical/index.htm**

Kirk, Elizabeth E. Milton S. Eisenhower Library of Johns Hopkins University, Homewood Campus. "Evaluating Information Found on the Internet": **milton.mse.jhu.edu:8001/research/education/net.html**

Rice University, Fondren Library. "Internet Searching Strategies— Evaluating Internet Resources": **www.rice.edu/Fondren/Netguides/strategies.html#evaluate**

Smith, Alastair. VUW Department of Library and Information Studies, New Zealand. "Evaluation of Information Sources": **www.vuw.ac.nz/~agsmith/evaln/evaln.htm**

---

quietly indicates an acceptance of the theory. View pages like these with a certain amount of skepticism.

■ *Look for bias in self-described balanced, neutral "resource" sites.* You'd expect oil companies to oppose the global-warming theory and Green Peace to embrace it. Even so, organizations like these provide "resource sites," which implies a wide range of links reflecting different opinions. Instead, they may have carefully filtered out the opposition.

■ *Look at the information itself.* How much careful research is evident in the Web site? If links point to other well-established sites, if the information tries to present both sides, if the author cites sources, or if the information is detailed and provides plenty of support for its assertions, these are all good signs. However, if the information is old, if you can't find the date for it, or if it is weak on facts and full of generalizations and emotional rhetoric—watch out!

■ *Find out about the Web site.* If the Web site is owned by an educational institution, government agency, or professional organization, you can view its information with some confidence.

■ *Find out about the author.* Look for information that authors of Web sites provide about themselves, particularly their affiliations with organizations. If they provide no information about themselves, that's a problem. Use a meta-search engine like Inference Find at **www.infind.com** or one of the many "people finder" search sites like WhoWhere? People Finder at **www.whowhere.lycos.com**, or try e-mailing the author directly.

WHAT ABOUT ENCYCLOPEDIAS AND OTHER REFERENCE BOOKS?

Good encyclopedia entries give you a sense of the "landscape" of a topic—key terms, main issues, major categories, historical names and events, and so on. Background reading in encyclopedias also helps to narrow and focus a topic.

1. *General encyclopedias.* Start with a current "general" encyclopedia such as the *Encyclopedia Britannica*, *World Book*, or *Americana*. For "global warming," the index of the 1995 *World Book Encyclopedia* lists Greenhouse effect G:383; the 1998 *Encyclopedia Britannica* lists seven different articles. Skim the main and cross-referenced articles; make a note of books, articles, or other sources cited. New, "hot" topics may not be covered. For example, as of February 2000, the online *Encyclopedia Britannica* or *Encyclopedia Americana* had no entries for "Internet 2" or its variants ("Internet2" and "Internet II").

2. *Yearbook supplements to encyclopedias.* Also take a look at any of the "yearbook" supplements available with some encyclopedias, particularly multivolume ones. Look for your topic in the index. If you find it, you'll find some excellent updated information.

3. *Specialized encyclopedias and reference works.* For a technical-writing project, don't stop with general encyclopedias. Look at subject-specific encyclopedias, handbooks, and dictionaries. To locate these encyclopedias, find out the call number range for your topic, and then browse the reference stacks in that range. For example, music will be in the M's, art in the N's, and psychology in the BF's. Most library reference areas have handouts or charts on the Library of Congress classification system. Librarians can direct you to specialized encyclopedias, but try a keyword search on your library's online catalog. For example, the keywords "engineering" and "encyclopedia" should retrieve a list of the library's encyclopedias related to that field. Here are some examples of what you might find:

Encyclopedia of Crime and Justice

Encyclopedia of Educational Research

Encyclopedia of Religion

Encyclopedia of World Art

Guide to American Law

International Encyclopedia of Sociology

McGraw-Hill Encyclopedia of Electronics and Computers

McGraw-Hill Encyclopedia of Physics

McGraw-Hill Encyclopedia of Environmental Science & Engineering

McGraw-Hill Encyclopedia of Quality Terms and Concepts

McGraw-Hill Encyclopedia of the Geological Sciences

McGraw-Hill Encyclopedia of Engineering

McGraw-Hill Encyclopedia of Science and Technology

McGraw-Hill Encyclopedia of Astronomy

McGraw-Hill Encyclopedia of Environmental Science

AMA Encyclopedia of Medicine

4. Increasingly, encyclopedias are appearing in full on the Internet, for example, *Encyclopaedia Britannica* at **www.britannica.com**. Here are some ways to find others:
   - Internet Public Library. Provides a good list of online encyclopedias: **www.ipl.org/ref/RR/static/ref32.00.00.html**
   - Refdesk.com, Encyclopedias. Also provides links to online encyclopedias: **www.refdesk.com/factency.html**
   - Michigan Electronic Library (MEL). Provides an extensive list of links to free online encyclopedias, dictionaries, and almanacs: **mel.lib.mi.us/reference/REF-encyclopedias.html**

These free online sources are useful more for quick reference than in-depth research. That's because they are older, abridged, or concise versions of the print editions and their fee-based electronic counterparts. Go to your library for the more recent and most complete versions.

WHAT ABOUT BOOKS?

Before starting a search for books, make sure that books are what you need. If your topic is new, no books may be available yet. Instead, articles, reports, or other kinds of publications may be what you need. Books treat a topic in-depth and can take a year to research and write and another year to publish. The information in books is not so much outdated as it is conservative in its approach.

Searching for books will become increasingly easier. The next few years will see all but the smallest and most under-funded libraries have their entire collections searchable on the World Wide Web. That means you can or will soon be able to sit at home and search your local library for books on a topic (and see whether they are checked out). Here are some suggestions for finding books:

1. *Start with local libraries.* Your local library is the best "first stop." Obviously, you can use the World Wide Web to find books, but they may be sitting in a library in London, England, while you are down home in Alabama. When you get search results on your topic, print them out, and go take a look at those books. Skim through them, checking the footnotes and bibliographies for additional titles that might be useful.
2. *Check online library resource pages.* These provide specialized library resources as well as links to online libraries all over the world:

- Try the Library Web-Based OPACS page provided by webCATS at **www.lights.com/webcats.** Click either Geographical Index or Library Type Index. Library Type Index provides two categories: consortia, cooperative libraries whose catalogs you can search all at once; and special libraries, such types as hospital, legal, and corporate libraries, as well as libraries of organizations and other special collections.
- Visit lib-web-cats, maintained by Marshall Breeding at Vanderbilt University: **staffweb.library.vanderbilt.edu/breeding/libwebcats.html**
- Also try Berkeley Digital Library's Libweb at **sunsite.berkeley.edu/Libweb**
- Take a look at Library Information Services from Refdesk.com at **www.refdesk.com/factlib.html** for links to libraries all over the world.

3. *Check the Library of Congress.* Check a major library for books on your topic, such as the Library of Congress at **catalog.loc.gov.** Click on "Use the Online Catalog" and select the "keyword" search button. Enter a keyword, such as Internet2 in the search box, and click the search button (see Figure 20-1).

4. *Search commercial books.* Take a look at what is available commercially on your topic. See what you can find at one of the well-known online bookstores: as of February 2001, Amazon.com produced one direct hit on Internet2 *(Internet2: The Future of the Internet and Next-Generation Initiatives)* and one on Internet II *(Internet II: Quality of Service and Future Directions).*

```
Records 1 through 1 of 1 returned.
_____

Author:        Cameron, Debra.
Title:         Internet2 : the future of the Internet and other
                  next-generation initiatives / Debra Cameron.
Edition:       1st ed.
Published:     Charleston, SC : Computer Technology Research
                  Corp., 1999.
Description:   v, 164 p. : ill., maps ; 28 cm.
LC Call No.:   TK5105.875.I57C35 1999
Dewey No.:     004.67/8 21
ISBN:          1566070643
Notes:         Includes bibliographical references.
Subjects:      Internet (Computer network)
                  World Wide Web.
Control No.:   1200480

Tagged display | Brief Record Display | New Search
_____

This display was generated by the CNIDR Web-Z39.50 gateway, version 1.08, with
Library of Congress Modifications.
```

FIGURE 20-1

Search results from a Library of Congress query. See what's available from the biggest library in the world!

5. *Use Interlibrary Loan, if necessary.* How do you get books that are far away? When you find such books through an online catalog, print out the information you'll need to acquire it. Your local library may be able to borrow it for you through Interlibrary Loan (ILL). In the ILL process, your librarian acts as your agent, requesting a book from another library for you.

WHAT ABOUT MAGAZINE, JOURNAL, AND NEWSPAPER ARTICLES?

If your focus is a "hot" topic, your best or only information may come from magazine, journal, and newspaper articles. Even if your topic has "cooled," see what magazines, journals, and newspapers have to offer.

Magazines and journals. Periodical indexes are the keys to finding articles. An index like *Reader's Guide to Periodical Literature* covers a broad range of subjects, whereas other indexes are devoted to a single discipline or field (for example, *Engineering Index*). Indexes called "abstracts" provide summaries of the articles listed (for example, *Chemical Abstracts* and *Psychological Abstracts*).

Although not very long ago indexes were available only in printed form, most libraries now have at least one index available in an electronic format—either on CD-ROM or on the Web. *Readers' Guide to Periodical Literature*, for example, is available in both electronic formats. Do the following to use a periodical index:

1. *Make sure you have a good set of keywords.* If you were looking for articles on Internet 2, use phrases like "Internet2" and "Internet II" also. Perhaps try "Internet" just in case good materials are hidden under a phrase like the "new Internet." For a search on global warming, try "greenhouse effect" and "global climate change" as well.

2. *Start with a general periodical index.* General indexes help you find articles for general audiences: these are good starting points. Most electronic indexes let you mark citations so that you can look more closely at them and start choosing the best ones. If your library subscribes to two or three online periodical indexes, try them all. Here are some examples:

   ■ *MasterFILE Premier*, an online general periodical index, provided full-text for nearly 1,960 periodicals covering nearly all subjects, including general reference, business, health, and much more as of 1999. A search for "e-commerce and security" results in 138 hits, many full-text and in such journals as *American Banker*, *Information Systems Security*, *Management Accounting: Magazine for Chartered Management Accountants*, and *Security Management*.

   ■ *Periodical Abstracts*, another online general periodical index, produces 71 hits for a search on Internet 2 OR Internet2 OR Internet II. The publications cited range from the general and popular (*Rolling*

Stone, Smart Computing, US News & World Report) to the technical (*IEEE Network, IEEE Software*) to the special audience publication (*Training & Development, Journal of Academic Librarianship*).

3. *Search the most active time frame for the topic.* If your topic has a specific time frame, start with index entries in that period. For example, you'd find more articles on the most recent visit of Halley's Comet or the nuclear-reactor disaster at Chernobyl in months just following those events. Online periodical indexes cover articles published from the late 1980s or 1990 forward. For material published in the early 1980s or earlier, use a print index.

4. *Examine the actual articles.* Take a look at the articles you find, especially the references to other articles or to reports and books. If the full text of your article is available online, you may be able to e-mail it to yourself or copy it to a diskette (but libraries typically charge for printing articles).

   If your library doesn't subscribe to the periodicals you need or if the articles aren't available online, read the abstracts of those articles to see if they are worth acquiring. For the articles you really need, try ILL.

5. *Check specialized indexes.* If you haven't found the right articles or enough articles, or if you are curious as to the content of the more specialized articles, take a look at one or more specialized indexes related to your topic, such as the following (the numbers in parentheses are the total periodicals indexed):

Applied Science & Technology Index (485)	*General Science Index* (190)
Art Index (377)	*Humanities Index* (451)
Biological & Agricultural Index (292)	*Library Literature & Information Science* (292)
Business Periodicals Index (528)	*Social Sciences Index* (520)
Education Index (478)	*Readers' Guide to Periodical Literature* (270)
Essay and General Literature Index	*Biology Digest*

6. *Check field-specific indexes.* Finally, take a look at the articles for your project in indexes that cover specific fields. Find these field-specific indexes by consulting a reference librarian or by searching the library's online catalog (for example, type something like chemistry indexes in the word search field).

7. *Search online magazines and journals.* Another possibility is to check "e-journals," which have no counterpart in either print or full-text online indexes. NorthernLight.com at **www.northernlight.com** provides indexing for some online magazines and journals in its "Special Collections." Internet Public Library has an extensive listing of periodicals at **www.ipl.org/reading/serials**; click on Computers & Internet, then on Internet.

Newspapers online. Many newspapers provide the complete text of their current issue online, although most charge for back issues. See the Internet Public Library for an extensive list of online newspapers by country, state, and city. (For the online edition of the *New York Times*, click on New York State, then on New York City.) Online newspapers offer some features you don't get in print: searchable archives and links to background information that never made it into the print edition. Here are some links to online newspapers:

- Internet Public Library provides a list of online newspapers by continent, country, state or province, and city: **www.ipl.org/reading/news**
- Refdesk.com offers a good selection of newspapers in its Current News and Facts section: **www.refdesk.com**. If you searched *San Jose Mercury News* for Internet2 on December 23, 1999, you would have found 6 articles. You have to pay for the entire article, but you do get to see the abstract.
- AJR Newslink from *American Journalism Review* links to both print and broadcast sources and provides search capability: **www.newslink.org**
- TotalNews is searchable; archives include content from gated sites you might find with a search engine. Link to **www.totalnews.com**, click U.S. Local, then browse by state.
- Newspapers Online has a broad range, including specialized news sources such as ethnic, minority, and religious publications: **www.newspapers.com**

In addition to newspapers online, visit the Web sites of television broadcast news and network news sites. These are online equivalents to TV news broadcasts:

- ABC News has headlines and in-depth stories in such categories as travel, world, entertainment, and sports. Link to **www.abcnews.com**, and click Contents for a listing of recent stories or Search for a particular story.
- CBS News asks for your zip code and presents local news whenever you log in. Link to **www.cbs.com** and click CBS News.
- NBC News has headlines, quick news, and stories in clickable categories as well as local news that you can select from a region on a map: **www.nbc.com**
- CNN has top news stories by category, with in-depth coverage of individual issues: **www.cnn.com**
- C-SPAN mirrors its television counterpart with in-depth coverage of topics and source material on events currently in the news: **www.c-span.org**
- CBC, the Canadian Broadcasting Corporation, at **www.cbc.ca**, and BBC, the British Broadcasting Corporation, at **news.bbc.co.uk**, provide international coverage.
- ZDNet, at **www.zdnet.com**, is a hybrid news/magazine site, providing Ziff-Davis magazine online equivalents as well as news articles and

product reviews. See the Breaking News, Business & Tech, and Tech News for particular industry developments.

For finding particular news content, there are some additional search sites that may be useful. Newslibrary, **www.newslibrary.com**, provides searchable archives of articles published by U.S. newspapers. A search for words that appeared in those articles produces a list of dates, headlines, and the first few lines of each article. (There is a charge to download the full text.) News Index, at **www.newsindex.com**, is another Web-based newspaper search tool.

WHAT ABOUT GOVERNMENT DOCUMENTS?

The depth and variety of information collected by government agencies or published as government-funded research is astonishing. The U.S. government publishes more information than any other entity. Luckily for the trees, though, the federal government—and state governments—are publishing this material on the World Wide Web.

Certain large university research libraries, state libraries, and large public libraries serve as "depositories" for these government publications. They are often placed in special areas, forming a "government document" collection. Government documents are often shelved by Superintendent of

U.S. Government Documents: Common SuDoc Divisions

A	Department of Agriculture	C	Commerce Department
C3	Census Bureau	C21	Patent and Trademark Office
CC	Federal Communications Commission	CR	Civil Rights
CS	Civil Service Commission	D	Defense Department
E	Department of Energy	ED	Department of Education
EP	Environmental Protection Agency	FT	Federal Trade Commission
GA	General Accounting Commission	GS	General Services Administration
HE	Health and Human Services	NH	Department of Housing and Urban Development
I	Department of the Interior	IC	Interstate Commerce Commission
J	Justice Department	L	Labor Department
L2	Labor Statistics	P	Postal Service

Continued

PrEx	Executive Office of the President	S	State Department
SBA	Small Business Administration	T	Treasury Department
T22	Internal Revenue Service	TD	Transportation Department
VA	Veterans Administration	X	Congressional Record
Y3	Congressional Commissions, Committees, Boards	Y4	Congressional Hearings

Documents (SuDoc) numbers, which groups documents by the agency that issues them.

U.S. government documents were difficult to search and access just a decade or two ago. The process has improved but it is still different. Try these suggestions:

1. Think about which agencies of the U.S. government would likely have the best material on your topic. Also, find out if there is a depository library somewhere near you.
2. Start with FedWorld, at **www.fedworld.gov**, the gateway to U.S. government publications, regulations, and statistics. Click on the category link, and use the first search box to search the entire FedWorld network and then narrow your search to the most appropriate agency.
3. Also search for your topic in the National Technical Information Service, at **www.ntis.gov**. This collection of nearly three million titles is the federal government's central sales point for scientific, technical, engineering, and related business information produced by or for the U.S. government. For interesting items, go to a nearby depository or library, or order them for a fee.
4. Try Thomas Legislative Information on the Internet at **thomas.loc.gov**. For example, you can search committee reports for "global warming," click report titles in the result list, and then "Best Sections" to access the prepared statements of expert witnesses and others who have testified before Congress on the subject.
5. For additional help in finding U.S. government documents, see the following:
   ■ Federal Government Information Resources, developed by Jonathan Buckstead at Austin Community College: **library.austin.cc.tx.us/ research/w3/Soc_Sci/gov/govfed.htm**
   ■ Columbia University Libraries. U.S. Government Documents Ready Reference Collection. But you have to pay to get the entire article: **www.columbia.edu/cu/libraries/indiv/dsc/readyref.html**
   ■ FedStats. Access to statistical information from more than 70 federal agencies, provided by Federal Interagency Council on Statistical Policy: **www.fedstats.gov**

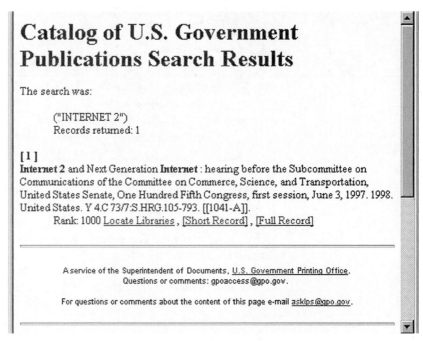

FIGURE 20-2

Search results from the online Catalog of U.S. Government Publications. (This screen capture has been edited to reduce the overall size.) The lack of a highlighted URL means that this document is not available online. Instead, you must either go to a federal depository library where it is kept (click "Locate Libraries") or order it from the Government Printing Office.

■ U.S. Government Printing Office, "Official Federal Government Information at Your Fingertips": **www.access.gpo.gov/su_docs** (see Figure 20-2). However, not all the government documents indexed here are online:

■ See **bookstore.gpo.gov** for a topic listing.

■ See **www.access.gpo.gov/su_docs/locators/cgp/index.html** for a listing of U.S. government Internet sites by topic.

■ Catalog of U.S. Government Publications—the mouth of a Mississippi of information: **www.access.gpo.gov/su_docs/dpos/adpos400.html**

6. Once you've found potentially useful government documents, try to get a look at them. Some government documents may be fully online and therefore downloadable. Others may be available in government-depository libraries (indicated in the government catalogs and indexes). If you don't know where the nearest such library is, ask a librarian. For all other government documents, you have to order and pay for them.

WHAT ABOUT BROCHURES AND OTHER PRODUCT LITERATURE?

Some projects may require product literature. For example, imagine you were working on a comparison of wind turbines used to generate electricity from the wind. To survey this equipment, you'd want manufacturers to send you their brochures and related literature. Here are several ways to do that:

1. Try using the *Thomas Register of American Manufacturers*, available both in most libraries and at **www.thomasregister.com** on the Web. A search for "wind turbines" would produce results similar to those in Figure 20-3.
2. Also try using any of the search engines on the Web. If you searched **www.yahoo.com** for "wind turbines," you'd get results similar to what you see in Figure 20-4. Most search engines divide the results into areas, one of which is "Companies" in the case of wind turbines.

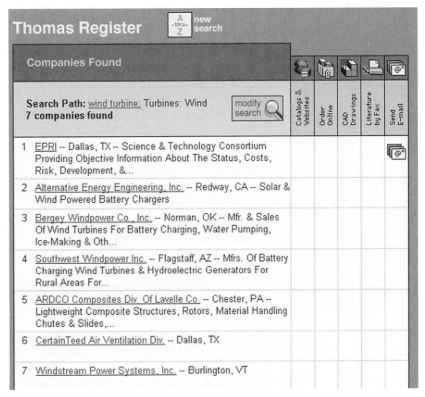

FIGURE 20-3

Thomas Register of American Manufacturers. A fine tool for looking up manufacturers who can provide you with information about their products and about the technologies used in those products.

Business and Economy > Companies > Energy > Renewable > Wind Power

- Vestas Wind Systems A/S - specialize in the manufacture of **wind turbines**. Located in Denmark.
- Windmission - develops and markets **wind turbines** and hybrid systems, components such as rotors, generators and controllers.
- Nordex Balcke-Dürr - produces **wind turbines**.
- Bergey Windpower Co - manufactures small **wind turbines** for remote power, water pumping, and grd-connected applications.
- Southwest Windpower, Inc. - supplier of small battery charging **wind turbines**. Products are used to bring electricity into rural areas of the world.
- DMP Mølleservice - service and repairs on **wind turbines** in Denmark and Germany.
- Windland, Inc. - sales and installation of reconditioned **wind turbines**.

FIGURE 20-4

Search engine results. The search engine **www.yahoo.com**, for example, divides search results into categories—in this case, companies that manufacture wind turbines.

WHAT ABOUT INFORMAL, UNPUBLISHED SOURCES?

If you get information from a salesperson, an expert, or someone generally in the know about your topic, treat these sources the same as you would a published book or journal article. In fact, citing phone interviews, in-person conversations, e-mail, or responses to inquiries shows what careful, thorough, professional research you have done. Readers are far more likely to be impressed with the research you've done and confident about your information and your conclusions. (See Chapter 21 for style and format in citations of these informal, unpublished sources.)

Interviews and Inquiries

Interviews and inquiry letters or e-mail can be good sources of information for a technical-writing project.

Interviews.   Consider interviewing local experts or otherwise knowledgeable people on your topic—but *only after* you've reviewed your published information sources. It's not a good idea to go asking questions of a busy expert when you could have found the answers in any general encyclopedia or introductory textbook on the subject. To get ready for an interview:

1. Get in touch with the interviewee by phone and set up a date and time. Don't expect to be able to walk in any time you choose and hold the interview.
2. Make sure you've done your homework before going to the interview; don't ask questions with answers you could have found in introductory textbooks.
3. Prepare your questions in advance and bring them with you. Make sure they are both specific enough to get the information you need and general enough to get the interviewee talking about the topic.

4. Bring some money for photocopying costs in case the interviewee has some potentially useful materials that you can't take away with you. Bring some diskettes in case the information is in electronic files.

5. At the beginning of the interview, explain who you are and what you are working on. If you have a cassette recorder, ask the interviewee if you can tape the interview.

6. Encourage the interviewee to tell you about any other resources, such as other experts, printed documents, or associations, that might be useful.

7. Don't allow the interview to run on longer than you had initially requested. At the end of the interview, offer to send a copy of your writing project to the interviewee.

Postal-mail or e-mail inquiries. Another good informal source of information is the inquiry letter or e-mail:

1. Find knowledgeable individuals to whom you want to direct inquiries, for example, authors of books, articles, or reports related to your project.

2. If necessary, search for these individuals' e-mail addresses on any of the search tools available on the World Wide Web such as Yahoo, Excite, AltaVista, or HotBot.

3. See Chapter 13 for ideas on content, organization, and strategies for writing inquiries.

WHAT ABOUT SURVEYS AND QUESTIONNAIRES?

Some technical-writing projects lend themselves to direct information gathering—not from published sources but straight from the "real world." In ordinary language, there's not much difference between the terms "survey" and "questionnaire." For this discussion, however, the following will apply:

- *Survey.* A type of direct information gathering in which you directly observe and record. For example, the city might assign you the task of counting traffic at an intersection to determine whether a stoplight is needed there.
- *Questionnaire.* The kind of direct information gathering in which you gather people's opinions, preferences, or demographic data through in-person, print, or electronic means. For example, if you were a member of a recycling action group, you might send out questionnaires to ascertain your fellow citizens' opinions about curb-side recycling.

When you develop forms for surveys or questionnaires, include them in the appendix of the document that includes the data you gathered with those tools.

WORKSHOP: INFORMATION SEARCH

Here are some additional ideas for practicing the concepts and strategies in this chapter:

1. Pick one of the following topics and list as many synonyms for it as you can think of. (These might come in handy as additional keywords to use in an information search on this topic.)

Media violence	Rain forests
Workplace discrimination	Renewable energy sources
Childhood diseases	Big Bang Theory
Narcotic addiction	Aging
Native Americans	Aerospace medicine

2. Consider the following topics, and make a list of the order in which you would search the different types of information resources (books, articles, encyclopedias, government documents and reports, product literature, informal resources):

Media violence	I LOVE YOU virus
Remote sensing	Privacy legislation
Renewable energy sources	Aerospace medicine
Human Genome Project	Toxic waste sites
Family planning	Disappearance of the Mars Polar Lander

3. Choose one of the topics in the preceding exercises, think of as many keywords as you can, and then find up to six books on that topic. Use one of the online libraries discussed in this chapter.

4. Choose one of the topics in the preceding exercises, think of as many keywords as you can, and then find up to 12 articles on that topic. Use one of the online periodical indexes discussed in this chapter.

5. Choose one of the topics in the preceding exercises, and find six online newspaper articles related to that topic. Use the suggestions in this chapter for finding online newspaper articles.

6. Choose one of the topics in the preceding exercises, think of as many keywords as you can, and then find up to six articles on that topic in one encyclopedia. Try using one of the online encyclopedia discussed in this chapter, but also use an encyclopedia, such as the *Britannica* or *McGraw-Hill Encyclopedia of Science and Technology*, in your library.

7. Choose one of the topics in the preceding exercises, and find six Web sites related to that topic in some way. Use the strategies discussed in this chapter to find these Web sites. In particular, try to find at least one "guide" site. Use suggestions in this chapter to evaluate each of the Web sites you find: rate them on a scale of 1 to 5, with 5 being highly reliable and 1 being highly unreliable.

8. Choose one of the topics in the preceding exercises, and find six government documents related to that topic, using the strategies discussed in this chapter.

    Choose one of the topics in the preceding exercises, and try to find three manufacturers or companies associated with that topic, using *Thomas Register* or some similar resource as discussed in this chapter.

9. Choose one of the topics in the preceding exercises, and make a list of the unpublished, nonprint information resources you might need to research that topic.

10. Consider experts, technicians, executives, product users, site visits, questionnaires, surveys, experiments, and so on as sources.

Citing Sources of Borrowed Information

EXTRATERRESTRIAL INTELLIGENCE AND UFOS

Next time you sight a UFO, be sure to document it using a proper citation method such as one of the documentation styles presented in this chapter:

About.com. UFOs/Aliens. **ufos.about.com/culture/ufos/mbody.htm**

Beginner's Guide to UFOs & Aliens.
ufos.about.com/culture/ufos/library/bldata/blguidea.htm

Gregg Easterbrook. "Are We Alone?" *Atlantic Monthly* (August 1988).
www.theatlantic.com/issues/88aug/easterbr.htm

Search for Extraterrestrial Intelligence at U.C. Berkeley.
albert.ssl.berkeley.edu/opticalseti/

Carl Sagan. "The Quest for Extraterrestrial Intelligence." (Cosmic Search Vol. 1 No. 2.): **204.240.36.10/radobs/vol1no2/sagan.htm**

The Active Mind's SETI Web site.
www.activemind.com/Mysterious/Topics/SETI

Area 51. **www.ipcress.com/area51/**

Journal of Scientific Exploration: research-style articles on "fringe science."
www.scientificexploration.org/jse.html

US Government and Unidentified Flying Objects.
www.hq.nasa.gov/office/pao/facts/HTML/FS-017-HQ.html

Accessed February 3, 2001.

This chapter shows you how to acknowledge information sources you've used to write your technical documents. Not acknowledging those sources, as you probably know, is called *plagiarism*. You may have already encountered the MLA system or the APA system, in which you indicate the sources of borrowed information in parentheses. This appendix reviews those and adds one other—the number system, which is often used in technical and scientific fields.

To provide a frame of reference for this process of acknowledging the sources of borrowed information, we'll review the idea of *intellectual property*. The individual's intellectual property includes the ideas of an individual and the words that the individual uses to express those ideas. Intellectual property may not have the same concrete reality that a house or an automobile has, but it can be just as valuable, if not more so.

That's what you are doing when you indicate who you have borrowed information from, put quotation marks around the exact words of someone else, asked for permission to use a direct quotation from an author, affixed trademark symbols to product names—honoring, protecting, and respecting the intellectual property of others, as well as your own.

Note: Some examples of book, articles, and other information sources in this chapter are fictitious.

INTELLECTUAL PROPERTY AND PLAGIARISM

Before getting into the details of citing borrowed information sources, take a moment to understand the concept of *intellectual property*. When you cite the source of borrowed information, you are honoring the creator or originator of that information. You are also preventing people from thinking you were the creator or originator of that information. What are some of the forms of intellectual property that can be borrowed?

- Someone's exact words, or a similar rendition of them
- Someone's carefully researched data

- Someone's graphic (photo, drawing, chart) or an exact, or almost exact, replica of someone's graphic
- Someone's musical composition, or a similar rendition
- Someone's design, for example, a building, a software interface, or a Web site

It's hard to think of someone's words, data, images, and sounds as property the same way we think of land, automobiles, and other physical things as property. But they are—and every bit as valuable.

For more information on intellectual property, trademarks, copyrights, patents, and related issues involving the Internet, see these resources:

- Uncle Orson Scott Card's Writing Class: On Plagiarism, Borrowing, Resemblance, and Influence: **www.hatrack.com/writingclass/index.shtml**
- Brad Templeton. A Brief Intro to Copyright: **www.templetons.com/brad/copyright.html**
- Brad Templeton. 10 Big Myths about Copyright Explained: **www.templetons.com/brad/copymyths.html**
- Jennifer Kyrnin. Copyright Issues and Intellectual Property: **html.about.com/compute/html/msubcopyright.htm**

When you are taking a technical-writing course and are using information from other writers, what does intellectual property mean to you? What's the difference between copyright violation and plagiarism? Both are violations of the intellectual property rights of others. You can be sued for plagiarism, but plagiarism is more of an ethical offense. Copyright violation is both an ethical and legal offense, often involving a direct intention to use someone else's copyrighted material for monetary gain. While you are more likely to be sued for violating copyright, plagiarism—although it's free—will merely cause you to be haunted by shame and other such moral anguish for the rest of your life. For example, in the 1980s, a U.S. presidential candidate was discovered to have plagiarized some of his law school work. He suffered shame and embarrassment and dropped out of the campaign, but was never sued.

NUMBER SYSTEM (IEEE, CBE)

In many areas of science and technology, some version of the number system is the commonly used documentation style. Two widely used versions of the number system are those of the Institute of Electrical and Electronics Engineers (IEEE) and the Council of Biology Editors (CBE).

In the *number system*, you create a numbered list of your information sources, arranged in order of use in the text, and place it at the end of your document. At the point where you borrow from one of those sources in your regular text, put the number of that source in brackets:

Because the Condon Report [1] is the only unclassified investigation of the UFO phenomenon carried out by an established scientific organization under contract to a U.S. federal agency, it constitutes a landmark in the study of the UFO phenomenon, to which all later work must be referred.

The history of the UFO phenomenon in the United States is long and complex. Jacobs [2] has given a comprehensive account of this history up to 1973 in his book *UFO Controversy in America.*

You can also indicate the page where the information occurs:

Condon argues that a civilization from a planet attached to a nearby star would not set out on a journey to Earth until that civilization knew that an advanced technology had been established here. Thus, he estimates that there is no possibility of such a civilization visiting Earth in the next 10,000 years [1:28].

You indicate that you are borrowing from a combination of sources:

Soon after it was published, the Condon Report was widely reviewed [2,3,4,5].

Full details about the information sources should be provided in a list called "References" at the end of the document, as illustrated in Figure 21-1:

- Items are arranged in the order that they are first cited in the text—not alphabetically.
- The author's name is shown in regular order: first-name initial, period, middle-name initial, period, then last name, followed by a comma. (Full first and middle names are not shown, only initials.)
- The title of information follows the author's name: italicized if it's a book, in quotation marks if it's an article. The title is followed by a period if it's a book, a comma if it's an article.
- For books, the book title is followed by the city of publication, name of the publisher, and year of publication. The city is followed by a colon; the publisher's name is followed by a comma.
- For magazine or journal articles, the article title is followed by the name of the magazine or journal in italics. Depending on the type of periodical, volume and issue numbers, page numbers, and date are handled in one of the following ways:
  - J. McMurrey, "Photographic techniques and UFOs," *Journal of UFO Research*, vol. 51, no. 2, 1999, pp. 113–117.
  - P. McMurrey, "UFO personalities," *UFO Monthly*, Jul. 1999, pp. 51–52.

References

1. E. U. Condon (Proj. Dir.) and D. S. Gillmor, D. S., Ed., *Scientific Study of Unidentified Flying Objects*. New York: Bantam, 1968.
2. D. M. Jacobs, *The UFO Controversy in America*. Bloomington: Indiana University Press, 1975.
3. J.E. McDonald, "The Condon Report: Scientific Study of Unidentified Flying Objects," *Icarus*, vol. 11, pp. 443–447, 1969.
4. H. Y. Chiu. "The Condon Report, Scientific Study of Unidentified Flying Objects," *Icarus*, vol. 11, pp. 447–450, 1969.
5. J. S. Hynek, *The UFO Experience*. Chicago: Henry Regnery, 1972.
6. P. A. Sturrock, "Report on a survey of the American Astronomical Society concerning the UFO phenomenon." Stanford University Report SUIPR 681R, 1977.
7. L. Hannesonne. <remlynn@eathlinx.net> 1999 July 7. No UFOs here [Personal e-mail communication. 1999 July 8.]
8. J. P. Petit. "Shockwave cancellation in gas by Lorentz force action," In Proc. 9th Meeting on Magnetohydrodynamic Electrical Power Generation, 1986.
9. Celestron International. Ultima 2000-8 Schmidt-Cassegrain Telescope. Product brochure. 1999.
10. G. Easterbrook. "Are We Alone?" *Atlantic Monthly*, August 1988; <www.theatlantic.com/issues/88aug/easterbr.htm>. Accessed 1999 December 19.

FIGURE 21-1

Number-style references page. This example references page shows you the most common types of bibliographic entries using the number style.

■ For Internet material, cite the author and title as in the preceding, the date of publication, the URL within angle brackets followed by a period, followed by the date you, the writer, accessed that Web site.

NAME–YEAR SYSTEM (APA)

The *Publication Manual*, 4th ed. (1994) of the American Psychological Association (APA) has long been used as the documentation style by a wide range of disciplines, such as medicine, nursing, and sociology. In APA style, you put the name of the author whose information you are borrowing and the year that borrowed information was published in parentheses at the point in your text where you borrow that information. Because its focus is author name and publication date, the APA style is often called the "name–year" style:

```
Because this study is the only unclassified investiga-
tion of the UFO phenomenon carried out by an estab-
lished scientific organization under contract to a U.S.
```

Practical Ethics: Plagiarism

In 1994, singer Michael Bolton was found guilty of plagiarizing a song by the Isley Brothers and was ordered to pay them $5.4 million.[1] When an instructor at a Vermont college asked her students to write about John F. Kennedy's inaugural address, two out of sixteen students unwittingly handed in the same papers. They had both copied an article from *The New York Times* and turned it in as their own work. Both were given Fs for the class (although one student contested this grade).[2]

Simply stated, plagiarism is using someone else's words and passing them off as your own. Perhaps it's competition that leads us to steal phrases, paragraphs, or entire documents and claim ourselves to be the original authors. Then again, maybe it's just laziness or panic—writing is hard work, especially under deadline.

Plagiarism obviously poses some serious risks. However, avoiding it shouldn't be simply a matter of avoiding the consequences. It should be a matter of respect. Acting with integrity as a student in college or a professional in the workplace means giving others credit for their work; you should expect no less from them. If you want to take a totally selfish point of view, citing your sources (avoiding plagiarism) actually makes your work appear more professional and authoritative. Citing sources indicates you've done your homework, know your stuff, and take a professional attitude toward your work.

Respect others' intellectual property, and take some simple precautions. Cite your sources clearly and accurately. Ask permission to use copyrighted material. When in doubt, ask for a second opinion; an instructor, supervisor, colleague, or lawyer would be happy to help.

[1] Farhi, Paul. *Washington Post,* 22 February 2000, p. C01.

[2] Lieberman, Trudy. "Plagiarize, Plagiarize, Plagiarize . . ." *Columbia Journal Review* (July/August 1995). www.cjr.org/year/95/4/plagiarize.asp

federal agency, the report based on this study (Condon & Gillmor, 1968) constitutes a landmark in the study of the UFO phenomenon, to which all later work must be referred.

You can also show the page number:

Condon argues that a civilization from a planet attached to a nearby star would not set out on a journey to Earth until that civilization knew that an advanced technology had been established here. Thus, he estimates that there is no possibility of such a civilization visiting earth in the next 10,000 years (Condon & Gillmor, 1969, p. 28).

If you've already cited the name or the year, or both, in the text, you can omit those elements in the parenthetical citation:

The history of the UFO phenomenon in the United States is long and complex. Jacobs (1975) has given a comprehensive account of this history up to 1973 in his book *UFO Controversy in America.*

Cite p## for quotations

References

Celestron International. (1999). Ultima 2000-8 Schmidt-Cassegrain Telescope. Product brochure.

Chiu, H.Y. (1969). The Condon Report, scientific study of unidentified flying objects (book review). *Icarus*, 11, 447–450.

Condon, E. U. (Proj. Dir.), & Gillmor, D. S. (Ed.). (1968). Scientific study of unidentified flying objects. New York: Bantam.

Easterbrook, G. (1988). Are we alone? Atlantic Monthly. URL www.the atlantic.com/issues/88aug/easterbr.htm (visited 1999, December 19).

Hannesonne, L. <remlynn@eathlinx.net> (1999, July 7). No UFOs here. [Personal e-mail]. (1999, July 8).

Hynek, J. S. (1972). The UFO experience. Chicago: Henry Regnery.

Jacobs, D. M. (1975). The UFO controversy in America. Bloomington: Indiana University Press.

McDonald, J. E. (1969). The Condon report: scientific study of unidentified flying objects (book review). *Icarus*, 11, 443–447.

Petit, J. P. (1986, September). Shockwave cancellation in gas by Lorentz force action. Proc. 9th Meeting on Magnetohydrodynamic Electrical Power Generation, Tokyo.

Sturrock, P. A. (1977). Report on a survey of the American Astronomical Society concerning the UFO phenomenon. Stanford University Report SUIPR 681R.

Sturrock, P. A. (1994a). Report on a survey of the membership of the American Astronomical Society Concerning the UFO problem: Part 1. *Journal of Scientific Exploration*, 8, 1.

Sturrock, P. A. (1994b). Report on a survey of the membership of the American Astronomical Society Concerning the UFO Problem: Part 2. *Journal of Scientific Exploration*, 8, 153.

FIGURE 21-2
APA-style references page. The items in this example references page show you the most common types of bibliographic entries using the APA style.

You can indicate that you are borrowing from a combination of sources:

```
Soon after its publication, the Condon Report was
widely reviewed (Jacobs, 1975; MacDonald, 1969; Chiu,
1969; Hynek, 1972).
```

Full details about the information sources should be provided in "References" at the end of the document, as illustrated in Figure 21-2. Notice the following details that are displayed in Figure 21-2.

- Items in the list are arranged alphabetically but not numbered. Notice the "hanging indent" format: following lines are indented, not the first line.
- Last name comes first, followed by initials (not full names).

- Following the name is the year of publication in parentheses, which is followed by a period.
- The title of the book or article comes next—not italicized or enclosed in quotation marks. Notice that only the first word of the title is capitalized.
- For books, notice that the city of publication comes first, followed by a colon, followed by the name of the publisher.
- For articles, notice that in the title of the article only the first word is capitalized and is *not* enclosed in quotation marks. The name of the magazine or journal is italicized. Depending on the type of periodical, volume and issue numbers, page numbers, and date are handled in one of the following ways:
  - McMurrey, J. (1999). Photographic techniques and UFOs. *Journal of UFO Research 51*(2), 113–117.
  - McMurrey, P. (1999, July). UFO personalities. *UFO Monthly*, pp. 51–52.
- When more than one source was published in the same year by the same author, differentiate them with lowercase letters attached, as shown in Figure 21-2. In text, you would cite one of the Sturrock sources like this: (1994b).

NAME–PAGE SYSTEM (MLA)

As a college student, you may have learned the documentation style of the Modern Language Association (MLA). In MLA, parentheses are used for the name of the author whose information you are borrowing and the page number where that information occurs at the point in your text where you borrow it. For example, notice the style of the following:

> Most scientists who study UFOs, however, adopt a more restricted definition that rules out reports that are readily explainable (Hynek 3-4).

If you've already cited the name in the text, omit it in the parenthetical citation:

> Hynek, however, adopts a more restricted definition that rules out reports that are readily explainable (3-4).

If you don't cite a specific page, MLA doesn't expect you to create a citation at all (but you would still list the source in works cited):

> The history of the UFO phenomenon in the United States is long and complex. Jacobs has given a comprehensive account of this history up to 1973 in his book *UFO Controversy in America*.

If no author's name is available, use the first meaningful words of the title:

Works Cited

Celestron International. Ultima 2000-8 Schmidt-Cassegrain Telescope. Product brochure. 1999.

Chiu, Hi Y. "The Condon Report, Scientific Study of Unidentified Flying Objects." *Icarus* 11 (1969): 447–450.

Condon, Edward U., and Daniel S. Gillmor, ed. *Scientific Study of Unidentified Flying Objects.* New York: Bantam, 1968.

Easterbrook, Gregg. "Are We Alone?" Atlantic Monthly, August 1988. URL www.theatlantic.com/issues/88aug/easterbr.htm (visited 1999, December 19).

Hannesonne, L. <remlynn@eathlinx.net> (7 July 1999). No UFOs here. [Personal e-mail]. (8 July 1999).

Hynek, J. Allen. *The UFO Experience.* Chicago: Henry Regnery, 1972.

Jacobs, David Michael. *The UFO Controversy in America.* Bloomington: Indiana University Press, 1975.

McDonald, J. E. "The Condon report: scientific study of unidentified flying objects." *Icarus* 11 (1969): 443–447.

Petit, Jean-Pierre. "Shockwave Cancellation in Gas by Lorentz Force Action." Proceedings of the 9th Meeting on Magnetohydrodynamic Electrical Power Generation. Tokyo, 1969.

Sturrock, Peter A. Report on a Survey of the American Astronomical Society Concerning the UFO Phenomenon. Stanford, CA: Stanford UP, 1977.

"Tis the Season for UFOs." *UFO Times* July 19, 1990: 3–5.

FIGURE 21-3

MLA-style references page. The items in this example page show you the most common types of bibliographic entries using the MLA style.

The past fifty years have seen several distinct periods of heightened interest in UFOs ("Tis the Season," 3).

For multiple authors, use the following format:

Because this study is the only unclassified investigation of UFOs carried out by an established scientific organization under contract to a U.S. federal agency, the report of this study (Condon and Gillmor, 28) constitutes a landmark in the study of the UFO phenomenon, to which all later work must be referred.

Provide full details about your information sources in "Works Cited" at the end of the document, as illustrated in Figure 21-3.

Notice the following details, illustrated in Figure 21-3.

- Items in the list are arranged alphabetically and are not numbered. Notice the "hanging indent" format: following lines are indented, not the first line.
- Last name comes first, but the MLA shows first names and middle initials.
- After the name comes the title of the book (in italics) or article (in quotation marks). Notice that headline capitalization style is used (all main words).
- For books, after the title comes the city of publication (and state unless it is a large, well-known city such as New York), followed by a colon, the name of the publisher, a comma, ending with the year of the publication.
- For articles, the name of the magazine or journal is italicized. Depending on the type of periodical, volume and issue numbers, page numbers, and date are handled in one of the following ways:
  - McMurrey, Jane. "Photographic Techniques and UFOs." *Journal of UFO Research*. 51.2 (1999): 113–117.
  - McMurrey, Patrick. "UFO Personalities." *UFO Monthly*. July 1999: 51–52.

FOR ADDITIONAL INFORMATION

The scope of this chapter can cover only the most common types of information sources. For additional information on the CBE, IEEE, APA, and MLA styles of documentation—in particular for unusual or complex sources—see the following resources:

- Institute of Electrical and Electronics Engineers. IEEE Transactions, Journals, and Letters Authors. 1996
- Perelman, Leslie C., James Paradis, Edward Barrett. *Mayfield Handbook of Technical and Scientific Writing*. Mountain View, CA: Mayfield, 1998.
- Harnack, Andrew, and Eugene Kleppinger. *Online! A Reference Guide to Using Internet Resources*. New York: St. Martin, 1998.
- Modern Language Association of America. *MLA Handbook for Writers of Research Papers*, 5th ed., New York: 1999.
- American Psychological Association. *Publication Manual of the American Psychological Association*, 4th ed., New York: 1994.

LINKING CITATIONS AND BIBLIOGRAPHIC ENTRIES ON WEB PAGES

Whichever documentation style you use, if you prepare your document as a Web page, you can create hypertext links from the citations in the main text to the bibliographic entries at the end. That way, readers can click on

Because the Condon Report [<A
HREF="#source1">1</A> is the only uncla[...]
investigation of the UFO phenomenon carri[...]
out by an established scientific organization[...]
under contract to a U.S. federal agency, it c[...]
stitutes a landmark in the study of the UFO
phenomenon, to which all later work must [...]
referred. Starting from the assertion that an[...]
civilization must originate on a planet of the[...]
sun or some other star, Condon argues that[...]
civilization based on a planet attached to a
nearby star would not set out on a journey
to earth until the civilization knows that an
advanced technology has been established h[...]
From this consideration he estimates that th[...]

<H1>REFERENCES</H1>
<OL>
<LI><A NAME="source1">E. U. Condon (Proj.
Dir.) and D. S. Gillmor, D. S., Ed., Scientific
Study of Unidentified Flying Objects. New York:
Bantam, 1968.</A>
<LI><A NAME="source2">D. M. Jacobs, The
UFO Controversy in America. Bloomington:
Indiana University Press, 1975.</A>
<LI><A NAME="source3">J.E. McDonald, "The
Condon Report: Scientific Study of Unidentified
Flying Objects," Icarus, vol. 11, pp. 443-447,
1969.</A>

FIGURE 21-4

Linking citations to bibliographic entries. The A NAME tagging on the bibliographic
entries create a "target" at which to aim A HREF links.

the citation and go directly to the full bibliographic detail about the
source. Study the HTML tagging in Figure 21-4 to see how to create these
hypertext links.

WORKSHOP: SOURCE DOCUMENTATION

The following exercises give you some practice with the concepts, tools,
and strategies presented in this chapter:

1. Create a reference or works-cited list by formatting the bibliographic information available at **www.io.com/~hcexres/power_tools/documentation/
   exer1.html** using the number (IEEE, CBE), name-year (APA), or name-
   page system (MLA).

2. Using the text at **www.io.com/~hcexres/power_tools/documentation/
   exer2.html,** revise the citations according to the documentation style
   you picked in the preceding exercise.

3. Reformat the text and reference list available at **www.io.com/~hcexres/
   power_tools/documentation/exer3.html** for hypertext links using
   HTML tags.

CHAPTER 22

Managing Team Projects

As the workplace has become less formal and as hierarchies have become less defined, people are increasingly working in "teams"—shifting groups that are reformed at practically each new project (or crisis). In fact, "teams," "teamwork," and even "teaming" became quite the buzzwords in the 1980s and 1990s. In a team, hierarchy is ill-defined. No one is officially the boss of anyone else; you don't do your work because the boss told you to, but because you feel loyalty to the team.

The modern workplace wants "team players" (another buzzword): people who know how to work effectively within teams. Teamwork is essential in completing large-scale projects, including technical documents. Some computer software products require several thousand pages of documentation. To get that amount of material out on time, writers must work in teams, which also consist of editors, graphic artists, testers, technical reviewers, product specialists, document designers, managers, and production and distribution specialists.

In response to the emergence of teams in the workplace, colleges and universities have increased the amount of team projects students do. To reflect the workplace movement, this chapter reviews the roles typically played in the production of technical documents and then explores how you can develop writing teams in your technical-writing courses.

HOW DO INDUSTRY WRITING TEAMS WORK?

Before developing your own writing team, spend some time getting to know how writing teams function in the workplace and what their roles and tasks are.

Teams in Industry

Technical documentation is handled in many different ways in industry. The following list reviews the organization of a typical well-staffed and

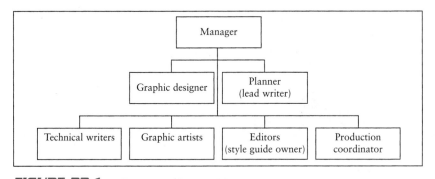

FIGURE 22-1

Typical organization for a documentation group. Remember that in smaller, or "down-sized" organizations, some of these roles are combined into individual team members.

well-organized writing team such as you might find at IBM, Dell, Hewlett-Packard, Adobe, or Microsoft. See Figure 22-1 for an organizational chart of a well-staffed documentation group. The point of this discussion is not to get you ready to work in a technical-writing department but to see the roles and tasks required in the production of a technical document—whatever the organization.

- *Managers.* Needed to make decisions, settle disputes, and ensure that the organization runs smoothly (despite what Dilbert thinks).
- *Planners.* Handle overall technical responsibilities for documentation projects, such as scheduling, library design, contents, and delivery media. Planners are also referred to as "lead writers" and "information architects." (In small "shops," the manager and planner may be the same person.)
- *Document designers.* Make decisions as to a documentation project's color, graphics, page design, type style, headings, media, and so on. (These people often handle graphic-artist responsibilities as well.)
- *Writers.* Create, revise, and maintain the documents for a product, often specializing in certain kinds of documentation, such as Web pages, online helps, or print, or in certain technical areas, such as electronics, graphics, or networking. (In downsized organizations, a writer often must handle design, editing, and graphics as well.)
- *Technical reviewers.* Plan, develop, and test the actual product as well as write "specifications" that describe product functions. They review writers' documentation to ensure that it is technically correct and complete.
- *Graphic artists.* Develop and maintain "artwork" for a documentation project: illustrations of the products and other such graphics.
- *Editors.* Copyedit and proofread drafts of the documentation, assess whether it meets the needs of the intended readers, maintain the style guide, and ensure documents meet internal requirements (such as for legal notices).
- *Information testers.* Supervise individuals typical of the target audience who try using the documentation to perform product tasks. Testers summarize this feedback, which writers can use to improve their documents.
- *Production specialists.* Coordinate the scheduling, delivery, and inspection of completed documentation projects. They put it "into production."
- *Distribution specialists.* Handle the logistics of how the product and its documentation are distributed to customers. They coordinate how the product and all of its pieces, including the documentation, are packaged, or "kitted."

In most smaller documentation teams, many of these roles and tasks are combined and handled by the same individuals.

Teams in the Technical-Writing Classroom

In your technical-writing course, you won't have such a complex writing team as just described. Even in an introductory technical-writing course, you still must think about the functional roles performed by your team members. See Figure 22-2 for an idea of how you can structure your own technical-writing team.

- *Writing.* Everybody on your writing team gets to do some writing for the project. Divide the writing tasks evenly among the members of your team—after all, it is a *writing* course!
- *Reviewing.* Likewise, everybody on your team should get some experience reviewing—an important skill often lacking in the professional world. Review each other's drafts to enable your team to produce a better document; to help your team reach consensus on content, organization, and style issues; and just generally to help you think as one about the project. In this context, reviewing means looking at documents in terms of technical accuracy, completeness, comprehension (understandability), organization, and usability.
- *Editing.* Editing is a specialized skill. Try finding that one team member who has a sharp eye for typos and grammar, usage, punctuation, and style problems. Reduce this individual's other project responsibilities

	Team writer 1 (Kerry) *Library/interview specialist*
	Team writer 2 (Jim) *Graphics coordinator*
Team leader (Julie) *Production coordinator* *Team writer 5*	**Team writer 3** (Sterlin) *Chief style/edit guru*
	Team writer 4 (Anh) *Technical lead*

FIGURE 22-2

Team for a technical-writing class. Make sure that individual team members get their fair share of the writing, but find out if anybody on your team has special skills as editors, proofreaders, or graphic artists.

accordingly. In this context, editing means looking at documents for spelling, grammar, usage, and punctuation errors, as well as other mechanical and style problems.

- *Revising.* When your team members revise, individual team members use the feedback they get from other team members and do their own revising. To produce a consistent document that does not read like a patchwork written by four very different individuals, assign the final revision to one individual (and reduce that individual's workload accordingly).
- *Developing graphics.* As mentioned in Chapter 11, your technical-writing course is a *writing* course—not a graphics course. You can use various techniques to produce effective, professional-looking graphics without being a professional graphic artist. If one team member does have graphics talent, have other team members draw rough sketches of the graphics they need and get your designated graphics specialist to develop the final graphics.
- *Researching.* It's a tricky problem to plan who will research project information and how and when this can be accomplished. Without some planning, individual team members may duplicate each other's effort, each finding the same information on their own.

Practical Ethics: Groupthink

Being assigned to a group project is not only a reality in the classroom, but in many workplaces as well. When groups of people get together, conflict is almost inevitable. For many people, conflict is a negative thing to be avoided at all costs and, to them, a group without conflict is a successful one.

The author of *The Art and Science of Leadership* points out that a lack of conflict can actually indicate that members of a team are reluctant to disagree with the person in charge. "In some cases, the subordinates follow the leader because of personal commitment . . . or they may truly respect their leader's expertise and personal integrity. In other cases, the compliance is simply due to fear of retribution."[1] When people are afraid to voice their opinions, "groupthink" can result—a situation in which team members keep their concerns to themselves, alternative ideas are frowned on, and bad or even unethical decisions are made.

The Team Handbook teaches that consensus decision making can prevent groupthink.

Consensus doesn't mean that decisions are unanimous, but rather that everyone has the opportunity to speak and test one another's ideas: "Consensus decision making is not just a way to reach a compromise. It is a search for the best decision through the exploration of the best of everyone's thinking. As more ideas are addressed and more potential problems discussed, a synthesis of ideas takes place and the final decision is often better than any single idea that was present at the beginning."[2]

A truly successful team is not necessarily one that lacks conflict. Rather, it is one that encourages all members to brainstorm, raise concerns, and hold one another accountable so poor or unethical decisions are not made.

[1] Nahavandi, Afsaneh. *The Art and Science of Leadership, Second Edition.* New Jersey: Prentice Hall, 2000, p. 87.

[2] Scholtes, Peter, Brian Joiner, and Barbara Streibel. *The Team Handbook, Second Edition.* Madison, WI: Oriel Incorporated, 1996, p.4–23.

■ *Designing the document.* Early in your project, get your team to design the document: margins, type style, heading and list style, highlighting, terminology, and so on. Have each team member create a document prototype separately, and then have a group meeting to compare designs and choose one.

■ *Producing the document.* Producing the final copy is no simple step. Once team members have produced their final drafts, the parts must be assembled in one complete, integrated document. Final graphics must be inserted. Getting the page breaks right may take some time. Front and back matter elements—such as title pages, covers, and tables of contents—have to be added. And you must get the document bound. See Chapter 15 for details on producing a final copy.

■ *Overseeing the project.* Even your project may need a manager or overseer—someone to settle disputes and to ensure that everything is running smoothly. As a team, anticipate what disputes may arise and how to settle them. Solutions for typical problems are suggested in the next section.

Anticipating Problems in the Team Project

In any team effort, you must anticipate problems and plan how to deal with them. Think about the kinds of problems that might occur when four or five college students (who are not majoring in English or technical writing) attempt to team-write a technical document.

■ *One team member ends up having too much or too little to do.* The overworked team member gets sulky and less cooperative. The underworked team member is resented by the others. What to do? Here's a solution: have team members fill out weekly project time sheets and have an overall project coordinator watch for and resolve problems. (See Figure 22-3 for examples.)

■ *One team member just doesn't do her or his part—either out of laziness, personal problems, or inability.* What to do about slackers and incompetents? What if a team member has a personal crisis and can't finish the course? Develop "by-laws" that address these possibilities. Ask your instructor: if one team member doesn't produce, what will be the effect on the rest of the team?

■ *Team members disagree about some aspect of the writing project and can't reach a compromise.* For example, team members may be unable to reach agreement over whether contractions should be used (sad, but truly possible). Try getting potential arguments like these settled early and recording them in the style guide. Also, agree on a process for resolving disputes. For example, decide on a 20-minute maximum for discussion followed by a vote, or present both sides to the instructor who will decide.

■ *Some team members are shy and nonassertive; others, loud and aggressive.* How do you bring out those quiet members of your team who have lots to contribute? How do you keep loudmouths and bullies from taking

```
Name _____
Team-Report Project: Week of _____

        W=writing          G=graphics       P=production
        R=reviewing        I=research       M=meetings
```

Date	Start	End	Code	Comments

FIGURE 22-3

Example of a project log. To ensure that team members are doing their fair share and keeping to the schedule, consider having everyone keep a project log like this one.

over? Appoint a discussion leader whose responsibility is to ensure that everyone is invited to contribute and to put the overly aggressive members in their places.

Anticipating problems like these at the beginning of your team-writing project, agreeing on ways to resolve them, getting those agreements in writing, and then ensuring that everybody "buys into" those agreements can help. Build your instructor into the process as the arbiter.

HOW DO YOU TEAM-WRITE A TECHNICAL-WRITING PROJECT?

Let's put all these ideas together into a scenario for a team-writing project.

1. *Assemble and get to know your team.* Find a way to get a good mix of writing, editing, design, graphics, and technical skills for your team. Get your instructor to stage some sort of getting-to-know-you event in the classroom. Once you've formed a writing team, find out about the skills each team member has. Just for fun, give your team a name, a logo, or a slogan.
2. *Agree on general procedures and "by-laws."* When you divide up team roles, make sure each team member has a fair share of writing to do. As a team, anticipate problems, reach agreements, and write them down. If your team is concerned about individual members doing their fair share of the work, have individual team members keep project journals or time sheets in which they record what they do and how much time they spend doing it.
3. *Decide on your writing project.* Get together with your team to develop a project, preferably one addressing a real workplace problem. Analyze the audience, decide on a focus, and plan other details. Get these in writing, too.

4. *Do some initial research and develop an outline.* To define your writing project thoroughly and to outline it, spend some time scanning information sources, talking to experts, and brainstorming as a team. Decide on an effective way to create that outline: should everybody go off and take a stab at it separately (a tactic that brings out your quieter, less assertive teammates)? Should you get together for a big brainstorming session?

5. *Assign the team roles and tasks.* Perhaps once you've developed the rough outline, your team will be ready to decide who writes which parts of the outline and who handles which tasks. Get these in writing too.

6. *Develop a detailed schedule.* If you've assigned team roles and tasks, you can develop a schedule. (See the example schedule in Figure 22-4.) In it, include due dates for the drafts of the different sections, due dates for completed reviews, due dates for completed editing, due dates for final production, and so on. Work backwards from the final due date—that date when your instructor expects you to turn in the finished project.

Individual prototypes due	October 1
Team meeting: finalize the prototype	October 1
Rough-draft style guide due	October 5
Team meeting: finalize style guide	October 5
Twice-weekly team meetings: progress & problems	October 5–26
Graphics sketches due to Jim	October 14
Rough drafts of individual sections due	October 26
Review of rough drafts due	October 28
Team meeting: discuss rough drafts, reviews	October 28
Update of style guide due from Sterlin	October 31
Revisions of rough drafts due to reviewers	November 3
Final graphics due from Jim	November 5
Completed drafts to Sterlin: final edit/proof	November 7
Team meeting: review completed draft with final graphics and editing	November 12
Completed drafts due to Julie for final production	November 15
Team meeting: inspection of completed project	November 15
Project upload due to McMurrey	November 16
Party at Julie's	November 19

FIGURE 22-4

Document project schedule. Develop a schedule with tasks, completion dates, and the names of team members who are responsible for those tasks. If you want to get fancy, try developing a Gantt chart, which shows the relationship of concurrent tasks and their different start and stop dates.

7. *Design the document; create a document prototype and style guide.* Agree as a team on how you want the final document to look. Create a prototype—a "dummy"—of that document. See Figure 22-5 for examples of document prototypes. In the prototype, include examples of every type of page or format: covers, title pages, tables of contents, graphics, tables, headings, lists, highlighting, notices, and so on. Agree on page size, margins, fonts, type sizes, color, and other such issues. Make sure that all team members have a copy of the prototype to reference as they develop their parts of the document.

Also, develop a style guide that records team decisions about terminology; rules for punctuation, capitalization, and hyphenation; rules for italics, bold, alternate fonts, and color; format for bulleted and numbered lists; design for headings and notices; and so on. Also record rules such as when to use digits or words for numbers in regular text; whether to use decimals or fractions; how to use abbreviations; and

Chapter 1. Chapter Title

Lorem ipsum dolor sit amet, consectetuer adipiscing elit, sed diam nonummy nibh euismod.

Heading 1

Tincidunt ut laoreet dolore magna aliquam erat volutpat. Ut wisi enim ad minim.

▼ To veniam, quis nostrud exerci tation:

0. Ullam corper suscipit lobortis nisl ut aliquip ex ea commodo consequat.

   soluta nobis eleifend

1. Duis autem vel eum iriure dolor in hendrerit in vulputate.

   Note: Vvelit esse *molestie* consequat, vel illum dolore eu feugiat nulla facilisis at vero eros.

2. Duis autem vel eum iriure dolor in hendrerit in vulputate dolore eu feugiat nulla facilisis at vero.

3. Eros et **accumsan** et iusto odio dignissim qui blandit praesent luptatum zzril delenit ague duis dolore te feugait nulla facilisi. Nam liber

4. Tempor cum soluta nobis eleifend option congue nihil imperdiet doming id quod mazim placerat

Chapter title– ##

Lorem ipsum dolor sit amet, consectetuer adipiscing elit, sed diam nonummy nibh euismod.

Heading 1

Fugeat nulla pariatur. At veos eos etim accusam et iuosto odio dignissim qui blandit praesento lupatim delenti aigue duos color et mole.

Table 1. Table title			
Tempor	*Dolor*	*Vvelit*	*Assum*
Commo	aguel	odio	23
Eumi	vulpat	iusti	12
Quisi	luptum	nulla	0
Feugat	nobis	robo	456

Fugeat nulla pariatur:

• At veos eos etim accusam et iuosto odio ignissim qui blandit praesento.

• Lupatim delenti aigue duos color et mole stais exceptur sint.

• Ut enim ad minimim veniami.

– Book Title

FIGURE 22-5

Sample pages from a prototype for a writing project. The prototype, consisting of "greeked" text, illustrates every unique feature of the document: each unique section (title page, table of contents, body page, etc.), headings, lists, tables, graphics, and so on. These sample pages show only two body pages.

Highlighting

1. Use bold for interface elements that function like commands (for example, the **Exit** button).
2. Use bold for menu options that get you to commands (for example, **File→Open**).
3. Use the → symbol to abbreviate menu traversal.
4. Use Courier New for example text that users type in (for example, `myfile.doc`).
5. Use italics for variables—placeholder text for which users substitute their own information (for example, *filename*.doc).

Hyphenation

1. *Individual words.* Turn automatic hyphenation off. Do not hyphenate words except in tight places like tables or graphics.
2. *Compounds.* Mr. Hyphen (Sterlin) will keep the hyphenated-compounds list. Use only those in his list, and submit new ones to him for approval and inclusion on the list. (Hyphenate compounds only when they modify [for example, "back-up copy"], not when they act as nouns or verbs (for example, "to back up your files.")

Terminology

1. Use only the words in **graph_project.dic**. Sterlin approves all new words for that database.
2. Use the same word for the same object, same process, or same action. No elegant variation, please!

FIGURE 22-6

Sample from a style guide for a team-writing project. Style guides help team writers agree on things like whether to use contractions or Latin abbreviations, how lists will be punctuated, how to handle abbreviations and numbers in text, and which terms are preferred.

so on. Record these decisions along with examples illustrating them in a style guide, as shown in Figure 22-6.

8. *Write the rough drafts.* Writing projects are not neat, tidy affairs where one task stops and another starts without any overlap. When you start writing the rough drafts of your individual sections, you may need to rethink the outline, do additional research, or change the document design. These kinds of events necessitate that you get back together with your team. For these reasons, schedule regular meetings during the rough-drafting phase—if not in person, perhaps by phone, e-mail, or Internet chat.

9. *Review each other's drafts.* Ensure that team members provide each other with good thorough reviews of their drafts. Remember that a review generally does not include picky grammar, usage, and punctuation issues. A review focuses more on content, organization,

```
From hcexres36:05 1999 -0600
Date: Sun, 5 Dec 1999 15:36:04 -0600 (EST)
From: "David A. McMurrey" <hcexres@io.com>
To: julie@colltech.com
cc: xgraphic_team
Subject: Review of your section of Xgraphics HTML project
Content-Type: TEXT/PLAIN; charset=US-ASCII

Julie, your section of the guide is super! You've
done several things the rest of the team ought to
incorporate in their sections.

1. I do find places where it feels like there is too
much text -- for example, in "Using Gravity and
Snap." It's not a major problem, but I'd be looking
to see if I could cut a few lines from the longer
paragraphs without sacrificing detail.

2. Your labels for the screen captures are really
nice. You'll have to show the rest of the team how
you do it.

3. You leave out generic buttons on several pages --
I think the group was in agreement that *all* pages
would have them at the bottom.

4. I notice in some areas you use italics for some
interface elements, bold for others. Our style guide
states that we wanted bold for any screen button or
similar element that makes something happen when you
click it. Maybe we need to discuss the distinction
you are thinking about here at our next meeting.
```

FIGURE 22-7
Review memo for a team-writing project. Notice that this sampling of comments focuses on contents, audience, organization, comprehension, and other such "high-level" matters.

comprehension, flow, and general suitability for the audience and situation. Summarize your review comments in a memo to the writer whose section you reviewed. (See the example review memo in Figure 22-7.) Attach the memo to the reviewed draft, which includes your markup and marginal comments.

10. *Revise and review again.* The review-and-revise phase is essential in producing any document. And it's not a once-only event. Reviewers review; writers revise; and then reviewers review again to ensure problems were fixed. Keep reviewing and revising until everyone is satisfied, or time runs out.

11. *Edit the full draft.* You must leave time between the completion of the rough drafts (including their review) and the production of the final copy for a final thorough edit of the complete document.

12. *Assemble and "produce" the final copy.* When you've got the complete document drafted, reviewed, and edited, it's time to put all the pieces together into the final copy. Now's the time to insert the final graphics and get the pagination right. Now's the time to put on the front- and back-matter elements. When you get that done, make a good clean photocopy, get the photocopy bound, and hand in the bound photocopy. (Put the original copy away for safekeeping.)

13. *Throw a party and celebrate!* Unless your team has had so many disagreements that everybody hates each other (which reflects inadequate up-front planning), get together and celebrate the completion of the project. Have some laughs over things that went wrong, and try to imagine how the problems might have been avoided. As a matter of fact, this sort of event is an actual stage in formal projects, often called a "postmortem" (although "postpartum" might be a better name). Team members in industry, business, and government typically go on to work on other projects together. They need to reflect on what went right and what went wrong with the project and use those insights to improve their process for the next project.

WORKSHOP: TEAMS

Here are some additional ideas for practicing the concepts, tools, and strategies in this chapter:

Teamwork for a nonwriting project. Find some nonwriting project requiring multiple individuals, such as putting up a tent or cooking a spaghetti dinner. Approach that project in one or both of the following ways:

■ *Plan nothing!* Without any planning whatsoever, just dive in and try to get the job done. When the smoke has cleared, step back and reflect on who did what and why. Recall what problems occurred, such as tasks getting done out of order, tasks being duplicated, or people stepping on each other's toes (or turf). List the roles that were assumed by the members of your team and the steps in the process. Devise a plan for doing the same project that will ensure efficiency and effectiveness next time.

■ *Plan everything!* Try to plan everything up-front. Decide who will do what and when, whether there should be an overall boss, how to resolve problems, and so on. Get everything in writing. When you've planned it to death, do the project. When you've finished the project, step back and have a "postmortem" and identify what worked and what didn't.

Teamwork for a writing project. To explore the dynamics of teamwork in a technical-writing context, find a writing project in which the actual writing has been done. For example, convert a document to a hypertext mockup or to a Web site as discussed in Chapter 17 (in particular, see the exercises). Or use the unformatted text available at the Web site for this book: **www.io.com/~hcexres/power_tools/teams**. Use the suggestions in this chapter to plan your process, assign roles, and accomplish other aspects of the project. Plan it to death; get it all in writing—remember that the point is to experience teamwork and to observe what works and what doesn't work.

PART V

Writing Tools: Mechanics and Style

Abbreviations, Symbols, and Numbers

TIME TRAVEL AND SUPERLUMINAL MOTION

Thinking about time travel and faster-than-the-speed-of-light transportation? You'll need plenty of abbreviations, symbols, and numbers.

Michael Crichton. *Timeline.* New York: Random House, 1999.

NOVA Online: Time Travel.
www.pbs.org/wgbh/nova/time/index.html

Superluminal Motion: Fact or Fiction?
lal.cs.byu.edu/ketav/issue_3.2/Lumin/lumin.html

Time Travel home page.
freespace.virgin.net/steve.preston/Time.html

John Gribbin. "Time Travel for Beginners."
epunix.biols.susx.ac.uk/home/John_Gribbin/Time_Travel.html

Time Travel Research Center. www.time-travel.com

Worm-Hole Network. worm-hole.net

Jurgen Vannoppen. "Travelling through time . . .": from a first-year college student at Katholic University of Louvain (Belgium).
gallery.uunet.be/vannoppen/science1.htm

Einstein: Image & Impact. From the American Institute of Physics.
www.aip.org/history/einstein

NOVA Online. "Einstein Revealed." www.pbs.org/wgbh/nova/einstein

Cambridge Relativity. "Relativity and Cosmology."
www.aip.org/history/einstein/einlinks.htm

Accessed February 3, 2001.

In technical writing, you face numerous situations in which you must decide whether to use an abbreviation or write out the word, whether to use a symbol or the word for the symbol, and whether to use digits or words for numbers. Styles vary from field to field and profession to profession. Find a style guide for publications in your field or profession. It will show you the rules for annoying things like abbreviations, acronyms, symbols, and numbers. (See "Find a Guide" in Chapter 20.)

Here are some common examples of standards and style guides for specific fields and professions:

Symbols.com—Claims to be the world's largest online encyclopedia of graphic symbols: **www.symbols.com**

University of Exeter. A Dictionary of Measures, Units, and Conversions: **www.ex.ac.uk/cimt/dictunit/dictunit.htm**

Electric Library. Concise Columbia Electronic Encyclopedia: **www.encyclopedia.com**

Russ Rowlett, University of North Carolina, Chapel Hill. *How Many? A Dictionary of Units of Measurement:* **www.unc.edu/~rowlett/units/index.html**

ABBREVIATIONS, ACRONYMS, AND INITIALISMS

The official difference between acronyms and initialisms is that you can pronounce acronyms (for example, AIDS, NAFTA, and NASA). "Acronym" is the term commonly used for both, while "initialism" seems to be a favorite of the hypercorrect. Here are the essential guidelines for abbreviations and acronyms.

1. Use abbreviations that are standard. Check a good general dictionary or a specialized dictionary, handbook, or style guide in your field. Don't make up abbreviations, and include a space between a number and its abbreviation unless your field or profession dictates:

```
For most work, much higher frequencies are needed
such as the kilohertz (kHz) and megahertz (MHz),
named after the German physicist Heinrich Rudolph Herz.
```

```
Traverse City Light & Power enrolled about 25 small
businesses, which represent 12 percent of the total
participants and account for 38 percent of its 600 kW
wind turbine output.
```

```
In 1996 in some states, grid-connected-system owners
were eligible for a tax credit of 1.6 cents per
kilowatt hour for the electricity they sell back to
the utility. In some Midwestern states, the credit is
very low (less than $.02/kWh).
```

```
Earth's gravitational field is 1 g (9.81 m/s per second).
```

```
To get to Andromeda at 1 g using Newton's theory
would take some 2,065 years.
```
(Notice that the abbreviation "g," representing gravity, is used without a period and is written with a space after the numeral.)

```
Our own galaxy is moving at about 600 km/s toward a
distant object dubbed the "Great Attractor." This
lies at a distance of 45 Mpc and has a mass
approaching 5 × 10 solar masses.
```

2. In documents containing lots of abbreviations such as inches and feet, use the symbols ′ and ″:

```
To build a purple martin birdhouse, you'll need to get
a 4' × 8' 1/4" sheet of plywood and a 14' 4" × 4"
post.
```

```
Cut a 25" × 25" floor from the sheet of plywood.
```

Note: To get the "×" (multiplication symbol) for "by" in the preceding:
- In Corel WordPerfect, choose **Insert→Symbol** and look in Math/Scientific.
- In Lotus Word Pro, choose **Text→Insert Other** and look in Math B.
- In Microsoft Word, choose **Insert→Symbol** and look in Math B.

3. Watch out for abbreviations beginning with a capital letter. Words like angstrom, joule, and tesla were named after people. Therefore, according to some styles you must use the initial cap; in others, you don't:

```
Named for James P. Joule, a joule (J) is the energy
expended by a force of 1 newton acting through a
distance of 1 meter.
```

> An angstrom (Å) is a unit of length equal to 10^{-10}
> meter; it is used to measure wavelengths of visible
> light and other forms of electromagnetic radiation.

Note: To insert the Å for angstrom, see the preceding steps, but look in "Current Font" in Lotus Word Pro and in "Normal Text" in Microsoft Word.

4. Use periods on abbreviations only if they spell a word. Usage varies; check a dictionary or style guide in your field. Acronyms and initialisms are rarely punctuated with periods, but again there are exceptions (as always). If an abbreviation ends the sentence, you only need one period:

> What would be the sense in determining that a table
> is 80 cm long if the very act of measuring it changed
> its length?

> At Traverse City Light & Power, 25 small businesses
> account for 38 percent of its 600 kW wind turbine
> output.

> In Vancouver, British Columbia, a 30,000 sq ft office
> complex uses composting toilets and urinals for human
> waste disposal.

> Because carrots usually have a slow and relatively
> poor germination rate, they should be sown about
> 3/4 in. apart and thinned to about 11 in. apart.

5. Don't use an abbreviation if it occurs without a value:

> On the American football field, the yard is the
> primary measurement, not the meter.

> The newton was named for Sir Isaac Newton, whose
> second law of motion describes the changes that a
> force can produce in the motion of a body.

> The dyne is a unit of force in the centimeter-gram-
> second system of physical units. One dyne equals
> 0.00001 newton.

> As a unit of mechanical power, the horsepower is
> equal to 33,000 foot-pounds per minute, or 6,600
> inch-pounds per second.

6. Do not add an *s* to make abbreviations plural (but check your dictionary or style guide for the few exceptions). To show the plural of an acronym, just add *s*:

> We do not know the if the universe contains any
> closed timelike curves (CTCs), although the German
> mathematician Kurt Gödel, among others, have
> performed calculations that predict CTCs.
> *(Notice that you do not use an apostrophe on plurals of acronyms.)*

> In the United States, each state has its own regula-
> tions for labeling produce as organic, and there are
> 36 non-governmental organizations (NGOs) that can
> certify produce as organic.

7. Don't overwhelm readers with abbreviations. For example, if an unfamiliar acronym occurs 4 times in a 6-page document, why not just
   write it out those 4 times rather than burdening your readers' memory?

> The kilohertz and megahertz were named after the
> German physicist Heinrich Rudolf Hertz (1857-94).
> *(No reason to use kHz or MHz here, unless you want to establish the
> abbreviation in parentheses.)*

> The 16,000 wind turbines in California produce 1,500
> megawatts, the equivalent of 3 to 4 large coal-fired
> plants.
> *(If this is the only occurrence of megawatts, why use the abbreviation Mw?)*

8. Always write out acronyms and unfamiliar abbreviations (placing the
   acronym or abbreviation in parentheses immediately after the spelled-
   out term) on first use. Thereafter, use the abbreviation:

> By following a closed timelike curve (CTC), we could
> meet ourselves in the past, or if the loop were large
> enough, visit our ancestors.
> *(The written-out version occurs first, followed by the acronym in
> parentheses. The written-out version uses lowercase—it's not a proper
> noun.)*

> We do not know if the universe contains any CTCs,
> though there have been several calculations,
> including one by the German mathematician Kurt Gödel,
> that predict CTCs.
> *(Notice that you do not use an apostrophe on plurals of acronyms.)*

> Internet Relay Chat (IRC) is a distributed client-
> server system, with more than a hundred servers
> scattered across the Internet.
> *(This one is a proper noun; therefore initial caps are used.)*

9. Don't use initial caps on acronyms unless they are proper nouns.
   NAFTA stands for "North American Free Trade Agreement"—a
   proper noun. ROM stands for "read-only memory"—not a proper noun.

SYMBOLS

A symbol is something like ′ (foot), ″ (inch), @ (at), # (pound), ¶ (paragraph), © (copyright), ° (degree), or Å (Ångstrom). Computers have made inserting symbols into regular text much easier.

■ In Corel WordPerfect, choose **Insert→Symbol** and look in Math/Scientific.
■ In Lotus Word Pro, choose **Text→Insert Other** and look in the current font, Symbol, or Math A or B.
■ In Microsoft Word, choose **Insert→Symbol** and look in (normal text).

1. For potentially unfamiliar symbols, write the symbol and, on first use, put the name of the symbol in parentheses just after.

```
To "comment out" a line in a Perl program, start the
line with # (pound).

To access your home page on a computer running Linux
Apache, use the ~ (tilde) followed by your user name.

Named after James P. Joule, a joule (J) is equal to
the work done or energy expended by a force of
1 newton acting through a distance of 1 meter.

An Å (angstrom) is a unit of length equal to 10⁻¹⁰
meter; it is used to measure wavelengths of visible
light and other forms of electromagnetic radiation.
```

2. Avoid using # (pound) for numbered items. Just use the word followed by the numerical digit:

```
The Anti-exe virus overwrites the first 8 sectors of
every head and track on the hard drive starting at
side 0, sector 4.

If the software does not perform correctly, return to
step 4.

Highlighting is covered in Chapter 12.
```

3. Don't use a symbol unless it is next to a value:

```
The primary unit of currency in the United States is
the dollar.
```
(No $ symbol here.)

```
What's the difference between a centimeter and an inch?
```
(No cm and no ″ here.)

4. If there are just a few occurrences of the symbol in the document, write out the name of the symbol instead of using the symbol.

The ohm is the SI unit of resistance of an electrical
conductor, named after the German physicist Georg
Simon Ohm.
*(No reason to use the symbol Ω or ω, the Greek letters for omega, in this
instance. However, if you want to establish the meaning of the symbol for
later use, show the symbol and put its definition in parentheses.)*

NUMBERS

Although mathematics may be an exact science, choosing between digits
and words is not. In the technical-writing context, where precision is
important, use digits for numbers, even for numbers you've been taught to
write out (such as one through ten). But because there are so many exceptions, keep a style guide of all instances where you use or could have used
digits. (See Chapter 22 on style guides.)

1. Use digits for exact numbers that express an important value, even if
   they are 10 or below (this same rule applies to percentage values):

   Earth's gravitational field is 1 g (9.81 m/s per second).

   To get to Andromeda at 1 g using Newton's theory
   would take some 2,065 years.

   One of the problems associated with time dilation is
   that when we return from Andromeda we would have aged
   less than 4 years while the Earth would have aged
   around 4.4 million years.

   More than 85% of all viruses are boot sector (Master
   Boot Record - MBR) related viruses.

   Macro virus population diversity has gone from 1 to
   more than 800 in the last two years.

   It started with 12 "bad" files and grew to 166 by 1987.

   The Planck epoch, calculated by quantum processes as the
   earliest time that classical space-time is conceivable,
   is set at 0.000000000000000000000000000000000000000001
   seconds.

2. Use words for nonexact, nonimportant numerical values. Obviously,
   this guideline involves judgment calls. Take a look at the following
   examples:

   For some, there are two main categories of galaxies,
   the spiral and elliptical galaxies. Others make it
   four, including lenticular and irregular galaxies.

Practical Ethics: Trusty Numbers

 Take out your driver's license and notice all the numbers on it. Besides the official license number, there's your birth date, address, weight, and height. These numbers are obviously concrete—either you weigh 150 pounds or you don't. A quick jump on the scale will set the record straight. Not all numbers are so easily established. In fact, when it comes to using numbers for advertising or conveying data, numbers can be manipulated to appear more informative and credible than they actually are. Take a look at the following claims and try to determine what might be wrong with them.

"9 out of 10 dentists surveyed prefer Granite brand toothpaste."

"Our herbal supplement improves memory 14%."

"This modem speeds up Internet connections by 16.13 percent."

So what's wrong with these claims? Perhaps nothing. But then again, maybe they've been treated to a sleight-of-hand in order to convey something that isn't true.

For instance, it's important to know the context of any survey. If an independent organization surveyed 3,000 randomly selected dentists, had a 90% response rate, and found that 9 out of 10 preferred Granite toothpaste, the claim is credible. But if the Granite Corporation sent out 100 questionnaires to which only 10 dentists responded, then its claim is questionable at best.

The problem with the herbal supplement claim is that memory is a difficult thing to measure. Before you believe the claim, what questions would you want answered? For starters, how was memory improvement tested? What other factors were considered? Who conducted the research? Has the scientific community established a credible way to test memory? Is it possible to quantify memory improvement with a percentage? It can be misleading and even unethical to use precise numbers for something that is not really quantifiable.

Then there's the modem claim. The fact that two digits are used after the period in 16.13 percent indicates a high degree of accuracy and impressive performance. This is not problematic unless the speed can only be measured within ±2 percent.

Being an informed consumer means recognizing suspicious numbers. Being an ethical communicator means that the numbers you offer your audience will be trustworthy; they must be presented within their proper context, used to define something quantifiable, and applied accurately.

The disk of the Milky Way has four spiral arms, and it is approximately 300 pc thick and 30 kpc in diameter. It is predominantly made up of Population I stars that tend to be blue and are reasonably young, spanning an age range between 1 million and 10 billion years.

The study of large-scale structure, currently being made by the Hubble Space Telescope, show galaxies just a couple billion years after the Big Bang. *(Just round "ballpark" numbers here; no digits!)*

Research indicates that there may be up to ten times more dark matter associated with each galaxy than the previous estimate. *(Here "ten" is an estimate—not a good spot for a digit.)*

The diversity of macro viruses has gone from 1 to
more than 800 in the last two years.
(The "two" years in this case is an estimated, ballpark value—not exact.)

The idea that our universe might have more than the
three familiar spatial dimensions was introduced more
than half a century before the advent of string
theory.

3. For rounded numbers in the millions or greater, use digits followed by
the word "million," "billion," and so on.

Imagine a journey to Andromeda, some 2.2 million
light years away.

One of the problems associated with time dilation is
that when we return from Andromeda we would have aged
less than 4 years while the Earth would have aged
around 4.4 million years.

To get to Andromeda at 1 g using Newton's theory
would take some 2,065 years. The same journey in an
Einsteinian universe, at the speed of light, would
take 30,000,000 seconds, or a little under 354 days.
*(The writer probably chose to use digits instead of "30 million" to make a
sharp contrast with 2,065 and for emphasis.)*

Each year, automobiles are responsible for some 57
million bird deaths, more than 97 million birds die
by flying into plate glass, and about 1.5 million
birds die from collisions with structures *(towers,
stacks, bridges, and buildings)*.

Businesses worldwide have lost a total of $7.6 billion
in U.S. dollars in the first two quarters of 1999 at
the hands of Melissa, the Explore.Zip worm and other
viruses, according to a new study.

4. Avoid starting a sentence with a digit; rewrite so that the digit occurs
somewhere within the sentence:

Avoid: 3960 miles is the Earth's radius.
Revised: The Earth's radius is 3960 miles.
Avoid: 70% of concrete mix is made up of
          aggregates.
Revised: Aggregates constitute 70% of concrete mix.

5. Hyphenate numeric-measurement compounds; leave a space between
numeric-measurement compounds:

Heisenberg presented his discovery of the uncertainty
principle and its consequences in a 14-page letter to
Pauli in February 1927.

For the Newtonian version, the power requirement is
enormous, even assuming perfect efficiency. The energy
required would be 5.1×10^{26} joules for a 10-ton
spaceship.

6. Use digits for numbered items (but omit the #):

The Anti-exe virus overwrites the first 8 sectors of
every head and track on the hard drive starting at
side 0, sector 4.

If your software does not perform correctly, return
to step 4.

Highlighting is covered in Chapter 12.

7. Use digits for one or the other of a pair of numbers that occur side
by side:

To build the 16-plant hydroponic garden, you will
need to collect 16 two-liter bottle caps.

Panel coverage will be 36″ to the weather with 1-1/4″
deep major ribs every 12″ and two 3/16″ deep minor
ribs between.

The six 80-foot wind towers are estimated to produce
50,000 kilowatt hours (kWh) per year, or 4500 kWh per
month.

The specifications call for 38 six-liter biohazard
containers.

8. Spell out fractions occurring by themselves without whole numbers
or measurement names, unless either the numerator or the denomi-
nator is more than 10. Use digits if the fraction is associated with a
measurement.

The first sky Einstein ring is an invisible line two-
ninths of the way to the top of the plot above the
photon sphere.

A meter is the distance light travels, in a vacuum,
in 1/299792458th of a second.
(No "s" at the end of "th.")

Ensign wasps have three pairs of legs, two pairs of
wings, and are 1/4 to 3/4 inches long with a general

body shape that makes them easily distinguishable
from other wasps.
(Use digits here because of the "inch" measurement.)

WORKSHOP: MECHANICS

The following exercises give you some practice with the guidelines and rules presented in this appendix. For additional practice, see **www.io.com/ ~hcexres/power_tools/mechanics**.

1. *Abbreviations.* In the following sentences, convert the appropriate written-out words and phrases to abbreviations, acronyms, and initialisms, using the guidelines presented in this appendix—or add abbreviations, acronyms, and initialisms, as necessary. (Careful! Not all of these items should be converted to abbreviations, acronyms, or initialisms.)
   a. The CheapTech BikeLite is simply a battery-powered light source that uses light-emitting diodes to provide its light.
   b. The bike light is about 7 centimeters by 5 centimeters by 4 centimeters, and it weighs approximately 60 grams (including the battery).
   c. For example, NIST-7, a cesium clock at the National Institute of Standards and Technology, is accurate to five parts in 1015 (meaning it will lose about one second in 6 million years).
   d. For example, goldfish enjoy water temperatures of 69 degrees Fahrenheit or less.
   e. In March 1998, astronomers warned that an asteroid could come within 30,000 kilometers of Earth or even strike Earth in 2028.
   f. It's rare that asteroids are more than a kilometer across.
   g. According to Donald Yeomans, head of the near-Earth objects program office at the Jet Propulsion Laboratory, there are no known near-Earth objects that will threaten Earth in the next century.

2. *Symbols.* In the following sentences, convert the appropriate words to symbols, using the guidelines presented in this appendix. (Careful! Not all words in the following that could be converted to symbols should be converted to symbols.)
   a. For example, goldfish enjoy water temperatures of 69 degrees Fahrenheit or less.
   b. NASA has just doubled its asteroid search budget to 3 million dollars.
   c. To build the purple martin birdhouse, you'll need to get a 4 foot by 8 foot by one-quarter inch sheet of plywood and a 4 inch by 4 inch by 14 foot cedar post, among other things.
   d. On a diamond's surface, the distance between adjacent hydrogens is about 2.5 Angstroms.

    e. A micron is one millionth of a meter.

    f. Currently 95 percent of all energy produced in the world is made by one or another method of burning carbon dioxide in the atmosphere.

3. *Numbers.* In the following sentences, convert the appropriate words-for-numbers to numbers-for-words, using the guidelines presented in this appendix. (Careful! Not all words-as-numbers in the following should be converted.)

    a. In the United States today there are an estimated fifteen million people who have been diagnosed with Diabetes Mellitus.

    b. Diabetes is known as the 7th leading cause of death in the United States.

    c. Microsoft's popular software programs Word and Excel include within their hidden software code a 32-digit number, called a Globally Unique Identifier, which is transmitted to Microsoft whenever a customer registers a copy of Windows 98 using its automated Registration Wizard.

    d. At six o'clock the five men made their way to 435 2nd Street where they began remodeling the small house.

    e. Not until the 1999 bonfire tragedy that killed 12 students did the university seriously question whether the tradition should continue.

    f. 5'1 inches tall and only 90 pounds, the gymnast nevertheless dominated the arena.

Punctuation: Commas, Semicolons, Colons, Hyphens, Dashes, Apostrophes, and Quotation Marks

COMPUTER VIRUSES

The similarities between the various marks of punctuation and computer viruses are strictly accidental. However, the following links enable you to explore the possibilities:

Symantec AntiVirus Research Center. **www.symantec.com/avcenter**

About.com's Antivirus Software page. **antivirus.about.com/compute/software/antivirus/msub7.htm**

CNET's virus page. **www.cnet.com/Content/Features/Howto/Virus**

Computer Virus Myths. **kumite.com/myths**

IBM Thomas J. Watson Research Center. Computer Viruses: A Global Perspective. **www.research.ibm.com/antivirus/SciPapers/White/VB95/vb95.distrib.html**

Accessed February 3, 2001.

For a complete review of most grammar, usage, and style problems, see *The Pocket Holt Handbook* by Kirszner and Mandell (Harcourt, Inc., 2000). If you are not sure which are your grammar favorites, try using a sentence diagnostic such as the one available online at **www.io.com/ ~hcexres/power_tools**. Also, take a look at a sampling of your papers from previous writing courses.

In any case, most writing teachers—certainly those teaching technical-writing courses—are likely to agree that the grammar and usage problems covered in the following are their "favorites."

For complete coverage of grammar, usage, and punctuation topics, see the following sources:

■ Grammar Handbook at the Writers' Workshop, University of Illinois at Urbana-Champaign. **www.english.uiuc.edu/cws/wworkshop/ grammarmenu.htm**

■ Grammar, Usage, and Style Resources, from refdesk.com. **www.refdesk.com/factgram.html**

■ Charles Darling, Capital Community College. Guide to Grammar and Writing. **webster.commnet.edu/grammar**

■ Reference Guide to Grammar: A Handbook of English as a Second Language. **www.acusysinc.com/English**

■ Jack Lynch. Guide to Grammar and Style. **andromeda.rutgers.edu/~jlynch/Writing**

■ David McMurrey. Grammar & Usage Study Guides. **www.io.com/~hcexres/tcm1603/gram0_plan.html**

INTRODUCTORY, COMPOUND, SERIES, AND RESTRICTIVE COMMAS

In the technical world where documents have multiple writers and multiple editors, all these document "co-owners" must produce some sort of stylistic consistency. For that reason, rules such as those for commas are as simple as possible.

Introductory-Element Commas

An introductory element is any word or group of words that comes before the main clause. To simplify matters, use a comma after any introductory element, no matter how few words or how short the pause. Go ahead and use a comma after words and phrases like "Today," "By tomorrow," "During the first few weeks," and "Generally" at the beginning of a sentence. Here are some examples:

```
Like a biological virus, a computer virus invades
other organisms, causing those organisms to
proliferate and spread the virus.
```
(The introductory element is a simple prepositional phrase.)

<u>Once the virus has been executed,</u> it can exploit weak points in the Windows system.
(The introductory element is a dependent clause.)

<u>Once executed,</u> a virus has free reign on all normal and high memory.
(It's only two words, but still introductory.)

<u>Typically,</u> this code will at first do little else than install the virus in high memory.
(Here is a single adverbial introductory element.)

<u>To understand anti-virus programs,</u> consider the basic behavior of known viruses.
(Here is an infinitive-phrase introductory element.)

<u>Limiting the number of initial virus infections in an organization</u> is important.
(There should be no comma after "organization"; the entire phrase is the subject of the verb "is.")

Compound-Sentence Commas

Use a comma to punctuate any compound sentence joined by a coordinating conjunction, regardless of the length of the individual clauses. A compound sentence is two or more complete sentences joined by a coordinating conjunction (*and, or, nor, but, yet, for*). Problems arise with those pesky sentences that look like compound sentences but are only compound predicates. Also, some compound sentences don't seem long enough, like this example: "Type your name, and press Enter." Here are some examples of the compound-sentence comma rule in action:

A virus might start reproducing right away, <u>or</u> it might lie dormant for some time until triggered by a particular event.
(The conjunction "or" occurs between two independent clauses, so use a comma.)

Virus programming does not demand special skills; there is no "black magic" about it.
(There is no conjunction between these two independent clauses. Use a semicolon, or start a new sentence.)

There are fewer boot infector viruses than file infector viruses, <u>but</u> most of virus-infection damage is caused by the boot infector viruses.
(The conjunction "but" occurs between two independent clauses here.)

The payload can alter individual figures in files or delete files.

(There should be no comma here because this is a compound verb phrase, not a compound sentence.)

```
A virus should never be assumed harmless and left on
a system.
```
(As in the preceding, there are two verbs here but only one subject. Commas not welcome!)

Series-Element Commas

A *series* of elements is a set of words occurring one after another. For example, "apples, oranges, and bananas" is a series; so is "in the den, behind the couch, under the rug." Even whole sentences can occur in a series. Punctuate series elements only if there are three or more such elements. Put a comma before the *and* occurring before the last element—it's not optional. Omitting it can cause reading comprehension problems, but including it does not. Here are some examples of the series-element comma rule:

```
A virus may infect memory, a floppy disk, a tape, or
any other type of storage.
```
(A series of four items with a comma before the "or.")

```
Once executed, a virus has free reign on the entire
memory-interrupt vector table, normal memory, and
high memory.
```
(A series of three items with a comma before the "and.")

```
Viruses can display obnoxious messages, erase files,
scramble a hard disk, cause erratic screen behavior,
or freeze up the computer.
```
(This example has five verb phrases, each having "Viruses" as its subject.)

```
A computer virus can cause damage simply by
replicating itself and taking up scarce resources.
```
(There should be no comma after "itself" and before "and" because there are only two series elements, "replicating . . ." and "taking up . . .")

Special problems occur when you have a series of adjectives before a noun. When is it appropriate to use commas between those adjectives? Although there is probably no sure-fire rule, you can try using these two tests:

- Try reversing the order of the adjectives. If doing so doesn't make the sentence sound strange, that's one clue that you can use commas.
- Try putting *and* between the adjectives. If doing so doesn't make the sentence sound strange, that's another clue that you can use commas.

If you can apply both tests without making the sentence sound strange, use commas. But watch out! Don't put a comma between the last adjective and the noun. Here are some examples of the series-adjective comma:

This best protection can be accomplished by installing <u>resident anti-virus</u> programs.
(You can't switch "resident" and "anti-virus" so no comma is needed.)

Viruses are usually transmitted within an organization by innocent people going about their <u>normal business</u> activities.
(You can't say "business normal activities"—no comma!)

A virus is simply a program containing <u>harmful, disruptive</u> instructions.
(You can switch these two adjectives, so use a comma.)

Try to limit the number of <u>initial virus</u> infections in an organization.
(There should be no comma because you can't say "virus initial infections.")

Junkie is a <u>multipartite, memory-resident, encrypting</u> virus.
(You could probably mix and match these adjectival elements; therefore the commas are appropriate.)

Restrictive- and Nonrestrictive-Element Commas

A challenging area of comma usage involves restrictive and nonrestrictive elements. If it's restrictive, don't punctuate the element; if it is nonrestrictive, punctuate it. Here are some examples:

A virus is a code fragment <u>that copies itself into a larger program and then modifies that program</u>.
(This refers to not just any "code fragment," but one that copies itself and modifies its host.)

A partition-sector infector is a virus <u>that infects the partition record on hard disks</u>.
(This is not any old virus, but one that does a particular kind of damage.)

Viruses modify software in an uncontrolled way, <u>which can damage the software</u>.
(You could delete this clause from the sentence; that means it's nonrestrictive and takes a comma.)

The partition sector/boot sector contains a small program, <u>called the partition record/boot record</u>, that is executed each time the computer is turned on.
(The information on what it's called is just thrown in as extra, potentially useful material.)

This program, <u>like normal files infected by the file infectors</u>, can be modified by a virus and thus be infected.

(You can delete the nonrestrictive phrase without causing problems to the sentence.)

```
All boot sector viruses infect disks, both floppy
and hard disk, by replacing the boot-sector program
with a copy of itself.
```
(This is just more nice-to-know information, which means it's nonrestrictive; thus commas are appropriate.)

End-of-Sentence Modifiers

A gray area in the world of punctuation involves dependent clauses and verbal phrases at the end of sentences. Two rules seem to apply: the absolute rule not to punctuate any dependent clause at the end of a sentence, and the nonrestrictive rule to punctuate only when the element is nonessential. Look at the following examples:

```
The virus then replicates itself, infecting other
programs as it reproduces.
```
(The underlined participial phrase could be deleted without harming the sense of the main clause. The main clause doesn't say much—but the phrase doesn't add anything to it.)

```
A virus can lie dormant for some time, until it's
triggered by a particular event.
```
(This is the same situation as in the preceding sentence.)

```
It is important to realize that viruses can only
reproduce if they are run.
```
(This sentence would be wrecked if the underlined dependent clause were removed. The dependent clause is essential to the meaning and the grammar of the main clause and it is restrictive; therefore, it should not be punctuated.)

```
A computer cannot become infected unless an infected
program is started on it.
```
(This is the same situation as in the preceding sentence.)

```
A virus is a computer program that copies itself when
an infected program is run.
```
(Notice how the dependent clause "restricts" the action of "copying itself." It's restrictive! No commas!)

```
A virus is inactive until the infected program is run
or boot record is read.
```
(Imagine this sentence without the italicized dependent clause—it doesn't make sense. The dependent clause is essential.)

Comma Combinations

Comma rules often combine within individual sentences, as in the following examples:

Like a biological virus, a computer virus invades other organisms, causing those organisms to proliferate and spread the virus.
(This sentence has an introductory element at the beginning of the sentence and a nonrestrictive verbal phrase at the end of the sentence.)

Of course, DOS has the file-protection flag, set by the DOS command **attrib r** filename; however, a virus can easily modify this attribute.
(This is a compound sentence joined by a semicolon; the first clause contains an introductory element and a nonrestrictive element; the second contains an introductory element.)

They search the disk for files to infect, and when one is found, they simply change it to include the virus.
(Here's a compound sentence; the two independent clauses are joined by "and"; the second begins with an introductory element. Apply the introductory element rule to the second independent clause.)

From the resident state, a partition-infector virus keeps monitoring disk operations at all times, and if at some later time an operation on a floppy disk is detected, it can then infect it.
(This is a compound sentence, both clauses of which have an introductory element.)

When a PC starts up, the partition sector on the disk is read, and the code there is executed.
(This sentence begins with an introductory element—another dependent clause—followed by compound independent clauses.)

As early as 1916, less than a year after Einstein had formulated his equations of the general theory, the Austrian Ludwig Flamm had realized that Schwarzschild's solution to Einstein's equations actually describes a wormhole connecting two regions of flat space-time—two universes, or two parts of the same universe.
(This big sentence starts out with two introductory elements, followed by the main clause, followed by a nonrestrictive phrase that uses other words to restate an idea in the preceding. Overly precise types would put commas around "Ludwig Flamm," but the sentence already has too many commas.)

SEMICOLONS

You can think of the semicolon as a strong comma—a comma with muscles. You can also think of it in musical terms—a shorter rest than a period. (If a period is a whole rest, the semicolon is a half- or three-quarter rest.)

1. Use a semicolon between two sentences that are not joined by a coordinating conjunction but seem so closely related that a period seems wrong or too much of a stop. (This situation causes the infamous error known as the comma splice, covered in Appendix C.)

    ```
    Female virus writers are few and far between; so far
    Sarah Gordon has encountered only five.
    ```
    (Notice how close these two independent clauses are—a half rest!)

    ```
    Appropriately used, user prompts can be valuable;
    however,they are frequently abused, overwhelming the
    user with questions or asking questions the user
    cannot answer.
    ```
    (A semicolon is commonly used when complete sentences are joined by words like "however," "therefore," and "furthermore.")

    ```
    Two major trends in Internet technology will have an
    impact on virus spread in the next few years: one is the
    increasing ubiquity and power of integrated mail
    systems; the other is the rise of mobile-program systems.
    ```
    (In this sentence, the semicolon joins the two sentences following the colon that explain the major trends.)

2. Use a semicolon between sentences that are joined by a coordinating conjunction but contain other commas. Here, the semicolon acts as a stronger comma, emphasizing the point at which the two complete sentences join:

    ```
    For $10.00, users could obtain the most up-to-date
    Dirty Dozen virus list; and for a self-addressed
    stamped disk mailer and disk, they could receive a
    current copy of the list.
    ```
    (To help clarify where the first independent clause ends and the next begins, a semicolon is used in front of the coordinating conjunction "and.")

    ```
    Often, Internet service providers already have IRC
    installed, available to all users; but if not, IRC
    clients are widely available on the Internet, and
    any user can download one.
    ```
    (Both independent clauses contain their commas; we need a semicolon—a comma with muscles—to mark the joining point of the two clauses.)

Like many computer games, Sim City creates a world
that the player may manipulate; but unlike a real
game, it provides no objective.
(Once again, this is a compound sentence, both independent clauses of
which contain commas of their own.)

3. Use semicolons between series elements in which some of the elements
   contain their own commas—again, the semicolon acting as a strong
   comma:

In 1998, IBM researchers examined several types of
Trojan Horse viruses that had been spread on the
Internet: the Trojanized PKZIP, which was widely discussed but rarely found; the Trojanized PGP, found
very rarely; Trojanized IRC scripts and clients, both
found rather frequently; applications that had been
rootkitted and systems that have been Trojanized
systems, numbering in the thousands.
(Each of the four list items have their own internal punctuation—thus
semicolons are needed to ensure that you see where each list item ends and
another begins.)

In his comparison of computer viruses to life, Spafford
defines "life" as having a "pattern in space-time";
being able to self-reproduce, grow, expand, evolve;
having an interdependence of parts; being able to
convert matter to energy; remaining stable under
"perturbations of the environment"; being capable of
functional interactions with the environment; and
being capable of information storage of its own self-
representation.
(Not meant for those with "short little attention spans," this sentence
presents a phrase for each of the six characteristics. Several of the phrases
contain commas of their own, necessitating semicolons to mark the
boundaries between the six characteristics.)

COLONS

The primary use of the colon is to punctuate the point between a lead-in
and the items introduced by that lead-in. The lead-in and the items
following it can be in the form of a regular sentence or in the form of a
numbered or bulleted list. Don't use a colon if the lead-in is not a complete sentence. Also, don't use a colon unless the items have to occur at the
end of a sentence. Here are some examples:

There are two main groups of viruses: the boot sector
and the infector of executable programs.

(The introductory element, the "lead-in," is complete in itself; use a colon.)

Two major trends in Internet technology will have an impact on virus spread in the next few years: one is the increasing ubiquity and power of integrated mail systems; the other is the rise of mobile-program systems.

(This lead-in tells you that two statements about "trends" are about to be presented.)

Honorable mentions included Stealth C, Wazzu, NPad, One Half, Parity Boot, and Ripper.

(The sentence is not complete at "included"—don't use a colon.)

The top seven viruses of 1997 were NYB, Anti-exe, Concept, Anticmos, Form.A, Junkie, and Monkey/Stoned/Empire. Honorable mentions are: Stealth C, Wazzu, NPad, One Half, Parity Boot, and Ripper.

(The sentence is not complete at "were"—no colon.)

This section gives a brief introduction to computer viruses: what they are, how they can spread, and what they can do.

(The lead-in sentence prepares you to hear about the contents of the introduction and is grammatically complete—use a colon!)

This section discusses what computer viruses are, how they can spread, and what they can do.

(In this version, the sentence is not complete at "discusses"—no colon!)

A computer virus can cause damage simply by replicating itself and taking up scarce resources, such as hard disk space, CPU time, or network connections.

(No colon either before or after "such as"!)

HYPHENS

Hyphenation may seem like some fiendish version of Trivial Pursuit, but careful hyphenation increases readability and comprehension. Good hyphenation practice is particularly important in technical writing. Because hyphenation usage is loaded with exceptions, writers and editors use style guides (see Chapter 22): these list every instance of hyphenation (as well as instances where hyphenation was considered but not used). The following examples illustrate common hyphenation usage rules. (For hyphenation of word breaks, see your dictionary.)

1. *Don't* hyphenate words with the common prefixes such as *re-, anti-, de-, un-, mal-, dis-, co-,* and so on.

> The best strategy is to make sure that the antivirus program operates automatically.
> *(Not "anti-virus.")*
>
> Nonresident programs look for and deal with viruses on your entire system at one specified time.
> *(Not "Non-resident.")*
>
> The control on the Web page is downloaded and reinstalled every time you visit a page that uses it.
> *(Not "re-installed.")*

2. *Don't* hyphenate a compound in which the first word ends in *-ly.*

> A competently coded version of the Sharefun virus exploiting modern e-mail systems could spread very quickly.
> *(No hyphen between "competently" and "coded.")*
>
> Viruses can combine possibly damaging code with the ability to spread.
> *(No hyphen between "possibly" and "damaging.")*
>
> The area Directory X serves has a large agriculturally based population, many of whom are future AGRICON suppliers and consumers.
> *(No hyphen between "agriculturally" and "based.")*

3. Hyphenate compounds in which the two words are an abbreviated version of a longer phrase or clause.

> Virus applets can open hundreds of windows rapidly on the user's display, make annoying and difficult-to-silence sounds, and try to fool the user into disclosing his user name and password.
> *(The sounds are difficult to silence.)*
>
> Malicious Java or ActiveX programs posing a danger to innocent users on the Web could become a more serious threat in the not-too-distant future.
> *(The future is not too distant.)*
>
> Virus instructions can have event-driven effects or time-driven effects.
> *(The effects are driven by time or event.)*

IBM antivirus software uses a patent-pending technology
from IBM that distinguishes infected disk boot
records from normal boot records.
(The technology has a patent that is pending.)

The International Computer Security Association is a
for-profit corporation specializing in certification of
security-related software products.
(The corporation is in business to make profits—that's a hard one!)

Password-stealing Trojan horse viruses are a much more
sophisticated form of virus.
(The virus tries to steal your password.)

A platform-specific virus is one that affects either a
PC or a Mac, but not both.
(The virus is specific to that platform.)

The NYB virus is a memory-resident virus.
(The virus stays resident in memory.)

The Junkie virus spreads quickly because of its
ability to spread as a file-sharing virus.
(It's a virus that shares files.)

4. Hyphenate most compounds that use *self-, cross-, -like, well-,* and so on.

   Most antivirus software includes heuristic methods to
   detect common virus-like signatures.

   A cross-platform virus is one that can infect either
   a PC or Mac. Concept (Word) and Wazzu are two
   examples of well-known macro viruses.

5. Be careful with compounds like *back up, print out, and mix up.* If they
   act as adjectives or nouns, use hyphens or compound them (check a
   dictionary for the correct usage); if they act as verbs, don't hyphenate
   or compound them:

   Make sure you are using an up-to-date signature file
   with your antivirus program. If it isn't up to date,
   you will be vulnerable to new viruses.
   (Notice that the first instance of "up-to-date" modifies "signature file"
   whereas the second simply modifies the verb.)

6. Hyphenate number-measurement compounds when they act as modifiers:

   The four-person team of security researchers jointly
   unearthed a vulnerability to the virus during a
   brain-storming session last month in Palo Alto,
   California.

Plants inoculated with Rhizobium leguminosarum showed a 7-percent increase in growth compared with the noninoculated ones.

The report is based on data collected during a 12-week period on separated greywater/blackwater plumbing in an apartment complex of ten apartments.

Leaching facilities require that beds or trenches be dug 24 inches deep and filled with 6 inches of gravel, with 4-inch distribution pipes laid on the gravel and covered by 2 inches of gravel followed by 12 inches of soil.

The typical 3-pin transistor has pins for the emitter, base, and collector.

Purple martin houses should have an 8-foot elevation above the ground and a 30-foot clearance on all sides.

7. Hyphenate adjective-noun compounds that can be misread:

Multipartite viruses are a cross between file and boot-sector viruses, infecting both files and boot sectors.
(It's not a sector virus—there is no such thing; it's a virus affecting the "boot sector.")

Microsoft uses a digital-signature technology called AuthentiCode to verify who has signed an ActiveX control.
(It's not a "signature technology" that happens to be "digital"; rather it's a "signature" that happens to be "digital." The hyphen ensures we know what modifies what.)

The fluctuations that seeded the large-scale structure of the Universe were primordial in origin, that is, associated with some of the very earliest times after the Big Bang.
(It's not a "scale structure" that happens to be "large." Even though it's not likely to be misread, the writer hyphenates this compound for readability anyway.)

8. Don't hyphenate compounds that occur after a linking verb. You may have "up-to-date virus protection," but your "virus protection is up to date."

Out-of-date antivirus software is useless. Don't let your signature files get out of date.

VRML is really just a computer language that describes three-dimensional objects. HTML has no way of addressing objects that are three dimensional.

Enhanced-reality software may provide us with more true-to-life information than our "natural" perception of reality. Not all of our perceptions are true to life.

Advanced real-time video filters may some day be able to remove wrinkles and pimples from your face! Although this is possible with programs like Adobe Photoshop, it's not yet possible in real time.

9. Avoid hyphenating an adjective-noun combination not acting as a modifier. However, hyphenate phrases like "back-up" and "print-out" when they act as nouns or adjectives. Here are some additional examples:

The Planck epoch is the earliest time that classical space-time is conceivable, as calculated by quantum processes.
(Physicists and astronomers hyphenate "space-time" to indicate the Einsteinian perspective.)

Life is a pattern in space-time rather than a specific material object.
(Just too good to pass up.)

Netscape plug-ins raise some similar concerns about virus hazards on the World Wide Web.
(Count on technology to wreak havoc on the English language. To prevent misreading, "plug-in" must be hyphenated when acting as a noun or adjective.)

Some antivirus programs try to achieve an acceptable trade-off by balancing acceptable false-negative and false-positive rates.
("Trade-off" acts as a noun in this sentence, necessitating the hyphen.)

Virus writers range from teenagers to college students to professionally employed grown-ups.
(The phrase "grown-ups" doesn't make sense without a hyphen—an "up" that is "grown"?)

To view the list of known viruses, select Virus descriptions from the Help pull-down on the main window.
("Pull-down" is a noun; it would be confusing if it weren't hyphenated.)

10. Watch out for compounds with punctuation that has not become established. If you cannot find a standard, just be consistent:

    ```
    As early as 1916, barely a year after Einstein had
    formulated his equations of the general theory, the
    Austrian Ludwig Flamm realized that Schwarzschild's
    solution to Einstein's equations actually describes a
    wormhole connecting two regions of flat space-time—two
    universes, two parts of the same universe.
    ```
    (In other contexts, you'll see "space-time" and "worm hole.")

11. Use an en dash (or hyphen) on "balanced" compounds. A balanced compound is one in which neither word is modifying the other (such as "blue-green sea" or "client-server model." Notice that the en dash is twice as long as the hyphen but half as long as the em dash. To get an en dash:
    - In Corel WordPerfect, click **Insert→Symbol→Typographic Symbols,** and select the en dash from the list.
    - In Lotus Word Pro, click **Text→Insert Other→Symbol,** and select the en dash from the list.
    - In Microsoft Word, click **Insert→Symbols,** and select the en dash from the (normal text) set of symbols.

12. In Microsoft Word, press **Insert→Symbols,** and select the item (–) that is shorter than the full em dash (—) but longer than a regular hyphen (-).

    ```
    Internet Relay Chat (IRC) is a distributed client-
    server system, with hundreds of servers scattered
    throughout the Internet.
    ```

DASHES

The dash is a form of punctuation similar to the comma and the parenthesis. Use it to introduce abrupt comments or to differentiate text when commas are also being used. Don't use a single hyphen as a dash. Either create a dash with two hyphens, or create the real thing with your word-processing software:

- In Corel WordPerfect, click **Insert→Symbol→Typographic Symbols,** and select the em dash from the list.
- In Lotus Word Pro, click **Text→Insert Other→Symbol,** and select the em dash from the list.
- In Microsoft Word, click **Insert→Symbols,** and select the dash from the (normal text) set of symbols.

    ```
    Paris's choice—to marry Helen—like most choices, was
    not without its consequences.
    ```

(Don't use just a single hyphen to create a dash!)

In the remainder of this paper, we will talk about "Trojan horses" of a different kind—the digital Trojan horses users are encountering today.
(Come on, use a real em dash!)

A simple addition over all the luminous material—stars and hot gas—within the optical radius of galaxies yields a non-dynamical estimate for the mass density, Omega ~ 0.005.
(That's more like it!)

A Trojan Horse virus sent through e-mail will be executed as soon as the message is viewed—without any prompting.
(The dash here adds emphasis and dramatic effect.)

To suggest that computer viruses are alive also implies that some part of their environment—the computers, programs, or operating systems—also represents artificial life.
(These dashes act as a different form of comma. If commas were used instead, we might read this as a list of five elements—not as three examples of "their environment.")

APOSTROPHES

Apostrophes are the endangered species of punctuation marks. Before the eighteenth century, they were scarcely used (yes, a world without apostrophes). But the correct use of apostrophes can prevent great amounts of confusion and ensure precision—something definitely needed in technical writing.

1. If the word is singular and does not end in *-s* ("employee," "computer," "disk"), add *'s* to make it possessive:

   If the employee's personal computer is connected to the organization's network, the virus can spread throughout the organization.
   (One employee—one organization.)

   At risk are Windows users who use programs like Microsoft's Outlook and Qualcomm's Eudora, which use Microsoft's viewing software and have fairly recent versions of its Java virtual machine.
   (Lots of opportunities to make apostrophe mistakes here!)

2. If the word is plural and ends in *-s* ("viruses," "computers," "disks"), add an apostrophe to the end of the word to make it possessive:

Political virus writers write programs that merely
display a key word such as Macedonia, their creators'
names, or the name of a group as a way of marking
turf.
(Multiple virus creators.)

If employees' personal computers are connected to
their organizations' networks, viruses can spread
throughout those organizations.
(Multiple employees—multiple organizations.)

3. If the word is singular but ends in *-s*, add *'s* to make it possessive
   (pay no attention to the styles that give you the option to add just the
   apostrophe):

   Paris's choice—to marry Helen—like most choices, was
   not without its consequences.
   *("Paris" is a singular noun ending in -s; just add an apostrophe s to the
   end of the word.)*

   The bus's role in computer architecture is central.
   *(Some argue that you should avoid making inanimate objects possessive.
   In this example, they would prefer "The role of the bus.")*

4. If the word is plural but does not end in *-s* ("geese," "men," "children"), add *'s* to the end of the word to make it possessive:

   Virus-creation kits make creating new viruses mere
   child's play.
   *(If you are not sure, you can rephrase it as "the play of a mere child."
   Therefore, the apostrophe is necessary.)*

   Children's computers are as vulnerable to virus
   attacks as are grown-ups'.

   The goose virus causes a computer to emit sounds
   resembling geese's honking.
   (Granted, "the honking of geese" would sound better.)

5. If you change the spelling of the word to make it plural ("pansy" →
   "pansies"), add an apostrophe at the end of the plural version of the
   word:

   Many universities' Web sites provide direct links to
   antivirus software for student and faculty use.
   *(Convert the singular word "university" to the plural "universities"; then
   add an apostrophe.)*

   High-tech companies' security systems will be
   challenged by next-generation Internet-borne viruses.

(Convert the singular word "company" to the plural "companies"; then add an apostrophe.)

6. The grand exception: *its* is the possessive, and *it's* means "it is" (who made up this language anyway?):

> If you want to protect your computer against viruses, it's essential that you follow the five guidelines below.
> *(This "it's" means "it is"—use the apostrophe version.)*

> When a virus is started on a workstation, it can run any instructions that its author chooses to include.
> *(This "its" is possessive—the "author" of "it." Don't use an apostrophe.)*

> The Junkie virus spreads quickly because of its ability to spread as a file-sharing virus.
> *(This "its" is possessive—the "ability" of "it." Don't use an apostrophe.)*

> IBM tests its new antivirus software on its more than 250,000 PCs before releasing it to help ensure that problems are found and corrected.
> *(The word "its" here refers to "IBM," which is singular.)*

7. For possessive pronouns ("yours, "hers," "theirs"), don't use an apostrophe:

> He believes that the fault for allowing the Melissa virus to spread throughout their company was hers.
> *(Don't you dare put an apostrophe between the "r" and the "s"!)*

> The responsibility for protecting your home computer is entirely yours.
> *(Don't touch that apostrophe key!)*

8. For plurals of acronyms (CPUs, CD-ROMs), don't use an apostrophe:

> IBM tests its new antivirus software on its more than 250,000 PCs before releasing it to help ensure that problems are found and corrected.
> *(It's PCs—not PC's.)*

QUOTATION MARKS

As Chapter 12 on highlighting points out, quotation marks are often used incorrectly for emphasis. Quotation marks are primarily for punctuating direct quotations; technical-writing contexts rarely require quotations. Instead, quotation marks in technical writing more commonly indicate words referred to as such or words used in unusual ways.

For our purposes, the term "click" refers to a single click of the left mouse button. The term "double-click" refers to two quick clicks of the left mouse button. *(We are referring to the words "click" and "double-click" as words; we are not using them as verbs.)*

Polymorphic viruses are well named, with "poly" meaning more than one or many and "morphic" meaning shape or body. *(The word "poly" is referred to as a word—actually, as a prefix.)*

A computer "virus" is simply a program that contains unwanted instructions that change files on a computer. *(A computer virus is not a real virus in the original biological sense of the word.)*

Antivirus software checks files for virus "signatures," which are identifiable byte sequences of known viruses. *(Viruses can't sign anything.)*

A computer virus is a program that can "infect" other programs by modifying them to include a copy of itself. *(Viruses can't infect anything in the original biological sense.)*

Virus detectors that look for these abnormal patterns of bytes not found in normal programs are called "scanners."

Note: The standard rule of punctuation of quotations is that commas and periods go inside the closing quotation mark; semicolons and colons are placed on the outside.

WORKSHOP: PUNCTUATION

The following exercises give you some practice with the punctuation rules presented in this appendix. (For additional practice, see **www.io.com/ ~hcexres/power_tools/punctuation**.)

1. *Introductory-element commas.* Punctuate the following sentences that have introductory elements. (Careful! Some do not have introductory elements.)
   a. In Bandelier National Monument raging fires threatened several cliff dwellings and other ancient ruins left by Native American tribes who formerly lived in the area.
   b. Donated by the non-profit Vietnam Veterans Memorial Fund the new computer lab at a university in Hanoi will help economically disadvantaged Vietnam gain access to the World Wide Web.

    c. With an increasing number of technology-related jobs in the new economy, experts fear girls who lack computing skills might be left behind.

    d. This fall, a project called "Home Access to the Internet and Learning" will provide Appalachian students with free computers and Internet access.

    e. Wheelbarrows were first used in Europe during the Middle Ages although they appear to have been common in China beginning around 230 A.D.

2. *Compound-element commas.* Punctuate the following sentences that have compound elements. (Remember that only compound sentences—compound independent clauses—are punctuated with a comma.)

    a. The 1950s have been called the "Golden Age of Science Fiction", and for the most part, Hollywood's view of technology and technological process was positive and optimistic.

    b. Novelists in the 1920s and 1930s predicted much of our technology and its impact on our world and anticipated advancements such as miniaturization.

    c. Sometimes science fiction inspires science fact, and a case in point involves a Texas Instruments engineer who came up with an idea for a new use of technology after watching an episode of *Deep Space Nine.*

    d. A number of books and World Wide Web sites have been written offering weird theories about the purpose of the pyramids and why they are here.

    e. Many people still believe that women are not interested in technology, but women like Ada Byron Lovelace and Rear Admiral Grace Hopper are testaments to the technological abilities of women.

3. *Series-element commas.* Punctuate the following sentences that have series elements.

    a. In the 1950s, science fiction movies reflected the common idea that technology brought political, social, and personal advancements.

    b. Admiral Hopper possessed a variety of talents: in addition to her outstanding technical skills, she was a whiz at marketing, repeatedly demonstrated her business and political insight, and persevered despite obstacles.

    c. A young cyber rights activist posted criticism of Internet filtering programs on his Web site and accused the software developers of having a hidden political agenda.

    d. When the software developers responded to the activist's criticism, excerpts from their correspondence were posted to anti-censorship e-mail lists, Web sites, and newsgroups.

4. *Restrictive- and nonrestrictive-element commas.* Punctuate the following sentences that have nonrestrictive elements. (Careful! Don't punctuate the items with restrictive elements.)
   a. When you're holding an online conversation whether it's an e-mail exchange or a response to a discussion group posting don't forget that the other person has feelings that might be hurt by a rude or thoughtless post.
   b. Seven astronauts were killed when the space shuttle they were piloting the *Challenger* exploded early in the flight.
   c. In order to protect the air, Congress enacted the Clean Air Act of 1970 and amended it in 1977.
   d. The "digital divide" defined as the gap between people who can afford to gain access to information technology and those who cannot has the potential to further isolate uneducated and poorer people from the prosperity of the "information age."

5. *Semicolons and colons.* Punctuate the following sentences with semicolons and colons as necessary. (Careful! Some of the sentences do not need semicolons or colons.)
   a. Even preschoolers are becoming familiar with the jargon of their generation floppy drive, CD-ROM, mouse and Web.
   b. Some experts believe that growing up with information technology will change the personality of this generation by making them collaborators and innovators.
   c. Generation Xers are considered cynical and negative the digital generation is expected to be worldly and optimistic.
   d. This digital generation is the biggest ever they outnumber even the Baby Boomers.

6. *Commas, semicolons, colons.* Punctuate the following sentences with commas, semicolons, and colons as necessary:
   a. Cookies are small pieces of information that a Web site can store in your browser the Web site can then recognize you when you return.
   b. Web site developers like cookies they can be useful in marketing online ordering and remembering passwords.
   c. Other people worry that cookies might help a Web site invade a users privacy in a variety of ways by keeping a record of where the user goes, by stealing personal information, or maintaining a list of purchases.
   d. Many Internet users have heard of "cookies" they just don't have a firm idea of what this term means.
   e. While revealing personal information on the Web can sometimes bring benefits to consumers there are other situations in which people would prefer to remain anonymous.
   f. Many countries already have privacy-related regulations others will be considering whether such regulations are necessary.

7. *Hyphens.* Punctuate the following sentences with hyphens as necessary:
   a. Most technology-driven companies make extensive use of the World Wide Web.
   b. Many travelers take advantage of duty-free shops overseas, where they can buy products without paying taxes on them.
   c. Employees for the start-up company were hand picked by the CEO.
   d. The old monitor took on an eerie shade of yellow-green, which its owner found irritating to the eyes.
   e. Because the data-carrying capacity of telephone lines, known as bandwidth, is low, receiving electronic data can take a long time.
   f. In February, 1999, a next-generation network, called Internet 2, went online.
   g. While computers are now the primary means of accessing the Internet, we're already seeing other Internet-enabled devices, such as pagers and cell phones, which can send and receive e-mail and access the Web.

8. *Dashes.* Punctuate the following sentences with dashes as necessary:
   a. Luddites—a group of workingmen who rioted and destroyed new technology that they felt threatened jobs and wages—named themselves after a mythical King Lud.
   b. Outbreaks of Luddism—which occurred mostly in Lancashire, Cheshire, and Yorkshire, England—were harshly suppressed by the British government.
   c. Enemies of the Luddites claimed that the men were irrational, that they had an unfounded fear of science and technology.
   d. However, their supporters had another viewpoint—the men were defending their jobs and lifestyles from technology which would displace them.

9. *Apostrophes.* Punctuate the following sentences with apostrophes as necessary:
   a. It's a popular myth that viruses can invade your computer when you open a piece of e-mail.
   b. In fact the viruses' deadly effects happen only if you open a file that comes attached to the e-mail.
   c. Even very good virus protection programs can't protect computers from every new virus.
   d. Therefore it is a user's responsibility to be vigilant.
   e. A virus can do its dirty work only if computers owners let down their guards.

10. *Combined punctuation.* Punctuate the sentences available at **www. io.com/~hcexres/power_tools/punctuation** with commas, semicolons, colons, hyphens, dashes, and apostrophes as necessary.

Grammar Favorites

COMPUTER ANIMATION: GAME DESIGN

Someday, kids will learn grammar and usage strictly through animated games. Sesame Street got it started with "Lolly Lolly Adverb," but there's much left to do. Here are some good links to get your grammar-animation career started:

Anna McMillan and Emily Hobson, Animation Tutorial. **www.hotwired.com/webmonkey/multimedia/tutorials/tutorial1.html**

Dyske Suematsu. Introduction to After Effects. **www.hotwired.com/webmonkey/99/14/index2a.html?tw=multimedia**

Animation Learner's Site, provided by a former Disney animator. **come.to/animate**

Larry's Toon Institute. From Animation World Network. **www.awn.com/tooninstitute/lessonplan/lesson.htm**

University of British Columbia. Imager Computer Graphics Laboratory: take a look at the Imager gallery in particular! **www.cs.ubc.ca/nest/imager**

About.com. Interactive Fiction. **interactfiction.about.com**

Chris Crawford. The Art of Computer Game Design. **www.vancouver.wsu.edu/fac/peabody/game-book/Coverpage.html**

Accessed February 3, 2001.

No doubt, most people are not likely to use the words "grammar" and "favorites" in the same breath. The grammar and usage topics covered in this appendix are "favorites" in the sense that they occur more often than others. For a complete review of most grammar, usage, and style problems, see *The Pocket Holt Handbook* by Kirszner and Mandell (Harcourt, Inc., 2000).

If you are not sure which are your grammar favorites, try using a sentence diagnostic such the one available online at **www.io.com/~hcexres/power_tools**. Also, take a look at a sampling of your papers from previous writing courses.

For complete coverage of grammar, usage, and punctuation topics, see the following Web sites:

- Grammar Handbook at the Writers' Workshop, University of Illinois at Urbana-Champaign: **www.english.uiuc.edu/cws/wworkshop/grammarmenu.htm**
- Grammar, Usage, and Style Resources, from refdesk.com: **www.refdesk.com/factgram.html**
- Charles Darling, Capital Community College. Guide to Grammar and Writing: **webster.commnet.edu/grammar**
- English as a Second Language (provided by Rong-Chang-Li): **www.rong-chang.com/grammar.htm**
- David McMurrey. Grammar & Usage Study Guides: **www.io.com/~hcexres/tcm1603/gram0_plan.html**

FRAGMENTS

Fragments are "sentence wannabees" because they lack a subject or a complete verb. We tend to write fragments because we use fragments in our conversational speech. While fragments are easy enough to understand or clarify in conversation, they present potentially serious communication problems in writing. A fragment is not necessarily a short sentence. "It is" is a sentence—not a fragment! True, we don't know what "it" refers to, nor what it "is." Such a sentence might occur like this: "You may wonder whether global warming is a reality. It is." Here are some examples of fragments along with revisions:

Version with fragment	Revised version
Blasting each other to pieces in Quake or Delta Force doesn't constitute a social experience. *Unless you meet the other players afterwards and share your stories.*	Blasting each other to pieces in Quake or Delta Force doesn't constitute a social experience, unless you meet the other players afterwards and share your stories.
For example, fantasy is a popular setting in almost any computer game genre. *No matter whether it is an adventure, role-playing, strategy, or action game.*	For example, fantasy is a popular setting in almost any computer game genre—no matter whether it is an adventure, role-playing, strategy, or action game.

Continued

Version with fragment	Revised version
Many independent studies in various professional fields conclude that seven is the highest number of objects that a person can comfortably keep in mind at once. *A theory that applies equally to computer games as well.*	Many independent studies in various professional fields conclude that seven is the highest number of objects that a person can comfortably keep in mind at once. This theory applies equally well to computer games.
Some games violate all the guidelines for intellectual manageability and still somehow reach a wider group of players. *Civilization 2 being a good example of how successful computer games can violate "established" guidelines.*	Some games violate all the guidelines for intellectual manageability and still somehow reach a wider group of players. Civilization 2 is a good example of how successful computer games can violate "established" guidelines.
A license with a sports league will entitle you to use the league's own logos, plus the team names, logos, and colors. *Assuming the league owns all those rights.* Of course, different leagues have different rules.	A license with a sports league will entitle you to use the league's own logos, plus the team names, logos, and colors, assuming the league owns all those rights. Of course, different leagues have different rules.
To break into computer game design, you can and should write a fully functional demo game. *One of about 10,000 lines of C++ code with at least one and preferably several features not found in commercial games.*	To break into computer game design, you can and should write a fully functional demo game. Your demo game should consist of about 10,000 lines of C++ code with at least one and preferably several features not found in commercial games.
These days, a typical commercial game might take 100,000 lines of C++ code written by a team of 3 programmers over a period of 18 months with a budget of a million dollars. *Not something an individual trying to break into the game design business can easily accomplish.*	These days, a typical commercial game might take 100,000 lines of C++ code written by a team of 3 programmers over a period of 18 months with a budget of a million dollars. Obviously, a game of this magnitude is not something an individual trying to break into the game design business can easily accomplish.

COMMA-SPLICE SENTENCES

A comma-splice sentence is two or more complete sentences joined by a comma, but without a coordinating conjunction—that is, *and, or, nor, but, yet,* or *for.* The following examples show that you can fix a comma-splice sentence by (a) adding a coordinating conjunction, (b) using a semicolon between the complete sentences, (c) making each of the complete sentences a separate sentence in its own right, or (d) reducing the words to one complete sentence.

Version with comma splice	Revised version
In a role-playing game, certain icons may move the character, other icons cause the character to pick up items, rest, cast spells, and so on.	In a role-playing game, certain icons may move the character; other icons cause the character to pick up items, rest, cast spells, and so on.
In a role-playing game, enabling players to see the dice that determine the outcome of a combat is impractical, it slows down the game or takes up valuable screen space.	In a role-playing game, enabling players to see the dice that determine the outcome of a combat is impractical. It slows down the game or takes up valuable screen space.
People prefer multiplayer board and card games to solitaire games, multiplayer games are a social experience.	People prefer multiplayer board and card games to solitaire games because multiplayer games are a social experience.
In computer games, the opposite situation has prevailed, most computer games have been single-player games.	In computer games, the opposite situation has prevailed. Most computer games have been single-player games.
Using a boring game for socializing isn't exciting, get together with a couple of friends and play tic-tac-toe for an hour to see what I mean.	Using a boring game for socializing isn't exciting. Get together with a couple of friends and play tic-tac-toe for an hour to see what I mean.
There are many reasons why Civilization 2 managed to attract novice gamers, the most important is that players start with a simple, easily manageable situation (one settler unit), build the first city, and add various units and cities progressively.	There are many reasons why Civilization 2 managed to attract novice gamers. The most important is that players start with a simple, easily manageable situation (one settler unit), build the first city, and add various units and cities progressively.
To be honest, many of the science-fiction and fantasy worlds that appear in computer games aren't that creative either, they're rehashes of old ideas and borrowed genres.	To be honest, many of the science-fiction and fantasy worlds that appear in computer games aren't that creative either. They're rehashes of old ideas and borrowed genres.

PRONOUN-REFERENCE PROBLEMS

Pronoun-reference problems are the bigots and the misogynists of the sentence world—or else they just can't count. As you know, a pronoun is a word like *he, her,* or *theirs,* and it refers to nouns such as *Patrick, Jane,* or the *McMurreys.* Problems arise when the noun is human but neutral (either masculine or feminine). For example, "Everyone opened her (or his?) briefcase." Because we don't know whether these people are male or female, we mistakenly use "their." The traditional rule of using "he," "him," or "his" in these neutral situations is considered sexist writing. Of course, constructions like "she or he" and "him or her" are options, although they are awkward and pedantic. (And always putting the "he" in front of the "she" in phrases like "he or she" is also considered sexist by some.) Instead, change the noun to a plural; then references to it with "they," "them," and "their" are grammatically correct. Thus, instead of saying "Everyone opened their briefcase" or "Everyone opened his or her briefcase," you can write something like "The board members opened their briefcases."

Problems also arise when the noun is a collective thing such as the *team*, the *Orlando Magic*, the *company*, *Dell Corporation*, or the *U.S. Coast Guard*. Because we know these entities represent multiple people, we want to refer to them with pronouns like *they*, *them*, or *theirs*. The traditional grammatically correct way is to refer to such collective entities with *it* or *its*. And as the examples below illustrate, words like *any*, *none*, *each*, *either*, or *neither* also cause pronoun-reference problems:

Version with pronoun problem	Revised version
To help ensure that problems are found and corrected, *IBM* tests *their* new antivirus software on their more than 250,000 PCs before releasing it.	To help ensure that problems are found and corrected, *IBM* tests *its* new antivirus software on its more than 250,000 PCs before releasing it. *(Also note that it's PCs—not PC's.)*
The *customer* must be aware of the kind of software *they* are downloading and take the necessary precautions to prevent virus attacks.	*Customers* must be aware of the kind of software *they* are downloading and take the necessary precautions to prevent virus attacks.
To avoid the risk of contracting the Melissa virus, it is recommended that the network *administrator* upgrade *their* antivirus software to include detection and cleaning for W97M/Melissa.	To avoid the risk of contracting the Melissa virus, it is recommended that network *administrators* upgrade *their* anti-virus software to include detection and cleaning for W97M/Melissa.
In Lebling & Blank's Zork, the game *player's* sole objective is to solve a puzzle: *they* must find objects and use them in particular ways to cause desired changes in the game state.	In Lebling & Blank's Zork, game *players'* sole objective is to solve a puzzle: *they* must find objects and use them in particular ways to cause desired changes in the game state. *(The word "players'" is a plural noun.)*
To adhere to the seven-object rule, a role-playing game can confront a *player* with choices to move, rest, fight, or administrate *their* character. If the *player* chooses to fight, *they* can attack, guard, shoot, or use an item. At any level, the *player* is never faced with more than seven alternatives from which *they* must choose.	To adhere to the seven-object rule, a role-playing game can confront *players* with choices to move, rest, fight, or administrate their character. If *players* choose to fight, *they* can attack, guard, shoot, or use an item. At any level, *players* are never faced with more than seven alternatives from which *they* must choose.
Stories are inherently linear. However much *a character* may agonize over the decisions *they* make, *they* make them the same way every time we reread the story, and the outcome is always the same.	Stories are inherently linear. However much *a character* may agonize over the decisions *she or he* makes, *that character* makes them the same way every time we reread the story, and the outcome is always the same. *(Plural "characters" would be better here.)*

Continued

Version with pronoun problem	Revised version
A game is a form of art in which a *participant,* called a "player," makes decisions in order to manage *their* resources through game tokens in the pursuit of a goal.	A game is a form of art in which *participants,* called "players," make decisions in order to manage *their* resources through game tokens in the pursuit of a goal.

PARALLELISM PROBLEMS

Sentences with parallelism problems are the psychiatric cases of the sentence world. By using different forms of grammatical phrasing, they become sentences with multiple personalities, schizophrenia, or just bad dressers. Problems with parallelism can occur any time you have two or more elements in a series. The problem involves using different types of grammatical phrasing for those items—you're supposed to use only one! For example, look at the following sentence that has series items that don't use the same style of phrasing:

Parallelism problem: In Sim City, some of the goals you can set include *building* the grandest possible megalopolis, to *maximize* how much your people love you, or *you can try designing* a city that relies solely on mass transit.

The three italicized phrases use different types of phrasing—namely, gerund phrase, infinitive phrase, and independent clause. The following table shows you some of the common types of phrasing that, when mixed, produce parallelism errors:

Phrasing type	Example
Complete sentences	One of the essential elements of a game involves decision making. Another involves managing your resources. A third essential element involves reaching a goal.
Noun clauses *(who, what, when, where, how, that)* clauses	*How you make decisions, how you manage your resources, and when you reach the goal*—these are the essential elements of games.
Participial and gerund *(-ing)* phrases	*Making decisions, managing resources,* and *reaching the goal* are the essential elements of any game.
Infinitives *(to* + verb phrases)	The essential elements of any game are *to make decisions, to manage resources, and to reach the goal.*
Noun phrases	*Decisions, resources,* and *goals* are the essential elements of games.

You can use practically any one type of phrasing as long as you don't mix types. Here is one good way to revise the preceding sentence:

Revised version: In Sim City, some of the goals you can set include *building* the grandest possible megalopolis, *maximizing* how much your people love you, or *designing* a city that relies solely on mass transit.

In the following parallelism problems, notice that in almost every case you can revise equally well with a different style of phrasing:

Version with parallelism problem	Revised version
As game designers, we need a way to analyze games, *what their basic elements are,* and to understand what works and what makes them interesting.	As game designers, we need a way to analyze games, to discuss their elements, and to understand what works and what makes them interesting. *(A series of three infinitive phrases)*
This guide will give you an overview of how the forum is set up, maneuvering in it, as well as methods for posting, replying and editing messages.	This guide will give you an overview of how the forum is set up, how to maneuver in it, and how to post, reply to, and edit messages. *(A series of three noun clauses)*
The creativity in computer sports games is found in more subtle areas: user interface design, player behavior AI, *how character animations interact,* and intelligent audio, to name a few.	The creativity in computer sports games is found in more subtle areas: user interface design, player behavior AI, interaction of character animation, and intelligent audio, to name a few. *(A series of four noun phrases)*
In developing a computer sports game, just consider all the events that appear in a team's annual calendar: hiring rookies, trading players, holding training camp, *exhibition games,* playing regular season games.	In developing a computer sports game, just consider all the events that appear in a team's annual calendar: hiring rookies, trading players, holding training camp, scheduling exhibition games, playing regular season games. *(A series of five gerund phrases)*
Consider the game of chess. It has few of the aspects that make games appealing: no simulation elements, *you don't have characters involved in role playing,* and little color.	Consider the game of chess. It has few of the aspects that make games appealing: no simulation elements, no role playing, and little color. *(A series of three noun phrases)*

WORKSHOP: GRAMMAR

As mentioned at the beginning of this appendix, we can't cover all grammar, usage, punctuation, and style problems in this book—just your favorites. For complete coverage, get a grammar reference book like *The Pocket Holt Handbook* by Kirszner and Mandell (Harcourt, Inc., 2000).

To find out which are your favorites, review your past writing or use a sentence diagnostic like the one at **www.io.com/~hcexres/power_tools**.

Here are some exercises to give you some practice recognizing and revising the grammar and usage problems covered in this appendix. For additional practice, see **www.io.com/~hcexres/power_tools/grammar**.

1. *Fragments.* In the following, identify the fragments and revise to eliminate them:
   a. At the meeting, the speaker explained how to maintain the environment within an aquarium. What types of pumps and plants are best, and how to introduce new fish to the new aquarium.
   b. Not only meeting once a week to discuss schedules but also keeping in constant touch by e-mail.
   c. The Internet has allowed many people access to information they never had before.
   d. Despite opponents' claims that Internet privacy legislation would hinder the ability of corporations to satisfy the customers' demands.
   e. Large numbers of corporations are still collecting information and tracking Internet users without the customers' consent or knowledge. Even though these corporations claim to regulate themselves.

2. *Comma splices, run-ons, and fused sentences.* In the following, identify the comma-spliced, run-on, and fused sentences, and revise to eliminate them:
   a. The inconveniences of being diabetic are indisputable but the benefits of proper self-care can outweigh these inconveniences.
   b. Student Bonfire workers are trained in the proper use of axes, machetes, and chain saws, however there are still many risks involved in preparing the logs.
   c. At the meeting, the speaker explained how to maintain the environment within an aquarium—what types of pumps and plants are best, and how to introduce new fish to the new aquarium.
   d. Privacy guidelines have been very successful in Europe, it seems logical for the United States to adopt similar guidelines for Internet privacy.

3. *Pronoun-reference problems.* In the following, identify problems with pronoun reference, and revise to eliminate them:
   a. The tutorials for Microsoft Excel tables show the user where they are to click or type.
   b. The World Wide Web has given the ordinary person access to information they never had before.
   c. In the documentation department, they keep in constant touch by e-mail.
   d. At the meeting, the speaker explained how to maintain the environment within an aquarium, what types of pumps and plants are best, and how to introduce new fish to the new aquarium.

4. *Parallelism problems.* In the following, identify problems with parallelism, and revise to eliminate them:

   a. To solve the communication problem, the managers agreed to relay information about personnel changes, updates for major projects, and to make announcements aimed at the entire company through weekly meetings.

   b. The judges evaluated the Web sites based on content, style, how interactive it was, and the quality of the graphics.

   c. In a Japanese garden, designers use many techniques to ensure that the garden is attractive, as well as in harmony with its surroundings and does not sacrifice the sense of privacy.

   d. Some financial magazines have warned readers about brokers who advise them to move money into variable annuities from 401(k)s, retirement plans that are tax deferred, or IRAs.

Index